A history of
OTTOMAN
ARCHITECTURE

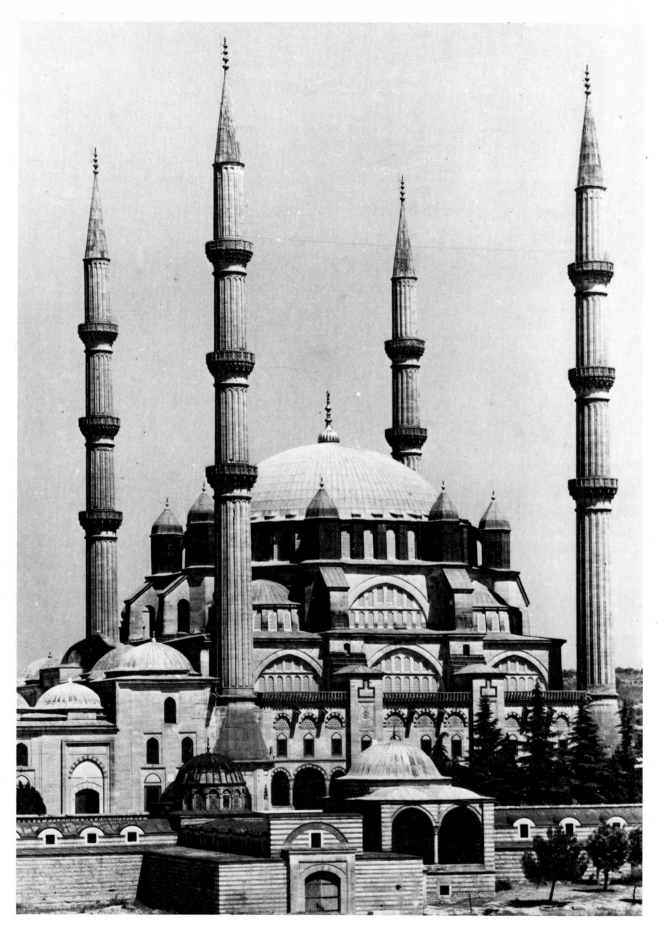

Selimiye Cami, Edirne.

A history of OTTOMAN ARCHITECTURE

GODFREY GOODWIN

with 4 color plates and 521 illustrations, including 81 plans

THE JOHNS HOPKINS PRESS · Baltimore

To Gillian

Endpapers: nineteenth-century engraving showing the Azapkapı mosque with Süleymaniye across the Horn

PUBLISHED IN THE UNITED STATES OF AMERICA
BY THE JOHNS HOPKINS PRESS, BALTIMORE, MARYLAND 21218

LIBRARY OF CONGRESS CATALOG CARD NUMBER 79-124947
ISBN O 8018 1202 X

FILMSET IN GREAT BRITAIN BY FILMTYPE SERVICES, SCARBOROUGH
PRINTED AND BOUND IN GREAT BRITAIN BY JARROLD AND SONS LTD,
NORWICH

Contents

Foreword

THE AIM OF THIS BOOK is to show that Ottoman architecture, far from being merely a decadent mixture of Persian, Byzantine and other styles, is a historic style in its own right. Its aim is, also, to show Ottoman baroque as a creative period; for, although many Turkish writers deny it any virtue, it did have considerable influence on the Romantic movements of the West and for many Europeans epitomized the architecture of the Sultanate. It clearly had individuality and zest.

It is undoubtedly true that early Ottoman architecture was influenced by the Byzantine and Armenian traditions; it can also be seen as the issue of Roman engineering, which had been transmuted into the poetry of space with the building of Hagia Sophia and Hagia Irene in Constantinople. Ottoman builders, like their predecessors, were disciplined by religious symbolism – the great garden of Islamic abstract design which is so entangled with Eastern and Western forms, from the lotus to the vine. They came from many regions and not all of them were believers in Muhammed; among those who were, many were unorthodox. So, like all creative art anywhere, Ottoman architecture was derivative and acknowledged no frontiers: it fed on the compost of other cultures in order to develop its own individual style. It was finally killed by nationalism.

If this book, through the analysis of this style, its history and its symbolism, helps towards an understanding and respect for Ottoman architecture, then its purpose will have been achieved.

I have had the help of many people, friends, colleagues, strangers and members of my wife's family. It is impossible to thank all those who have been kind to me like the imam at Samanbahçe who feasted us on the steps of his mosque or the innumerable children who have run in search of keys. There have been students like Bay Faruk Pekin who gave up time in their vacations to check information, and guests like Miss Marianne Straub, Miss Margaret and Miss Dorothy Pilkington who have seen familiar monuments with a fresh and critical judgement. There are all those who patiently walked Istanbul with me on Saturday after Saturday whatever the weather, like Mr and Mrs James L. Brainerd, Mr and Mrs Michael Waar, and Professor Elbow. I have been able to ply my Turkish colleagues like Professor Fahir İz or Professor Bahadur Alkım with questions. Bay Mehmet Ali Pazarbaşı has always been ready to help me with translation from the Ottoman. It is astonishing how rarely I have been frustrated or met with discourtesy of any kind. I must perforce be selective or the list would cover many pages.

I owe a great debt to the directorate of Topkapısaray and many other museums and libraries, and a very personal one to the architect of the saray, Bay Mualla Anheggar, to Bay Cemil Atilgan, the poet Sabahittin Batur, Dr Sabahittin Eyüboğlu and Dr Erol İnelman. I have enjoyed the inestimable friendship of the Şakir Pasha family and most particularly of Bayan Aliye Berger-Boronai. There has been the wisdom of Professor Ercement Atabay to draw on and the vision of the painter Özer Kabaş and of Bayan Ayma Kabaş in whose company buildings live again.

Friends like Professor and Mrs Keith Greenwood, Professor and Mrs David Garwood, Professor and Mrs John Freely and Dr Mehmet Rona have been a continual support for year after year. I owe a particular debt to Dr Howard P. Hall, formerly Vice-President of Robert College, for his faith in me which resulted in grants from the College to aid travel and the preparation of material. It has been my privilege to learn from Mr Robert Van Nice and from the foremost scholar of Ottoman architecture, Dr Aptullah Kuran. There has been the stimulus of long conversations and correspondence with Mr Arthur Stratton and Mr John H. Harvey.

I am most grateful for the patience and endurance of the photographer Mr Michael S. Thompson whether in the heat of August in Anatolia or in a January blizzard at Edirne. I must acknowledge the gift of photographs taken by Mr Sedat Pakay, now at Yale, and my brother-in-law, the Hon. R. R. E. Chorley. I would like to thank very sincerely the Turkish Ministry of Tourism for their lavish help on many occasions. Mrs Pauline Baines and Miss Helen Walliman have had the task of preparing this book for publication, and I have deeply appreciated their sensitive treatment of it, their vigilance and their care.

I have had the advice and understanding of Dr and Mrs Geoffrey Lewis for nine years. Mr Lee Fonger, Librarian of Robert College, has been selfless in his sustained help however busy he may have been. My father- and mother-in-law have encouraged and sustained me for many months in their house, in ideal conditions for work and reflection. None of these will begrudge my very special thanks to Professor Hilary Sumner-Boyd whose unique and authoritative knowledge masked by his urbane modesty made him my principal mentor.

Finally, no one else but she can ever truly know how much this book owes to my wife.

8

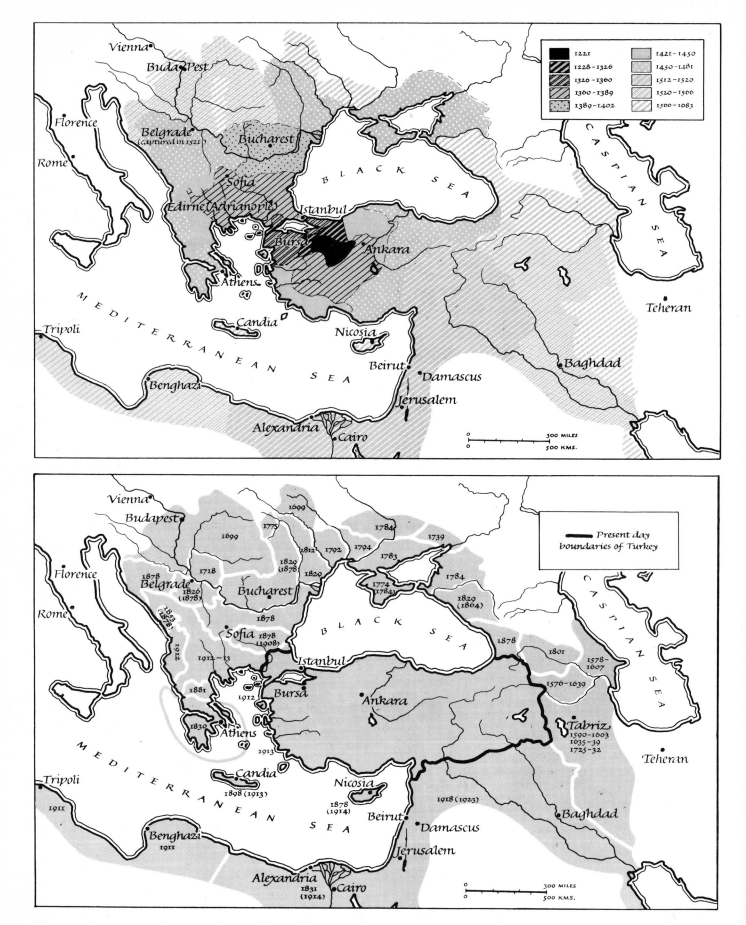

The expansion and contraction of the Ottoman Empire. These maps do not take account of minor fluctuations

Introduction

THE EARLY RULERS of the House of Osman, the Ottomans, were chieftains of a small tribe of shepherds and Gazis (warriors) on the frontiers of the Faith. Their followers were the Kayı clan of the numerous Oğuz Turkish people who fled from Central Asia into Anatolia before the onslaught of Genghis Khan. They eventually settled in the region between Bursa and the Black Sea. The Ottomans were heads of this Turkish family and absolute masters of their subject peoples and this relationship continued throughout their history although with gradually diminishing force.

For nearly 250 years they produced a line of gifted soldiers and rulers who achieved conquest after conquest, from that of Bursa in 1324 to that of Constantinople in 1453 and Syria and Egypt in 1517. Süleyman I was to add Belgrade and Rhodes to the Ottoman Empire but he failed to capture Vienna, and it is convenient to see this failure as the first serious manifestation of the decline of the empire. It was precipitated by the absence of any creative thinking and by the imposition of an intellectually stagnant educational system. Great men continued to arise but they could not overcome the forces of superstition and sterile conservatism, although some perished in the attempt. After the death of Süleyman, there were some great vezirs, such as the members of the Köprülü family, but few important sultans except Murat IV, and Mahmut II who overthrew the tyranny of the Janissary Corps. Even in the nineteenth century, reformist movements were frustrated and the Ottoman House could not survive the insurgent nationalism of the twentieth.

The Ottoman conquests brought them into contact with many different peoples, such as Greeks, Armenians and Slavs who formed millets or quasi-independent communities under their own religious leaders within the state. The Christian levy, or devşirme system, which is so important to the understanding of the establishment of the government is discussed in Appendix I. The point to be made here is that the ruling classes were mainly selected from the subject peoples until the sixteenth century, and that there were few hereditary noble families although there were some, such as the Candarlı. The subject races also supplied craftsmen of all kinds, from architects to cooks (not to mention bedfellows), since soldiers and administrators tended to regard such people as their inferiors.

The sultan was assisted in his rule by the Divan, or Council of State, and the highest office was that of the Grand Vezir who was, however, subordinate to the Şeyhül-İslam, or Grand Mufti, who had to be a true-born Moslem and whose spiritual power included, in theory, the right to counsel the deposition of the sultan. It was for the Grand Vezir that the architects of the household worked when not engaged in building for the sovereign. This was even more the case after the conquest of Constantinople when the power of the Vezir greatly increased.

This was due to the overwhelming burden of administration resulting from the increased size of the empire which made it impossible for the sultan to supervise details of daily rule or to continue to preside over the Divan as a court of final appeal. It was also due to increased seclusion of the sultan behind high walls after Mehmet II had accepted a number of Byzantine concepts of majesty as well as the Asian belief in a chosen family that was fit to rule the world.

The great provinces were ruled by Beylerbeys or Viceroys in the sense that communications were slow but events often pressing so that the Beylerbey had to act before instructions could arrive from the Divan. The smaller provinces were ruled by Sancaks or Governors who, like the Beylerbeys, combined civil with military authority. This authority was tempered by that of the local kadı who would be a graduate of a religious college and a true-born Moslem. There was little division between secular and religious rule in practice, and the grouping of quarters for pilgrims, officers of state, dervishes and orthodox students, among others, round a mosque, especially in the period prior to the conquest, is witness to this.

The Ottoman world was medieval in its obedience to order and precedence and this governed architecture also. Only a royal mosque, for example, might have more than one minaret. When faith in the established hierarchy faded it was natural that eclecticism should grow as an architectural movement and equally natural that a reactionary attempt at revivalism should come to nothing. It is customary to talk of Tudor or Georgian architecture but Ottoman architectural fortunes more than any other were inalienably linked with those of the ruling family and their household. The türbe or mausoleum of the last sultan of any conceivable importance, Mehmet V Reşat, at Eyüp, therefore, can be seen as the last monument in that style, a style which in the sixteenth century had achieved monuments which were the wonder of the world.

Note on Turkish characters, spelling and pronunciation

So AS TO BE CONSISTENT, modern Turkish spelling (but mainly in the nominative case) is employed throughout this book, and Turkish terms are used where necessary. Where names are frequently used in English the familiar form of spelling is adopted; thus Istanbul and Iznik are written without a dot on their capital letters, and pasha and kiosk are spelt in the Western manner. The Turkish language is in a continual process of change and its spelling and usage here cannot claim to be either fashionable or expert: it seeks to be rational.

THE FOLLOWING TURKISH CHARACTERS ARE USED:

ç	pronounced *ch* as in church
ğ	lengthens a preceding vowel
ı	is akin to the pronunciation of the *u* in radium
ö	is pronounced as in the German word *König*
ş	is similar to the *sh* in shall
ü	is as the German *ü* in *Führer* or the French *u* in *tu*

OTTOMAN SULTANS	POLITICAL EVENTS		ARCHITECTURE	
Osman Bey, 1281–1320(?)	1308	Break-up of Selçuk Empire	1331	Süleyman Pasha Medrese,
Orhan Bey, took title of	1321	Ottomans reach Sea of Marmara		Iznik
Sultan, 1324(?)–62	1326	Orhan Gazi takes Bursa	1333	Haci Özbek Cami, Iznik
Murat I (Hudavendigâr, or The	1349	Ottomans cross into Europe	1334	Orhan Cami, Iznik
Ruler), 1362–89	1361	Murat I captures Edirne	1339	Orhan Cami, Bursa, begun
Beyazit I (Yıldırım or Light-	1371	Ottomans reach the Adriatic	1365	Hudavendigâr Cami, Bursa,
ning Beyazit), 1389–1402	1378–85	Ottomans occupy Anatolia		begun
		from Kütahya to Amasya	1370	İsa Bey Cami, Selçuk
	1389	Murat I's victory at Kosova	1376	Ulu Cami, Manisa
	1390	Ottomans establish a navy	1390	Yıldırım Complex, Bursa,
		in the Aegean		begun
	1397	Yıldırım Beyazit enters Athens	1396	Ulu Cami, Bursa, begun
Süleyman, İsa, Musa, Mehmet	1402	Beyazit defeated at Ankara by	1419	Yeşil Complex, Bursa, begun
dispute the throne until		Timur who overruns Ottoman	1437	Üç Şerefeli Cami, Edirne, begun
Mehmet I prevails, 1413–21		Anatolia	1452	Rumeli Hisar, Bosphorus
Murat II, 1421–44 and 1445–51	1448	Murat II with the second	1463–70	Fatih Complex, Istanbul
Mehmet II (Fatih or The		victory at Kosova consolidates	1472	Çinili Kiosk, Istanbul
Conqueror), 1444–5; 1451–81		Ottoman power in the Balkans	1484	Beyazit Complex, Edirne, begun
Beyazit II, 1481–1512	1453	Ottomans take Constantinople	1486	Beyazit Cami, Amasya
	1481	Revolt of Beyazit's brother, Cem		
Selim I (Yavuz the Inexorable;	1509	Great earthquake in Istanbul	1501–6	Beyazit Cami, Istanbul
in Europe known as Selim the	1517	Conquest of Syria and Egypt	1518–20	Fatih Pasha Cami, Diyarbakır
Grim), 1512–20	1521	Süleyman I takes Belgrade	1536	Hüsrev Pasha Cami, Aleppo
Süleyman I (known in Europe as	1529	The first siege of Vienna	1543–8	Şehzade Cami, Istanbul
the Magnificent), 1520–66	1537	Raids on Puglia and Corfu	1550–6	Süleymaniye Complex, Istanbul
Selim II (known in Europe as	1555	Peace of Amasya (with Persia)	1562–5	Mihrimah, Istanbul
the Sot), 1566–74	1570	Capture of Cyprus	1567–74	Selimiye, Edirne
Murat III, 1574–95	1577	War with Persia renewed	1586	Muradiye, Manisa
Mehmet III, 1595–1603	1589	Mutiny of the Janissaries	1597	Yeni Cami, Istanbul, begun
Ahmet I, 1603–17	1622	Janissaries depose Osman II	1609–16	Sultan Ahmet Cami, Istanbul
Mustafa I, 1617–18	1623–40	Murat IV restores order and	1639	Baghdad Kiosk, Topkapısaray
Osman II, 1618–22		captures Erivan and Baghdad	1663	Completion of Yeni Cami,
Murat IV, 1623–40	1648	Janissaries depose Ibrahim I		Istanbul
Ibrahim I, 1640–8	1683	Second siege of Vienna		
Mehmet IV, 1648–87				
Süleyman II, 1687–91				
Ahmet II, 1691–5				
Mustafa II, 1695–1703				
Ahmet III, 1703–30	1730	Murder of Sadrazam Damat	1728	Ahmet III Fountain, Istanbul
Mahmut I, 1730–54		Nevşehirli Ibrahim Pasha and	1748–55	Nuruosmaniye Cami, Istanbul
Osman III, 1754–7		deposition of Ahmet III, after	1759–63	Laleli Cami, Istanbul
Mustafa III, 1757–74		popular uprising against taxes		
Abdülhamit I, 1774–89		and Western ideas		
Selim III, 1789–1807	1766	Great earthquake in Istanbul		
Mustafa IV, 1807–8	1824	Massacre of the Janissaries by	1800	Rebuilding of Eyüp Sultan
Mahmut II, 1808–39		Mahmut II		Cami
Abdülmecit, 1839–61	1894	Severe earthquake in Istanbul	1826	Nusretiye Cami, Istanbul
Abdülâziz, 1861–76			1853	Dolmabahçe Saray, Bosphorus
Murat V, 1876				
Abdülhamit II, 1876–1909				
Mehmet V, Reşat, 1909–18	1922	Deposition of the last Sultan	1918	Türbe of Mehmet V Reşat, Eyüp
Mehmet VI, Vahdettin,				
1918–22				

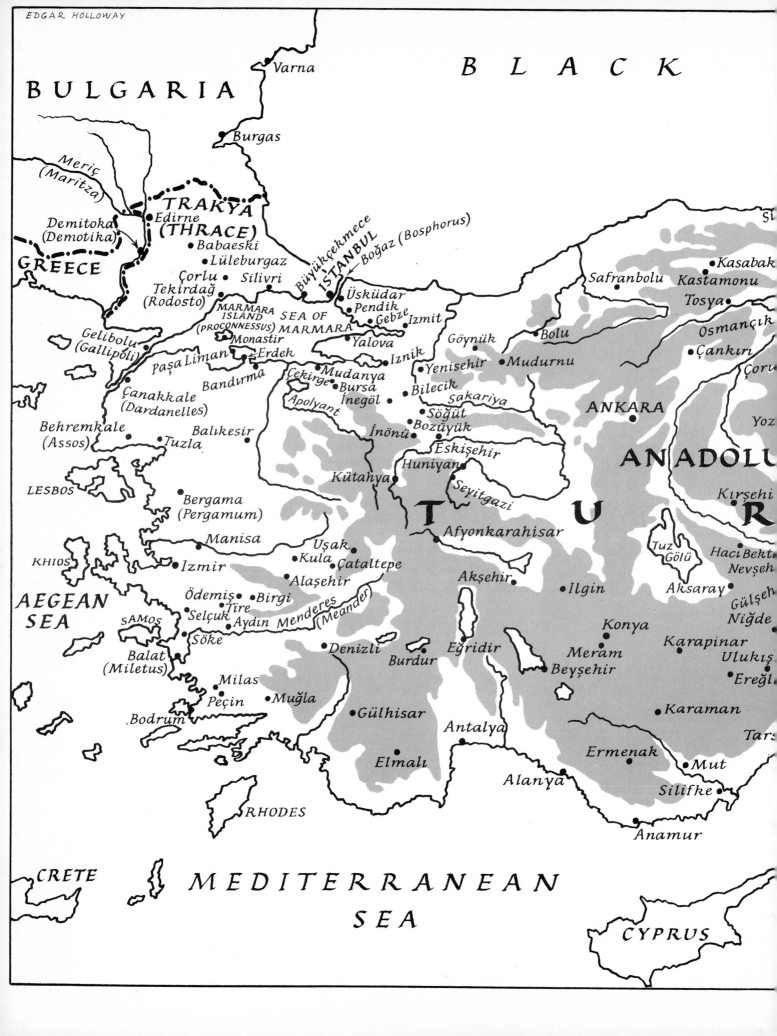

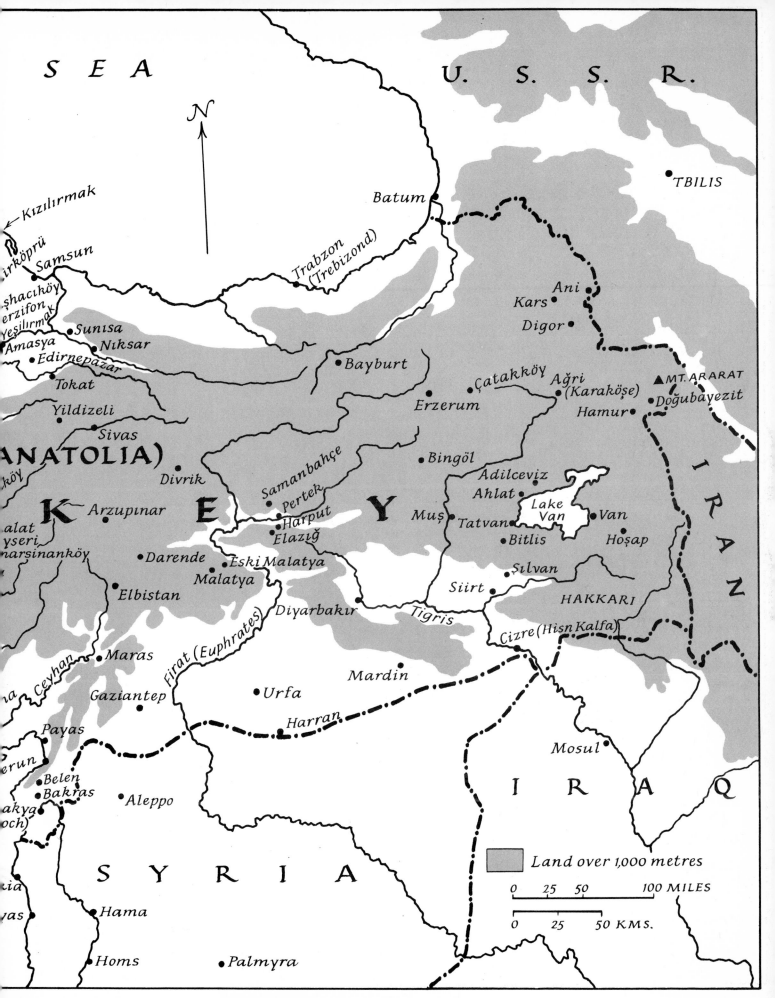

SEA

U. S. S. R.

Kızılırmak

·TBILIS

Batum

Trabzon (Trebizond)

irköprü

·Samsun

·Ani
Kars
Digor

shacıköy
erzifon
Yeşilırmak

·Sunısa
·Nıksar

·Bayburt

Çatakköy Ağri (Karaköşe) ▲MT. ARARAT

·Doğubayezit

·Amasya
·Edirnepazar

·Tokat

·Erzerum

Hamur

·Yildizeli

·Sivas

·Bingöl

(ANATOLIA)

·Divrik

Samanbahçe

Adilceviz
Ahlat

köy

K ·Arzupınar **E**

Pertek

Lake Van

Y

·Van

alat
yseri
marsinanköy

·Darende

·Harput
·Elazığ

·Muş Tatvan

·Hoşap

·Bitlis

·Eski Malatya

·Malatya

·Şılvan

·Siirt

·Elbistan

Diyarbakır

HAKKARI

Tigris

IRAN

na

Ceyhan ·Maras

Firat (Euphrates)

Cizre (Hisn Kalfa)

·Gaziantep

·Urfa

·Mardin

·Payas

Harran

erun

·Mosul

·Belen
·Bakras

·Aleppo

I R A Q

akya
och)

S   **Y**   **R**   **I**   **A**

as

Land over 1,000 metres

·Hama

0   25   50   100 MILES

·Homs   ·Palmyra

0   25   50 KMS.

Anatolia, showing the chief sites of Ottoman architecture

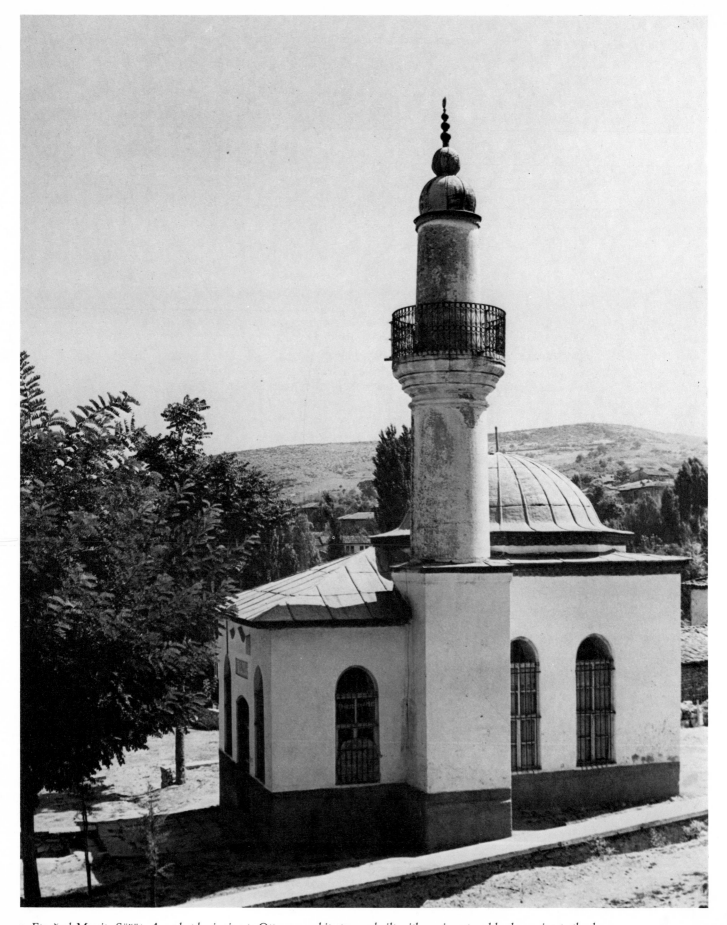

1 Etruğrul Mescit, Söğüt. A modest beginning to Ottoman architecture, rebuilt with a minaret and lead covering to the dome.

I

Before the capture of Bursa

THE DISINTEGRATION OF THE SELÇUK STATE in the late thirteenth century and
the convulsive condition of Anatolia under Mongol emirs resulted in the break-up
of the region into small communities attached to local leaders; but Ibn Battuta
shows that travel was still possible and some trade survived, although both were
greatly reduced. The guilds also preserved the basic skills necessary for the continuation of a simplified form of civilization. They were as much responsible for
its survival as were the monasteries in the Dark Ages of the West and they had a
religious significance bound up with the concept of chivalry which was related
to the socialistic Brotherhood of Virtue and which made guildsmen members of
the Ahi sect.

The oldest emirate was that of the Menteşe who won their lands on the western coast round Balat[1] by attacks from the sea, for they had first been pirates
based on Antalya. Others were the Karacı Hans who had control of the Dardanelles, the Germiyan at Kütahya, and the Candarlı, who were to unite with
the Ottomans, towards the Black Sea. The leading emirs were the Karamanlı
who won the old Selçuk capital of Konya and whose architecture was rich but
conservative, the Saruhan at Manisa, and the Aydınoğulları[2] who ruled the rich
Meander valley and who dared to raid the Balkans.

If Islamic Anatolia was weak, so was the Byzantine Empire and in the conflict
of small units lay some of the same creative stimulus that thrived in Renaissance
Italy. The Turkish beys or princes built modestly, but it was out of the cross-
fertilization of their styles that the Ottoman arose.

The Ottoman story starts at Söğüt, a small town set back into the hills. There
is the türbe of Ertuğrul[3] which is now rebuilt and larger, perhaps, than it was
originally. There also is his mosque which has been replaced by a nineteenth-
century structure built by Abdülâziz in an attempt to glorify his family. It faces
a large school of the same period. These buildings have lost their significance but
a brief walk from the centre of the town, across a brook bordered by mulberry
trees, is Ertuğrul's mescit which stands upon a small mound. This too has been
altered and restored, domed with lead in place of tiles, and whitewashed. Large
windows have been cut into the thick walls and the interior is light and fresh.
Nonetheless, this building has an authentic atmosphere because it is so small; yet
the interior is fittingly lofty to be the oratory of a champion of the Faith.[4]

The spiritual leaders of the people of Turkestan and eastern Anatolia, şeyhs
and dervishes, were there to cheer the Ottomans on, for they had been driven
out by the Mongols, whose invasion of Asia they had fiercely resisted, and who
did not tolerate their unorthodox beliefs. The early Ottomans were not bar-
barians; nor were they conservative, yet tradition was, one might say, to be the
most prominent Ottoman architect at all periods. They had the natural demo-

1

cracy of soldiers who share dangers, and were uninhibited by the laws of their faith concerning wine and the subservence of women. Ertuğrul's grandson Orhan[5] married a Greek princess whom he left in control at Bursa when visiting his five hundred towers and castles. The Ottomans themselves tended not to be architects or artists, but they succeeded in imposing their concepts on those who built for them; and at this stage of their rapid advance to imperial greatness, they had on their side the Brotherhood of Virtue. The clubs or zaviyes of these Ahi artisans and merchants were evening meeting places where hospitality was offered to travellers and where refugee dervishes found particular comfort. The Ahi lived his own family life but pooled his income with his fellows and was united with the Gazis, the traditional Moslem warriors of the frontiers, and with the dervishes by their mutual subscription to the canon of rules by which the Islamic mystical life could be led.[6] Their meeting houses, which also served as hostels, could have one room or several. They were the centres of provincial life and even government, and were a serious check on the despotism of a local lord. Ibn Battuta[7] speaks warmly of his reception at Alanya on his arrival in Anatolia and again of the hospitality of other houses of the brotherhood at Gülhisar, Denizli, and Bursa among many other towns.

At this period the Ahis were important to the Ottoman Gazis because they followed in the rear of the victorious armies,[8] took over such strategic points as crossroads, and established civil rule – besides effecting the conversion to Islam of those who might be acceptable. At Konya, Battuta lodged in the hospice of a Young Ahi who was the governor of that city.[9] Ahis had, moreover, to travel to the capital, which was wherever the sultan's horsetails were flying, to report and to co-ordinate the administration of the new provinces. They were essential to the development of the early Ottoman state, the supreme stabilizing element. But they were the enemies of the orthodox doctors of the sacred laws, the Ulema, to whom their banqueting, singing and dancing was anathema. After the conquests of Iznik and Bursa, the building of law schools, or medreses, threatened their supremacy but, because Ahi and dervish ideas fed on older beliefs than those of Islam and incorporated the symbolic drinking of wine and other practices, they continued to have a strong hold on the conquered people and on the soldiers: the notorious corps of Janissaries were members of a guild and spiritually led by the Bektaşi dervish sect.[10] The Ahis also became the trade guilds of the empire, retaining until recent times a number of mystical practices and still trading fraternally and individually rather than in a Western commercial style.

There is neither medrese nor zaviye at Söğüt, but the Ertuğrul mescit still stands. It has a tiny forehall before the room[11] for prayer, entered through a tall rounded arch with a window on each side. On the right of the entry is a well. Water, significant for any traveller or nomad, was particularly so for a Moslem, and even more for those who came from Shamanist Asia, for water was one of the five sacred elements; waterworks were highly developed in Transoxania, as they were later to be by the Selçuks and the beys of Anatolia.[12] This well, therefore, meant more than just the ritual cleansing of the worshipper before he prayed to his god; it also represented refreshment, and was therefore symbolic of a zaviye and of the portico or son cemaat yeri, the place of prayer for late-comers which in the hot south can act as the summer mosque. The inner room is in the form of the domed square of the Zoroastrians, which survived the Arab invasions of Iran. The perfect circle set in the perfect square is symbolic of heaven, of eternity (for a circle has neither beginning nor end) and of the universe with its four corners. Under the dome at Söğüt it would be difficult for more than twenty people to pray but here is the nucleus of all Ottoman architecture.[13]

The road from Söğüt to Bilecik runs for thirty kilometres through undulating hills with views over the Sakarya valley to the mountains and the gorges where the crags are made for strongholds. It is scenery of great beauty and it was good grazing land for Ertuğrul's flocks. At Bilecik, his grandson Orhan was to build a royal mosque which was destroyed in an earthquake but built again and, in spite of the more recent tremor damage, still stands. It is probably later in date than his mosque at Bursa but earlier in plan.[14] It is at Iznik[15] that the first Ottoman mosque with an inscription survives, that of Hacı Özbek, dated *734/1333*. It is noteworthy that the zaviyes of Iznik are bigger than any of the mosques of the town, all of which are small. This was because upon capturing the town in 1331, Candarlı Kara Halil Pasha immediately converted the large church of Hagia Sophia into a mosque in accordance with custom.[16] The city shrank back from its beautiful lake and became a village well within the Roman walls. Orhan's army was still an intimate troop of comrades although success and the panache of the Ottoman Gazi life attracted more and more adventurers. Candarlı and Mikhaloğlu, the renegade, formed an early aristocracy and a detachment of the Catalan Company of mercenaries sent by the Byzantines to destroy it, instead joined the Ottoman cause.

The interior of Hacı Özbek Cami is nearly eight metres square[17] – not much bigger than a large drawing-room.[18] It has suffered from restoration and the building of a hideous porch but its essential form survives. The dome which is a little too large to be a true hemisphere is supported on a belt of Turkish triangles as sharp as arrowheads.[19] It sits very low in the manner of the time so that one is immediately aware of its dimensions and always conscious of it above one's head. The mihrab niche, which is off the true kıble axis,[20] is set between two slightly lower bays. The mosque is well lit by five casement windows at lower level[21] and three set in the belt. There is no upper window on the west because here was the original portico, wantonly destroyed when the road was widened in 1939. It was unorthodox for this portico not to be placed on the north side of the mosque, but this variation occurs elsewhere at this period, noticeably at the Akça mosque at Ermenak dating from *700/1300* although there it is more a place for summer prayer than a son cemaat yeri.[22] The destroyed portico of the Hacı Özbek mosque had three bays with pointed arches[23] carried on two marble columns with Byzantine capitals. The door, preceded by a groined cross-vault, was in the north corner; the other two bays were covered by a barrel-vault.[24] There were walls with wide niches on either flank to protect those praying there from the weather when the mosque was full or the door was locked.

The logic of structure is constantly exploited in the development of Ottoman architecture not only creating useful, intimate areas such as small eyvans between piers or in the deep recesses of casement windows, but also governing the decorative forms. Niches economize in masonry and also form useful sofas for the repose of the faithful or the poor. They had been the centre of life in a Turkish yurt or home in Central Asian times.[25] In effect, a sofa or mastaba is any form of platform for sitting or kneeling on; it can become a bed or can form the floor of a portico and the core of a prayer hall. It is the equivalent of the early Chinese K'ang, a two-foot-high brick platform across one end of a room raised as a protection against the winter cold. This was warmed by flues running under it. Stiff cylindrical cushions, called yastık in Turkish, were used for arms and back. Nobody in Eastern Asia except the Chinese used chairs before modern times.[26] The Mongols used carpets and the Iranians used cushions and divans. The influence on architecture of this lack of furniture is marked, for instance on the height of windows. Floors had to be clean, and preferably polished for fear of splinters,[27] wood was preferred to stone which can be cold and damp; shoes had to be removed, so as not to make dirty the place where one sat (so that shoes with laces would have been tedious), and robes had to flow over extended knees.[28]

The walls of the Hacı Özbek mosque are of cut stone flanked by single bricks and sandwiched between three courses of brick. Although the Umayyads had used this formula at the palace at Anjar, it seems in this case to derive directly from Byzantine models. Externally, the dome is covered with terracotta tiles moulded specially to face a spherical surface and this was the rule with early Ottoman buildings although many have since had their tiles replaced by leaves of lead. The Ottomans had a variety of tiles and bricks of different shapes; the Byzantine brick was of standard size and had if necessary to be broken to fit, but it was superior to the Ottoman in quality whereas the Byzantine mortar was not.[29]

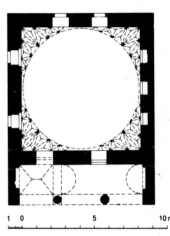

1 0   5   10 m

2, 3 Hacı Özbek Cami, Iznik. Plan (scale 1 : 250) and exterior view. The portico, which was destroyed when the road was widened, accounts for the dissymmetry. Many roof tiles are original.

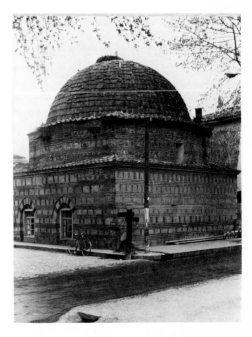

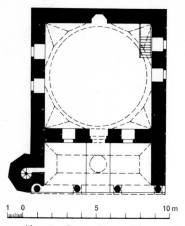

4 *Alaettin Cami, Bursa. Plan, scale 1 : 250.*
The irregularity is probably due to repairs.

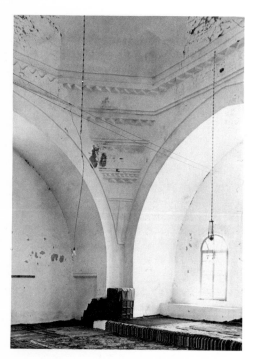

5 *Orhan Gazi Cami, Bilecik, showing the*
springing of the arches. The mihrab wall is on
the right.

In Karamania, the tradition of stone domes of Byzantine and Armenian times, such as can be seen at Binbirkilise, continued until after the Ottoman conquest for stone was a traditional material of the Anatolian plateau. The domes were supported by corbels and squinches of Iranian and Central Asian derivation, the pendentive being primarily a Byzantine form.[30]

The single-domed mosque reached early perfection during the reign of Alaettin Bey. This prince, the brother and vezir of Orhan Gazi,[31] built his mosque at Bursa *736/1335* after its capture by the troops of the dying Osman, who was to be buried in a Byzantine chapel in its citadel.[32] The interior of the mosque is 8·20 metres square[33] and the walls, which are over a metre thick,[34] are pierced by pairs of casement windows at lower level on all but the south side where one window is set above the mihrab niche. There is no other recess. The dome is carried on a belt of sixteen triangular planes. With these early mosques, the dome is like a lid on walls pierced for light; later, pier and buttress brought about a new conception of architectural structure, and space was found for fenestration between dome and wall. The near-perfection of the Bursa mosque lies in the simplicity with which an ideal space is expressed. A curious deformity is caused by the east and west windows not being set opposite each other, but this is due to the major restoration of 1862 (there was another restoration in 1890). The door is set in the centre of the north wall on the mihrab axis. The portico is formed by four columns with Byzantine capitals creating three bays with three lightly pointed arches and it was once surmounted by a decidedly Greek pediment added during the restoration of 1862,[35] which misled both Kızıltan and Gabriel.[36] It has now been rebuilt in what may have been its original form of a triple saw-edged cornice. The portico is covered by a long, flat-topped barrel-vault, with a small central dome which can be seen from outside above the roof level. This feature was much used by the Ottomans, but externally the odd little dome is a weak element both here and when more elaborately developed at the Yeşil Cami at Iznik. When seen from within the son cemaat yeri it makes a satisfactory, indeed, noble accent. The portico is walled on the west and on the east masked by the minaret, which is set on a brick and stone base and is entered from the portico. The shaft is brick and the triangulated supports of the şerefe or gallery are unusual. If this is the original minaret, then it is the first known Ottoman minaret still complete,[37] but the octagonal base is set at an awkward angle and is weakened at the north-west corner to accommodate the fourth column, so it is likely to be a later addition.

The mosque of Orhan Gazi at Bilecik represented a notable advance in size and in the understanding of structure. The prayer hall measures 14·30 × 15·30 metres along the axis of the mihrab, and the dome is approximately 16·50 metres in height.[38] This mosque is twice as big as that of Alaettin or Hacı Özbek, possibly because there was no large church which could be converted. But its central area is only 9·50 × 10·50 metres; the extra space is due to the depth of the recesses – four metres square – under the four great arches which spring from the prodigious corners of the building.[39] The wall is approximately 10·50 metres high and the dome 6·00 making a total of 16·50 metres from the floor to the crown of the dome, which is close to the golden mean. This proportion recurs in Ottoman architecture, which is not surprising since the geometry and algebra taught in the medreses and the palace school were Greek in origin. Were it not that the central area under the dome on the kıble-entry axis is a metre longer than it is east to west, it would form a perfect square.[40]

The slightly elliptical dome is set on a low octagonal drum which rides on broken pendentives and not the usual triangles. There is a large window with a smaller one set above it on the east and west sides and two large windows flank the mihrab which has a small one over it. This became traditional. Partly because of the whitewash, the mosque is filled with a pleasing soft light. The massive thickness of the walls was a precaution which was not misplaced in an area subject to earth tremors. It results in wide recesses which extend the interior giving an air of spaciousness added to the loftiness of the dome, while the springing of

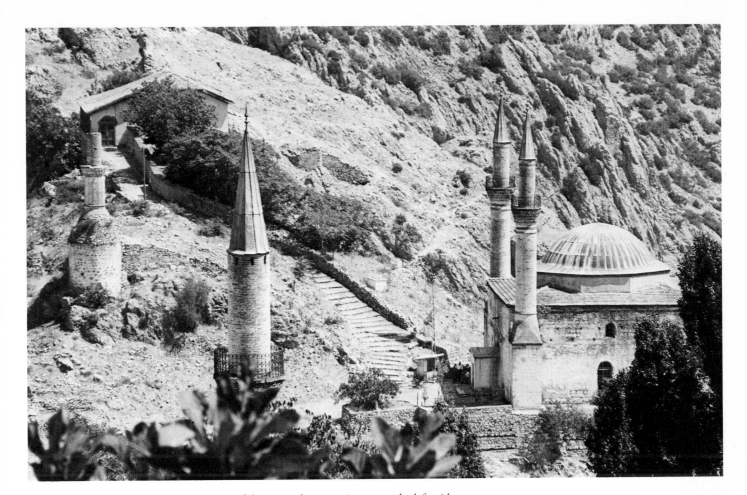

6 Orhan Gazi Cami, Bilecik. The stump of the original minaret is seen on the left with the tekke above. The twin minarets and the porch are nineteenth-century additions.

the arches from floor level awakes a sense of movement and grace. Across the south wall on each side of the mihrab niche is a solid stone bench for rows of candles. This occurs in other mosques even as late as the Abdülâziz Cami at Söğüt built in the latter half of the nineteenth century.[41] The shallow, low recess cut into the springing of the arches is also interesting because it will become the richly carved Bursa arch, discussed on page 48, with the building of Yıldırım Beyazit two generations later. Moreover, the four strong corners of this mosque are forerunners of the four independent piers of the classical, centralized mosque such as Şehzade. The area under the south arch, before the mihrab, is raised and so set apart from the rest of the mosque.

6   There is no trace of a portico and the minarets are later than 1882.[42] The original minaret, built fifty or sixty years after the mosque, stands in ruins on a rock to the north. Its base is remarkably thick in relation to its shaft and this accounts for its survival. The şerefe, according to Ayverdi,[43] is the oldest one of the Ottoman type known, but the minaret of Orhan's mosque at Yenişehir may be older.[44] Only the base of his minaret at Gebze appears to be original. The Orhaniye at Bilecik is built of brick and stone courses which alternate irregularly – one course of stone, one of brick, then one of stone and three of brick. It is set above a ravine, on the opposite side of which, among the trees of a little plateau, is an imaret or hostel with a kitchen. It has no inscription or date and is in a state of ruin, but was once a building of great size, consisting of a double-domed hall with two flanking chambers behind a five-domed portico. If these are the remains of Orhan's building, it is the grandest imaret of the period both because of its dimensions and the remains of the decoration; the building covered an area approaching 190 square metres and the carved plasterwork was clearly elaborate with patterns on a grand scale. The principal domed unit inside is approximately eleven metres high

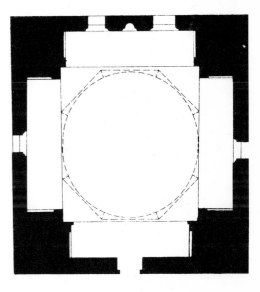

1 0   5   10

7 Orhan Gazi Cami, Bilecik. Plan, scale 1 : 250. The deep recesses under the arches introduced a new dimension to Ottoman architecture.

and the floor 6·60 metres square, proportions which are close to those of the golden mean as are those of the dome itself, when combined with the chevron friezes five metres high, in relation to the wall which is eight metres.[45]

On the neighbouring height, commanding splendid views over the verdant but craggy landscape, is a tekke, frequently repaired, with a sepulchral chamber housing the tomb of Şeyh Erdebalı under a slightly oval dome. The tekke is built largely of wood and has a deep porch instead of a portico, together with three other rooms, one of which is used as a mescit for women. Some steps down from the little entry hall is a very small masonry türbe containing the graves of two of Orhan's aunts. The setting is ideal for a dervish retreat, above but not apart from the world. Although it stands among trees, there is today no single grand tree such as dominates the zaviye of Doğin Baba at Kara Belen or the Geyikli Baba Sultan Zaviye, where there are also symbolic stags' horns.

Orhan drove westwards and conquered Assos, on the Aegean coast, where a mosque somewhat larger than the one at Bilecik was built or converted from an existing church. There is no inscription, but it is likely to be the work of his son, Murat I for, like his mosque at Bursa, it bears the royal name of Hudavendigâr. Here the dome is eleven metres across, a remarkable achievement.

The Yeşil Cami or Green Mosque at Iznik shows several new developments. It was built between 780/1378–794/1391 by Candarlı Kara Halil Pasha, prince in his own right, one of the first to bear the title of pasha (paşa), and founder of a hereditary line of first vezirs. It is the first surviving Ottoman mosque of which the architect's name is known:[46] it was Hacı bin Musa; but no more than his name is recorded.[47] The mosque was mauled in the 1922 war which destroyed the geometrically patterned balustrades and miniature stalactite[48] window-frames[49] of the portico. The frame of a false door to this deep son cemaat yeri area is set in the central arch as it is at the basilica of the Studion or of the Kilise Cami at Istanbul. The portico is roofed by three flat-topped cross-vaults but the dome in the central bay before the door is tall and fluted, riding on a high octagonal drum of plaster cut sharply in a diamond pattern, recently restored, and pierced by four windows. The arch of the door springs from four sets of stalactites reminiscent of the şerefe of the Alaettin Cami and it is flanked by two fine antique columns.

On entering, there is a vestibule of three bays, again with flat-topped cross-vaults and a second small dome, with the same diameter as that of the portico but less lofty and ending with a lantern. Two very thick columns with heavy stalactite capitals bear the three pointed arches which divide the vestibule from the hall where the dome (11 metres in diameter) is carried on a belt of triangles. The marble revetments on the wall reach to a height of 3·30 metres[50] and the finely chiselled mihrab is also of marble. There are ten casement windows at

8 Yeşil Cami, Iznik.
The ornate false door to the portico.

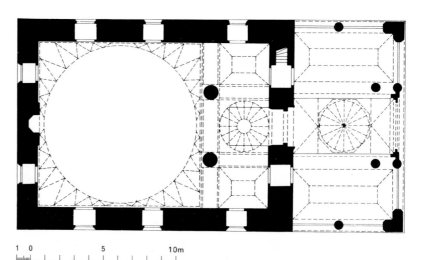

9 Yeşil Cami, Iznik. Plan, scale 1 : 250. The prayer hall and the portico interlocked under the gallery by the forehall.

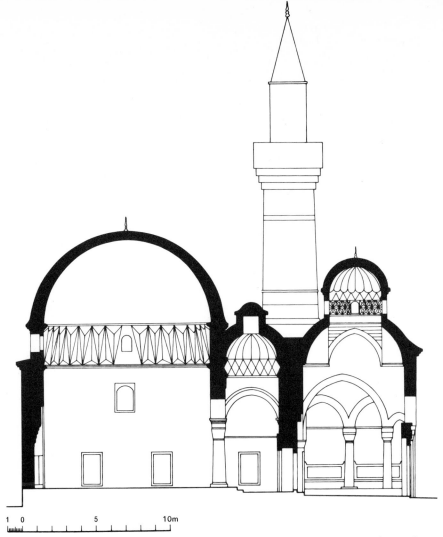

10 Yeşil Cami, Iznik. Elevation, scale 1 : 250. The sophisticated division of space does not arrest the ritual drive towards the mihrab. The rise and fall of the domes adds a new rhythm.

ground level, two right and left of the door and of the mihrab, three on the east and west walls which have an additional light above; and there are also three windows in the drum of the dome. The effect is noble but cumbersome.

The Yeşil Cami is unique among fourteenth-century mosques in having the drums of its domes exposed internally and in having part of the weight of the main dome supported on columns. Again the architect was cautious, which is why he made these piers so sturdy. The addition of an ante-chamber opening on to the prayer hall extends its length and provides a gratifying pause before entering the harem, adding to one's appreciation of the relatively lofty dome (17·50 metres) above one. The architect has organized his plan so that the area of the portico and the vestibule together equals that of the prayer hall, thus creating a unity between the exterior and the interior at the expense of some confusion in the organization of the extra long vaults of the portico. The lateral columns between pier and wall fit comfortably in the centre but the pairs of central columns and the door-frame in between cause confusion. The framing of this space is odd and gives one the curious sensation of stepping out of the world through a mirror into another dimension.

The windows at casement level were not glazed and probably not all the upper grilles for light had bottle glass in either. An interesting feature is the external expression of the inner frieze of triangles by a simple pattern on the outer face of the drum. This drops to the next course of stones when it meets with each of the three windows. It is, indeed, a true drum but not Byzantine in feeling because it is not circular but has sixteen facets. There are thin reinforcing buttresses with relieving arches at each corner. Outside, the mosque is built of ashlar stone.

An interesting rosette is carved into the east wall and the lateral windows have ornate dogtooth frames.

The minaret is set in the north-west corner of the mosque which was by this period the rule. It is reached by means of the window west of the door up stairs set in the thickness of the wall, which is more than two metres thick because of this, i.e. one-third thicker than the other walls. The restoration of the minaret has been catastrophic. The beautiful matt-surfaced original tiles whose thick slip oozed and undulated over the bricks have been replaced by the most vulgar machine-shop, commercial glazes from Kütahya. The patterns of chevrons of green, blue and red which encircled the trunk have lost their quality.

The dome of the Yeşil Cami, which is five metres high, combined with its frieze of 2·60 metres is close to half the total interior height of 15·50 metres. The wall is just 7·90 metres high. This relationship occurs earlier with the Orhaniye at Bursa and at Gebze. It occurs again with the massive Yıldırım Cami at Mudurnu where the dome height and the wall height are each 8·50 metres. Another excellent example is the tomb chamber of the Hayrettin Pasha Türbe at Iznik p 71 where dome and drum combined are half the height of 12·50 metres. These ratios are related to the concept of the perfect circle in the perfect square which was to continue into the period of Sinan and after. The Yeşil Cami floor area is in the proportion of three to two and so are the two bays of the portico. The two to three relationship is a common one and can be seen in the floor area of the Orhan Gazi at Izmit or the relation of dome to wall height at the Hudavendigâr at Tuzla. At the Nilüfer Hatun İmaret at Iznik, the courtyard dome and frieze p 44 are also related in proportions of two to three to the height of the wall. On the other hand, the proportion of the height of the mihrab of the Yeşil Cami (5·20 metres) to the total height of the wall is quite different: five to eight.

While the Ottomans were developing their particular mosque form from the limited concept of a domed square towards a deeper intellectual approach to the division of space, building in the other Beyliks also evolved. The old ulu cami

11, 12 Yeşil Cami, Iznik. The mutilation of the window frames has weakened the façade. The minaret is still Selçuk in form.

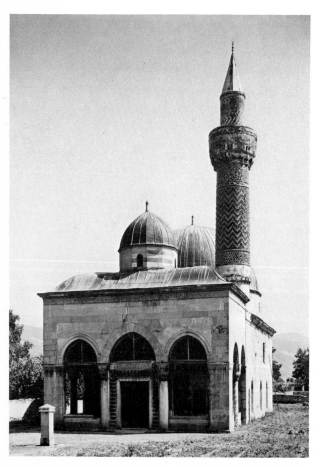

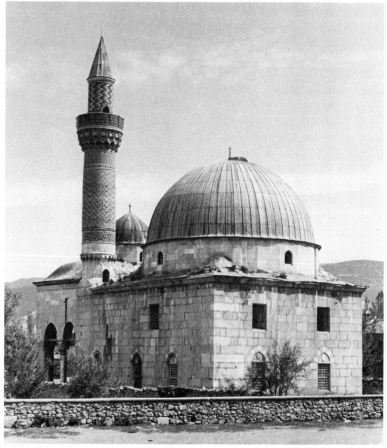

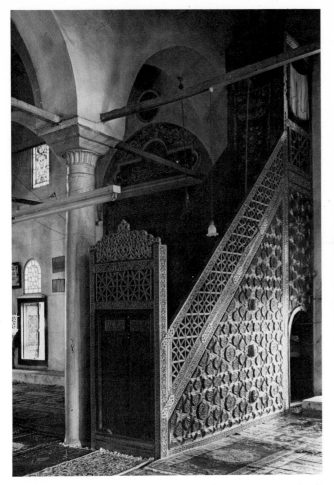

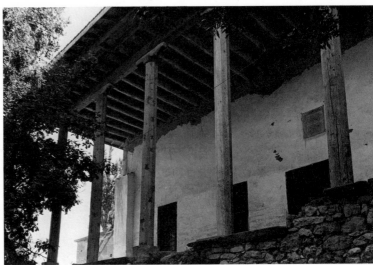

13 Ulu Cami, Birgi. The wooden mihrab with a re-used column and capital.

14 Meram Mescit, Konya. The wooden portico, in the tradition of Central Asia and Iran.

form was slowly dying even in the Karamanoğlu lands. The Ulu Cami at Ermenak, *700/1300*, with its three aisles running east-west belonged to the Damascus type except for the porch, which reappeared at Iznik, as we have seen, with the Hacı Özbeck Cami. But as late as 1376, or thereabouts, the Arapzade Cami at Karaman was built with ten stone piers and two columns making four aisles. It also had inside stairs to the minaret in the Selçuk manner and as late as *840/1436* the Dikbaşan Cami, also at Karaman, was similar in form.[51] Smaller versions abounded, e.g. the Akça mescit at Ermenak where the columns were reduced to two posts like poor relations of the Yeşil Cami at Iznik. In *800/1402–*
14 802/1404, the Meram mescit near Konya had three rows of three posts and a vestibule besides a portico looking out over the valley. It is an agreeable country mosque but cannot compare with the Ulu Cami at Birgi built for the Aydınoğullar in *712/1312*[52] with its four rows of four columns[53] and its domed sanctuary before the mihrab, rich with the last manganese black and turquoise tiles in the
13 Selçuk style. The stars in the magnificently carved minber and shutters of walnut wood were picked out in yellow paint, probably in the nineteenth century, but possibly following an old tradition since such delineations in paint occur on minbers elsewhere including that of Süleymaniye in Istanbul. The effect at Birgi is lively although the paint is crude and the varnish worse. In accordance with tradition, the carving of the shutters gets finer the nearer it is to the mihrab. A high portico precedes the steep descent into the mosque through the restored north door, and the mihrab glowing at the end of the shadowy vista is impressive after the daylight outside. The east flank on to the square is decorated in carved stone in the manner of the Gök medreses of forty years or more before. Opposite the mosque is a modest and much restored medrese still used as a school. The family türbe which has an inscription dated *734/1334* is set on the west side of the mosque and overlooks the gorge down which the town spreads. It, too, is much restored but its proportions are as grandly spacious as those of the mosque.

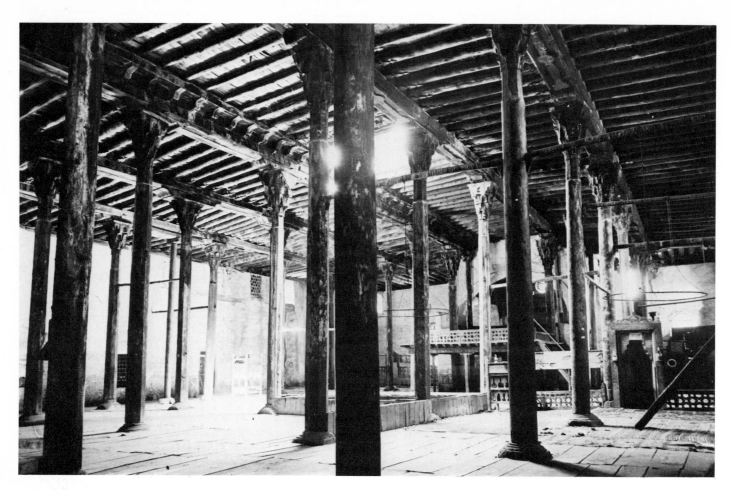

15 *Eşrefoğlu Cami, Beyşehir. View towards the mihrab from the north-west.*

The greatest of the wooden Beylik mosques is the Eşrefoğlu Süleyman Bey Cami at Beyşehir by the broad lake with its romantic islands. Its portal and its elegant fountain inset in the wall retain the master carving of the Selçuk era. The great door, set at an angle, opens into the north vestibule, strikingly like a narthex, from which stairs lead up to the gallery and the minaret. Two doors admit to the body of the mosque from which there is access to the türbe on the east. The court in the centre aisle has been reopened, but glassed over, thus recreating the original light effects among the six groves of columns. Thus far it will be seen that it is a mosque in the Selçuk manner but its wonder is in the magnificent use of wood. It is more of a forest mosque[54] than any other in Turkey, for not only are all the columns and their capitals (now replaced by copies) of wood but so are the furniture, the large galleries and the dramatic balustrades. Light filters through the high columns (7·50 metres), both from the central aperture and from the many windows set high up in the walls under the flat roof, like sunlight through a glade onto an autumnal floor, which is covered with some of the most interesting kilims still to be used in a popular mosque. The dark wood is a proper setting for them while the mihrab glows grandly back with the turquoise, black and white of tiles which were almost the last of their type. The front rank of the mosque is screened by a bold fence with high doorways both sides of the harem before the mihrab, beside which is a splendid wooden minber of the period; while the müezzins' mahfil, or singing gallery, stands immediately before the mihrab supported on four of the nave piers with one extra central post beneath. To the west, a long flight of stairs leads up to the emir's box which is screened almost to the level of the capitals. At the back is the gallery over the north vestibule. The eye moves fascinated from level to level and the mihrab, with its stars does indeed seem to be the great gate to the universe. The centralization of the müezzins' mahfil was to be exploited by Sinan for quite different reasons in the Selimiye at Edirne. Also significant was the mihrab area dome which is inset under a conical roof. This reappears in Ottoman architecture and is discussed later.[55]

After a time one is intensely conscious of stars everywhere – star formations in the tiles of the inner doorway into the mosque and of the mihrab; little four-pointed stars formed by the interlacing chevrons of the rail of the müezzins' mahfil; eight-pointed stars made by the double square pattern in one part of the south fence, and by interlacing sun-wheels in another; intensely brilliant central stars in the panels of the royal lodge; and a milky way all over the minber. The interlacing of wooden wheels to form stars and other patterns are all part of the visual vocabulary of Islam; but here it is spoken with astonishing clarity. All together they express that dualism which is a force of Ottoman creativity: the clash between orthodoxy and mysticism.

Among other wooden mosques the much repaired Ulu Cami at Bayburt is related to the Eşrefoğlu but is smaller and simpler. Its mihrab dome reverts to the most primitive type and is built up on layers of beams laid across the angles of diminishing octagons until the roofing can be completed by a single beam.

The mosque of the Mongol emir of Eretna, Sungur Bey,[56] at Niğde has suffered from restoration as well as from the lack of it.[57] The plan has been altered, but its basilica form must always have been unusual and closely related to the very beautiful Selçuk Alaettin mosque of the citadel above it. There is plenty of decoration and ordering of the structure which is Selçuk, from the magical animals on the door to the placing of the türbe. The design of the windows is
16 Gothic in feeling and in fact they are directly related to those of the monastery of Bellapaise in Cyprus. Wheel windows are not Selçuk in origin[58] although round windows appear at Armenian Ani in the seventh century and in Ottoman
38 architecture as early as the Süleyman Pasha Medrese at Iznik.[59] It is possible that stonemasons from Cyprus were brought over to assist in the building of this mosque since there is a significant inscription relieving the strangers of taxation.[60] This could only be due to a lack of local craftsmen resulting from the turbulent state of Anatolia, but it does show that Christian workmen had nothing to fear by working for a Moslem – if this particular Mongol lord were a true Moslem – and that there was practical intercourse between the cultures in the fourteenth century.

The tendency to width in the larger mosques of Karamania has been noted and two little Karaman fourteenth-century mosques in Niğde, the Şah Mescit and the Hanım Mescit, reflect this trend. It is not found elsewhere and when it came to Ayasluğ and Manisa it took a very different form. Among the wooden mosques of the Candar family at Kastamonu there was a contrary liking for length, and four out of the six more important mosques built between 1363 and 1454 were of this long type. They are modest enough, yet are important as fore-runners of the Candarlı Yeşil Cami at Iznik. In 765/1363, Halil Bey built the mescit at Kemahköy.[61] It has a small portico and then a long prayer hall with a central window at ground level east and west and, oddly enough by comparison with the Ottoman tradition, two small windows above each central window set slightly northwards and so out of true.

20 The Mahmut Bey Cami at Kasabaköy dates from 768/1366[62] and, although similar in plan, is more interesting. It has suffered various additions at later dates including a second tier of small galleries on the east and west of the north wall. The mosque is a rectangle due to the gallery and the narthex beneath being part of the square area before the mihrab, and there are four central piers to support the roof. The north pair abut the gallery which has four slender piers to support it. The piers have splendid wooden stalactite capitals and carry two large beams running the length of the mosque. These support two tiers of avenues of brackets, which cantilever the support outward to carry a phalanx of smaller traverse beams down the centre of the ceiling. Brackets are used between the piers supporting the gallery to create hipped archways and the narthex is balustraded off.

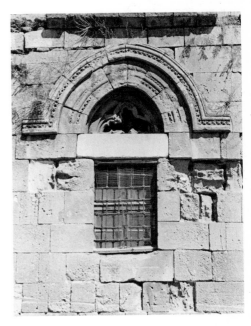

16 Sungur Bey Cami, Niğde. Side window with Gothic elements.

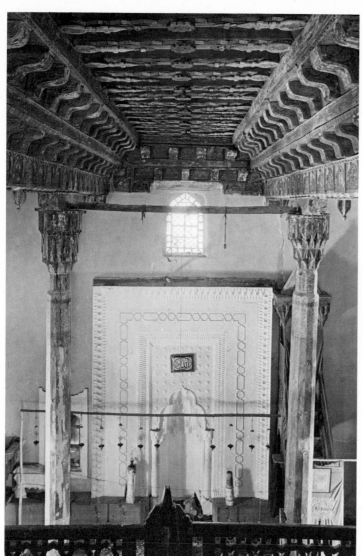 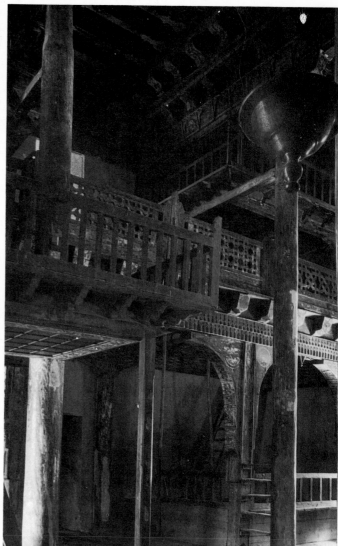

17, 18 Mahmut Bey Cami, Kasabaköy. The mihrab and galleries.

The diagonal of the stair up to the gallery across the right side of the north wall adds a new dimension and the balustrade of the gallery is projected on a line of consoles. At ceiling level there is a pelmet of three shallow stepped arches. The beams are ornamented by fretwork devices which begin as circles and end as fleur-de-lys; and in the centre are hexagonal stars; the balustrade follows traditional Islamic interlocking patterns. Under the roof along the walls is a frieze of foliate arches in miniature. Everywhere the woodwork is richly painted in orange, red and blue and some of the circular designs contain devices of heraldic importance while in places there are hints of heads and faces. The large mihrab is flanked by pillars and a wall of shallow stars above; it is set in a large plaster frame with successive bands of ornament in shallow relief. In such a small and intimate room the emphasis on height and axial movement is very powerful and the richness of the woodwork and its paint[63] adds nobility and splendour. The relationship to Beyşehir is discernible particularly in the design of the main piers and their stalactite capitals. The portico is inset between windowless walls under the shed roof of the mosque and has a new minaret on the north-west side. Four wooden columns support the traverse beam above and there are sofas on each side. The door is small but of very fine workmanship and there is a small window at roof level above it. The later mosques of Beyköy and Küreihaditköy follow the tradition in simpler form with minor variations.

19

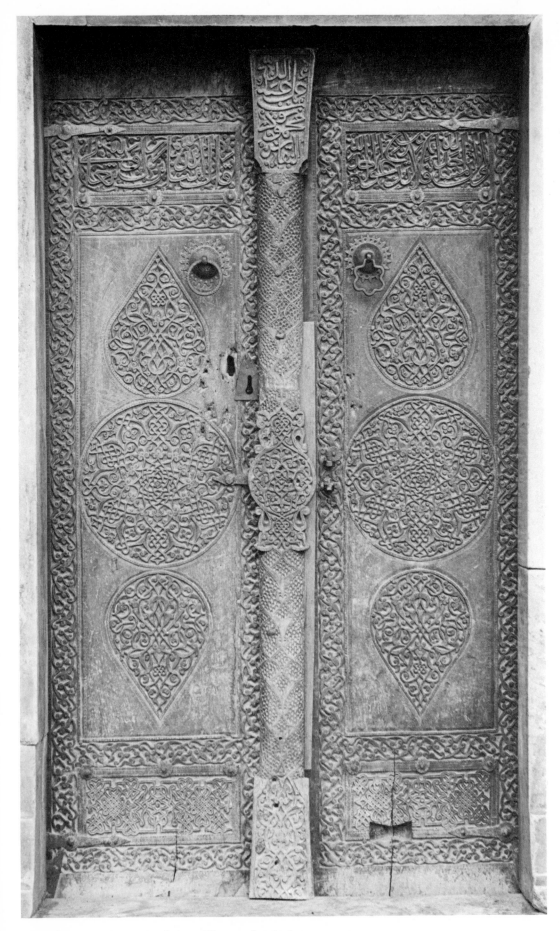

19 Mahmut Bey Cami, Kasabaköy. The carved main door.

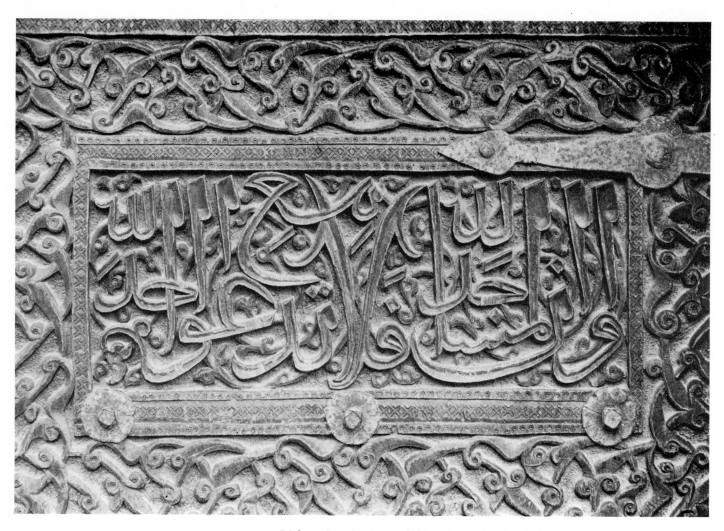

20 Mahmut Bey Cami, Kasabaköy. Detail of an inscription on the main door.

There are a few other long-naved mosques such as that of Ahmet Gazi at Milas dating from 780/1378,[64] which is of the ulu cami type or, even, a converted church. It has eight supports for the roof and three longitudinal aisles. The interesting array of dome and cross and barrel vaults have been covered up by a new ceiling.[65]

Of all the foundations belonging to the Beylik period, that of Gazi Ahmet Bey, in ruins, on the height of Peçin within sight of Milas, is the most romantic. The buildings are set on a separate knoll outside the walls of the little town which crowns a conical hill. It is a green haven with fine trees shading brooks and rivulets, and has become a retreat for mystical contemplation; the tomb of the Gazi is tended as a Sufi shrine. The path leads up to a modern cistern and along a stream which forms a little moat along the north side of the two-storey medrese, still close to the Selçuk style. Steps act as a bridge and one enters by the back door into the eyvan which is also the türbe. The walls of this medrese were once cut stone. Little trace is left of the upper floor except for the stairs in the south corners. There are four cells each side of the eyvan and two each side of the principal entrance opposite, which has now been walled in. The portal has a good if small stalactite half-vault in the Selçuk manner and the cell doors are also of excellent workmanship. The cells were barrel-vaulted. The dome of the türbe was originally of stone, but has been repaired in brick, and was supported by pendentives. A second grave under a tree is walled round and placed in the northeast corner of the courtyard which is small and intimate, and must have felt more so when the upper storey still stood. A great variety of five-stones boards and chessboards, adding to the mystical atmosphere their perpetual questioning 21

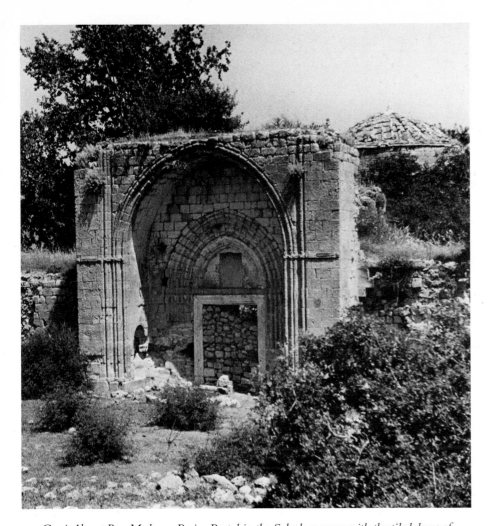

21 Gazi Ahmet Bey Medrese, Peçin. Portal in the Selçuk manner with the tiled dome of the eyvan-türbe behind.

of fortune, have been engraved on the steps and even on the çeşme which is north-west of the medrese amid criss-crossing streams full of green-faced frogs.

South-east of the medrese is the ruin of the gateway, built of re-used Byzantine material including a relief of peacock and grapes, opening into the complex which must once have been walled; beyond this is a square brick-domed hamam and the remains of what was probably a mescit. Farther south is a large building which was a two-storey han, the lower floor barrel-vaulted and the upper probably triple-domed, with the main door in the centre of the west side beyond the outside stairs to the upper storey. It is a very grand building indeed and fit to be a palace. The domes are supported on triangular squinches which spring just above the level of the floor. The east and west walls have a parade of strong buttresses. There is no other han of this form in existence, and the setting of Ahmet Gazi's tomb in the eyvan of the medrese is also extraordinary. Although the mysticism which is so strongly planted there now is in part due to its dilapidated state and the beauty of the meadow and the stream beneath old trees, its association with dervish and other heretical sects may date from its building in 777/1375.[66]

The really fertile mosque plan remained the square and is naturally mostly to be found on Ottoman territory, such as the Hoca Yadigâr Cami at İnönü dating from 776/1374. Inside, this mosque is kin to the Orhan Cami at Bilecik, but the east and west windows are gracefully grouped, with the upper ones centred between the lower casements. On the south side, there is a window above the mihrab, as one has learnt to expect. The recesses are shallower but help make a more spacious setting than is found in the more pedestrian single-domed

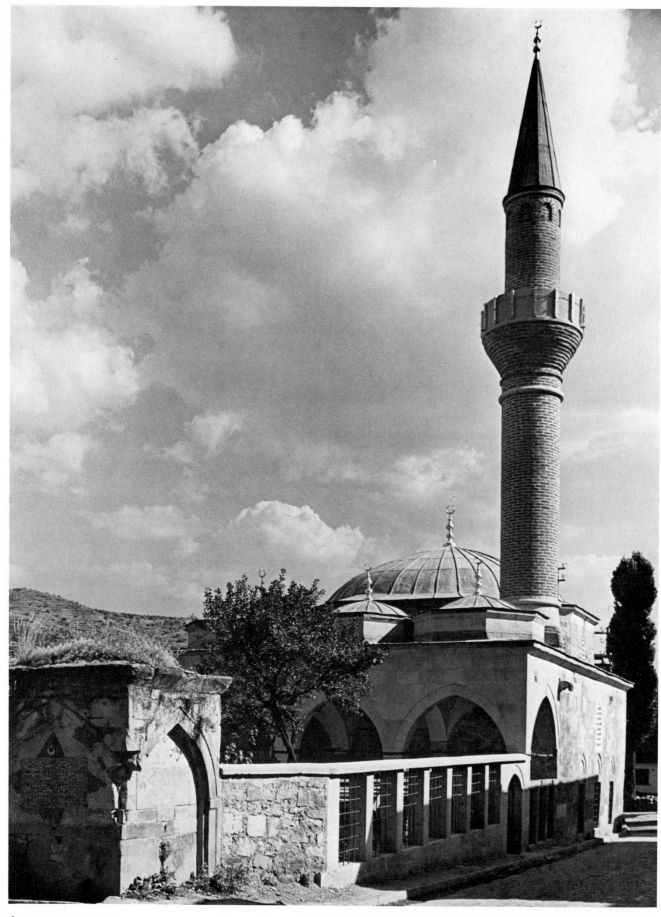

22 İbni Neccar Cami, Kastamonu. The brick minaret has been restored in the Selçuk manner, but the triple-domed portico is a newer style.

mosques. The cupola is borne on pendentives, perhaps due to restoration. Outside, it sits on an octagonal drum which carried a tent-style tile roof. Here, too, the minaret's base is almost as high as its trunk and şerefe. It is set into the north-west corner and half incorporated in the wall. There is now no portico but only a platform and an external mihrab niche beside the east window flanking the central door.

22   In 754/1353[67] İbni Neccar Dülgeroğlu built a very small square mosque at Kastamonu with a triple-domed portico open at the east end while the west faces on to the street and so is masked by a triple lattice window. The main dome and those of the portico are inset in tiled conical roofs which stand upon polygonal drums. The minaret is incorporated into the north-west corner of the mosque and the stairs are cut into the added thickness of the north wall as are those to the gallery on the north-east side of the central door. The 8·50 metre dome is carried on semicircular squinches which were to be accepted as part of the canon by Sinan. Moreover, the mosque has a surprising number of windows in comparison with its contemporaries. There are casements cramped between the central door and the minaret and gallery stairs, and three on each flank with two each side of the mihrab. There is also an upper window above the middle casement on the east and west and one on each side of the octagonal drum of the main dome, making sixteen in all. In front of the portico is an open area which presages the return to the courtyard.[68]

At Afyonkarahisar and Kütahya, the square-domed type was well established. At the former, the Kubbeli Cami dates from as early as 732/1331 when it was under Germiyan rule.[69] The room (7·30 × 7·40 metres) has a dome under a conical roof carried on a decagonal drum. The door is set off-centre, because of the north window, and the workmanship is of the simplest. These little neighbourhood mosques multiplied both at Afyon and Kütahya, added porticoes and minarets and also ordered their windows more exactly. The Ak Mescit at Afyon built in 780/1379[70] is set on a hillside; instead of a portico it has, because of the landfall, a fine flight of eight stairs leading up to a door set on the west flank. A short minaret with internal stairs is stuck on the south-east shoulder for the same reason. The Kurşunlu Cami at Kütahya, built in 779/1377,[71] has a three-bay portico with domes on each side of a central smooth-topped cross-vault. The arches are more pointed than usual and carried on piers, not columns, and the step up to the area comes immediately after the entry. The minaret, comparatively thick and lofty for so small a mosque, is on the north-east and reached by internal stairs. Its name, Kurşunlu, suggests that its tiled domes were early replaced by lead. The exigencies of the uninspired plan result in the central dome of the portico being lower than those which flank it and in the arch being narrower, while the north windows cannot be central in their bay or inside they would be too far to right and left. This was to continue to be a problem with

166 small mosques and will be discussed in relation to the Firuz Ağa Cami in Istanbul.[72]

,24   There remains one example of particular beauty at Balat, amid the ruins of the ancient city of Miletus, founded by İlyas Menteşeoğlu in 802/1404 to celebrate his return from exile at Timur's court.[73] It could have been built by masons of the same school as was responsible for the carving in the Firuz Ağa mosque at Milas. The ruins of the ancient city of Miletus supplied the marble with which it is dressed but the fresh carved Islamic motifs are particularly fine. The walls are over two metres thick which makes it pleasantly cool in hot weather and the windows are organized in pairs, as large above as below, on the east and west walls and on each side of the mihrab above which a smaller opening occurs. The upper windows have fine grilles made up of radiant spokes. The dome is fourteen metres in diameter and is thus one of the largest of the Beylik period. It is partly marble and partly brick and is carried on four arches, set in the flanking walls, and four squinches across the corners, which are composed of a row of chevrons, a row of small stalactites, and, on top, a shallow shell. Sprung between the eight shoulders of these arches are eight arcs above a fan of three stalactites. This

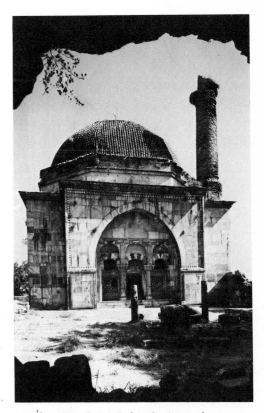

23 *İlyas Bey Cami, Balat. Owing to the climate there is a screen wall instead of a portico.*

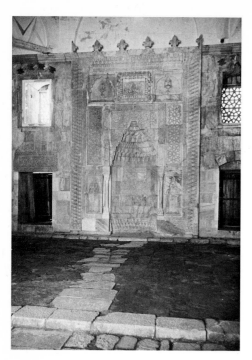

24 *İlyas Bey Cami, Balat. The mihrab wall.*

elaborate band occupies a quarter of the wall area under the eighteen-metre-high dome and begins only four metres above the floor. The dome, therefore, is basically low, in the tradition of the time. The walls have marble revetments to the springing of the arches; they have to be thick to carry so much weight. The grandiose marble mihrab (7·37 × 5·15 metres)[74] is carved with hanging lamps each side of the inscription over the niche and surrounded by a four-tier stalactite frame. It is surmounted by a nine-tier arch with bold cresting. The handsomely carved walnut minber has been removed to the new mosque in the rebuilt village. The window frames are also carved, particularly outside where some carry stone inscriptions foreshadowing the calligraphic tile of the sixteenth century. The façade is unique in Anatolia. A broad portal frames a great arch beneath which are set three framed, hipped and stilted arches carried on columns with interlocking voussoirs in alternating coloured marble. In the centre is the door to the right and left of which are marble grilles so that cool air may circulate continually. This, in disguised form, is the usual window on each side of the door of less exotic mosques. Under the deep arch there are niches in each side, while steps ascend to the central door. Remains of glazed tile and inlaid marble decor occur in the window frames and façade, and various bosses and stars in the walls are related to similar emblems at Bursa. The brick minaret is reached by a broad entry in the north-west corner of the mosque. In front of the building is a large paved court flanked by a series of domed buildings all in decay and set haphazardly.[75] But here is the germ of the concept of the mosque and medrese sharing the same court with a şadırvan, though the well is not in the centre of the group of buildings and thus the ruined fountain looks as if it were a later addition.

By the fifteenth century it had become orthodox in all Beylik territories to set the door in the centre of the north façade on the axis of the mihrab. When deviations occurred it was because of the terrain. This was evidently the case with the Akça mosque, but the Sungur Bey main door follows the precedent of the Alaettin Cami in the citadel. At Ermenak, in Karaman domains, there was a trend towards irregularity, for even where the door was set on the north side, as at Sipas Cami, it was opened well west of centre and the son cemaat yeri was on the west flank. The two doors into the Ulu Cami there were on the east and west. But out of some forty representative mosques built between 1300 and the mid-fifteenth century, thirty-five possess central doors.

The span of the dome was doubled in the period between the building of the Kubbeli Mescit at Afyon, *732/1331*, where it averaged 7·40 metres, and 1404 with the fourteen-metre dome of İlyas Bey Cami. The dome of Emir Sultan at Bursa, originally built between 1366 and 1429, is 15·20 metres wide but it is not certain that the proportions of the present building are exactly those of the old. During the fourteenth century the achievement of a diameter of eleven metres was a considerable task and the approximately twenty-metre dome of the Yıldırım mosque at Mudurnu (*784/1382*), is exceptional and is carried on thick walls which distort its proportions. If this mosque and that of Emir Sultan are excluded, then the first dome to reach fifteen metres is that of the Yeşil Türbe at Bursa in 1425. There was nothing to rival it until the astonishing achievement of the twenty-four-metre dome of Üç Şerefeli Cami in the middle of the fifteenth p 97 century. It is noteworthy that elliptical domes appeared in Ottoman architecture as early as the Orhaniye at Bilecik. They continued to occur whenever structural problems demanded them.

Triangular dome supports eventually gave way to the Byzantine pendentive. They were best exemplified in Selçuk times by the splendidly elegant tiled fans which support the dome of the Büyük Karatay Medrese at Konya, but were capable of many modifications including equilateral and isosceles triangular forms. Moreover, they were set at a slant so that a sense of the circular, one following upon the other, could be achieved. Squinches were more rarely employed and then mainly in Candarlı mosques.

The placing of minarets at the north-west corner was not yet established, although common. Sometimes there is the impression that minarets could wander where they pleased like queens over a chessboard. The staircase minaret[76] of Hacı İlyas Bey Cami at Milas, dating from *730/1330*,[77] rising up the length of the left flank of the building, is an elaboration of a very humble type. The Ulu Cami at Birgi has its minaret set at the south-west corner and the Akmescit at Afyon has it at the diametrically opposite end, in the north-east. This and the north-west were the commonest positions. Many minarets were detached completely from their mosque as has been seen with the first, built for the Orhaniye at Bilecik, which stands thirty-five metres up the hill. Twin minarets did not

93 appear until the İsa Bey Cami at Ayasluğ. In Selçuk times the entry to the shaft had usually been from inside the mosque and always through the base. During the fourteenth century the door moved out into the portico or into the open entirely. A considerable number of mosques could afford no minaret at all and many which now have minarets did not have them originally. It is significant that even a royal mosque such as the Hudavendigâr at Assos first made use of a natural shelf in the hill nearby to avoid the expense and skill required in building these elegant towers.

96   The courtyard was hesitantly reappearing in the form of a more or less defined
93 space in front of the mosque but was not established clearly until the İsa Bey Cami and the Ulu Cami at Manisa were built in the 1370s. The early mosque porticoes tended to be walled in at the ends, doubtless for protection against wind and dust, or else the minaret base acted as a wall. Indeed, the first, that of the Ulu Cami at Ermenak, dating from *702/1302* is a room with a loggia forming a western extension to the mosque.[78] A few were walled on one side only and windows also developed at the end, while completely open son cemaat yeris occur at Karaman in the Akçasar mosque, the Akmescit at Afyon, the Ulu Cami at Birgi and also at Kastamonu, Iznik and Bursa. Some mescits had no porticoes at all.

A significant type, resulting from the gradual disappearance of the forest hall type of ulu cami, was the mosque with four centrally grouped columns. This is a simplification of the centralized plan, derived from domestic houses,[79] which had begun in Iran and in Central Asia as long before as the early eleventh century with the Degarron Cami at Hazar in the province of Bokhara.[80] It was to reach its apotheosis in the Şehzade Cami in Istanbul, the first major work of Sinan. The Kasabaköy mosque was an example of this form and the Hacıbeyler Cami at Karaman, along with the Kemerosu Kebir Cami at Ermenak, approached it.

Nothing that the other Beyliks built was seminal, although they might have stimulated the enrichment of Ottoman forms, particularly in the Saruhan and Aydınoğullar provinces which were soon to be conquered or overrun. The next positive step could only be the expansion of the domed unit, which was to be initiated by Orhan Gazi and his remarkable wife, Nilüfer Hatun, at Bursa and at Iznik, as the logical response to the needs of a strong central government as well as a victorious army. It is to the first major mosque built in Bursa, then, that this enquiry must now turn.

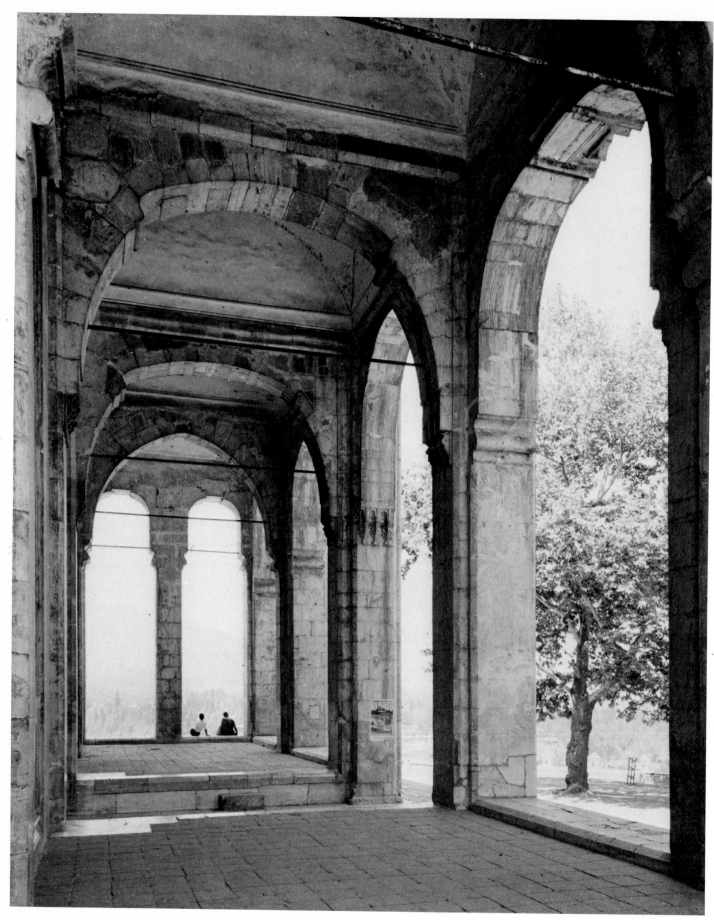

25 *Yıldırım Beyazit Cami, Bursa. The first major Ottoman portico.*

2

Bursa – the first mosques

ON THE SLOPES OF ULUDAĞ, or Mount Olympus in Asia, is the first true capital of the Ottomans, Bursa, the city that Osman was only to enter after his death to be re-buried in a chapel in the palace grounds on the heights of the citadel. He lived long enough to learn that it had fallen to his son, Orhan, in 1326.[1] The capital was still, officially, the place where the Khan pitched his tent or the castle he happened to be visiting, but during his absences much of the business of government was conducted from Bursa by his wife, Nilüfer Hatun.[2] Here was a city worthy of a victorious dynasty. The citadel was nearly impregnable, and on the many spurs along the mountainside successive princes were to build their own palaces and neighbourhoods with medreses, imarets or soup kitchens, hamams and türbes set about the central mosque.[3] The sarays were built of wood and none has survived.[4] Each looked down on the broad well-watered plain, rich with trees, that formed the stomach of a wealthy province. The city has falls and streams which divide its quarters, and in its centre below the citadel is the great market where Yıldırım Beyazit built the Friday Mosque. Here was one of the most important trading posts in Anatolia and the centre of the silk industry. The Ottomans had revenue now with which to build in style.

Orhan's palace was in the citadel[5] but he built his royal mosque in the market. It is descended from the Selçuk medrese type which approached its end with the Cacabey Medrese at Kırşehir, in 1272.[6] This medrese was built round a court with a large pool under a dome which was open to the sky, for like the Büyük Karatay Medrese at Konya its waters reflected the stars and it was possibly an observatory.[7] The building is divided into cells and rooms and eyvans without much symmetry, but it is based on the four-eyvan type of medrese which evolved in the Friday mosques of Isfahan, Ardistan and elsewhere;[8] introduced from Horasan, it represented the universal Asian concept of rooms set round an inner court. The ideal form of such a college is the Gök Medrese at Sivas where the centre of the court is formed by the cross-axis of the four eyvans. The southern eyvan forms the dershane and the northern the vestibule, while the lateral eyvans can be used for classes or meditation in summer. The Cacabey Medrese is set in the heart of dervish country where the traditions are so much alive that even a stranger today can become aware of their emotional continuance.

It was with the dervishes and the Ahi brotherhood in mind that Orhan built his zaviye-mosque in Bursa in 1339.[9] It was burnt down by the Karaman horde and quickly restored by Beyazit Pasha (who built his own mosque in Amasya) for Çelebi Sultan Mehmet I[10] in *820*/1417. The Orhaniye was severely damaged in the earthquake of 1855 and restored by Parvillée for the vali, Ahmet Vefik Pasha,[11] in 1864. There was another restoration in 1904 but the basic plan does not appear to have been greatly modified.

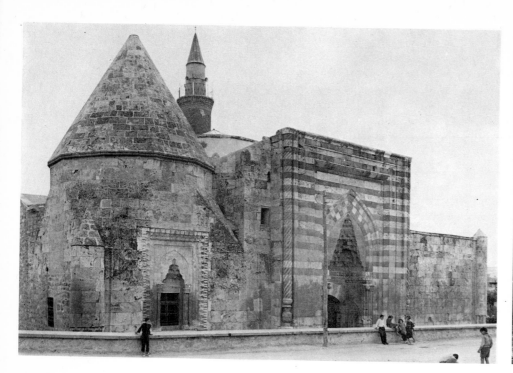

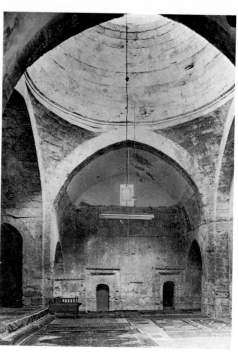

26, 27 Cacabey Medrese, Kırşehir. The view, left, shows the türbe and the great door, between which the rim of the once open dome of the inner court can be seen. Right: interior view of the medrese.

The door admits to a small but loftily domed vestibule which represents the shrivelled remains of the northern eyvan.[12] Inner halls left and right lead to narrow chambers which are lit by windows on to the portico and have doors to the eyvans. From the central vestibule one enters the inner court, the dome of which $(8\cdot45 \times 16$ metres)[13] is now closed but it may once have been partly open over a pool beneath. It is set on a band of triangles broken by eight windows. On either side of the court are domed eyvans, one step up from the court, made rectangular by deep arches on their north and south sides. On the south, and two steps higher, in order to emphasize its detachment, is the mosque itself.[14] Excluding the area two metres in depth below the pointed arch, this hall is $9\cdot30 \times 8\cdot60$ metres and the dome is therefore oval; but it is likely that the ceiling was vaulted, at least until the fifteenth-century repairs following the raid on Bursa. The dome is supported by squinches filled with trihedral designs which, significantly, form five-pointed stars. Three windows are pierced in the dome and the prayer hall is lit by pairs of casements with smaller windows above them in the east and west walls and on each side of the mihrab. The eyvans could be used for teaching and debate and also as tabhane rooms[15] for Ahi and dervish pilgrims and administrators, just as could the smaller rooms which would be warmer in winter.[16] It could be that these were small because travelling would be restricted during the rainy season. I believe, however, that most of these rooms were part of small dervish convents or tekkes, a point which will be discussed in relation to the mosque of Beyazit Pasha at Amasya.[17]

p 78

An important formal relationship is maintained between the higher dome of the court and the lower dome of the prayer hall, for the string-course, which is the base of the frieze, or drum, of Turkish triangles which support the courtyard dome, also forms the upper rim of the frieze of the inner hall. It is likely that, when the court dome still had its oculus or lantern, the unifying light effect, which Le Corbusier noted in his sketchbook before the First World War, was apparent at the Orhaniye. The court dome is brilliantly lit by the aperture and the ring of windows in the drum, while the floor area is in soft shadow, for it receives its light from the eyvans and the prayer chamber. But the prayer hall has a dim dome and is well lit at floor level, so that the movement of light and shadow from north to south crosses where the two halls meet. The courtyard area is nearly nine metres wide while its dome is sixteen metres high and so approximates to the golden mean; the frieze and dome together are six metres high and the wall height is ten metres, a proportion of three to five which again approximates. The wall of the prayer hall reaches 6·75 metres which is the height of the dome and frieze together. The dome, with an height of 13·50 metres in relation to the floor area of 8·75 also approaches the golden mean.

The portico has five bays with three middle domes and cross-vaults at each end. The arches are supported on stone piers but the rest of the building is of alternating courses of stone between three layers of brick. In the upper corners at each end of the façade are sun discs in brick and these recur, together with brick rosettes, on each side.[18] The central arch is taller and narrower than the rest, and a lively three-dimensional surface is achieved by dog-toothing. The remaining arches are equal in dimension, those right and left of the main arch have alternating courses of brick and stone for voussoirs while the end arches are lightly dentilated. The severe rectangular casements are shallowly recessed under arches and the doorway is modest. The large wing arches are divided into two by a Byzantine column and base, and a chequerboard pattern enlivens the inner tympana. Externally, the windows are set in relieving arches; this is characteristic of architecture in Bursa. The central dome of the portico is raised higher than those on its right and left which emerge from barrel vaults. The wing vaults are even lower. Behind them, the large eyvan domes can be seen while the court dome in the centre is raised over all on a high octagonal drum. The resulting impression is one of bubbles rising and falling, which gives a sense of movement to the mosque. The minaret is a nineteenth-century construction set awkwardly at the north-east corner. It is clear, from the plan, that there is no strengthening of the wall anywhere, unlike the mosques studied in the last chapter, and it is reasonable to assume that originally there was no minaret or that it was an independent structure set in front of the mosque.

The Orhaniye is the first of the Bursa-type T-plan mosques. It developed logically in the same way as the zaviye had done. It was not an ulu cami, or Friday mosque for all the town, but the court mosque and convent and it was essentially a formal arrangement of independent units. A small version, possibly built in 735/1333,[19] but more probably a century later, was the beautiful Yeşil Cami or

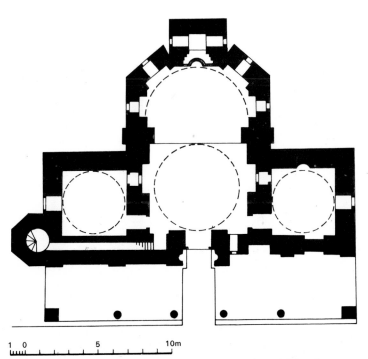

28

1   0   5   10m

28 *Yeşil Cami, Tire. Plan, scale 1 : 250. An example of the elementary zaviye-plan with hostel rooms right and left of the forehall and an unusually recessed mihrab.*

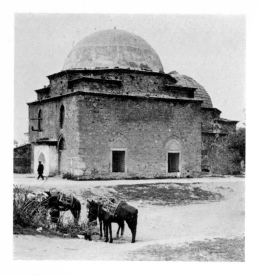

29 *Hacı Hamza Hamam, Iznik. An early Ottoman bath illustrating the versatility of the domed unit.*

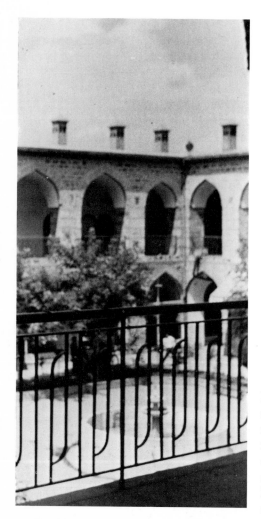

30 *Bey Han, Bursa. Looking across the heavily restored courtyard towards the Ulu Cami.*

Zaviye at Tire which has over the mihrab at the south end, the first half-dome (albeit of shell formation) in Turkish Anatolia.[20] Externally it is expressed not as a half-dome but as half a polygon. The mihrab itself is a remarkable plaster screen set forward from the actual niche like that of the Great Mosque of Cordova.[21]

The combining of several domed units was the turning point of Ottoman architecture. The desire to create unity of space and form was inevitable from that moment, however long delayed it might have been.

In conjunction with his mosque, Orhan built two hamams and an imaret which has vanished.[22] The Eski Hamam has been rebuilt after a fire but the Bey Hamam remains, although much restored, more or less as it was in 1339.[23] It is the first recorded Ottoman hamam and already orthodox in plan.[24] It was a double bath until the restoration of 1934[25] and the surviving section for men consists of the usual camekân or dressing-room, a soğukluk or cool-room with a privy, and a domed chamber off it, and a cross-form harara or hot-room with a central dome and four private hücre or cells for depilation at each corner. The user hung his towel over the entry to show when one was in use. At the end, serving both sections, were the furnace and the water-tank. The women's section was a modest version of the men's.

Orhan also built a fine han, the Bey Han, which has suffered from earthquake and fire and bad restoration alike.[26] It was originally a very grand building indeed, almost square (45 × 50 metres) with a stable at the rear. While the door into the stable from the great court is central, the great gate into the han from the street is set slightly to one side and is therefore off the true axis, the centre of which is marked by a hexagonal pool. The thirty-six cells of the ground-floor are sheltered by a colonnade which supports the covered gallery in front of the thirty-eight cells of the upper storey. One cell on the ground floor is recessed to take two latrines and this device is repeated immediately above them on the first floor. The south-west corner of the stables was mutilated to make room for the second minaret of the Ulu Cami at the beginning of the fifteenth century. The great gate has a niche with a sofa on each side for the gate-keeper to relax in by day and there are even larger sofas just inside the doors. These doors were of wood and studded with coach nails. A postern was cut into the right-hand panel in the traditional manner. In between the outer arch and the rectangular door-frame was a pattern of small crosses. The han was built of courses of rough-cut stone between double layers of brick set between thick mortar. The lower cells were for storage since they possessed no windows, but those at the upper level had one each – except for those at the corners which had three – and also a fireplace. They were reached by stairs cut in shallow eyvans which masked the porticoes. The lower arches were round while those above were ogee in shape, and both these and the arch of the gate had brick voussoirs. The long, shaded vaults of the upper storey formed attractive vistas. The domes of the lower floor were built in a series of spiralling brick courses descending to a decorative ring of small arches with a herring-bone pattern just above the crown of the arches. These are Byzantine in style. Externally, the lines of small chimney flues added an interesting dimension to the bold façade of this austerely grand building.

The original medrese which used to stand here has disappeared and the oldest Ottoman medrese still standing is that of Orhan's son Süleyman Pasha at Iznik.[27] His vezir, Candarlı Kara Halil Pasha, was appointed kadı or Chief Justice of Iznik upon the capture of that city and he had converted a monastery to a medrese but now a building newly built for the purpose was opened.[28] Its three-sided court must once have been walled in. The east and west sides consisted of four cells, the corner ones having their doors set at an angle while the dershane, or lecture and study room, in the centre of the south side had a cell on each flank. It protrudes behind the building in a manner alien to the Selçuk medrese and is very much smaller than the great open eyvan of that period; besides which, it is a room. The portico in front of the cells had three arches on the south side and two each on the east and west. There was a pool in the middle of the little court, and the cell to the east of the dershane was likely to have been reserved for the şeyh for it

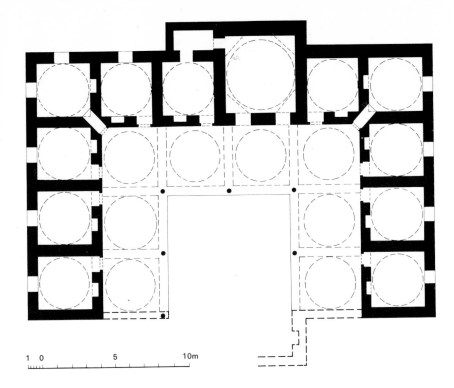

1   0   5   10m

*31, 32, 33 Süleyman Pasha Medrese, Iznik,
the embryo of future Ottoman colleges.
Left: plan, scale 1 : 250. Below: the typical
three-sided courtyard and (below right) the
projecting dershane with the round windows
of the cells.*

possesses an inner lobby due to a need for symmetry. A school for the orthodox
teaching of the shariat or law under Sunni doctors was urgently needed, for Sufi
doctrine was rampant and Shamanism latent besides; yet it is probable that at
this period it was possible to be three-faced and thus a good Sunni although a
member of a dervish order and also honouring the ancient faith of a distant past.
The grave of Davut of Kayseri, who was the first regular teacher at the medrese,
lies beneath the Büyük Çinar or the Great Plane Tree in Iznik which is of magnificent size and an unorthodox religious symbol.[29] The cells have a casement at
lower level with strikingly large circular windows above to admit the light of the
sun, and through these circles the symbolism must have been as clear as the daylight itself.[30]

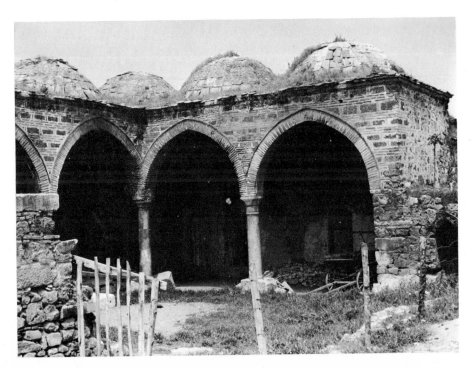

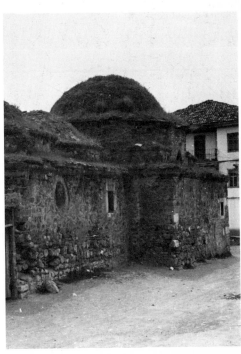

The death of the Orhan Gazi in 1360, at the age of sixty, brought Murat I to the throne. The tradition of conquest went on flourishing and the new sultan entered the Balkans. In 1366, he began his mosque at Çekirge west of Bursa, a truly splendid site. But his life was that of a warrior, and the building was not completed until 787–8/1385.[31] It seems remarkable that a royal mosque took nineteen years to build even if Murat was often far away. He was only to survive four more years after its completion. If it was begun in 1366 in honour of his son's circumcision then he must have shown little interest in it. The date 1385 is that of the vakfiye which is not always a reliable guide to the beginning or end of the building of a foundation.

The Hudavendigâr or royal mosque is an astonishing tour-de-force: not only *34,* does it combine a zaviye with a mosque on the ground floor but it also has an orthodox medrese on the first. The door into the building is plain and opens into a hall from which broad stairways ascend, partly through the thickness of the wall. The first two flights of the east staircase are broader than the last, while on the west it is the middle flight which is the narrower. Confusing elements, such as relieving arches which were added later, indicate alterations, but it is hard to determine what these could have been.[32] Past the stair hallways, doors open to corner rooms which appear to have been stores, since they have two slits instead of windows. The first hall leads into a second, narrower lobby which is the north eyvan. It is now covered by a wooden balcony. On each side are broad passages leading to fine chambers (5·50 × 6·50 metres) which have doors into the court and into the wing eyvans as well as into the store-rooms. These are the rooms with ocaks, or chimneys, which are now replaced by side entries with windows on either side. From the central eyvan, one steps immediately into the court under a dome eleven metres in diameter which once had an oculus over its basin for ritual washing. On the east and west are the large cradle-vaulted eyvans, and level with the four steps up to the prayer hall are doors into two more smaller rooms without ocaks. The prayer hall itself is a rectangle under a barrel vault. This was surely always the case but the eyvans may once have been domed.[33] The building suffered severely in the 1855 earthquake and this has led to disagreement over the extent of any alterations. The facts are fully discussed by Kuran and, although he argues cogently for a reconstruction of the upper floor in 1417, for the first time I find myself in disagreement with him and believe that the rebuilding did not greatly alter the plan.[34]

Nineteenth- and twentieth-century decoration and additions, including the central fountain, have damaged the interior. The worst additions are the wooden gallery above the north door and the bricking in of the pairs of arches of the medrese galleries under the lateral and north arches which carry the great dome. This may have been done when the medrese became a lunatic asylum.[35] The wall of the chamber over the mihrab has also been mutilated. It was once only a stone rail like the medrese arches. The effect is still grand owing to the height of the dome and the depth of the eyvans and the mosque; and this is further accentuated by the deep recession of the large mihrab under a circular arch in order to support the room above, thus introducing the apsidal form to Ottoman architecture. However, the present mihrab does not appear to be the original one.

Upstairs, the gallery is remarkable for its good plasterwork in dome and vault and for its magnificent and inspiring view over the plain. In the centre, between the stairs, is a large room which must have been a fine dershane. It once had arches open on to the corridor exactly opposite those facing the mihrab. On the far side of each stair is a passage with two double cells probably for the preceptors. The first bays of the ones on the north have windows on to the gallery as well as east or west. The passages lead into the C-shaped corridor which was originally lit by the light coming through the arches from the court; now the light comes through a window at the south end on each side. There are eight cells for students on each side.[36]

Elaborate though it may be, this is really an orthodox medrese form even if the avlu lies nine metres below. The barrel-vaulted corridors are nothing but the portico before normal medrese cells. What is astonishing is the metre-wide corridors each side, each lit by four slit windows which are cut into the thickness of the upper wall of the prayer hall, and bend round the corner to reach the chamber above the mihrab. This room is octagonal in shape and has a dome of which only the tip bearing the alem or symbol of the crescent emerges from under the roof. It may have been a cell for a recluse or for the şeyh but it is hard to believe that so much trouble would have been taken for this purpose. Indeed, the room is smaller than the four principal cells. No authority has yet been bold enough to suggest a function. There is no other example of such a room, and it is infinitely more surprising than the façade, which has led to the suggestion that this very Islamic building is the work of an Italian. It could have been an oratory, although there is no trace of a mihrab but only a window on the south side. Yet a window was employed as a mihrab by Sinan in the hünkâr mahfil or royal loge, of Selimiye at Edirne. Moreover, it is strange that there is no provision at the Hudavendigâr for a royal box such as exists at the Yeşil Cami. The sultan would be well able to follow the prayers led by the imam below him, and there would be symbolic significance in the head of the people, and therefore imam of imams, being set above the lesser man. At the Yeşil Cami the royal box is in the centre above the court, but in later mosques it reappeared in the south-east corner with its own mihrab parallel to the main kıble below.

The main construction of the building was in the now traditional form of three courses of brick to one of stone. The façade handsomely unites the upper and the lower buildings by placing a fine gallery over the five-bay portico with its five concealed domes. The gallery has a cross-vault at each end and three domes in the middle appearing above the level of the roof, the central one being the highest. Large stone piers carry slightly pointed arches. Above the lower range of arches are small windows which can only be decorative and put there to break the monotony. Like the lateral arches at a lower level, the gallery arches are divided into two smaller ones, carried on the piers, and a central Byzantine column and capital. Byzantine capitals are also used as bases as they often were in more primitive Islamic work. A stone band forming the upper half of a rectangle above the central arch successfully suggests the grandeur of a pishtak doorway.[37] It has a simple pattern of hexagonal wheels which also occurs above the lateral arches of the gallery. The minaret which rises clumsily through the north-east corner of the gallery is a later addition.[38] Following the Karaman attack in 1417, when Kuran[39] believes the upper storey to have been reconstructed, an earlier minaret may have been added.

The portico is joined to the zaviye and eyvan walls by a line of five small decorative arches at roof level which become four times wider under the medrese roof to spring exactly below the eight chimneys of the cells whose span they mark. Assuming that Gabriel[40] and Çetintaş[41] are correct in their reconstructions, there were also chimneys each side, where now a door has been cut, to warm two lower zaviye rooms. Their flues still exist in the corners of the second of the smaller medrese cells on each side. The arch pattern diminishes to its original size and continues until broken by the room above the mihrab apse which cuts into the roof line; but it reappears at the higher level. The great square base beneath the hipped roof from which the dome springs has two such bands, one above the other. Thus the building is unified externally. This is necessary because each element is independent still, and it would have been possible for different master-builders to have had teams working on separate sections in competition with each other.[42]

Why did Murat I decide to put his medrese on top of his zaviye in this strange fashion when there was no lack of land around his complex? It is true that the plan did escape the problems of building on a terrace or a slope; nor was it quite as revolutionary as at first appears, since the two-storey medrese had existed in Selçuk times at Sivas, Erzerum, and elsewhere. It could have been that, because of remonstrances by the growing Ulema about the influence of heretical sects, the sultan was engaged in a delicate policy of balance of power and so put the Ulema

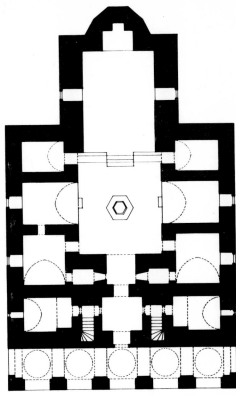

34, 35 Hudavendigâr Cami, Bursa. Plans, scale 1 : 500. Above: the zaviye floor with open court, open eyvans and retiring rooms. Below: the medrese floor with the portico serving as a court and the room over the mihrab.

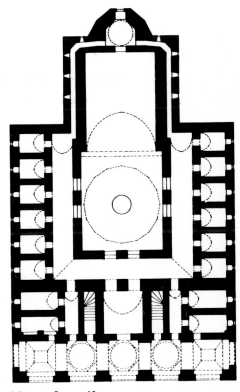

1 0   5   10m

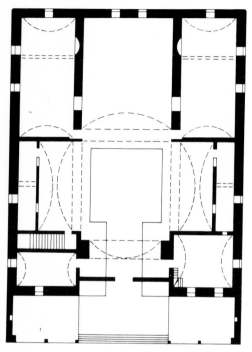

36 Mevlevihan, Manisa. Sketch plan. This is a strong expression of the cross-axial treatment of space.

in a superior position. It might also have been because the division between orthodox and heretic in a society of free men had not yet set fast. This at once worried and pleased Ibn Battuta. But though this building may represent a conservative victory, standing at a distance and imagining grey smoke rising from those chimneys about the great dome and its alem, one might feel that the spirit of mysticism rose supreme after all. However, one influence, perhaps that of the doctors of law, ensured the correct alignment of the mihrab with Mecca.

A zaviye of the Mevlevi dervishes on the mountainside above Manisa, built by İshak Çelebi at the same period as he built his Ulu Cami there, offers evidence of the close association of dervishes with royal foundations and their strong influence on their architecture. This is a bold, plain, almost square box of a building with a portico walled at each end and a shed roof carried on four wooden piers. There is a niche in each wall and an asymmetrical arrangement of the large high windows, one on the east and two on the west of the deeply recessed door. The flanking walls are better ordered, having two low casements towards the south and a pair of high windows towards the north, while there is a symmetrical range of four casements along the south wall but no projection for a mihrab for it does not exist. The plan of the interior is based on a sunken domed court about seven metres square surmounted by a dome which appears to have served as the sema-hane or ritual hall. It is reached by a vestibule, which like all the other sections of the building is barrel-vaulted. Off it are two lofty rooms, that on the left being very narrow because a wide stairway on the south side takes a third of its area. The west side room must have had some sort of stair within it because the shallow, unlit east and west eyvans have doors into windowless cells across their exterior walls, above which are galleries each with a large arched aperture looking down onto the court. Beyond the court is a deep and broad barrel-vaulted eyvan closely related to that of the Hudavendigâr mosque built at approximately the same time. (It may even have preceded it.) Flanking it are two large, somewhat narrow chambers with large arched windows onto the south eyvan as well as three to the outside world, and in their southern halves against the inside walls are large ocaks for cooking which must also have warmed the central area to some extent. This is not a mosque but the second most important Mevlevi tekke or zaviye in the country and the graves of the members of the great dervish order founded by Celâlettin Rumi at Konya lie under the trees all the way down the hillside. The close relationship of its cruciform plan to that of the lower floor of the mosque of Murat I at Çekirge is all the more significant.

At the foot of the hill at Çekirge, Murat built or rebuilt the Eski Kaplıca. A kaplıca is a thermal bath built over one of the hot springs which made Bursa famous from antiquity until the present day. The building is large and grand and only overshadowed by the Yeni Kaplıca built by Rüstem Pasha in the sixteenth century. It is probable that the foundations are Byzantine, and Roman before that. Ibn Battuta who was in Bursa in 1333[43] implies that the bath existed at that date and provided free lodging for three days (which was the traditional period for charity and long continued to be so). The use of Byzantine columns and capitals is not definite proof of the rebuilding but certainly evidence. Evliya attributes the bath to Murat but the building is not mentioned in the archives until 1456.[44] The inscription over the door refers to restorations in 917/1511 which were obviously extensive. The two half-domes supported on squinches in the camekân must be presumed to have been added then, or else the Eski Kaplıca would antedate the use of the true half-dome in Ottoman architecture by one hundred years. They may have been Byzantine and their influence never absorbed, but this is improbable. The bath, which had been freely open to rich and poor alike, closed at some point in the sixteenth century, perhaps because the revenues of the endowment had diminished; but popular clamour ensured its re-opening in 1616, hastily it would appear, because repairs had to be made in 1617 and again in 1680. The bath is not typical of Ottoman hamams, and the site on the edge of the hill, ordained by the hot springs, is unusual too, but the use of wooden annexes for lodgings is very Ottoman indeed.

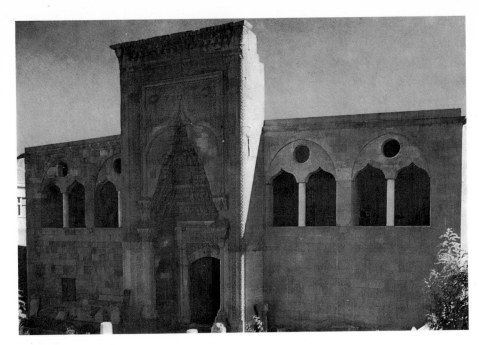

37 Ak Medrese, Niğde. Portal and loggias.

Murat's türbe, in front of his mosque on the cliff edge, has been rebuilt rather than restored. His body was brought back by his son to be housed with honour after his assassination on the field following his great victory at Kossova. The plan is more or less the original concept. The room is seventeen metres square with eight columns set about the cenotaph to carry a dome six metres in diameter. The proportions are noble but the decor is not. A kitabe (an inscriptive plaque) records a restoration in *1154*/1741, and another followed the earthquake of 1855.[45] The building was influenced by the mausoleum of Osman, which was known as the Gümüşlü Türbe because the lead plates of its dome shone like silver; it was a large chapel taken over by Orhan when he decided to bring his father's remains to the new capital. The tomb of Orhan himself was part of the same monastery. Both sepulchres were ruined in 1855 but Osman's new türbe was built on the old foundations and part of the Byzantine pavement has survived.[46] Alas, Orhan's beard, seen by Miss Pardoe, could not be re-grown.

The large imaret west of the mosque has disappeared.[47] The sıbyan mekteb, now a primary school, has been utterly transformed and so have two kiosks between it and the türbe. An engaging little monument which still survives in constant use is the handsome latrine that serves those who frequent the foundation. It consists of a domed court over six metres square with a fountain in the middle, two narrow washrooms, and five closets. Gabriel[48] says that traditionally it was built as a small hamam for bachelors, presumably students at the medrese. This would appear to have been superfluous since the Eski Kaplıca is so near. Çetintaş calls it the Kimsesiz Hamam as opposed to the Bekârlar (Bachelors). But since the word means the Bath of the Bereft it has much the same connotation.

There is only one building in Anatolia with a façade comparable to that of the Hudavendigâr mosque and that is the Ak Medrese built by the Karamanoğlus at Niğde in *812*/1409.[49] It is a two-storey medrese with finely framed arches onto the central court. The carving is particularly lavish as was the Karaman custom. The façade of the Ak Medrese is divided by an enormously high pishtak portal which contains a complex stalactite half-dome within an ogee arch which cuts into a field of wheels dominated by two large bosses, seemingly representing the sun and moon. On each side of the small entry eyvan, just as at the Hudavendigâr, are the stairs to the upper floor. They lead into loggias which are divided from each other by the vast portal. Each has two large arches divided by columns into two ogee arches with a circular element above, perhaps influenced by the

Sungur Bey Cami nearby. Much of the detail of this monument, including its facing of cut stone throughout, differs considerably from the earlier one at Bursa but it is hard to believe that its architect had not seen the Hudavendigâr, or its Byzantine inspiration, if he was not actually the same man. He was unlikely to have been an Italian but he may have been a builder from the Balkans, for this form of loggia, derived from the Venetian palaces of Dalmatia as it may be, appears in the principal church of Philippopolis which was converted into a mosque after its capture.[50] Far more important are the alterations undertaken in the church of Hagia Sophia at Ohrid, dating from 1313-14, a town taken by Candarlı Hayrettin Pasha in 1385. There is an upper gallery above the portico between two towers with triple arches supported on columns. Left and right, just above the door are two small windows which recall the decorative windows over the porch of Murat's mosque. At Ohrid, the gallery is divided from the portico by a band of blind arcading. The likeness is striking.[51] There is much re-use of Byzantine material in the Hudavendigâr and the stone and brick courses are in the Byzantine manner.

A medrese built by Murat in the name of his tutor, the Lala Şahin, in the citadel at Bursa represents the simplest form of medrese of all. It consists of a covered forecourt with an oculus and a mescit beyond. Off these on each side are one large and three smaller cells. The only interest in the coarse workmanship is the re-use of Corinthian capitals and the simplicity of the plan which is as elementary a combination of mosque and medrese as that of the Hudavendigâr is complex.

Murat built a number of mosques elewhere, including the subsequently rebuilt mescit at Tuzla and the Hudavendigâr at Assos.[52] The most important development architecturally at this time was the attempt to unify the dome and the walls by canting the corners so that they slope up to the exterior drum. The call to prayer seems to have been made from a crag alongside the Assos mosque, thus eliminating the need for a minaret and suggesting how it was first made at the Orhaniye at Bilecik.

In 790/1388,[53] Murat honoured his redoubtable mother, Nilüfer Hatun, by building a large zaviye close to the Yeşil Cami at Iznik, apparently her favourite city. It is known now as the Nilüfer Hatun İmaret and although the term imaret simply means a charity kitchen, something of its function is conveyed by that term. A modest door admits one to the court area under a lofty dome with a lantern. Right and left are two large rooms, with ocaks, which could serve as kitchens or dormitories. In front is a raised chamber subdivided into two by a great arch; each half has its own small dome rising out of concealed cradle-vaults. The stalactite plasterwork of these vaults is elaborate yet strong. The internal mihrab niche is well off the true kıble axis. The building is preceded by a fine, deep portico related to that of the Yeşil Cami but grander in dimension if simpler in decoration. Built of a single course of stone alternating with four courses of brick, its domes are still tiled. The façade of the portico is carried on four piers with the central arch slightly higher and more pointed than the two on each side which are divided into two by columns. A column also divides each side arch just as at the Orhaniye or the Hudavendigâr. The two pairs of side bays are flat-topped cross-vaults but in the centre the usual small dome is hidden in the roof. The external walls have inset sun discs like those of the Orhaniye and other devices set into the brickwork in the manner of the time, like so many amulets or charms. These zaviyes were richly furnished with beautiful Anatolian rugs, large numbers of glass lustres and brass candelabra, and oil lamps.[54] Ibn Battuta is full of praise for Ahi kindness and hospitality not to mention the excellence of the food and the cleanliness of Anatolia.[55]

A smaller zaviye of the period, that of Yakup Çelebi, has been converted into a mosque,[56] a fate which that of Nilüfer Hatun escaped because it is orientated west and its modest mihrab is placed in the side wall of the meeting hall of the Ahis and the dervishes. Probably, the cooking at Yakup Çelebi was done outside, as in a military encampment or in the meadows of the Sweet Waters of Asia beside the Bosphorus to this day. Both imarets are planned in the Bursa T-plan tradition.

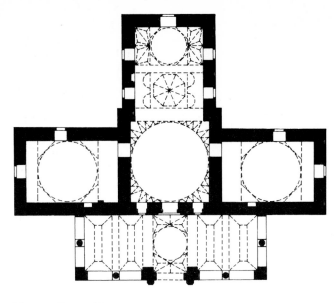

*38 Nilüfer Hatun Zaviye, Iznik. The plan (scale 1 : 500) shows
a clear relationship with the royal mosques of Bursa.*

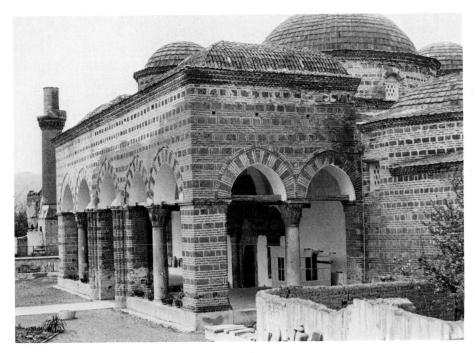

39 Nilüfer Hatun Zaviye. The large portico which served as a summer room.

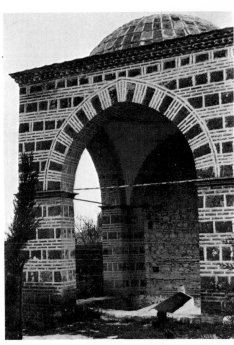

*40 Yakup Çelebi Zaviye, Bursa.
The open türbe of the founder.*

40   Yakup Çelebi's türbe lies to the west in front of his imaret. It is a domed unit,
carried on four huge corner piers of courses of stone between three courses of
brick, and is an early example in Anatolia of the open form of türbe. The Ottoman
türbe until the later fifteenth century cannot compare with those of the Selçuks
41 for beauty nor with such Beylik examples as that of Aşık Pasha at Kırşehir
probably built in 733/1333, the year when he died. This strange marble monument has a fine doorway into a small vestibule and the funeral chamber is very
much a room, in contradistinction to the symbolic cylindrical or polygonal
towers of the Selçuks. The curious faceted dome is not hemispherical, seemingly
by intent and not because of lack of skill.

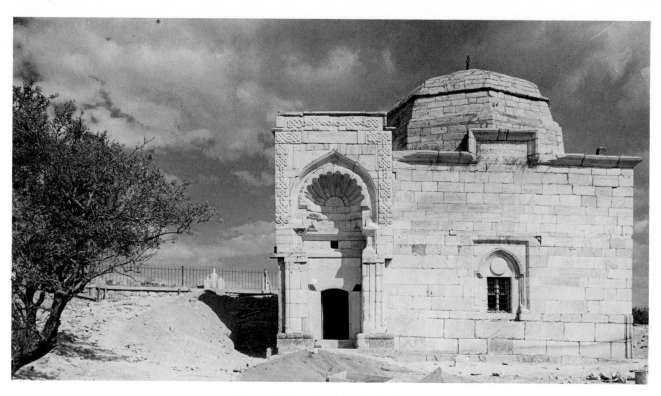

41 Aşık Pasha Türbe, Kırşehir. The elaboration contrasts with the severity of the classical Ottoman style.

A third important zaviye of the period was that of Posteyn Puş Baba at Yenişehir; and the list could be extended considerably. The Posteyn Puş Baba Zaviye consists of a central domed hall off a long narthex which acts as a corridor to the flanking rooms. It is of interest because of the strongly expressed relieving arches and because the sealed-off lateral chambers lend support to the theory that the side eyvans of some Bursa mosques were also walled off, hence the vestibules which otherwise appear purposeless at Murat II's mosque.

Murat I also built a palace and a royal mosque at Dimetoka which was captured in 1357 and served as the Ottoman capital from 1363 to 1366 in which year Edirne became the first real seat of government.[57] The mosque has suffered miserably over the years but retains some nobility of appearance in decay. The pitched roof suggests that originally a wooden dome may have been set within it.

Murat I's successor, Yıldırım (Lightning) Beyazit, so nicknamed because of the speed with which he moved his armies, began his mosque and its dependencies in 793/1390[58] or 1391[59] and it was completed in 798/1395. It was repaired in 1848 when Halil Ağa, the architect of the Empire, came to supervise the releafing of the lead domes, a task which had been necessary also in 1634 when a gale had skinned them.[60] It was not until 1878 that repairs followed on the earthquake of 1855, and further works had to be carried out in 1948 and more recently; yet the original form appears to have been little altered. Once again, the architect is unknown.

The interior of the mosque, at ground level, is related to that of Beyazit's father. There is only a small threshold, off which are two stairways, before one enters the courtyard under a high dome (22 × 12 metres). Facing one is the mosque which is raised two steps above the avlu as are the two eyvans. The domed prayer hall has large casements each side of the heavy mihrab as well as forward along the east and west walls. This is because there are two rooms both sides of the eyvan and those on the south project halfway down the flanks of the prayer hall. They are the more interesting pair because of the magnificence of the plaster shelving which fills their south walls which have ocaks in their centres. The plasterwork is painted white at present but must have been multicoloured when erected and it is tragic that the crispness of the carving has been blunted.

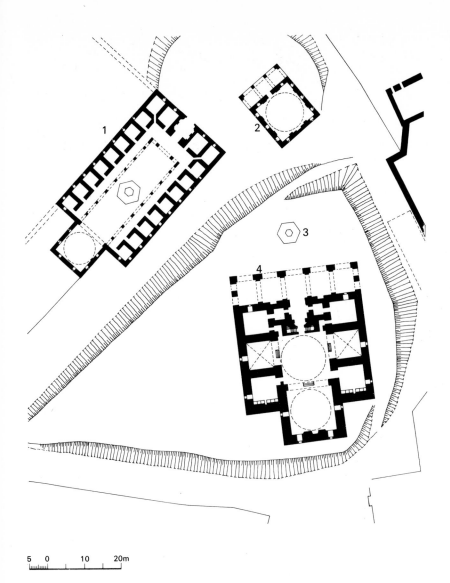

5 0   10   20m

*42 Yıldırım Beyazit Complex, Bursa. Plan, scale 1 : 1,000. 1 medrese; 2 türbe;
3 fountain. The mosque (4) shows a clear relationship with the plans of zaviyes, but
the prayer hall has enhanced importance.*

The mass of shelving offers some problems because of the variety of shape and
size. The tall, narrow slit on the right of the ocak in the west room looks designed
for a poker and it is a form which occurs in the same position elsewhere. Some
shelves were for pitchers of water, flasks of attar of roses, candles and lamps, and
even flowers. Others may possibly have held turbans, and others were simply
designed to complete a grand ensemble without specific use in mind, but due to
the horror vacui of Islam. The niches are framed in multifoil arches and over all
is a pattern of flowers. This is the earliest grand example of such a piece of furniture in Turkey; such shelves were to be an important object in domestic houses
until as late as the nineteenth century. An excellent wooden version with beautifully painted flower motifs can be seen in the ethnographic museum in the so-
called Muradiye Konak opposite the foundation of Murat II.[61] The two rooms on
the north side of the eyvan also have such furniture. These rooms are reached
by way of a small lobby behind the stairs which also give access to small cells,
each only three metres square, which have fireplaces and very high windows
onto the inner porch before the great north door. The stairs reach a passage only a
metre wide with a window centred on the axis of the mihrab. It leads to two open
loggias above the little cells. From these, by stepping out where a balustrade

might be expected and circumventing a pilaster carved out of the wall, one reaches two stairs set at an angle of forty-five degrees and then four more which lead into the thickness of the wall of the upper façade. Here the corridor is barely two feet wide and leads past a window to the minaret stairs.

At one time there was a minaret at each corner;[62] that at the north-west fell as recently as 1949 while the other collapsed at some indeterminate date in the nineteenth century. There is no special strengthening of the fabric at the corners and the approach is so tortuously contrived that one can only agree with Gabriel that the minarets were probably later additions just as were those of the Hudavendigâr Cami, the Yeşil Cami at Bursa, and certainly Beyazit Pasha at Amasya. Minarets, because they sway under stress, may survive earthquakes when domes fall or, if they do collapse, snap well above the base. It is significant that all those minarets which collapsed at Bursa prior to 1855 were placed in improbable positions and were not firmly anchored to the earth. The mosque plan does not indicate any other likely position for minarets at Yıldırım Beyazit Cami and it is possible that the terrace in front of the mosque was used for the call to prayer for this was a royal chapel and a hostel for pilgrims and not a neighbourhood mosque. It stands on an eminence which commands the whole assembly of buildings so there was no call for tall minarets.

The mosque inside has grandeur resulting from the freedom of space already achieved at the Orhaniye and the Hudavendigâr; the chevron or triangular band supporting the second dome is boldly expressed; but the most interesting innovation is the niche under the great arch that divides the prayer hall from its court. The slight recess which appeared at the Orhaniye at Bilecik has become a deep incision like a miniature mihrab above which rises a scaffolding of stalactites which reach a climax with two truly pendant forms. These eleven layers of carving are an intricate console from which the huge hipped arch springs. This is the first appearance of the Bursa arch.[63]

Even more splendid than the mosque are the façade and portico, which are partly of marble;[64] the latter is particularly important because the portico of the later[65] Yeşil Cami was never built since the sultan died before it could be added. Seen from the front, each of the five compartments is clearly framed so that the piers are totally disguised. The outer frames, which each section shares, reach to the ground; the inner, after an interval of nearly a metre, have handsome stilted arches on consoles. Those of the central arch are embryonic of the elaborated Bursa arch within the mosque. Subtly, the inner frame of the central arch is contiguous with the outer, thus slightly enlarging the space. Above, the five domes are equal but behind the middle one the lesser dome of the exposed vestibule is carried on a drum and so acts as a visual step towards the major dome over the court. Through the wing frames can be seen casement windows crowned with ogee tympana and, above these, smaller casements. Each is set in a ribbed frame which is divided across the centre. The inner arches reveal a fascinating three-dimensional vista. Below, where one would expect conventional exterior mihrabs, are deep recesses roofed in a cave of stalactites almost as rich as those inside the building. They form patterns of stars and rosettes and three thunderbolt symbols[66] which Çetintaş supposes to have been picked out in paint.[67] Above, triangularly recessed, are the arches of the stairways, the first three steps of which can be glimpsed. Again, each opening is clearly defined by a tall ribbed frame. A double-stilted and faintly hipped central arch leads into the open vestibule where doors have been cut into recesses whose stilted arches culminate in miniature stalactite cones. Beyond is the porch itself with a step up to another framed and elaborated niche in which are small sofas for doorkeepers or other mosque officers. This area is marked off by two columns with capitals made up of eight tiers of honeycombing. The door itself is modest, with keyed voussoirs of alternating marbles common in Syria, but a second hipped arch rises above it to double its height and above this is a small marble window[68] based on three interlocking wheels one above the other. This will recur at the Yeşil Cami. The whole ensemble, again, is strongly framed.

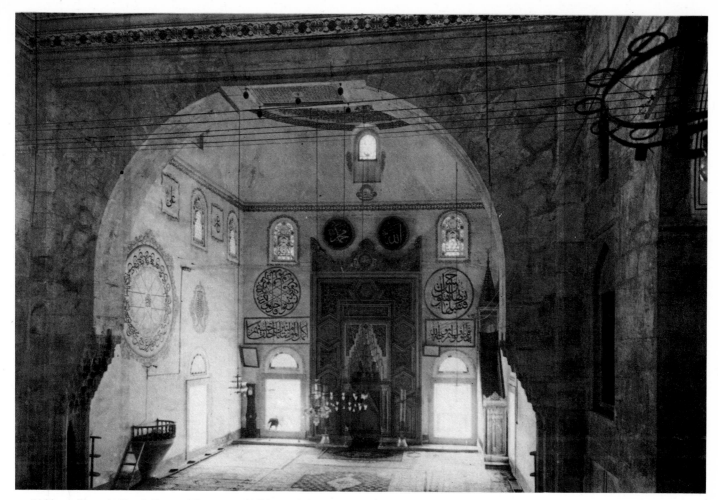

43 Yıldırım Beyazit Cami, Bursa. The prayer hall beyond the 'Bursa Arch'.

The wings of the porticoes are divided into two by an extra pier which creates two dramatically narrow arches. In the centre of each of the arches there was once a keystone from which an iron boss protruded. Lanterns used surely to be hung along the arcade and before the central door; moving with the breeze, they would add another dimension to an already grand architectural achievement.[69]

Seen from the side, the mosque is long and low and there are only two casements and one smaller window at ground level, but there are eleven just below roof level. Excluding the mihrab wall, it resembles the Hudavendigâr Cami except that it is built of marble and cut stone.[70] The frames of the casements are deeply dentilated and set into ogee recesses which are cut into the wall but otherwise the building is plain, reserving everything for the drama of the portico. Because it has been shut in recent years, and perhaps because it is out of the town centre, it is neglected. Yet the façade alone makes it the first truly royal Ottoman monument.[71] Moreover, it is an Ottoman building clearly distinguished from Selçuk or other ancestry.

42   Some of the complex has crumbled away including the small imaret below the mosque on the east and the modest palace perched on the cliff edge above the türbe. The second medrese listed in the vakfiye, which dates from as late as 1400,[72] has left no trace. The remaining medrese set below the north front of the mosque along a second shelf of cliff, which falls away precipitously on its north-west flank, is interesting because of its unusual length. The college is reached through a square porch, again the fourth eyvan disguised, with two large niches with sofas on each side suggesting much gossip at the gate. This porch is covered by a dome under a tall octagonal drum with a double pitched roof. Beyond the porch

is a triple-bayed portico with a central arch taller than those which flank it and carrying a small dome on a less elevated drum.[73] Right and left are the larger cells for the faculty or guardians which had windows onto the porch; and, with doors set at an angle, on the north-east are the latrines and on the south-east a room the use of which can no longer be determined since this place has been converted into a clinic and greatly altered – the fate of many medreses. Before one, a long garden court (28 × 8·50 metres), with a hexagonal şadırvan or fountain in the centre, leads to the dershane which is approached up two steps. The complex state of its dome is attributed by Çetintaş[74] to bad restoration. The double tier of drums is rare in Ottoman work but not unknown.[75] The revaks in front of the cells for students[76] which run along the sides of the garden were carried on seven arches borne by columns; they were undomed but, instead, covered by the short side of a shed roof (the apex of which was above the inner cell walls) with barrel-vault inset. Except for the end ones which had two windows, all the cells were identical, with one window and an ocak with a niche on each side of it, but the cliffside cells are two steps lower than those opposite. They all had cradle-vaults.[77] The building is constructed of two courses of brick to one of stone. On the entry wall, sun symbols and other devices are cut.

The medrese lies long and low between its gate and dershane domes. The exterior walls have shallow blind arcading. The effect was repeated at the ruined darüşşifa or hospital[78] which follows a similar plan but with ten cells on each side and a large chamber flanking the central hall which may have been an operating theatre or waiting-room. This was a teaching hospital.[79] The gate was modest but the court rises in a series of steps, which total thirty in all, towards the principal hall, in a manner which Sinan was to exploit when designing the two easterly medreses at Süleymaniye. The ascent from the entry to the highest level is as much as three metres. An interesting feature is the drain which runs under the middle of the east cells and makes a small loop to join the four latrines in the north-east corner room. A sewer with access from the cells also occurs in the rank of outer cells at the hospital of Beyazit II at Edirne built nearly a century later. These rooms were probably for patients who were too ill to make use of the ordinary closets.

In the north-west wall, facing the court of the great chamber, is a square plaque which is copied frequently in Ottoman architecture and elsewhere with stylized devices deriving from Kufic script and, possibly, weaving patterns.[80] On the façade to the right of the entry is a large brick sun disc with a hole in its centre and another, much smaller, is set on the left, perhaps representing the moon. Above this is a rectangular plaque with a pattern made up of four sets of interweaving diagonal lines. Elsewhere, plaques of brick and stone or plaster produce stars from myriads of hexagons in a form which tilemakers were then using. These can be read in several ways, principally as white stars with six red triangular rays but also as overlapping triangles of varying sizes. The result is that Islamic form of cubism which retains one's interest because the eye cannot rest after summing up the pattern structure, in the Western manner. Once this effect is accepted, it is as if the stars begin to shine and this elementary Op art is no less effective because it is simple.[81] Another star pattern can be read from diamonds either seen as independent units grouped in threes or united as hexagons. A modest tree of life also occurs. These simple brick patterns are distinctive of the period.

The vakfiye of 1400 ordained that this hospital should be staffed with three doctors, two chemists, a cook, a baker, and ten servants.[82] The question which always arises is how many patients were crowded into the twenty cells and how many out-patients used the hospital.

The türbe of Beyazit has a history as troubled as his own. Timur delivered the corpse of his royal prisoner to Beyazit's son, Musa Çelebi, but the state of civil war in the shattered Ottoman territories in Anatolia delayed the erection of the mausoleum by Süleyman Çelebi, until 1406.[83] It was sacked by the Karamanoğlus in 1414 and restored by Mehmet I. In the seventeenth century, Murat IV came to kick the sarcophagus and insult an ancestor who chanced to meet defeat. One can think of many others more worthy of that kick. In 1855 the türbe fell with the earthquake but was competently restored. It recalls a mescit more than a tomb because of its three-domed portico supported on piers at the corners and two fine but slender Byzantine columns, set on clumsy blocks of stone for bases. If the windows are authentic, they surprise because they are trefoils with seven-petaled shells in the centre. An inscription records that Ali bin Hüseyn was the architect and the central kitabe states that this tomb was erected by Süleyman Han son of Beyazit Han for the very great sultan, master of the kings of the Arabs and the Persians, the very happy sultan who seeks the blessing and indulgence of God, Beyazit Han son of Murat Han. Süleyman begged God to preserve his power but God was deaf and Mehmet I prevailed over his brothers in the struggle for the throne.

-49   Beyazit had been a prodigious builder[84] and was responsible for the Ulu Cami or great Friday mosque which stands above the bazaar as proof both of the increasing power of the Ulema over the Sufis and of the prosperity of the city. After the victory of Niğbolu (Nicopolis) had supplied him with caravans of booty with which to pay for it, work began in the autumn of 1396, or possibly the following spring if one takes the winter rain into consideration, and it was completed with remarkable speed by *802*/1399-1400, for the minber carries an inscription to Beyazit of that date.

The mosque is the grandest of all the ulu camis which arose in a dignified line from those of the eleventh century in Sivas and Malatya – although the latter is strictly Iranian in form – to Konya and Kayseri through some two hundred years of Şelçuk rule. Sivas is a simple copse of fifty piers arranged in ten ranks which carried heavy beams supporting a mud roof.[85] It is lofty and the windows small yet the aisles are spacious and so it is especially impressive in the evening when vista after shadowy vista opens before the wanderer. Its ancestors were the Samarra mosque of 852 and the Al Azhar at Cairo, among others. The Danişmend Ulu Cami at Kayseri, dated 1140, has one dome over the mihrab and minber and a second which was once open to the sky.[86] There is an organic development here due to the influence of Selçuk Iran[87] which divided the mosque into areas which could be defined and yet remain fluid. Thus the centre of prayer was under the south dome, but on Fridays the faithful could spread out over the entire building. At other times each teacher would have his pillar with his pupils squatting around him. The most grandiloquent of all the Selçuk monuments in Anatolia, the Ulu

44   Cami at Divrik, dated 1229, organized the interior into a balanced whole with a highly inventive system of ribbed vaults abreast of the Gothic.[88] The piers are reduced to two rows of four each side of the wider central aisle but the dome with the oculus still sits in the middle, although the opening is reduced and the impression of a court has faded. The İplikçi Cami at Konya built in 1162 is more closely related to the Bursa Ulu Cami because its twelve cruciform piers, in two ranks, divide the building into twenty-one more or less equal parts. The far larger Bursa mosque has twelve such piers in three ranks of four, carrying, together with those piers inset in the walls, a total of twenty domes.[89]

The story goes that Yıldırım Beyazit had vowed that he would erect twenty mosques if he were victorious at Niğbolu but was wisely advised by the noble dervish Emir Sultan, the most eminent of his counsellors and his son-in-law, to build a mosque with twenty independent domes instead. They cover an area of approximately 63 × 50 metres.[90] The mihrab dome in the centre of the south aisle is no larger than the others but all the domes on the central axis of the north door and the mihrab are set on higher drums and that over the court is highest of all. This is the middle of the second rank where the kıble axis is crossed by that of

46   the east and west doors. Under it is a splendid nineteenth-century marble pool[91] and fountain for ablutions and the whole area, which is two steps down, is paved in marble and railed off. The large oculus in the dome above is now glazed. Powerful pointed arches spring from the piers and pilasters in the walls. An impression of strength prevails, although the mosque is light and spacious. There are many windows because the walls between the arches only carry their

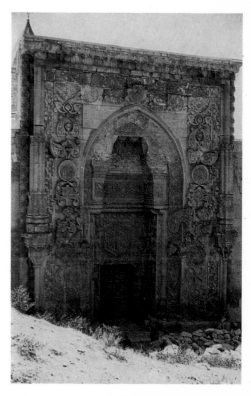

44 Ulu Cami, Divrik. The north portal with its fantastic swollen decoration translated from Iranian brick into Ottoman stone.

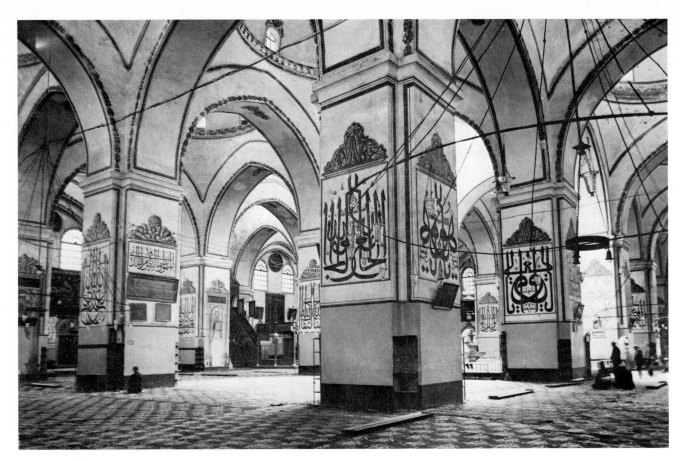

45, 46 *Ulu Cami, Bursa. The interior from the north-east, and the fountain court seen from the main portal.*

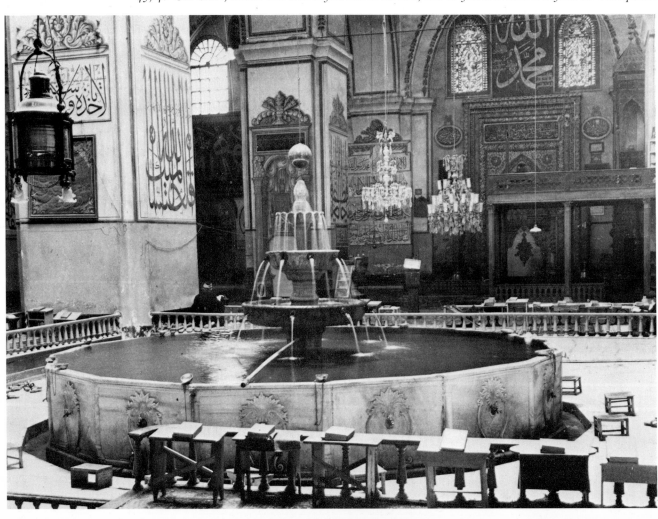

own weight, a principle fundamental to the development of twentieth-century architecture. The drums of the domes are also pierced with lights. The four domes of the central aisle are 21·50 metres high and their width is about 10·70 metres or half their height. The total area of the mosque is approximately in proportions of four to three, and the domes and their friezes are in proportion of one to three in regard to the height of the walls, 5·50 to 16·00 metres.[92]

The nineteenth-century whitewash[93] has been removed from the exterior to reveal the beautiful honey-coloured limestone of Olympus: but, inside, there is a plethora of tedious decoration which is either assertive, like the enormous inscriptions on the four faces of the piers or the massive chandeliers, or weak like the floral motifs that edge round the arches. The writing follows a tradition, since Evliya Çelebi[94] reported earlier examples in the seventeenth century; and he also stated that in his day the bases of the piers were gilded up to a metre high.[95] Replace the incongruous chandeliers with beautiful mosque lamps which can only be seen in museums today, and some idea of the original splendour can be imagined. In the mid-nineteenth century some Italian must have set out to refurbish mosques all over Turkey and, contemplating the dome of Sinan's Süleymaniye Cami, one wonders if it may not have been the younger Fossati. In the Ulu Cami there is that fake baroque drapery which is particularly inapposite in so masculine a building. The mihrab is also desecrated by poor paintwork. It is more closely related to the Selçuk type than to the Ottoman and so represents the final evolution of the handsome kıble of the Ulu Cami at Kayseri rather than forerunning that of the Yeşil Cami or those of Istanbul to come. The restored mahfil, which has a fine eighteenth-century wooden rail, is set a little off-centre before the mihrab, masking it in much the same way as does the mahfil at Beyşehir. The walnut minber is one of the finest in Islam. It is an elaborately carved piece of furniture of interlocking pieces needing neither nail nor glue, and the glow of the walnut has blackened with age and staining. It, too, belongs to the Selçuk tradition and its pyramidal roof stands high above the arch at the top of the stairs but not on a drum, in the later, Ottoman manner. The basic pattern arising from the involved geometric design creates a field of stars interspersed with plaster bosses of varying sizes, some smooth and some hollowed and grilled, many set in the centre of larger stars.[96] The two sides are not alike and the impression given is of suns and moons and planets and of some magic stylized constellation, perhaps Yıldırım Beyazit's lucky stars. With Timur on the march, the Khan had need of them.

Outside, the building is impressive because of its size and order. Its structure is clearly defined by the five great arches rising from ground to roof level on the south and north walls, and the four on the east and west. The windows are set beneath these arches. Both the upper and the lower pairs of windows in each arch are rounded but the lower ones are set in pointed frames. Small ventilators, if this is what these apertures are, have been opened above them. Sinan was to use polygonal ones in the Şehzade Cami in Istanbul. The new mosque was damaged during the conquest of Bursa by Timur in 1402 (Timur may have built the great north door[97]) and later by fires which frequently devastated the bazaar, particularly in 1493 and 1889,[98] while the earthquake of 1855 was also disastrous. The north façade was recently considerably restored as a result of the conflagration of 1956 which destroyed half the bazaar. The recent work has revealed that the grand portal attributed to Timur was once preceded by a flight of marble steps which may have started in the bazaar below. The top of these steps and an additional metre at the base of the minarets, together with the skirting of the façade, have been uncovered and show that this entry was very imposing indeed.

The minarets stand on bases faced with marble.[99] That on the north-east was probably added by Mehmet I between 1413 and 1421.[100] It is detached from the mosque wall[101] and set on a square base, while the north-west minaret stands on an octagonal base contiguous with the wall through which access to the mosque is obtained. It has also a stangely low outer wicket-gate preceded by high

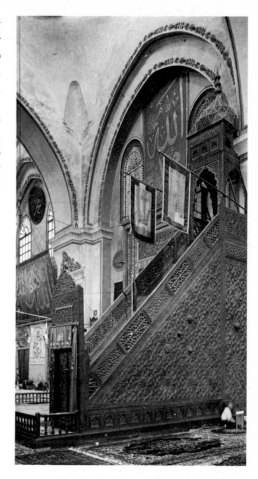

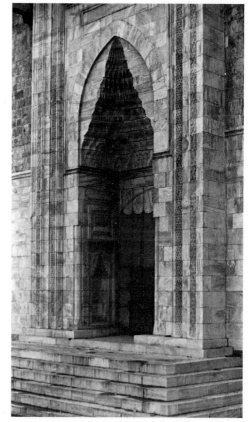

47, 48 *Ulu Cami, Bursa. The minber (above) and (below) the reconstructed main portal.*

47

48

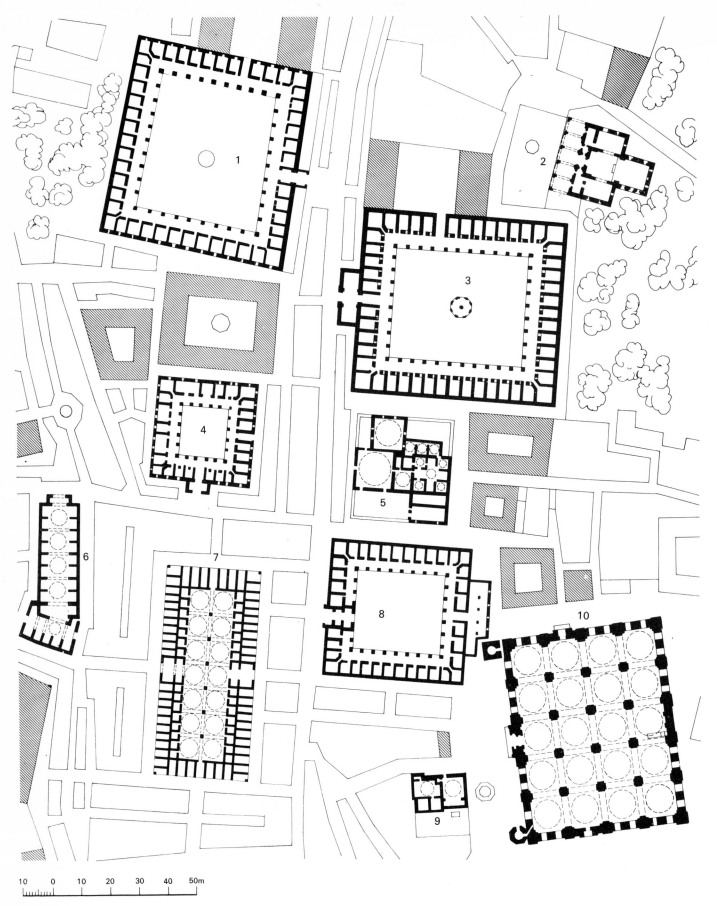

49 *Bursa. The central area of the market. 1 Fidan Han; 2 Orhan Cami; 3 Koza Han; 4 Geyve Han; 5 Bey Hamam; 6 Sipahiler Çarşı; 7 Bedesten; 8 Bey Han; 9 Şengül Hamam; 10 Ulu Cami.*

steps on the east facet, forcing those who enter to double forward uncomfortably as they mount. The north-east minaret has a door in the alley between it
and the mosque. The trunks of these minarets are of brick[102] but the marble
facing on the bases has been restored recently, along with that of the dado
of the north wall. The stone balconies are carried on severely stylized stalactites
common to the restored minarets of Bursa. The once round caps are now of stone,
and baroque in manner, because of their rebuilding after the earthquake of 1855.[103]
65 Parvillée was responsible for these as well as those of the Yeşil Cami and, due
to the lack of skilled craftsmen, he was reduced to using a frieze of bricks with
their corners projecting at an angle of forty-five degrees.

Yıldırım Beyazit was responsible also for the Ulu Cami at Bergama (18 × 22
metres) which dates from 801/1398[104] and is of cut stone with three axial domes
and lateral cradle vaults. The minber may be the first built of marble by the
Ottomans. The exterior of the mosque resembles a church and this mosque, like
that at Assos, may originally have been one. This could also be true of his mosque
at Balıkesir (22 × 24 metres) which is in basilica form with three aisles and two
rows of columns, but it is also related to the Beylik ulu cami form and I believe
both these mosques to be mainly Ottoman work. The Beyazit mosque at
Alaşehir is so rebuilt that it offers little indication of its original plan. The prayer
hall (23·50 × 10·50 metres) now has a plain roof; but the retention of two
columns and the actual dimensions support Ayverdi's theory[105] that it once had
a ten-metre central dome flanked by pairs of small cupolas in a manner closely
associated with mosques of the Saruhan beylik. Thus as early as the fourteenth
century local developments of the ulu cami form in Ottoman terms may have
appeared.

51 The final true ulu cami of the Bursa type was begun at Edirne by the Emir
Süleyman Çelebi in 805/1403, after the defeat of Ankara, to be completed only
in 816/1414 by his brother, Mehmet I. It was damaged by fire in 1749 and by
earthquake in 1752.[106] Repaired by Mahmut I between 1730 and 1754, it was
restored afresh in 1924 and 1934.[107] An inscription over the door states that the
architect was Hacı Alaettin of Konya and that the master mason was Ömer ibn
Ibrahim. The mosque is a perfect square of 49·50 metres. The piers are reduced
to four, each 2·80 metres square, and the domes to nine of equal size. They are
larger than those at Bursa, their diameter reaching 13·50 metres as opposed to
10·60,[108] and so there is a great feeling of space and ease. The hexagonal domes are
borne on pendentives, and have circular drums expressed externally. The mihrab
dome is on triangles, the central dome on stalactites, and the dome with the
oculus on simple squinches. These three, which form the main axis of the
mosque, are set on octagons as are all the domes of Bursa Ulu Cami independently of their inward form of support. There is a small opening in the dome in
the centre of the north side immediately before the door but the şadırvan has
gone, to be replaced by ugly rows of faucets outside the portico. This is of five
domes above six heavy piers and since it is not bonded is likely to be a later
addition. In the centre is an empty marble door frame in the Iznik manner but
because the arch is so wide, wing grilles have been added. The minaret on the
north-east side has one şerefe and a stumpy trunk on a square base. It is of stone
and if not a replacement is the earliest Ottoman minaret of its kind and something of a freak. The whole mosque is faced in cut stone apart from the brick
courses between the arches of the later portico. A second, much larger minaret
99 was added at the time of the building of the main minaret of Üç Şerefeli Cami
which it closely resembles, and it is therefore likely to have been built by the same
architect.[109] It has unusual projecting decorative turrets on its square base above
door-level and stands slightly aloof from the north-west corner of the mosque.
This could suggest how minarets were added to the mosques of Bursa. The
ground falls steeply on the west side of the mosque resulting in a sweep of stairs
up to the fine west door with its double arches and polychrome voussoirs beneath
a handsome cornice of arabesques. As this wall has to stand up to the prevailing
wind and the frequent winter rain of Edirne the gutters are fitted with water-

50 *Eski Cami, Edirne. Plan, scale 1 : 500.*
The court was originally the domed area
immediately beyond the portico which is a
later addition.

51 *Eski Cami, Edirne, from the south with*
the exterior of the Rüstem Pasha Han on the
left. The distant minaret belongs to Üç
Şerefeli Cami.

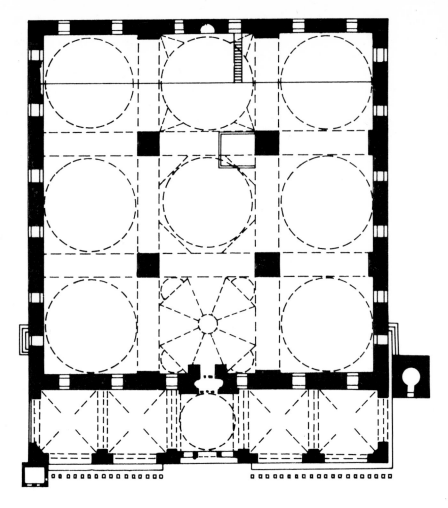

1 0   5   10m

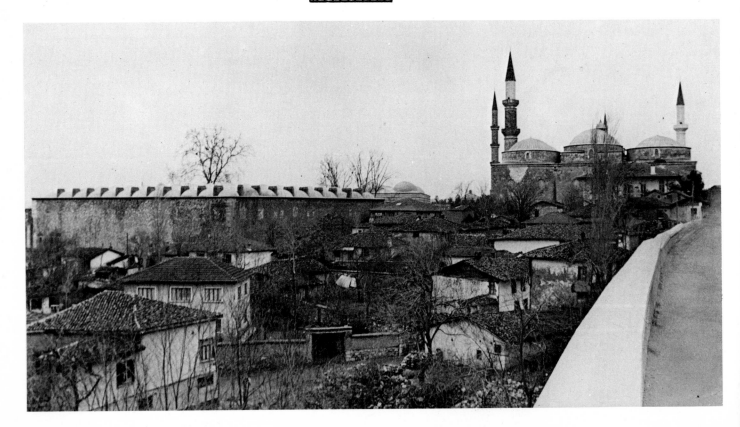

spouts, which are prominent but not prominent enough; the water is driven back against the wall, principally in the south-west corner where, consequently, veils of lichen eat into the stone. With the rise of Üç Şerefeli Cami in the later half of the fifteenth century this mosque ceased to be the biggest and surrendered its title to become the Eski or Old Cami.

The ulu cami form did not disappear but was adapted for civil use, with such exceptions as the mosque of Piyale Pasha, built in the classical period, which will be discussed later.[110] Minor mosques continued to follow the tradition. That of Zincirlikuyu was built by the Eunuch Vezirazam or Chief Vezir Atik Ali Pasha at the end of the fifteenth century between Fatih Cami and the Edirne Gate at Istanbul. The piers were reduced to two and there are six equal domes and no interior şadırvan. The three-bay portico has fallen.[111] A mosque belonging to the second half of the fifteenth century is that named after Abdal Mehmet, a cele-brated mystic of the reign of Murat II, whose tomb was built nearby in 854/1450 by order of this sultan.[112] The prayer hall has only two domes and can be seen either as the final diminution of the ulu cami form or simply as the doubling of the single unit type. This room is 15·20 × 7·70 metres and each unit is 7·00 × 7·70 metres, the arch dividing them being 1·20 metres thick. They are therefore slightly elliptical.[113] There is a triple-domed portico with access to the north-west minaret which hugs the corner of the façade. So as to have the exterior mihrab placed on the axis of that inside, it is centralized and two small doors are set, unusually, each side of it. There is also a sound, and probably decisive, structural reason for this, for if the door had been central it would have seriously weakened the support of the arch spanning the main axis of the building. The mosque was erected by a pious and wealthy butcher who specialized in the sale of sheeps' heads and who built another mosque which bears his own name, Başçı Ibrahim Cami.[114]

The Molla Arab Cami,[115] which was mutilated by the 1855 earthquake at Bursa, is later still. Only two of the nine cupolas survive. They were once all of the same dimensions and carried on four piers in the same way as those of the Eski Cami. Its portico has also gone but the fact that it once had one is interesting. Molla Arab served Selim I and Süleyman I and died in Bursa in 1531. One would suppose that he built his mosque in his old age and one wonders if his judgements were impartial, for the building was an expensive one. Just or unjust, he was a worthy member of the Ulema since by that late date his mosque must have been the ne plus ultra in conservative architectural taste except for the Adilceviz Ulu Cami on the shores of Lake Van. The ulu cami form refused, indeed, to die out. It reappears for example, in 1022/1613 in Urfa with the Yusuf Pasha Cami which has six domes[116] and in the nineteenth century with the Abdülâziz mosque at Söğüt, modified by the baroque experience. But the true future of the Ottoman mosque lay with the Bursa type.

52

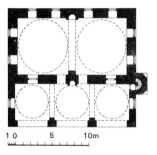

52 *Abdal Mehmet Cami, Bursa.*
Plan, scale 1:500.
An ideal solution to the
double-domed mosque.

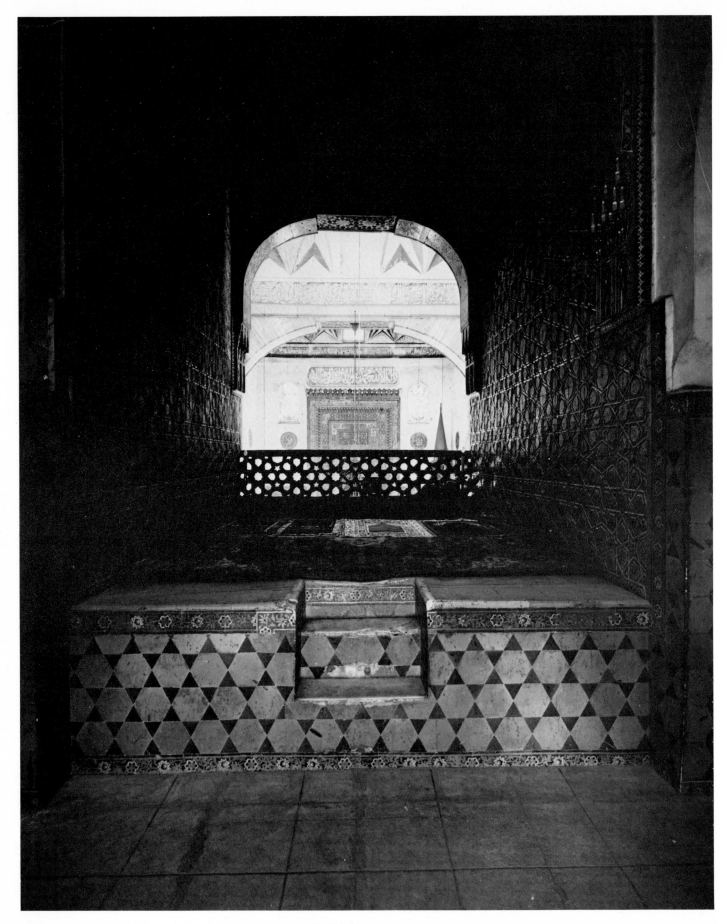

53 *Yeşil Cami, Bursa. The royal loge looking towards the mihrab below.*

3

Bursa – the Green Mosque and after

WITH TIMUR GONE and the fratricidal civil war over, Çelebi Mehmet Han set about the recovery of the Anatolian provinces and the building of his mosque in Bursa, the Yeşil Cami – which, because of its tiles and carved marble, is the most famous of them all – and his türbe, now standing among cypresses above it.[1] This foundation suffered severely from the earthquake of 1855, and the mosque domes were only rebuilt because the Vali, the cultured Ahmet Vefik Pasha, was a man of determination. As he was unable to find a Turkish architect qualified to carry out the repairs, he called Léon Parvillée to Bursa in 1863[2] to restore this mosque and the Ulu Cami together with the Orhaniye and the Muradiye. Parvillée was a man of sensitivity and had great powers of observation, although he did have occasional inexplicable lapses. That he saved the mosque is beyond dispute, but he was handicapped by shortages of money and skilled labour and by his lack of experience of the Selçuk and early Ottoman periods. Gabriel[3] has censored him for not restoring the original decoration of the vaults and walls of which vestiges survive, but his whitewash was preferable to most nineteenth-century attempts to copy old paintwork, or the recent picking out of the stalactites of the Süleymaniye.[4] These traces of paint in some of the Yeşil Cami's rooms, however much retouched, are warm and rich and show that the dome and stalactite squinches were once covered in foliate arabesques of a predominantly terracotta colour. One can also get an idea of the painting in mosque interiors from the türbes of Cem and of Süleyman Sultan in the Muradiye cemetery in Bursa, the Hacı Cami at Iznik, and the mosque of Murat II at Edirne where there is an astonishing mixture of styles. In the Cem mausoleum, pattern is imposed upon pattern in varying colours, especially where calligraphy forms the base. These designs are related to those used in wood and stone. There was nothing sober, white and cool about them, but every attempt was made to create splendour.

On entering the Yeşil Cami, one finds oneself in a foyer with a broad hall on either side, from which stairs lead up through the thickness of the walls to the royal apartments. In each of these lobbies are two Byzantine columns with basket capitals which add to the impression of a narthex; but this the lobbies are not, for the area is strictly secular: you are not yet in the mosque at all. The tradition of the vestibule goes back to the Selçuk medreses like the Hatuniye at Kayseri or the Gök Medrese of Tokat; it is disagreeable to pass directly from the street into the court. At the Gök Medrese at Sivas or the Sırçalı at Konya, doors admit directly to the flanking rooms from the hallway, but this was not a rule. The Karatay Medrese had its entry at the side, doubtless to avoid draughts which could ripple the surface of the pool and disturb the reflection of the stars. There is no room off the central hall of the Ince Minare Medrese, also at Konya. At the Hudavendigâr mosque, the rooms off the hall had no way into the mosque itself. At the Yeşil Cami the side extensions were essential because of the throng of officers of state, courtiers and humble men who wished to petition their sultan. Moreover, these vestibules admit to small lobbies which lead to two independent corner rooms like those at the Hudavendigâr. They are fitted with ocaks and recesses and were either dervish rooms or offices of government. Their function obviously varied according to circumstances.

At the ends of the vestibules on the north are flights of stairs leading to the upper rooms which open off the landings. These rooms have lattice windows on to the inner court, ocaks and shelves, but are detached from the place for prayer. They also have windows on to the loggias, each of which has a small fountain with a slender jet like those in the portico of the mosque of Beyazit p 7* Pasha at Amasya. An antechamber leads to the symbolic steps up to the hünkâr mahfil or royal box.[5] This splendid loge, in effect the fourth eyvan raised into 53 the air, is panelled with tiles and has a noble gilded ceiling and a ceramic balustrade pierced with stars. The west loggia has the outline of two boards for games of chance or casting horoscopes engraved into its marble sofa.[6] Beyond the balustrade, a step up into the thickness of the wall (2·25 metres), there is a splendid view of the Bursa plain, but the loggia is protected from all but the north wind and is a place of delight and relaxation. At the corner, a small door leads to corkscrew stairs which give access to the extensive and complicated lofts. From outside it looks as if there were two more loggias but this is a rare case of deception deliberately contrived in Ottoman architecture. They are false and mask a small upper window of the great room below and there is no means of access to them. The suite on the north-west is said to have been the haremlık and that on the north-east the selâmlık but there is no proof that they were other than dervish rooms.

Descending the stairs to the central hall again, one steps into an inner vestibule the walls of which are covered with deep green tiles in which great wheels of blue, white and yellow arabesques of tendrils and flowers are set. The splendour

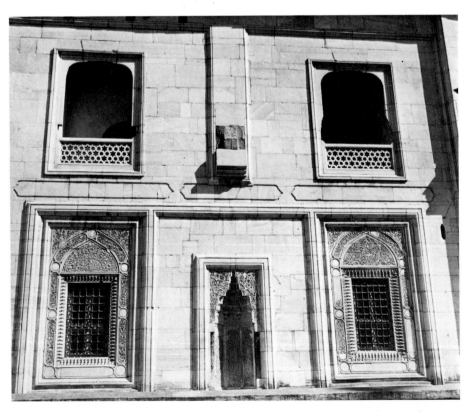

54 *Yeşil Cami, Bursa. The springing of one arch of the unbuilt portico can be seen above the mihrab.*

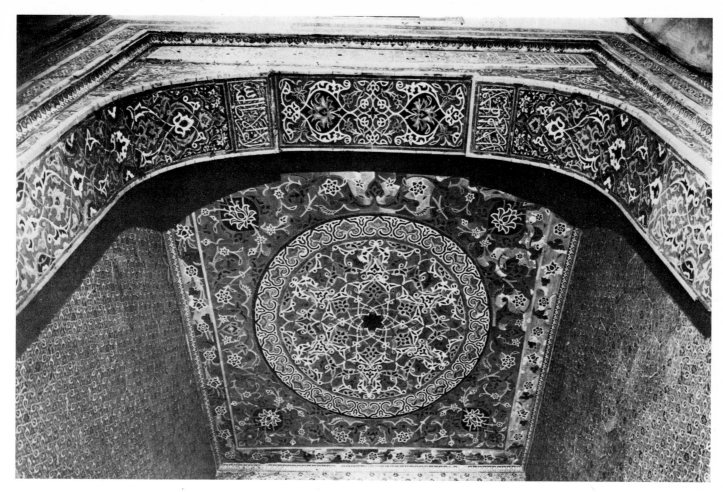

55 *Yeşil Cami, Bursa. Detail of the ceiling of a tiled eyvan facing the mihrab across the inner court.*

of these panels lies in the variation of their intensity. The dimness of this passage lures one away from the outside world and prepares one for the vision of the mihrab in all its glory as the gate of paradise beyond the court. This has a fountain with an onyx cup, under a dome (12·50 metres), the oculus of which Parvillée closed with a lantern.[7] Right and left are the two large eyvans and, recessed on each side of the vestibule, are richly tiled mahfils in the centre of whose ceilings are wheels of roseate arabesques of fantastic complexity. The wainscot tiles of the eyvans are simpler although their original deep green hexagons were gilded after firing and gold traces lie over the cloudy surface like a fragile veiling. Beyond the eyvans are two tabhane or tekke rooms complete with ocaks and niches which are now painted a tasteless brown. The south-west room has a fine ribbed dome and handsome stalactite squinches and has the best preserved paintwork; this follows the tile designs. The carving of the plaster of the ocak wall is related to work in wood, and its division into three sections by dentillated frames imitates the casements outside. A polygonal ocak hood projects into the room. The wall is panelled with hexagonal and triangular tiles forming stars, and over the door is a fine arch carrying an inscription in three lines of calligraphy. An interesting feature is that there are windows in the drum but also blind windows in the stalactite squinches. The habit of referring to these rooms as libraries persists, but books were kept in chests and boxes in that period and were far too precious to leave casually on a shelf by the fire. Korans were stored in coffers of inlaid precious woods, such as cedar and ebony, and ivory and mother-of-pearl. Under the domed lid the painter sometimes copied the patterns used in the domes of the mosques themselves.[8] Some dervishes were rough and even wild, but many

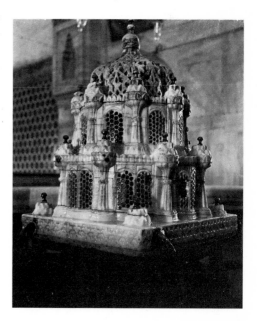

56 *Yeşil Cami, Bursa. The fountain in the basin of the interior court.*

were men of culture and refinement who might well find pleasure in relaxing in these noble rooms before a warm brazier. It is noteworthy that each sultan belonged to his own dervish order right down to Mehmet V Reşat in the twentieth century.

One ascends three steps from the court to the prayer hall. As was often the 57 custom with the Bursa-type mosque, these stairs are flanked by rows of papuçluk niches for the sandals of the faithful, thus proving that the court was paved, not carpeted, and that the fountain was for use.[9] Before one, in all its glory, is the mihrab with its moulded tile frame and niche, twelve rows of stalactites high, culminating in a six-ribbed shell. Above its flanking columns, ribbed to appear like trees of life, the flat surface is full of flowers and entwining stems, their abundance a symbol of a fertile reign.[10] Two bosses like cages on either side represent the sun and moon. Their intricate three-dimensional work, as with that of the prismatic columns and the castellations, is achieved by the potter applying the *cire perdue* technique of a sculptor to his tiles. In the firing, at the point when the glaze begins to set and the clay harden, the molten wax vanishes away to leave an effect of fretwork behind. Otherwise, the Bursa tiles are colourglaze tiles on a terracotta tile base with small flecks of siliceous matter in it. The four or five colours are separated by a thread which turns to ash in the firing, the *cuerda seca* technique. This mihrab is more than the gate of paradise: it is paradise itself.[11]

The Selçuks never created such ceramic splendour as is to be seen in this sanctuary, although their tiles did achieve greater brilliance. The union of deep blue and green which forms the chief field of the walls is enriched with white and a superb yellow. The use of gilding has already been noted. The royal loge 53 has the most beautiful tile balustrade made up of traditional polygons and stars. Although there are many nineteenth-century replacements among the wall tiles, the brick and plaster stars of the Yıldırım Cami here awaken to light and life. Abstract, but sensual, their variety sustains unbroken interest. The ceiling is full of stars and stalactites which make yet more stars, flowers in bloom, or lotuses like radiant suns. Everything is significant in Islamic decoration and there is constant reference in stone and brick, tile, wood and plaster on walls, ceilings, squinches or doors to the night sky, symbol of a greater world and all wisdom, until one is forced to accept the message and see the mosque as an image of heaven and men as the slaves of the cycles of the spheres. At the same time, one is consoled and uplifted by a vivid vision of the parterres of paradise.

In the royal box is an inscription, significantly in Persian, stating that this splendid tiled room with its glowing gold ceiling is the work of Mehmet the Eccentric,[12] who must therefore be responsible for the tribunes below since their style is identical. In what lay his eccentricity one wonders? On the right of the mihrab above the capital of the column is a simple statement written in white on the deep blue ground of the ceramic: The Work of the Masters of Tabriz.[13] On the other side are two verses of Sadi referring to tyranny and injustice.[14] Tabriz had long been a centre of Persian pottery production[15] but one is intrigued that these men should have been called refugees and that they were glad to work for the Ottoman khan. It cannot be assumed that they were ill-treated Turks and there is no justification for Ünsal's statement[16] that the tiling carries on Selçuk traditions and techniques. Ünsal's attribution of all the tiling in the mosque to Mehmet is equally unwarranted although he could have supervised that part of the work. The style of the work is not exclusive to Tabriz or to Bursa, but represents a fashion which spread over Central Asia and Iran.

Gabriel[17] implies that the tiles are related to Selçuk work and the first from the kilns of Iznik. Lane's authoritative work[18] makes it clear that there was a break after the collapse of Selçuk rule and during the fight for life among the petty Beylik princes. Such pottery as there may have been in Anatolia was coarse so-called Miletus ware. Suddenly, work of a skill that implies generations of transmitted experience occurs between 1419 and 1424 in this mosque, in 1421 in the türbe above it, and in 1433 in the Muradiye at Edirne where some tiles in blue

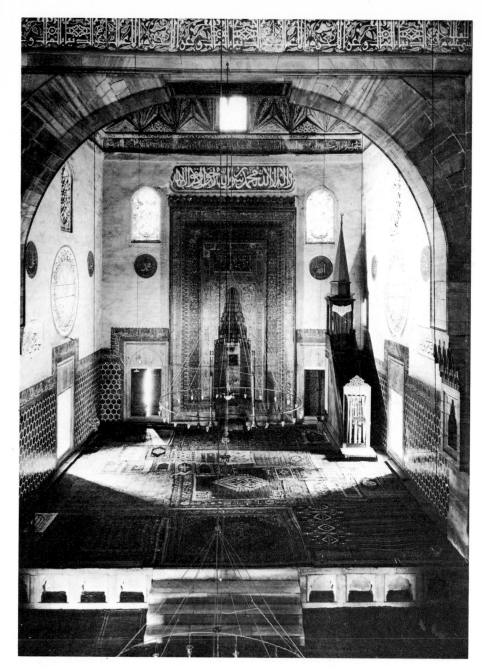

57 Yeşil Cami, Bursa. The prayer hall with the steps up from the court. The decoration above tile-level is late in date.

and white show strong Chinese influence. There are tiles which probably date from 1429 in the Cem tomb. The last tiles which can be attributed to this school are two pointed tympana sets carrying kufic inscriptions in the courtyard of Üç Şerefeli, which cannot be dated later than 1447.[19] However, the *cuerda seca* technique was to be revived.[20]

Above the royal box is yet another inscription in honour of Ali bin Ilyas Ali, known as Nakkaş Ali or Ali the Designer. He was born in Bursa and built his own mosque in the citadel, where a quarter still bears his name.[21] He was likely to have been in charge of the decoration in tiles, wood, plaster and paint. Although it is possible that he was only a painter, the size and position of his inscription in tiles makes this unlikely. He must have been either the director or else a master of considerable eminence, and no minor artist, to be honoured there or to be able to afford to build for himself.

The tiles are the glory of the mosque interior. The domes outside are no longer green but covered in lead in the classical Ottoman manner. Gabriel states that the use of lead dates from the fifteenth century but the Green Mosque retained its original dome tiles into the seventeenth century for Evliya – whose evidence Gabriel[22] accepts a trifle cautiously – states that the dome and the crowns of the minarets were still covered in tiles which sparkled like emeralds in the rays of the sun.

The tragedy of the Green Mosque is that the portico was never built because work would stop on a sultan's private mosque when he died. The removal of the fake marble, wooden addition of the nineteenth century was essential. The frontispiece to Dutemple's *En Turquie d'Asie* dating from the 1880s shows a ponderous canopy projecting over the entry. The revealed façade centres on a large and grand door[23] with a long inscription in bronze above it, and above that, set into the cascade of its stalactite crown, a small window similar to that at Yıldırım Cami which lights the floor of the foyer to the royal box. Fine recessed sofas on each side of the doorway have steps over twin papuçluks[24] while above is the magnificent stalactite half-dome, the flat face of which, set in a strongly ribbed frame, is a plantation of arabesques and inscriptions in Hattı and Rumi scripts. Above and behind, a small dome emerges from the sloping roof over the royal apartments as a prelude to the major dome of the inner court. On each side, where the two wing domes of the portico should be, are set two grand casements with belts of inscriptions punctuated by circles round their deeply toothed frames.[25] These are also framed in embryonic-stalactite toothing.[26] The tympana of the windows are enriched with arabesques as are the sets of three windows down the east and west walls of the tabhane rooms; the four which light the harem were framed additionally in blue tiles. Beneath the springing of the arches that divide the two missing domes each side of the portico is a small mihrab, forming half of a decagon. It has a rich stalactite ceiling faced by an elaborate arch which in silhouette resembles a stupa; its facets are alive with leaves and tendrils. These arches spring from porphyry colonnettes. Above the casements, at the upper level, are four loggias with balustrades of interlocking rosettes from which rise stilted arches. Their recession is important because it brings the whole face to three-dimensional life. Externally the building is still a group of defined units drawn together under the sloping of the roof over the flanking tabhanes and, by the progression of the lesser domes, towards the great cupola over the court. This unification was increased by the marble facing which once was elegantly ordered in courses of thin and thick blocks which were disrupted by the earthquake. They were replaced, but without respect for the graining of the Marmara (Proconessian) marble.

The mosque was complete, but not the decoration, in December 1419 or January *822*/1420, for there is a splendidly boastful inscription above the north door which states that: 'In the name of God, in whose universal mercy is refuge, work of the Craftsman and the Creator of Power, this noble place, reflection of the Infinite Garden of Delight, copies by the Will of the All-Powerful and Omnipotent, the Dawn of the Other World, woven with the lustre of life here below, which proudly advances across the land and without which the great towns fall into disorder: here is a building such as no nation has been presented with since the sky began to turn. The very great Sultan and most noble Sovereign, King of East and West, Overlord of the Persians and the Arabs, aided by the support of the Lord of the Worlds, Ghiyath al-Dunya Al-Din, the Sultan son of a Sultan, the Sultan Mehmet son of Beyazit son of Murat son of Orhan, may God perpetuate his power in the Caliphate of the Earth and let his ships sail hopefully on the Seas of Aspiration, has built this house when he ordered the digging of its foundations, its sturdy erection, the strong setting of its courses, and its building. This was achieved in 822.'

Above the niches each side of the door are inscriptions to Hacı İvaz son of Ahi Beyazit who designed the mosque and fixed its proportions. The Ahi connection here is of interest. It is clear that he was the overall architect but he was also a vezir and Subaşı or Prefect of Bursa, later its governor, and had much else to do. He had built a mosque, medrese and a han of his own. He was dismissed by Murat

II in 1426 or 1427, probably blinded, and died in 1428.[27] It is possible that the potentate had begun life as an artisan which the title Ahi, borne by both his father and his son, implies. Since he had made the pilgrimage to Mecca, he seems also to have been a devout and more or less orthodox Moslem. He would have ordered the general structure and have been concerned with the overseeing of the work. It is less likely that he had the time to be the working architect. The Masons' Guild which had been responsible over the years for a succession of monuments from the Orhaniye to the Yeşil Cami must have educated many experienced masters. Moreover, Ottoman plans were elementary[28] and the builder relied on the craftsman to apply his experience. The masons worked in standardized sizes of stone and lengths of wood and could incorporate special decorative features without undue difficulty. Uniformity of design was the result of conformity and also leadership and teamwork between plasterers and stone-carvers, tile-makers and bricklayers. The sculpture of the stalactites of this mosque could not be planned but only based on a traditional formula known to the craftsmen skilled in this work.

The Yeşil Cami presents the familiar problem of the placing of the minarets. They were both rebuilt, the north-westerly clearly on an old base with traces of glazed brick decoration from an early period, by Parvillée. They stand most awkwardly on the corners of the façade where the wall is in no way strengthened to receive them and where access can only be gained through the royal apartments and then up the winding stairs to the attics; these then have to be crossed and the actual minaret ascended. It could hardly have been worse contrived had that been the deliberate purpose. One is forced to conclude that they were a later addition and that at first there were no minarets or else they, or a lonely one, stood somewhere else. I find it hard to picture Bursa full of independent minarets – like that of the Ulu Cami – which with only two exceptions have all vanished without a trace. The most important exception is that of the Timurtaş Cami dated *806/1404*,[29] the minaret of which stands twenty metres in front of the mosque. But I find the resemblance to a zaviye so marked in the plan of this mosque that I would confirm Gabriel's reservations concerning its history, and suppose that the minaret appeared at a later date, when it was converted at a time when the Ulema was reducing the powers of the dervishes and Ahis. Kara Timur-taş was a Gazi, the commander-in-chief of Murat I and Yıldırım Beyazit and likely to favour the Ahis who supported the Ottoman conquest of the Balkans as opposed to the pan-Asiatic policy of the orthodox. It is significant that there was once an imaret attached to this mosque on its north-west side. When the time came to build a minaret, none of the mosque walls was strong enough to carry the weight and a building already occupied the appropriate site. There was good reason therefore to erect it in the only vacant place which was the small piazza in front of the zaviye.[30] It seems plausible that when the royal mosques like the Yıldırım and the Yeşil were chapels attached to the palace they had no minarets and when the sultan died his successor built a new mosque for himself. The old was left to the widows while the good works prescribed in the vakfiye were paid for out of the revenues of its endowment. The royal apartments would lose their importance and the mosque become fully public. The need for a minaret would then arise.[31] But since the foundation was still royal, there had to be two of them and this created an immediate problem because they ought to be set at the north-west and north-east corners of the façade. It has been argued that the first minarets were placed like those of the Gök medreses, each side of the entry, or rather each side of tribunes where there is a thickening of the masonry and where corkscrew stairs originally may have been set where are now little lobbies. This would imply, however, that the mosque was designed to carry minarets from the start. They would, indeed, be in the right position, that is to say at the corners of the mosque or, at least of its courtyard. But this theory pre-supposes considerable structural alterations. It is regrettable that Parvillée dis-cusses none of these problems in his book.

Near the entry to the Muradiye mosque and again at several points in the

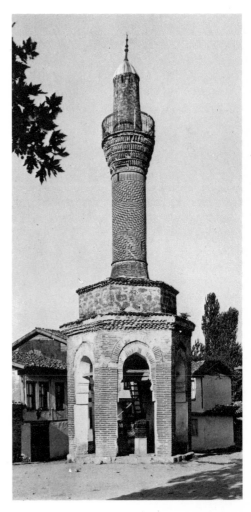

58 Deliktaş Minaret, Bursa. An example of an independent minaret set above the şadırvan.

Yeşil Cami there are a number of symbols in tile or lead inset into the wall, some of which recall those already mentioned in connection with the Balat mosque. Stars with five, six or eight points predominate but tile circles and lead ovals appear. The tiles are always blue and the most interesting symbol of all is the blue bar with half a star at each end at the Muradiye which is found in the west wall of the entry bay and, in truncated form, again lower down. This thunderbolt is like the centres of motifs of interlacing zigzags found in the türbe of Sahip Ata at Konya dating from 1282 and, to a lesser degree, at the mosque of Divrik.[32] It also relates to one of the basic forms which radiate in the façade niches at Yıldırım between the pendent stalactites[33] which were also once blue.

The same device occurs once at the Green Mosque at the northern extremity of the west side, but here it is elaborated in the middle by the addition top and bottom of small trefoil shapes. The position of the symbols appears to follow no logical ordering. They are to be found in the arch of the west loggia and its door to the stairs leading to the attic or at the east end of the façade. There are several in the marble of the south wall of the hall of prayer and one on its west side. Some may have been moved and some damaged, since fragments of tile occur elsewhere. Gabriel tentatively suggests that they are superior masons' marks or signatures of the Brotherhood, but it does not seem very likely. They are not made by masons but by potters and lead workers, nor are they like masons' marks in form. One is aware that, apart from the oval of lead, the majority are in the shape of stars and planets and that the more elaborate designs represent a flash of lightning or a thunderbolt.[34] There does seem to be a relationship with the planets and stars of the minber of the Ulu Cami and the hierarchy of symbols of the sky that dominates Islamic design to an extent which approaches obsession.[35] Nomads are familiar with the sky and astrology is the groomsman of fear. It is a pity that these signs may have lost their original positions which could have helped towards discovering their elusive significance. It seems that they may have been potent talismans and have nothing to do with masons, whose names are written legibly elsewhere.

The Yeşil Türbe high above the mosque was completed under the orders of Hacı İvaz at the command of Murat II following Mehmet I's death in May, 1421. This tomb is much nearer to the Selçuk type than that of the earlier Ottoman sultans and, through the Selçuks, is nearer to the Iranian kümbets and the fragile yurts or tents of the people living in Central Asia. It was the noblest tomb that the dynasty had yet achieved, but the disastrous earthquake has shorn the exterior of its faience which has been replaced with Kütahya tiles in varying shades of blue which succeed in making pleasing abstract designs.[36] Formerly, these walls were likely to have been faced with turquoise tiles, apart from the floral frames and tympana of the windows. Some of the old tiles of the portal have survived. The doors themselves are of exceptionally fine workmanship, the wood richly carved and the bronze handles particularly elegant and neat. The interior floral panels are closely related to those of the mosque as are the green tiles inside the door. The mihrab rivals that of the mosque and is crested with bouquets like flamboyant aces of spades cut out of multifoil arches.[37] Similar forms are seen in the shallow carving over a window in the east wall of the prayer hall of the cami. The bands of inscription in long panels between circles surmounted by bosses are also related to those of the mosque windows. One is constantly made to see the careful co-ordination of all the work of this complex. Triple toothing borders the mihrab, followed by the inevitable intricate pattern of stars. A pair of ceramic columns guard the stalactite niche and the central panel. Inset within a multifoil arch is a complex garden of hyacinths, marguerites, carnations and roses growing in paradise.[38] On either side decorated candles burn in gold bell-bottomed candlesticks inscribed with the names of Allah and Muhammed respectively, while in the centre hangs an elaborate representation of one of the beautiful mosque lamps of the period. Each window is surmounted by an inscription and in the ceilings of each casement is a multi-coloured mosaic of tile.

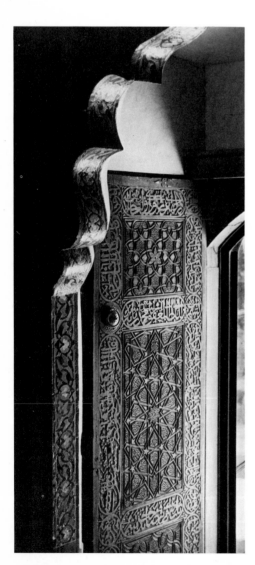

59 Yeşil Türbe, Bursa. A panel of the doorway through the multifoliate arch.

61   In the middle of the mausoleum is an octagonal tiled platform in the centre of which Mehmet once lay all alone in symbolic majesty surrounded by candles and their message of light, but three of his family have joined him on his eminence and four others together with his nurse lie behind. The royal catafalque is mounted on a second rostrum which is bordered by an arcade of flowers with all the exquisite colours employed in the mihrab, including ultramarine, turquoise, the unmatched fresh yellow and deep green, white and black and grey and, in addition, a pale mauve tinged with rose which seeks to excel them all. The coffin is glazed with gilded inscriptions, bold elifs and a lively, running naskhi script.[39]

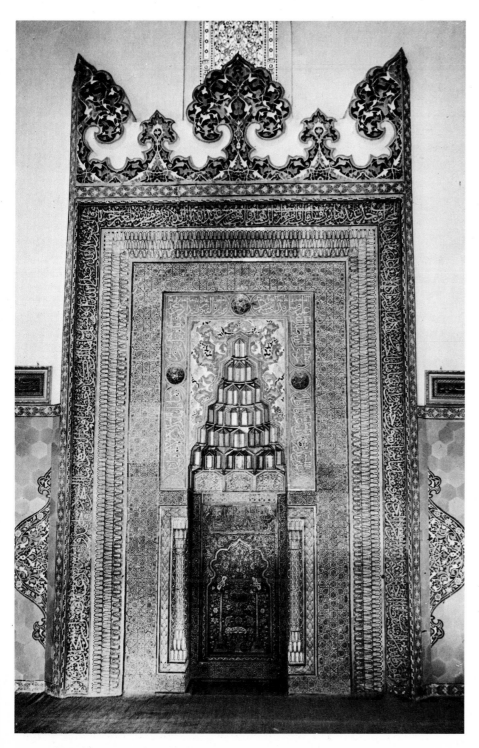

60 Yeşil Türbe, Bursa. The mihrab.

The only misfortunes are the modern pink chandelier and coloured-glass windows. The sultan was buried in the low vaults beneath – which are divided into five compartments – because Islamic law forbids burial above the ground. An entry was discovered below the east face of this sepulchral octagon, but nothing was found of the sultan and the twenty-three other men, woman and children buried there, except a few bones which rats had scattered.[40] There was no longer mummification under the Ottomans as there had been in Mongol times at Amasya or at Manisa under the Saruhan, where Ibn Battuta[41] found the Emir at his son's türbe and states that the boy, who had died some months before, had been embalmed and placed in a wooden coffin with a lid of tinned iron. This was raised on light trestles in a chamber without a roof so that the smell could escape.[42] Later it was domed and the coffin set at ground level and his garments laid upon it. Here was an early instance of the türbe with an oculus and of the habit of covering the sarcophagus with grave clothes in rich materials.[43]

The Yeşil foundation was endowed with fertile lands from Izmit[44] to Pendik.[45] There are still some signs of the imaret which these funds supported. It was a mixture of brick and uncut stone and consisted of a long chamber (approximately 22 × 10 metres) with an ocak and an inner room beyond. Near the door which opened into the principal room were two bake-ovens on the east side. Next to these was the twin-domed kitchen (about 10 × 3·50 metres) with the cooking ranges.

The medrese, now the local museum, is more conventional in plan than that of Yıldırım. Apart from the dershane, it is nearly square and the cells are set round a spacious garden with a large polygonal basin in the middle. The arches of the porticoes are carried on an assortment of Byzantine columns and capitals. The dershane is very lofty and approached by a double flight of eight steps. It is surmounted by a dome (9 metres) on a moderately high octagonal drum. There is a large mihrab niche so that the room could be used for prayer. The dershane is

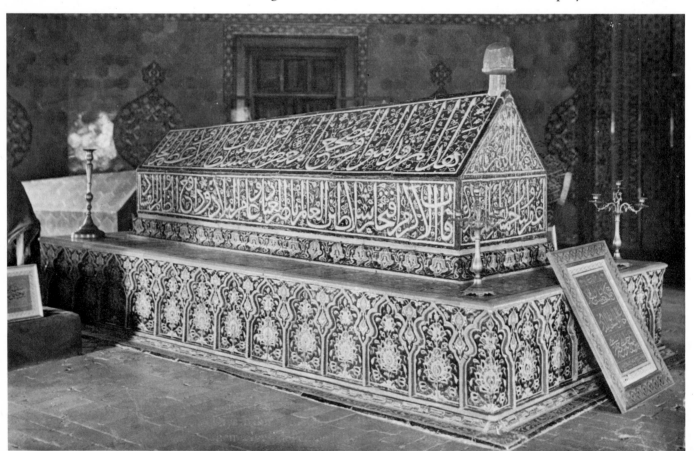

61 Yeşil Türbe, Bursa. The symbolic tomb of Mehmet I.

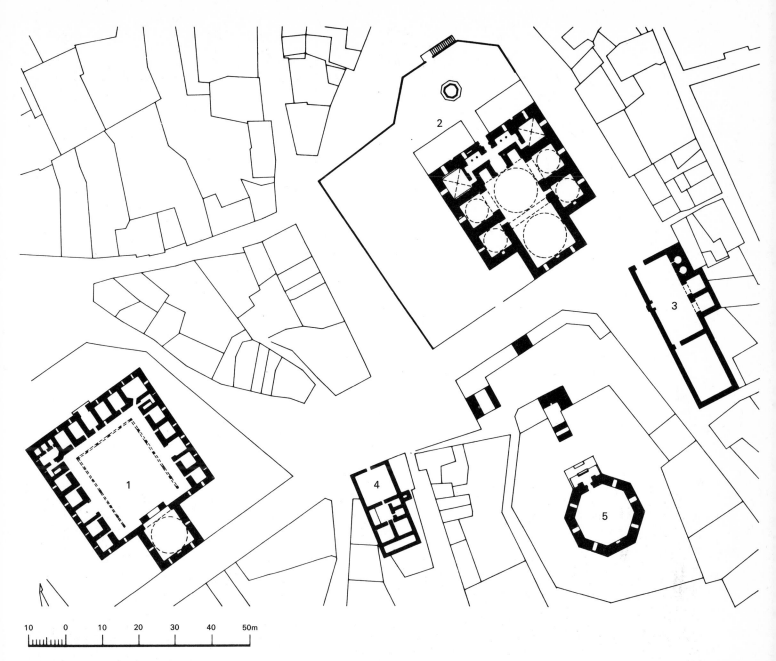

62 *Yeşil Complex, Bursa. Plan, scale 1 : 1,000. Account must be taken of the disappearance of the wooden structures. 1 medrese; 2 cami; 3 imaret; 4 hamam; 5 türbe.*

high above the court, and the area between it and the cloister is filled with an extension of the wall which is merely a screen to improve the proportions. A similar solution was used at the Yıldırım medrese. It recalls the much more extravagant masking achieved by the façades of Romanesque churches in Italy such as the Duomo at Cremona. There are pairs of cells on each side of the eyvans on the east and west and two more each side of the entry. The cell in the north-east corner is larger than the others and presumably was used by a teacher. The corresponding cell in the north-west corner forms a commodious marble wash-room with three closets. There are the remains of tiles over the door, which is set back in the fourth eyvan in the centre of the north front, and in the small west eyvan which has a beautiful example of a solar ceiling resplendent with twenty rays springing from a central boss. In the tympana of the windows is an interesting series of simple reversible patterns in brick and mortar.[46] On the north side, above the four windows on the right, are careful reversals of the patterns on the left.

Hacı İvaz bin Ahi Beyazit, the minister responsible for this great complex, also built the Çelebi Sultan Mehmet Cami at Dimetoka in *823*/1420.[47] Kadı Seyıd Ali Efendi was the administrator in charge of the supply of materials and Toğan Bey was the controller. Ayverdi suggests that he could have been Toğan bin Abdullah who worked on the Beyazit Pasha Cami at Amasya.[48] The Çelebi Cami is a large square mosque with a pitched roof which may have been the first of a series to have a wooden dome inset under it. The arch of the south door has fine zigzag chevron frames and the inscriptive target is strikingly dominated by tall, vigorous elifs which became traditional. The minaret has claim to mark the first Ottoman use of two şerefes. Another monument of the reign is the Çelebi Mehmet Medrese at Merzifon which has an inscription dated *817*/1414 and was built by Abu Bekir bin Mehmet. It is a fine example of a classical square medrese with four eyvans and twenty cells, beautifully logical and compact in plan. Its very grand entrance porch had a cumbersome clock tower added in the nineteenth century.

p 7

As soon as the workmen were freed by the completion of his father's complex, and he was established in power, Murat II began his own foundation in the centre of which is his medrese, which was the most beautiful in Bursa. Its architect was intellectually superior to that of the Mehmet I medrese for the square plan is perfectly controlled. There is the same recessed porch embracing the north eyvan but this has new interest because it is cut into by a half-flight of stairs. The court forms a perfect square with five cells east and west and with larger cells in the corners, which avoid awkward angled entries. There are small rooms between the cells each side of the gate.[49] The dershane has a bolder screen-wall to carry it across to the revaks and this is rivalled by the superb pishtak door of the porch. Both achieve dramatic effects out of the interlocking of hexagonal patterns. But everywhere varying patterns are designed with a mastery that excels the other monuments, while the little dershane is brilliant with tiles.

Hardly anything now remains of the imaret, but the plan shows many improvements on that of the Green Mosque. A long corridor leads past the refectory to the kitchen and a small room, which may have been an office or a store. The kitchen has a large central pier round which its life revolved, and a big oven, a fireplace, and a fountain with a small domed scullery beside it. Beyond was a second kitchen divided by two piers with three large ranges and four small ones lined up across the north wall. While the kitchen arrangements were capacious, the dining hall was small and it would look as if most of those fed carried their food away with them.

Behind the medrese and the mosque was the great burial ground of the Ottoman House, although Murat was the only sultan to be buried there. Besides the sepulchres of many princes were the graves of servants, friends and favourites. In the intimate park are twelve türbes, of varying dates but similar style, forming a small boulevard. The largest is that of Murat himself who died on 3 February 1451.[50] It was completed before 1437 and may have been built immediately after the completion of the mosque in *830*/(30 November) 1426. It follows the tradition set by the tombs of Osman, Orhan and Murat I, and it is left as was first intended, with the single grave of the sovereign set in regal loneliness in the centre under its dome.[51] This is open to the sky so that the water of heaven might keep fresh the flowers which grew in the soil of the grave: a simple mound of earth enclosed in marble.[52] The dome is carried on four piers and four Byzantine columns with Byzantine capitals from which spring eight pointed arches bearing an octagonal drum made up of four squinches and four ogee arches. There is a broad ambulatory round the tomb and the square chamber, lit by casements each side of the door and the mihrab. There are three down the west and three down the east side. But in the east side there is an annexe in which are four graves, two of them of Murat's sons who predeceased him,[53] so that the first window has become a door and the central window looks into this annexe. Between the door and the window is a porphyry column, curiously placed, with re-used Byzantine capitals both for capital and base. The dome is carried on stalactite squinches. There is a handsome baroque canopy over the entry with a pretty wooden painted ceiling, which detracts from the original austerity; the paint-work and the chandelier inside are even more unfortunate.

The inscription over the door refers, among other things, to Murat as Captain of the Warriors and the Champions of the Holy War.[54] This was not the only side to his character. Alderson discusses his abdications in the light of Babinger's *Mehmet II*,[55] for he twice sought to give up the throne. At the end of 1444 he retired to Manisa[56] – a western town attractively set on a hillside of gardens, captured by the Ottomans in 1425[57] – leaving his heir, Mehmet II, three months short of thirteen, sovereign in Edirne. He was weary of twenty years of wars and his victories over the Karamanoğlus in the east and the Crusaders in the west had assured the safety of the frontiers. He appears to have been dispirited and in search of a contemplative life in the company of mystics. Hasluck,[58] quoting Phrantses, states that he went to Manisa as a dervish. In May, 1446, he had to return to power because the Sadrazam Candarlı Halil Pasha was alarmed at the restiveness of the Janissaries. He returned reluctantly, still possessed of that melancholy that from time to time overcomes followers of Islam, and lingered at Bursa throughout August. There, significantly, he made his will. In September, he reached Edirne and sent his now fourteen-and-a-half-year-old son, Mehmet, whom he did not love, to Manisa to learn wisdom.

What is of interest in the context of architecture is the importance that Murat attached to the contemplative dervish orders. It substantiated their position in the hierarchy and shows the likelihood of their constant attendance at his court. In contrast to the sumptuous worldliness of Mehmet I's catafalque, the symbolic earth which covers Murat comes from another kingdom.

His türbe was neither the first to have two rooms nor was it the last. The ghoulish sixteenth-century annexe to that of Murat III served the same function, although it had a separate entrance, because so many princes were strangled upon their elder brother's accession that extra room had to be created for their corpses, in spite of the vastness of their father's sepulchre.[59] At Iznik, one of the earliest Ottoman türbes is known as the Hacı Camasa or Kırk Kızlar Türbe, the tomb of the Forty Maidens.[60] The building, even in decay, is interesting. The main room is square with a duodecagonal drum bearing a conical tiled roof but in addition there is the small but vaulted anteroom: constructed of two courses of brick to three of stone, the holes in the façade suggest that it may have been, or was intended to have been, faced with marble. It is difficult to determine whether it is a Byzantine building adapted or if it was built after the capture of the town.[61]

63 The very large türbe of Candarlı Hayrettin Pasha dated 789/1387[62] just beyond the Lefke Gate is certainly Ottoman; it is still visited by women in pursuit of blessings from older gods than Allah. The large square hall under the higher dome is empty, but like Murat II's tomb there is a door into a second chamber and also a window with a low sill. The floor level is lowered so that the plinth on which the two richly carved sarcophagi rest is level with the floor of the first room. Under the dome, which has an oculus, are the emir and his son Ali Pasha. There is no mihrab. It is a reversal of the Muradiye tomb, for one would have expected the potentates to have rested under the greater dome.[63]

The city of the dead in the garden of the Muradiye held traditions older than those of Islam, just as did the dervish orders. It was to grow through the years but the masonry followed the form of Murat's own türbe, three courses of brick to one of ashlar blocks flanked by tiles. There is variation in detail, but the earlier tombs established the elements of the classical tradition, chiefly the octagonal plan and the simplification of the exterior details which enrich the türbes of the Selçuks. Austerity is present in the tomb of Mustafa, son of Fatih the Conqueror, which dates from 1430[64] and which was originally built for Ahmet Çelebi, the son of Mehmet I, who died of the plague in 1429 at the age of twenty-seven. He had been blinded nine years before, together with his brothers Mahmud and Yusuf, then aged seven and six,[65] when Murat II ascended the throne.[66] The sultan atoned for the brutal necessities of state by building them this handsome

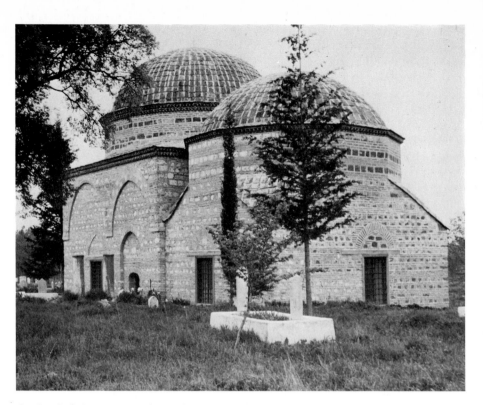

63 Candarlı Hayrettin Pasha Türbe, Iznik. The graves lie under the lower dome.

sepulchre. It is a spacious octagonal türbe with a white marble porch of grace-ful, hipped arches and has marble window-frames. The panels of tile which form the high wainscot are of the same period as those of the mosque and are set in floral borders. They are hexagonal and austerely blue and black. The graves are in neat ranks of two and four, and all are open and filled with earth.

Set apart east of the mosque are two türbes, the larger of which is that of Hatice Hatun, the alleged mother of Mehmet II who built it for her during the lifetime of his father.[67] She was a Candar and daughter of Mehmet's aunt, Selçuk Sultan, and therefore his first cousin, not his mother. The tomb is known as the Hatuniye and it was completed in the early autumn of *853*/1449. Since Hümâ Sultan died in September 1449, it would be reasonable to suppose that this türbe was constructed for her and that it was she who was Mehmet's mother, but beside Hatice's sarcophagus there is another one, which is unidentified and could be that of Hümâ. The inscription[68] shows that the work was clearly that of Mehmet. Outside, this hexagonal building is plain but inside six tall and elegant arches lead up to the six pendentives which carry the dome. The fifteenth-century paint has been replaced by fake marbling, but the soft red and blue motif in the dome could approximate to the original. There is room for a third sarco-phagus on the plinth. A star in lead each side of the door recalls those of the Green Mosque and the mosque of the Muradiye complex itself.

Beside the Hatuniye is the Cariyeler Türbe or Tomb of the Odalisques or Concubines. Its date is not known, but it could be of the Murat period. It is a humble open square pavilion with a dome supported on eight piers with two pointed arches on each flank. The original tomb is set in the middle with a smaller one added towards the north. Here there could be no mihrab niche. Open türbes of this kind originated at Söğüt[69] and were common at a later date. Elsewhere in Bursa is the tomb of Ömür Bey, dated *865*/1461[70] with a dome three metres in diameter carried on four piers, which leave just enough room for his sarcophagus. The türbe of Devlet Hatun, the mother of Mehmet I, dated *816*/1414,[71] is also open and is a more elaborate version of that of the Cariyeler. The dome is carried on a trihedron frieze and is set under a conical roof recalling those of Selçuk mausoleums.

The mosque of Murat is the climax of the cross-axial eyvan type in Bursa, and is simpler than those built by his predecessors. The door is recessed and admits immediately into the court with the prayer hall six stairs up and with an eyvan on each side. The corner tabhane rooms are small and reached by passages along the north wall which end at doors into the eyvans. This suggests that the eyvans were closed, and Gabriel[72] argues cogently in favour of this. The dominant colours of the tiles are a fine deep blue and white arranged not in star patterns only but, on the kıble wall in particular, in bold crystalline clusters. This strength of design is found in the chevron honeycomb squinches which support the court-yard dome and the astonishing convex consoles in the corners of the prayer hall, which belly forth to carry three tiers of large stalactites. Above these, the drum of the dome is pierced by eight windows set between Turkish triangles and the future chevron or baklava capitals of the classical Ottoman period can be clearly seen in this building. An important development is the move to unity between the two main domes, for they are almost equal in diameter. The drum of the courtyard dome is still the greater of the two – twice as high. Its chevrons turn into stars, also found in the honeycomb formation of its squinches.[73]

The portico of five domes is carried on piers and two antique granite columns. The finely patterned façade designs include the usual interlocking wheels and also the Asian weaving pattern of right-angled castellations round a square. The strange blue ceramic symbols have already been discussed in relation to those of the Yeşil Cami. It is notable that here they concentrate about the door and, apart from those already mentioned, there are five more which form fragments of stars and which look like pieces of a cleanly cut jigsaw. Since some of the pieces are lead it is clear that their shapes were carefully designed.

The mosque has two minarets, but at the beginning of the nineteenth century there was only the east one, so the north-west minaret with its stone is a later addition. The minaret at the east end of the portico is built into the corner of the wall and is set on a weak base. It has a lead cap and it may be supposed that it was added in the sixteenth century. Gabriel[74] believes that twin minarets originally stood right and left of the door, and in his reconstructed plan[75] he closes the eyvans and thickens the masonry each side of the entry at the expense of the doors into the passages. But his approach is cerebral not visual since it is impossible to be-lieve that two minarets rose from behind the portico only two metres apart from each other. As for the closed eyvans, they exist among minor mosques such as the Timurtaş or Ebu İshak Kazeruni, but both of these are small and could have no tabhane rooms if they had eyvans instead. The mosque of Hamza Bey retains the eyvans but has a small tabhane room at the north-west end of the portico. It also has a minaret at the north-east corner which extends from the façade and looks as if it were original. This appears to confirm the theory that ordinary mosques normally needed minarets while royal foundations did not and made no provision for them.

The conventional axial eyvan Bursa mosque was certainly ideal for the grow-ing empire because the form was repeated all over Anatolia and the new Balkan provinces. It was also capable of great variation and could adapt itself to the needs of the ultimate capital, Istanbul, during the early years of Fatih's reign. At Edirne, in 824/1421, Murat built a mosque in a suburb[76] which was badly damaged by an earthquake in 1751 and heavily repaired. It was associated with the Mevlevi order of dervishes and clearly started as a tekke before a separate building was added. The mosque is remarkable for its setting and particularly for its beautiful tiles, to which reference has already been made,[77] which include not only those of the Yeşil Cami order but hexagons with a multitude of blue designs on a white ground which derive from Chinese models.[78] There is also a plethora of painting of all periods on the walls indicating the lavishness of the original decoration.

At Milas,[79] an early example of the axial eyvan Bursa type is the mosque of Firuz Bey or Ağa dating from 797/1394.[80] He was the Ottoman vali of the town.[81] The door admits to a hall off which, right and left, are two tabhane rooms while up two stairs is the mosque beyond a large arch. The arch span, however, is only

64

67

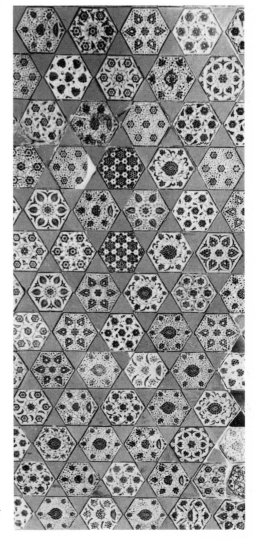

64 Muradiye Cami, Edirne. A section of the tiles.

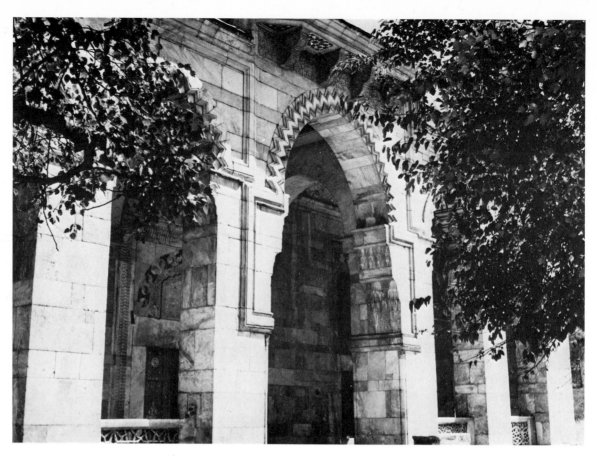

65 *Firuz Bey Cami, Milas. The central arch of the portico.*

66 *Yakup Bey Zaviye, Kütahya. The fountain court. The springing of the arches recalls Orhan Gazi Cami, Bilecik.*

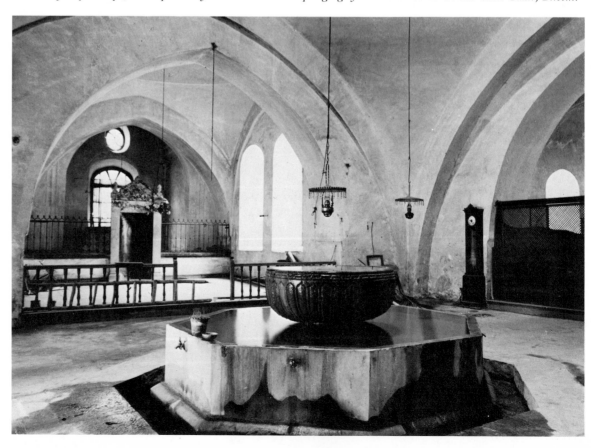

half the width of the mosque – four instead of eight metres – which makes for compactness. This was a private governor's mosque in the manner of the royal foundations at Bursa.[82] The mosque is small but of stone and has a wide barrel-vaulted porch carried on piers with a large dome rising out of its centre. This is of considerably better proportions than the little middle domes of the porticoes of Iznik and early Bursa.

The carved decoration is masterly and varied. It is faced in grey and white marble which once formed bands and frames, but it has suffered from hasty restoration. The star patterns on the portico balustrades are strikingly bold and each is different; equally bold is the chevron frame of the central arch. The other arches are sharply dentilated on their undersides. The piers which carry the central arch are heavily honeycombed on the inner sides to form a quarter of a capital, but they are cut clean off at each corner and this sharp definition of areas of pattern is a feature of Firuz Bey Cami. The ends of the portico are walled but there are two windows at each end. The upper one is surmounted by a marble mosaic radiating from a small central star like the casement ceilings of the Yeşil Türbe at Bursa of later date. Above these is a shallow stalactite frieze of four tiers firmly set in a rectangular frame and the width of the window. This recurs with the other, upper, flanking windows of the mosque. These are far larger than usual and some also have elaborate interlocking bands of marble above them (instead of voussoirs), particularly those on the mihrab side. The casement windows are very deeply set. The inscription over the great door is in an elaborate relief of vegetation patterns bound in an ogee arch formed of interlocking voussoirs of light and dark marble like I-beams flanked with tongues of fire. Above is a frieze of polychrome reversal patterns based on horizontal chevrons and circles; above this again is a fine tamgâh. The main dome – and it is notable here that the mescit dome and not the court dome is the larger – rides on a prominent double octagonal drum with a large circular window on each of three exposed sides. The prayer hall has squinches with bold ribs rising from two tiers of honeycombs while the mihrab is set in a strongly dog-toothed frame and its marble niche is finely engraved with an inscription and candles. It is lofty and crowned with flamboyant cresting, which again seems to prelude the great mihrabs of the Yeşil Cami and the Yeşil Türbe at Bursa. The proportions of the building are interesting and are based on a square of some 22·50 metres. The prayer hall is 8·40 metres square which is also the height of the wall (6·40 metres) together with that of the frieze (2 metres); thus a perfect cube is achieved. The height from the frieze to the summit of the dome is 4 metres, implying a sphere of 8 metres. Here is an excellent example of a perfect circle in a perfect square.

The minaret is set back to the north-west of the prayer hall and is later in date. It is of interest that its position is where Gabriel suggests the original minarets of the mosques of Bursa were set. The medrese or possible tekke cells lie back against the hillside to the west and are unique in that they deliberately follow its serpentine contours. There are other buildings of the complex beyond what is now wasteland to the south, and a jungle of a graveyard with pleasant trees spreads up the hill to the north.[83]

A variation on the Bursa type is the zaviye built at Kütahya by the Germiyan Emir, Yakup Bey (or Çelebi) II, which later served as a medrese before becoming a library. The recessed entry is a simpler form of that of the mosque at Balat. It opens into a very large court with a pool and fountain which are equally grand. This is covered by a ten-metre dome whereas those of the other five rooms are just over 6·50 metres. They ride on very large pendentives and are approximately the same in their dimensions. There is no mosque area any more than at the Nilüfer Zaviye at Iznik, and the building is orientated west. In the central eyvan there is a mihrab in the side wall. The south and north eyvans extend like arms, but the former has a raised annexe, which is the founder's türbe, and ends in a window and not a mihrab. In the crooks of the arms of these eyvans and against the porch are two rooms. This zaviye serves to show how much this architectural form has to do with hospitality as opposed to worship.

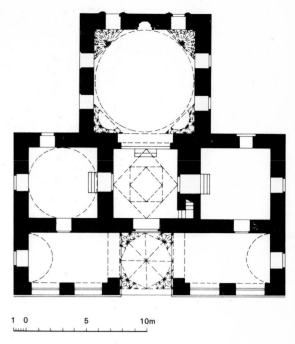

67 *Firuz Bey Cami, Milas. Plan, scale 1 : 300.*

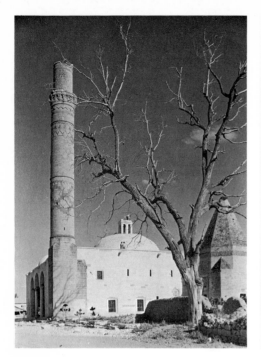

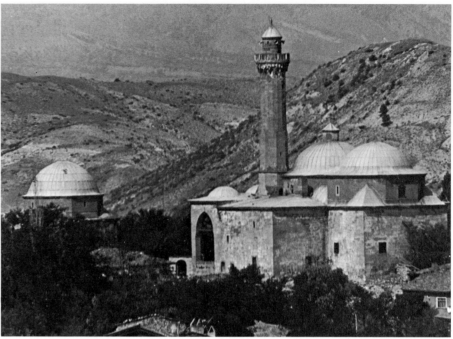

68 Ibrahim Bey İmaret, Karaman. This monument is heavily but austerely restored.

69 İsmail Bey Complex, Kastamonu, with its three related domes and severely geometric organization of forms.

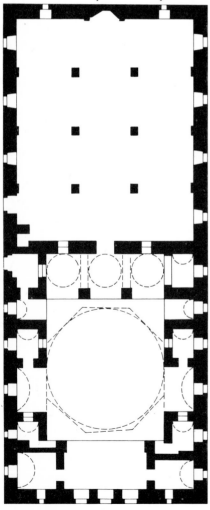

70 Karabaş Veli İmaret, Karaman. An elaborate form of zaviye-mosque. Sketch plan.

At Karaman, the Ibrahim Bey İmaret of *837*/1433 is built of stone and has a closed court derived from the Karatay Medrese tradition as is the tall fan-shape of its squinches. It is a handsome foundation but a later Karaman zaviye of greater interest is the Şeyh Alaettin Karabaş Veli İmaret with its now roofless congregational mosque dating from *870*/1465.[84] The vakfiye was issued by Pir Ahmet, son of Ibrahim Bey, and an aunt of Fatih Sultan Mehmet. The mosque, built of stone, was large and covered by a flat roof carried on piers. Its three-domed portico, which was reached by a screened entry, opened northwards on to the zaviye court as well. The zaviye was also of cut stone and has small cells covered by cupolas round its grand central court with a twelve-sided şadırvan under a fine stone dome. These stone domes were common to the Karaman Beylik and continued to be built after it became an Ottoman province, as can be seen at the very plain mosque at Davgandos. What is interesting at Karabaş Veli is the unification of elements and the fact that the court of the zaviye is also that of the mosque and that the son cemaat yeri is sandwiched between them, thus necessitating an oblique east entry. This can be regarded as a stroke of genius, or else as a freak, because the evolution of the ideal unification of mosque and medrese round an open court was to take much longer.

The İsmail Bey complex at Kastamonu, built in the mid-fifteenth century on a spur of hillside, is interesting because it is a clearly designed complex, but without true unity, and because of the imaret rooms which flank the mosque. That on the east is approached by a ramp as if someone important might ride up to the door. It is a single-domed chamber, but on the west are a pair of barrel-vaulted rooms of which that on the south appears to have been the kitchen with a separate entry and a large chimney. The room beside it is smaller because it incorporates the minaret at the north-west corner of the mosque. This is the only instance I have met with where the kitchen of the imaret is set against the mosque. The tabhane rooms have no doors into the mosque in the Bursa style. The mosque is a double-domed rectangle with good stalactite squinches and a central dividing arch. The four casements of the east, west and south walls have to be concentrated in the mihrab area and there is a window over the mihrab as well as on each flank; but there are no windows or casements in the façade of the mosque beneath the five-domed portico which is carried on six square piers but with honeycomb squinches and carved responds. There are two very high sofas, and the central dome is ribbed. Recently a romantic perspective drawing of an imaginary mosque has been inscribed on the blank wall west of the door. The snub cap of the minaret belongs to the pre-lead cap tradition.

The complex is entered diagonally due to the lie of the land. Behind a wall is the mekteb which is a small domed room with a foyer and its own garden. The founder's türbe has a lofty octagonal drum with triangular buttresses at the four shoulders and a ribbed dome. There is one lonely stalactite over the door but shell squinches inside. On the extreme north of the complex is a han which is no more than a large rectangular stone barn, but the small medrese to the east on the cliff edge has a pleasant court with eight single cells and one double. These are joined by a stretch of wall to the dershane in the centre of the south side. There is no room for porticoes. The complex feels spacious, its precinct is full of trees and there is a splendid view on the east thanks to the careful diagonal layout of the overall plan, which at one point brings the south-west end of the mosque to the cliff edge on one side and the north-east side of the medrese to the other edge opposite.

71   An example of the simplified Bursa type is the mosque of Yürgüç Pasha at Amasya, which shows the adaptability of the plan. It was built in October, *832/1428*[85] and is therefore almost contemporaneous with the Muradiye. Inside it is not remarkable, but the north façade is unique. The east side is a large room, access to which is obtained by means of a door inside the porch. This door, like all the other windows and doors, is surmounted by an arch of large red and white voussoir blocks. Above this, just as over the main door, only larger, a blind window delineated in plasterwork is painted. The dome above is carried on four powerful arches and four pendentives formed of converging triangles. Balancing the room on the east, two massive piers carry a second dome above the raised open türbe of the pasha, whose tomb is flanked by two other adult and one child's grave. The spandrels of the central arch are divided by a handsome disc between consoles. The floral decoration of this disc is related to that of the thirteenth-century Turumtay Türbe and of the Gök Medrese, which loom above this mosque. In the arch is a finely carved miniature stalactite niche. The dedication is to Yürgüç Pasha, son of Aptullah al-Atabey. He was one of Mehmet I's vezirs.[86] Apart from a ruined four-cell medrese or tekke, easy to overlook among the weeds, there is now no trace of the other buildings intended for the comfort

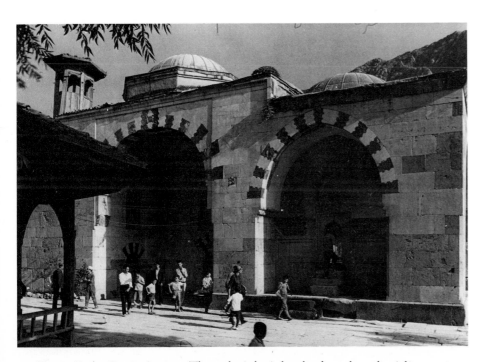

71 Yürgüç Pasha Cami, Amasya. The pasha is buried under the arch on the right.

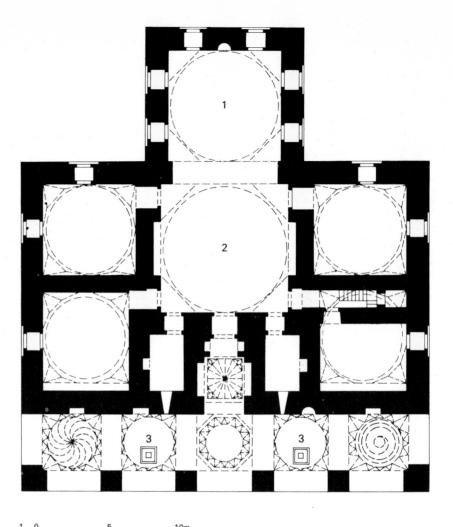

72 *Beyazit Pasha Cami, Amasya. The Bursa zaviye-mosque plan with additions. Scale 1 : 250. 1 mosque; 2 semahane; 3 fountain.*

of the poor. Gabriel[87] suggests that the room off the porch could have served as a place where alms were distributed, but it is surely a conventional tabhane room for pilgrims and dervishes.

Amasya has many architectural monuments of importance and of these the 72 Beyazit Pasha Cami and the Pir İlyas Tekke deserve close attention. The mosque of Beyazit Pasha was built between *817/1414* and *822/1419*,[88] and at first appears to be a typical Bursa-style mosque with some variations. Beyazit Pasha, after the capture of his sultan and namesake at the Battle of Ankara, fled with Mehmet Çelebi, the heir apparent, to Amasya and became his chief minister.[89] The inscription over the door of his large mosque calls him the Great Emir, the Vezir of Sultan Mehmet. Near the inscription to Beyazit is a second one which states that the mimar or builder was Yakup bin Aptullah, one of the Mameluks of the Pasha, who constructed it in *822/1419*. Opposite this is an inscription, which states that the builder was muallim (master) Abu Bakir bin Mehmet, surnamed Muşaymiş, of Damascus, who built the Mehmet I Medrese at Merzifon.[90] Another inscription on the Beyazit mosque may refer to Mimar Kağhan or Fiğ Tuğhan, son of Aptullah, slave of Beyazit Pasha.[91] If he was a slave he was not a Turk, and it is worth noting that Aptullah is a Moslem name frequently adopted by Christians under Ottoman rule upon their conversion.[92] Other inscriptions refer to Yakup, son of yet another Aptullah, and one more muallim or master, Zeynettin bin Zakariya. Inscriptions in honour of Sultan Mehmet I and his

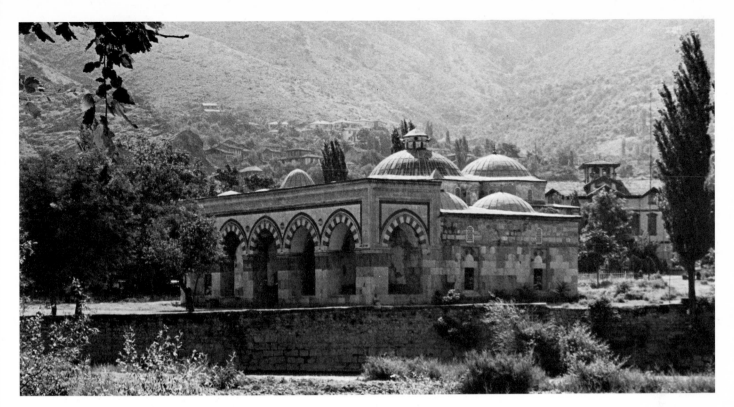

73 *Beyazit Pasha Cami, Amasya. View from across the river.*

pasha create no problems. The only trouble with this mosque is the excess of information which it offers, not all of which can be seriously studied because part of the mosque is in active use. To possess four architects or master-builders, when Ottoman architecture has often left no trace of even an usta or overseer, is riches indeed and supports the theory that they worked as a team. The two mimars are likely to have been master-masons overseeing the complete construction, while the muallim were responsible for the craftsmen including one indeed worthy of record, Mustafa the Carpenter, for the woodwork is very fine. He hid his signature in the traditional ornamentation of the door.[93]

The office of Architect of the Empire had not yet become the department of state that Sinan was to create in the sixteenth century. As with the Yeşil Cami at Bursa and so many other mosques, one is driven to wonder if Beyazit Pasha may not have been a forerunner of Lord Burlington dabbling in architecture, but there is little evidence to support this attractive thesis. Yet someone had to design the whole complex and the mosque in particular. It is double-domed with lateral rooms (but no eyvans) simply and satisfactorily ordered. The first and larger dome over the inner court – if it was a court – carried a lantern which Gabriel[94] believes to be of recent date. But from inside it does not in the least resemble the lanterns of Parvillée, for there is elaborate plasterwork, like that to be found in the little turrets of Üç Şerefeli at Edirne, under the minuscule dome. This plasterwork is akin to the rest of the plasterwork in the mosque. Moreover, the carpets and straw matting when rolled back reveal large stone flags, apparently of the fifteenth century, evenly distributed over the whole floor area. There is no trace of a basin nor of any hole for drainage below the cupola.[95] Although he records the two small fountains right and left of the central dome of the portico, related to those of the upper loggias of the Yeşil Cami at Bursa, Gabriel[96] states, poetically, that they were used by birds. He does not mention the row of taps set into the sides of the stone sofas of the porch under the central dome. While these are recent additions, the little fountains are original. Indeed, the sofas look undisturbed, and the fountains neatly set in place indicate a water-system which could, from its origin, have supplied water to the faucets of the main door. Gabriel[97] refers to the inscription on the rock by the river which runs

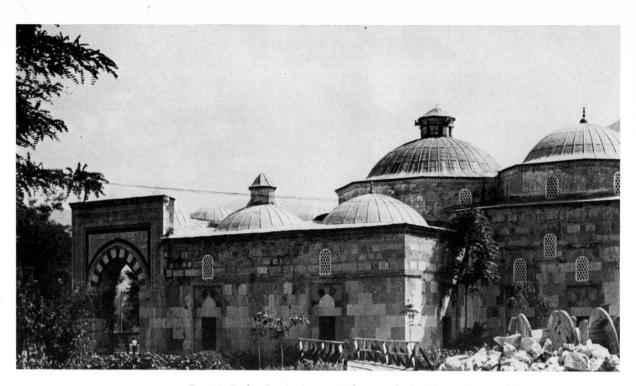

74 Beyazit Pasha Cami, Amasya. The west flank. The sections combine to create a sense of unity.

beside this mosque. It is near to the Kuşköprü or Bird Bridge and gives *820/1417* as the date of the vakfiye and then a list of the estates of this foundation. It also refers to a misafirhane, or guesthouse, and a hamam. Nonetheless, the date over the door of the mosque is *822*. This reinforces my belief that the registration date of an endowment is no sure guide to the date of the completion of a building. The money needed for the construction and early maintenance came directly from the purse of the noble donor or else he chose to establish a trust before work began, although this seems rarely to have been done. It is probable that at Beyazit Pasha the faithful washed in the shallows of the river, just as small boys were doing when I was there; to this day there are such crowds at Ramazan that they fill the meadow before the mosque and would overwhelm the resources of the largest şadırvan. It must also be recorded that this mosque is built over a large cistern, which I was unable to inspect, but which is likely to date from Byzantine or pre-Byzantine times. It could be that the mosque replaced and used some of the materials from a church. This mosque could represent a transitional stage between the buildings of Bursa and those of Üç Şerefeli, since there would have been no need for an inner court.

Where, at the Green Mosque there are two tribunes right and left of the door, at Beyazit Pasha there are two cells which are very ill lit,[98] but which appear to have had ocaks, though Gabriel[99] calls them service rooms. In the north-east corner is a large room with an east window, which is nowadays very much a store, and next to it is a room with windows south and east. Both these rooms are matched on the west side but the north-west room is unusual. The south-east and south-west rooms are similar, both possessing ocaks in walls of shelves, the latter of stucco over thin brick and wood, carved or moulded into Islamic motifs, and having the usual multiplicity of arched niches for lamps and jugs in the Bursa manner. There can be no doubt that these were residential chambers, but whether for travellers or for the dervishes of a tekke is another matter. The large chamber on the north-east is ordinary enough although one cannot be sure of its precise function, but that on the north-west has had a floor added, and the door from the central hall now leads to a passage whence steps descend to a cellar, unmentioned by Gabriel, with a small west window which appears only a little above the level of the ground outside. This could, indeed, have been a store, but only in summer, and one hopes that no human ever had to live there, even as a penance, for it must be cruelly damp in winter.[100] Above it is a stairway which turns into the thickness of the party wall, which Gabriel shows to have been an addition. He assumes that the minaret, which has fallen, was added later. It was perched on the corner of the cell to the right of the entrance and the north-west room. Its base was never secure, and the approach through the north-west room is as clumsy as are the external stairs into the trunk (which has a normal spiral stairway) from the open loggia west of the north porch. Yet there must always have been stairs to permit access to the two loggias which are connected by a narrow passage in the thickness of the wall above the north door itself.[101] This passage was once lit by a square window on to the mosque in the middle of the north wall – a repetition of that of Yıldırım Beyazit at Bursa. Above the arch of the main door another window was set at ankle level so that one might see where to put one's feet, which is difficult now that both these windows are blocked up.

75 What is astonishing is that the loggia set on the east above the porch has an ocak. Moreover, neither loggia looks into the mosque nor could either ever have done so; thus they could never have been places where the müezzin relayed the prayers to those outside for this would have called (preposterously) for a go-between. Although the north-west loggia no longer has an ocak it possesses niches usually found in cells. The two robust arches which look down into the portico or to the north are now thickly plastered, so that it is impossible to tell if once they were walled in. This is unlikely if the Yıldırım at Bursa offers a clue. Yet it seems absurd to waste fuel on cells exposed to the winds. That on the north-east clearly had a specific function, which that on the north-west lost when the minaret was erected. It is almost as puzzling as the room at the end of the passages above the mihrab of the Hudavendigâr Cami[102] or could these loggias be related to those of the Yeşil Cami?

During the period with which we are concerned, Timur's victories and the death of Yıldırım Beyazit resulted in much disorder. The throne of Mehmet Çelebi was far from secure and the dervish orders were in the ascendant.[103] It could be that the mosque of Beyazit Pasha was unorthodox and used as a tekke as well. The odd room or loggia above the porch might have served a fanatic and the central hall was not an avlu but a place of assembly, a room in its own right. In the great arched recesses on the east and west sides of this hall there is supporting evidence which was pointed out to me by the müezzin: through the top of each arch, back-to-back with the ocaks of the south-east and south-west rooms, are two additional flues for the ocaks which served this central area. Unless these people had a mania for wasting fuel, it would seem unlikely, therefore, that there was ever an oculus in the dome above. I would suggest that there could always have been a lantern here out of deference to conservative traditions in architectural forms.[104] It is also possible that the building was a zaviye, but Beyazit Pasha also built a kervansaray, or misafirhane,[105] and a hamam beside his mosque as we have seen from the vakfiye.

The fine mihrab has been garishly painted. In a frame of familiar interlacing polygonal wheels, the stalactite niche is supported by elaborate pilasters made out of many segments of polychrome marble which reach their climax with a banded ball before repeating, in reverse, their convolutions to the ground, and so resemble the bulbous legs of Jacobean furniture.[106] Gabriel supposes[107] that the windows retain their ancient glass, extraordinary though this would be in an area subject to earth tremors; they look more like worthy copies less than a century old, and the imam is of the same opinion. Their colours are of mediocre quality and their designs are based on those of needlework transfers consisting of flowers growing out of pots alternating with plain translucent panels.

The traditional portico has five domes springing from five pointed arches borne on six piers. The vault on the north-east is in the form of a whorl, that on 44 the north-west is spiral, anticipating those of Sultan Beyazit II's complex at Edirne; but neither form is an innovation in Islamic architecture. The piers are

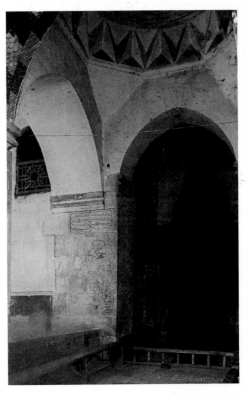

75 *Beyazit Pasha Cami, Amasya. The north door, with a glimpse of the upper loggia.*

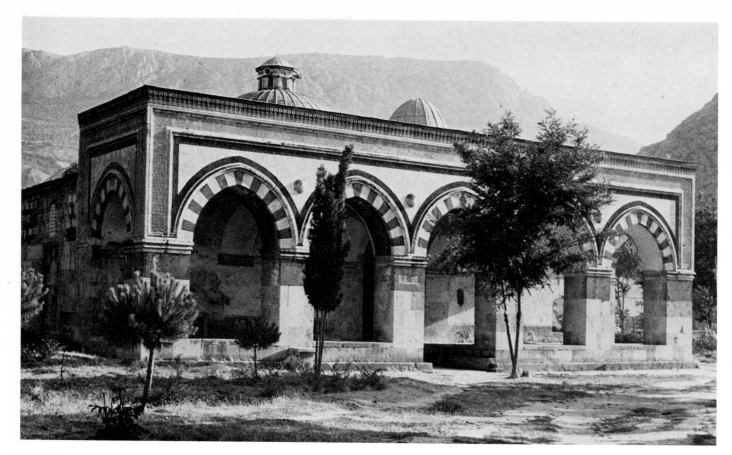

76 Beyazit Pasha Cami, Amasya. The portico in the powerful fifteenth-century manner.

stout and strong and constructed of huge blocks of stone which are not at all typical. There is one white block to sofa level followed by a band of red and then two bands of alternately white and red up to the cornice. Each of the arches supported by these piers has nineteen voussoirs of alternating Marmara marble and red stone. In each spandrel there is an elaborately carved calligraphic boss. Above the arches is a high marble screen, rather than an architrave, so that the portico is like a mask behind which the mosque lies hidden. It is edged in red stone with a cornice of arabesques based on the two-lobed leaf pattern. Inset between the two firm marginal bands of red is a ribbon of geometric pattern, which rises from the far arches to be carried straight across the top of the façade. Finally, a shallow stalactite band projects over the façade, as it does over the east and west sides of the portico, which are treated in a similar manner. This mask, therefore, is of considerable strength;[108] it is a form frequently used at the time.

Mustafa Usta's north door is deep-set under a stalactite vault with two stalactite alcoves each side, both with semicircular consoles projecting at foot level. According to Gabriel,[109] these consoles were meant to help one remove one's shoes in comfort, but he must have been thinking of shoes with laces and not slippers which are so easily kicked off. It would be equally incorrect, but more logical, to suggest that the high sofas[110] under the portico served this purpose. The imam of the mosque said that two sentries guarded the door when the Vali was at prayer. This suggestion has caused distress to other good Moslems who would deny the presence of a soldier at the door of any mosque; but these two men would have been as much symbols of Beyazit's authority as his protectors. Remembering the gory fate of the early caliphs and the need to screen the ruler even in the first decades of the Faith, the call for a guard is not easily dismissed.[111] It is still more probable that these sofas were functional and decorative, for there was no need for solid masonry at this point; but that they are useful seats for gatemen, guards or gossips is true to this day.

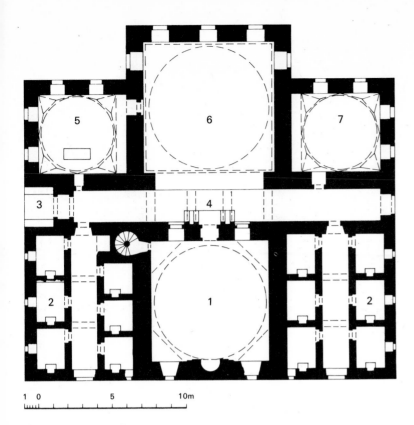

1 0   5   10m

*77 Pir İlyas Tekke, Amasya. Plan, scale 1 : 250. 1 mosque; 2 cells; 3 main entry;
4 corridor; 5 türbe; 6 semahane; 7 oda. The placing of the minaret defines the mosque area
flanked by the cells. The principal halls of the tekke are across the corridor which is open to
the public.*

77 Above Beyazit Pasha is the tekke of Pir İlyas built for the Halveti order of
dervishes.[112] The evidence is that it was founded by Yakup Pasha in *815/1412*
although the only dated inscription, in Persian, is of *903/1497*. It is, or was, known
as the Yakup Pasha Medrese or that of Aşaği Pir, the College Below as opposed
to the College Above of the same order.[113] The tekke is now a ruin. It was cut in
half by a corridor leading straight from the main portal on the west to a smaller
entry on the east. In the centre of the north side is an eyvan with a large arch
open on to the corridor, which projects back so far beyond the two flanking
rooms as to have a window east and west as well as three facing north. The tekke
stands on the hillside and this room affords a fine view over the town, trees and
gorge of Amasya, which was the favourite city of Süleyman the Lawgiver. The
north-west room has two casements on the north, and on the west is the türbe
of Pir İlyas' great-grandson, Celâlettin Abdurrahman Sani (or the Second). The
large room on the north-east was reserved, according to the vakfiye,[114] for the
şeyh of the convent. The central room was used for reunions of the brotherhood.[115] Each of the three chambers was vaulted.

Across the corridor and up four steps through a door flanked by two windows
was, significantly enough, a slightly smaller hall with a dome carried on four
arches and four stalactite squinches; it had a window each side of the mihrab in
the south wall. On the north-west, set into the wall, were steps leading up to
the stumpy minaret.[116] This was clearly a mescit or mosque to which the public
were allowed access, else the minaret would not have been built. Another point
of interest about this tekke is the unusual grouping of six cells each side of the
mescit, in threes facing each other across the corridors. Those on the east or west
outer sides had ocaks and windows, but those on the inner sides backing against
the prayer hall could have no windows, except for the end cells to the south.
Thus four cells got all their ventilation from the corridors and no daylight ever
entered them at all. The tekke is symmetrically planned but it is most unorthodox.

Not of the Bursa type but multi-domed are such small mosques as the Güdük Minare or Rüstem Çelebi Cami at Tokat, probably built in the first half of the fifteenth century, mainly of brick with some stone piers. It has a central dome, with pairs of cupolas to east and west forming the domes of the porch.[117] The mosque has been severely damaged and haphazardly repaired. The truncated minaret appears to be of an early date.[118] Had the door been on the north side, this mosque would have been related to the Manisa Valide type. In this quarter of the old town there are two or three mosques which, like the Güdük Minare, have leadless domes under a hipped roof of tiles which is hoisted over them like a canvas hood. The purpose is to protect the dome; double domes originally developed in Selçuk and İlhanlı Iran for the same reason. Double domes are only rarely used in Turkey, and then mainly with türbes, and also, in a very elementary form, with some of the kiosks of the Topkapısaray such as the Revan and the Sünnet built in the seventeenth century.

It was natural that the Bursa type of zaviye-mosque should appear in conquered Balkan territories as soon as new areas came under civil control. An example is the İshak Bey Cami at Üsküp,[119] dated *842/1438*.[120] The plan resembles the Nilüfer Zaviye at İznik, but the side rooms are open and there is less elaborate vaulting of the apse, while the dome is only 6·70 metres in diameter. It is, therefore, a thoroughly provincial building. The same style is to be found later. İsa Bey Cami, dated *880/1475*,[121] had two pairs of side rooms and twin domes to the prayer hall in the manner of Mahmut Pasha in Istanbul. The stalactite capitals and the tall, polygonal minaret indicate stability and prosperity. The Bursa-type mosque can also be found in Egypt for example in the Hasan Rumı Cami built, after the Conquest by Selim I, in 1523.[122]

Although most of the larger foundations conformed to the Bursa mosque-zaviye or tekke plan, a great many smaller square mosques with triple-domed porticoes were built in the early half of the fifteenth century; an example is the Davgandos Cami[123] near Karaman which has a simple stone dome over an austere structure.

Returning to Bursa, certain public buildings dating from the time when it was the capital are the best examples of their period and type. The Eski Kaplıca has already been referred to,[124] but it was exceptional because it was a thermal bath. A more traditional hamam, where water had to be drawn and heated in a tank, was that of Emir Sultan, built by Hundi Hatun, daughter of Yıldırım Beyazit, after her marriage to this saintly man in the year of the Battle of Ankara, 1402. Her husband Şeyh Bokhara Şemsettin Mehmet Emir was greatly revered and his mosque was built on an eminence above that of Mehmet I; since it was rebuilt by Selim III, it will be discussed later.[125] His hamam was much more logically ordered than that of Orhan.[126] It has a large square camekân under a now damaged dome from which a lobby leads to the soğukluk which has a splendid whorl vault. It admits to the sıcakluk with three small eyvans and two private rooms set in the corners. Behind is the furnace, Hell or Cehennem. Because the elements interlock, no space is wasted.

There are many other hamams of the period but most are in such poor condition that they have become curiosities; for example the Meyhaneli or Central Hamam, also called the Tavuk Pazarı Hamam, the bath of the Chicken Market. There it is adventuresome, but not very instructive, to climb among tins of oil, old rags and shoes, in pursuit of fine vaulting and to see how the Ottomans constructed their stalactites of brick edges and plaster.[127] It is quite impossible to gain a true idea of its original state; when Murat II completed it about 1425 it was considered the most handsome hamam in Bursa.[128]

Hamams were the centre of civic life and princes frequented them. It was in the entrance of Murat I's hamam that the Karamanoğlu burnt the bones of Yıldırım Beyazit as an act of public vengeance. In Europe they would have been incinerated in the market place, but such an open space never exists in a bazaar, for han and bedesten crowd one upon the other, and any room between the rows of workshops and one-man stalls is filled with jostling pedlars and purchasers.

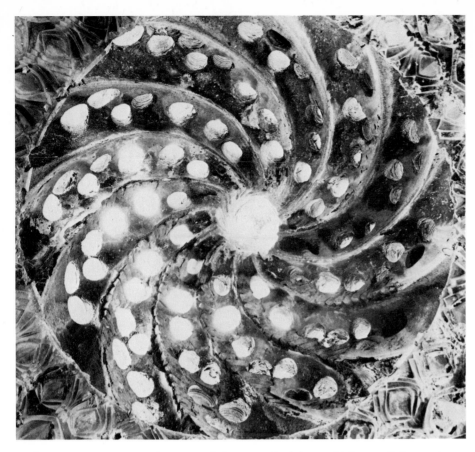

78 İsmail Bey Hamam, Iznik. A typical Ottoman whorl-dome with hamam lights.

Besides the public hamams there are several small private baths surviving in Bursa such as the Gönlüferah Kaplıca with its narrow vestibule – a mere passage – admitting to a hot-room with a domed washing-place (3·25 × 2·50 metres) and a waist-high bath filled with hot, constantly flowing, spring water. And there is the Keçeli Hamam which is altogether grander and has a large disrobing chamber with five windows, a soğukluk (nearly 5 metres square) and a domed pool chamber (4·50 metres square) with two additional recesses with basins for ablutions. These are thermal baths. At Iznik there is the pretty private hamam of İsmail Bey, which may be as late as sixteenth-century although built of brick and plaster. It has four small rooms, an eyvan for its entry, and much bold and handsome decoration in relief, even in its present state of ruin. It derives from the ruined royal hamam of Orhan Gazi in the Saray at Yenişehir.

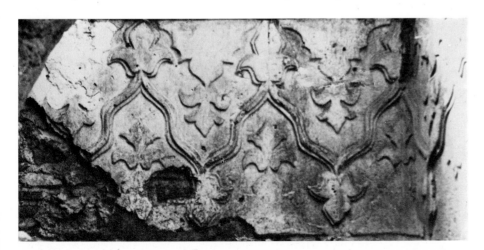

79 İsmail Bey Hamam, Iznik. Plasterwork surviving in the hot-room.

The bones of Yıldırım did not set the bazaar of Bursa alight, but it has suffered from many fires and earthquakes. The fire of 1955 devastated its heart, and the first attempt to rebuild it to the old pattern and to make a thorough historical survey of the foundations of the destroyed hans has been handicapped by the urge to get the market in full working order again.[129] The bedesten was restored *49* with care by experienced masons and the form has been preserved. It is the most imposing civil building in the town, the belly of the market, and was its treasure house during the fifteenth century. It covers an area 70 × 33 metres and has fifty-six exterior shops extending on all four sides. It is faced by subsidiary buildings with more shops.

The main doors of the bedesten are in the centre of the north and south sides and, in the nineteenth century, a road was driven clean through them through the middle of the building. It was meant to lead, straight as a Roman road, to Yalova, but peters out after a few kilometres across the plain. To this day, its green line can be seen cutting across the landscape. Perhaps because of this road, the two main doors are slightly off axis, although the east and west doors are directly aligned with each other. Only two of the six piers have escaped restoration. Round arches carry fourteen domes, two of which are slightly smaller than the rest. Along the north and south sides are thirty-two strong-rooms in front of which the merchants set up their platforms or sofas. Others set up booths round the piers. At the sides of both the outer and inner porches of the main doors are pairs of eyvans for yet more traders. The concentrated economy of space at ground level is only to be matched by the luxury of the height of the buildings. There is a close relationship[130] between this bedesten and that at Edirne built by Mehmet I. It, too, is covered by fourteen domes supported on six piers of which, today, only one is larger than the others. There are thirty-six strong-rooms including four groups of three at the corners. Here both pairs of doors are set truly on their respective axes and all the domes are the same size. The corners outside were cut diagonally to create triangular shops which serve to carry the movement of the building on and round. The same technique was employed at the entries so that the customer is ushered inside by the structure. The multi-dome concept was continued at the Büyük Bedesten and the Sandaliye Bedesten of the Kapalı Çarşı, or Covered Bazaar, in Istanbul, but in the former there are four rows of four piers and in the latter four rows of three carrying fifteen and twenty domes respectively. Thus it was in these commercial buildings that the ulu cami form flourished.

The bedesten was the commercial centre of a city and not to be confused with *49* a çarşı or market, nor with an arasta or a range of shops beside or even under a mosque. Bedestens are associated with bazaars because the word may derive from bazzazistan or bazistan. Their function was to be a strong-room and display hall for jewellers and brocade merchants and such, and only the major trading centres possessed them.[131] Their high rents, like those of the shops, usually provided endowments for pious foundations. Some were very large and flanked by shops like those of Bursa and Edirne or the Mahmut Pasha Bedesten at Ankara which is now the Archaeological Museum. Others were small and free-standing like that at Gelibolu (Gallipoli).

Close to the Bursa Bedesten is the Sipahiler Çarşı, the Market of the Cavaliers.[132] This is a logical enough covered bazaar built by Mehmet I. From the east gate extends a passage covered by four domes with eight bays for individual shops on either side. At the west end the market twists at an angle of twenty degrees. This second part of the building running north to south is higher and had one dome and three cradle vaults. It contrives five bays on the west and one in the angle of the north door. While the ordering of the joint where the two sections meet shows great ingenuity it also demonstrates the limitations that property rights imposed, and also emphasizes the value of land in a town and the constant ingenuity with which builders made the best possible use of it.

The hans and markets of Bursa were not only important for trade, especially in silks and other fabrics, but also as endowments for mosques and social services

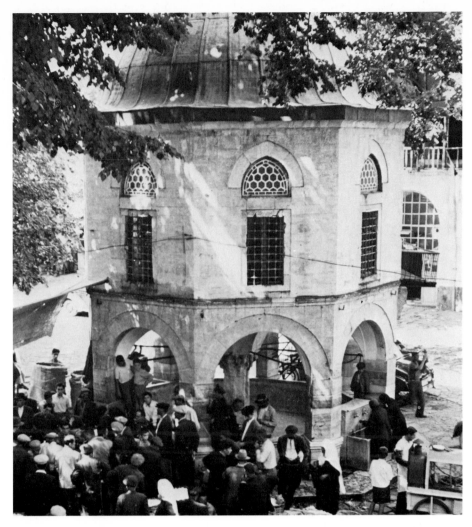

80 Koza Han, Bursa. A classical Ottoman mescit raised above the şadırvan in the manner of Selçuk royal hans.

not only in Bursa but in Edirne, Istanbul and elsewhere. The Emir Han has already been considered;[133] among others, there was the İvaz Pasha or Geyve Han built by the Vali responsible for the Green Mosque, which had a pleasantly shady eyvan in the centre of its east side. Later hans of this market type designed for trade, and not like kervansarays as post-houses, continued the tradition. Such was the Fidan or Sapling Han built by Mahmut Pasha, the chief vezir of Mehmet II, round a courtyard filled with trees. This has been much altered, but originally the building was not quite rectangular and built of two courses of brick to one of stone. Above the pointed arches of the arcades, the roof of the upper floor is set on a series of shallow domes. From the handsome gate the ground slopes gently down to the court, in the centre of which is a duodecagonal basin, six metres in width, above which was a mescit supported by twelve columns so that the traveller might wash and say his prayers – of thanks upon his safe arrival or for protection upon departing.[134] This harks back to kervansarays of the Selçuks and the Sultan Hans near Kayseri or Aksaray where much more elaborate mescits were raised clear of possible trespassing by pack-animals. Another example of the simpler form of fifteenth-century mescit is raised on eight piers in the court of the Koza or Cocoon Han which dates from the reign of Beyazit II. The Fidan Han had over one hundred rooms. Beyazit Pasha of Amasya also built a han near the Ulu Cami,[135] but only its foundations survive.

An interesting han, which continues the Selçuk tradition, stands above the lake of Apolyant on the road from Bursa to Bandırma and the west. It was built in 797/1394[136] and is the oldest known Ottoman kervansaray outside a city, and

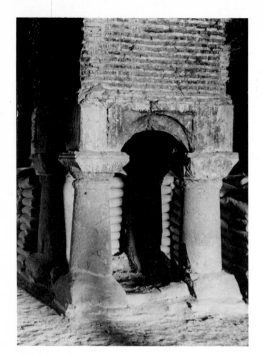

81 İssiz Han, Lake Apolyant. One of the two
central chimneys.

here the chevron capital appears in embryonic form. The external proportions
are approximately two to one (42·25 × 21·50 metres) and the interior is very
lofty and grand (20 × 35 metres). The hall is preceded by two small chambers
each side of the door and a room above. The great hall is divided into a nave and
two aisles by thick piers and was lit by windows which were small and high to
keep out the cold. Its unique feature is the pair of huge hearths in the raised central
area one third and two thirds the way down its length with the Herculean brick
chimneys spreading into huge hoods carried on stout supports. Usually the
drovers and muleteers slept down the side of such a hall and the animals were
tethered in the middle, but here the positions were reversed. This han was
known significantly as the İssiz Han or the Inn that has no Smoke[137] and the
traveller must have blessed Yıldırım Beyazit for his expensive improvement on
the older, smoky, type. Its door faces the lake and it would seem that the old road
ran by the shore and that travellers were also ferried across the water.

Of other public buildings in Bursa or elsewhere, little remains. Houses there
are none. The bridges were mainly of wood although some had stone bases;
but all have been ruthlessly rebuilt except the Koyun Köprü at Bergama built
by one Erne Bey. Gabriel[138] suggests that the Maksem Bridge west of Bursa may
have elements which date from the reign of Mehmet I. The great loss was the
ancient Irgandı Bridge, blown up by the retreating Greek army in 1922. The
bridge had a single great arch which carried rows of shops each side of its highway.[139] Linking, in miniature, Bursa with Florence and London, it was a charming
relic of the great days of this town.[140]

An early bridge of great elegance is the Ala Köprü over the Göksü Gorge at
Ermenak built in 706/1305.[141] It has one large span central arch and a subsidiary
arch on each side. Farther down the river is the Bıçakçı Köprü, which is undated
but similar in style and which also has a wide span central arch and a pair of
subsidiary arches on each side. These are divided from the main arch by big
circular apertures in order to relieve the weight. The bridge is narrow and rises

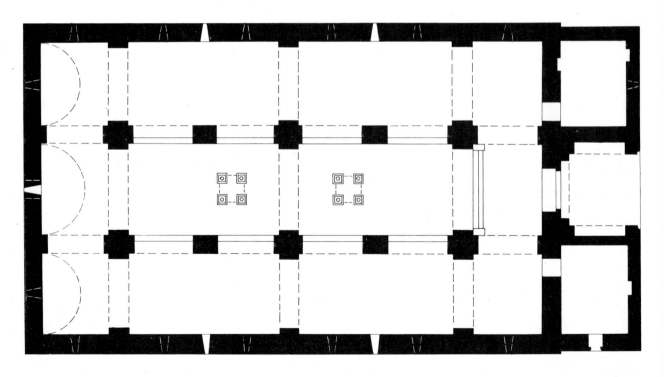

1 0   5   10m

82 İssiz Han, Lake Apolyant. Plan, scale 1 : 250. There is a platform for travellers with
two chimneys in the centre. Later such platforms would be set along the walls and there
would be several flues.

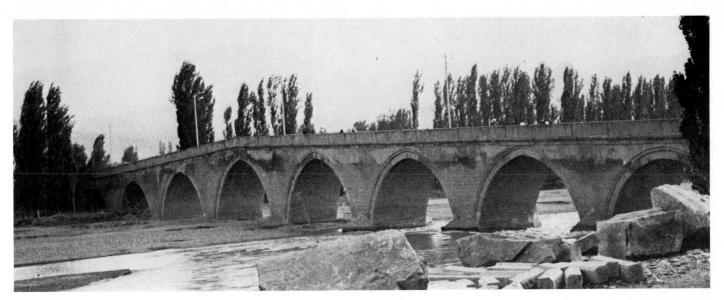

to a slight hump. It is still Selçuk in feeling, and this is also true of another undated
84 hump bridge of great beauty at Çataltepe between Uşak and Kula. But again
its balanced proportions suggest that it belongs to the transitional period between the asymmetrical Selçuk form (which reached its grandest dimensions at
Hisn Kalfa with a bridge sixty metres above the Tigris, which was the wonder
of the Venetian merchants who crossed it) and the more Roman or Persian
style of many arches which became the distinctive Ottoman form. This style
83 appears with the long stone bridge over the Kızılırmak at Osmançık carried on
a noble series of pointed arches. It is very much restored and attributed to
Yıldırım Beyazit locally but, more credibly, to Beyazit II by Hammer-Purgstall[142] for it is highly sophisticated both in aesthetic and structural terms.

*83, 84 Beyazit Bridge, Osmançık and, below,
the bridge at Çataltepe. The elegance of the
Selçuk tradition contrasts with the strength of
form of the Ottoman which is related to that of
Roman bridges.*

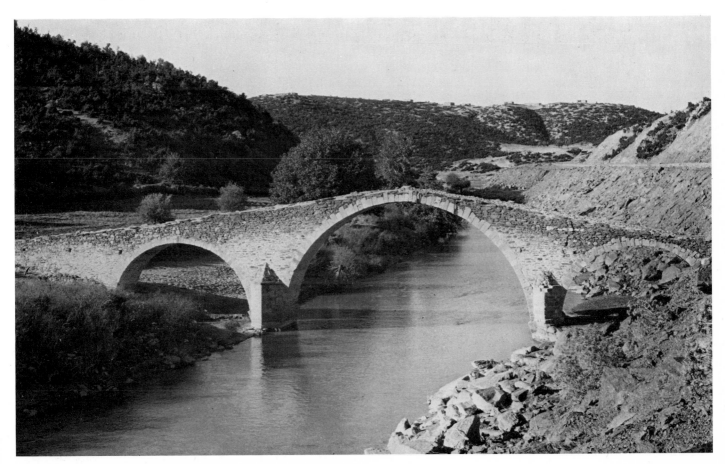

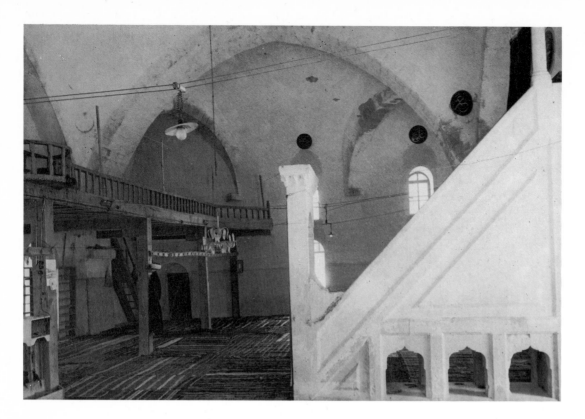

85 *Lâl Ağa Cami, Mut.*
Interior from the west.

The conservative Karaman emirs did not follow the Bursa style, but at Mut·
they attempted an innovation which sought to unify a rectangular interior
while retaining a central cupola. The moderately large Lâl Ağa Cami is built   *85*
of ashlar with the stone dome common to the area. It was endowed by Çelik
Mehmet Pasha and the vakfiye is dated *847/1444*.[143] It has narrow wings on the
east and west which are not eyvans of the Bursa type but integral to the domed
chamber. The central area (11 metres square) is minutely overlapped by the
recessed circumference of the blind dome. The wings (2·85 metres each) bring
the overall width of the mosque to 18·70 metres.[144] They are exceptional because
they are semicircular half-vaults over pointed arches set diagonally across the
corners beneath a sloping roof at an angle of forty-five degrees. The portico of
five-domed bays extends from the minaret – which had once been a small tower[145]
and opens on to the portico – to a classical Ottoman window. The four columns
of the portico are set on stone bases twice their width; the illusion that the central
arch is wider than the others is created by setting the two central pillars on the
edge of their bases which are turned towards the flanking columns. These are
correctly placed in the middle of their own bases. The effect mildly upsets the
symmetry of the casements on either side of the door. The door itself looks as if
it had been rebuilt in Ottoman times. A small door on the east opens into a
women's section. Inside, there is another asymmetry because the windows west
of the mihrab have been displaced to accommodate the lofty stone minber.[146]
The türbes beside and behind the mosque, with their octagonal, lofty conical
roofs and their low walls, are like tents. The smaller türbe is square with a hemispherical vault of stone but the larger octagonal türbe has an ogee dome inset,
which is unrelated to either the Selçuk or Ottoman traditions.

Mut had no successors, and the future lay with the Ottomans in Edirne where
Murat II established his capital, and where the important architectural developments emerge.

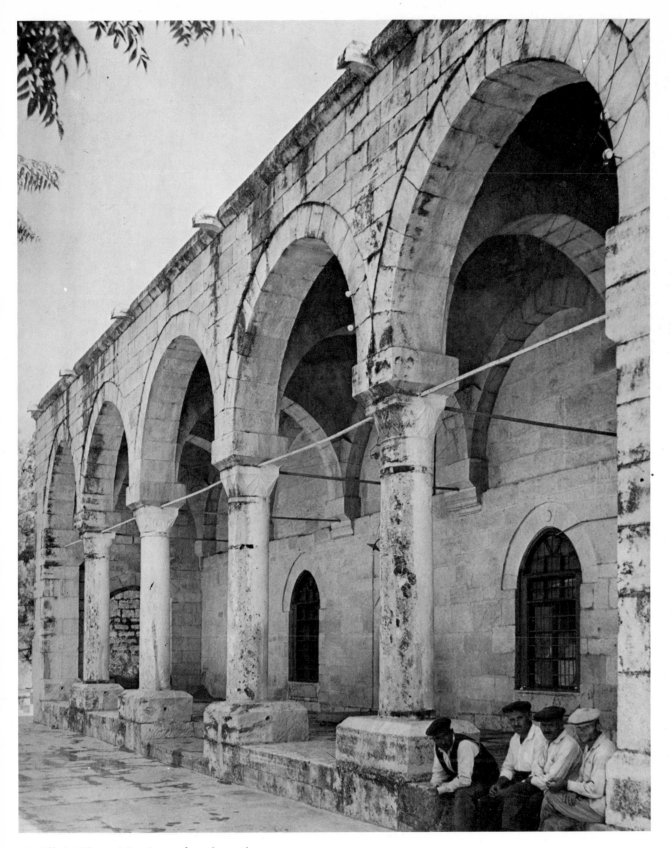

86 Lâl Ağă Cami, Mut. Portico from the north–west.

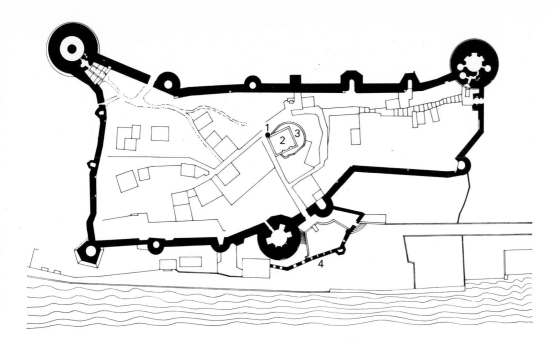

10 0 10 20 30 40 50m

97 Rumeli Hisar. Plan, scale 1 : 2,000. 1 minaret; 2 mosque; 3 cistern; 4 barbican.

98   For so young a man, he was exceedingly cautious; he first took absolute command of the Bosphorus by raising the castle of Rumeli on a spur opposite the fortress of Yıldırım. Rumeli Hisar, which has been known variously as Boğazkesen (Cut-Throat),[44] Yeni Hisar (New Castle) and Nik Hisar (Good Castle),[45] was built by expert artisans rather than architects, although the Office of Works or Mimarbası's department must have furnished engineers. It is possible that the rough ground-plan was by the sultan[46] since it is logical and it required no great experience to recognize the strategic dictates of the terrain. Evliya Çelebi[47] is responsible for the myth that is was shaped like an Arabic M after Mehmet's own initial: but it merely follows the contours of the site and the towers are offensive and not symbolic – offensive, more than defensive, since it is difficult to see what threat Constantine XI Palaeologus could offer a puissant prince although the possibility of Papal troops approaching from the Danube and the Black Sea did exist.

The operation was planned with that exactitude which characterized Ottoman organization at this period. Before work on the site began, in the winter of 1451, governors were ordered to assemble workmen for the spring.[48] Mythology has added the story of ten thousand men divided and subdivided into units of one thousand and one hundred, and the same story existed concerning the building of Hagia Sophia and, later, the building of Ahmet I's mosque in the Atmeydan. In all three cases, the work was surely farmed out to ensure speed in execution, and so each section was in part prefabricated. The supplies of Rumeli Hisar arrived from all directions without let or hindrance by the Byzantines; stones came from Anatolia and wood from the forests of the Black Sea and from Izmit, formerly Nicomedia,[49] probably already hewed and planed into standard lengths. More supplies of stone, conveniently cut to size, were quarried from the already decaying churches of the Bosphorus, including that of St Michael Archangel at Arnavutköy.[50] Hammer-Purgstall[51] mentions columns from this church, and several can be seen in the towers acting as bonding agents. Columns were also used to repair the city walls at various times, Byzantine and Ottoman, and can be seen at frequent intervals. Four furnaces for cement were set up at Çubuklu across the water[52] where the woods offered plentiful fuel. The castle was completed in August 1452[53] for the only inscription[54] to Mehmet gives the date as

Recep of 856. It also refers to his magnificent vezir, Zaganos Pasha,[55] who must have had overall charge of the work. Zaganos had been banished by Murat II, but was restored to favour by Mehmet II and was his closest companion at the time. The masonry shows signs of haste with much waste of mortar and roughly cut stones. The great tower by the water, however, has decorative brick panels and is built of alternating layers of brick and stone. All the vaults were brick. It was the strongest castle then existing in Mehmet's realms, and was armed with guns which closed the straits to all hostile shipping. On 10 November 1452, two Venetian galleys from the Black Sea passed in spite of the guns but sixteen days later a Captain Antonio Rizo was impaled after his vessel had been sunk. A galley from Trabzon got through on 2 December 1452.[56] None other appears to have succeeded, which is hardly surprising since the castle was equipped with small and large mortars, javelots, siege batteries, balls, arrows and stone shot. The large artillery was mounted on the ground and was doubtless removed and put to serious use the following year. Rumeli Hisar was more a base than a fortress, and after the fall of the city it became a prison and finally a museum. It would seem to have been as much a waste of effort and materials as it was a feat of engineering.

The great tower at the waterside and the barbican that curtained it had been built by the Vezirazam Candarlı Halil Pasha, who corresponded with the Byzantine governement and was beheaded for treason immediately after the fall of the city when his letters were allegedly discovered.[57] The heights on the south and north were defended by two other formidable towers, the Black Tower on the north, Karaküle, built by Saruca Pasha, rising through eight high storeys, and the Rose Tower, Gülküle, on the south, which was built by Zaganos. The padişah is said to have reserved the construction of the curtain walls for himself. This division of labour clearly simplified the operation and may have encouraged a healthy rivalry although, doubtless, no one outstripped Mehmet himself.[58] Thirteen smaller bastions offered full fire cover at the angles of the connecting battlements along which runs a continuous guard walk, up hill and down dale, with many steps and access stairs from the inner enclosure at frequent intervals. Inside the walls, among the trees, wooden houses were built as residences for the officers and as barracks. Whatever buildings replaced these have been cleared away together with the mosque (of which the stump of the minaret remains) to be replaced by an open-air theatre. Firuz Ağa was the first commander of the garrison of four hundred men, all of whom needed shelter.

The mosque at Rumeli contrasts with the namazgâh outside the walls of Anadolu Hisar which is still walled off but abandoned. The upper towers are round but the sea tower is duodecagonal. They are of considerable height with rooms and privies set into the thickness of the walls which varies from five to seven metres.[59] They culminate in broad terraces, which were once covered over, set round the base of the top terrace which had a conical red roof until the nineteenth century.[60] They are so strong that a battery could be mounted on each of them. The heights of the towers vary from over twenty-three metres to twenty-eight metres (that of the Black Tower).[61] The rooms were vaulted, reasonably well lit, and several had ocaks. The vaults were all of solid masonry supported by pointed arches. The thickness of the curtain walls varied, according to their position, from three to five metres. The sentry walk was five to ten metres high and protected by ramparts eighty centimetres thick. The building was castellated throughout. There were five gates of which the principal one was protected by the barbican and the sea tower, and their names describe their function: the Commander's Gate, Ravine Gate, Mountain Gate, Barbican Gate and the South Postern. Each was properly flanked and protected.

This fortification owes much to the experience gained from the great Armenian and Syrian fortifications such as castles at Pertek and Bakras, the walls of Diyarbakır with its Ulu Badem, and the Kraks of the Crusaders, which had themselves developed from a Christian study of Islamic defences as well as Roman. Rumeli Hisar is, strictly speaking, no more an Ottoman building than the great Karaman-cum-Armenian fortress on the shore at Anamur; it belonged

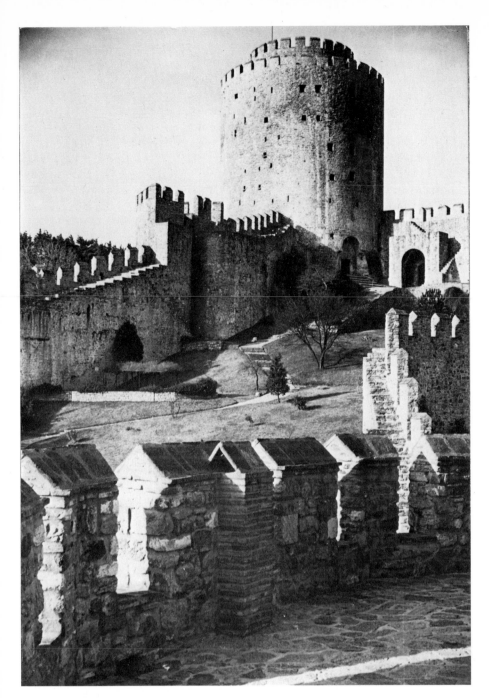

98 Rumeli Hisar. The Karaküle or Black Tower.

rather to the international style which had spread all over the Near East and Europe. Detached from its setting, it would be hard to find many details which were not universal.[62] It is significant that two great towers are round and not multifaceted in the Ottoman manner. But only the Donjon of Coucy exceeded the three towers in size at this period and their ancestry includes the Red Tower at Alanya and the White Tower in Salonika. The resemblances must have been greater before the roofs were lost in about 1830.[63] These roofs were built round wood frames like the caps of minarets and roofs of şadırvans. That the Hisar type of roof is Western in origin is confirmed by the similar capping of the Galata tower, now restored.[64] Tursun Bey specifically calls the water tower the Frengi (Frankish) Küle. The fortress also owes something to Yıldırım's fortress opposite, but this has been so altered in restoration – some walls were torn down and rebuilt as late as 1928 – that it is reduced to little more than a silhouette of a dungeon and curtain wall. This may have been all that there was of the original castle set on what was once the rocky point at the mouth of the Gök Su.[65] The gate is designed so that, should the enemy force it, they would have to enter the keep by a flight of stairs which exposed them to the fire of the defenders. This angled entry had honourable antecedents as long before as the gates of Mansur's circular walls of Baghdad.[66] Rumeli Hisar has also been heavily restored but not disfigured. Where Mehmet II bridged the Bosphorus with walls of shot and fire, Darius, far less fortunate in his campaign, had built his bridge of boats.[67]

In 856/1452[68] Fatih built a formidable fortress to protect the Dardanelles at Çanakkale, their narrowest point, known as Sultan Kale or Kale-i-Sultaniyye and a second one, on the Thracian shore, called Kilidbahir Kale. The two are 1,250 metres apart and each was defended by thirty cannon. They were restored in 958/1551 by Süleyman, and Mehmet Köprülü added two more in the seventeenth century. All four were overhauled by Selim III. The Sultan Kale had three floors and a terrace which sloped for drainage. The ground floor was raised four metres above the ground level of the inner bailey, and two flights of wooden stairs inside led up to the living floor, which was made up of ten circular dormitories. The outer walls, heavily battlemented and in places eight metres thick, formed a rectangle one hundred by one hundred and fifty metres and were defended by bastions at the corners and salient angles between. The wooden beams supporting the upper floors of the keep were thirty to forty centimetres thick in keeping with the massive masonry. The Kilidbahir Castle was protected by trefoil walls and its tall curved triangular keep reached by three bridges from the battlements. There was a large all-embracing outer bastion and a squat round corner tower. Even more sophisticated in plan than the Sultan Castle, it was as strong a defence against marine artillery as could be devised. Extensive work was carried out by such engineers as the Baron de Tott in later centuries.[69]

After the capture of Constantinople Fatih Sultan Mehmet, during his repair of the land walls, was to add another five to the two existing powerful flanking towers of the Golden Gate and thus he created Yediküle, the Castle of Seven Towers, with curtain walls twelve metres high.[70] He cannot have expected any serious attack, but the precaution was doubtless wise; moreover he needed a treasury, and the revenues of the Evkaf, or the Office of the Pious Foundations, were collected there until a late date.[71] It is to be noted that the defences faced inwards to the city as much as outward. He was also responsible, and very understandably since this was a frontier town, for the repair of the citadel at Kayseri which he also strengthened.

This solid background of military engineering dominates palace, mosque, and other civil architecture of the period, the larger mosques and bedestens being formidably strong and their proportions mathematically severe and straightforward.[72] During the reign of Mehmet II, there was a slowing down of the development of the basic conception of the form of the Ottoman mosque; his engineers, however, achieved an advance in sheer size which was the necessary prelude to aesthetic development: ideas had to await the accession of Beyazit II. It has already been noted that the expressive leap forward represented by the Üç Şerefeli Cami and Beylik mosques of Western Anatolia was not yet understood.[73] The Sultans' mosques in Bursa were to look puny beside those of Istanbul and this advance was due to the increased understanding of structure and the experimentation with stress that led to a dome which eventually enclosed a space as great as that of Hagia Sophia. The approach was characteristically cautious and painstaking: there was no jerry-building in the Byzantine manner. Mehmet II was a man of enquiring mind who debated religion with the Patriach Gennadius and who enjoyed the friendship of the Gentile Bellini (to whom he presented the golden armour of Enrico Dandolo, the first conqueror of Constantinople in 1204, as his mark of esteem when, dying, he sent him back to Venice because he was aware of his son's hositility to the pictorial arts); yet his reign was architecturally conservative. He deeply admired Hagia Sophia and had it converted into the first royal mosque immediately. A wooden minaret replaced the cap of a turret of the west façade,[74] a medrese was built, and the Sirkeci Tekke, the first in Istanbul,[75] was established just inside the gate.

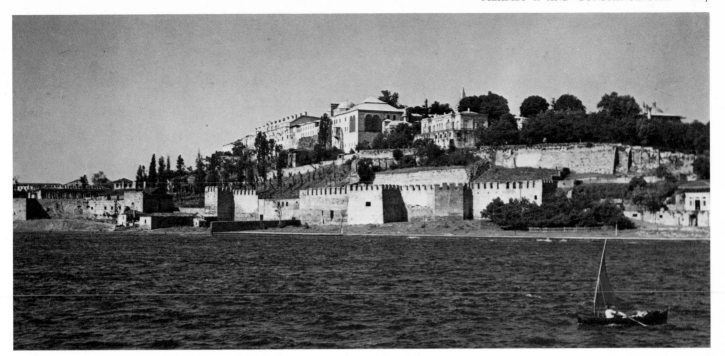

99 Topkapısaray, Istanbul. The Fatih Pavilion, now the Treasury, is in the centre, with the chimneys of the kitchens on the left and the nineteenth-century Mecidiye Kiosk on the right.

Istanbul did not immediately become his capital.[76] Mehmet left the city in the hands of a vali[77] twenty days after its fall, and returned to Edirne[78] after a visit to Bursa.[79] The walls of his first saray, later the Eski or Old Saray, were built in 1454 by the Vezirazam Mahmut Pasha and, according to Sanderson,[80] rose to the height of fifteen yards (if this seems an exaggeration, one can remember the walls of nineteenth-century palaces such as the Dolmabahçe and Çıragan, which are still standing and can be little less). Thus were the Ottoman monarchs to ape the Byzantine and be cut off from their own people. Within these walls[81] – after the old palace had been abandoned to become the House of Sighs for the discarded harems of dead sultans – were orchards, fountains, hamams and fair lodgings and also the burial ground for women, which by the mid-sixteenth century covered a large area.[82] The saray was built in the space between the ruined Forum Tauri and the markets which descended to the Horn. Here was the teeming haunt of footpads and other base fellows, and the prince intended to clean up the quarter by giving land free to his court in order to encourage them to build their own houses there, and thus rout out the infamous population. Topkapısaray, on the site of the old acropolis of Byzantium overlooking the three seas, was not completed until 1472, and not until then could Istanbul truly be called the centre of government. The Ottoman capital continued to be Edirne or wheresoever the sultan pitched his tent. The great mosque of Fatih was not begun until ten years after the conquest, in 1463, although plans went forward in 1459,[83] but small mosques were built all over the city from the first.

It was also in 1459 that Mehmet invited back the former inhabitants of Constantinople who had taken refuge in Edirne and Bursa and elsewhere and especially the learned and, significantly, the useful, giving them houses or building plots. He directed work on his mosque and the palace on his own account and was not only concerned with collecting materials but made sure that they were the most expensive and rare. He summoned masons, stone-cutters and carpenters from everywhere, together with all sorts of other craftsmen of experience and skill. He wanted to give back to Constantinople its former power and glory and brilliancy, and for this he employed many overseers who were exceptionally wise and he himself continually inspected the work.[84] One can sense the common anxiety of all rulers that the labour be swift, because crowned heads are never secure. The chronicler goes on to record that Mehmet spent the winter of 1464-5 in the city and finished his palace of Topkapı (The Gun Gate) then.[85] This contradicts Turkish tradition but, except for the Çinili Kiosk which bears an inscription dated 1472, conflicts with no recorded fact. There is no reason to suppose that the early pavilions and halls of the palace were not completed then. What emerges from the account of the work initiated in 1459 is the obedience of the vezirs, such as Mahmut, Murat and Rum Mehmet, in founding public buildings, and one detects an embryonic Department of Architect of the Empire. Fatih is also reported to have commanded hamams and aqueducts and other public works and he was responsible for the square nine-dome bedesten at Galata which is related to the Eski Cami at Edirne.

The oldest dated mosque in Istanbul is the Yarhisar Cami which was built in 865/1461[86] by Yarhisarlı Mustafa Efendi. It is representative of many other Ottoman mosques of its size. Destroyed by fire in 1917, it has been restored recently in unfortunate taste. Originally the walls were ashlar but are now courses of brick and stone. The two domes of the portico are carried on brick ogee arches springing from two corner piers and a classical column in the centre. The north side is walled in against the prevailing wind. The minaret collapsed during the fire but its classical base remains, with five external facets and a sixth set against the north-west corner of the building. It does not rise above the level of the roof. Inside, there is a square room with a single dome set on an octagonal drum and it is clearly the descendant of the typical Edirne mosque such as Kuş Doğan Cami, dated 830/1427[87] or Selçuk Hatun of 860/1456.[88]

The Ayşe Kadın Cami built in 873/1468[89] for a daughter of Mehmet I is also a variation of this Edirne type. Her mosque has a frieze in the Byzantine manner above the second row of windows while the octagon is exceptionally high with squinches at the four corners carried on bases of their own and with four sets of three very tall and slender Byzantine type windows under the arches on the other four sides. The dome itself reaches eighteen metres in height and is eleven metres in diameter.[90] The north-east wall and sofa, but not the portico, remain. It was built of stone. The door into the mosque is on the north-west side and is not set on the mihrab axis. The polygonal base of the minaret is strongly ribbed and the panels are inset with rosettes where the base slopes inwards towards the springing of the shaft.

More typical is the Sittişah Hatun Cami, also in Edirne. She was the daughter of Zülkadıroğlu Süleyman Bey[91] and the first wife of Mehmet II, and her mosque was built in 887/1482, fifteen years after her death, by her stepson, Beyazit II. Fatih appears to have had little affection or regard for her and his name is not mentioned in the inscription. Again, the portico, together with its east wall and slender columns, has disappeared. The dome measures 13·13 metres in diameter[92] and is set on the usual octagonal drum with four squinches at the corners of the square room. Chevrons lead up from the simple square base of the minaret – which rises above the lower casements – to its polygonal shaft.

Returning to Istanbul, a mosque to which Ayverdi attached considerable importance is the Yatağan Cami built by Hacı İlyas Ağa, Master-Gunner of Fatih. It is stone but has a wooden narthex which, with its second storey and its porch above five stone steps, looks like a house. It may once have had a portico like that of Kasım Pasha Cami at Edirne which was built in 883/1478[93] and which is twelve metres square and, so, much the same size. But this mosque has a dome and the Yatağan has not. Inside the latter are two wooden pillars which sustain three arches creating an area like an inner narthex over which is a wooden gallery supported by eight slender shafts. Whether the original construction was similar to the present one is uncertain. There are many mosques of this type, such as that attributed to Sinan at Kanlıca on the Bosphorus. In every case the weatherboarding has been renewed. The entrance to the minaret of the Yatağan mosque is from gallery level. It is set in the thickness of the north-west corner wall and this would indicate that, while the gallery is not still of the original material, this was its position from the first. The mosque may have suffered from fire or rot at some period, for the roof today is flat and decorated in the Empire style. It may well have had a small inner wooden dome like that of the late sixteenth-century

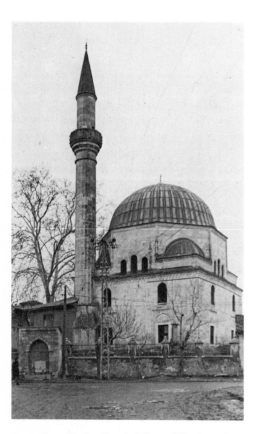

100 Ayşe Kadın Cami, Edirne. The dome is unusually high.

Takkeci Ibrahim Ağa[94] which was not replaced. Nonetheless, Ayverdi maintains[95] that this mosque is the only one of its type remaining intact, and claims that the woodwork is equally old. The prayer hall is thirteen by ten metres in area and six metres high.[96] It is so strikingly well lit by its large upper windows that its atmosphere is more late eighteenth-century, when it was obviously extensively restored, than fifteenth; but its basic plan belongs to that earlier period.

The little mosque of Timurtaş Ağa, restored in 1964, is also well lit and it is just possible that large windows were a freakish characteristic of the time. This mosque has a heavy terracotta cornice and the stumpy minaret has an unusual enclosed şerefe with four windows.[97] It, too, was preceded by a wooden narthex with a fine flight of stone stairs rising from the north-west and turning at right-angles on a line with the mihrab. There is a sofa on either side. For so small a building the effect of space in this hallway is quite grand. This mosque, like so many in the market quarter of Istanbul, was built above the vaults used as shops, the rent of which helped to maintain the foundation, forming a part of its vakfiye. Samanveren Cami, the mosque of the Strawmaster, near the Uzun Çarşı and the Merdivenli Cami, or mosque of the Stair, both in ruins, are other examples of mosques of these early years after the conquest which are set on vaults above the tumult of the market quarter. They are square rooms with domes at first floor level. The Samanveren had once a small but charming court which is now a midden.

Foremost among the early mosques of Fatih's reign was that of the Chief Vezir Mahmut Pasha which was the first large mosque to be completed within the city walls as opposed to the sultan's mosque at Eyüp. Mahmut was the son of a Greek father and a Serbian mother who had been a child of the devşirme.[98] Entering the Pages' School, he became the favourite of Mehmet II. In 1453 he was appointed Viceroy of Europe and after a period during which Mehmet was his own first minister, following on the execution of Halil Pasha, he was awarded the kaftan of Vezirazam in 1454.[99] He was known as Adeni, or Poet of Eden, because of his talent for writing verse and was a patron and protector of poets, musicians and learned men, many of whom fed at his table. He corresponded with the poet Mir Ali Shah, Grand Vezir of Iran. He was universally popular.[100] Besides his külliye in Istanbul, he built a mosque at Sofia. He was deposed from his high office in 872/1467[101] as a result of the treacherous scheming of the Second Vezir, also a Greek by birth, Rum Mehmet Pasha, but he was restored to office briefly in 1473.[102]

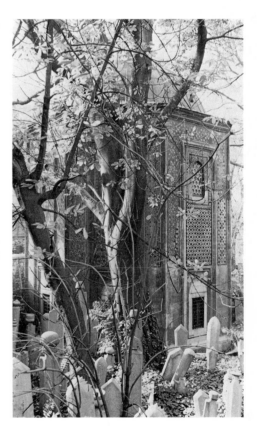

101 Mahmut Pasha Türbe, Istanbul.

The Mahmut Pasha complex[103] was large and included a medrese, his türbe, a mahkeme or law court, a han, an imaret and a sıbyan mekteb. Only the dershane of the medrese remains and it is noteworthy that it was built well east of the mosque. The courtroom, imaret and mekteb disappeared at different periods. The han, mauled though it has been, is still in use, and the plan of the rectangular first court survives although that of the second and lesser court demands an energetic imagination. It was distorted in order to fit into a constricted and far from easy site. This court still existed when Gurlitt photographed it. The picture shows with what simple logic the span and height of arches were altered in order to fit the shortest side which was set between larger ones at awkward angles. An entrance has now been made in the centre of the shops between the two courts but the original access was through the revaks at either side. The inner court has no egress of its own even today and there is still only one entrance to the great court from the Mahmut Pasha highway which passes the handsome domed gatehouse. Entering beneath its vault and then the dome of the arcade, between twin flights of stairs – once the only way up to the first floor cells – one is faced with a hideous modern construction which replaces, doubtless, the original fountain and its mescit. Although two-storeyed, the han lies low and is spacious. It once contained 167 rooms.[104] It is closely related to the hans of Bursa[105] and its contribution to Ottoman architecture was to adapt the general rule to the particular requirements of an awkward site in this crowded heart of the city where land values were high. It was completed in 871/1467, four years after the mosque, and is still known as the Kürkcü Han (the entrepôt of the fur merchants), creating a romantic vision of Tatars and Magyars on stallions of the Steppes. It now sells cheap materials and shoddy bric-à-brac.

The türbe[106] is octagonal and has windows on seven sides and a door without a *10* porch on the eighth. Each of the eight sections is set in elegant, tall frames but the great height leads to a disproportionate amount of space between the small windows whereas at Üç Şerefeli Cami and elsewhere the usual custom had been for the sill of the upper light to form the top of the frame of the casement below. The türbe is remarkable for the indigo, blue and green glazed bricks which decorate its exterior walls forming interlocking wheel and star patterns reminiscent of the painted mihrab wall of Üç Şerefeli Cami, and of the ceramic work of Tabriz in general and of the Timur dynasty at Samarkand in particular. At this period, however, the number of kilns working within the Ottoman dominions was few, for tilework is sparse in the reign of Fatih. It was not to become an important element in architecture until the growth of the Iznik kilns and their turn to tiles from dishes and jugs during the reign of Süleyman I, when the potters, of many nationalities, were increasingly brought under the control of the Court. Underglaze was also to be revived by the Iznik potters. In the türbe of Mustafa Sultan, son of Fatih, at Bursa there are excellent tiles of the period. Mustafa died in 1474.[107] The decorations of Mahmut Pasha's tomb belong to the old order rather than to the start of a renaissance. They could also be imports or gifts from Persian friends of this cultivated vezir but are probably from Anatolia. They were restored in 1950.[108] The türbe is dated *878*/1473 by the fine inscription set inside the traditional double arching of the door.

The mosque was completed in *869*/1464,[109] nine years before, and belongs, as *10* we have seen,[110] to the Bursa type considerably modified. It is very large and spacious. It was repaired in 1755[111] and again in 1828 and 1936. The nineteenth-century restoration followed on a fire which ravaged the district in 1827 and it is then that the most extensive alterations are likely to have been carried out. The unhappiest event was the encasement of the six fine columns of the portico within monstrous stone piers. Gyllius[112] reports that they consisted of two central columns of porphyry, two of verd-antique, and two of Proconessian white marble. It would be a reasonably easy task to strip off the stone and reveal these columns beneath. The mosque has recently been refurbished and is now spruce and its officers are proud of it; but the interior has suffered over the years. Originally, one entered a vestibule or narthex under a square stalactite vault with two domed areas right and left whose plaster shells were carried on stalactite squinches. Half these lateral areas are raised on sofas and beyond them on the north-west and north-east are rooms which were probably only eyvans. That on the north-east has a polygonal vault made up of Bursa triangles while that on the opposite side gives access to the minaret by an exposed flight of stairs. It would seem that the architects were concerned that the base of the minaret should be as solid as possible. Three steps lead up from the narthex to the twin-domed harem. Mahmut Pasha has no walled court and the present şadırvan is a later addition. I have been unable to inspect the floor under the first dome for traces of a fountain there but it is improbable that one ever existed. The dome is sealed and has no lantern and, although this could be due to repairs, the two areas are equal and the domes alike and strongly suggest that the whole of this central part of the mosque was always united. The domes are twelve and a half metres in diameter[113] and divided from each other by a broad arch. The inner avlu concept has gone.

Both the mihrab and minber are restored. The sultan's box set to the south-east is early nineteenth-century and is a pleasant but incongruous addition wedged awkwardly under an arch in the structure of the wall. Archways on each side of the central area admit to passages which lead directly from the vestibule to windows in the south wall and were once cut off from the prayer hall. Each of the passages has a suite of three rooms on its outer side. Those in the centre of these wings had oval domes[114] which are now round. They thus recall the proto-baroque of many early Ottoman mosques. They are followed by two smaller

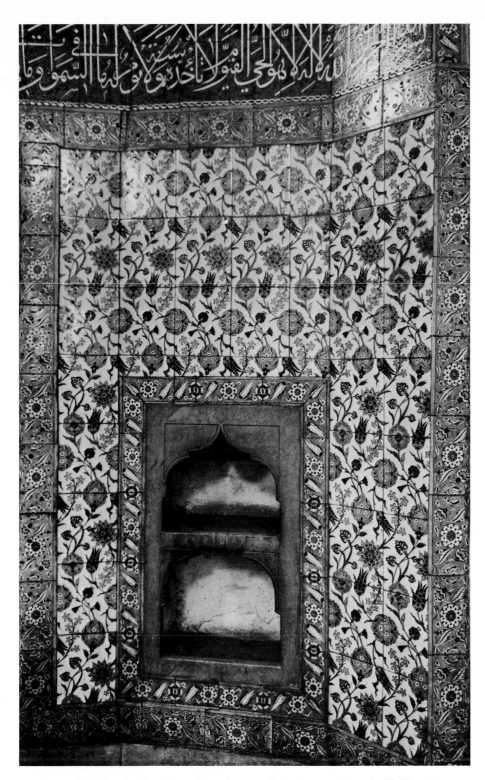

102 Mustafa Sultan Türbe, Bursa. Tiles from Iznik dating from the second half of the sixteenth century.

arched rooms which lead, down three stone steps, to narrow corridors between them and the walls of the north-east and the north-west eyvans which have doors on the east and west, so that it was possible to enter the tabhane area without disturbing those at prayer in the mosque itself. All the corridors have cradle vaults. The original dividing walls, if walls so thick can be so designated, may have had arches cut into them later on; but it would be just conceivable that these wing areas were open in sequence just as they are today, if it were not that the inner corridors would then have been unnecessary. It is also probable that

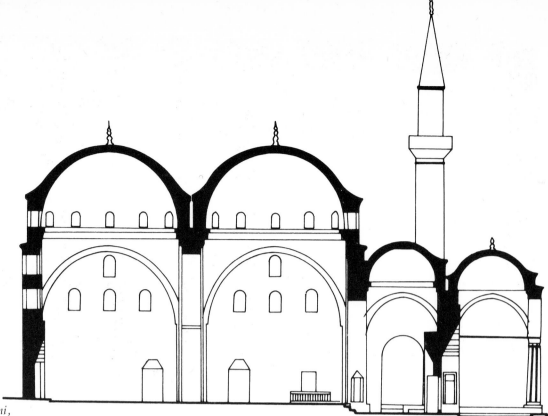

103, 104 Mahmut Pasha Cami,
Istanbul.
Elevation and plan,
scale 1 : 250.

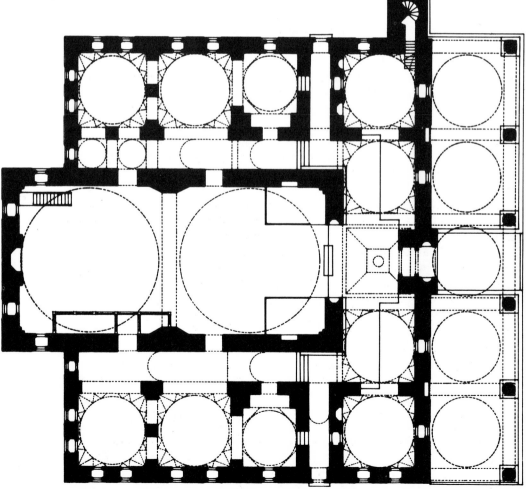

1 0   5   10m

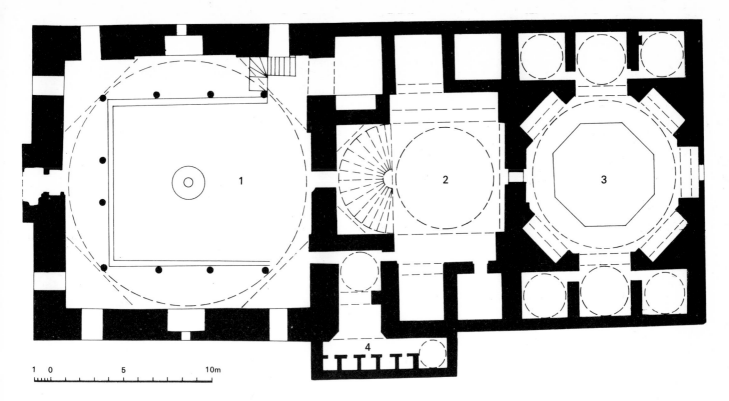

the rooms under oval domes were open and served as eyvans. Mahmut Pasha Cami is clearly of the Bursa type and I regard it as transitional in its cutting off the tabhane or tekke from the central area for prayer. The smooth pendentives of the two major domes of the mosque of Mahmut are likely to be due to restoration. Those of the vestibule are original, or have been restored to their original state. Typically, the drums of the lesser domes are all octagonal.

05   The hamam of this complex was completed in *871/1466*, three years after the erection of the mosque, thus challenging the belief that it was customary to build the hamam first for the refreshment of the masons and other workers on the construction of a complex. It is the oldest Ottoman hamam in the city and was damaged in the fire of 1755. In 1953 it was restored with reasonable care.[115] It is approached from the midst of Mahmut Pasha market through a splendid doorway with a handsome stalactite vault. The depth of the cutting of the stone makes it clear that these stalactite formations are, in effect, half-domes and follow the traditional division and multiples of two which underlie so much Ottoman scale. It leads into a very splendid camekân under a dome seventeen metres in diameter[116] on an octagonal drum carried on simplified stalactite squinches. The dome is, therefore, larger than any in the mosque and would indicate that the proportions there were controlled by function and not by any lack of engineering skill in the architects. There is trace of a small ocak, for making coffee or other hot drinks, near the door to the soğukluk which is finely vaulted with a whorl of ribbed plaster preceded by a multi-ribbed half-dome. This was the first Ottoman half-dome in Istanbul. Two eyvans and two private rooms for personal ablutions are all richly vaulted. In the centre, a narrow door admits to the hot room which has an octagonal marble göbektaş, or navel stone, on which to recline and to be massaged.[117] Above is another finely ribbed dome, set with the usual bottle-glass lights.[118] In the Surname of Ahmet III, attributed to Vehbi, is a miniature showing that hamam lights were sometimes coloured, and it is likely that they would have been in one as fine as this. The glass for this purpose, along with that for the windows of mosques and palaces, was imported from Venice.[119] The result must have been pretty with the various colours playing over the many facets of the plaster vaults and the marble revetments and the floor. There are two deep eyvans on the left and right, also finely vaulted, from which two private rooms give off to form the four corners of the chamber. There are also five shallow public

105 Mahmut Pasha Hamam, Istanbul. Plan, scale 1 : 250. The half-dome in the cool room is a logical development. 1 disrobing hall; 2 cool room; 3 hot room; 4 latrines.

eyvans with basins and taps for washing. In some of the domes there are plaster flowers in which the lights are set. More than in any other Ottoman building, these hamam domes must have shone and twinkled like the sky at night although they were only used by day.

The Murat Pasha Cami is related to that of Mahmut. It was built by a renegade member of the Palaelogos family, the son of one Vitus,[120] and an impetuous young man. In 877/1472, while Viceroy of Europe under the future Sultan Beyazit II, he took command of the right wing of the Imperial army in a fatal battle against Uzun Hasan. Disobeying the sagacious orders of the Chief Vezir, he led his cavalry in a wild charge worthy of the Crimean War and fell into a relatively simple trap which cost him his life. At least this was not because the orders had been muddled in the manner of those given the Light Brigade![121] He built his mosque in 870/1466.[122] The first dome (10·50 × 21 m.)[123] is supported at each corner by a set of three Bursa triangles to make a twelve-sided polygon together with the four walls, in the centre of each of which is a window. The slightly lower south dome is carried on pendentives decorated with large-scale stalactites. Externally, both domes are set on duodecagonal drums. There are only two rooms on each side and there the domes are set on plain pendentives, probably of a later date. The south-east room can only be reached through the one facing the north-east, but that on the south-west now has a door into the prayer hall. There is an entry into the minaret in the north-west corner. The portico retains its six columns, unblemished, but the interior has been completely renovated after many vicissitudes including use as a polling booth. It is another transitional form of the Bursa mosque but less elaborate than Mahmut Pasha Cami although it is large and lofty. Whereas the Mahmut mosque is faced in cut stone, Murat Pasha has alternating courses of two layers of brick to one of stone and, recently refurbished, the mosque is vivid among the trees of its enclosure.[124] In the reign of Mehmet II, the use of brick was frequent and this would indicate that the quarries were better organized later in the classical period than at this period rather than that the architects or their patrons preferred to use brick. During the 1960s stone was in short supply in Istanbul because of the extensive restoration of Ottoman monuments.

Like the mosque of Murat Pasha with its lateral rooms was the mosque built at Üsküdar by Rum Mehmet Pasha, another renegade Byzantine general and, due to his evil counsel, the usurper of the office of Vezirazam for a brief period (1467-70) after the deposition of Mahmut Pasha.[125] The mosque was built in the nick of time in 874/1469[126] and has been restored from its miserable condition of a few years ago. It has been a refugee hostel, a squatters' cavern and a chicken farm. Inside there are traces of old paintwork. The great door leads to a brief flight of steps between the open tribunes to the area under the main dome. Beyond are the mihrab and the minber, after two more steps, under a half-dome. The plan is thus related to that of the first Fatih and also to its development twenty years later in the mosque of Atik Ali Pasha at Çembelitaş. The half-dome unites the mosque area in a way that the twin domes of Bursa, after the first had ceased to be a court area (as at the mosque of Mahmut and the mosque of Murat Pasha) did not. With the great semi-domes of Hagia Sophia facing him across the water, the architect, whoever he may have been, took the hint; or half of it. It was not until the mosque of Beyazit II that the other half was taken[127] and the south semi-dome balanced by a second on the north.

Each side of the mosque were pairs of square tabhane rooms. Those on the south-east and south-west have ocaks and intercommunicating doors into the north-east and north-west rooms. The rebuilt porch, which may first have been tiled, now has five domes above its enormously high sofa with its superb view over the three seas. They are supported on six antique columns which are something of a job lot and which now, if not originally, have debased capitals. The minaret is conventionally set at the north-west corner and is approached from outside, but its door is not connected to the sofa of the son cemaat yeri. This was to be more and more the custom until a canon was established. A very plain

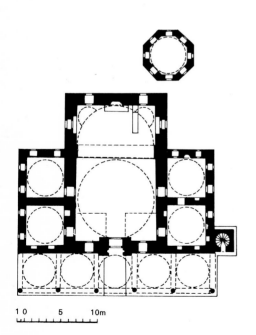

106 Rum Mehmet Pasha Cami, Üsküdar. Plan, scale 1 : 500. Except for the half-dome, this is a Byzantine building subdued by Ottoman concepts.

1 0   5   10m

octagonal türbe, which indeed could not be simpler, is nicely proportioned in ashlar. It lies south-west of the mosque in the cemetery behind. The dome, which is ten metres wide, is supported on a true Byzantine drum although it is of lead over a layer of brick in the Ottoman manner derived from a Byzantine practice. Even more distinctively Byzantine are the cornice and the four great arches of the central base, on which the drum rests and which achieve their crests above the level of the emergent roof. This and, less probably, the half-dome suggest that the architect, like the vezir, was a Greek, but the plan is strictly Moslem and traditional. The stalactites of the half-dome and the pointed arches of its windows are Ottoman in contrast to the four in the tympana which are Byzantine again in treatment as they are, indeed, at Mahmut and Murat Pasha. If it is accepted that these tympana windows show Byzantine influence, then it must be agreed that the fenestration of Sinan's vast mosque of Mihrimah at Edirnekapı owes something to this influence as well. More interesting is the origin of the half-domed apsidal form at Rum Mehmet's mosque and it is pertinent, therefore, to look at the later Atik Ali Pasha Cami especially since the first Fatih Cami was destroyed in the earthquake of 1766.

But, before considering Ali Pasha's building, it is helpful to inspect a signifi-
cant development which occurred at the mosque of Davut Pasha, Viceroy of Asia and a sounder soldier than Murat Pasha.[128] He was an Albanian and eventu-
ally Vezirazam from 888/1483 until deposed by Beyazit II in 903/1497 after nearly fourteen years in office.[129] His mosque was built in 890/1485.[130] It was the assembly point of the army before going on campaigns in Europe.[131] Here also was one of the four mahkeme or district courts of Istanbul. It was in use in Le Chevalier's time at the end of the eighteenth century but has since been destroyed. The simple early classical octagonal türbe survives. The mosque was damaged by earthquake and the interior restored. This consists of a square room with a grand dome eighteen metres in diameter[132] set on an octagonal drum borne on four stalactite squinches. The stalactite arch over the north door has a distinctive and attractive shell formation. In sum, all the aspects of this mosque are conventional. It is all the more surprising, therefore, to find that the mihrab is set in a deep five-sided niche which is clearly apsidal in origin.[133] Moreover, the niche is under a small but high half-dome. It is a direct Byzantine influence rather than a sudden disappearance of Rum Mehmet Pasha's half-dome. This feature remained part of the catalogue of Ottoman architecture. It had already appeared once before in the Hudavendigâr's mosque at Bursa, occurs at the Sultan Beyazit Cami at Amasya and is frequently found in the mosques of Sinan and his pupils.[134]

The portico was composed of the conventional five domes and six antique columns of granite (0·95 metres in diameter) some of which still stand with baklava (chevron) capitals which so closely relate to the Bursa plaster triangles. There are the usual two, domed rooms on each side with intercommunicating doors. The southern rooms have ocaks and, since successive mosques have this feature, it had become the rule for a tabhane to have an inner sanctuary or winter room. The minaret, fat as an earthenware jug, is set at the north-west corner and has been restored. The trunk springs from its base at the level of the lateral domes.

The alternative development – seen at Rum Mehmet and first Fatih – of a full semi-dome over the mihrab area[135] is repeated at Atik Ali Pasha, built in 902/1497.[136] Atik Ali Pasha was a slave and a eunuch who rose to be the Vezirazam of Beyazit II from 907/1501 until deposed in 909/1503 and again in 912/1506 until he was killed in battle in 917/1511.[137] This chancellor was a great builder and the mosque is of good workmanship. Of its dependencies, the medrese, mutilated by the widening of the Divan Yolu, remains. Inside, while the main dome, which is an almost standard twelve and a half metres in diameter,[138] and the half-dome, set on large and finely wrought pendentives, are not innovations, the wings are now open. The two, domed rooms have become fluid areas only divided from the prayer chamber by the broad pier which helps support the arches which serve in the place of curtain walls. It is just conceivable that these areas were originally detached[139] but there is no trace of the conventional ocaks

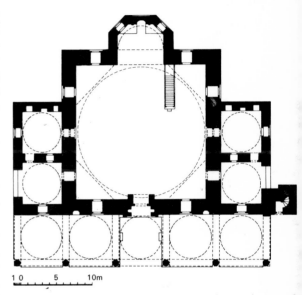

107 Davut Pasha Cami, Istanbul. Plan, scale 1 : 500. The mihrab niche shows the influence of Byzantine apsidal forms.

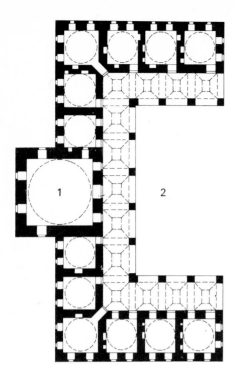

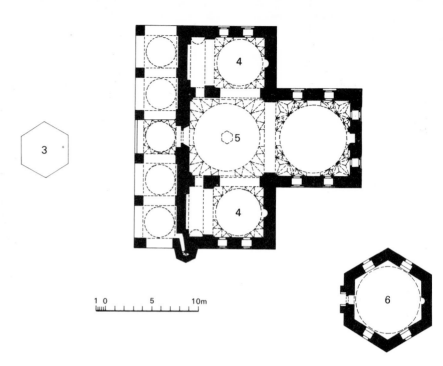

108 İshak Pasha Complex, İnegöl. Plan, scale 1 : 400. 1 dershane; 2 medrese; 3 şadırvan; 4 tabhanes; 5 inner court; 6 türbe. Note how the mosque and medrese are united by a single courtyard.

in the southern sections either in wall or roof. The porch is lofty but the columns are unattractive because of the rough chipping of the granite and the Marmara marble, and of varying width, to make them fit the well-carved stalactite capitals. This crude workmanship makes it probable that such architectural details as capitals were ordered from a workshop and were not always cut on the spot as is done when restoring mosques today.

I believe that this mosque has never been altered but that it was always open at the wings. There have been a number of Beylik examples (cited previously) to support such a theory and the conception of a fluid interplay of areas in a mosque is as old as Islam and the House of the Prophet at Medina, the first of all the mosques.[140] It is the basic concept which was so important in the development of Üç Şerefeli also. It is not likely that the walls were cut away and arched at a later date if only because of the work involved. It was not a common Ottoman habit to adapt existing buildings, except churches immediately after a conquest; instead, they rebuilt and, indeed, lack of maintenance of old buildings is one of the most trenchant criticisms levelled at the Ottomans by travellers and others at all periods down to the coming of the Revolution. It is true that the piers of Atik Ali Pasha have mouldings which look surprisingly eighteenth-century but this sophistication occurs in other buildings including the Ulu Cami at Manisa or Sultan Beyazit and Sinan Pasha in Istanbul.

The small, Bursa-type, mosque of the Vezirazam İshak Pasha, who was the chief minister to Fatih and Beyazit II, was built at İnegöl in *887/1482*.[141] It has one room on each side. These, unlike Atik Ali Pasha, may have been altered, since each has an addition on its north side which could have been a store but more likely was a lobby with a small separate arch giving admittance to this area. Yet the inside walls of each room have wide arches so that both are very much part of the whole interior space and the floor level is uniform throughout. It would be possible to conceive of the lobbies as separate small rooms[142] were it not that the plan of the mosque so closely resembles that of the now ruined Karaca Bey Cami seventy kilometres from Bursa where the rooms are walled off and their only entry was through similar vestibules, the function of which is quite logical. But at Karaca Bey Cami the rooms also possess ocaks and I found no trace of these at İnegöl which, however, was twice repaired. As at the mosque

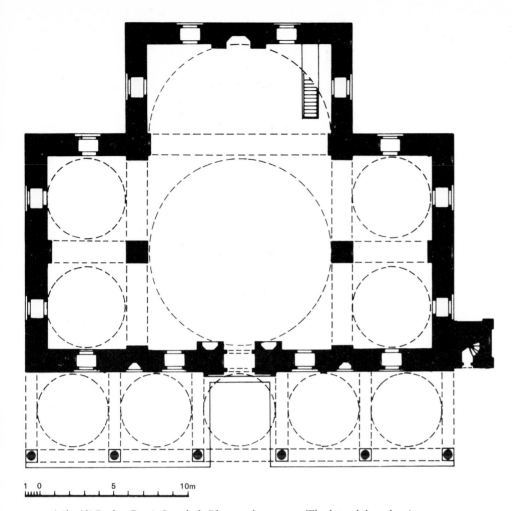

1 0   5   10m

*109 Atik Ali Pasha Cami, Istanbul. Plan, scale 1 : 250. The lateral domed units are
incorporated into the body of the mosque.*

of İsmail Bey at Kastamonu there is no window in the wall on to the portico
which could not, therefore, have served as a son cemaat yeri. There may have
been a şadırvan under the first dome inside as a consequence. The course of
brick and stone and the vertical bricks between each stone give this mosque a
rustic appearance.

The İnegöl complex is important because of the relationship of mosque and
medrese which face each other across a court and do not stand side by side as at
Murat I in Bursa or Mahmut Pasha and Davut Pasha in Istanbul. The unification
is not complete because the C-shaped medrese of twelve cells has its own area
of court between its cradle-vaulted revaks and there are no lateral revaks to the
larger area of the mosque precinct. The şadırvan is set midway between the
mosque portico and the medrese on the axis of the mihrab and the dershane in
the centre of the medrese. Today, when the medreses at Amasya have been
demolished, İnegöl is the best example of the approach to unification of mosque
and medrese with vezirs' foundations which began in the latter half of the
fifteenth century. It will be noted that while the first mosques after the conquest
reflected the Gazi spirit of the Bursa mosque, this was dying. The supreme
victory, the capture of Constantinople, undermined comradeship and egali-
tarianism and replaced it by a hierarchical bureaucratic system – that pomp and
paper which had already destroyed the Byzantine Empire.

The Atik Ali Pasha Cami gives some idea of the form of the first Fatih Cami
but a far more pronounced relationship was achieved in the larger mosque of
Selim at Konya, to which the mainly seventeenth-century Şerefettin Cami in
the same city is remotely related. The Selimiye is attributed by the directorate
of the Mevlana Museum at Konya to Sinan but it is impossible to believe that

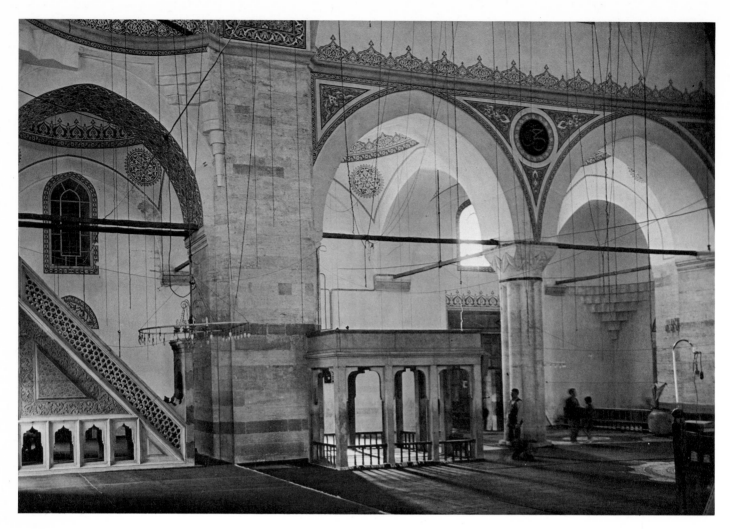

110 Selimiye Cami, Konya. Interior from the south-east.

he was the architect, for if the plan were his, however excellently contrived, it would show a signal atrophy of his creative powers since it is a throwback to the later fifteenth-century style and a deliberate copy of the Conqueror's mosque on a reduced scale. It is incredible that the division of the two central areas of the mosque would have been re-introduced after its abandonment at the end of the fifteenth century. Nor, after Sinan, were the wings detached in the Bursa tradition except in a handful of rural mosques in obscurer corners of the empire. The portico is also similar to those of the Beyazit period. The squinches of the exedra each side of the mihrab, moreover, are simplified versions of the huge forms seen in the mosque of Murat II at Bursa.

The conclusive proof that it is not Sinan's work is that it is not listed in either of the tezkeres or lists of his buildings. It is inconceivable, even to someone blinded by local pride, that an imperial mosque could be erected without the approval and guidance of the Architect to the Empire. It was what he was there to do. Fortunately, in *Illustrasyonu Türk* No. 67/1 (23/4/1938), which issue is devoted to Konya, an unsigned article of some interest on the monuments of the city states that this mosque was raised by Süleyman I for the soul of his father,[143] a soul in great need of prayers, and that his son Selim II endowed it with other pious foundations and organized by the vakfiye.[144] The article gives no authority for any statement about anything, but those which are verifiable are correct, or more or less correct, and the proposition is most probable, fitting all the facts that can be found. Certainly Süleyman had a deep regard for his father, and his first buildings such as the Selim I mosque in Istanbul were dedicated to him. The Selimiye at Konya helps to fill the curious gap in building activity in the first quarter of the sixteenth century caused partly by the extent of the Ottoman campaigns in Asia and in Europe. It was clearly a deliberate and pious copy on a reduced scale of the Fatih mosque and as such an invaluable record of that lost monument. It is for this reason that it is discussed so fully here, out of chronological order.

12 Inside, the four hefty piers from which the relatively small pendentives spring to support the dome,[145] and partly to support the half-dome over the mihrab 10 and minber, are ugly. The pillars, between which are eight tori or pilasters grouped round a star shaft, an interesting but not an original idea, only serve to underline the toris' dumpiness and a disturbing bulk![146] Mehmet Ağa was to use fluting on a far larger scale when he built the Sultan Ahmet Cami in the Atmeydan. Sinan abandoned the concept after he had built Şehzade. In Konya, it would seem inspired by the fluted drum of the pyramidal dome of the türbe 11 of Celâlettin Rumi which stands opposite the east door of the mosque.[147] The toris' baklava capitals are also, necessarily, large and cumbersome. The north door is spanned by a deep segmental arch which carries a tribune. This does not project and is reached by stairs set into the flanks of the two piers where two

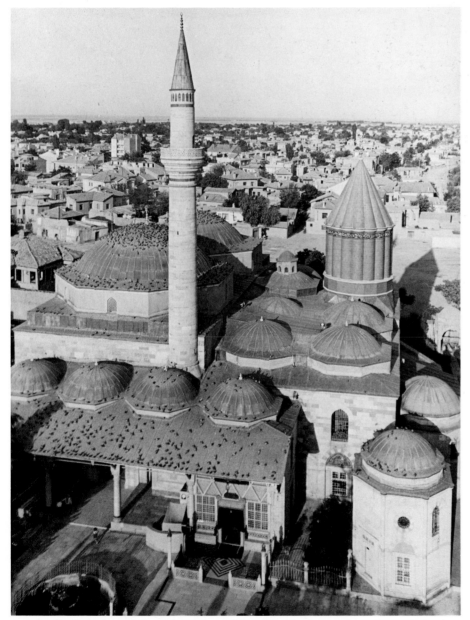

111 Mevlana Türbe and Complex, Konya. The conical dome over the tomb is Selçuk; the rest of the buildings are Ottoman.

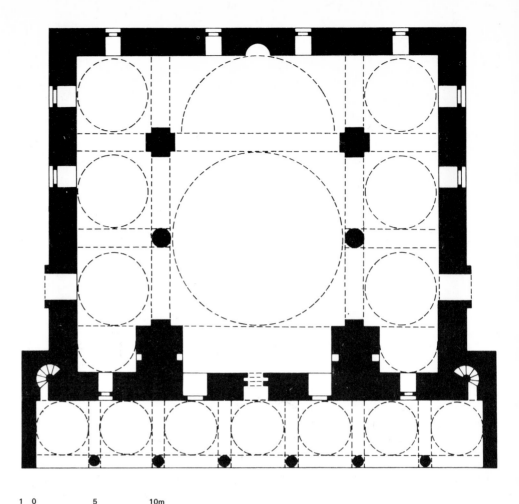

1 0   5   10m

112 Selimiye Cami, Konya. Plan, scale 1 : 300. Its form is a tribute to Mehmet II.

narrow passages are pierced in the Byzantine manner either side of the door
from which the arch springs. Under three smaller and lower cupolas and a half-
vault to the north, both west and east aisles are detached elements just as they
are at the Selâtin Cami or Imperial mosque of Beyazit II and at the first Fatih,
harking back to the overgrown Bursa type. The south-west and south-east
domes are borne on stalactites, much given to bleeding over the voussoirs, and
so are the north-west and north-east vaults. The interior is well lit with six
windows in the drum of the central dome, three tall windows with smaller
circular lunettes between them in the north tympanum, two more large windows
with circular ones flanking them east and west, partly masked by the lateral
domes, while the south tympanum includes one restored stained-glass window.
The mihrab is finely carved dark grey dappled marble while the white marble
minber is intricately carved with an elaborate multifoil papuçluk below and
hexagonal figures which create stars in the triangulation of the balustrade above.
The tall drum of the conical hood which is painted blue repeats the form of the
conjoint pillars – which make up the thick piers – and of the Mevlana dome.[148]
There is a plain free-standing marble mahfil near the south-west pier.

All the woodwork in the mosque is new but inoffensive as is the paintwork,
which is predominantly ochre and black, possibly copying a tradition.[149] The
forepart of the prayer hall under the semi-dome is two steps higher than the
rest of the mosque, another throw-back to the Bursa style; indeed, the steps are
between the walls of the aisles and the piers as well as across the centre of the
chamber. There the present shoe racks fortuitously suggest that direct access to
the upper part of the room was not meant to be made from the central area.

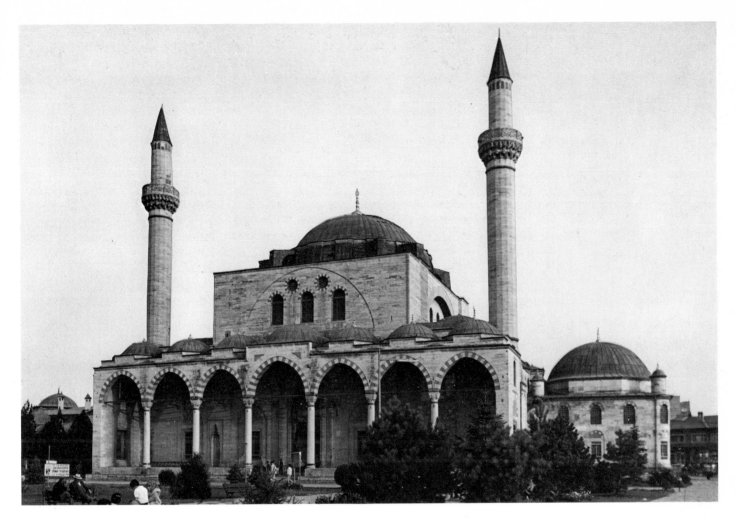

113 Selimiye Cami, Konya. The seven-domed portico with the square mass behind is a guide to the original appearance of Fatih Cami, Istanbul. The library (right) is a later addition.

It could be that there was a direct connection between the mosque and the Mevlana Tekke and that this central area was used by the dervishes. The mosque has no courtyard, which is surprising in a royal foundation since the Üç Şerefeli Cami had established the custom. It has a fine portico, however, with seven arches carried on six white marble columns with stalactite capitals of the best workmanship such as one associates with the period of Beyazit II. There are walls at the east and west ends of the broad, high sofas which are pierced by two tiers of windows which would suggest that a court was once contemplated. The lower window is under a pointed arch and has a grille while the upper is ogee and open to the sky. The minarets to which there are doors at the south-west and south-east corners carry single şerefes on stalactites and are ringed just below their shallow sixteenth-century caps with imitation windows of black stone. Between the two windows east and west of the door are simple niches which correspond to the two cupboards set in stalactite niches inside. The south wall is reinforced by two strong buttresses with stalactite niches to lighten the effect, for this side is as much exposed to the public view as is the north; and presumably it always was. This again is of fine quality. The drum of the central dome has four flying buttresses to support it.

The mosque of Sultan Fatih Mehmet itself, whether planned in 1459 or not, was begun on 21 February 1463 and completed in December, 1470.[150] It was the first great social unit of Istanbul and the largest in the empire. The architect was the first Sinan, known as Atık (Old) Sinan to avoid confusion with the great master of the sixteenth century. Demetrius Cantemir, Voyvode of Wallachia, in his history of the Ottoman Empire,[151] on the other hand, says that the architect

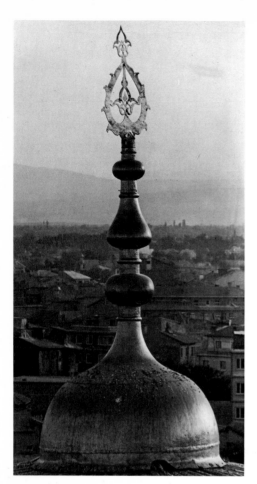

114 Selimiye Cami, Konya. The alem or bronze finial of the main dome.

was a Greek named Christodoulos. Yet there is nothing Byzantine in the architectural style for it was, as has been shown, an enlargement but not a development of the orthodox Ottoman style emerging from the Bursa period. But whether Sinan was a former slave or a Janissary who had been a devşirme is another problem. Konyalı[152] clearly uses the term Azadlı or one who is at liberty, a freedman, instead of Atık to avoid any confusion. Eyiċe[153] writing of the Kumrulu Cami or Mosque of the Doves built by Sinan Atık as his own and the place where he is buried, refers to him as Sinan l'Affranchi and ignores the meaning ancient, a term unlikely to be applied to anyone still living except the Ancient Mariner or the Ancient of Days. The second Sinan, who was indeed ancient, was called Koca Sinan when it became necessary to differentiate him from a student who shared his name. Koca has the connotation of old or ancient but also of great or large or famous, of being an elder. So it may be accepted that the implication surely is that the first Sinan was a freed slave and therefore not a Moslem by birth. A Byzantine plaque, carved with two doves drinking from a fountain of life, gave his mosque its name. Atık Sinan died or was executed, on 3 September 1471.[154] His assistant was one İyas, or İlyas, who died in *892/1487* and is buried by the mescit of the saddle market near the great mosque.[155]

The courtyard – which has the same area as the mosque itself – and the portico survived the devastating earthquake of 1766. Together with the cemetery behind it, the mosque is surrounded on three sides by a large precinct where the caravans could pitch their tents. This was raised up in the manner of the şahn of the Dome of the Rock at Jerusalem over specially built vaults and the Byzantine cistern of the monastery of the Holy Apostles. In places, these vaults are four metres high. The whole precinct is enclosed by a wall and by the ranks of medreses on the east and west. The mosque and its dependencies were damaged in the earthquake of 1509 when Beyazit took the opportunity to rebuild the royal loge. The medreses and the tabhane survived most of the vicissitudes except neglect, restorations, and the widening of the highway to the Edirne gate which destroyed a secondary range of buildings. The Saraçhane, or leather market, disappeared in one of the many fires.[156] This was probably built where the great funeral church of the Holy Apostles, model for St Mark's and St Front (Périgueux), stood.[157] It is likely that materials for Fatih were quarried from this dilapidated building which for a brief period after the conquest of the city was the patriarchal cathedral.[158] The legend that a murder on the steps of the church led to the prudent departure of the Greeks from the neighbourhood may or may not have substance: that Mehmet II coveted the fourth hill for his own mosque is the more probable reason. Gyllius[159] states that there were two hundred saddlers' shops and workshops making horsegear, leather buckets, trunks and quivers and that he saw the remains of the cistern of the church of the Holy Apostles and the prophyry sarcophagus of Constantine the Great. Most of the other sarcophagi, which had been broken open and plundered by the Crusaders in 1204, were transported to Topkapısaray and all have been accounted for. The saddle market was an endowment of the mosque and its considerable rents helped maintain the schools and charities.

On the north of the precinct were the Boyacı and Çörekci[160] gates. They faced the steps leading up to the platform which preceded the east and west doors of the mosque and were, therefore, off the main axis of the building. The result was that the central gate of the avlu, or inner courtyard, carefully set on the axis of the great north door into the mosque and the mihrab, was not in alignment with a gate out of the precinct. Between the Boyacıkapı and the Çörekcikapı were two square pavilions, traditional in form, the sıbyan mekteb[161] and a kütüphane or library. In an excellently delineated picture in sixteenth-century manuscript[162] the latter is shown as raised above the wall west of it. The room was domed and had three casement windows on to the precinct with three small triangular lights above. Presumably it was supported on consoles on the south side and had an anteroom and stairway to the north, outside the wall. The manuscript also shows a kiosk and a sebil or çeşme nearby and the sofas which still exist against the north

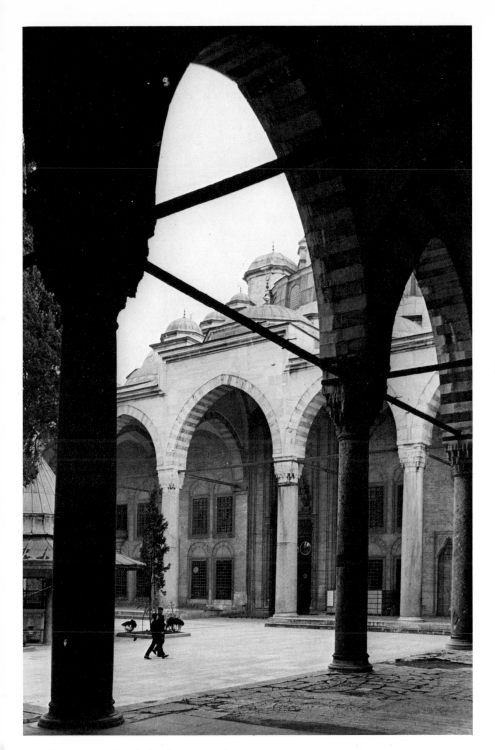

115 *Fatih Cami, Istanbul. The courtyard.*

wall of the avlu. The north-east sofa was altered by the addition of a cistern.[163]
16 Each side of the cemetery were the Türbekapı and the Çörbakapı, the Soup Gate.
Some of the old cemetery wall remains, with its grilled arches reminiscent of
those of the türbe of Murat II at Bursa and so does the Soup Gate with a multifoliate arch and elaborate arabesque stonework crowning it. It also has fine
inlaid coloured marble linear arabesque decoration in the spandrels and above.
The Türbekapı admitted to a lane between the wall of the mosque precincts
and that of the square garden in which the large darüşşifa or hospital was set.[164]
Evliya[165] says that there was a separate hospital for infidels and that music was
played to the sick and insane.[166] The doctors were all Jews. This building was
completely destroyed in the earthquake and the site built over. The closed winter

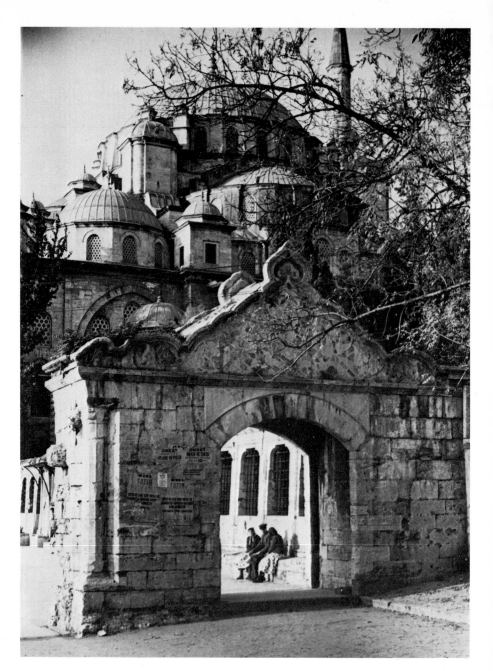

116 Fatih Complex, Istanbul. The Soup Gate, with the mass of the eighteenth-century mosque of Fatih beyond.

dershane, the Demirciler Mescit, had an apsidal form related to that of Davut Pasha[167] and it possessed two domed eyvans and two large domed chambers at the north-east and north-west corners. There were also fourteen large cells or wards, and it was a model for the still existent darüşşifa at Süleymaniye.[168] It had a kitchen of its own.

Beyond this hospital, to the south-east, stood the double hamam which was the largest in the city. It was known as the Irgatlar or Labourers' Hamam[169] and was destroyed in the conflagration of 1916. It was a very fine bath indeed. The sofa of the men's camekân was three feet high and five feet broad and stood against a wall thirty-seven feet high. The great hall under the cupola was seventy feet square with a huge marble basin in the centre three feet deep with a bubbling fountain fed by a spring. The pavement was of marble and, passing through the soğukluk with its cells and lavatories cleansed by waste water from the bath, and places for washing linen, the bather came to the hot room where the dome was supported above eight arches. The octagonal göbektaş was wide and high above the floor. In the corners were four cells or sweating-rooms. There were six open recesses for washing, one of which possessed a stately marble throne. The water was piped to the stokehole directly from a rivulet. The domes were starred with glass and amid the steam and gloom gave an excellent impression of the heavens at night.[170]

The Çorbakapı led to a second lane off which was the imaret which has also been destroyed. Plans and reconstructions indicate, improbably, that it was a simple two-room kitchen without a dining-hall, from which food was issued to be taken away just as it is today at the only three Istanbul imarets still open to the poor, those of Haseki Hürrem, Şah Sultan at Eyüp, and of the Valide at Üsküdar. Beyond the imaret was a tabhane and elsewhere there were several kervansarays with large gardens which have now been lost.[171] Sanderson states[172] that Fatih had one hundred lead-roofed houses for travellers,[173] by which he means cells, 'in round cube fashion', in which a three-day free stay was permitted. There were also, interestingly enough for there appears to be no contemporary Turkish record of this, one hundred and fifty lodgings for the poor outside the precincts where the inmates received food and one asper a day. Nicolay[174] says that although fed, the poor were not happy there and so most of the cells were empty. He also states that the foundation was endowed with many shops as far as the saray but he fails to state which saray it is that he means. The Eski Saray or the Vefa Saray near the Şehzade mosque was the most probable. Eyice[175] points out that in the towns the kervansaray was intended for the beasts and the merchandise which they carried while the tabhane was reserved for their masters and for itinerant dervishes. At Fatih it has been asserted that there was stabling for three thousand animals[176] which is surely exaggerated even if all the vaults under the precinct were employed. These include the cistern and although Gyllius[177] refers to it without suggesting that pack animals were ever tethered to its large columns, I believe these vaults to be the missing building. The school above, none the less, may occupy the site of the main kervansaray of which the sketch plans are so inadequate.[178] Both the imaret and the kervansaray are likely to have been much larger than such plans suggest, including that of Ali Saim Ülgen of 1938, and they would have been in proportion to the other grand buildings of the complex, at least until 1766. The suggested size of the imaret[179] is unrelated to the needs of the many hundreds who were fed each day; and hundreds is no exaggeration for there were the mosque servants, the faculty and students of the eight colleges and the eight tetümme or subsidiary schools, cooks and scullions and perhaps some of the staff of the hospital, gardeners, washerwomen, porters, the travellers and the poor.[180] Storage space alone must have required many hundreds of cubic feet. This will be discussed in relation to the imaret of the Beyazit II foundation at Edirne.

The one important building still standing which belongs to this part of the complex, now heavily restored afresh, is the hospice or tabhane.[181] It is a large building (64 × 43 metres),[182] and it incorporates a kitchen which could have been the fodlahane or bakery of the imaret. The large chamber, the equivalent of a dershane in a medrese, which could have been used as a common room in winter, as well as being the mescit, is about twelve metres square and is thus the size of the average mosque of the period. The noble court (35 × 26 metres) is heavily restored. It has revaks of twenty domes supported by sixteen arches on antique columns with both baklava and elaborate stalactite capitals. Three distinct periods of rebuilding can be read easily along the east side and the extent of these and other alterations makes any firm conclusion concerning this grand building impossible.[183] The rectangular piers in the centre of the open side of the double-domed east and west eyvans are of exceptional interest. They are flanked by rosettes set under arches which echo the stepped arch, or crow-step gable, of the great door of the avlu of the mosque, and the same stepping was applied to the four great arches which span the tympana of the present mosque as is the case with, among others, the Yeni Cami, Ahmediye, Süleymaniye and, to a lesser degree, the mosque of Mihrimah at Edirnekapı. This feature of the first Fatih is

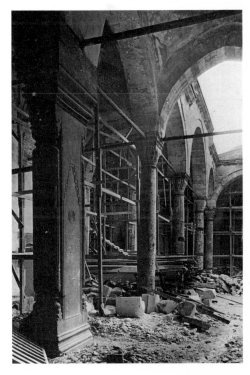

117 Fatih Complex, Istanbul. Work on the restoration of the tabhane courtyard in 1968.

43

17

II

not shown by Lorichs who depicts a simple pointed arch inset in a square block *11* of masonry as is the case at Selimiye at Konya[184] and this is accepted as accurate by Ayverdi in his reconstruction.[185] Although hard to decipher, Matraki's miniatures would also support this view; yet the last drawing made before the earthquake, dated 1669–70, which I have been able to see,[186] and which was made in conjunction with repairs or reconstruction of certain waterworks, while inaccurately depicting the domes and windows of the court and the minarets, shows odd details that caught the eye of the draughtsman including the contraction of the minaret trunks above the galleries, the height of the cypress trees poking above the domes of the courtyard, the terrace between the gates of the court and the doors of the mosque east and west and the stepped arch of the west flank boldly defined.[187]

At the corners of the piers of the tabhane there are inset fluted shafts with *11* slender necks held between identical base and capital which commonly appear at the angles of mosque portals or mihrabs, often as inset shafts of marble which can revolve.[188] Here they are sculpted as if they were material and so look as if they were slender bolsters bound at the end to create a tassel.[189] The rosettes of this building like those of the courtyard gate are boldly carved, and it was evidently a feature of the first Fatih that the stonemasons were skilled and experienced. Their genius was beautifully expressed in the stalactite half-arch above the north door of the mosque which from its three-dimensional base to the scalloped summit rises in nine tiers of honeycomb. It is set back under a shouldered arch which is purely a decorative screen throwing a significant shadow and stands in turn beneath an ogee arch set in a ribbed frame. The rosettes are formed of two circles of eight petals each which suggests mystical significance.

East and west of the mosque, seventy-five metres away across the paved *11* precinct, where the caravans once camped under the trees and youths now play football, are the eight colleges[190] which were the highest schools of the empire until those of Süleymaniye were built nearly a century later.[191] From this moment the Shariat, or sacred law, was dominant but much Byzantine jurisprudence was incorporated.[192] The Ottomans were no longer Gazis but Emperors. The medreses on the east side formed the Karadeniz or Black Sea group and those on the west the Akdeniz or Mediterranean group. On both sides, the four large units are parallel to the mosque and are identical in size and entered by a door in the centre of the wall facing the precinct. Each possesses, or possessed, nineteen cells,[193] an eyvan the same size as a single cell, and a dershane with a high dome on the south side with a washroom beside it. These rooms were built round the traditional porticoed court with stone piers supporting brick arches and spandrels of two courses of brick to one of stone and a şadırvan. The medreses on the north and south are divided from the central pair, which are contiguous, by a broad walk leading to a narrower stone passage which divided the larger schools from the subsidiary ones now destroyed, although those on the east have been replaced by primary schools occupying the same area. These had no courts and only nine or ten cells with a portico facing a high wall. The larger corner rooms may have been used for studying or by the teachers, in which case each of these eight medreses had only eight cells.[194] The medreses are faced in cut stone and their doorways have the traditional double arch, the lower of polychrome voussoirs, and the upper rising above the level of the cells. These had varying simple and effective brick reversal patterns in the tympana of their arches in the early Ottoman tradition and are related to some in the Samanid mausoleum at Bokhara, dating from the ninth century. The walls are of three courses of brick in thick mortar to one of stone. The Akdeniz medreses are raised high above the street on vaults because of the fall of the land and these formed part of the vaults extending under most of the precinct. A curious feature of the dershanes are their side entrances between two small open plots for trees and flowers; these minute gardens divide the reading-rooms from the revaks of the courtyards in an unusual way and are a later development. All the medrese domes are set on hexagonal bases and drums except for one which was probably repaired care-

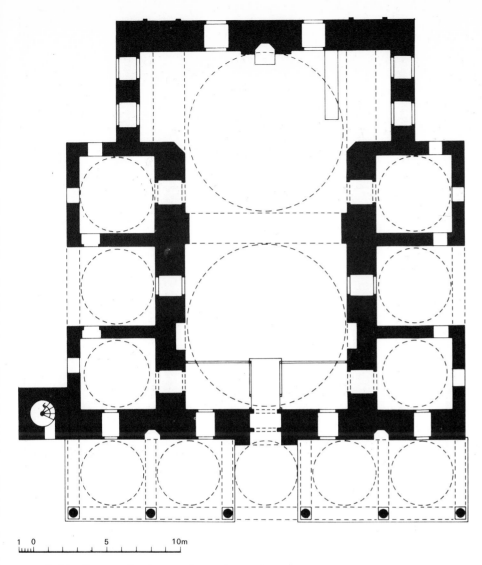

130 Gedik Ahmet Pasha Cami, Afyon. Plan, scale 1 : 250. There is a relationship between this plan and that of the Çinili Kiosk.

side under thick arches with double tie-beams reminiscent of those of Üç Şerefeli Cami. The corners of the two lateral rooms on the south-west and south-east are cut at an angle of forty-five degrees to lead the eye into those unusual extensions beyond the shouldered arches which, in this position, are themselves strange. The mosque had four small flanking tabhane rooms with ocaks set on either side of the eyvans on the east and west from which their doors open. The eyvans and the rooms each have a window which opens into the prayer hall. The stalactite niche of the mihrab is of white stone set in a vivid frame of alternating bands of stone and local marble. The minaret, which is on the north-east and set behind the portico, has a base as high as the lateral rooms with an unusual joint between it and the shaft, because it projects slightly and is not divided into receding triangles but, instead, has its corners cut into petal shapes. The trunk is spiral like that of the Selçuk Burmalı Minare Cami at Amasya and the north-west minaret at the Üç Şerefeli Cami, and the ribs are particularly deeply incised. At the top, they unexpectedly make a double zigzag, before the stalactite – as is usual – mushrooms under the balcony.

One of the tragedies of Ottoman architecture was the decay of the palace at Edirne[256] for, set among the trees, was a collection of garden courts and pavilions some of which were of fantastic and inventive shapes and forms. But to a believer, as we have seen, the proof of God is in the perishable quality of that which is not

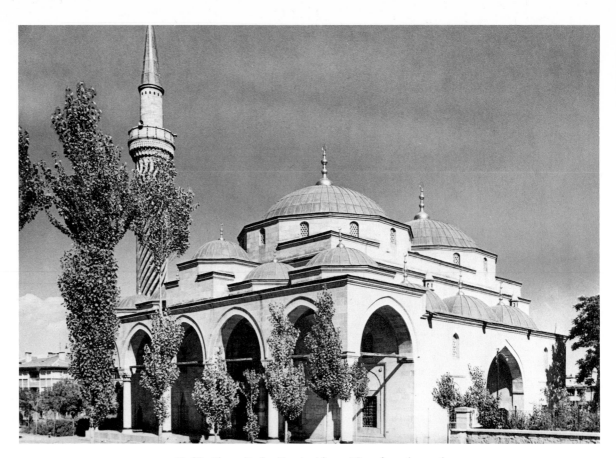

131 Gedik Ahmet Pasha Cami, Afyon. View from the north-west.

Him.[257] The setting was ideal. Villehardouin in the thirteenth century described it as 'beside the river in some of the most beautiful meadows in the world'.[258] It remained the favourite residence of the sultans, who mostly cordially hated Istanbul, and they sought it as their home until the Janissaries forced Mustafa III to abandon it. Here they could relax and hunt and here they were free of the mob about the gates of Topkapısaray. Yet even here, Fatih, infected by the Byzantines with the concept of the sanctity of monarchy, had built a great wall. A photograph of 1873 shows his father's extraordinary Cihannümâ Kasrı which was a rectangular building then reached at first-floor level by two sweeps of nineteenth-century baroque stairs. Square in the centre was another tall storey as sparsely fenestrated as the first with, above it, a circular drum or neck which carried a polygonal turret with eight windows and a conical roof. This large upper chamber must have commanded wide views and, indeed, it looked almost as if made to revolve.[259] In 1829, the additional wings still stood on each side of more elaborate stairs. The Kum Kasrı[260] was tiled throughout including the ocak, or hearth, of the grand salon, and it had an inset, domed ceiling richly painted and embossed. The small salon had an unusual cone-shaped plaster stove inset with circles of coloured glass like those of the domes of a hamam. Many of the pavilions were of wood on stone basements, summer houses of many windows, and they were clearly the forerunners of the yalıs of the Bosphorus. But they were so extensively repaired that the nineteenth-century records in the form of drawings and photographs are of dubious historical value.[261] The kitchens, however – a series of eight, domed halls with large chimneys – were clearly the model for those of Topkapısaray. Their vastness at both palaces indicates the considerable establishment that the sultan and his governement maintained at Edirne just as at Istanbul.

Fatih also purchased the land necessary to form the Okmeydan[262] above Kasımpaşa on the Horn. This grand archery ground was used for training and also formed a sacred club, because archery had a religious significance from long before Islam and the elaborate and arduous training was a ritual to which the sultan willingly submitted. Indeed several princes, like Murat IV, were great marksmen.[263] This club was called ocak or hearth as were Janissary platoons, a concept based on that of the camp fire. The pillars set up to celebrate outstanding feats of marksmanship and lengths of flight are mainly eighteenth-century.[264] There was also an archery ground in the gardens of Topkapısaray. At the Okmeydan, besides a tekke associated with the cult of archery there was a military namazgâh,[265] similar to that at Anadolu Hisar, with its grass sofa and minber surviving but its mihrab lying shattered. Very much earlier in date but in much better condition is the namazgâh at Gelibolu (Gallipoli) constructed from antique marble blocks and panels, today the finest example of its kind in Turkey.[266]

The reign of Mehmet II, which ended at Maltepe in May 1481,[267] was architecturally conservative but it was constructionally bold, as has been shown. The splendid plaster of the Treasury and the Tiled Pavilion at Topkapısaray, where the tiles are not strictly Ottoman at all, reflect the all-ranging interest of a cultivated Renaissance ruler. What was new and peculiar to the Ottoman school was the breadth and height of the dimensions and the confidence with which blocks of masonry were reared one upon the other. The search for craftsmen by conquest and by invitation was significant.[268] The transferring and regulation of the palace school was not only significant, it was to be the major influence in the empire until the nineteenth century in all aspects of government, including building and town planning. Murat II had decreed that he would only eat with ten guests at his table; his son ate alone or with one of royal blood.[269] Padişahs and vezirs, who in the great decades were mostly recruited from the Balkans and later Anatolia as children of the devşirme, became a race apart, a miniscule élite that governed vast dominions. Within the bureaucratic confines of this palace system was the office of the Şehr-Emini, the Minister of Works, and his first officer, the Royal Architect. Ottoman architecture was truly established.

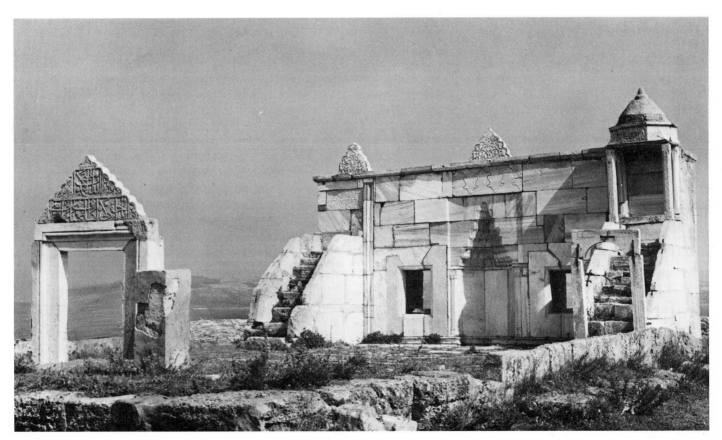

132 Namazgâh, Gelibolu. Note the twin minbers – an unusual feature.

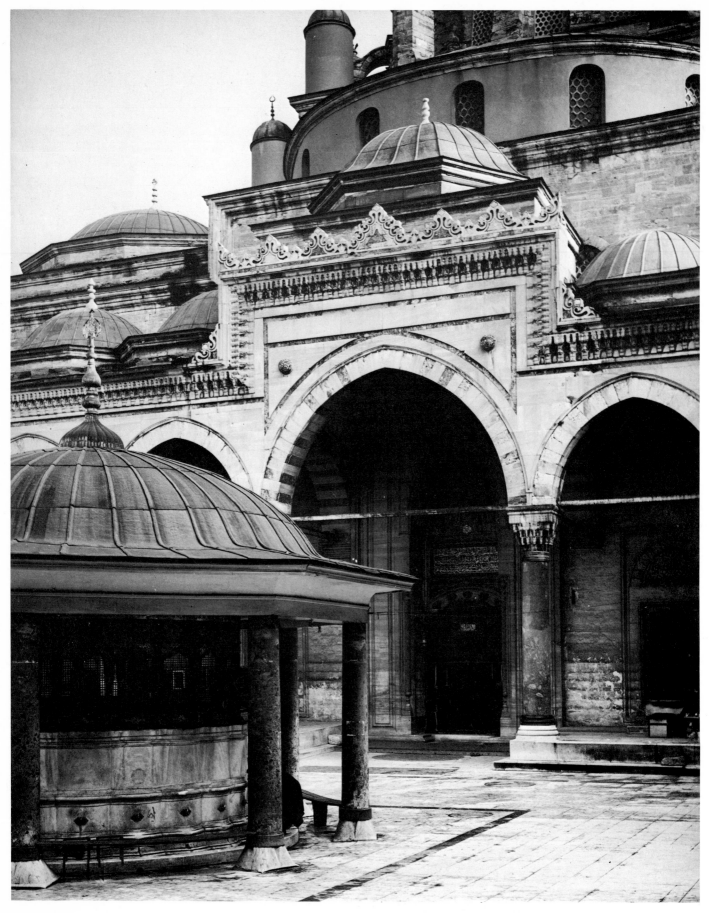

133 *Sultan Beyazit Cami, Istanbul. Courtyard with şadırvan canopy added by Murat IV.*

5

Prelude to the Grand Manner – Beyazit II

IN THE LATE SPRING of 1484, Beyazit II arrived in Edirne on his way with his army to the Balkans. He was thirty-seven and in his full maturity. He ordered the construction of a number of works, the chief of which was his own mosque and medical centre. The Royal Architect at that time is said to have been Mimar Hayrettin,[1] who was at one time supposed to have constructed the great mosque of Beyazit and its dependencies in Istanbul but this misattribution has been corrected. Hayrettin in 1484 had presumably succeeded İlyas Ağa although Ünsal[2] states that the latter did not die until 1486; he could have been ill and unable to travel. This unfortunate architect is distinguished only by the lack of any recorded work and, although he may have been responsible for any major building dating from the last years of Fatih's reign, none was particularly remarkable and none is even rumoured to be his. It could be that he was an administrator rather than a creative artist. Hayrettin is more fortunate because, although the complex at Edirne is the only important work associated with his name, and then with reservations, it is a masterpiece and of such influence that the architect of Selim I mosque in Istanbul, completed in 1522, followed his plan very closely.

39   The Beyazit foundation lies below the Tunca river and was completed in 895/1488.[3] The fine stone bridge may have replaced a wooden predecessor or have been built already. It is a traditional and classical structure with small, pointed, widely-spaced arches which carry it across a small island. The first concern of the architect must have been to strengthen the dykes before laying the foundations of any buildings. Even so, high as the dykes are, the mosque and its sister buildings have been damaged frequently by flood. Today, the Beyazit Külliye is in the country, but at the time of building the city extended all about it and it is probable that the layout of the complex was influenced by the lanes and adjacent houses.

35   It was clearly intended that the main approach should be from the land, not from the river, and consequently the buildings strangely turn their backs to the water and face the road. Doubtless, this is partly due to the height of the embankment which cuts off any view of the Tunca which with its willows, its tamerisks, and its shallows is particularly attractive at this point. Instead, a stone gateway admits to a small park where once the caravans camped. The five principal units of the complex are carefully walled off because of the number of horses, mules and camels that would be grazing there.[4] These buildings form an irregular U-shape, with the mosque and its court in the centre. This layout is as orderly as that of Fatih though less pedestrian; but it could not achieve that freedom from the orderliness of the Islamic mind which the hillsides and spurs of Bursa enforced.

Because the land on which the Beyazit Complex was built was not a symmetrical plot, the main gate is set in alignment with the street wall, which was at a slight angle and so is not on the axis of the portal of the mosque courtyard fifty metres

beyond it.[5] This slightly rectangular, paved court has a double tier of the deep-set, 13
finely framed windows which are common to the whole foundation, and is
bounded by revaks carrying twenty-two cupolas including those of the portico.
Some of these still retain the original lively plasterwork inside, with shells and
whorls instead of sober hemispheres. All are set on octagonal drums, except for
the central arch of the portico which has a square base superimposed on a larger
one. The antique marble columns which support these cupolas include fine
examples of verd-antique in the son cemaat yeri and each contains an excellent
example of the traditional stalactite capital; from these spring slightly pointed
arches. The large şadırvan was covered at one time by an octagonal canopy but
now only the shallow bases of the supporting columns remain. In the north-east
and north-west corners of this avlu are two well-heads. The central door has a
circular arch with polychrome serpentine voussoirs below a handsome stalactite
niche in a firmly delineated marble frame.

The mosque itself is uncompromisingly square, half the width of the fifty- 13
metre-broad court, but the dome is so lofty and grows so dramatically out of the
walls that there is no anticlimax or disappointment. The pendentives rise
straight out of the corners of the room to form massive arches, linear descendants
of those of the Orhaniye at Bilecik, on which the lamplighter's gallery and the
drum of the dome are carried. High above the casements at ground level – of
which there is one each side of the great door and two each side of the mihrab –
are the windows in the tympana in three rows of five and three and two which
recall Byzantine models and presage, if timidly, the highly festooned tympana of
the Mihrimah Cami at the Edirne Gate in Istanbul.[6] The dome is just over twenty
metres in diameter,[7] but because the pendentives spring from half way up the
walls it appears considerably larger. This interior is the climax of the single-dome
unit which, as we have seen, forms the nucleus of all Ottoman architecture.

The spacious, open imperial box is carried above the level of the casements on
four rows of three arches, each of which is set on slender antique columns. It is
the first of its type still standing and it clearly influenced that of the Beyazit
mosque in Istanbul and the rebuilt mahfil in the first Fatih.[8] The mosque was
shockingly redecorated, probably prior to 1830, in the sloppiest and most banal
rococo style by some Italian who has been forgotten but not forgiven. As has
so often happened, even the light fittings have been destroyed. There is no longer
a large central wheel carrying three tiers of oil lamps, ostrich eggs,[9] and corn
symbols, suspended by a single chain, nor the two smaller wheels on the west side
nor the single one on the east – only one here because none is suspended over the
hünkâr mahfil – nor the rectangular pair east and west of the main door, nor
even the very handsome independent lamps which were doubtless of coloured
glass.

Flanking the mosque are two square tabhanes with nine domes each, each with
four corner rooms opening onto four eyvans off a central court. This plan, as has
already been shown, is closely related to that of the Çinili Kiosk and therefore,
distantly, to the concepts of Central Asia. These buildings take up two-thirds of
the area of the mosque itself and extend beyond the width of the portico so that
there is access to the rooms on the extreme north-east and north-west without
need to enter the courtyard at all; they also have doors into the mosque. The
corner rooms beside the mosque also have casements opening into the prayer
hall. This intimate contact is important for an understanding of the eventual
development of the tabhane in relation to the mosque, for after the consolidation
of Imperial power and the waning of Ahi and dervish influences, these rooms
were to become, first eyvans and then fluid areas. Like the mosque itself, the
tabhanes of Beyazit are closely related to those of the Selimiye at Istanbul although 17
the latter was not built until thirty-five years later. Indeed, the only great change

I Çinili Kiosk, Istanbul. The portico and the restored arcade.

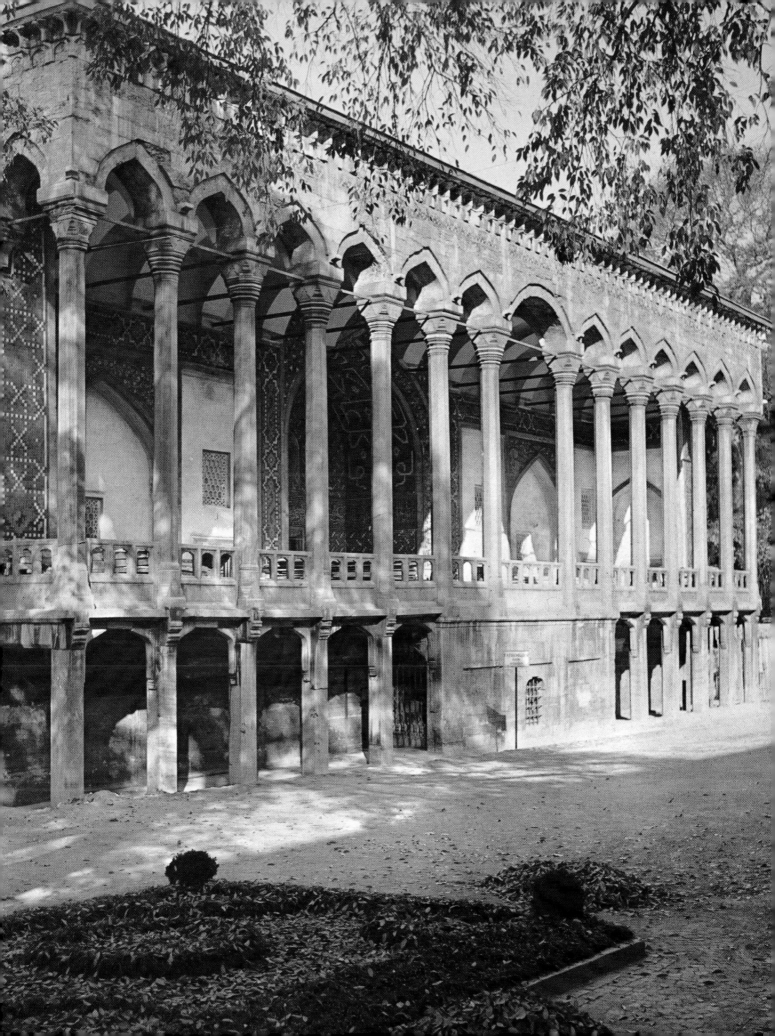

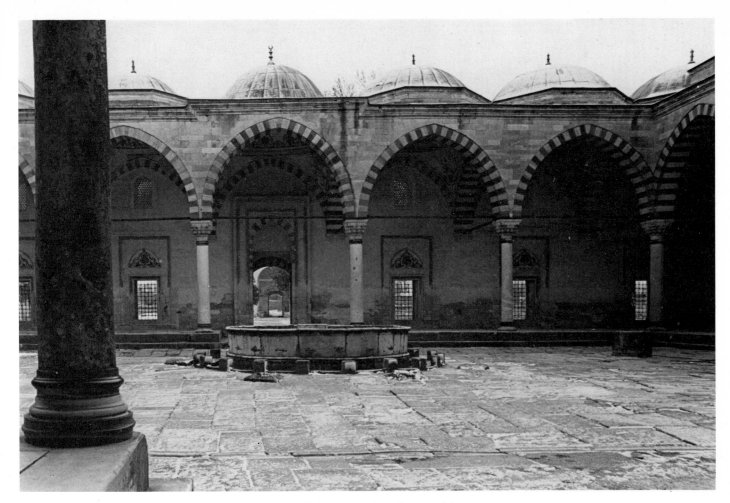

134 Beyazit Complex, Edirne. Courtyard of the mosque, looking through to the gate of the outer precinct.

there is that the minarets are set at the angle of the court and thus the tabhane walls effectively block out either a window or a door at the north corner of the corridor. The minarets of Beyazit Cami are set at their north-east and north-west extremity, and so permit an extension of the court and the opening of windows onto it from the north corridor, and still leave space for the doors into the north-east and north-west rooms.

The ruined Böreği Büyük Tekke at Niksar is a precursor in Anatolia of this form of tabhane which appears Ghaznevid in plan. This tekke is tentatively dated as fourteenth-century[10] because of the floral motifs in the decoration of the main portal which are related to the Tımarhane at Amasya of *708*/1308, but this is deceptive evidence, since the Hasbey Darül-hadis at Konya – because of the conservatism of all Islam and of the Karamanoğlus in particular – continued to use motifs from two centuries before. In the tympanum of the tekke is the elegant carving of a stag;[11] animals are frequent decorative elements in the Niksar region, set over doors as they are at the much later hans of Tokat. It is unfortunate that the inscription over the door, which may well have included the date of this building, has perished. The tekke consisted of four corner rooms and three eyvans; the fourth arm of the cross became the vestibule. Here is exactly the plan of Beyazit and Selim tabhanes.[12] This form is also linked to that of the Çelebi Mehmet Medrese at Merzifon,[13] dated *817*/1414 to *822*/1419.[14] Ünsal relates it to the Selçuk form of medrese but it is closer to examples outside Anatolia.[15]

This tabhane form was a step towards its severance from the mosque itself which followed logically on the development of the Mahmut Pasha Cami. The final achievement of total detachment had come at Fatih. It was inevitable, once the Ulema had established primacy over the heterodox orders.[16] The question

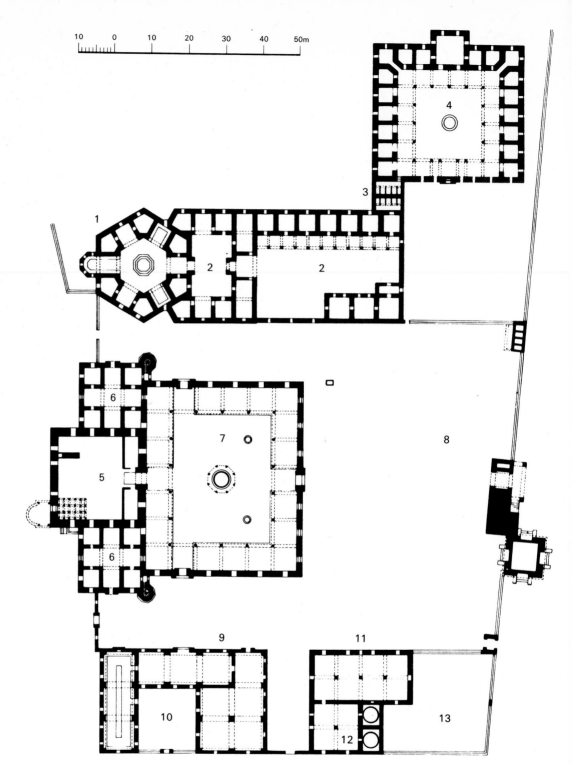

135 Beyazit Complex, Edirne. Plan, scale 1 : 1,000. 1 daruşşıfa (hospital); 2 tımarhane; 3 latrines; 4 Tip Medrese; 5 mosque; 6 tabhanes; 7 mosque courtyard; 8 precinct; 9 imaret; 10 courtyard; 11 store; 12 bakery; 13 courtyard.

arises as to what was the function of such annexes in the late fifteenth century.[17] Ünsal defines a tabhane or taphane as a convalescent home for Moslem religious officers.[18] In other words, they are retreats. Eyice[19] calls them lodgings for travellers. Kuran[20] shows with well-reasoned arguments that they were indeed zaviyes or hostels for wandering, though not necessarily ailing, dervishes and also other travellers. Their use was surely modified by time and varied according to locality, as is clearly apparent at the Fatih tabhane which once lodged the Conqueror and later the litter of the twentieth century.[21] Travellers who were not merchants or traders, above all the poor, were given a roof and could stay for three days without payment and could also draw food from the imaret. Certainly there is now no kervansaray attached to the mosque and without travellers the size of the imaret would be excessive. Astonishingly, Babinger[22] mistranslates tabhane as medrese and corrects Gurlitt (who was right[23]) and he even defines a medrese as teaching rooms. There is a relationship between *tip* and *tab* and *tap* which invites confusion[24]

The dervish orders increased in number in the fifteenth century, and Beyazit had mystical leanings just as had his grandfather, Murat II.[25] He was pacific, poetic, studious and contemplative by nature and was indeed, nicknamed 'Sofi' (or a man who loves simplicity, peace and retreat).[26] One may suppose that he would be likely to order lodgings for itinerant and resident members of the Sufi sects in addition to those for the orthodox. The annexes of his Edirne mosque are the logical development of the Bursa form which had been heavily dependent on a Persian past, just as the mosque itself, with its massive walls and pendentives, was the apotheosis of the Alaettin at Bursa.

Like Fatih and other sultans' mosques, that of Beyazit had two minarets but there is no trace of influence from the Üç Şerefeli Cami; indeed the mosque might never have existed, as far as they are concerned, although it was the ulu cami of the city in Hayrettin's time. The minarets represent the new classical style of Istanbul, built in cut stone with polygonal shafts rising from parallel bases which reach the level of the tabhane roofs and have only one gallery each. They are tall and more slender than those of the Eski Cami or of the mosque of Üç Şerefeli, which look immediately out of date by comparison. It is odd that the structure of the latter mosque was, however, both more inventive and altogether more grandiose. Beyazit's minarets, set fifty-five metres apart, are important architecturally not only in relation to the mosque, nor because of the elegance of their panelled bases, but because they unify the whole complex.

When discussing the Hudavendigâr at Bursa, it was said that Ottoman building depended on simple, unelaborated plans, tradition in workmanship and standardization of lengths of timber and stone blocks. At Beyazit, the point where the courtyard walls meet those of the tabhanes provides evidence in support of this thesis: they are not bonded and collide most uncomfortably with the edge of the corner windows. This clumsiness gives a strong impression that two teams of builders worked independently of each other and were practical fellows with little respect for aesthetics.

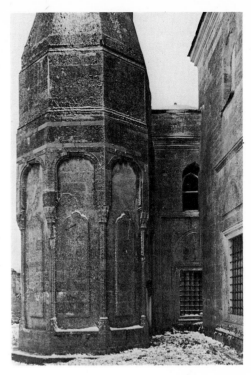

136, 137 Beyazit Complex, Edirne. Above: collision of the tabhane windows and the mosque wall. Below: the foodstore.

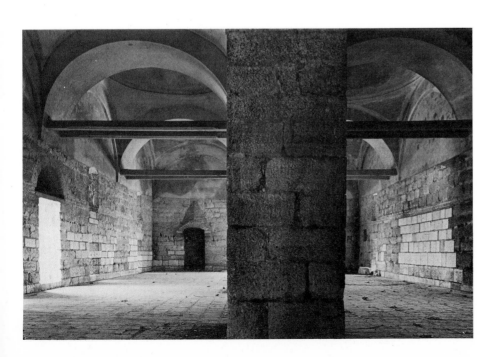

To the east of the mosque are two large buildings, one with twelve and the other with eleven large domes round a square courtyard into which there is a door from outside the precincts. The latter building contains two refectories over twenty-five metres long, both with three domes, and handsome rooms. Çetintaş shows the one on the south side to be divided into a suite of rooms of equal size and one of these might be the mumhane listed in the vakfiye. Since the making of candles is not unlike simple cooking, it might be reasonable to look for such a room near the kitchens when no other place can be assigned to this task. The courtyard has no portico but it must have been an important assembly point for those who ate at the canteen, particularly in summer. It would seem – since there is no shelter in the form of a portico against the unpleasant winter weather of Edirne – that food was eaten in the imaret and not issued at the door to be taken away. The kitchen has four domes over a square area which possesses a large flue in the traditional manner, and also a fifth, to the west, in the form of a vestibule. This is similar to the plans of the kitchens of Süleymaniye and elsewhere and in each case the areas are kept fluid to ensure the maximum of space when the bustle of serving occurs. Opposite the imaret is a foodstore of considerable size, *137* the main hall of which opened onto a large enclosure or yard with its own postern gate into the street for the assembly and handling of the great quantity of provisions and fuel required. This hall (25 × 12·50 m.) has eight lofty domes and three central supporting piers in the manner of a small bedesten. Even in its present lamentable condition, it is splendidly proportioned and is one of the finest rooms of the Ottoman period. An interesting feature is the pair of handsome ocaks left and right of the main door at the north end. The windows are mere slits, else one might wonder if this hall had other functions. Presumably the fires kept the stocks dry and the porters warm.

The smaller room has four domes and a central pier. Gurlitt showed the two rooms as one L-shaped hall but here Çetintaş appears to be correct in supposing that there was a dividing wall, for this lesser chamber was always on a higher level. It was the bakery and it contains the ruins of two capacious ovens side by side to the north. However debatable the use of certain areas at different periods may be, it is interesting that the imaret had twenty-three domes and much unroofed space besides – a far larger area, relatively, than that allowed on the extant reconstructed plans of Fatih which Evliya said had seventy-five cupolas and which fed three or four times as many people. Moreover, the Beyazit imaret did not necessarily supply the hospital staff and patients at all, for the hospital had its own building in the north-west corner of its private garden. This consisted of a porch and three domed rooms, one of which may have been the porter's lodge. The other two may have been for the preparation of special vegetarian diets and medicines.[27]

This hospital has been called an asylum but was intended to be a refuge for *13*... every type of sufferer since there does not appear to have been any other general hospital at Edirne when it was built. A gate east of the mosque courtyard admits to a green plaisance with the kitchens on the right and the handsome inner gate on the left. Across the lawn is a long colonnade of antique marbles supporting eleven domes set before six cells and a large vestibule to the lavatories, in which the five cabinets are set back to back with those of the medical school, thus forming an important architectural link as well as some indication of the number of inhabitants of both institutions. They could hardly have exceeded one hundred and twenty or so without inconvenience. Gurlitt[28] asserts that the tımarhane section, or actual asylum, was the six cells in the outer court only.[29] Ünsal[30] says that the rest of the foundation was reserved for psychiatric cases. However, a darüşşifa was intended for all manner of patients.[31] He goes on to speak of the music used in the cure of mental patients, but this service could well have been for everybody, while any more refractory mental patient was unlikely to be admitted within the inner hall of the hospital. The Ottoman treatment of mental disease was in advance of Western Europe at that time but Turkish texts are apt to overlook reports that difficult patients were chained. Nicolay de Nicolay[32]

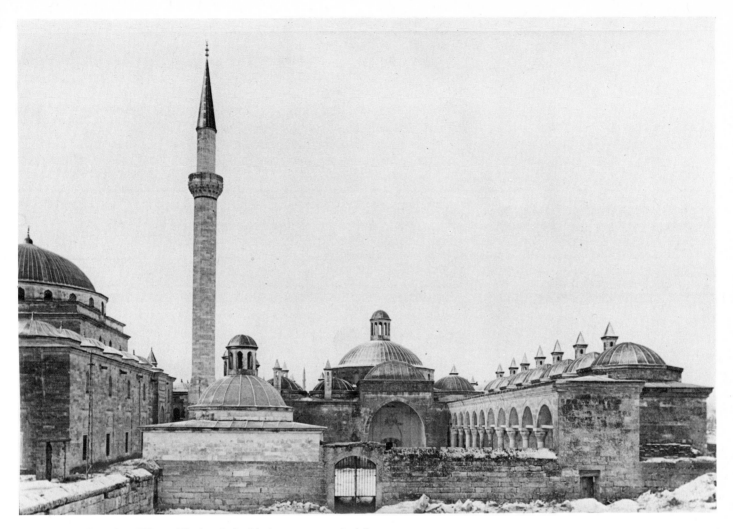

138 Beyazit Complex, Edirne. The hospital with the mosque on the left.

describes their being subdued with whips at Fatih, but states that the other sick were gently treated. Evliya[33] describes them in the Procession of the Guilds as being beaten or boxed by their keepers, who numbered two hundred, but others were drugged with medicines. Some were naked, some cried, laughed or swore or attacked their keepers and put the spectators to flight. Ünsal, therefore, may be said to exaggerate. The truth is that both societies were capable of brutality and a certain heartless humour that idiocy can arouse in those of baser feelings.[34] However, ten musicians came three times a week to soothe those of distraught mind or suffering pain, and a diet of fruit and vegetables was prescribed.

The hospital was lavishly staffed, if the orders in the vakfiye were obeyed, for there were three doctors, two eye specialists and two barber surgeons – which alone is evidence that this was not merely a mental hospital – a dentist, and one who washed the dead, implying that Ottoman hospitals were as prone to failure as those anywhere else. The grisly function of the laundering of the corpses may have been performed on the river bank or in one of the three rooms beside the garden gate. Since there was only one cook on the list, presumably only one of the rooms would have been a kitchen. A clerk, a steward, and a major-domo were also listed and would need an office, which would account for another room by the gate. Only one sweeper was appointed, which can only imply that convalescents helped maintain the wards or else that the hospital was intolerably dirty. This list is not complete, however, since Aslanapa says that there were twenty-one people on the staff but only accounts for thirteen.[35] The whole complex employed 167 people, all of whose posts were inscribed on the vakfiye, and these included the imam and the müezzins as well as the scullions in the imaret.

This vakfiye is an impressive document which lists a great number of houses[36] – including some as far away as Kavalla – villages, and farms; those endowed by the sultan alone produced one and a half million akçe each year in the sixteenth century. His family and vezirs, agas and beys added their gifts until the roll covers over a hundred pages and names over a hundred donors.

As one leaves the first compound of the daruşşıfa, an inner court is reached through a large domed gate with doors on each side into the two double-domed rooms which could have been operating theatres, administrative rooms or dormitories. The small grassed court has four other domed rooms, two set neatly into the hexagon of the inner hall, with domed eyvans between for summer use. Thus the first pair of halls could be kept separate from the inner court and the court separate from the innermost hall, which suggests intelligent flexibility of accommodation. They are unique in having an ocak for each of the two domed areas. The western room has one ocak on the north wall and one obliquely on the south. A second domed vestibule admits to the heart of the hospital through another handsome portal. This great chamber has a central dome, over fourteen metres in diameter, above a şadırvan, now smothered in feathers and the droppings of pigeons which infest the place. It is crowned by a lantern similar to those over the central courts of the tabhanes. This hall is hexagonal and is set within a larger hexagon which accounts for the two lopsided cells in the corner of the second court already described. Corresponding to the domed entry, and on its axis to the south, is the main eyvan which has a deep apsidal extension of the same width but with a lower dome and is therefore a microcosm of such mosques as Davut Pasha in Istanbul. Between it and the doorway, which forms the sixth eyvan, are pairs of lateral eyvans which complete the symmetry of this hall and which incorporate the engaged support of the dome. This has twelve windows in its drum. Its hexagonal support is related to that of the dome of the Üç Şerefeli mosque. Out of the six arches grow stalactite squinches which develop into the cornice on which the dome is set. The eyvans have doors into six pentagonal fan-shaped inner rooms which have no direct access to the hall and which have ocaks for winter use. They have only one window each, thus creating an unexpected dissymmetry outside. This is also reflected in the disposition of the windows of the kitchens. Evliya states that the musicians played under the central dome but it seems more probable that they made use of the sofa of the principal eyvan which forms a stage; under the central dome is a fountain. The hexagonal form of the hospital which merges so successfully with the rectangular inner court is related to the only octagonal medrese in Anatolia, that of the Kapıağa at Amasya, built in 894/1489; but whether Hayrettin built the Kapıağa Medrese or not is unknown.[37] An interesting feature at Edirne is the acute angle where the hexagon meets the rectangle, for the architect has thickened the walls of the two cells at the south-east and south-west angle of the inner court in order to reduce it more nearly to a right-angle without altering the square shape of the cells themselves, thus ensuring their perfect symmetry in relation to the north-east and north-west corners. This small detail is indicative of the care employed in the building of this part of Beyazit's foundation, but it is not an invention because it was traditional in fortress towers and also appears at, among other buildings, the Yeni Kaplıca at Bursa.

Although, as has been shown, the Tip Medrese is united to the tımarhane by the lavatories at right angles to it, it is reached either from the street or through a small postern in the wall which is a continuation of that of the hospital kitchens and behind which was the medical students' private precinct. Considerable restoration is in progress after years of neglect. The square courtyard is flanked by cells on three sides to form a U in the established tradition. The dershane, with a dome seven metres in diameter, is flanked by two cells and there are six cells on the north and south sides, making eighteen in all. The east side has no cells but only a wall. In each case the cells possess one window except for those at the corners which enjoy two views. The three windows on each side of the entry are irregularly placed, interest being added to the domed colonnade, which

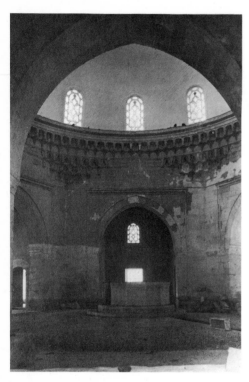

139 Beyazit Complex, Edirne. Basin under the great dome of the hospital hall.

runs along all four sides, by setting a vault half its width each side of the dome before the gate.

Beyazit's great foundation establishes Hayrettin as an architect, if the architect he be, of importance and some inventive powers, although his use of the hexagon may have been due to the influence of the Üç Şerefeli mosque. He may also have been responsible for the Beyazit foundation at Amasya built at the same time as that at Edirne but completed earlier, in 891/1486.[38] It may have been planned when Beyazit II was still heir apparent, for he had been governor of Amasya for a long period before he was called to the throne in 1481.[39] The ground could have been cleared and the sheds and workshops erected. There the position was the exact reverse of that at Edirne for the complex is set at the foot of the hill facing the Yeşil Irmak. Its arms, indeed, are wide open to it. The reason for this reversal is simply due to the fact that at Edirne the river is on the south and at Amasya it is on the north.

Amasya in its green ravine is exceedingly beautiful even now when modern building is mutilating the river banks. It was loved by its governors who were usually the eldest sons of the sultan and it was the preferred city of Süleyman Kanunı, illustrious among princes. In the sixteenth century when Busbecq visited it[40] most of the private houses were very simple flat-roofed mud dwellings, and the river and the streets were not romantically overhung with casements and kafes[41] as they are still in part today. But the citadel and the saray were then intact, together with such Selçuk or Ilkhan monuments as the Burmalı Minare Cami, the Tımarhane by the water and the Gök Medrese on the hill. In the town was the Sultan Meşud Türbe influenced by the cliff tombs of the Mithridates family above the citadel across the river. Here Mehmet Pasha was completing his mosque in the year that his sovereign's mosque was finished, 1486.

140 Mention has already been made of the Kapıağa Medrese across the Kuş bridge opposite the Beyazit Pasha Cami. It is now being rebuilt after falling into a miserable state of ruin after use as an industrial school, a state which reflects the neglect of the Ministry of Public Instruction and not the architect's for it was a splendidly robust building. It was built in 894/1488 by Hüseyin Ağa, the Büyük Ağa or Kapı Ağa, the Great Captain or the Captain of the Gate, Seneschal and Prefect of the White Eunuchs, who were the preceptors of the Enderun College, 152 the Palace School. He also converted the church of SS. Sergius and Bacchus into the mosque of Küçük Aya Sofya towards 1500, built the Kurşunlu Cami at Sunısa in 892/1487 and had already, in 888/1483, endowed Amasya with its bedesten.[42] He was adept at sublimating his creative frustrations into stone. The medrese courtyard is grandly spacious, the more so because the cells are relatively low. Octagonal inside as well as out,[43] the large dershane on the south had the unusual addition of two shorter wings with semi-domes on each side so that the chamber occupies all that eighth section of the building without resorting to half-size additional cells. There is an echo here of the vaults flanking the domed threshold gate of the Tip Medrese at Edirne just described, but by using semi-domes on a small scale this dershane has the right to claim to be the first occasion where two were used symmetrically in Ottoman architecture. There are six sets of three cells and two more each side of the gateway in the north-west angle carefully not set on the dershane axis. Where the segments of the octagon connect, the walls fan outwards to a considerable thickness like slices of cake, once more recalling Edirne and its hospital. These angles are of unnecessary strength in spite of the niches cut into them. The portico had twenty-three cupolas and one square vault in front of the door to the dershane. At each of the eight corners it was logical to construct an interesting ribbed vault which opened like a fan. While the arches and the outside walls of the medrese were of cut stone, the inner walls were of brick. Until recently, on the river bank there was a mill with a wooden water-wheel which surely dates from the fifteenth century and is related to the great wheels of Syria.

The river runs through the heart of the city, and all along its banks it is green with trees. In fulfilment of a vow made when heir to the throne, Beyazit built

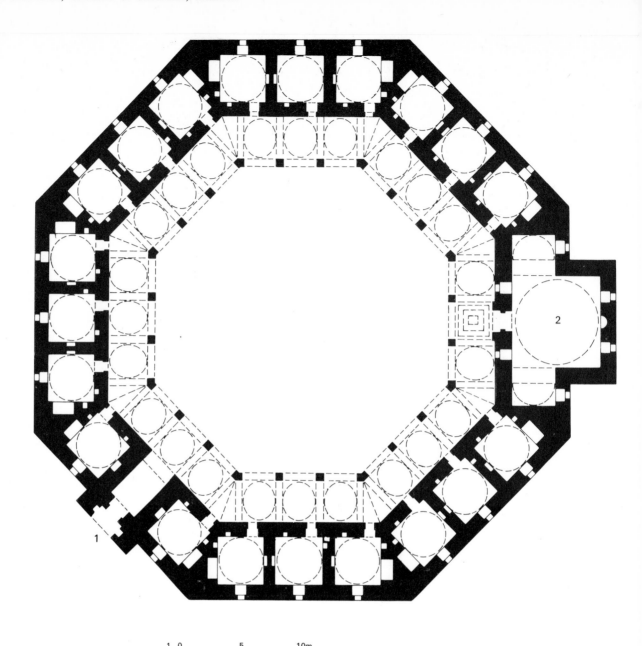

1 0   5   10m

140 Kapıağa Medrese, Amasya. Plan, scale 1 : 300. 1 entrance; 2 dershane.

not only a mosque but also a school of music, philosophy, theology, astronomy   *141*
and cosmography. The mosque is in the centre of the complex and is, as it should
be, the finest in the town. Beyond the portico there are two domed central areas
in the manner of the Mahmut Pasha Cami, but grander. The domes were ruined
by the earthquake of *1079/1668* and later restored. One is approximately thirteen
metres and the other fifteen metres in diameter. The two aisles each have
asymmetrical piers with inset colonnettes and three domed areas. The immediate
effect inside is of height and space and openness because, unlike Bursa, there is no
sense of detachment between the two main areas, and the wings are integrated
with the central spaces. Only a very low step divides the two areas for prayer
and appears to be nothing but a vestigial remnant. In order to reduce the size of
the third dome, on each side the arms of the cross-shaped piers are lengthened on
the inside and shortened on the outside, but this distortion cannot be observed
unless one walks deliberately round the piers to inspect how the sense of flow

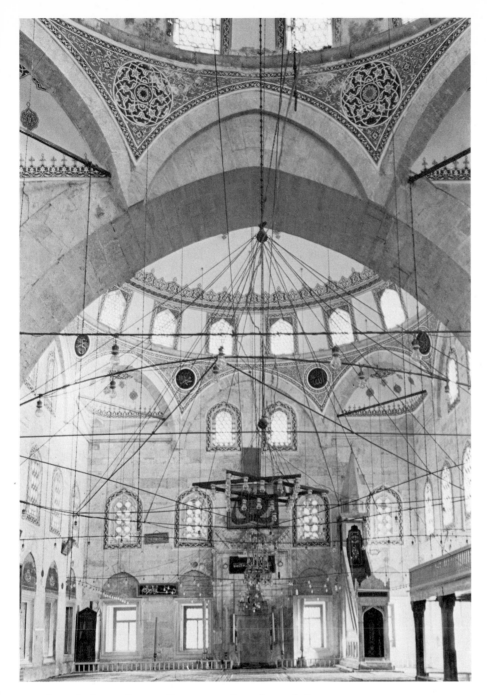

141 Beyazit Cami, Amasya. Interior seen from the north door.

and movement in this mosque is achieved.[44] Gabriel[45] argues that the need to receive light from the windows on the east-west axis of the mihrab area necessitated a larger dome and the diminution of the south-east and south-west bays followed because of the need to retain exterior symmetry. But an additional reason could be that the increase in the size of the second hall, contrary to the Bursa custom, gives a great sense of volume and grandeur, while nothing is lost by the reduction of the area of the bays. The mosque took five years to build and antedates Atik Ali Pasha Cami by ten years. It was one more attempt in the manner of Mahmut Pasha to break down the compartmentalization of the Bursa-type mosque and to this extent the innovations of Üç Şerefeli Cami had been absorbed.

The stone mihrab of Sultan Beyazit Cami, handsomely restored, has a pair of revolving marble colonnettes. The design of the grey marble minber is very restrained with only a single modest medallion on each side, now unhappily

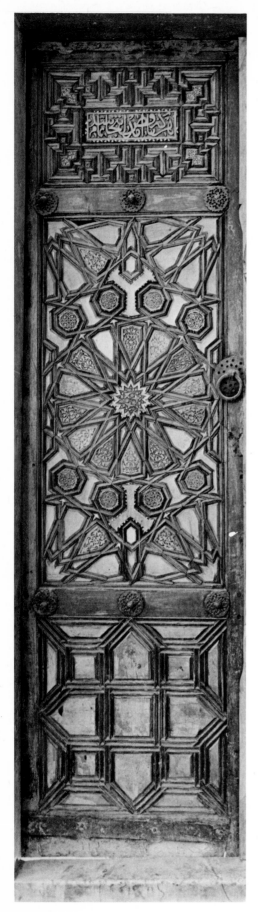

142 Beyazit Cami, Amasya. Casement shutter.

painted over in buff and black. Compared with the sultan's, the mihrab of Beyazit Pasha Cami along the river is very ostentatious and belongs to a baroque and not the puritan tradition. The windows of the Sultan Beyazit mosque are coarsely restored and so is the paintwork and the woodwork, together with the workaday mahfils and the wooden gallery across the north wall which is carried on consoles related to those of the Eski Cami at Edirne. There is no trace of the hünkâr mahfil, nor was there a gallery for women who still said their prayers at the back of the harem. There are three tiers of windows; square dark-blue tiles in arches of green glazed brick are set over the lower casements, except for the three on the east and west of the inner harem and those of the portico, which have white inscriptions on a blue ground. They are of such poor quality that they can only be replacements. There are no tiles over the windows of the mihrab wall. In the vicinity of the new kürsü (teacher's chair), in particular, are fine silk hangings embroidered in gold. One pair of shutters on the east of the entry is a *142* splendid original.

The five domes of the porch are carried on marble columns with fine marble *143* stalactite capitals ornate with roundels and various motifs. There is an unusual inset black marble pattern outlining the arches to give, not altogether successfully, an effect of lace. On each side of the portico, placed with exactitude, are two very large stalactite capitals which serve as coffin rests.[46] It would look as if the very sensible use of Byzantine capitals for this purpose had become so accepted that, where none were available, Ottoman capitals were specially cut instead. While the mosque is of soft saffron stone, the doorway which was *144* damaged in the earthquake of *999/1590*[47] and restored and the window-frames are of marble. Like those of many mosques of this period the sofas of the son cemaat yeri are very high – Beyazit at Edirne requires two steps and Fatih no less.[48] Before the door is a fine tooled nineteenth-century leather windshield.[49] In the porch are two small, but beautiful, verd-antique colonnettes with bright white stars and jet black punctuation in the veined field of deepest green. Above, is a remarkable vault of brick and plaster carved into strong three-dimensional forms only rivalled by those of the mosque at Edirne, perhaps by the same craftsmen.

The exterior south wall has the unexpected addition of a stone apse with a minuscule dome on a high drum which is, in fact, the mihrab niche. Like that of Davut Ağa Cami, it presages the apsidal mihrabs of Sinan.[50] There are four stabilizing turrets at roof level, parents of the four, and later eight or more, which were to help anchor classical Ottoman domes; but here they are set at the extreme corners, while two powerful buttresses take the thrust of the bridge between the main domes in the centre. The bases of the minarets at each end of the north wall of the mosque are incorporated into the portico on to which their doors open. The minarets are not a pair. A geometrical terracotta design covers the twenty facets of the north-west trunk and that on the north-east has alternating thick terracotta and stone ribs which spring from the base as if about to become another corkscrew or burmalı type of minaret. Each minaret has only one balcony. They were restored after the earthquake of *1079/1668*.[51]

An interesting precedent for this mosque is the Germiyanoğlu Ulu Cami at Uşak with an inscription, which probably came from the şadırvan,[52] dated *822/1419*. This mosque has been heavily restored and the five-domed portico rebuilt and glassed in. The interior consists of a vaulted forehall united to a prayer area under a dome ten metres in diameter with three-domed aisles on each side. Four massive and distorted piers carry the thrust of the dome and vault, in conjunction with four engaged in the north and south walls. The piers are also shared by the lateral domes. Externally, the building forms a single mass. It is transitional from the divided Bursa-type mosque to the Amasya Beyazit and Mahmud Pasha. At the same time, from outside, it is strikingly Byzantine in appearance.

The Amasya complex was built round a small park which extends to the present highway along the waterside. On the west is the U-shaped medrese

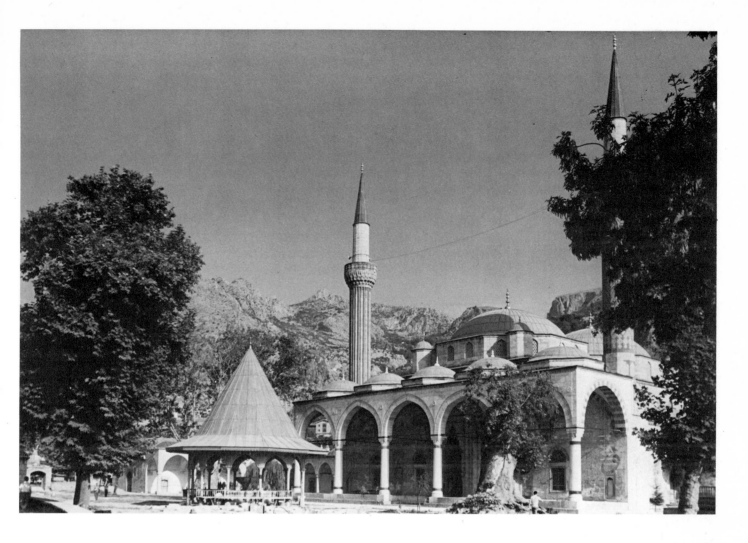

which is entered through a fine doorway. Its courtyard has become a luxuriant garden which overwhelms its modest fountain. The medrese and its dershane in the middle of the south side turn their backs on the town and face in the direction of the river. The medrese is axial, across the lawns and the trees, to the north-west outer gate. It has the traditional eighteen cells and its revaks have seventeen domes. The restored arches and capitals are rounded, but the original capitals were octagons with the four corners cut away, and at first sight look like a debased seventeenth-century form but are actually more closely related to the embryonic Ottoman capital used by the Selçuks at Kayseri and elsewhere long before. They represent a last attempt at the acanthus leaf of old,[53] but here they are also the stalactite in embryonic form. The door of the dershane is arched with red and white voussoirs. The close likeness of this medrese to the medical college at Edirne (just as was the case with the thickened corners of the octagonal Kapıağa Medrese) suggests, but does not prove, that this is the work of Hayrettin or his team. Faced with identical structural problems, Ottoman architects could be expected to apply established formulas and achieve identical solutions. At Beyazit's medrese at Amasya we have examples of the calligraphy of Şey Hamdullah, who died in 1520. He was the first great Ottoman calligrapher and with him Ottoman calligraphy as a separate and creative entity may be said to have come into being.[54]

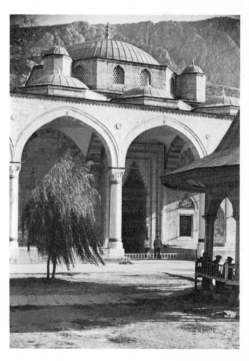

On the south-east is an L-shaped group of buildings, recently restored, which included the imaret, muvakkithane[55] and a library. The imaret was the richest in the province and fed the students and the poor twice a day. Local tradition claims, or rather insists, that there was a saray, or at least a kiosk, near the south-east corner of the mosque; this would have been in the traditional position in

143, 144 Beyazit Cami, Amasya. The portico and the eighteenth-century şadırvan.

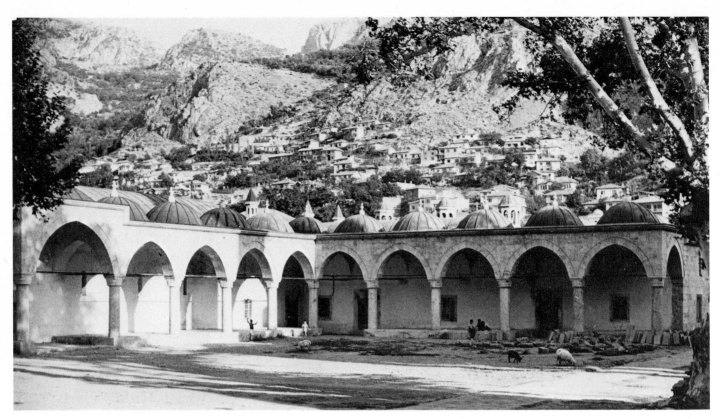

145 Beyazit Complex, Amasya. The restored imaret.

relation to the imperial tribune inside. The whole rectangular precinct was walled and had several gates and many walks. The present şadırvan is eighteenth-century and is splendidly hooded with a steeply pitched cone descending to sweeping eaves. There was once a second fountain built by Ayşe Hatun in 1227/1812[56] not to mention other baroque luxuries such as taps which flowed with hot water and a sebil which dispensed ice and snow.

The construction of the integral tabhanes at the flanks of the Beyazit mosque at Edirne was, as has been shown, the prelude to the complete detachment of these annexes which were becoming outmoded. It was therefore a logical development at Amasya for the rooms to be set apart from the parent mosque. It was not a new step since Fatih's complex had brought about the severance twenty years earlier. Yet Amasya Beyazit retained the Bursa form of double dome and rejected the unifying half-dome of Fatih as unsatisfactory; which it was. The error was to be corrected with the building of Beyazit's mosque in Istanbul where the second half-dome makes its appearance in the correct position over the entry. At Amasya, the architect was unable to break free of the tyranny of the domed unit.

The complex is strictly ordered except for the trees, just as was the complex at Edirne, but this at Amasya is not so large. The setting is even more beautiful and this sanctuary is one of the most civilizing and tranquil in Islam, worthy of the melancholy sultan for whom it was built.

The mosque of Mehmet Pasha farther down the river is less happily placed because the Germans have built a school in front of it and its medrese has been destroyed. It once faced the mosque, and if it was U-shaped – which it almost surely was – it was a forerunner of those mosques of Sinan such as Sokollu Mehmet Pasha at Kadırga and Mihrimah at Edirnekapı, both in Istanbul, where the revaks of the medrese also formed the revaks of the mosque court and the şadırvan was common to both worshippers and students. The present imam of Mehmet Pasha states, however, that the medrese had only one row of cells, set parallel to the mosque and its annexes, to the extremities of which it was connected by walls with handsome gateways. These walls are to be restored but will merely join the nineteenth-century school wall and make research work even more difficult.[57] The area at present is a waste which offers no clue to the original plan of the medrese. Gabriel says that it disappeared prior to 1934[58] while the imam says that it stood until the earthquake of 1938. Since Gabriel, even if erroneously, drew up a plan of the mosque, it is hard to believe that he overlooked so large a building unless he had expected an orthodox U-shaped medrese. It is just conceivable, I suppose, that the wings had been demolished earlier and that the remaining cells and dershane, its door axial to the north door of the mosque, had been so misused that they were unrecognizable; for it is clear from his text, and some unavoidable errors, that the complex was in a bad state and difficult of access when Gabriel was there. If we accept that the medrese was simply a row of cells each side of a dershane – in itself a strange form to take – the plan is still embryonic of Sinan's, for the courtyard and şadırvan would have served both mosque and college. If there were no wing cells to the latter this courtyard would have been a queer mixture of those of İsa Bey and Üç Şerefeli and also exceedingly spacious.

Of much the same date 887/1482, is the mosque of İshak Pasha at İnegöl already cited[59] where the U-shaped medrese does face the mosque across the court and its fountain, but it is still detached. It has its own inner court within the embrace of its wings, exactly like the Süleyman Medrese at Iznik, and a south wall with a gate in the centre cutting it off from the principal court. None the less, the future union of the two areas can be foreseen.

Another development of the courtyard concept occurs at Bursa with the mosque of Başcı Ibrahim[60] which in itself is of little interest, for it is simply a domed square, and was built in 896/1491.[61] The square court which has a hexagonal şadırvan was, however, surrounded by a zaviye rather than a medrese, set under four domes on each side. At the south-east and south-west corners two eyvans are framed within the portico, and two longer ones, each tripledomed, run down the east and west sides. Each side of the vaulted north doorway there is a cell and the building is, therefore, related to the Hünkâr Cami at Sarajevo.[62]

Another mosque belonging to this period of building activity at the beginning of the reign of Beyazit is the Hatuniye Cami at Tokat, built by the sultan, who appears to have rid himself of many frustrations through architecture. It was to honour his mother, Gülbahar Sultan, whose türbe is at Fatih, and it is dated 890/1485.[63] The mosque is relatively small for a royal foundation and has a ruined medrese across the garden in which is the şadırvan. Beside it is the great market, and the size of its garden is immediately apparent at noon of a Friday when it is filled to such capacity that its trees seem to grow out of a human paddock. Walls the length of the meadow complete the seclusion of the sanctuary. The possession of a courtyard had previously been the prerogative of a sultan's mosque just as much as the erection of twin minarets: now the pashas could wall their precincts and build arcades.

46 The Hatuniye is now commonly called the Beyazit Cami and is a square room with a high dome, twelve metres in diameter, supported on finely wrought stalactite pendentives at each corner. The workmanship of the mihrab has been obliterated by thick layers of recent paint, and the minber is brand new. The floor has handsome traditional terracotta flagstones. There is a tabhane room on each flank and these are heavily buttressed, as is the south wall. There is the usual tribune carried on consoles above the north door. All the proportions are good but those of the fine marble portico are grandiose. The central pair of columns are of Marmara marble while the other columns are of stone. On each side an early baklava type of capital, made up of alternating acute-angled triangles, is set between two of stalactite form. The bases are simply carved embryonic stalactites like the capitals of the Beyazit Medrese at Amasya. The door of black and white marble is stately and the stalactite niche above it as fine as any of the period. It has circular inscriptive plaques above the flanking niches which are enriched with rosettes. The pendant and intricate keys are not marble or plaster

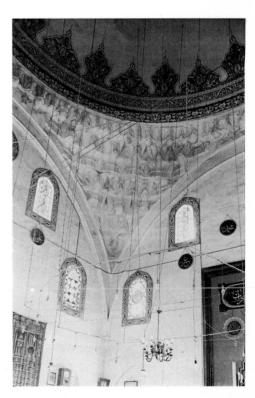

146 Hatuniye Cami, Tokat.
The stalactite support for the dome.

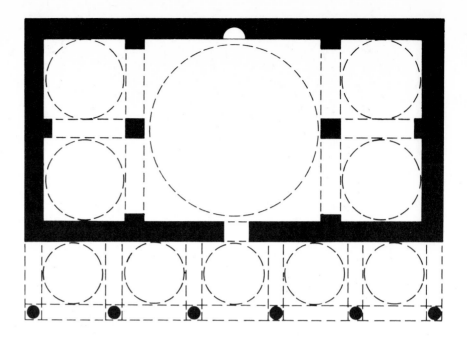

147, 148 *Hatuniye Cami, Manisa. Right:*
Plan, scale 1 : 250. Below: the interior from
the north-east.

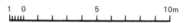

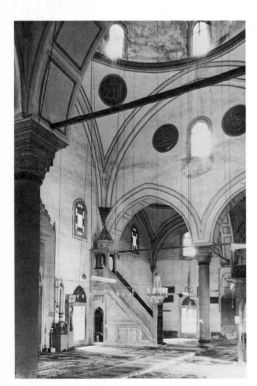

but bronze painted to look like marble, as in other royal foundations of the period, and this gives their stalactite portals their peculiar elaboration and distinction. There is only one minaret (perhaps because the mosque was dedicated to a mere princess) and this is set at the extreme north-west end of the portico.

In 894/1489,[64] Beyazit also built the lofty and spacious Hatuniye Cami at Manisa in honour of his wife, Hüsnü Şah Hatun, when Şehzade Şahin, her son,[65] was governor of the province. The plan follows the Saruhan tradition. There is a central dome[66] with two domes half its dimensions on each side. It clearly shows this style's relationship with Üç Şerefeli Cami and also with Atik Ali Pasha Cami in Istanbul but has no apsidal half-dome. Other examples of this plan are the Çesnegir Cami built ten years before and the pretty İvaz or Ayas Pasha Cami dated 889/1484[67] which used much Byzantine material. This little mosque is remarkable for its fine stalactites as well as for its proportions. An odd aspect is the very high base to its minaret, which rises above the level of the dome.

Also at Manisa, and similar in plan, is the mosque of the Valide Ayşe Hafize, widow of Selim I and mother of Süleyman the Magnificent[68] who built it in her honour in 929/1522.[69] It has had many baroque features added but its rectangular, high exterior in red stone is uncompromisingly solid and shows how important the half-dome was to the flow of the external mass. (In some later mosques this rigidity can be felt in spite of the half-dome, for example Mihrimah at Üsküdar by Sinan, and Beyazit II at Istanbul. It is a measure of the advance of such Sinan mosques as Süleymaniye that the feeling of a solid central cube is so diminished that it ceases to assert itself externally at all.[70]) The eighteenth-century stucco work on the mihrabs of the portico is very delicate. Inside, the mosque is lofty and spacious consisting of a central dome with twin flanking cupolas a quarter of its size, which was the typical plan of the region. Over the windows flanking the mihrab are two very fine sets of dark-blue tiles inscribed and decorated in white. They are made up of square and restangular tiles shaped to fit the pointed relieving arch. The floral borders are pretty but the design is weak compared with the mastery of tile design which was to develop at Iznik.

The complex is now being restored after having been allowed to decay to an extent where the work required is closer to rebuilding. It has a low-lying and

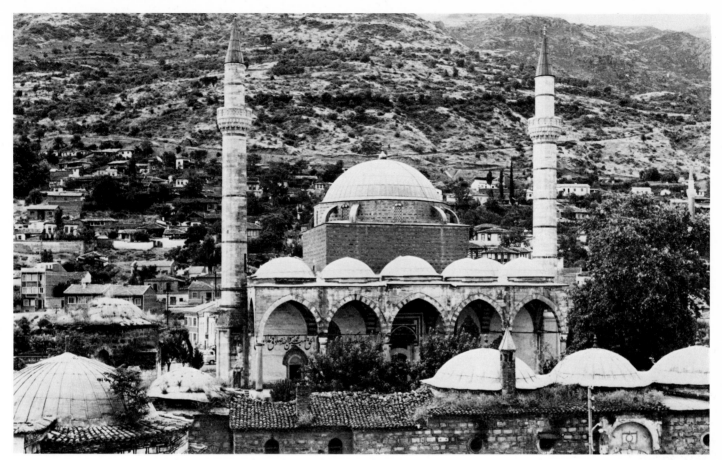

149 *Hatuniye Cami, Manisa. The view across the medrese and the court from the hamam.*

simple tımarhane or insane asylum in a modest four-eyvan form. Neither modest nor simple is the grand but heavily restored double hamam with its vast dome over the hot room pierced with hundreds of stars. The battered medrese across the capacious court from the mosque portico is united to the mosque by a wall, as in Mehmet Pasha at Amasya and İshak Pasha at İnegöl. Here at last mosque and medrese share their court and fountain for the first time, but the cells sprawl each side of a central north door and it is more as if they shared a garden than a court; this is true also of the more formal precinct of Sinan's Kara Ahmet Pasha. Nevertheless, the shared court is achieved here, for Sinan to perfect by bringing it to its taut and logical conclusion at Sokollu Mehmet Pasha.

To return to Amasya and the mosque of the Vali Mehmet Pasha, who was a general of Beyazit II's and tutor to his son:[71] this was built in filial piety, with tabhane rooms on each side and with the türbe of his father at the eastern end. He reserved a humbler grave for himself in the little garden plot at the door of the tomb. The mosque and its fine, plain marble doorway have been restored since Gabriel wrote, and all the domes have been stripped of tiles and covered in lead. Inside, the mihrab has been rebuilt of marble instead of plaster.[72] The original marble minber[73] resembles none other in Turkey, because the richness of its carving leaves no interval anywhere and because it possesses two carved marble doors which still swing effortlessly on their hinges. They are preceded by a multi-faceted semicircular cantilevered step closely related to those of the portal niches of the Beyazit Pasha Cami close by, making it even more probable that there were steps up into the niches for guards or porters. The imam of the Mehmet Pasha Cami was adamant that no radical changes had been made to the interior, and one is at a loss to understand Gabriel's plan.[74] The room beyond the inset minaret, which must have contributed to his theory concerning the placing of the original minarets of the great Bursa mosques, is presently divided by a

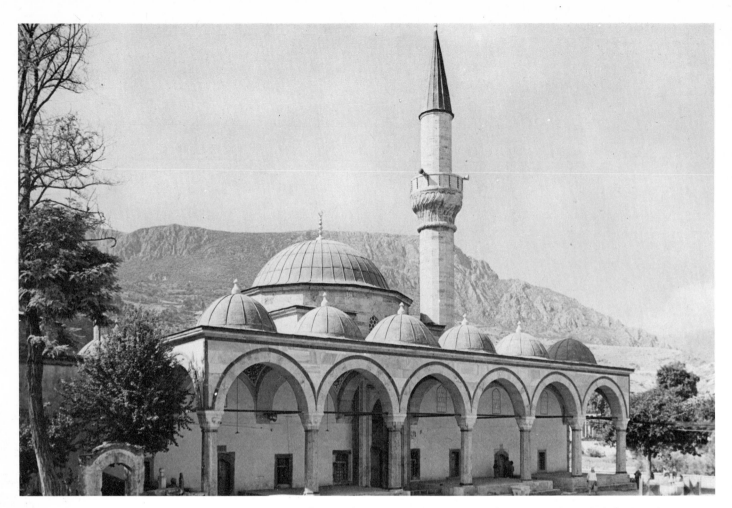

150 Mehmet Pasha Cami, Amasya, showing the portico and, on the left, the türbe.

thick wall into which a window has been cut. The first, north-west room has a door on to the porch and the inside room possesses an ocak in the south wall which has been blocked and is used as a mihrab.[75] Unlike Gabriel's plan the eastern pair of rooms are similar in every way to those on the west and the first room is walled off from the prayer hall and not open in the manner shown. What is missing on this side, naturally, is the broad passage behind the large base of the single minaret, and this disproportion of about four metres is only partly balanced by the addition of the türbe.[76] There is, therefore, an inevitable lack of balance which disturbed Gabriel. The result is that there are only two arches east of the central arch of the portico and three on the west. If a third had been added on the east it would have placed a column full in the face of the türbe door. The plan omits an important feature in the sequence of sofas, which are divided by the area under the domes before the main door – as is usual – and also before the tabhane doors east and west – which is not. The door to the minaret, however, is reached directly from the level of the sofa. The most unusual feature is the continuation of the porch and sofas before the tabhane rooms, although a broad raised skirting or podium frequently surrounds mosques. One such can be sat on all the way round the Green Mosque at Bursa or Firuz Bey at Milas while there is a deep sofa along the north face of the inner court of Fatih. This skirting was clearly useful and continued to appear throughout the Ottoman period as it does at Ahmet III's Valide Cami at Üsküdar. But at Mehmet Pasha the intent

II Mihrimah Cami, Istanbul. View from the Edirne Gate.

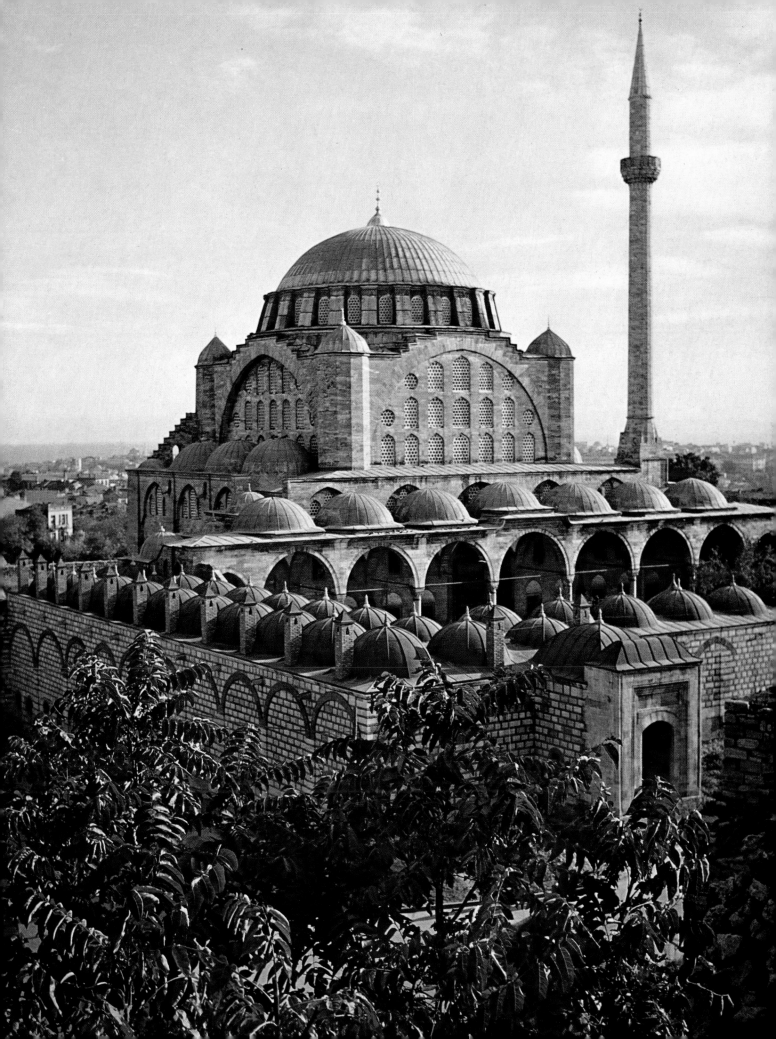

was to create a grand portico, although the actual mosque is small. It is the two cells and the two rooms of the tabhane which add so much to its graceful width. The construction is logical and, on the kıble side, is balanced; the architect could not hope to resolve the problems of the court face without altering established, ritual forms. In the elementary mathematics of an architecture based on the conjunction of traditional component parts, one türbe cannot equal one minaret base.

The seven decagonal columns which support the portico show that at Amasya the quarrying of antiquity had come to an end while nobody had the skill to round new columns.[77] Their capitals are decorated with motifs like those of Sinan at the Rüstem Pasha Medrese, Istanbul, and elsewhere; but he had no craftsmen of like skill to employ. All six domes are slightly elliptical. The windows are very recent copies made for the present restoration. It is intended to reconstruct the şadırvan, and the basic stone components have been reassembled. The new paintwork is a misfortune which the small but charming mosque does not deserve.[78]

The period was one of diversity all over Anatolia. Ahlat in the east was not yet a part of the Ottoman dominions, but it may be helpful to note the extreme conservatism of the region which was eventually to have its own form of Ottoman architecture. The mescit of the local Emir, Bayındır, dates from 882/ 1477,[79] and is but a chapel with a deep porch and an apsidal mihrab built of looted cut stone and almost certainly the work of Armenian masons. The türbe only escapes being a slavish copy of those of the thirteenth-century Selçuk period because it presents a stumpy colonnade instead of a wall on its southward face, so being at once a closed and an open türbe. It is also notable that it is set on the axis of the mihrab of its mescit. This local respect for the historic past was to develop later at the İshak Pasha palace at Doğubayezit into a genuine movement towards revivalism.[80]

Towards 902/1496, when he died, Geyikli[81] Ahmet Pasha, who was a poet as well as a high functionary, built his medrese at Bursa near the Muradiye, with the unorthodox number of eleven cells, due to his desire to exploit the panorama opposite the dershane. The domed gate occupies the site of the twelfth cell on the east side. There are two cells facing north so that the open side is slightly enclosed lest the sense of seclusion might have been dissipated. Equally inventive was the college at Merzifon known as the Küçük Ağa Medrese built in 900/1494[82] which was raised on a terrace and approached by stairs. It was left completely open on the east side. Indeed, the dershane, which is now a mescit, emphasizes this by being set back behind its three-domed portico on the south-east. The fall of the land causes problems which puzzled Gabriel; but it is awkwardness of terrain, as we have seen, which inspired the pragmatic Ottoman architects by liberating them from convention and permitting an imaginative approach which plain or plateau stultified. The cells number seventeen or seventeen and a half which is, again, an irregular number and the revaks did not stretch the length of the north side.[83] The end of the fifteenth century was a highly formative period and, whether due to dervish influence or not, escaped servility to tradition when it could. Novel use could be made of established forms and clever treatment of an interesting site. Whether this inventiveness was due to the influence of one or two creative men is impossible to assert.

It is tempting to believe that Beyazit II had no great love for the capital of his dominion because it is difficult to trace much work there during the first twenty years of his reign, that is to say for two-thirds of it. There was, however, little need for building in Istanbul at this period, for the population was not to expand alarmingly until the sixteenth century. In 1453 there were already some Turks residing in Constantinople, else Beyazit I, in 1391, would not have obtained permission for them to build a mosque and install a kadı in their quarter of the city, possibly on the Marmara shore below where Cerrah Pasha Cami now stands. The conquered metropolis was repopulated by Turks from Yenişehir, Aksaray, Balat,[84] Manisa, Eğridir, Karaman, Tire and Bursa, Trabzon, Çarşamba,

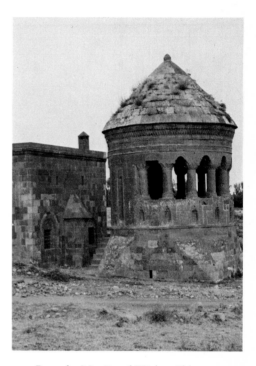

151 *Bayındır Mescit and Türbe, Ahlat.*

Samsun, Sinop and Çanakkale, among other places, while Armenians came from Tokat, Sivas, Kayseri, Amasra and Bursa, and Greeks from the Morea and the islands. Beyazit II and Selim I continued the practice of sending people from the conquered territories to Istanbul. Selim, in particular, brought craftsmen from Tabriz, the Caucasus, Syria and Egypt including ceramicists, particularly from Azerbaijan and Syria.[85] This influx was to explain some of the excellence of Ottoman craftsmanship in the sixteenth century. Süleyman I brought in Serbs besides Moors and Jews expelled from Spain.[86] In 1477, the Kadı Mühüettin states that 9,000 houses were inhabited by Turks, 3,000 by Greeks, 1,500 by Jews, 267 by Christians of the Crimea, 750 by Karamans and 31 by gypsies. There were also 3,667 shops, certain to have been of one room only, and this would indicate a population of little more than 70,000.[87] By 1520–35, however, Ömer Lufti Balkan[88] estimates there to have been 46,635 Moslem hearths, 25,292 Christian hearths and 8,070 Jewish hearths, making a total of about 80,000 houses and 400,000 inhabitants of whom 58 per cent were Moslem. These figures are supported by Cristobal de Villalon, private physician to Sinan Pasha, who, in 1550, seems to have accurately estimated there to be 40,000 Christian houses, 4,000 Jewish and 60,000 Turkish and also 10,000 suburban houses, making a total of 114,000[89] which implies a population of about half a million of which, again, 58 per cent were Moslem. The increase over the preceding figures is a reasonable one.[90]

Prior to 1500, therefore, there can have been little need for many new mosques in addition to those already cited and the many mescits dating from the first creative impulse following on the conquest. And there were still churches to convert in addition to those already taken over by Fatih and which had not decayed and been exploited as quarries. A number of these were to be sequestrated in the reign of Beyazit, the most famous being the Church of St Saviour in Chora, Kahriye Cami. There the magnificent mosaics and the frescoes of the paraclesion were whitewashed over and so not greatly harmed. The conversion was carried out at the expense of the Vezirazam Atik Ali Pasha. The new mihrab p was small and in keeping, for it was made of grey marble identical to that of the revetments of the apse.

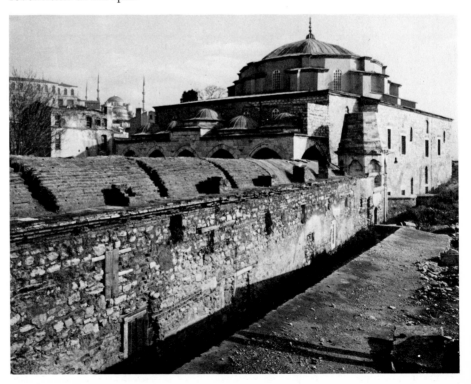

152 SS Sergius and Bacchus, now the Küçük Aya Sofya Cami, Istanbul. The portico and cells round the courtyard are Ottoman additions.

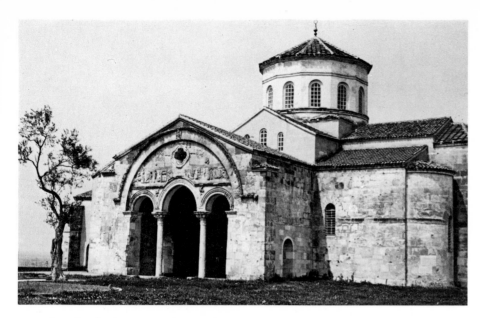

153 *The Church of Hagia Sophia, Trabzon.*

The basilica of the Studion was more extensively remodelled by İlyas Bey, the Master of the Horse, from which office it derived its title of İmrahor Cami and it has already been noted that SS Sergius and Bacchus, Küçük Aya Sofya, was converted by Hüseyin Ağa.[91] At about this time, Mesih Ali Pasha, who died in 1501, converted the Bodrum Cami, while the Church of St Andrew in Krisi had been radically altered when it was made into his mosque by the subsequent chief vezir, Koca Mustafa Pasha, a Greek who was destined to betray Beyazit II to his son Selim I and be a cause of the deposition and death of his sultan. Selim the Grim had no reason to trust such a man and his reward for treachery was his own execution in the same year, 1512.[92]

Hayrettin Ağa[93] took the Khalkoprateia for his mosque, while the monastery of Constantine of the Lips, sepulchre of the Paleologos dynasty, was appropriated by Fenarizade Alaettin Ali Efendi who died in 1496. The cells of the monastery became a tekke. It has already been noted that some unspecified churches were given to the vezirs as residences. The battered, but still repairable, last chapel of the Great Palace, clearly depicted on the map of 1450,[94] was taken by the sultan who used the vaults for his zoo and the church above as a hostel for his artists, thus housing two sorts of lion in the same residence, which was known as the Aslanhane. Whether the beasts below or the artists above were responsible for the deterioration of this monument is of no importance: it has totally disappeared. With more dignity, Hagia Irene became the armoury of the saray and the principal building in the First Court while St Theodosia, who failed so lamentably to answer the prayers of her followers on that last night before the city fell, was a naval depot until converted into the Gül Cami in the reign of Selim II.

Hagia Sophia and the Pantocrator, Molla Zeyrek Cami, were the two largest churches converted in the Fatih era together with the Kilise Cami, perhaps St Theodore, and Toklu Ibrahim Dede Mescit. It has been shown that the first imaret of Fatih was installed in St Saviour Pantepoptes. Other small churches and chapels were also appropriated. Fethiye Cami, the church of the Theotokos Pammacristos, was not converted until 1591 after the transfer of the Patriarchate to the Phanar. Other minor churches were converted in the seventeenth century, such as the Odalar Cami by the Sadrazam Kermankeş Mustafa Pasha. By then, however, such conversions were few, for little was left to take over, and in the reign of Murat IV those seeking ready-made mosques were reduced to the cellars of the castle of Galata, founded by Tiberius II, which became the curious Yer Altı Cami or Subterranean Mosque.

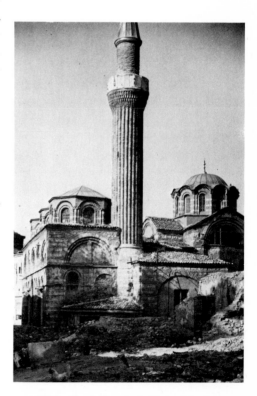

154 *Kilise Cami, Istanbul. The original church may have been St Theodore.*

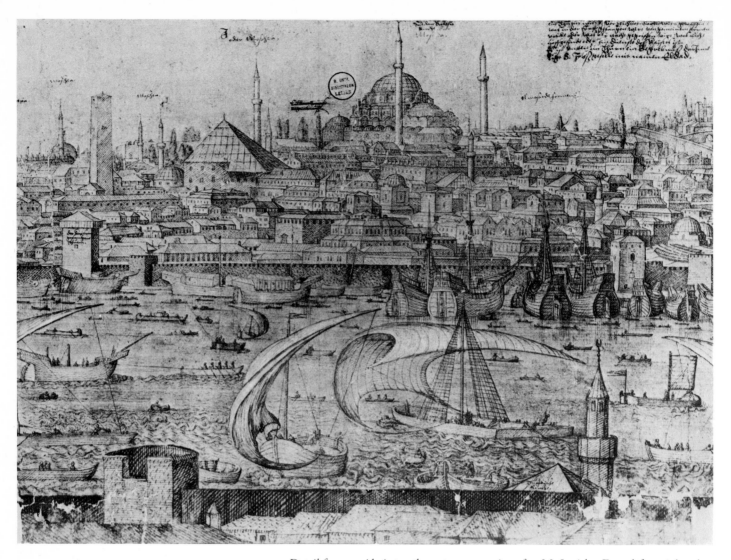

155 *Detail from a mid-sixteenth-century engraving after M. Lorichs. From left to right: the Atik Ali Pasha Cami, Byzantine tower, Candarlı Ibrahim Pasha Cami, Beyazit Complex, and the wall of Eski Saray.*

Surprisingly few churches were taken over in the provinces, except as quarries, but at Amasya there was Fethiye, of modest proportions, and at Edirne the foundations of the ruined church on which the zaviye mosque of Yıldırım Beyazit was set askew.[95] At Trabzon examples are the Ortahisar or Fatih mosque and Hagia Sophia. The Ramazanoğlus converted a monastery into the Yağ Cami complex prior to 1510[96] and built a grand gateway inscribed 960/1553 as well as such churches as that at Tarsus where they added a squat and fat minaret at the north-west corner. Another good example of a monastery converted into a tekke is the Burmalı Medrese on Rhodes. What is surprising is the small impression these churches made on the now established Ottoman code. The use of mixed courses of brick and stone had been absorbed in the earliest period together with the pendentive and the apsidal projection for the mihrab, although this could represent a gradual disappearance of the main eyvan of the four-eyvan type of medrese. After 1453 there was the borrowing of the second half-dome from Hagia Sophia, and a part of the exedral form, but otherwise the domed-square unit continued to govern the development of Ottoman structure. In the entangled world of symbol and decorative detail, patterns bounce from court to court but the only influence of fallen Constantinople on Ottoman decor appears to have been the deplorable use of crude fake marbling on plaster panels. Later this was adapted to skirtings and fake columns in Iznik tile.[97] Whitewash came like January snow to any appropriated building and, not only were mosaics submerged, but abstract reliefs were coarsened and choked just as the elaborately carved cornices of SS Sergius and Bacchus are choked to this day.

Beyazit II also added the stone, south-east minaret to Hagia Sophia to balance that built by Fatih in brick in the south-west.[98] It was a curious position to choose, because, by the reign of Beyazit, minarets were usually set to the north-west, but, at this time, as has been shown, there was still the wooden minaret raised on the west turret of the west façade immediately after the conquest.

It will be seen from the foregoing that the capital was not so neglected as might at first appear and that each neighbourhood inhabited by Moslems had its Friday mosque and many mescits for daily prayers. Moreover two vezirs' mosques belonging to this period, Davut Pasha and Atik Ali, have been discussed already. Before these, in *882*/1477, Candarlı Ibrahim Pasha had made an important contribution to Ottoman architecture. This first minister of Beyazit II died during an attack on Lepanto in *905*/1499.[99] He built his mosque off the Uzun Çarşı, the main artery of the outer bazaar and the former Byzantine market street of the Makros Embros. It stands out in a drawing by Lorichs because of its vast hipped roof which seems to have been tiled and which is now restored to its correct shape outside after being gutted by a fire. Of the wanton disregard for its original interior form, no mention shall be made, nor shall the use of concrete be described. The mosque is extraordinary for two main reasons apart from its size. It provides the first example in Istanbul of a double revak of marble columns – a form often to be employed by Sinan in the country and in Istanbul where space was too restricted to build a court, as it was at Rüstem Pasha and at the İskele Cami. It is not the first example of such a portico, for it appeared in embryo at the darül-hadis at Edirne, but it is the first still standing which was fully developed. In wood, the form may have been common by 1500, at least with small mosques. The court of the Ulu Cami at Manisa could be said to have double revaks but not of the grandeur of this double front, for at Ibrahim Pasha Cami the columns are exceptionally high and have governed the proportions of the whole building, just as they would an Italian Renaissance monument. The result is a son cemaat yeri which is princely in its spaciousness. The second unusual aspect of this mosque is its shed roof which extends not only over the inner row of arches but over the outer row as well and so dispenses with the need for domes such as a Sinan mosque would have. Consequently, the northern side of the roof is longer than the southern, and this demanded a steeper pitch than usual, which made the building prominent. Inside, there was originally a wooden dome inset under the rafters[100] which has not been replaced. This concealed cupola must have been very large, for the mosque is many times greater in area than Takkeci Ibrahim Çavuş or Ağa Cami built in *1001*/1592 on the Bakırköy road beyond Topkapı.[101] In the latter the double portico is of wood and very rough and simple, creating an unexpectedly Japanese effect, partly because the posts and railings are painted a dull red in the oriental manner. The mosque itself is of stone and brick. Inside, it has a splendid wooden dome painted a dark green and gold at a late date, and all the cornices and other woodwork are of fine workmanship which is not true of the Yatağan Cami.[102] This is apt to be overlooked because of the fame of the tiles which are, indeed, as fine as any in the country. This form of inner dome must have been common to many of the smaller mosques and made them a delight in comparison with the flat-ceilinged rooms which now obtain, let alone the concrete grille which straddles Ibrahim Pasha Cami. It was a form which was used in houses and palaces and can be seen in the royal pavilion of the Yeni Valide Cami and, spectacularly, in the recently revealed dome of the seventeenth-century salon of the Kafes, or Cage, or Princes' Apartments at Topkapısaray.[103] This has been excellently restored. The paintwork is rich and gorgeous and of great refinement in spite of the brilliance of the reds and blues and the gilding. Other examples are the Eski Cami at Mudanya dating from *1053*/1643,[104] the dome of the soğukluk under a pitched roof at the hamam at Niş,[105] and the salon of the seventeenth-century Köprülü Yalı at Kanlıca on the Bosphorus. Whether there were once

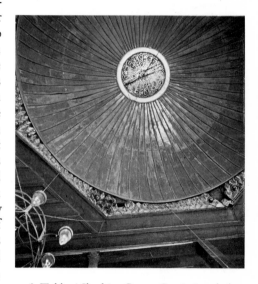

156 Takkeci Ibrahim Cavus Cami, Istanbul. The inset wooden dome.

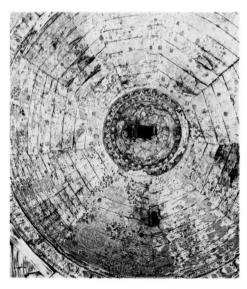

157 The wooden dome of the Köprülü Yali on the Bosphorus.

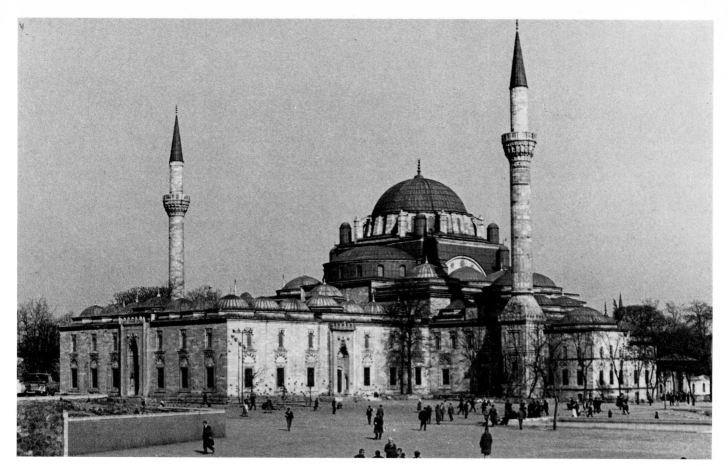

165 Sultan Beyazit Cami, Istanbul.

There is a careful division of the areas of the complex, such as the Sultan's garden and the cemetery, but the units are scattered over the spacious precincts, including the large medrese[145] now a library where a weekly lecture was given by the Şeyhül-İslâm himself, who was its müderris or Dean, so making it the foremost law college of them all.[146] It is a grand building with a nobly arched entry in the established tradition and largely faced in stone except for the dershane itself. The upper lights are placed between the casements below, creating an interesting effect but nothing more. The innovation, which stemmed from the growing habit of building tiers of mosque windows pyramidally, was not copied with later medreses. The court is large and encased in domed revaks and the dershane is still approached by a flight of steps but is not united to the lateral colonnades by a screen, as at Bursa, but by cupolas on arches. The relatively small imaret has a fine marble fountain in the pool of its forecourt and is also a library. The very grand hamam was partly founded on the debris of the triumphal arch of Theodosius which was uncovered when the road was widened recently, and of the Forum Tauri. It was certainly a valuable quarry and the roadworks have revealed a frieze of soldiers under the hamam walls, many ignominiously standing on their heads.[147] The hamam was permitted to fall into a deplorable state while being used as a store and a barrack for rats, but some restoration is now in progress. It was once among the grandest of the baths of the city. The kervansaray has totally disappeared unless it was the Şımkeşhane. It was within the walled area and included a fine fountain.[148] The outer precinct of the mosque was surrounded by stalls and small shops while below the mosque was the Beyazit Meydan shaped in something approaching a square with shops on all four sides including a row designed by Sinan which is now rebuilt under the graveyard. The mosque was, therefore, the centre of religious life for a great market area which, through the alleys of the Kapalıçarşı, or Covered Bazaar, and the open bazaar beyond, spread down the hillside to the sea. The türbe of the sultan was set on the south side beyond the mihrab. It is a fine classical mausoleum but has a heavy baroque porch added, which conflicts with the austere proportions of this grey, domed octagon. The sibyan mekteb is the first still standing in Istanbul to have the closed winter classroom set beside the open summer eyvan. It stands twin-domed above Sinan's shops at the end of the cemetery. The muvakkithane has disappeared but it was once used by all the shipping at Constantinople.[149]

At the same time as Beyazit II was being built, an important mosque was built by Huma Hatun, in honour of Damat Bali Pasha, her husband and the vezir of the sultan who was his father-in-law. The inscription plainly states that it was completed in 910/1504, but it was badly damaged in the earthquake of 1894[150] and was more or less rebuilt in 1938 after a fire three years earlier. It has been attributed to Esir Ali[151] but he would not appear to have arrived in Constantinople from Iran by that date, and if he were brought back by Selim from Tabriz would only have come ten years later. The mosque appears on the list of the works of Sinan and this attribution is the most puzzling of all. Ethem[152] has suggested that he carried out major repairs based on the old plan and this has been generally accepted. The mosque was very solidly built and it would be difficult to suggest reasons for so rapid a decay if it were not for the great earthquake of 1509 immediately after its completion. It might then have been left to rot for lack of funds with which to restore it. Nonetheless, its characteristics are more akin to those of the Beyazit period than that of Süleyman.[153]

Inside, the restored dome is set on an octagonal base. The three deep recesses on the east and west sides and the two flanking the door, exposed as exterior buttresses on the south, are a development which was to be used by Sinan in metropolitan and provincial mosques such as those of Hadım Ibrahim Pasha at the Silivri Gate and the Kurşunlu at Kayseri, and by his students with such mosques as that of Ali Pasha at Tokat. Thus Bali Pasha Cami is the prototype of many of medium size which would follow and has features which were to become the canon of the classical period. The casements and the windows are very large and in the tympana they collide with the arches. The windows are also cramped or awkwardly placed externally. The portico overlaps the width of the north front in order to achieve the grandeur of five arches carried on classical columns. The north-west extension of the façade is formed by the base of the minaret, and a corresponding base exists to the north-east which contains a stairway to the

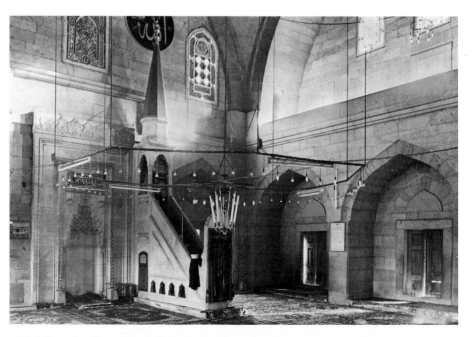

166 Bali Pasha Cami, Istanbul. Interior.

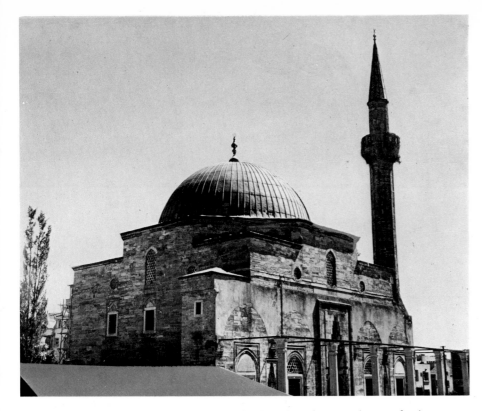

167 Bali Pasha Cami, Istanbul. The mosque has been heavily restored except for the portico.

42 gallery. This is a form used by Sinan to broaden his façades both at Mihrimah at
62 Edirnekapı and at Sokollu Mehmet Pasha at Kadırga and elsewhere. It may be
that the façade as well as the minaret were his contribution to an otherwise
modest mosque. The base of the minaret, however, is related to those of Beyazit
at Amasya. There could not be two minarets at Bali Pasha Cami because it was
not a royal mosque. The architect may have made a bid to solve the problem of
the vezir mosques, where a single minaret means a lack of symmetry, and built as
much of one as would give balance to his façade so as to avoid such distortions as
occur at Mehmet Pasha Cami at Amasya.

Most provincial mosques followed local building traditions, like that of
Karagöz Ahmet Pasha at Kütahya dated 915/1509[154] which has a triple tile-
lipped build-up of its central dome consisting of two twelve-faceted drums with
a round one inset between. There is a further frieze of tile forming a shallow eave
to the basic square block of the mosque. Tiles also roofed the portico. It is
likely that lead was not extensively used in the Kütahya region at this period.

At some time in the reign of Beyazit II, between 1479 and 1515[155] the Ulu Cami
was rebuilt at Elbistan in the territory of the Dulkadır family south-west of
Malatya. This remote plateau, difficult of access, lies at the foot of Şehri Dag and
is watered by the upper reaches of the Ceyhan river. It is poetically beautiful
in the clean air and light, but its history has been particularly bloody. The Arabs
conquered it when they took Malatya in the seventh century but the Byzantines
had control again in the tenth. The Selçuks arrived in October 1057, but from
1090 it was free until subjugated by the Danışmends in 1153. Timur conquered
it in 1395, Selim in 1515, and Mehmet Ali in 1838. The mountains round about
were strongholds of Kurdish nationalists from then on until the fall of the Ottoman
Dynasty. The mosque is evidence – but in no way as conclusive as Ünsal asserts –
of the emergence of the quatrefoil plan in Anatolia prior to Sinan's building of
Şehzade. Indeed, as has been shown, the quatrefoil plan existed in Central Asia
long before.[156] A great number of Early Christian, Byzantine, and Armenian
churches were centralized in plan including that of the Holy Apostles at Ani and

others in Syria and near Antalya. The Elbistan mosque is now more or less an Ottoman building, with its dome set on an octagonal and true drum above a square base.[157] It is supported by four flying-buttresses due to later restoration. Inscriptions refer to major repairs in the nineteenth century and the 1920s, while recent work amounts to rebuilding and mutilation.

Of the Selçuk Ulu Cami of Kılıç Aslan only the legend survives. The triple-arched, cross-vaulted porch supported by stone piers has been rebuilt using materials from an early period including fragments of brick patterns which look fifteenth-century in origin. (The nearby çeşme employs some Byzantine material, a little of which is still littered about the town.) The mosque inside has a central dome now supported by pendentives with four vaulted lateral areas, not half-domes as Ünsal suggests, and four small domed corner units. The central area equals four-sixteenths, each lateral two-sixteenths, and each corner unit one-sixteenth of the whole and thus achieves the classical division of space which modulates the plans of all quatrefoil mosques. The little domes in the north-east and north-west corners cover two high square sofas which are vestigial remnants of the Bursa tabhane rooms. Under them, with ventilators at floor level, are storage rooms. The area under the south vault before the mihrab was once raised thirty centimetres but is now level, thanks to the ruthless use of concrete on the old floor. The royal box was set into the thickness of the wall on the south-east and is no more than a niche with a rail. It is approached by stairs set into the wall which are reached from a window alcove, as are the two stairs to the two upper eyvans left and right of the north door. These now have protruding balustraded balconies. The mosque has a descendant in the Lala Mustafa Pasha Cami at Erzerum which dates from the sixteenth century and is also centralized with vaults, not semi-domes. It is probable that provincial masons were unable to build semi-domes, partly because they retained pointed arches. However, the Anatolian development of the quatrefoil mosque continued.

The unhappy last years of Beyazit's reign were heralded in 1509 by one of the worst earthquakes in the history of Thrace. His reign had already included many natural disasters such as famines and, after many vicious storms in Istanbul, an appalling explosion at the Arsenal due to lightning which killed five to six thousand people and blasted the dome into the sea.[158] In 1509 there were shocks and tremors for forty-five days. The town of Dimetoka, birthplace of the sultan, was reduced to rubble[159] and Çorum disappeared. In Istanbul, 109 mosques were brought to the ground and part of the walls and seven towers fell into the sea. The walls of Topkapısaray from the water to the garden gate were ruined. The dome of Fatih cracked, together with the capitals of the four largest columns and the domes of the şifahane and the eight medreses. The newly completed dome of Beyazit's own mosque collapsed. Thirteen thousand people were reported dead.[160] Three thousand officers and their mounts were entombed in the shambles of the palace of the Vezirazam Mustafa Pasha, who, unfortunately for his master, escaped to betray him to his son. Mortar and plaster fell in Hagia Sophia and the evangelists in the tympana reappeared somewhat vengefully. The padişah was forced to camp in his garden for ten days and[161] eventually he left for Edirne, only to meet with a new earthquake there on 10 November which was followed by an unparalleled tempest on the 16th of that month. The Divan met in council at Edirne, and the work of repair was begun immediately, although Evliya states that the Sultan was famed only for his lassitude at this period. Nearly seven thousand masons and workmen were set to work on the city walls[162] including those of Silivrikapı and Yedikule and also the towers of Leander and Galata.[163] There must also have been extensive restoration at Topkapısaray and at Edirne-saray. Thus there could have been few men available during this troubled time for new works, which would explain why there were so few. The end of the reign came with the rebellion of Beyazit's youngest son, Selim, who deposed his father at Çorlu. Beyazit was to die thirteen days later, aged sixty-five, on the road to Edirne and Dimetoka which had been selected as his retreat, either from infirmity, despair, or poison on 26 May 1512.[164]

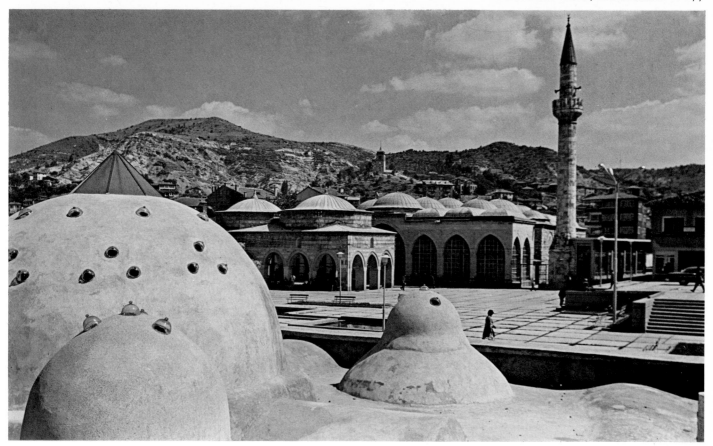

168 Nasrullah Cami, Kastamonu. The unusual double şadırvan is between the mosque and the hamam domes in the foreground.

68   It was about this time that the Nasrullah Cami at Kastamonu was built.[165] It is a very late example of a nine-domed ulu cami type, but too extensively restored to be representative. It has a large rebuilt portico of two sets of three vaults on each side of a central cupola before the north entry, in front of which is an extensive meydan which has risen considerably in level, even submerging an early hamam. Before the mosque is the largest şadırvan in Anatolia consisting of a grand arcade of six arches on the south and north and three on the east and west. These support two domes inset into high octagonal drums. Beneath these are two large pools. By this time, the concept of an internal fountain had died out but the present heavily restored şadırvan could have been added at a later date.

    Yavuz Selim, or Selim the Grim, could have had little time for building and perhaps even less inclination. His reign started with the disposal of his elder brothers and their offspring which, once accomplished, left him free to proceed to the conquest of Egypt and a part of the Persian dominions. These wars were to occupy most of his brief reign of eight years, a brevity which Evliya attributes to his father's deathbed curse. Like their padişah, the Chief Vezirs of Selim's reign had no time for building mosques nor, perhaps, did they have the taste of a man like Hadım Ali Pasha, the Vezirazam of Beyazit II, who was to die in 1511. Koca Mustafa Pasha survived only a few weeks before Selim prudently disposed of him. The next to hold office was too busy fighting and was to die on the battlefield in January, 1517. His successor returned from Egypt in the same year only to be greeted by his executioner.[166] Selim's last chief minister, Piri Mehmet Pasha, continued peacefully in office under Süleyman I, for whom he captured Belgrade in 1521, until he gave up the seal to the great favourite and first truly Grand Vezir, Ibrahim Pasha, in June 1523. Piri Mehmet built a number of interesting mosques and mescits; among these was the beautiful Bursa-type mosque of Silivri.[167] At Hasköy on the Golden Horn he built his major mosque which is now a dilapidated tobacco warehouse; it was heavily restored in the nineteenth century. It was built on a grand scale (in 930/1523, the year of his fall) and was the

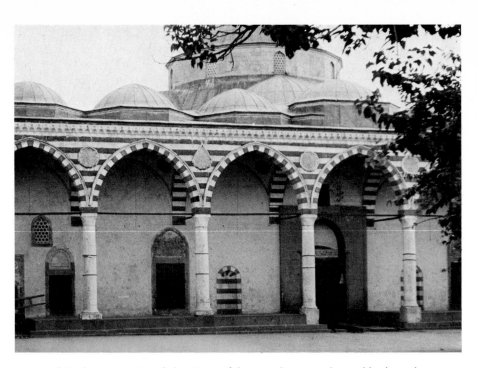

169 *Fatih Pasha Cami, Diyarbakır. Two of the semi-domes are discernible above the portico.*

first quatrefoil mosque in Istanbul. This centralized, four-leaf-clover plan was the accepted climax and perfection of the ideal Ottoman mosque which all previous architects had led towards and which only Sinan was to eclipse.

It was antedated by the mosque of Fatih Pasha at Diyarbakır built between 1518 and 1520, perhaps in the winters when the army was idle in its quarters. Selim had captured this key strategic city from the Akkoyunlu in 1515 and it became the headquarters of the Ottoman army in the south. The local architectural tradition had already taken the domed unit for its module, as with the Kasım Padişah Cami built in 1500, but the extensive use of broad black and white horizontal banding in the Syrian manner, due to the basalt quarries in the locality, gives the buildings of Diyarbakır their distinctive character; that, and the severe geometrical forms employed in obedience, perhaps, to a dictum like Plato's that exactitude is beauty. This was to be seen also with the Nebi or Peygamber Cami, built after the conquest in 1524. There the precision of the rectangular forms of the central area and subordinate wings and of the hexagonal drum of the dome together with the grimness of the black stone leaves a dry taste on the palate. Inside, there are haphazard panels of surviving tiles, some of which are of fair quality and appear to have come from Damascus at a somewhat later date than that of the mosque;[168] but none of them compare to the Iznik panels of the capital. Both mosques have square, detached minarets; that of Kasım Padişah is supported on four columns and can only be reached by a ladder.

To Diyarbakır came an unknown architect who, prior to his patron's death in 1521, was to achieve Büyük Mehmet or Fatih Pasha, the first centralized Ottoman mosque, with four semi-domes and not mere vaults.[169] The four corner areas are surmounted by four small cupolas and the central dome is supported on four piers. It is the logical conclusion to the form of such mosques as that at Elbistan. Apart from the domes, there is no relief from cubes and octagons[170] and the architecture is still austere despite the vivid zebra striping of the black and white courses of cut stone.[171] The squareness of the mosque at human level represents earthliness and the domes the heavens, in the same way as the square and the circle do in Chinese architecture, while the two-centred arch forms a spiritual limbo. The four corner domes and the semi-domes are carried on squinches. The interior is spacious and well-lit and nicely proportioned but the area of window is mean compared with that of Şehzade because of the need to exclude the strong southern light. The two upper tiers are of modern coloured glass. The step up into the harem area is only one inch high and comes immediately after the first pair of piers so that two-thirds of the floor area is raised. Sinan could enlarge the perfected concept of the Fatih Pasha Cami when he built his mosque a generation later, but no more. He reacted against its monotony and creative limitations and did not repeat the clover-leaf form. The portico of Fatih Pasha is seven-domed and the minaret on the north-west exceptionally slender.[172] There is a large precinct[173] with walls and gatehouse and a capacious şadırvan.

71   A problem is the mosque at Çankırı which is said to have been begun in 1522 and completed in 1558, a quite inexplicable length of time.[174] It is a centralized mosque with four semi-domes which are slightly pinched because they are set above pointed and not semicircular arches. It would look as if at first they were, or were intended to be, vaults, in which case the mosque would be a logical and grander successor to that of Elbistan. Unfortunately the mosque has suffered from earthquake, and its present administration is poor so that it is not well restored and the interior is in a shoddy state. The damage by earthquake was such that the repairs in 1302/1884[175] were partly a rebuilding in which the north side became an antechamber in place of a portico, and contemporary nineteenth-century casements were inset. On the south and west large buttresses were added and a new gallery built across the new north wall. The minaret is also new. In the south-east corner buttress, which may have been an original thickening of the corner, is inset a marble star. The interior, for all its turgid nineteenth-century paintwork, is very spacious and the recessed mihrab of good proportions. A curiosity is the support of the inset arches between the elephant feet and the south wall, which are carried on short, crude pairs of columns.

Of the men who formed the entourage of Selim I, Cezeri Kasım Pasha, who was among those who survived to serve Selim's son too, was the most eager builder. Besides a small mosque in Istanbul, he founded another at Eyüp in 921/1515 when he was a vezir of the Cupola. It is very modest and is remarkable for the fine tiles of the Tekfursaray revival under the Sadrazam Nevşehirli Damat Ibrahim Pasha in the earlier half of the eighteenth century.[176] The door is set on

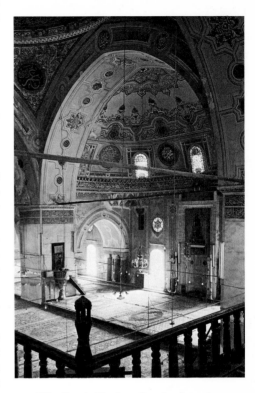

170 *Ulu Cami, Çankırı. Interior from the north-west.*

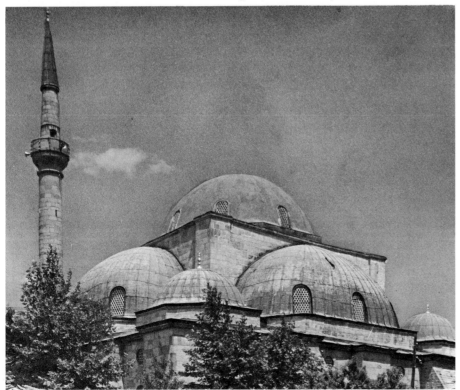

171 *Ulu Cami, Çankırı. Exterior from the south-west showing the bold organization of the four-leaf-clover plan.*

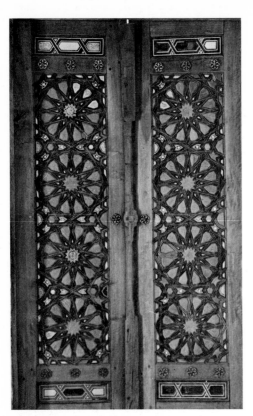

172 Kasım Pasha Cami, Bozüyük. Interior. Casement shutter.

the right of the three-domed porch, as at the Yarhisar Cami, and not in the centre, and the alternating brick and stone courses possess a certain boldness. At Bozüyük, however, he built a fine vezir's mosque[177] in the classical style of handsome red ashlar with a triple-domed son cemaat yeri with a fine garden precinct before it.[178] The mosque itself is a typical single-domed unit but spacious and well-proportioned. It contains remarkable tiles which appear to be Iznik and are certainly not from Iran; they form panels above the windows of the portico and over the interior casements as well as forming the balustrades of the hoca's chair and the tribune on the north-west. In the latter two cases, they seem to be later additions.[179] A second chair is carried on four small columns exquisitely carved with animals and birds among vegetation. This comes from Hama and could have been brought back by the conquering pasha. I have not seen its like anywhere else in Turkey. The shutters and the door are splendid examples of wood-carving while the simple but elegant mihrab, the exterior mihrabs and the stalactite capitals of the portico are all of excellent craftsmanship. Its inscription states that the mosque was completed in 935/1528 when Kasım Pasha was Beylerbey, Viceroy of Europe.

The cube plan (of fifteenth- and early sixteenth-century mosques) makes the prayer hall so aggressively geometrical as to be called an ugly box, unless it is seen as symbolic when it becomes too meaningful to be fairly criticized on aesthetic grounds since it was part of a living religious alphabet. With the mosque of Kasım Pasha, except for the tiles and the kürsü, the interior is sober and the mihrab plain but there was almost certainly lavish paintwork on the walls, which has been lost. The mosques of Kasım Pasha, and possibly the Peygamber at Diyarbakır, among others, show that the use of tiles inside Ottoman mosques preceded the building of the Süleymaniye in Istanbul and that this mosque was first only in the extent of their use on a mihrab wall.

Selim must have been at least responsible for remodelling the great chambers, the Hırkai-Serif Oda or Pavilion of the Holy Mantle,[180] in the Topkapisaray associated not only with the Robe of the Prophet but also with many other holy relics brought back by him from Egypt as the trappings of the Caliphate.[181] These were all stored in one of this suite of rooms until the reign of Mahmut II. The pavilion stands at the extremity of the harem and selâmlık upon a towering vaulted basement. The main entry and the dismounting block of the sultan are onto the third court because this was the dormitory of the most privileged senior pages of the palace school. The two south rooms open onto the colonnades before the marble terrace which overlooks the city and the Horn and commands the Fourth court of the saray. The pavilion has been altered frequently and, in

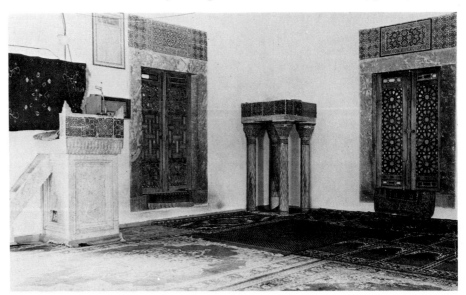

173 Kasım Pasha Cami, Bozüyük. Interior. South-east corner.

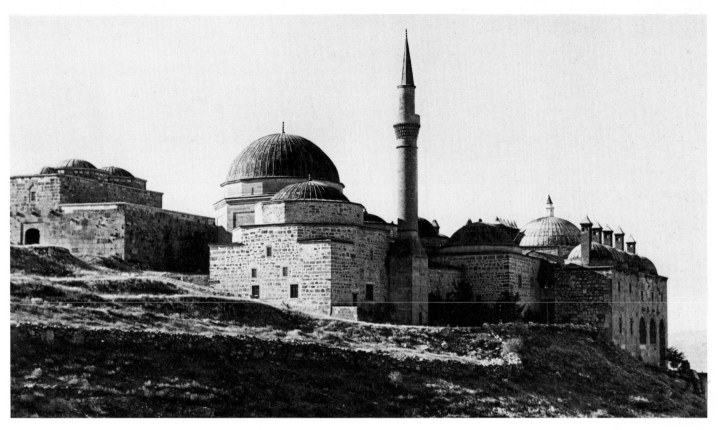

174 *Tekke of Battal Gazi, near Eskişehir, showing the original convent church left, the large türbe dome above the mosque centre, and a row of five cells right.*

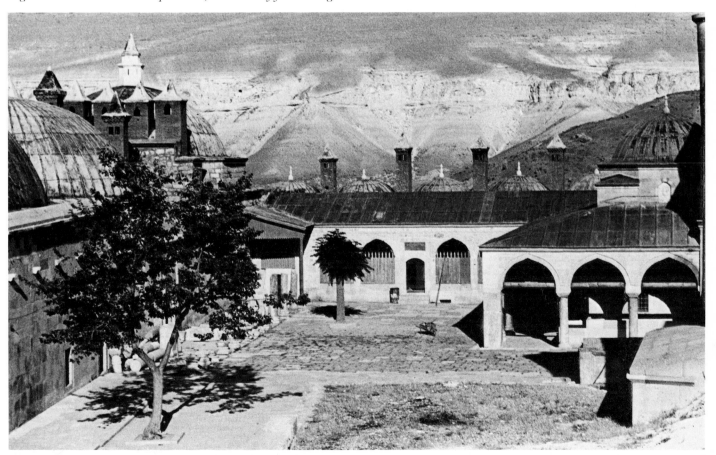

175 *Tekke of Battal Gazi. The courtyard from the west.*

particular, at the end of the sixteenth century, but the formidably thick and powerful walls are likely to be original. Its core is a great hall off which are two rooms on one side and one leading to the Golden Road on the other. It has a fine fountain, added by Mahmut II, before the door to the third court with a great eyvan at the far west end with a high stone sofa and a grand ocak. All four rooms are domed and lofty and at various periods were grandly clad in tiles of every description.[182] Selim brought back from Egypt the marble facings of the Divan-el-Kebir where the relics were preserved in Cairo and they were used to face the side protected by the colonnade of this sacred kiosk.[183] These rooms are the most holy in Istanbul and the Room of the Robe, although used by the sultans as a bedroom on special occasions, is a mosque. For this reason it has the first dummy minaret in Ottoman architecture, rising slender and high above its dome.

The principal architectural event of the reign of Selim I was the rebuilding of the complex on the Ankara-Eskişehir road of the legendary Battal Seyyit Gazi who was born allegedly in the 670s at Malatya and died in *122/740* and is said to have married a Byzantine princess.[184] The buildings are set on a hillcrest above the town and the plain, and were a centre of the Bektaşi dervish order. Originally there had been a convent on the site, and the church and its cells remain on the right of the entry while a terrace and group of cells overlooking the town were rebuilt on the old foundations, along with the rest of the complex, between 1511 and 1517, as many inscriptions show. On entering, the traveller descends to a long, irregular, paved court with some old trees for shade; the church is on his right, above, and the major public rooms are to his left. These are built over lofty and extensive cellars, some with split levels and some vaulted, while one is supported by wooden piers. They are lit by those funnel windows which are so common in the colder regions of the eastern provinces. Above them are a reception hall and two very large dershanes which are remarkable for the great size of their ocaks in which small trees could be burnt. The first of these rooms has eleven steps to the corbelled honeycomb squinches supporting the dome, which has a window on all but the outward sides. There are large casements each side of the ocak and the entry, onto which a porch was added at a later date. Seven big niches are cut down the side walls, and there are others each side of the casements.

The arrangement of windows, niches and alcoves in the second dershane is more complex, partly because the ocak is smaller and set to one side. It has pipes in the walls to carry hot air. Next comes a refectory with yet another ocak, this time on the outside wall. On the right of the entry is a çeşme, and along the east wall is a stone fosse with a small ocak and two very commodious bake ovens. A door in the north-east corner leads to a narrow chamber into which these protrude and which has an additional ocak and may well have been useful as a drying closet. Beyond this combination of dining hall and bakehouse – which was not uncommon and is also found at the Yeşil complex in Bursa – is the kitchen which is one more domed cube like the rest. What is unusual is that the dining hall and the bakery are on two levels. In the north-east corner, reached through a trapdoor like that of the Çinili Kiosk, are stairs down to the cellars. Opposite the door, side by side in the outside wall, are two large ocaks. There is also a remarkable line of seven hearths with triangular hoods the length of the west wall.

Between the imaret and the mosque are the reconstructed cells already mentioned. They are large (5 metres square) and off a broad landing approached by a ramp. Beyond them is the mosque and türbe which have been enlarged rather than totally rebuilt, for Selçuk period elements remain and the plan is unusual in that there is a double central hall with a woman's mescit off to the east and then subsidiary rooms, with the mosque at the south end. On the west is a small türbe fitted into the exterior angle of the octagon of the mausoleum of the Gazi and against buildings which were originally Byzantine. The portico is L-shaped in order to unite mosque and tomb. The loftiness of this tomb of Battal Gazi recalls those of Cairo sultans, but it is plain and octagonal and belongs

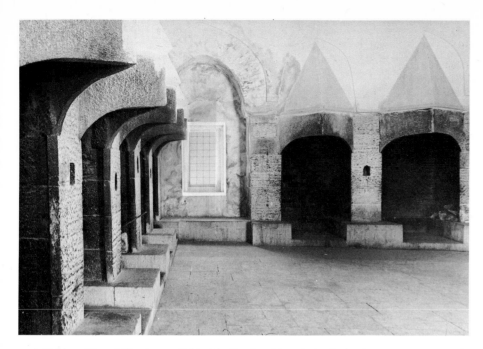

176 Tekke of Battal Gazi, near Eskişehir. Ranks of hearths in the kitchen.

very clearly to the reign of Selim I and the Ottoman tradition. What is astonishing is the tombstone, which is long in accordance with the belief that the greatness of the man must be expressed by the magnitude of his sarcophagus. This was to be true of Yavuz Selim's own but that of Battal Gazi, although thin and low in the Selçuk tradition, reaches more than twenty-five feet in length and its proportions are therefore preposterously distorted.

The foundation was lavishly built with grand rooms and with excellent masonry. The groupings of domed cubes in ordered ranks is offset by the contours of the site and the irregular spacing of the chimney stacks and ventilators, while the trees in the courtyard, by creating shadow and shade, break up the bare surfaces of the upper façades. It owes a great deal to the siting of the monastery which went before it. To some extent these foundations were alien to the Ottoman ideal, so that such a building could only have been erected by a Sufi and not a Sunni, i.e., orthodox authority. Apart from citadels and castles, conforming to the requirements of strategy and not religion, Ottoman architecture before Sinan, while crowning hills with mosques, preferred its monuments to be grouped within the city walls. Only the dervishes exploited the landscape – as with the tekke of Orhan at Bilecik – in their search for peace. Not that Seyyit Battal Gazi can have been particularly peaceful, for it must have been thronged with visitors. The shrines of great heroes and holy men attract others; of about the same date is the tomb and single-roomed tekke of Uliyan Baba at Huriyan a few miles away. The türbe is large, octagonal, but in no way exceptional except for its location in a modest hamlet on the plain.

The kitchen at Battal Gazi is rivalled by that of the Hacı Bektaş Tekke south of Kırşehir. This tekke is of great interest but was so rebuilt in the nineteenth century and restored in this that its historical importance is sadly diminished. Like Battal Gazi its two subsidiary areas and a major central court recall the form of Orthodox monasteries. The kitchen is approached by a passage past a small türbe and a large store. Off it is the meat store and the spacious apartment of the chief cook complete with ocak. The room is lit by windows set high up with sloping sills recalling those in the basement of the Çinili Kiosk. There are three large cauldrons across the back wall and subsidiary ones, sinks and carving blocks along the others. In the middle of the large room are the scales and a main chopping block. There are also cupboards and niches for lamps while the ceiling is supported by beams.

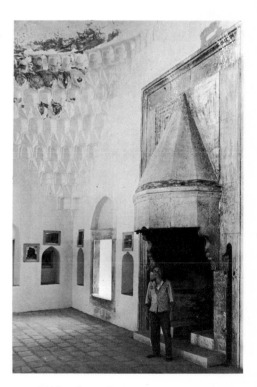

177 Tekke of Battal Gazi. Hearth and elaborate stalactite pendentive of the dershane.

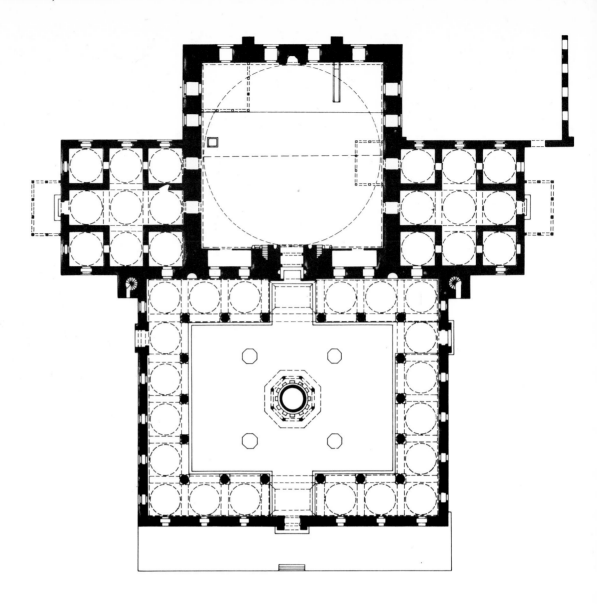

178 Sultan Selim Cami, Istanbul. Plan, scale 1 : 500.

Selim I's own mosque on the crest of Istanbul's fifth hill, was not strictly a *17*
congregational mosque nor was it completed by him: indeed, it may have been
built entirely by Süleyman I in his father's honour. It was completed in 929/1522[185]
but the date on which it was founded is unknown.[186] It has already been compared
with the mosque of the Beyazit Foundation at Edirne which in some aspects, p *1*
but not all, it strikingly resembles. The minarets were moved inwards from the
extreme north-east and north-west corners of the tabhanes[187] to be set in the
middle of their north sides. The relationship between the minarets and the great
dome of the mosque was improved, but it meant the blocking of the window
or the door of the north eyvans of the tabhanes. This, with the absence of doors
to the south, enhances the importance of the doors on the east and west and
so emphasizes the dominance of their east-west axis which is further underlined by the door which admits to the interior of the mosque itself. The south-
west and south-east corner rooms of each tabhane also have a window onto the
prayer hall but the corner chambers on the north-west and north-east do not.

The external structure of the drum of the central dome, which is in fact a belt *17*
of twenty small buttresses, includes pairs of flying buttresses at each corner of the
square structure together with embryonic corner turrets in the thickness of the

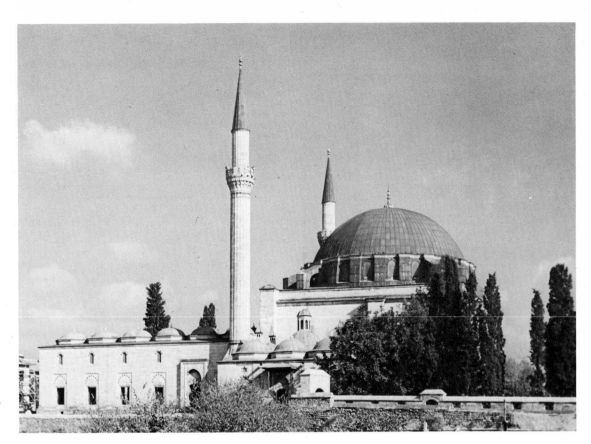

179 Sultan Selim Cami,
Istanbul.
Exterior from the west.

walls on the north-east and north-west, and two thick buttresses which rise from the ground to divide the south wall into three. These are all elaborations on the puritanical and uncompromising squareness of the Beyazit mosque. Internally, the differences are few except that, although Selimiye was subjected to a careless restoration in the nineteenth century, it has been far more carefully tended recently. There is a splendidly ornate multifoil arch[188] over the grand müezzins' gallery which dominates the west wall. In the south-east corner, accessible only by way of a stairway cut in the thickness of the wall and reached by a door onto the small, walled royal yard, is a handsome hünkâr mahfil carried on marble columns of several exotic varieties including jasper.[189] The circles of lights are recent but decently ordered and the limestone has been scrubbed clean of the ugly paintwork which is still offensively surviving at Edirne. What paint there is at Selimiye is predominantly white and this enhances the air of spaciousness. Under the sultan's loge is a splendid painted wooden ceiling. In part the work is certainly eighteenth-century at the earliest, because of the way in which the flowers depicted in lozenges are loosely tied with ribbons, but other more formal designs are traditional and hard to date at all. The dominant colours are, equally traditionally, red and gold. Over the windows, both inside and onto the arcades outside, are lunettes inset with fine panels of tile with floral patterns akin to those of the court of Fatih but which are likely to be very early cuerda seca work from the Iznik potteries.[190] Both mihrab and minber are in the trad-itional and grand manner. The recesses each side of the north door are deep and the usual gallery is set on consoles high above it, with access stairs in the supporting buttresses. The dome is 24·5 metres wide by 32·5 metres high[191] and is therefore as large as that of Üç Şerefeli and wider than those of Beyazit at Edirne (20·55 metres) and Istanbul (17·5 metres). It owes its spectacular eminence above the open cistern of Aspar to the splendid terrace which overlooks the Golden Horn; this could have been begun before Selim died and would thus explain the confusion over the date of this mosque's foundation.

The courtyard also resembles that of Beyazit at Edirne, except for the vaults over its main door and that of the mosque itself. This north door is very fine and

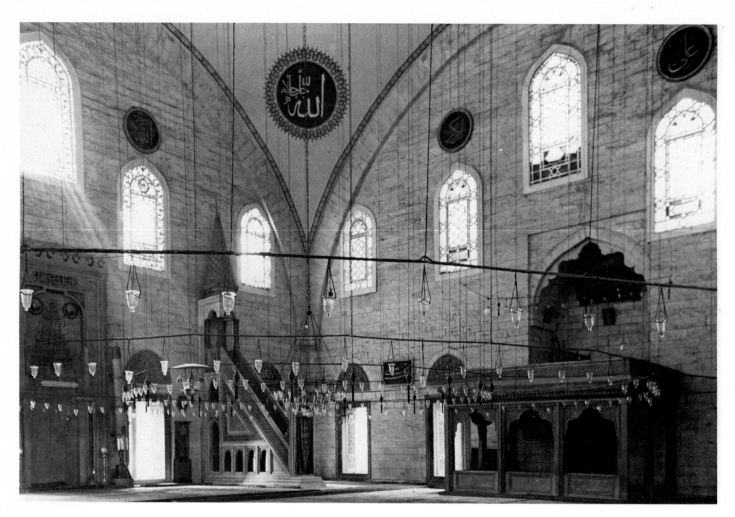

180 Sultan Selim Cami, Istanbul. Interior from the north-east.

inlaid with metal. The frame and its stalactites are of equal quality, but a curious feature is the pair of pendant breast forms where normally there would be bosses or stars. Including those of the portico, as at Edirne, there are eighteen columns. Lateral portals sever the revaks from the portico, unlike those at Beyazit in Istanbul which are set centrally on each side of the court. The portico is paved with a design of flowers which is exceptionally agreeable. The octagonal şadırvan is large and has an ungainly canopy added by Murat IV over one hundred years later.[192] The cypresses at the four corners continue the old and elegant tradition. The polychrome marbles of the voussoirs of the arches and the beautiful rose-coloured conglomerate stone steps and window-frames are finer than those of the parent mosque but its court appears the more spacious because there is no canopy to its şadırvan.

The imaret on the north was demolished and replaced by a girls' school designed by the revivalist leader, Kemalettin, and the medrese has also disappeared[193] while the mekteb with its pleasant portico has been completely but accurately rebuilt.[194] It is a smaller edition of that of Beyazit Cami in Istanbul with its shed roof extending over the porch to rest on arches in the way that p 1 Ibrahim Pasha Cami, on a far grander scale and with a double portico, extends 155 its roof before it. This mekteb once marked the gateway into the precinct, now a dusty football pitch. Sheep still stray there but only sweating youths sit on the outer sofa which runs along all three sides of the court wall. The Garden of the Dead on the south has escaped destruction. It can be entered from the royal yard behind the east tabhane and also from the east end of the precinct. Besides the türbe of Selim I himself there is that of his wife Hafsa or Ayşe Sultan, destroyed in the earthquake of 1894, and that of three young grandsons of Süleyman I.

There is also the tomb of the forthright widow of the ex-Sadrazam Lufti Pasha, Şah Sultan, and latterly that of Abdülmecit and four of his children and the grave of the brother of Mehmet V Reşat. The türbe of Selim is in the traditional form of an octagon preceded by a columned porch; it is very big but has been heavily restored in indifferent taste. The catafalque is exceptionally large. Selim, as many had reason to know, was an exceptionally mighty man who continued to inspire awe when dead. The tiles in the portico are of unusual design and the colours rich while the encrusted woodwork of the doors is noteworthy. The tomb was completed in 929/1523.[195]

The fine workmanship here and in the mosque might be due to the artisans brought back by Selim from Iran, Egypt and elsewhere.[196] After the capture of Tabriz, he also took to Istanbul from Azerbaijan Esir Ali or Acemi Ali (slave or Persian Ali),[197] and according to Ünsal and Öz[198] this mosque and that of Şefettin in Bulgaria are his characteristic works. Mayer[199] also attributes the Cezeri Kasım mosques at Eyüp and at Bozüyük to him, also the Çoban Mustafa Pasha Cami at Gebze, Piri Mehmet Pasha at Hasköy, the second gate of the saray (1523), Hüsrev Pasha at Sarajevo (1532), and the Hatuniye at Trabzon, together with the Valide at Manisa, the Selimiye at Konya, Ayas Pasha at Tekirdağ, and Bali Pasha, which is to be discounted on grounds of its date alone. The rest are as polyglot a mixture of Ottoman styles as possible and the only justification, aesthetically, for supposing all these buildings to be the work of one man is that they all ape other mosques before them and the character of Esir Ali emerges as that of a great architectural magpie. The attribution of a major sultan's mosque such as Selim to Esir Ali, royal architect, is reasonable but unsubstantiated. It would look as if there were no distinguished architects in Istanbul and that this forced Selim to look in Iran for a successor to Yakup Shah. The sparsity of religious building and the lack of invention was due to the sultan's need for a first-class military engineer, and that Esir Ali appears to have been, for the structures attributed to him are sound and extravagantly strong. He died in 1537.[200]

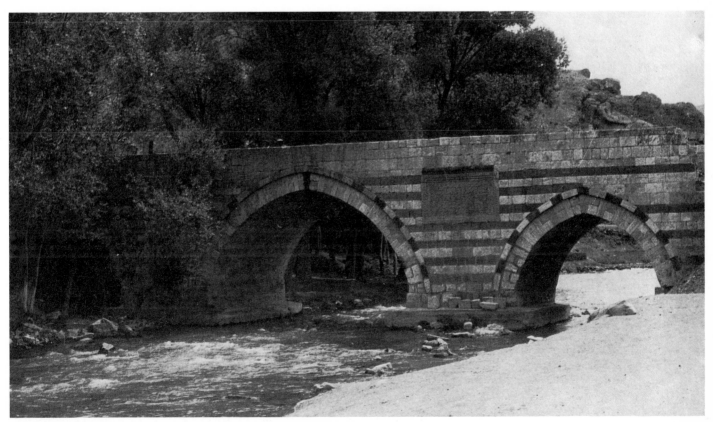

181 Bridge at Hoşap.

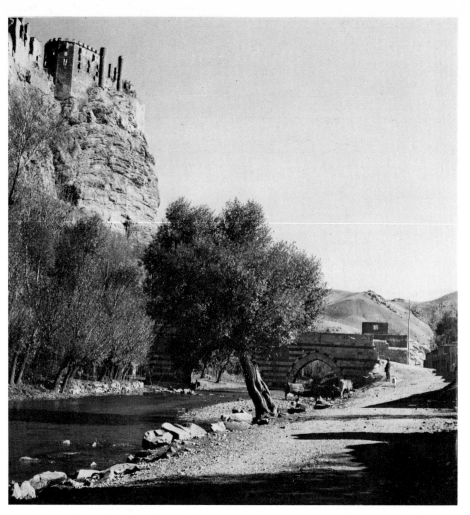

182 *Castle at Hoşap. The keep.*

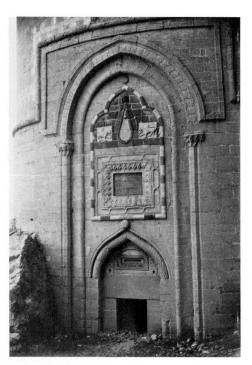

183 *Castle at Hoşap. The great door.*

Of Selim I's military architecture, of which one would expect there to have been a great amount, little that can be certainly attributed remains. This is partly because his work in Anatolia would consist of the repair of existing fortresses and city walls and partly because much of the rest would be in Iran or Syria or Egypt. This is also true of roads and of the causeway, now under water, which he drove across the Tuz Gölü or salt lake, south of Ankara. Hoşap Kale 181 on the Hakkarı border may have been strengthened by Selim I and Süleyman I, but it was firstly a Kurdish or Armenian stronghold probably mainly built in its present form in the fifteenth century, although of much earlier foundation. It stands on a lofty crag, one of many in the region, and is remarkable for its massive towers. The highest is that of the citadel; it has random peepholes like a dovecote made of terracotta pipes, pointing in every direction, probably so that the sentries were protected against the bitter winter cold. The grand gate of the angled entry has elaborate decoration above it which includes that leaf or tear device which is so common in Eastern Anatolia. The town has dwindled away, but extensive walls still stand with their large castellations like open wings. Neither these nor the castle are Ottoman in design or detail although the castle was heavily repaired in 1643 by Sarı Süleyman Bey. It was extensively damaged eleven years later when besieged by the governor of the province, Mehmet Emin Pasha.[201] The crag on which it is set was chosen because the river runs beside it, and this is crossed by a handsome twin-arched bridge of cut stone with 181 patterns in basalt and very fine inscriptive panels. It must be the most decorative bridge of its time and was built in *906/1500* by Zeynel Bey and is thus pre-Ottoman although related to that type.

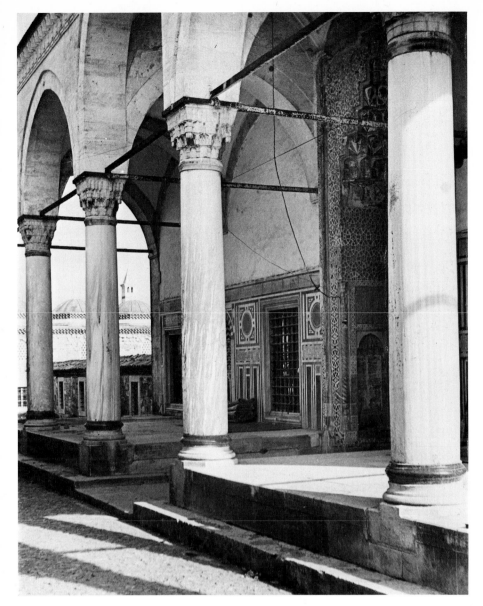

184 Çoban Mustafa Pasha Kervansaray, Gebze. Mosque portico showing the Egyptian marblework.

The vast complex of Çoban Mustafa Pasha at Gebze[202] is renowned for the splendour of its carved marble – the work of Egyptian craftsmen, which could have been brought back from his brief viceroyalty in Egypt or, more likely because they fit perfectly where they are required,[203] cut on the spot by the men still living in exile. The revetments within and without and all the furniture of the mosque form a mosaic of colours. The panels are made up of narrow strips and topped by long carved marble inscriptions; they are twin to the panels from the Divan-i-Kebir now in the north wall of the Hırkai-Şerif at Topkapısaray. It is surprising that the influx of foreign workers had no more than a transitory effect on Ottoman architecture and its development. They plied their trade but taught no one.

Mustafa Pasha had been viceroy of Egypt for a few months in 1522 when he was removed from the post of Serasker, or Commander-in-Chief at Rhodes where his strategy met with no success, and kicked upstairs by Süleyman. He did not remain in Cairo long because his royal wife, Hafise Sultan, complained bitterly that her father had widowed her by executing her first husband, the Vezirazam Ahmet Dukağinzade, in the field[204] and exiling her second. The pasha was an elderly gentleman burdened by rheumatism, twitchings and a habit of dozing, but with his virility unimpaired. He was not to die – perhaps

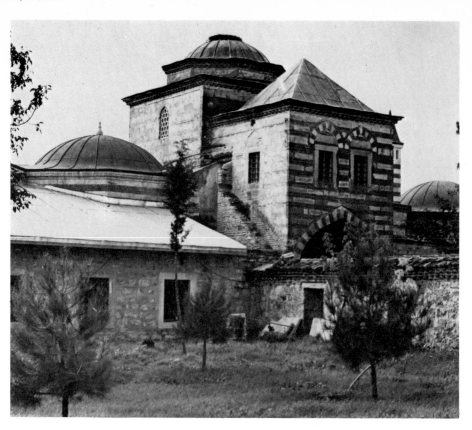

185 Çoban Mustafa Pasha Kervansaray, Gebze. The main entry seen from the garden.

because he spent so much of the day on a litter or in his bed – until over the age of eighty on 27 April 1529. His widow died in 1538, the year of Sinan's appointment as Royal Architect. This is important because the Gebze complex is attributed to him. It could be that he carried out extensive restorations there and even rebuilt some of the sections of the complex, since they are clearly of different dates; but the mosque which is specifically listed as his clearly is not his work, nor is the hamam which still stands in the centre of the town, if only because the squinches are in a style more archaic than any he employed. The work could have been under the direction of Şihabettin Ahmet, Chief Architect of Egypt in succession to his father, who was brought to Istanbul by Selim in 1517.[205] It is possible that Sinan may have had a subordinate job to perform, but not likely.

The Mustafa Pasha Kervansaray is entered through a handsome gatehouse to the west which has a two-roomed vezir's apartment reached by an exterior stair and a verandah with ocak and niches in the deep plaster of the walls. There is also a charming, restored, wooden-faceted cone ceiling under a pyramidal roof.[206] On the south lie the long suite of kitchens and store rooms and the bakery, which are walled off from the mosque garden and have their own door to the street, besides the passage between the wall and their line of doors. To the north are large cells for important guests. Across the north flank of the complex, facing the mosque through the trees of the precinct, are two great public halls, divided by a second gate and hall, which are built at a lower level and form a bulwark. Divided from the kervansaray on the east by a wall and a lane is a tekke and a medrese united by a line of supplementary cells. The tekke has tiny individual cells built round a small court which leads to a semahane in an independent yard. The dervishes, like Western monks, may have looked after the travellers. The annexe has a portico onto a wall across a small garden and is in the shape of a shallow-armed C. Its windows look out onto the lane and the precinct of the kervansaray beyond. There is access to the tekke through a door into the semahane yard and to the medrese through a slype into its courtyard, but the main entry to the court is across a wasteground, which once may have been a garden or orchard, from the road which bounds the south side of the whole complex.

The medrese is orthodox in form and has a handsome Byzantine well-head before its dershane which is set on the east and looks out over the country beyond. The complex has been extensively restored recently by an architect not conversant with its period.

In the garden behind the mosque is the türbe of the founder of the complex, if such he really was. It is set in front of the mihrab wall and is a perfect example of the classical Ottoman form and is most felicitous in its proportions. Each segment of the honey-coloured octagon is framed, and the two tiers of windows are also divided. The door beneath a vaulted porch is on the north, face to face with the mihrab niche.[207] A second kervansaray in the town has disappeared but not the big çeşme in the main square opposite the hamam. The latter has interesting squinches, archaic for the period, and some beautiful marble which still survives.

Some of the mosques at Diyarbakır of Selim's reign and the early years of Süleyman's, have already been discussed. It was the garrison town of the southern provinces of the empire and therefore the winter quarters of the army where the Janissaries were doubtless employed building and embellishing in order to keep warm and out of the mischief which was concomittant with their periods of idleness. In the 1520s, Hüsrev Pasha was governor-general and built his mosque near the Mardin Gate. There is a central dome with two wings under simple shed roofs and a very large pentagonal apse. The mosque opens into a courtyard without an intervening portico. The cells of the medrese are formed round the remaining three sides, except where they are divided by the gate on the north, and are contiguous with the mosque itself on the south. The tabhane extensions of this must have been the dershane. This is the first example of a mosque and a medrese completely united round a shared avlu and the only one I have found where neither gate nor son cemaat yeri divides the two. Hüsrev Pasha has the distinction of being one of the first of Sinan's patrons before he was appointed Royal Architect, and Sinan must certainly have visited Diyarbakır and doubtless studied its mosques.

The small but handsome Yakup Ağa İmaret Cami at Kastamonu was built as late as 904/1547,[208] but it belongs to the pre-Sinan period and to the regional architecture in style. The square mosque, much restored, with its triple-domed portico supported on octagonal columns presumably because no round Hellenistic or Byzantine columns were available any longer, its salient mihrab, and stepped relieving arches to the casements of its façade, is simple, but its setting on the hillside above the town is spectacular. The eighteen cells of the medrese have been broken up each side of the entry where there is a line of six cells on the east side with the dershane forming the foot of the L-shaped portico at the west end. Beyond the entry four cells are set apart in a walled garden and are larger than the rest. Facing the mosque along the west side of the park-like precinct is another L-plan group of eight cells making the standard eighteen in all. Because each section is at right-angles to the next, there is a unity to this group, although it spreads over a large area and has more the atmosphere of a tekke than a medrese.

An outstanding example of civil architecture is the palace of Ibrahim Pasha on the Atmeydan. The identification of this building presents numberless difficulties, some of which will never now be resolved; among these is the great number of Ibrahim Pashas who lived in this neighbourhood at various times. Clearly the Hippodrome was the Downing Street of the Ottoman Empire until the founding of the sadrazam's office and official residence down the hill opposite the Sokollu Mehmet Pasha Kapı of the saray wall. This is a small postern admitting to the park below the Alay Kiosk, so called because it was from this pavilion that the sultan watched the processions of the guilds.

The original Ibrahim palace is tentatively assigned to the fifteenth century by Ünsal[209] in which case it would have been built by that Candarlı who built the Ibrahim Pasha Cami and who was chief vezir at the end of the fifteenth century. Konyalı believed that this first palace was burnt down by the Janissaries in 1524, when it was already in the possession of the sultan.[210] The position of this great

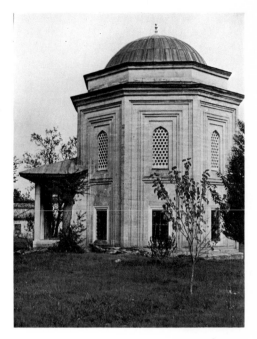

186 Çoban Mustafa Pasha Kervansaray, Gebze. The türbe.

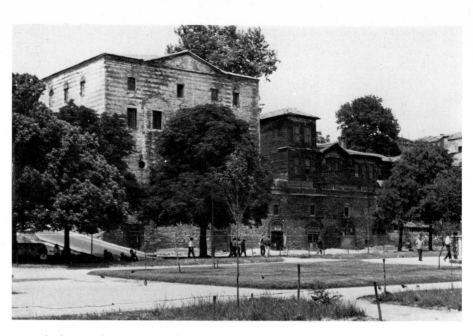

187 Ibrahim Pasha Saray, Istanbul. The Great Hall.

house with its many halls and rooms appears to fit the requirements regarding the placing of the public rooms of the palace of that Ibrahim who had been the Greek boyhood favourite of Süleyman and later his son-in-law and for whom a grand saray was completed on the occasion of his marriage to the princess in 1524.[211] This could be the existing palace. Travellers constantly referred to its splendour and continued to refer to it long after Ibrahim's swollen ambition drove Süleyman to order his strangulation in 1536.[212] To add to the confusion, in 1594 it was inhabited by the third Ibrahim Pasha, sadrazam and brother-in-law of Murat III, who died in office in 1601.[213] Upon the great Ibrahim's execution, the palace must have reverted to the crown.[214] Like the palace of the first Candarlı Ibrahim, those of the second and third were partly schools and associated with Galatasaray and Edirne which took the less successful candidates for the Enderun College in Topkapısaray itself.[215] But the problem of the school alone is confusing, for no authority is able to give the date of its opening. Since it may be that at one time it had to house two thousand youths,[216] but not in Sinan's day, it needed many halls, rooms and broad corridors with sofas for junior dormitories.[217] The eighteenth-century map drawn for the French ambassador, the Comte de Choiseul-Gouffier, often inaccurate, shows the Great Hall of this palace to be the Tuğrahane, or High Court of Justice,[218] and later the college sank to being a prison, a fact, for once, vouched for by reliable, living witnesses. At one time there may have been ocaks for unmarried Janissaries on the Atmeydan[219] which could have survived the destruction which followed on the suppression of the notorious corps because they were taken over by the new model army of Mahmut II.[220] There is also the ruin of a substantial mansion opposite Aya Sofya which spreads backwards into Byzantine structures and which tradition claims to have been the School of the Acemioğlans or Apprentice Pages.

When the diverse evidence is presented and summarized it confuses more than it helps. The wing containing the great hall was built in three separate, unbonded sections and projects at the end of a long wing of chambers too large to be called cells which are strung on two sides of a court full of fine old trees, and which open off a broad corridor with a stone sofa under the windows. They were built as an entity over magnificent vaults which, like those supporting the Yeni Valide Cami at Eminönü, are similar to bridges[221] and seem likely to date from the sixteenth century or earlier. Across the open side of the rectangular precinct, facing the meydan, wooden houses sprawled as early as the eighteenth century and probably before because they appear on engravings of the period.[222] Previously, this section of the palace was faced with tiles and so were the hall and

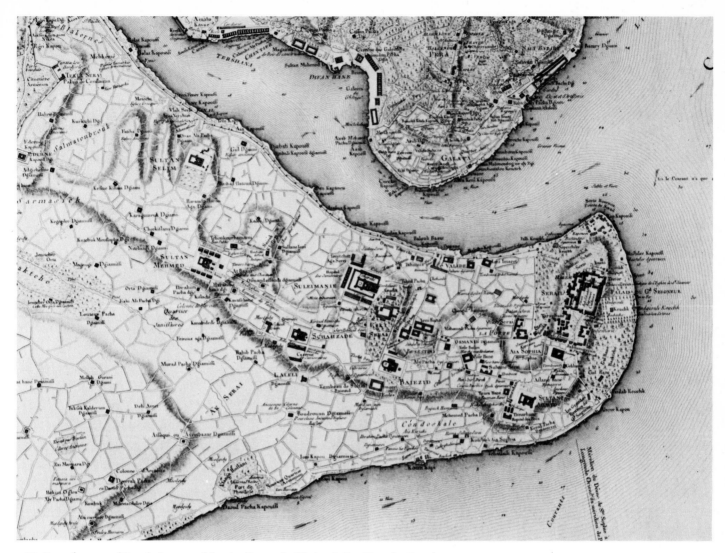

188 Part of a map of Istanbul prepared for the Comte de Choiseul-Gouffier, the French Ambassador, by Fr. Kauffer, 1776.

other kiosks for these can be seen plainly in the *Surname* of Mehmet III. The second part of the palace which closely resembles a double han has been greatly damaged and half demolished. It was built at a different period and stands immediately beside and parallel to the nobler wing but need never have been connected with it. Choiseul[223] marks only this part of the palace as that of Ibrahim; but this might simply mean that in the eighteenth century part of the state apartments was taken over as a court of justice – a function they would already have served as the Divan Hall of the Sadrazam – and an incredibly large court in comparison with the normal mahkeme surviving in Istanbul. It was partitioned in the nineteenth-century manner when the army occupied the palace, although the ante-room to the great hall may well have been refurbished in the previous century. It is no help to discover that the school was often opened and closed,[224] while at one time the residential portion was used to house ambassadors.[225] The *Hadika* this time contradicts all the other authorities by saying that the first medrese at Ibrahim Pasha Saray was founded in *1086/1675* in conjunction with that of Galatasaray;[226] it then goes on to state that in each case two more medreses were added in the same year. Then seven more were added to the Ibrahim palace, which would have made it vastly larger than Galatasaray.[227] The problem turns on what is meant by a school, and in this case the *Hadika* appears to suggest that the palace of Ibrahim was becoming no more than a superior barrack. The *Hadika,* moreover, can only be referring to a later re-opening after one of several closures.[228]

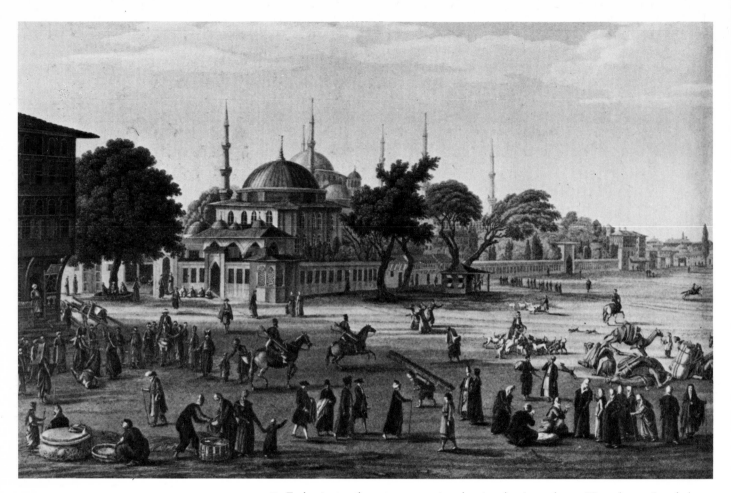

189 Early nineteenth-century engraving showing the Atmeydan or Hippodrome, Istanbul.

Perhaps the original palace was indeed the battered wing that now remains, together with a walled garden set with the private apartments of the harem and the selâmlık, kiosks and parterres, orchards and ponds which reached as far as Çemberlitaş. This palace could have been confiscated from the Candarlı princes upon their fall from favour and eventually presented to Ibrahim as a grace and favour residence, enlarged and embellished, upon his marriage to his royal bride. The private quarters and pavilions have disappeared leaving much of the school, which was also a barracks, and the Hall of the Divan together with the offices of the Chancellor's department. It is surprising that even so well-beloved and imprudent a subject as Ibrahim should raise a Divan chamber greater by far than any of his sovereign's, but it is plain to see on the miniatures, and it supports the theory that Süleyman hoped to delegate some of the supreme autocratic power to an unprecedented extent, because of the growth in the wealth and the territories of the Ottoman dominions. This hall, then, was the audience chamber of the Chancellor of the Empire – not a chief councillor or chamberlain, but the mirror of the shadow of God on earth. It was logical for this hall of authority to become a court of law when the Grand Vezir was granted the significantly large area now occupied by the Vilâyet and the Record offices. It was equally logical for the army to take over the quarters of the Janissary recruits.[229] Above all, the size of the palace and its indisputably correct position facing the Hippodrome is proof that these buildings are on the site of the Ibrahim complex.

The building has been cruelly mutilated and part wantonly pulled down. It was left ramshackle and bedraggled, its floor sleazy and dangerous, by the military, while the basements which are now used as a furniture workshop may equally have been stables[230] or dormitories for the children of the levy,[231] particularly upon their arrival in the city for inspection and circumcision before their dispersal. The great hall and its vaults are of cut stone and majestic in their

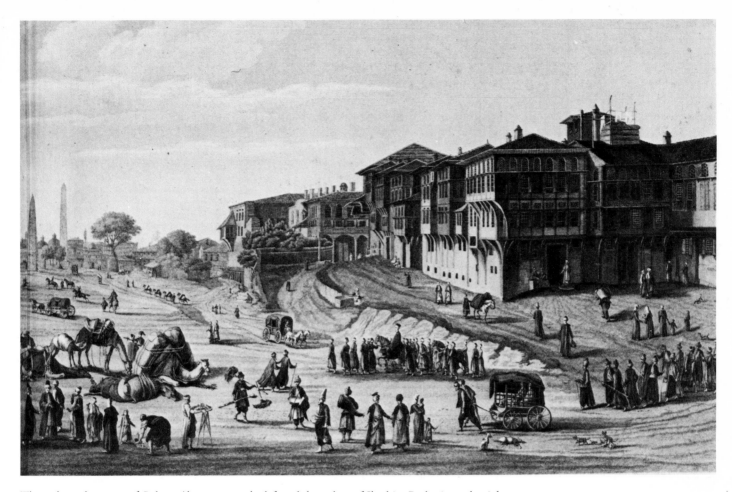

The türbe and mosque of Sultan Ahmet are on the left and the palace of Ibrahim Pasha is on the right.

strength and size. The brick and stone courses of the eastern section are timeless in style but very probably also sixteenth-century. The Divan Hall has been stripped of its many, quite pretty, two-tiered wooden partitions that cluttered its grand dimensions.[232] Under this hall, in the basement, are avenues of stone piers and muscular arches. The façade onto the Hippodrome, and the west side which faces a later Aslanhane or Lion Pit,[233] the remains of which deserve excavation, are austere, but the marks of various bowers and gazebos can still be seen on the south front and the structures themselves are depicted in the Melling engraving. It is hard to conceive of anyone but the Grand Vezir of Süleyman I achieving this great house or school, and one notes Hammer-Purgstall's assurance[234] for he had no doubt that this was the place. Gemelli-Careri, who saw it early in the eighteenth century, was told that it had six hundred rooms, which was probably no more than double their number.[235] It must have occupied a considerable area and could have been nowhere else on the meydan since there was no room. A significant date in its history was 1727 when the Sadrazam Nevşehirli Damat Ibrahim Pasha, favourite of Ahmet III, was established at the Bâbıâli. Until 1843, the palace was made of wood,[236] confirming one's impression that much of the first harem of Ibrahim's palace was also of wood and plaster although faced with tile and set on stone foundations. Thévenot, who was in Constantinople in the late seventeenth century, states that the private sarays were walled like monasteries and we may suppose that the plaisances of Ibrahim Pasha Saray sprawled up the hill and over the site of the present hideous law courts, the Cistern of One Thousand and One Columns, and the Church of St Euphemia besides, possibly, the depressing remains of the palaces of Laurus and Antiarchus. It could not rival Topkapısaray but it was the grandest private residence ever built in the Ottoman dominions; and in its permanence[237] it dared even to defy the laws of God.

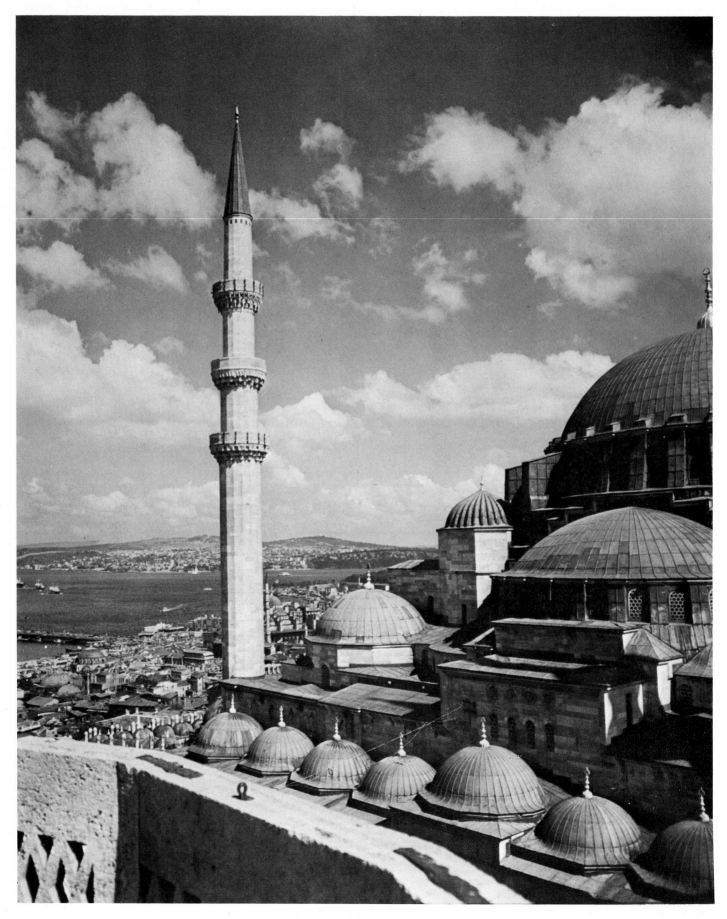

190 *Süleymaniye, Istanbul. Domes of the mosque and its portico.*

6

Sinan – the rise to greatness

THE MOST FAMOUS of all Ottoman architects was Sinan who held the office of Architect of the Abode of Felicity[1] for fifty years. So great was his personality that he extended the powers conferred on him with this office until he became far more than the Clerk of Works and senior engineer of Constantinople: he transformed the office into that of Architect of the Empire and himself into an officer of state superior to his Minister, the Şehir-emini.[2] He was responsible for every detail of city administration[3] including the sewers, fire regulations and the repair of all public monuments. He drew or supervised the plans of every important building in the city and all over the empire and listed more than three hundred buildings as his own – although some he could never have seen for himself – ignoring such minor works as sibyan mektebs which he considered unworthy of mention. He organized an elaborate government department and trained many subordinates, some of whom were men of distinction. He took established practice by the forelock and left the traditions amplified and transformed. His work is considered the climax of the classical period. It is more correct to say that he appeared at the end of that period and took it to its logical conclusion – Süleymaniye – and beyond, to leave it shaken to its foundations in the same manner that Michelangelo[4] shook the Renaissance like an earthquake; for the mosque of Selim II at Edirne was as revolutionary in conception as the Florentine's plans for St Peter's. Sinan had equal pretensions to immortality and he died in office in his ninety-seventh year, the result, it is said, of an accident.[5]

The only record of Sinan's origin are three brief manuscripts in the Topkapı-saray Museum which are attributed to his friend, Mustafa Sâ'i, who is said to have compiled them to Sinan's dictation. This was not unusual in the sixteenth century when many Ottoman statesmen had letters and petitions read to them and dictated their replies, possibly because some, but certainly not many, were illiterate. The three manuscripts are the *Adsız Risale* (Anonymous Text), the *Tühfetül Mimarin* (Architectural Masterpieces) and the *Risalet-ül Mimarin* (Book of Architecture).[6] They are accounts of Sinan's youth and military career and, while their information overlaps, it does not seriously conflict. There is no reason to suppose that they are more inaccurate than decent conceit might make them. Egli,[7] who has peered diligently into the stews of myth, and rendered a service by so doing, permits himself to fabricate a new account of Sinan's mother in captivity, the prisoner and slave of Candarlı Ibrahim Pasha. This enables him to suggest that Sinan might have been of Greek, Serbian, Albanian or even Austrian, origin.[8] The only sure and certain fact is that Sinan was an Ottoman. It is far from proven that he was educated at the Ibrahim Pasha School – a point essential for the support of Egli's hypothesis – since it may not have been open when Sinan was an apprentice.[9]

92

Before summarizing the information in Sâ'i's documents, it is helpful to give an account of the Ottoman Empire in its prime. The society was theocratic and, although the padişah was the Defender of the Faith, spiritual control was exercised by the Şeyhül-İslam, or Mufti of Constantinople, the head of the orthodox religious teachers and lawyers who were collectively known as the Ulema. The civil government was quite another matter. In the fourteenth Ap century a corps of Christian levies was created which was known as the New Army, the Yeniçeri,[10] and which was to attain world fame as the Janissaries. These youths were converted to Islam[11] and formed a formidable infantry force. The lands which the Ottomans conquered in Anatolia and later in the Balkans were heavily populated and, in the main, that population was Christian. It was plainly politic to win the best of the new subjects for the empire. Recruiting was usually organized once every seven years, when recruiting officers selected male children between eight and twenty-two[12] from among the Greek, Albanian or Slav peoples. This levy has caused more indignation than it warrants. It is true that sons were taken away from their families and were unlikely to see them again, but life was brutal everywhere in those days. If a son was unsuccessful in a career and if the family was poor, all contact was lost, but some families were only too glad that a son could go to the capital and seek advancement which would be totally denied him in his home town or village. The real objection was that the system deprived the provinces of their best men, for the recruiting officer sought out those who were the healthiest, the most intelligent and the best looking. From the point of view of the Ottoman government, this wisely reduced the possibility of unrest and rebellion since it deprived the Christian areas of their natural leaders.

By the reign of Mehmet II, after many reforms, these youths were recruited for more than just military duties. The Conqueror established the Imperial College College in his own saray because he wanted a trained civil service. We have seen that the idea was not original, but the school bore the imprint of his own sceptical mind. The numbers varied but there was always an excess of recruits so that they were classified on arrival in the capital according to their intellect and their looks. The élite went to the Enderun College where they would remain fourteen years.[13] The best of these, in their graduating year, already attained such offices as Gentlemen of the Bedchamber, or Falconer Royal.[14] One of the latter was to become the Grand Admiral and later Grand Vezir Sokollu Mehmet Pasha. Nearly all attained government offices of varying importance. The few who ran away tended to be converted prisoners-of-war, who would also be enrolled at the college if they were suitable. They included Italians, such as the Grand Admiral Kılıç Ali Pasha, Austrians, Poles or even French. If the recruit was not worthy of admittance to the palace school, he would be sent to one of the auxiliary colleges such as those of the Ibrahim Pasha and Galata sarays, while the least satisfactory of all were sent to the old palace school at Edirne or to Çanakkale to be raw recruits for the Janissary force. By the middle of the sixteenth century, the obvious advantage of being a devşirme, or child of the levy, was such that sons of Moslems contrived to be accepted and the Janissary ocaks swelled in numbers and declined in quality.

The reason why the system rejected Moslems before was that it was impossible for the son of a true believer to become a slave. For, great officer of State or not, Viceroy of Damascus, Governor of Belgrade, Lord Treasurer or Grand Vezir, these men were slaves, and proud to be slaves, with responsibility only to their sultan and to God. They were also their prince's family and more than his family and this quasi-mystical relationship, which was exceedingly complex, meant that if a man was due to be executed, although his friends might intercede for him, there was neither a popular nor a palace rebellion against the royal decrees. As late as 1730, a man of outstanding ability, such as Nevşehirli Damat Ibrahim Pasha, married to a daughter of his monarch, saw nothing extraordinary in his death being ordered so that Ahmet III might cling to his throne for a few days more. Such a society was hierarchical to the extreme and a code of behaviour existed that determined stance and costume in every detail. The highest officers of the realm stood with hands clasped as a sign of their submission whenever in public in the presence of their sultan, and the despot himself had to submit to elaborate rules of behaviour.[15] It was into this society that Sinan was admitted under Süleyman Kanuni – known in the West as the Magnificent – at its greatest moment when the Ottoman court was one of brilliance and ability in all departments.[16]

According to Mustafa Sâ'i, Sinan was the son of Abdülmenan,[17] whom he plainly calls the erring servant of God, meaning that he was not a Moslem and, indeed, the name was one taken by Janissary recruits on enrolment. He is said to have praised God for making him a Moslem Janissary and thus able to serve in the holy war for Rhodes and Belgrade. He came from the district of Karaman and the Greek lands, but he does not, it is true, specifically call himself a Greek,[18] which, in effect, he no longer was from the moment that he admitted that there was no other God but Allah. Yet after the conquest of Cyprus in 1571, when Selim decided to repopulate the island by transferring Greek families from the Karaman beylik, Sinan intervened on behalf of his family and obtained two orders from the Sultan in council exempting them from deportation.[19] It was Selim I who ordered the first devşirme levy in Anatolia in 1512 and sent Yaya-başıs to Karamania and this is probably the year in which Sinan came to Istanbul. Since he was born about 1491, or at the latest in 1492, he was old for a devşirme youth. He had almost reached the maximum age and this might well explain why he was not admitted to the Enderun College but sent to one of the auxiliary schools. By the sixteenth century the Janissaries were a *corps d'élite,* small in number, dedicated as gazis in war, and turbulent in peace. They were regarded with distaste by the orthodox Ulema because of their alliance with the mystical and heretical Bektaşi sect which had affinities with both the Shi'ites or Alevis and Christianity, and had a dangerous, socialistic popularity with the common people who were the descendants, for the most part, of the original dwellers in the hinterland and whose love for their old beliefs continues to this day. The recruits who failed to gain admission to the imperial school were circumcised, taught the rudiments of their new religion, and sent into the country until they had learnt the skills of a recruit, and Sinan bears witness to this custom.[20] These acemioğlans or cadets were farmed out to feudal Turkish landowners to learn basic skills, toughen up, help with the harvest, and learn Turkish. On their return to the capital, they were apprenticed to a trade before graduating as çıkma when a second selection might promote them to the saray school or send them to serve in the Janissary barracks, the great ocaks or dormitories near the aqueduct.[21] Sinan is alleged to have been trained as a carpenter but Ahmet Refik asserts that he was trained as an architect from the first and that he assisted in the building of important monuments under the leading architects of his day.[22] Only tradition supports this thesis, but it is reasonable to suppose that Sinan did learn mathematics and carpentry and he may also have been put to work on building sites in the winter – when the Janissary corps had too little to do – for the sake of civil peace.[23]

If Sinan was accepted into the devşirme at twenty-one, he must have demonstrated outstanding qualities of intellect and ambition which impressed the recruiting officer. He could not escape a period of barrack service as an ace-mioğlan or recruit before being accepted as a trained soldier in the Janissary corps. The exact date of his admission to the brotherhood of the Janissaries is not certain, but it must have been prior to 1520, when he states that he was fighting on Rhodes, because the acemioğlans were left behind to garrison the capital. This would indicate that he had received a full training over six years or so which was the usual span. Two years after the fall of Rhodes, he was present at the conquest of Belgrade. Promotion then began. He joined the Household Cavalry in time for the Battle of Mohacs in 1526. It is likely that he first came to the notice of Süleyman at that time, for he was promoted a captain in the Royal Guard before being given command of the Infantry Cadet Corps. He then served in

Austria where he commanded the Rifle Corps[24] and continued in this appointment until the Baghdad campaign of 1535 when he was transferred to the Guard again, possibly as commanding officer. When this campaign was over, he asked the sultan for permission to go on the expedition to Corfu and Puglia in 1537 and to this Süleyman graciously consented. Service in Moldavia followed. Then, suddenly, this seasoned soldier states that he was appointed Architect of the Abode of Felicity, that is, Constantinople or Istanbul, an office which he was so greatly to enhance.[25]

The puzzle is how the soldier suddenly became the architect. However, it is clear from Sinan's own account of his life[26] that he had ample opportunity to make himself known to his sovereign. The senior officers of the Household Brigade anywhere are known to their masters, and if any one of them has particular abilities that too is likely to be known. The old fraternal world of the early sultans had been constricted by etiquette, but on campaign protocol has to be relaxed. If Sinan had assisted with the building of defences and bridges, which is probable, then Süleyman would have known. It is claimed that Sinan had converted churches into mosques, built a bridge across the Danube, and launched floats or transports for artillery on Lake Van.[27] Both the latter achievements would demonstrate that he was a trained engineer. The conversion of churches need only have meant that he designed minbers and mihrabs for the existing buildings. These would have been of wood and the work of carpenters. By 1539 he was surely employed by senior ministers and he had built his first recorded mosque, for Hüsrev Pasha in Aleppo when that officer was Governor-General there. When Lutfi Pasha succeeded Ayas Pasha as Grand Vezir, it is probable that he had already noted Sinan's aptitude when he had served under his command. The appointment of Architect was vacant in 1538 and here was a man with two qualifications, for he had proved his practical ability as an engineer and his authority by his distinguished career as a soldier. Nor would he have held a post of trust and honour in the guard of his monarch if his courage and loyalty had not been long observed.[28] p 2

The question which remains is when Sinan learnt anything at all about engineering. It is not to detract from his eminence when it is emphasized that the job of architect was highly pragmatic in those days. The plans were rudimentary and all smaller buildings were repetitions of former types. By 1538, thousands of medrese cells, for example, had been built and those cells were the basic domed unit which was then universal in Ottoman architecture and this basic unit could be enlarged to cover the harara of a hamam or contracted to cap a revak. What is true of the dome is true of arch and vault and squinch and, even when bonded, Ottoman buildings were an assembly of parts in the manner already discussed in connection with the Hudavendigâr mosque at Bursa or the Beyazit II Külliye at Edirne. It was possible for the architect to draw up sketch plans and appoint an apprentice architect or foreman to carry out the work for him not only because there was nothing unusual demanded of the builders but also because of the standardization of measures and forms. Miscalculations could arise and also clumsy improvisations (and nowhere are these more evident than in provincial mosques misattributed to Sinan out of local patriotism), but these were not frequent because novel ideas were avoided. Moreover, Ottoman buildings were erected with an extravagant margin of safety, and this wasteful use of valuable material and labour is a measure of the conservative basis of engineering techniques in the first half of the sixteenth century. p 4
p 1

When he came to build the Aleppo mosque at the start of his career, therefore, Sinan did not need great experience nor does the work reveal much. His masons would advise him from their traditional lore, even if he had not been conversant already with the details of such elementary mathematical formulae as this relatively simple structure demanded. Above all, Sinan was a remarkable man who was able to learn and continue to learn until over eighty years old and who developed a capacity for achieving ideal proportion in the envelopment of space. He was forty-seven when he was appointed Royal Architect and within seven years he had solved the problem of centralized space in the traditional form with the Şehzade mosque, the first of his major works, and with it brought all previous Ottoman endeavour to a logical conclusion. It was not a puny mind which had impressed some of the ablest ministers in the history of any country, for the reign of Süleyman saw the full flowering and justification of the devşirme system, and men like Lutfi Pasha and Sokollu Mehmet Pasha, of Bosnian royal blood, or the Croat plebeian Rüstem, the financial genius, and a host of others were no more likely than Süleyman himself to overlook greatness and still less likely to fail to appreciate it.

Sinan was not appointed to a sinecure, nor only to display his creative abilities as an architect. He was to administer the Office of Works and train a team of subordinates. Throughout his life, Sinan delegated the construction of lesser buildings, else he could never have had the time for the personal supervision of those major works which, because of their magnitude, like Süleymaniye, or their inventiveness, like Mihrimah at the Edirne Gate or the great mosque of Selim II, required his constant presence. The long list of orders published by Ahmet Refik[29] reveal a remarkable diversity of tasks – some of which would have been familiar to a man who administered a military encampment – calling for considerable experience. Some jobs were straightforward and to be expected: he was to open new windows in the old mosque at Edirne, to build a new and modestly vaulted, as opposed to domed, room behind the palace kitchen, or to repair a bridge. He was also to supply architects to build a castle on the Danube or to support the Persian expedition. He was constantly concerned with the repair of drains and waterworks and worrying about the encroachments on city pavements by shopkeepers' counters and boxes, problems which harass the municipality to this day. He had to find four hundred master carpenters, which can have been no small task, and also have ocaks built in wooden houses so as to reduce the risk of conflagrations. He himself requested royal orders to be issued to bring carpenters in from the provinces. He had recourse to nomads for rough work and repairs. He was worried about the wages of his men and the idling of his Janissaries. He had to defend himself against the charge of filching water and lead for his home[30] beneath the Süleymaniye while complaining, himself, about an attempt by neighbours to grab some property of his own in the country. Meanwhile, some of his workers rioted in Edirne and people persistently threw dirty water into the street. He must have had nightmares about drains; the subject recurs like a theme tune: and all the while he would be building a masterpiece, such as the Selimiye at Edirne. Selim II, who appears to have been an attractive but weak personality whose heart may or may not have been broken when his wine cellar was destroyed in a palace fire, was interested in his architect's work down to the last detail.[31] His orders indicate that he, like other sultans, actively interfered in the choice of decoration and the design of every aspect of his mosque. Sinan was instructed to use certain marble at that moment on its way by sea, and he received orders about the calligraphy to be used and about the stairs and floors. All this while he was so short of skilled men that he had to recruit gypsies.

His concern for his relations, when it was decided to restore prosperity to Cyprus by repopulating it with Greeks from the Kayseri region, has been noted. He was equally concerned about vacant land in Kayseri which appears to have belonged to his family, and there is a royal order stating that it is to be restored to its rightful owners.[32] Nor did he forget his nephews and niece in his two wills. One nephew was converted to Islam and moved to Istanbul to become a hunter, doubtless taking advantage of the fame of his uncle. Sinan's brother, it appears, remained a Christian but his widow is listed as a potential beneficiary, just as is Sinan's own wife, along with Emine Hanım, who was left twenty-three thousand pieces, and Kamer Hatun, left four thousand; there is no knowing who these two ladies were. Sinan's own children predeceased him.[33]

From a little much has to be deduced; but this is fitting because the sixteenth century was an age of strictest protocol designed to diminish the importance of

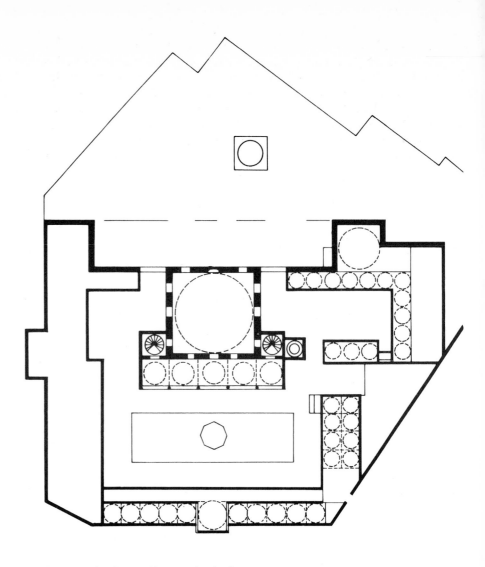

191 Hüsrev Pasha Cami, Aleppo. Sketch plan.

the individual before God. The Ottomans were still freer than other Islamic states, where the names of any artists are hard to find, but they were not concerned with individual rights however much some personalities contrived to emerge and radiate. It is, therefore, by means of the buildings themselves that the evolution of Sinan's genius must be traced. Even if he did assist in the building of Selim I Cami at Istanbul or the Gebze complex of Çoban Mustafa Pasha, there is no proof that he was entrusted with their design and every likelihood that he was not. The churches of the Balkans and the bridges repaired and built on several campaigns are unrecorded. It is therefore to Hüsrev Pasha's mosque that one must go to inspect the first attempt by Sinan to achieve an important monument. It was important because it was among the first Ottoman mosques to be built in Aleppo, and his patron was not only governor and commander-in-chief but of royal blood and great pride. When he fell from favour and was deprived of high office and the trappings and dignities which went with it, he turned his face to the wall and died. Sinan built a sumptuous türbe for him in Istanbul, which would seem to express his gratitude to a great patron. The mosque and its double medrese were built in the winter of 1536–37 between two campaigns and its coarsenesses were partly due to the haste with which the complex was constructed. The only inscription is dated 953/1545, but this is likely to be the date of the completion of the külliye, for Sinan could not have been in Aleppo after 1538. It was important to build an orthodox medrese in a city full of hetero-dox Moslems if only to assist in the support of stable government in a wealthy province.

The Hüsrev Pasha Cami is square and spacious but the dome is relatively low. Its present decor is plain and inoffensive. The workaday minber has a low and inelegant cap and the mihrab has patterns of fussy marble inlay in the local tradition. Although both were designed for the mosque, they are unrelated to each other. Each of the lower casements on both east and west has a rectangular window above it which is flanked by two round lights, a form popular in Syria. They are set out of alignment. The windows of the façade are also clumsily spaced and so awry that those each side of the central entry collide with the springing of the pendentives of the cupolas. Even the two external mihrabs are not centralized. This is because Sinan did not, or could not, resolve the problems created by his portico being wider than the main building.[34]

The portico has five domes, the centre arch and cupola being slightly higher than those on either side. The mosque dome has sixteen windows and, therefore, sixteen buttresses to form a drum, together with four pairs of flying buttresses at the corners. With his first mosque, Sinan had to cope with the extension east and west of his portico beyond the breadth of the mosque itself, else it would have appeared too narrow for its height. He masked the extremities of the portico with the addition of a vestigial tabhane room[35] each side of the mosque façade, and he was to continue to use this solution throughout his career at such mosques as Mihrimah at the Edirne gate, or with Sokollu Mehmet at Kadırga. The sofa at Hüsrev Pasha is very high indeed, even higher than that of Fatih in Istanbul, approaching a metre on average.[36] The polygonal minaret is thick and clumsy but reasonably lofty and it still has the stumpy sixteenth-century cap which in so many mosques was replaced by a tapering one in the eighteenth century. The gallery is supported on stiffly cut corbels which have a band of Damascus tiles beneath and lack the hanging finials which would make them into stalactites. The decoration at the base is crude and the base itself is high, so that the shaft begins at the level of the roof of the prayer hall. At the foot of the shaft is a crested black stone band which is due to Syrian influence; such bands will recur in Sinan's work in various forms, especially in the provinces.[37]

The broad, rectangular avlu with its relatively small Ottoman şadırvan and garden of fine trees is a delight, although its revaks and cells were savagely mauled when the present school was constructed in 1319/1901.[38] Indeed, this large medrese may not be the work of Sinan at all, or not any more, so greatly altered and mutilated has it been. The long north revak has shallow domes, except for the eyvan which now contains a staircase. It is groin-vaulted and so is mediaeval in feeling. The exigencies of the site enforced a distorted but practical juncture with the west wall. Indeed, the north revak overlaps so far that it was possible to cut a window facing south. This haphazard approach to problems arising from a not completely rectangular site was to occur again at Mihrimah and Zal Mahmut Pasha mosques. Through a gate on the south-west is a second small court and medrese, with a traditional dershane with six, large, vaulted cells onto an L-shaped portico. Beside the entry and directly opposite the dershane is a three-domed bay which could have served for summer duties. On the south-east side of the complex is a corresponding large dershane with a similar three-domed extension which served the principal, much larger college. The columns and capitals of the lesser medrese's portico are coarse and ugly. They are of interest, just as are the eyvans in the centres of the revaks of the main court, precisely because they are of such poor workmanship. The complex is roofed with a miscellaneous collection of vaults and domes made to fit awkward corners, the tabhane rooms being remarkable for their hexagonal and segmented form. The right-angle corners of buildings are cut away in order to relax the severity of the geometry. It is bold and tough and, in its Syrian setting, very Ottoman. Hüsrev Pasha succeeds in confronting the formidable citadel on the hill above it. With its pleasantly green principal avlu it is a forerunner of Mihrimah; none the less, any who looked on this and managed to see in it the spring and fountain of Sinan's genius would indeed have been gifted judges of their fellowmen.

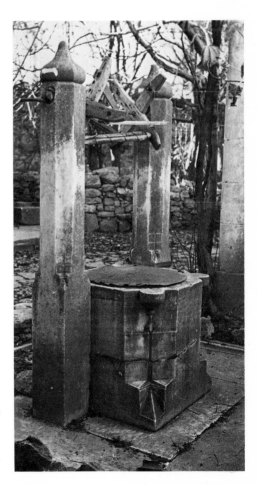

192 Haseki Hürrem Complex, Istanbul. The well-head.

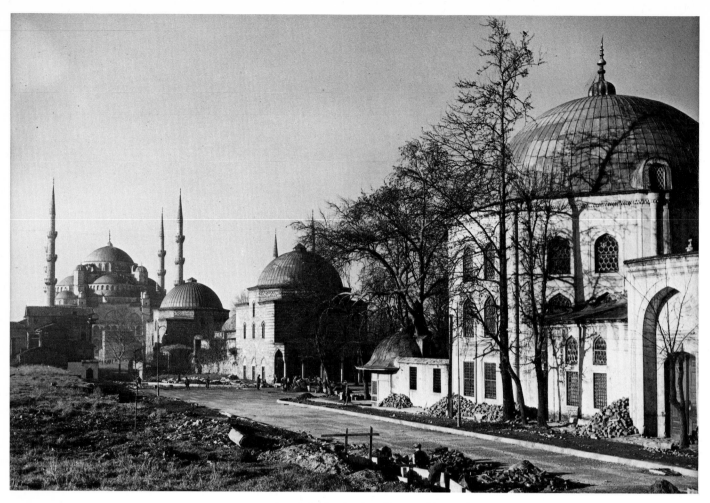

193 Istanbul, the city that Sinan and his students were to transform, showing the site of the Great Palace of the Byzantine Emperors, Sultan Ahmet Mosque and the hamam of Haseki Hürrem with, right, the türbe of Mehmet III.

It is probable, but not certain, that Sinan succeeded Acemi İsa in his office as Architect of the Abode of Felicity, and there was certainly some delay between the death of the old Persian and Sinan's taking up of his duties.[39] The first work attributed to him in Istanbul after his return in his new post is the health centre of Haseki Hürrem, Roxelane, the Russian wife of Süleyman,[40] at Aksaray. It was endowed for sick women of any colour or creed by this remarkable woman who had reached the height of her power and who was the last woman to be formally married to a reigning sultan.[41] The Haseki Külliye is a very large cluster of buildings, significantly not set out in order but conforming to the exigencies of the site and the streets which bound it. It is likely that it was not built all at the same time since the medical school, hospital and imaret are set shoulder to shoulder as if jostling each other.[42] The mosque across a lane was doubled in size in *1021/1612* by one Hasan Bey.[43] It was a simple domed unit with a wide five-domed portico, the west end of which was masked by the minaret. There is now no knowing what happened at the east end, because this is where the additional half was added, with the result that, inside, the mihrab clumsily faces the two supporting columns which replaced the original wall. The main dome is supported by elegant shell squinches.[44]

The medrese, consisting of sixteen cells, a dershane, washroom and a slype into the garden in front of the imaret, is U-shaped, flanking a square court with revaks totalling twenty columns and a wall with two windows on each side of the entry facing the street. It was, therefore, in the established tradition of the medreses of the reign of Beyazit II. The chevron or baklava capitals are decorated with rosettes and also serpents which could be a reference to Aesculapius and

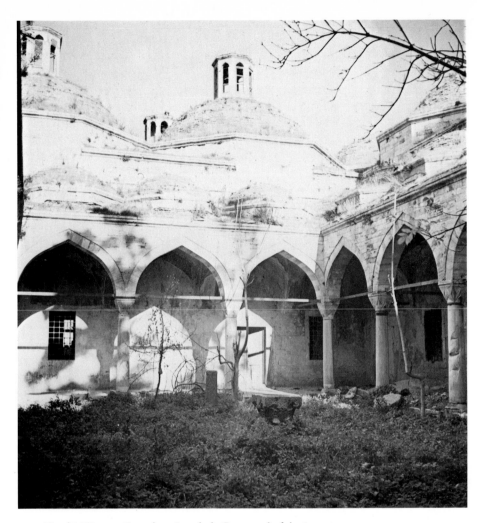

194 Haseki Hürrem Complex, Istanbul. Courtyard of the imaret.

the science of medicine. The spaciousness of the court is agreeable and suggests that the Syrian delight in capacious precincts had influenced Sinan. The hospital and the medrese were conceived as conjoint units, for they were built back to back with a narrow passage between them. This permits access from the imaret to an extension of the wards, now used as a boilerhouse and offices, for this hospital is still used as a clinic, while the bedridden are housed in a new building nearby. The imaret is large and planned simply. To the east and west, flanking the rectangular court, are four large halls, divided on the west by a passage to the hospital, and, on the east, by a second passage, now leading to nowhere in particular. The main entry into the court is in the middle of the south end and is approached by an attractive avenue. The four halls were storerooms and dining-rooms except for that on the north-west which houses the great oven of the bakehouse. Set centrally on the north side is the large kitchen with a range of fires and a huge table where nowadays two cooks cope with great piles of cabbages and carcasses of sheep. Externally, the four octagonal chimneys and the four ventilators of the kitchen are impressive and so are the large domes of the halls which tower over those of the daruşşifa.

The hospital is unusual and the court not Ottoman in form. It is possible that this building was begun by Sinan's predecessor and that Sinan only completed it, which would explain why the medrese is stuck on with some waste of space and why its gates are not aligned with those of the mosque precinct across the lane. The hospital entrance is preceded by a short, covered passage due to the need for privacy because it was for women.[45] It is for this reason, perhaps, that there is a small cell attached to the north-east corner of the imaret for use by the porter who had no need to invade the ritual privacy of the hospital itself. From the doorway in the angle of the octagon, one steps into the court, which is related to those of the Kapıağa Medrese at Amasya[46] and the later Rüstem Pasha Medrese in Istanbul. Opposite the entry in the equivalent angle to that of the porter's passage, the four privies are awkwardly inset. On the street side between these two areas there is simply a high wall, naturally without windows, and on the flanks are two large square eyvans that are now glassed in with a consequent unfortunate diminution of the original sense of space. Beyond, divided into two identical sections, is the main building containing a total of eight wards and four smaller rooms either for consultation, operations, or possibly private patients.[47] The design is compact and makes intelligent use of space, although thickening of the masonry to cope with fan-shaped corners occurs just as it did at Amasya and at the Beyazit hospital at Edirne. Because of the need for privacy, no consideration is given to the outlook; the only external windows are on the west and face the flank of the imaret a few feet away, and the north-west ward in particular must have been cold, dark, and depressing to live or die in.

The complex is much better built than that at Aleppo and it is compact if not well ordered. Unlike Hüsrev Pasha's foundation, Haseki Hürrem's is elegant as well as strong, and each individual building is a competent job of work. It has suffered from the extent of the restorations and the medrese has lost its splendid faience lunettes which once enriched its severe façades. The use of tiled lunettes first appeared in Istanbul at Fatih, where they may not have been original but added in the sixteenth century after the earthquake of 1509. They were used by Sinan with great discretion in order to add sufficient brilliance and so articulate the grave grey stone of his façades. Examples of his use of tile in lunettes are in the Hadım Ibrahim Pasha Cami at Silivrikapı, Kara Ahmet Pasha Cami, and the Atık Valide above Üsküdar. His lavish use of faience on the façade of Rüstem Pasha Cami is an exception and he never used it again in this manner, which suggests that he was there obeying the express orders of Mihrimah Sultan. He used decor to obtain the maximum effect and did not dissipate it with excesses as Mehmet Ağa was to do in the Ahmediye on the Atmeydan.

There is one more dated work built by Sinan prior to the Şehzade mosque, and that is the türbe, and possibly the hamam, of the Grand Admiral Barbarossa, Kaptan Pasha Hayrettin Barbaros. It was built in 948/1541[48] by the shore at Beşiktaş on the European seaboard of the Bosphorus where the fleet used to assemble.[49] The mausoleum is severely classical and is an octagonal hall preceded by a porch carried on four columns of Marmara marble with baklava capitals bearing a rectangular lead roof. The windows at both levels are set into the wall, the lower ones being rectangular beneath an incised arch and the upper set into the arch itself. The plainness of the tomb serves to emphasize that excellence of workmanship and accuracy of dimension which was the mark of the work of Sinan, in such vivid contrast to many Byzantine monuments which stand around. The interior has been totally restored, but the ceiling is related to that of the türbe of Süleyman and has ceramic bosses inset in flowers. The severe classicism of this türbe contrasts with the lavishly ornamented and much larger türbe of Hüsrev Pasha below Fatih Cami, which was built in 952/1545.[50] This use of cresting and ornate detail was abandoned by Sinan, except on rare occasions, after the completion of the Şehzade mosque. The türbe is tall and both the inner and the outer octagons[51] are ornamented with friezes, the former of arabesques, the latter of stalactites. Each corner of the octagon is ribbed with pilasters, and slender ribbing frames the two-tier windows. The interior is neglected and the rats have eaten the last of the brocade coverings of the plain deal sarcophagus while saplings push their way above the cresting which rims the dome.

Süleyman the Magnificent was approaching his capital in triumph on his return from the conquests of yet another Balkan campaign when he was greeted with the news of the death of the heir to the throne, his much loved son Şehzade Mehmet, at the age of twenty-two. The tragedy brought Sinan his first major commission, for in November 1543 his sultan commanded the building of a great

195 Türbe of Hayrettin Barbaros, Beşiktaş.

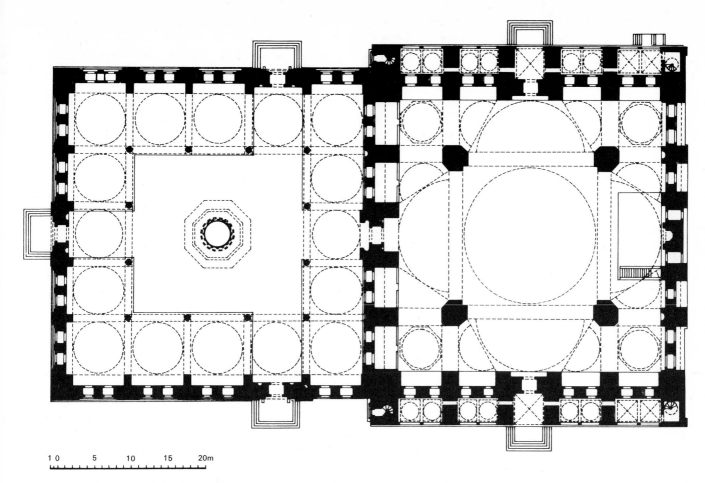

1 0   5   10   15   20m

196 Şehzade Cami, Istanbul. Plan, scale 1 : 500.

202 complex at Şehzadebaşı in honour of the prince.[52] At that time there were only
three major mosques in Istanbul besides the converted Hagia Sophia. Fatih Cami
was stiff and out of date,[53] Beyazit II Cami also lacked suppleness, and Selim was
merely a grand room. Sinan made no attempt to excel Hagia Sophia but was
78 absorbed by the concept of the centralized dome and turned to a plan like that of
77 Fatih Pasha Cami at Diyarbakır or Piri Pasha at Hasköy, and the ancient tradition
of which these mosques' form was then the climax.[54] Sinan built a firm and sturdy
pile with the thrusts of the central dome partly absorbed by four equal half-
domes, the four corners of the mosque strongly reinforced, and with four piers
incorporated into each lateral wall to help withstand the force of dome and half-
domes. Four stabilizing turrets serving as anchors rose above roof level from the
four interior piers, solid and four-square, from which the pendentives sprang.
The proportions were still based on multiples of two and the interior was still
divided into sixteen equal parts, four of which formed the central area beneath
the great dome. He avoided anything reminiscent of the tabhane rooms of the
Bursa period – as lingered still under the lateral domes of the Beyazit mosque –
since the government no longer depended on Ahis but on the centralized
98 organization of the Enderun College and the bureaucracy of Topkapısaray.
70 Nor had Şehzade any relationship with Hagia Sophia where the symbol of the
dome surmounted a processional way. In this monument Sinan had only to
express the earthly squareness of the gathering place of the faithful under the
canopy of eternity where as many as possible could see the mihrab and so follow
the leadership of the imam during prayer. The essential was to reduce any
obstruction to a minimum, whereas at Sophia the intent was to cut off the side
aisles, amounting to nearly fifty per cent of the interior space, completely. The
result was an apprentice work,[55] which was what Sinan acknowledged it to be,
which offers remarkably little obstruction but nonetheless offers some. This

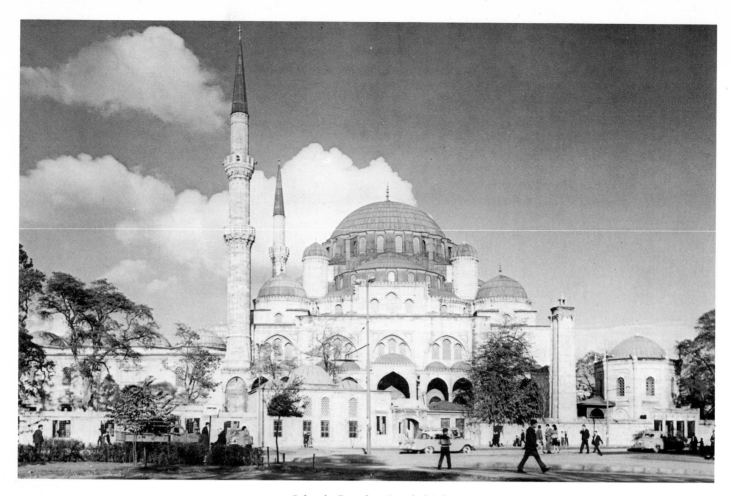

197 *Şehzade Complex, Istanbul. The mosque and türbe from the west, with the sibyan mekteb in the centre foreground.*

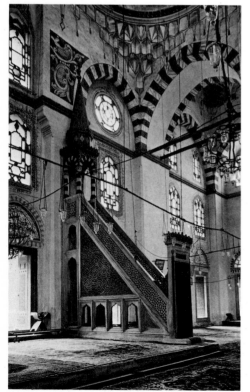

198 *Şehzade Cami, Istanbul. Minber.*

problem was to continue to fascinate him until he reached its solution, when the poet emerged from the chrysalis of the engineer and achieved the mosque of Selim II at Edirne thirty years later.

Şehzade is so often criticized, even by those who praise Sultan Ahmet Cami, that its merits need to be stated. It would be of first importance simply as the largest of the great cruciform mosques, but Sinan strove to modify the limitations of the proportions inherent in such a plan and there is as much variation inside the building as the formality of the vaulting would permit. The mihrab wall is hardly recessed at all in comparison with the north wall because the buttresses are external. The east and west lateral walls are brought half forward to make two outside loggias, only one storey high, which add a new dimension and interest to the exterior.[56] The north wall retains its complete buttresses inside to help carry the traditional gallery and to create the established recesses each side of the great entry. It was also essential in each instance to avoid any projection where the portico would be built after a mosque hall was completed. There are lateral doors in the centre of the east and west walls which over-emphasize the symmetry inside and divide the loggias outside somewhat clumsily. The four octagonal piers, from which the pendentives carrying the main dome spring, are fluted in an unsuccessful attempt to lighten their appearance and to add interest to them. It was a feature which Mehmet Ağa was to copy, less excusably, in Sultan Ahmet. Sinan rightly rejected such inorganic solutions to the problems of vitality in ornament, although columns continued to be faceted for religious symbolic reasons. The arches carrying the four corner domes necessarily had to be lower and smaller than those carrying the main dome,[57] and the problem of uniting these, which is masked in Hagia Sophia, was never to be solved. However, this inequality also gives movement to the arches and emphasizes the importance of the central dome. Because marble is heavier than stone and stone than brick, the voussoirs are of brick, painted in red and grey to imitate marble. An interesting interior feature are the grilled ventilator holes over the lower casements related to those of the Ulu Cami at Bursa. Slits for air appear above doorways in much older buildings, including the cells of the royal Selçuk kervansaray on the Aksaray-Konya road, but these ventilators are much more noticeable. Directly due to the influence of Hagia Sophia is the use of exedras in conjunction with semi-domes. They expand the area of vision and communicate with the isolated corners of the chamber. They also help destroy the feeling that the building is a conglomeration of units and so prepare the way for a fluid approach to interior space new to Ottoman architecture. Another Byzantine technique employed in Ottoman architecture at Şehzade is the use of urns in the shoulders of the pendentives in order to lighten their weight, in the manner of the Baptistery of the Orthodox and San Vitale at Ravenna.[58] The use of leaves of lead over a bed of mortar on a single thickness of brick, exemplified by Hagia Sophia, was by now an established Ottoman practice. The whole interior is thirty-eight metres square and the dome accordingly half this – nineteen metres – in diameter, but it is only thirty-seven metres high and not thirty-eight metres as one would expect.[59] This could be due to repairs.[60]

Even the columns of the courtyard are set at intervals which are equal to half their height, and there is no variation in the dimensions of the five domes of the son cemaat yeri, only in their greater elevation. The domes are large and there are therefore only sixteen covering more than three-fifths of the area of the whole avlu. The open centre is further diminished by the heavy canopy which covers the şadırvan, but this is an addition made in the reign of Murat IV. The great main door is in the centre of the portico which is divided by two equally large doors from the revaks on either side. The court covers an area equivalent to that of the interior of the mosque itself. The use of pink and white marble in the voussoirs is attractive as are the motifs in relief which cover the twin minarets (because although dedicated to Mehmet this is a sultan's mosque). This charm

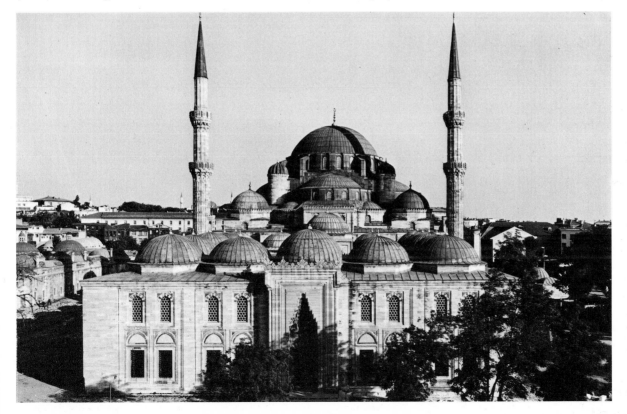

199 Şehzade Complex, Istanbul. The mosque and its courtyard from the north with part of the tabhane on the left.

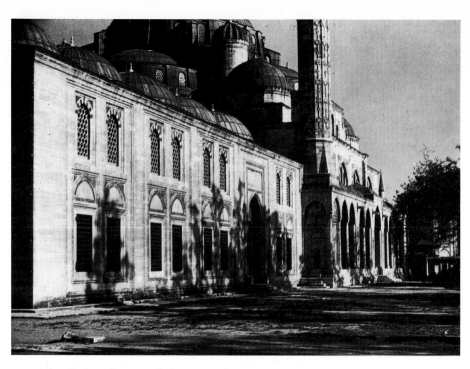

200 Şehzade Complex, Istanbul. Mosque from the north-west.

Sinan was to reject as dangerously sweet afterwards. The minarets are set at the extreme north-east and north-west of the mosque façade on bases which act as terminals for the lateral galleries outside. Their twin şerefes are carried on stalactite corbels. The caps are tall but they have been restored and the original ones would have been squat in the earlier sixteenth-century manner. They serve as fine foils to the upsurge of dome and semi-dome and robust decagonal turrets. This is the first formal, classical build-up in logical but aesthetic terms of the exterior mass of a great mosque's roofing. The use of cresting at lower levels is over-rich as is the segmenting of domes of the stabilizing turrets, but the grand contrast between the silhouette of the pyramid of the building to the cavity of the court is triumphantly achieved.[61] The windows of the court are framed and grouped in twos, and two pairs of arches sharing a central column are framed each side of the east and west doors; but the monotony is broken by five sets of flanking arches above the loggias into which three tall and slender windows are set. How much the four small corner areas are detached is clearly shown outside by the way in which they fit squarely against the great flanking buttresses.

With Şehzade, Sinan appreciated that a mosque preceded by a court equal in area, or nearly so, could present no true façade and that its flanks, therefore, serving as substitutes, required order and grandeur. This was also the case at Süleymaniye and Selimiye at Edirne where the side doors were the principal entrances for the public and the sultan and his court. This important contribution to Ottoman architecture was acknowledged by Mehmet Ağa at the Ahmediye. He extended the arcade along the flank of the court, but his style lacked spirit and failed to do justice to his concept. In the eighteenth century the east entry became markedly the true façade at Nuruosmaniye. The ambiguous orientation of such mosques is a cogent reason, in addition to aesthetic considerations, for the placing of the ablutions along the flanks.

The Şehzade complex is vast, for the outer precinct like that of Fatih had room for caravans to camp under the trees. The mekteb, on the west by one of the outer gates, is spacious and north of it is a side entry to the cemetery besides two su terazi (towers for carrying water by pressure up and down pipes) which are of later date.[62] The medrese on the north-east, now a women students' hostel, is large with a very fine courtyard containing a twelve-sided şadırvan in the middle, the usual range of cells on each side, eyvans, and dershane. The imaret, across the road on the south-east, is also of considerable size, with a large central yard between the kitchens and the refectory. There is a remarkably big tabhane which has been converted into the laboratories of the Vefa High School. But the garden of the dead is the heart of the matter, for here originally, among the cypresses, the tomb of Mehmet Sultan stood alone, approached down an avenue from a gate in the south-east wall.[63] The octagonal türbe is faced with marble enriched with green breccia and terracotta. The dome and its drum are deeply fluted with thirty-six ribs, and a richly carved frieze crests the octagon supported by multiple corbelling. Each facet has two lower casements and two upper lights recessed in panels and framed in alternating blocks of red and white marble. The porch has been glassed in against the weather with the inevitable loss in that sense of freedom and openness which is usually so attractive a quality in Ottoman or Renaissance architecture. The noble door is flanked by panels of Iznik cuerda seca tiles in which full blue, primrose, white and a fresh green predominate. The inscription over the door grants a foretaste of the overwhelming beauty of the interior, which is panelled to the level of the dome with a heavenly meadow of magnificent faience tiles in which are set the upper stained-glass windows delineated in fragile plasterwork under the painted dome of eternity. The sarcophagus has lost its brocade covers and the candles no longer burn, but a richly inlaid wooden cage still encases the symbol of man's death.[64] Doors and casements are equally handsomely inlaid. The tomb is not large and the tiles are overwhelming but without vulgarity or any weakening of their force. Sinan was able to use the finest work of the early Iznik period to create his mirror of paradise, and the unprecedented beauty of this sepulchre must have been a consolation to Süleyman when he came, in a kaftan of black watered silk, into this room of the apple-green colour of youth.

The complex was completed in 1548, but other minor work had been achieved at the same time. In November 1539 an event of importance for the future work

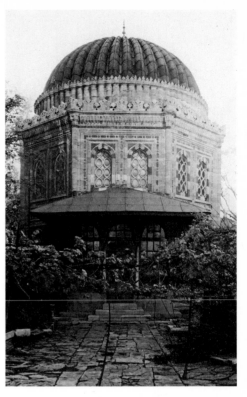

201 *Şehzade Complex, Istanbul.*
Türbe of Şehzade Mehmet.

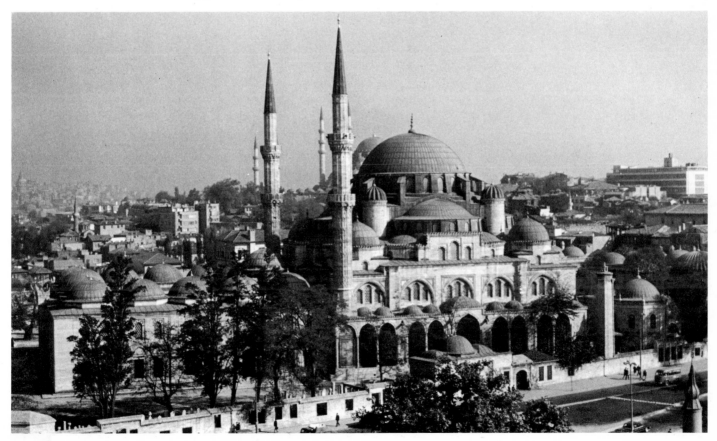

202 *Şehzade Complex with, behind, the Süleymaniye. The column left of the türbe is a*
su terazi or water-tower.

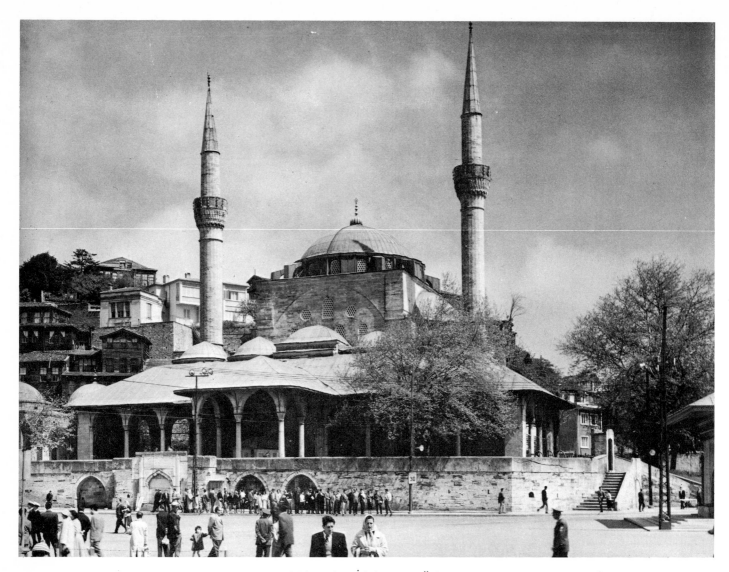

203 *Mihrimah or İskele Cami, Üsküdar. The second portico is preceded by the loggia of the şadırvan.*

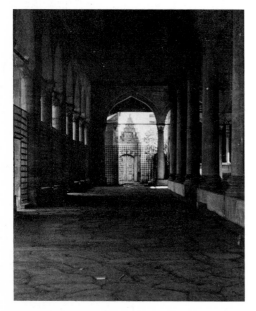

204 *Mihrimah or İskele Cami, Üsküdar.*
The outer portico to the west door of the medrese.

of Sinan took place. Mihrimah Sultan[65] married Rüstem Pasha, Viceroy of Karamania, who was to soar through the offices of fourth and second vezir to be Grand Vezir by 1544, an office which he was to hold, to his immense personal profit, until his death in 1561 except for a brief politic break between 1553 and 1554.[66] Involved in the overthrow and execution of Şehzade Mustafa, Rüstem's unpopularity, that gave him the nicknames of Mekri (Cunning Fox) and Kehle-i Ikbal (Lucky Louse), was increased due to the severity of his fiscal policy which accounted for the solvency of the expanding empire in spite of the ever-growing costs of its administration. His meanness and cupidity were said to be such that his father and brothers were left to beg in the street when they came, over-hopefully, to share in his prosperity. Yet his endowments were considerable and it would seem that he, as much as his royal wife, took pleasure in building.

It was for Mihrimah that Sinan built the İskele or Jetty Mosque near the shore at Üsküdar together with a medrese, now a clinic, an imaret, which has vanished, and a sibyan mekteb.[67] The exterior of the mosque is handsome and, together with the medrese lying alongside it, stands grandly above the water. The interior is clumsy in some of its details and the entry is abrupt and cramped. This is because Sinan had to build between the shore and the steep hillside into which he cut to place his large mekteb with its fine winter room and summer loggia above a spacious vaulted basement. The mosque and medrese are raised on firm foundations above the strand. Steps lead up to the platform on which the mosque

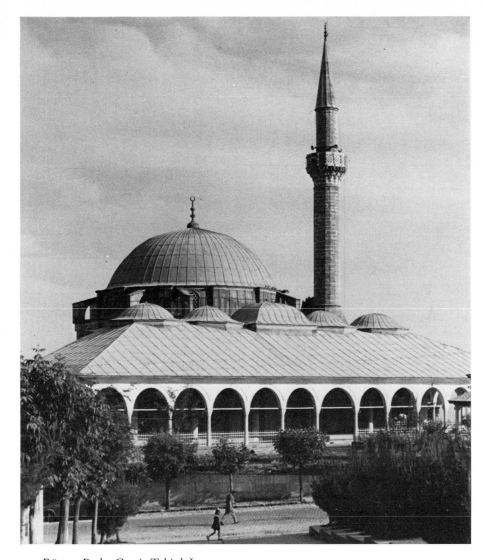

205 Rüstem Pasha Cami, Tekirdağ.

is built and to the precinct set to the west. The son cemaat yeri has five domes supported by columns with baklava capitals. There was no room for a courtyard and so Sinan added a second porch with which he enclosed the inner portico
04 with a shed roof borne on columns with stalactite capitals, for the sake of variety, and piers for reinforcement at the corners. From the centre of this second portico a square loggia, its shed roof supported by twin arches on three sides, thrusts
06 towards the sea to cover the ample şadırvan. East of this are türbes including that of the Grand Admiral, who, oddly enough, is not buried in his own complex across the Bosphorus at Beşiktaş. This is probably not the first classical use of a second portico in Ottoman architecture because there is one at the Adliye Cami in Aleppo which is dated 1517 and, therefore, earlier. It might have been added at a later date but this does appear most unlikely. Sinan, who worked in Aleppo, would certainly have been familiar with this mosque, but the Adliye second portico is heavy in form, compared with the more strictly Ottoman variety, even though large circular apertures were cut in the spandrels. A double portico existed, in effect, in the early form of mosques which were based on the plan of the Umayyad mosque at Damascus and so on the House of the Prophet at Medina where the mosque was effectively a series of porticoes.

Rüstem Pasha and Mihrimah seemed to have been particularly interested in the double portico, since all three of their mosques in Istanbul had them and the
05 Rüstem Pasha Cami at Tekirdağ has an outer portico thirteen arches wide.

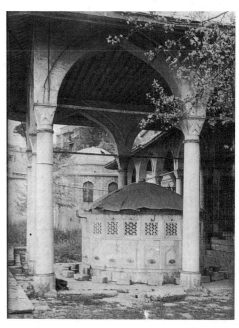

206 Mihrimah or İskele Cami, Üsküdar. The şadırvan.

This mosque may have set a fashion for the use of the double portico with country mosques and for the mosques of vezirs in particular. The mosque is small and the work was not supervised by Sinan, for the window frames are crushed against the central buttresses of the flanking walls and the lunettes of the octagonal support for the dome are set off-centre to catch the light. The capitals of the outer portico are unadorned and primitive in form. The foundations of this revak are not bonded and the mosque was extensively restored in *1257/1841* but the probability is that there were always two porticoes. As with later Sinan examples, the outer portico encloses the inner on three sides. Traditionally, the inner have stalactite and the outer porticoes baklava capitals.

At Üsküdar, Sinan had not exploited the form before, and it is noteworthy that he used it with ingenuity and achieved a frontage to his mosque which is both logical and elegant and, in the evening, poetic in its play of shadow. Moreover, the three-dimensional depth of the colonnades is contrasted with the long flat flank of the medrese. The square main block of the harem of the mosque is as uncompromising as that of the Valide Cami at Manisa. It rises starkly from *149* behind the broad roofs and domes, its main dome crowning all. The half-domes on the east and west are obscured to some extent, and this gives the impression that the elegant minarets are set unusually far apart, the whole effect being of stateliness which must have been greater still before the foreshore in front of the building was cobbled and crowded with taxis and trucks. The second minaret, which is so essential for the balanced design of the complex, shows this to be a sultan's mosque; the greater mosque which Mihrimah built for herself at Édirnekapı has *11* only one.[68]

The interior is a partial recession to Fatih on a small scale which is emphasized by the loftiness of the central dome which makes the lateral half-domes appear mean and strained; this would be true outside as well were they not obscured.[69] The two corner domes on the south-east and south-west fail to extend the kible wall but remain as detached as they are at Şehzade, a point which is made painfully obvious because they are lower and because of the coarse design of the elephant feet and their capitals.[70] The north wall is cluttered with recent mosque furniture and partitions, the müezzins' mahfil and such oddments as a model of an unnamed and improbable shrine. There is a door in the west corner onto the precinct, off which is a miniature graveyard with tombstones topped with carved *20* turbans with heavy coils and folds so strong in form that they are worthy of comparison with the sculpture of Picasso. The türbe of Kaptan Pasha Sinan is an excellent plain classical work next to the west door into the medrese where the tiny garden has been cluttered with a ponderous tomb in the nineteenth-century eclectic style. The medrese stretches, lean, along its bulwark, against the steep hillside. Steps from the present street level on the east lead to a terrace from which access is obtained to the courtyard through a lateral door beside the substantial dershane. The revaks are now glassed in but the fountain remains and the court is handsomely paved. The curve of the hill necessitated the setting of the medrese at a slight angle which increases the perspective and the sense of length, but this must be accepted as fortuitous and not design although a similar effect occurs at Edirne with the great han that Sinan built for Rüstem Pasha below the Eski Cami.[71]

The mosque with its three half-domes is no more than a truncated four-leaf-clover design and for this the site must partly be blamed. It is significant that Sinan never used this plan again, even when forced to build mosques on awkward sites which compelled a design broad rather than long. The accomplished workmanship and design externally reveals the considerable growth of his skill due to the exacting test that the Şehzade Cami had imposed, and thus far he responded ably to the requirements of a difficult site at Üsküdar. It is true of all his later work that the more difficult the terrain, the more Sinan's imagination could escape the trammels of tradition, just as was the case with Ottoman architects earlier at Bursa and elsewhere. Doubtless, Süleyman decided that Sinan was now ready to undertake the major architectural project of his reign.

*207 Mihrimah or İskele Cami, Üsküdar.
Tomb in the west wing of the portico.*

Seven years lay between the completion of the mosque of Hüsrev Pasha and the planning of the mosque of Şehzade on a simple flat plot in 1543. It was only to be seven more years before he was to plan the greatest imperial neighbourhood in Istanbul, the Süleymaniye Külliye above the Horn. In 1550, he had been royal architect for eleven years and had had time to build up his department and train the great number of assistants that the task demanded. He was nearly sixty but still in his prime.

By 1550, Süleyman had moved his private residence from the old saray at Beyazit to the seat of government and the college at Topkapısaray.[72] The kiosks and pavilions with their gardens and courts were abandoned to those women of the harems of dead sultans for whom no suitable husbands had been found. It was clear that the large park and women's cemetery that stretched down the hillside in the heart of the city covered an area that was too valuable to be left for old women to wander in now that the padişah had departed. Süleyman was fifty-four years old and past the height of his powers[73] and his glory but he was still Kanuni, the Codifier, by which name he was to go down in Ottoman history, and he was no less a Gazi, a victor for Islam. He could not expect to live for ever: the time had come to build his own imperial mosque and there was treasure accumulated from the loot of Belgrade, Rhodes, and Baghdad. He had already endowed one great mosque, but it was dedicated to his son; the new foundation was to be his alone. Moreover, the increase in the importance that he gave to orthodoxy in the latter part of his reign necessitated the enlargement of the university set up by Fatih Sultan Mehmet at his own mosque on the crest of the fifth hill.

When the Sultan sent for his architect, Sinan Ağa, the instructions must have been clear and comprehensive. The site of the new social centre was to occupy that half of the gardens of the old saray, now the House of Tears, that faced towards the Golden Horn. Besides the mosque, four major colleges[74] were to be built together with all the usual charitable services including the soup kitchen, a hospital and asylum, a hamam, kervansaray, tabhane and other appendages as well. How unlimited the funds placed at Sinan's disposal were is apparent when one inspects his monumental achievement today. It was the work of a man of matured experience, of a brilliant engineer who had a trained team at his command.[75] The accounts, which were faithfully rendered, are in Armenian and, besides the intendent responsible for them, many of the masons were probably Armenian or Greek.[76] An Armenian, Trdat, had repaired Hagia Sophia after the great earthquake of the tenth century, and Armenian workmanship was spread over Anatolia and the Caucasus and had penetrated into southern Italy.[77] It could only be due to the excellence of his workmen that Sinan was able to finish his task in less than seven years, although the tradition is that Süleyman was displeased with his slow progress.[78] It was the foundations of the terrace on which the mosque is raised which must have consumed the first months, because the site, which was admirable for parkland and gardens like that of the former plaisances of Topkapısaray, presented considerable problems to an architect who sought to erect an enduring monument.[79]

Sinan was not free. If he ever regretted becoming a Moslem, there is no reflection of this in his architecture nor was any hint of heresy attached to his name as was the case with Davut Ağa, his successor, who was to be executed in 1597 while engaged in building the Yeni Valide Cami at Eminönü. The Islamic tradition was bred into Sinan's heart and mind. Every aspect of the work is Islamic, from the mystical number of cells in a medrese to the centralized concept of the mosque itself which was divided into sixteen sections with four under the central dome in just the same way as Şehzade Cami had been planned. Yet the mosque and its complex are full of ideas and surprises and Sinan exploited every aspect of the site. The mosque had to stand in the midst of its dependencies, the spiritual centre of all the charitable and educational enterprises. Moreover, it was to be the most important mosque above the Horn. The uneven site had already made it clear that it would have to be set on a platform but this was also

symbolical: moreover, Sinan set it against the skyline so as to dominate the   *19*
city when seen from Galata. On the Beyazit side, the medreses and hospitals were
grouped at the same level so that the domes of the mosque rose out of a massive
concourse of smaller cupolas. But on the eastern, seaward side the platform ends
abruptly above the street where Sinan built his own house, to supervise the work
more easily, and later built his tomb at the corner of the garden. Here the two
lower medreses descend the hillside by a series of steps. The result is that, seen
from Galata, their lesser domes lead up to the mosque which rides unobscured   *22*
on the skyline together with the independent domes of the türbes of Süleyman
and of Haseki Hürrem. Thus he took advantage of the site to achieve that monumentality which is the dominant aim of Ottoman architecture, and, with
Süleymaniye, Sinan establishes himself as a personality emergent from the
anonymity of the Middle Ages.[80] It is impossible to discover how much he knew
of the Italian Renaissance and its ideals, but Süleymaniye has assimilated so
many aspects of Renaissance architecture that there appears to be more than a
parallel development. The elegant courtyard of the imaret is meaningful to   *21*
anyone brought up in the traditions of fifteenth-century Florence; less obvious,
is the relationship of the great mosque itself to the ideas of Alberti.

   Alberti was concerned with the ideal church which was to be raised above
the distractions of daily worldly life: his windows were to be so high that all that
could be seen through them was the sky. Sinan did not go so far as this, since the
casements had become an essential functional part of a mosque, but they were
so deep that they appear to be detached units. Alberti took from the Eastern
Church that cosmic conception of the dome which Sinan had also inherited,
seeing God as the centre of the circle, the symbol of the universe.[81] He believed
that Nature enjoyed the round above all other forms. The circle, therefore,
was the ideal form together with all others determined by it which he listed as
the square, the hexagon, the octagon, the decagon, and the duodecagon: all
forms common to Ottoman architecture. Harmony resided in the perfection of
geometry in architecture just as in music. The perfect building was one where
nothing could be added or taken away without destroying the harmony of the
whole. To such a canon, Süleymaniye also conforms. It is true that Alberti took
three because it is the divine number, but he makes use of the simplest multiples
in the same way that Sinan inherited multiples of two when working out the
proportions and ratios of his buildings.[82] The two architects shared a passion for
pure geometry as great as their devotion to the symbolism of the circle and the
dome.[83] Alberti learnt from Vitruvius; Sinan from the direct study of Hagia
Sophia in the light of his training in the Ottoman tradition. The two men also
share a puritanical approach to decoration, seeking the ideal of pure philosophy.
For both, the laws of harmonic numbers commanded universal conformity so
that the concept of God as the perfect geometrical figure, the circle, was as easy
for Sinan to grasp as it was for Alberti who accepted the teaching of Nicholas da
Cusa.[84] The Christian mediaeval expression of the cruciform church, in honour of
Christ the victim, had returned to the universal ideal of the Essence expressed as
the Pantocrator of the Eastern Church.[85]

   The similarity of the work of Alberti and Sinan is matched by the contrasts.
The monuments of the Italian Renaissance are the sum of their parts, whereas
with the works of Sinan the parts are subordinate to the whole because the
movement is always upwards to the central dome. Even the often compared
Santa Maria della Consolazione at Todi, built by Caprarola with the advice of
Baldassare Peruzzi, within and without is a conjoining of distinct parts.[86] Externally, the detachment of the central dome is three times underlined. Firstly, the
dome is set on a high drum; then the drum is drawn in from the edges of the
square central block on which it is set; and then its detachment is increased by the
balustrade which marks all four sides of this central block. In some sketch plans for
churches which were never built, however, Leonardo designs buildings which
externally show an integration of parts which, together with stabilizing turrets
nearly as tall as minarets, if much fatter, might well have served for mosques.[87]

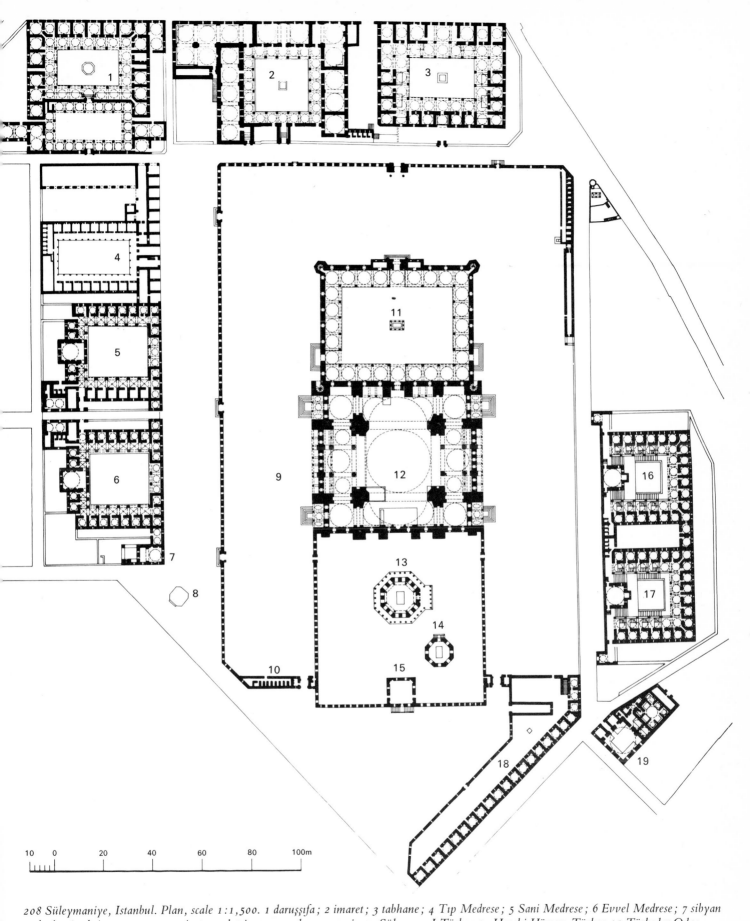

208 Süleymaniye, Istanbul. Plan, scale 1:1,500. 1 daruşşıfa; 2 imaret; 3 tabhane; 4 Tıp Medrese; 5 Sani Medrese; 6 Evvel Medrese; 7 sibyan mekteb; 8 taksim; 9 mosque precinct; 10 latrines; 11 avlu; 12 cami; 13 Süleyman I Türbe; 14 Haseki Hürrem Türbe; 15 Türbedar Oda; 16 Salis Medrese; 17 Rabı Medrese; 18 darül-hadis; 19 hamam. There are coffee houses in the ground floor of the Evvel and Sani Medreses.

The insurmountable dividing line between Sinan and the Italians lies in his concern with volume rather than form, with simplification not enrichment, and his consequent exposure of material rather than search for effect.[88] In the West, man remained the measure, at least in the imagination of the architect; in the East, the measure was a totally abstract conception of God. In Italy, however noble the dome may become, the great portal of the west façade is a tribute to the nobility of man whose God is man made perfect. Significantly, with a mosque there is no façade but a portico, and that is preceded by an enclosed courtyard. Its door is small and seems intentionally to diminish the importance of men, as do the doors of Salisbury Cathedral which, in relation to the magnitude of the west front, make midgets of those who enter in. None of this precludes Sinan from being aware of the ideas of the Renaissance where they were akin to his own, but there could be no universality in his approach because Mecca is not Rome. Süleymaniye cannot, therefore, be compared with Alberti's Sant' Andrea at Mantua except in certain details. It, in its turn, might influence, but could not be absorbed by the West. It is interesting that Hawksmoor first intended to base the Radcliffe Camera on Süleymaniye but abandoned the project because of the expense; fortunately, for sketch plans show that it would have been a travesty of its model.[89]

The noble foundation was endowed with hans and kervansarays, streets and villages, and a plenitude of farms. It needed them to support the mosque officers and servants, doctors, cooks, and many tradesmen, the students and scholars, the poor and the sick, their feeding and their shelter. This vast wealth was assured by the sultan and his family and also those who cared, conveniently, to prove their loyalty at the same time to God and to Süleyman Han. It was still sufficient to support three hundred people as late as 1900. Two streets of traditional one-man shops were set back into the foundations of the outer precinct and leased as small iron-foundries, while along the elegant piazza which runs from the taksim (a cistern where the water is channelled into its respective conduits) to the asylum, were cobblers' shops and coffee houses[90] specializing in the smoking and distribution of hashish.[91] It is known as the Tiryaki (Antidote) Meydan to this day.[92] The rent from these enterprises augmented the revenues of the foundation. The shops were built with two exits so that they could be divided into two.[93] The buildings round the mosque were kept low intentionally and the piazza was kept narrow in proportion. The eaves projecting over the shops help separate them from the colleges above them as well as providing shade. The whole of the outer court of the mosque and all the auxiliary buildings on the north side are set on a vast system of vaults, which contain a sewage system so large that it would be possible to drive a jeep down it. The medreses on the west side are raised on additional vaults against the gentle slope of the hill. These vaults had to be strong enough to bear the massive weight of the mosque and to absorb the roots of the many fine trees which bring shade to the precinct.

Behind and above the shops which face onto the piazza are the Evvel (First) and the Sani (Second) Medreses which today house the Süleymaniye Library.[94] Each had a rectangular court, which is now a garden, with a large dershane in the centre of the west flank and an open summer loggia occupying the area of three cells opposite. The dershanes stretch backwards behind the cells and also forward, and so divide the north revak into two. This creates a vestibule at the corner onto the flagged passageway which divides one medrese from the other. Another unusual feature is the narrow area between the alley wall and the cell windows which admit light while being shut off from the throng going to and fro between the colleges. The two entries face each other and both project to the level of the outer wall. At the far end of the passage, behind each college, is a house which Sinan built for the müderris or preceptor. These are the only two private houses by Sinan still in existence and, happily, they are still used as homes. Built of stone they form a unit with the medreses of which they are an extension.[95]

Contiguous to the Evvel Medrese is a small domed primary school, or sibyan mekteb, which is not recorded as the work of Sinan. It is reached through a

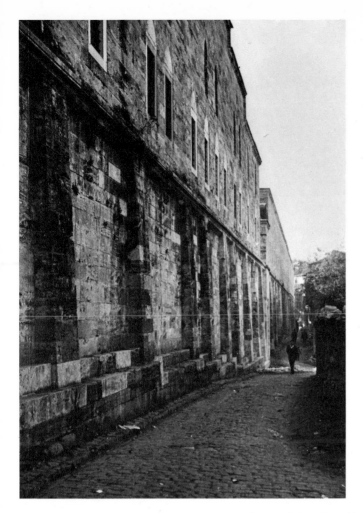
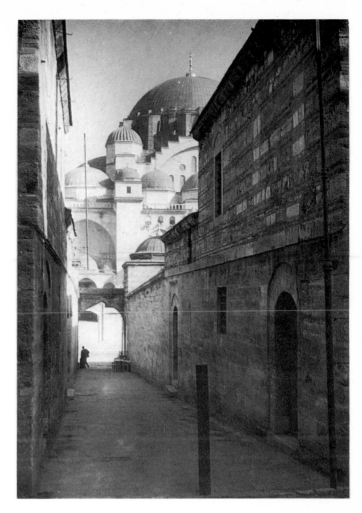

209, 210 Süleymaniye, Istanbul. Left: street of vaults below the tabhane, imaret and darüşşıfa. Right: the alley leading to the mosque between the two houses attached to the western medreses.

lobby, made out of a cell, and across another narrow yard divided from the school garden by a high wall so that the children should not interrupt the studies of their seniors. The mekteb is a domed hall with a large sofa under a second dome in front of it for summer lessons. Little papuçluks are cut into the sofa where children could leave their shoes.[96] From the Sani Medrese on the north-west admittance is gained to the vast space, now a pleasant garden, between the medical school and a modern maternity clinic. Like the east cells of the medreses, those of the medical school are raised above vaulted shops and on the north, the pharmacy, and are reached by stairs. There is simply a line of cells facing onto a corridor which is closed by a double cell at each extremity.[97] There is evidence that this, the foremost medical school in the empire, once had cells facing revaks on the other three sides of a square in the area of the present garden. Not a trace of these remains. An interesting feature is the complexity of the flues leading from the vaults below to the cells above. The Tıp Medrese has a postern gate onto the side street onto which the central gate of the tımarhane or hospital opens.[98] It is a building of considerable grandeur, standing on a huge rampart high above the lane beneath. Below it is a storey of rooms which may have harboured some of the insane[99] or formed part of the kervansaray, and below this are vaults now used as workshops, and stores which could originally have been stables. Similar great vaults lie under the neighbouring imaret and tabhane but their gates, which face each other across the enclosure between these two large buildings, are sealed and access is impossible. These, also, may have been stables.[100] The hospital has an outer court behind the blind wall which faces the street, containing three small halls. East and west two narrow passages lead to another lobby and to a garden.

Two other cells are difficult to explain unless they were latrines. On the north side a second door leads through a second blind wall into the inner court with its sixteen domed cells which are larger in their proportions than any other cell in the complex, for they are approximately five metres square and not three metres. It is to be supposed that they held more people. A passage into the garden on the west side upsets the rhythm of the arches. It is balanced, on the east side, by a cell so narrow that it is a mere wardrobe, one and a half by five metres. It is not exactly on the axis of the passage opposite, but it looks as if it was intended as a passage before its door was walled up. The inner court is oblong and had a fine pool with a fountain in the centre, and the arches of its revaks are broader than those of the first court and the effect is at once grander and more peaceful.[101]

The tımarhane is divided from the imaret, now the Museum of Islamic and Turkish Art, by a broad stairway which leads down to the astonishing street which runs behind the vaults of the complex on the north side. To walk there is to gain a true impression of the immense task which Sinan undertook, because the two buildings on the north side tower above one the length of the way which gently rises to the east. Between the imaret and the tabhane there is a large plain gateway into the yard between the stables under these buildings, which have already been described. The imaret has its main gateway parallel with that of the hospital and the hospice opening from the broad street which divides the social services from the actual precinct of the mosque. Steps lead down to the courtyard with a square pool and a typical Ottoman fountain in the middle, like an inverted stalactite capital, from which the thin jets of water bristle like the quills of a porcupine. In the corners four stricken plane trees shade the parterre of flowers. The court is thirty metres square and has five arches on each side which spring from carefully matched antique columns. The proportion of width to height at the crown of the arch is two to three, and of width to the springing is equal. The central arch is slightly wider, however, but not so much so that it breaks the leaping rhythm of the colonnade, which is carried round the court without interruption at the corner, where there are only columns and no strengthening piers. The rhythm is so powerful that a sense of the circular is present in the square. The decorative elements are sober in the extreme. A double border marks the conjunction of the voussoirs of the arches and the soffits, each of which is articulated with a projecting stone waterspout. The baklava capitals are echoed in the simple design which runs along the lip of the pool. The larger domes of the halls behind the domes of the porticoes change their spatial relationships as one moves and so sustain interest. The doors and the casements are ample but plain, stone rectangles, and the revaks depend on the cross arches and their springing, together with the tie-beams which are common to all Ottoman porticoes, for the articulation of their perspectives and the simple exactitude of their proportions. Each segment is a domed square and thus related to the great dome of the mosque and to every other dome, as opposed to vault, of the four hundred domes[102] of this complex.

To the right of the entry there is access to the kitchen yard with its separate gate, and to the latrines. The kitchens with their four immense ventilators lie behind the great refectory along the whole of the west side of the court under four domes. The refectory is thirty-two metres by eight metres and lofty in proportion. It is noteworthy that there is now no ocak; perhaps the crowds kept the hall warm. In the north-west corner is the door to a chamber almost as large with a stone sofa running the length of the north wall where casements look out across the valley and the Horn below. This room had immediate access to the kitchen but the walls have been reconstructed. In the centre of the north side is a second such hall in which is a mighty stone balance for portioning out food in bulk. This hall was therefore a store, as may have been the L-shaped room at the north-east corner. At the south end of the east revak is a huge grindstone, which suggests that all the east rooms were stores. It, and the massive balance like a crane, are indications of the vast quantity of foodstuff handled each day.[103] From the south-east corner there is access to the stable yards, latrines, and the tabhane.

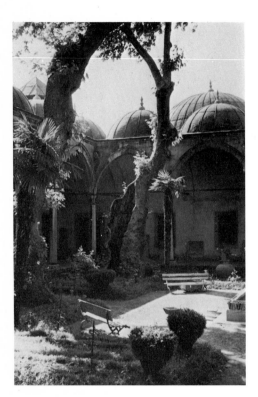

211 Süleymaniye, Istanbul. Imaret courtyard.

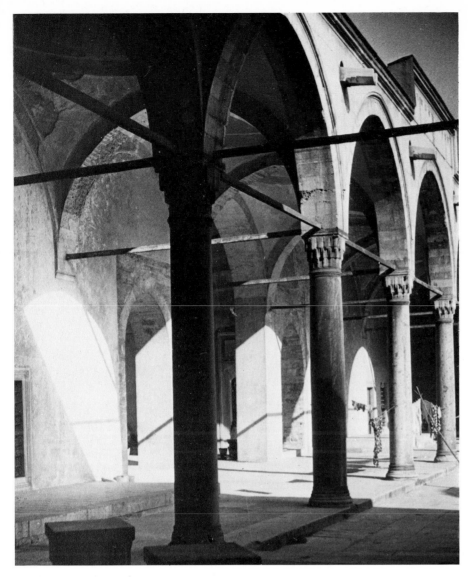

212 Süleymaniye, Istanbul. Tabhane courtyard.

The principal entry to the tabhane is through a masking wall like those of the upper medreses. The passage between the outer gate and the portal is broader than the others. It leads to a small walled garden on the east and to the latrines, imaret, and stable yard beneath the tabhane on the west. The rectangular courtyard of this hospice – the largest in Istanbul – is austerely grand and spacious. Across the oblong pool there is a fine open eyvan with three grand domes and with halls opening off on either side and windows which look out to the Horn and the hills beyond. The halls (6·50 × 5 metres) which have large ocaks, and the cells (5 metres square), on the east and west flanks, are spacious, while those each side of the entry are smaller (4 metres square). There are capacious open eyvans in the south corners so that there was almost as much covered area open for summer use as closed rooms with ocaks for winter warmth. Above the central arches of the south revak before the wide eyvan is an inscription in stone which is matched by a second over the entry facing it.

Beyond the tabhane is a triangular piazza with an enormous stone execution block, grooved by the blade of the sword, or so it is said, left carelessly under a plane tree. Obliquely facing the complex is the Müftülük (religious secretariat) which was installed there in 1826 after the destruction of the Janissaries. Previously, the palace of the Janissary Ağa, the General of the Brotherhood, had stood there; it was an irregular group of buildings, set four sides of a quadrangle, of which no trace remains.[104]

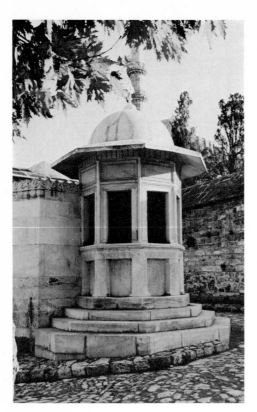

213 *Süleymaniye, Istanbul. The fountain built by Sinan at the end of his garden.*

Running from north to south along the east flank of the mosque precinct is a broad lane, at the north corner of which, on a triangular plot, is the open türbe of Sinan himself at the corner of his garden.[105] Nondescript buildings now occupy the site of his house. The tomb was built late in his life and was completely restored in 1922. It is reached through a little plot in which members of his family are buried. The open grave is set in a stone frame under a vault with a fine crested border. The tombstone itself is crowned by a typical great stone turban.[106] An elaborate inscription records a poem by Mustafa Sâ'i with an eulogy of the bridge at Büyükçekmece which more than any other of his monuments was felt worthy of recall; it is described as the Milky Way.[107] The triangular site, the division into two levels, the contrast of grass and marble, and the grille-work combine to make a dignified memorial. Below the tomb is the public fountain or çeşme which was the source of the enquiry into his misappropriation of the royal water supply to the medreses beyond.

The two lower colleges farther down the street are unique because they descend the hill more sharply than any before, although the concept had appeared in embryo at Bursa, as we have seen.[108] The Salis or Third Medrese is approached by a gate which leads to a pretty loggia overlooking a long garden running down the side of the cells on the north which now flowers with a collection of tomb-stones. From the loggia, a door leads to a vestibule from which steps lead up to the dershane. This is mounted on a high marble vault in which is set a fine çeşme within a hipped and foliate arch. Thus the central chamber stands aloft, the court and cells below. Short flights of broad stone stairs alternate with landings to take one down inside the revaks to the cells across the eastern end of the medrese court. There is a second broad set of stairs outside the revaks which are out of step with those inside. This system is repeated on the south side of the medrese as well. In the centre there is a pretty garden with trees. The stairs on the south lead up to latrines adjacent to those of the Rabı or Fourth Medrese next door, which is similar to the Salis Medrese except that its entry is from the south and not from the north. Between the two medreses, the width of two cells, one belonging to the Salis and one to the Rabı, is a narrow garden which gave light and air to the cells along the inner sides, just as the flanking gardens helped light the cells on the outer sides of each college.

It at first appears that these medreses follow the fall of the land, with such modifications as uneven terrain naturally enforces on any architect, but this is

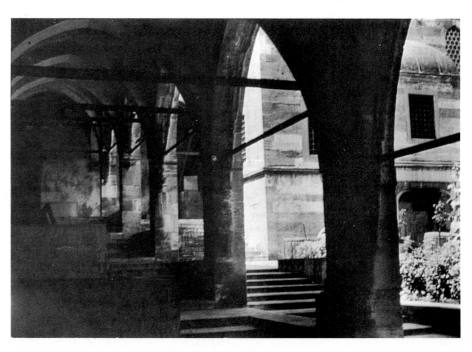

214 *Süleymaniye, Istanbul. Inside a step medrese.*

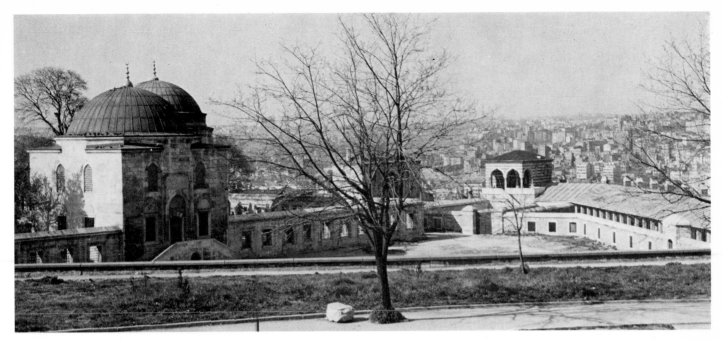

215 Süleymaniye, Istanbul. The restored Türbedar Oda with the türbe of Haseki Hürrem behind. Across the wrestling ground is the darül-hadis.

not the case. For a long time scholars were puzzled by the vakfiye which listed a fifth medrese for tyros, the Mülazimler Medrese,[109] of which no trace could be found because of the neglected state of the complex. It is interesting to see how wild guesses can become when a building totally disappears. This college has now been rediscovered and the area cleared of rubbish to reveal a unique set of cells running straight along in the vaults under the eastern cells at the bottom of Salis and Rabı medreses. There are double cells at either end, and they look across a broad and very long garden at a plainly vaulted wall with individual latrines curiously set into its buttresses. It is a most ingenious use of space and of the vaults which support the two medreses above. Stairs now lead from a cell in the Rabı Medrese to the preparatory school beneath, but it is improbable that there was access in this way originally. A gate at the end of the lower court opened into the street below the hamam.

Beyond the Rabı Medrese is a lane which divides it from the single hamam, which is small for so large a complex. It is in a deplorable state because it has been uncouthly used as a depot, but there is now hope that it may be restored. The site was a difficult one and as a result there is a twist in the plan which is bridged by a lobby between the cold room and the hot room in which there was no cell but screens with doors instead.[110] Opposite the side street is a flight of stairs leading up to the mosque precinct, and round the corner on the south side is the broad ramp up which the sultan rode to the area south of the cemetery beyond the mihrab wall and to the porch of the imperial loge.

Beyond the cemetery is an open space bounded by the vaults of the Moslem university which is on the site of the old saray. Once a week this served as a wrestling ground, its stones being covered in sand, and the sport was as dedicated in the religious sense as it was popular. The east side is bounded by another long line of cells, ham-fistedly restored, which face a wall against which latrines are set. Its revak consists of piers and vaults and is covered by a shed roof in the manner of the Yıldırım Medrese at Bursa.[111] The twenty-two cells, the last three of which turn the corner of the street opposite the hamam, have fine south views over the market quarter but cannot compare with those on the east sides of the Salis and Rabı medreses which look over the Horn and up the Bosphorus. At the north end of this college – which is the darül-hadis[112] and the foremost school of Prophetic traditions in the empire – raised above the ramp to the ironmaster's workshops under the cells, is a fine dershane with a pretty open loggia looking

15

out over the cemetery and the wrestling ground. In the centre of the south wall of the cemetery[113] is a türbedar's or tomb keeper's room which, like this loggia and study hall, has been extensively rebuilt. It is approached by a double flight of stairs from the wrestling ground and was probably the Koran chanting school or darül-kurra.[114] The cemetery is surrounded by the walls of the precinct and each side has a fine gateway with a room above for mosque servants, while that on the south-west has a phalanx of nine latrines. Another set of latrines, thirteen closets in all, is strung along the east side of the precinct where stairs lead down to a door which was opposite the house of Sinan.

The mosque and cemetery stand in an enclosure some 210 by 145 metres. The walls which surround this great area are lightened by grilled windows in the traditional manner. There is access on to the piazza through three gates and by a small postern facing the tabhane, as well as by the stairs described as leading to the road opposite the house of Sinan. But none of these could cope with a large throng. There is a larger gate, the İmaret Gate, with a room reached by stairs on each side in the centre of the north wall which faces the great portal of the courtyard. It is always shut nowadays and could never have been the principal gate, although highly important because it led directly to the hostel and the kitchen. One is at first surprised, for the gate from the piazza leading along the newly paved walk to the west door into the mosque seems to be the most important, because with the medreses and shops and cafés across the way this is the area where architectural unity is most intensely felt. But it is significant that this gate is faced only by the relatively narrow archway to the passage between the two medreses which leads in the direction of Vefa and Şehzade through a maze of humble by-ways and alleys. The approach past the north foundations, either by the tabhane and the Müftülük or by the tımarhane was more important for people coming from Fener, Unkapi or Fatih. But the main flood of people would have come up from the bazaar region on the south-east or Beyazit on the south-west. The two gates either side of the cemetery are the largest because these were the main approaches. It was also the way by which the caravans entered the precinct to pitch their tents and tether their beasts along the west side of the mosque itself.[115] The ramp on the east, as we have seen, is important because it leads to the great east gate beyond which is the royal door into the mosque, and this would have been the gate used by the sultan. The logic of the geography carries the faithful in past the latrines to the lateral washing spigots and then to the great doors on the north-east and north-west which give access to the mosque. Only when it was full would it have been necessary to enter the courtyard and pray there. At noon on Fridays when the mosque was still alive, in a way that it cannot be today, and the students crossed over from the colleges and the travellers from the tabhane, and a throng approached from the market, it must have looked like rivers flowing into an inland sea.

The precinct is now filled with trees, but at first they could only have been saplings except in the north-west corner where there is a large octagonal stone sofa carpeted with grass. In Islamic architecture, one is constantly aware of the importance of places for rest and meditation and also, from the Bursa period onward, of the importance of a view. Süleymaniye on the east has a raised stone walk beside the flanking wall from which to look beyond the descending domes of the Salis and Rabı medreses over the Horn and the meeting of the Marmara and the Straits to the hills of Asia. To appreciate the accomplished excellence of this precinct it is only necessary to compare it with that of the Fatih mosque or the Ahmediye. At Fatih, the medreses are set too far away from the mosque and, seen from its steps, lose their importance architecturally and become merely a boundary. At Sultan Ahmet the subordinate buildings are so scattered, apart from the imperial pavilion, that they are not complementary to the mosque at all. The Beyazit complex is equally loose and vapid, whereas at Süleymaniye every subordinate part contributes to the grandeur of the whole yet the mosque stands independently at the heart and can be seen from all sides in accordance with the precepts of Alberti or Leonardo.

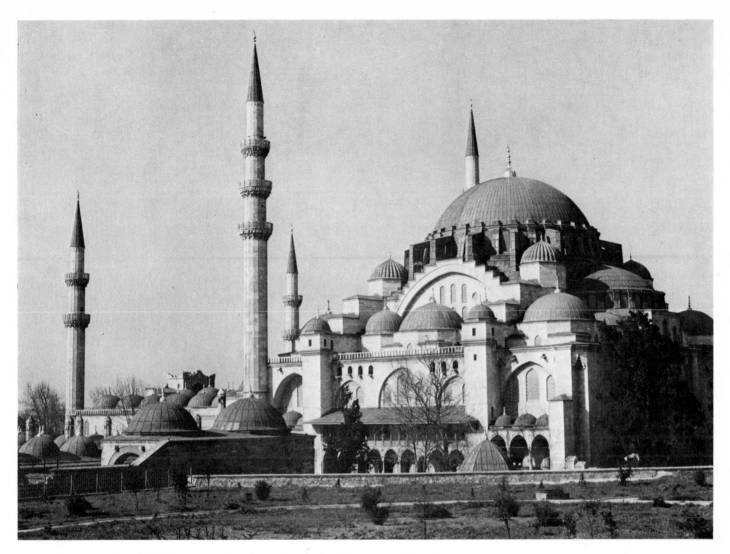

216 Süleymaniye, Istanbul. The mosque from the south-west with the domes of the sibyan mekteb bottom left.

The mosque itself, the crown of the third hill, must now be considered. The dome and the courtyard, which is its foil, are no new development, although Sinan has abandoned the square in favour of a rectangular court forty-four by fifty-seven metres; nor is his use of four minarets: both concepts are related to the Üç Şerefeli Cami at Edirne.[116] But there the minarets were archaic, whereas Sinan has achieved classical symmetry; moreover his are beautifully proportioned, with the two taller at the junction of court and building possessing three balconies[117] while the shorter at the extreme north corners of the court have only two. This contrast in size helps greatly to emphasize the powerful axial movement from north to south which is such an outstanding feature and also the underlying pyramidal form, strongest of all architectural statements, of the silhouette so grandly set above the Horn. The clover-leaf of the Şehzade mosque is reduced to two semi-domes north and south, while on the east and west, due to the direct influence of Hagia Sophia, two great arches are exposed. These are stepped towards the stabilizing turrets which anchor the dome. The buttresses which thrust boldly outwards from these towers do not become dominant features in the same way as those of Sophia because they are contained in part within the walls of the mosque itself.[118] They receive the thrust from the four major piers inside, which carry the pendentives that take the weight of the dome and part of that of the semi-domes across the great arches of the aisles and nave. On the south side within the cemetery walls, they are fully exposed as buttresses because they have to be placed externally in order to keep the kıble wall flat

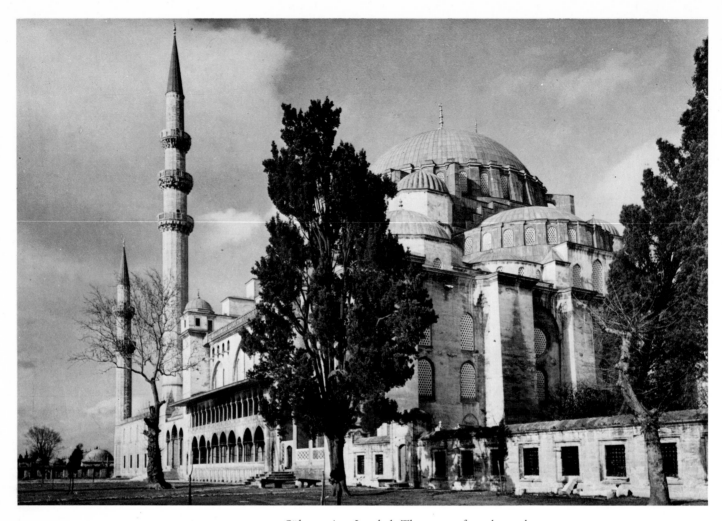

217 Süleymaniye, Istanbul. The mosque from the south-west.

inside. This pair of buttresses embraces a secondary pair, half their size because they only take the thrust of the south semi-dome. The corners on the south side are supported by further blocks of masonry which rise two-thirds the way up the south wall. All six of these great supports are slightly battered and their corners recessed and crowned with stalactites to add elegance to the power which they express and to give this wall its monumentality. The corresponding corner-blocks on the north side are incorporated into the bases of the taller minarets, while the four central buttresses avoid projecting into the portico by forming the traditional recesses inside the mosque itself. The south corner-blocks are excessively strong and their function is partly aesthetic, in that they balance those at the north corners which have to support minarets which reach the height of 63·80 metres exclusive of their lead caps. These may have been elongated in the seventeenth century, and bring the total height to seventy-six metres.[119] All four minarets are multi-faceted, and their ten galleries are borne by sharply carved and vigorously pendant stalactite consoles with balustrades designed in a diversity of traditional geometric patterns. Beneath the lead caps light-blue glazed tiles lighten the effect as if they were windows.[120] The square bases which are simply panelled on each face, with pilasters set into their corners, reach to the height of the portico over the west and east doors and their feet reach to the height of the courtyard wall. The huge and clumsy bases of the earlier periods are now reduced to harmonious proportions and the stone shafts are as lissom as they are strong. Moreover, the tapering of their trunks between and above their galleries is subtly handled so that their diminution is felt rather than perceived and so adds to their appearance of height.

216   In place of the east and west semi-domes of the quatrefoil mosque are domes eleven metres in diameter flanked by two smaller domes, while the four corner domes are eleven and a half metres in diameter. This establishes a rhythm along the flanks of the mosque which the semi-dome and central doorways on the east and west sides of Şehzade Cami obstructed. It is sustained by the large dome between two elliptical vaults over each lateral entry. Between the towering buttresses which flank these porches are set the twenty-one ablution taps in soberly decorated panels and above these rise two-storey loggias.[121] These galleries are accessible from inside the mosque and add an important third dimension, and so life, to the east and west flanks, but their function is to carry a heavy eave which protects the faithful washing below from sun and rain. The lower gallery has eight columns crowned with stalactite capitals which carry nine arches, the third and seventh of which are only half size. Their arches are only a third the height of the rest, above which plain porphyry circles are therefore inset which are matched by mere half-discs at each end of the colonnade. They have almost lost any symbolic significance as sun discs and have become mere ornament. The sixteen arches of the upper gallery spring from baklava capitals and they are all the same size as the smaller arches of the colonnade below. This is because this gallery is only two-fifths whereas the lower is three-fifths the height of the whole loggia exclusive of the panels of taps at the base. Above and behind the loggia roof and the portico domes are five arches which reflect the rhythm of the domes they help to support; that is to say that there are three large arches with smaller ones between. The windows and casements at the gallery levels and also above are likewise grouped in threes and twos and the external movement is continued with the lights in the larger arches at the upper level because one large is set between two small. The modulating movement of this mosque is based on the traditional division into sixteen parts in segments made up of one, two or four units combined but it is challenged by a counterpoint of divisions into three and into five. Because the minor domes usually cover half the area of the greater it will be seen that a group of three large and two small domes represents four sections of the ground plan, that is to say a complete aisle. There

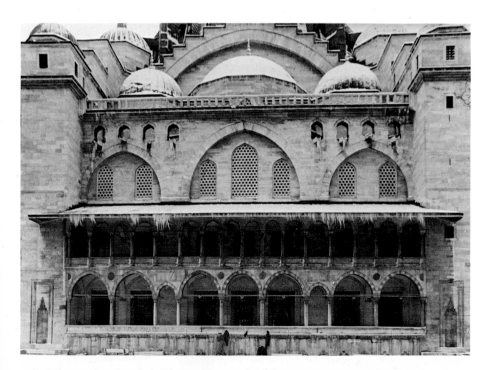

218 Süleymaniye, Istanbul. The western arcade of the mosque.

are other variations: the lateral porticos and the two major eyvans left and right of the north door inside are divided into three, but only because Sinan has distorted his domes and made use of elliptical shapes usually associated with baroque. This is fascinating because it shows that once an architect with a fertile mind seeks to introduce movement into a static classical concept, baroque forms will emerge. The use of gutters to accent façades was long established in Ottoman architecture and in the Süleymaniye Sinan uses them boldly, grouping four at each end of the central section and two less grandiose at the extremities of the building as well as along the courtyard façades and the kıble wall.

The royal entrance on the south-east and the corresponding loggia on the south-west have stone lattice balustrades and arched doors set in between pillars and the usual niche. The royal balustrades are grander and the steps lead up through the central arch instead of the north arch, which is the case on the west. The royal mounting block was cut into smaller units, unfortunately, during recent restorations. The doors of the taller minarets face north and have small porches with canopies supported by one free-standing column and the wall where the eaves cut into the end casements of the son cemaat yeri. They are there to protect the müezzin from a gutter spout beside the upper window. Set under rectangular inscription panels, the east and west doors which divide the son cemaat yeri from the revaks are only slightly recessed externally under their double arches into the sober and flat face of the wall. This contrasts with the three-dimensional character of the mosque, and the consequent chiaroscuro; this necessarily gives the walls an added strength which is important because, when the lower casements and the doors are open, there are dramatic glimpses into the daylight of the court.[122]

The north wall is dominated by the great gate which rises above the wall and the domes behind for a third of the width with three tiers of windows in pairs each side of the tall portal. The stalactite arch above the recessed door steps up sharply to a peak behind its flat façade supported on pilasters. Two much larger, but still slender, colonnettes soar to carry two alems and frame the outer portal which has a carved entablature. This, and the cornice of the ilwan behind, is richly crested. Beneath it is the traditional inscription stating that there is no God but God and that Muhammed is His Prophet. There is a second inscription beneath the stalactite half-dome of the porch above the door and richly carved niches on each flank of the recess. In the rooms inside the ilwan were the muvakkithane and lodgings for sextons and porters.[123] Beyond this door is the much repaired court itself.[124] Some of the capitals here, as at the tabhane, are of recent date but all are fine examples of stalactites with rose symbols which are smaller versions of the seven below the honeycomb above the north door. The twenty-four columns of the courtyard are said to come from the kathisma, or royal box, of the Hippodrome. The two before the great gate are tallest and of porphyry, ten are of Marmara marble, and twelve of pink Egyptian granite. They sustain twenty-four domes. The portico is higher than the revaks and the little rectangular fountain enhances the sense of spaciousness. There is a handsome marble pavement marked out with simple geometric patterns in the style of the tabhane court and perhaps, originally, those of the hospital, whereas the other courts are gardens. Tournefort, who was in the city about 1700, reports that trees once grew here, presumably in the manner of those at Fatih.[125] Sinan had the usual insuperable difficulty where the portico and gateway arches meet. Because the former are higher, the latter have to spring from below the true capital. But far worse confusion was caused by the three higher arches in the centre of the north revak due to the lofty ilwan and its portal. The lower arches each side are made conspicuous because the alternating colours of the voussoirs are expressed in the two-tier capitals, which are cut in half so that, while the top half carrying the higher arch faces the court, the lower half faces the revak wall and from the court is seen in silhouette with a result which is disastrous.[126]

Opposite, under the central dome of the portico lies a circular porphyry slab which was said, traditionally, to have been brought back from Baghdad for use

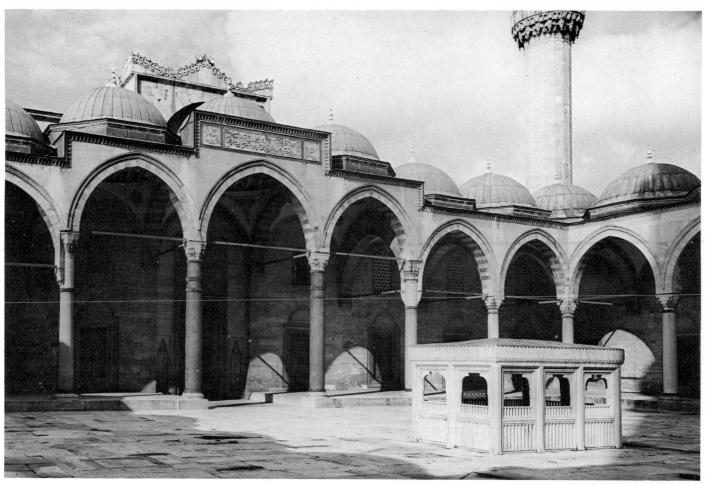

*219 Süleymaniye, Istanbul. The mosque courtyard and
fountain, showing the deformation of the capitals due to
the conflicting levels at which the arches spring.*

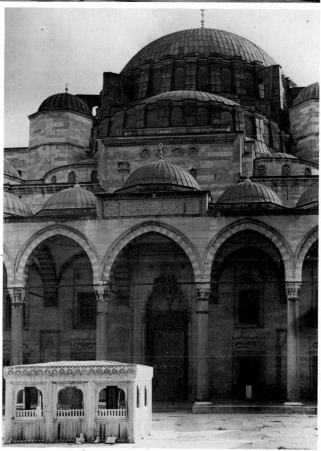

*220 Süleymaniye, Istanbul. The portico and north door
of the mosque.*

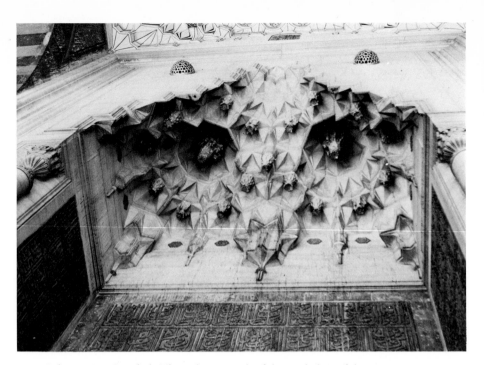

221 Süleymaniye, Istanbul. The stalactite vault of the north door of the mosque.

in front of the mihrab, which is an unlikely tale. It was probably to hand in Istanbul which was still an excellent marble quarry in Sinan's time.[127] The alleged reason why it was rejected for use before the mihrab, where it would have been most incongruous, is that it had been dropped and cracked. It is a fact that the Romans did not succeed in quarrying a piece of porphyry of this size without cracking it. Similar circular slabs in the Pantheon are all cracked in the same manner or else made up of segments neatly fitted together.[128] There is a second circular porphyry slab in the north entry to the court and there are rectangular ones before the lateral doors; similar marble paving is used elsewhere, including the court of Yavuz Selim Cami. The columns inside the building and much other marble was said to come from the church of St Euphemia at Chalcedon, now Kadiköy.[129] Gyllius,[130] however, saw one of the four huge porphyry columns which help support the lateral arches between the piers being cut to size. It appears to have been the renowned column of the Virgin which once stood near the church of the Holy Apostles and would sway when a maiden who had lost her virtue passed by. Matching columns were allegedly brought from Iskenderun.[131] Over the windows of the portico are rectangular tile plaques bearing white inscriptions on blue; similar ones were to recur throughout the second half of the sixteenth century in many mosques.

The doorway into the mosque is again narrow and the niche between two sun discs relatively modest. The actual doors of this mosque are in poor condition but are still fine examples of traditional Islamic patterns and inlay of ebony, mother of pearl, and ivory; their bronze appointments are also very fine. Upon entering the building, one is overwhelmed by the spaciousness. There is a definite axial drive towards the mihrab which is immediately counteracted by the centralized climax of the dome towards which one is inevitably drawn.[132] The sense of width is strong because the aisles are not masked by double rows of columns hung with curtains, as was the case with Hagia Sophia when it was a church. There are only two columns between the east and west elephant feet and one is never visually excluded from the space beyond them. Moreover, the axial drive is brought to a halt by the flat uncompromising screen of the kible-wall from which the vision rebounds.[133] The basic plan of the mosque is fifty-seven metres square,[134] but this is broken by the deep recesses of the north wall and of the doors on east and west where it is further diminished by the lateral galleries which, with their arcades below, are the inward expression of the exterior galleries over the taps for ritual washing. The gallery high over the north entry[135] and the tribunes lower down over the eyvans immediately left and right of it cannot counteract the axial drive because the recession under them gives an enhanced impression of length. This is abetted by the vestigial remnant of the raised area before the mihrab, now reduced to a sofa just long enough to support the minber and the width of the area between the two buttresses. But the central space is uncompromisingly twenty-six and a half metres square and it is exactly half the total area of the mosque, while the dome is fifty-three metres at its crown, or precisely twice its diameter.[136]

These measurements conform absolutely to the symbol of the perfect circle in the perfect square and it is so satisfactory a definition of space that it dominates the complexities which modulate the rigid form of the rest of the mosque, and so shows an advance on the innocent mathematics of Şehzade.[137] The underlying formula based on sixteen units has been noted as has the use of the half in order to introduce a new rhythm based on three, a number for which, as we have seen, the Renaissance had a deep respect. Three is inherent but not expressed in the exedras for there are only pairs, north and south, but each of these pairs is one-third the size of the half dome which it helps to support. The inward expression of the lateral galleries covers one-third of the central area of each aisle and these galleries are divided into three by the responds of their two major piers.[138] The north recesses and eyvans are one-third the area of the domed corner areas which represent one-sixteenth of the total interior space, and the three central recesses add up to one-third of the area of the half dome. These divisions may be pursued endlessly and include the royal tribune which fills two-thirds of the area under the south-east corner dome; or the use of two columns under the east and west tympana of the great dome which again creates a division of three, but only because the span of the central arch is twice that of the ones flanking it. Since Sinan continued the Ottoman tradition of adding masonry to his piers in exact proportion to the requirements of the conglomeration of arches of varying size which sprang from them in all four directions, these too express divisions based on two and two halves which add up to three.[139] The Süleymaniye is a remarkable advance on the static arithmetic of the mosque of Beyazit II. The handling of space is supple, not rigid, and Sinan could vary the size of elements like the lateral domes without destroying the clarity with which he expresses

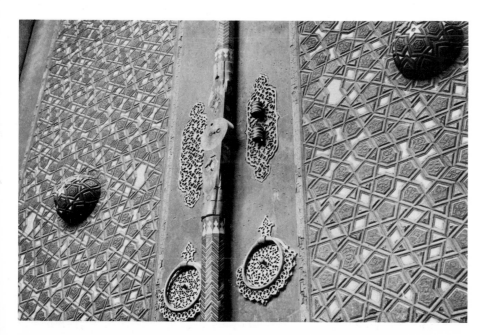

222 Süleymaniye, Istanbul. Detail of the mosque door.

the limits of space and the climax of volume.[140] Sinan legitimized the intractably detached four corner areas – which in Christian centralized architecture are either omitted altogether or turned into vestry or side chapel or diaconicon – by giving them the function of vestibules before his corner entrances, thus escaping the limitation of the central entrance of Şehzade Cami. While cut off from the central area they still form part of the aisles and their flowing vistas.

The most serious weakness is the reappearance of the problem of the stalactites which mask the disparity in height between the arches in the kıble wall and those joining it to the south piers in order to carry the exedras, and also the corresponding arches and exedras on the north side. The traditional use of the stalactite as a console has been noted at Bursa and it belongs to Islamic architecture as a whole. Normally, it is effective and more logical than its elaboration first suggests; an intractable square with corners of ninety degrees is moulded into a circle on which the dome can rest more effectively than on any ordinary squinch: indeed, it is much nearer to the smooth Byzantine pendentive than it looks. Once the height of the arch in each of the two walls varies, however, neither the Ottomans nor the Byzantines could resolve the problem of balance.[141] Sinan's exedras are inescapably slightly lopsided and, while springing directly from the pier, project from the kıble buttresses and those buttresses flanking the north door fractionally but enough to shift the centre away from the corner. The result, inevitably, is to create a lopsided stalactite which springs inside the right-angle, instead of exactly at it where the two walls meet. A second result is that the stalactites bleed into the voussoirs of the side arches. This clumsiness is overridden by the excellence of the workmanship and the boldness of the finials at each extremity and at the centre of each console.

There are a great number of windows, including thirty-two in the drum of the dome, thirteen in the semi-domes, and five in each of the exedras. Of the twenty-three in each tympanum, four are round and ease the stepping up of the three tiers. There are also a pair of rose windows in the kıble wall. The circular elements on the vertical faces and in the shoulders of the pendentives – made up of windows or inscriptive discs, or, in the soffits of the arches of the lateral galleries, simply plain marble sun discs – are important both symbolically and as minor planets round the great sphere of the central dome. While there are eight casements in the north wall there are only four upper lights, and the lofty eyvans without tribunes above them on the north-east and north-west have only two casements each, with the result that the height of the bare wall above them is even more emphatic than it might have been. There is no present indication that these great bare stretches of wall were ever purposeful. A possible explanation is that the lack of these four windows makes the total number in the mosque two hundred, a figure which may have had some significance.

The gallery which runs round the lip of the dome, and the lamplighter's gallery, borne on a handsome string-course supported on consoles, which runs round the building at the springing of the pendentives of the dome, semi-domes and exedra, underline the vital division of the temporal world of the wall and the spiritual regions of the spheres. The central light fixtures in the form of massed circles of lamps and ostrich eggs are less distracting than usual, but the ironwork is crude and cumbersome. The loss of the original mosque furniture is tragic, for the crystal lamps[142] and inlaid Koran chests and all the paraphernalia of religion were of unexcelled workmanship at this time. Only imagination can reconstruct the original splendour[143] but discipline can educate the eye to absorb the distraction of so many slender cords by which the lamp wheels, like wheels of the sun and therefore potent symbols, are suspended; the task is not made easier by the dirty electric light flex wound round them. In certain lights however – and the double windows ensure that at no time is the interior harshly lit – the threads dwindle into gossamer and enhance the sense of height disseminated from the dome. The rings and clusters of lamps themselves form a low roof over the heads of the congregation, and this must have been much more marked when the glass saucers were filled with oil which, even when unlit, must have glinted

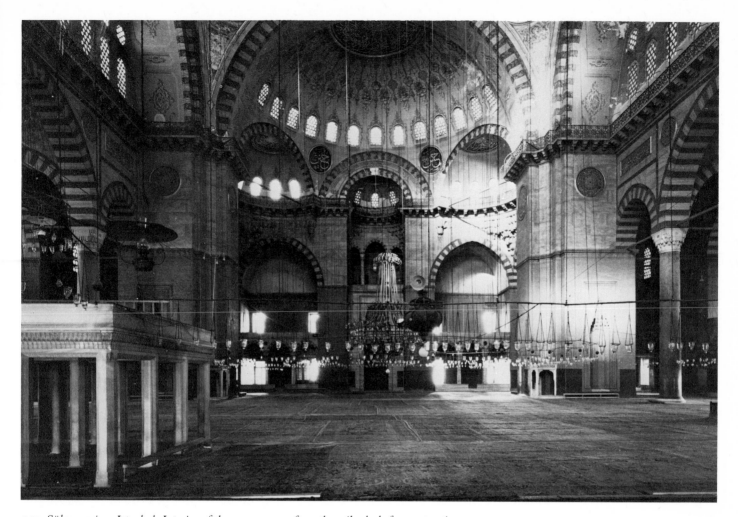

223 Süleymaniye, Istanbul. Interior of the mosque seen from the mihrab, before restoration.

like green gold. The lamps are hung so low for the practical reason that they must be easily reached for filling and cleaning, and also because oil light is soft and quickly diffused, but the sub-ceiling created is a part of the architecture and the mystique; it detaches the human beings below from the supra-human proportions of the pendentives and the dome. To this extent it enhances the grandeur of the piers and arches: but it is an effect which originally was fortuitous.

In the north and south side of each of the four major piers are framed beautifully proportioned stalactite niches, the silhouettes of which reach particularly sharp conical points that echo the hood of the minber and increase the upward thrust of the piers. Faucets for drinking-water are inset.[144] Many other details of the mosque are of fine workmanship, including the stalactite capitals of the great columns supporting the arches under the tympana, but here there is an unusual development. The central arch is flanked by two smaller ones which spring normally from the capital but end flush with the wall of the pier above the niches for drinking-water. Usually a pilaster would project but here their support is incorporated. This greatly enhances the setting of the niches which otherwise would be cramped for space; it also adds to the feeling of axial drive towards the kible wall: but the two wing arches are diminished in importance since the facets of some six voussoirs, or parts of them, are absorbed into the wall.[145]

The mosque has been restored and redecorated over the last twelve years. The stone has been scraped clean; what was a dark grey building is now softly milky and turns to honey under the floodlights, which is most becoming. Inside, and in the courtyard, the stalactite pendentives have been picked out in black and red paint and a sodden orange hue which is quite remarkable, and the voussoirs of the arches have been painted red and white in imitation of marble in a surer

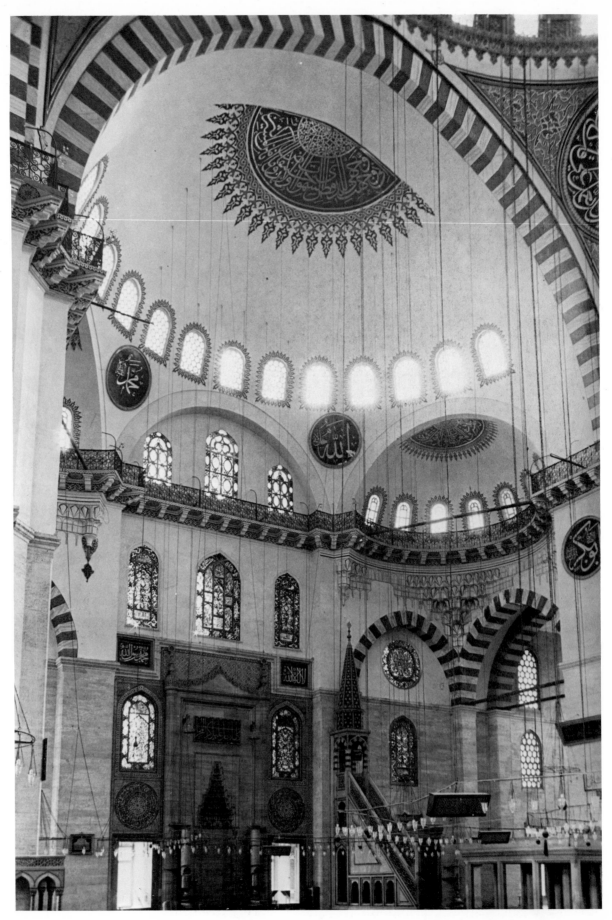

224 *Süleymaniye, Istanbul. Mihrab, minber and the south semi-dome of the mosque after restoration.*

tradition.[146] The real grey marbles of the arches and spandrels under the tympana are discrete and the fake therefore are all the more obtrusive. The dome, or part of it, fell in the earthquake of 1766[147] which had little mercy for the domes of any monument save that of Hagia Sophia which had fallen three times before the conquest. Whatever traces there may have been of the old decoration in Süley-maniye must have been largely obliterated during the subsequent repairs, but evidence has been found, during the recent cleaning, that Sinan first experi-mented with blue before making red the dominant colour in the dome. In the middle of the nineteenth century, the Fossati brothers – whose restoration of Hagia Sophia saved that monument from collapse, to their everlasting credit and glory – were ordered to repaint the dome of the Süleymaniye and they pro-ceeded to cover both it and the semi-domes with a debauched attempt at Ottoman baroque which, on the grounds that this is part of the history of the mosque, was recently faithfully restored, fake jewels and all.

24   The grey marble mihrab is traditional but with all decoration reduced to the strongly delineated inscription,[148] gold on green, the inevitable stalactite of the niche itself, and the arabesques at the summit. At the top of the two fluted columns which flank the mihrab are crescents and so this heavenly gate is related to the north portal of the courtyard. There is a pretty legend that the two great candles were brought back from a church in Hungary.[149] There are the marks of rings each side of the mihrab (and the rings themselves, as well as the marks, in the side of the portico sofa of the court) which look as if candlesticks were sometimes chained there, but there is no sure explanation of this odd feature.[150] There is handsome opus sectile work skirting the windows and niches in this area and each casement floor has its own individual design. In its traditional place, west of the mihrab, is a minber of Marmara marble which is tall and graceful and also puritanically plain. The balustrade is made up of the usual pattern of interlocking decagonal wheels. The lower portal is decorated with a stalactite pattern reduced to a simple series of angles. The stairs sweep up to the canopy which is supported on four piers of interlocking green and white marble complete with miniature tie-beams. The flanks form a perfect equilateral triangle in conformity with custom but the octagonal drum and spire are very tall and delight with their galaxy of gilded octagonal stars which crowd and sparkle on a dark blue ground. They must have been refurbished but it would seem that this deep blue approxi-mates to the shade of the original. The several müezzin, hünkâr and minor mahfils are in character with mihrab and minber; that is to say, they are decorated with sober versions of traditional patterns, are nicely proportioned, and of faultless craftsmanship. Their colonnettes are also of varied rarer marbles except for the piers supporting the müezzin's mahfil.[151] Any of the carpets that survived are in the museum and none of those now used on the floor is old. Egyptian matting once covered the handsome red tiles set in herringbone fashion divided by ribs of stone at intervals, but has been replaced by crude local rush.

The inscriptions are the work of Çerkes or Circassian Hasan Çelebi, a pupil of the most renowned of all Ottoman calligraphers, Ahmet Karahisarı.[152] Those engraved in stone are surely his design but those painted elsewhere must have been restored even if with care and felicity, while the famous verse beginning 'God is the light of the heavens and earth' (xxiv, 35) which adorns the dome, can only have been completely rewritten after the earthquake. The texts in the pendentives are transformed into flowers with sixteen petals and the letters spring and cavort with great vitality. In the dome they radiate like rays from a sun disc transformed into arabesques. The names of God, Muhammed, the first four caliphs, and Hasan and Hüseyin, sons of Ali, gave Hasan Çelebi scope to add animation to the established script. He may also have designed the inscrip-tions in tile left and right of the minber, the upper two rectangular, confident and clear-cut, the larger lower pair circular and complex in the manner of those of the pendentives.

The glass is gorgeous and attributed to Sarhoş Ibrahim (Ibrahim the Drun-kard). There is a legend that the two rose windows were trophies from Baghdad,

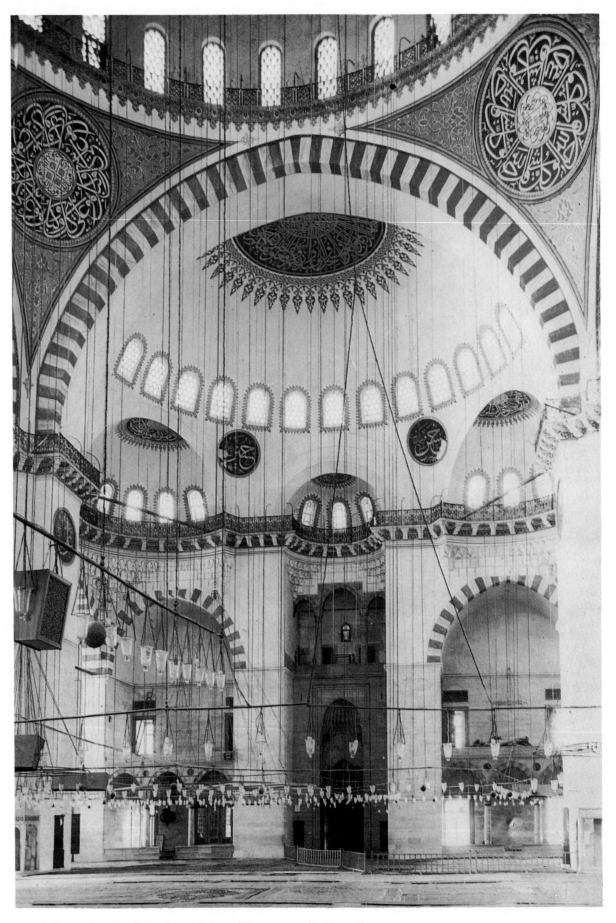

225 Süleymaniye, Istanbul. The north door of the mosque after restoration.

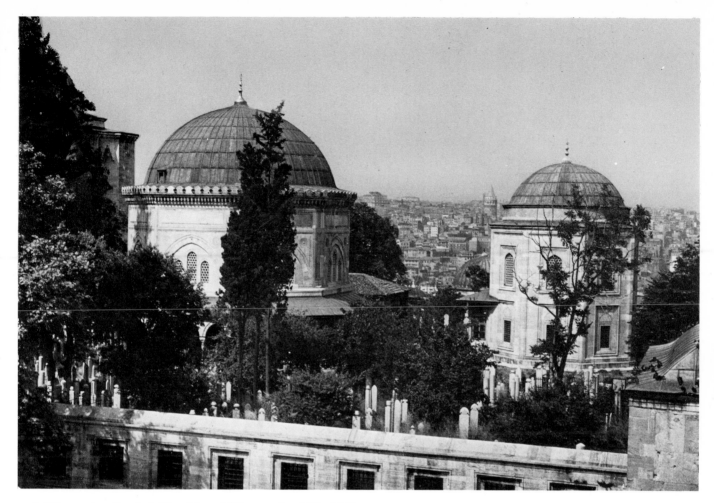

226 Süleymaniye, Istanbul. The türbes of Süleyman I and Haseki Hürrem.

but how they could survive the journey is beyond comprehension. It is interesting to note that the artist was excused his heinous sin of alcoholism. These
windows follow the original design but have been restored because the intricate
plaster ribs inevitably decay, even without the depredations of pigeons.[153] These
inner windows are protected by bull's eye lights set in lead outside; the latter also
soften the interior light.

   The mihrab wall is discreetly decorated with predominantly red on blue
Iznik tiles and this is the first extensive use of tile in this manner in an Ottoman
mosque. The pattern of flowers is somewhat lost in the dimness, but not the
powerful circular inscriptive plaques over the casements right and left of the
mihrab. Sinan seems to have used tile cautiously at first and then with enthusiasm,
41 lavishly, in the mosque of Rüstem Pasha. He rapidly abandoned this excess.

   South of the mosque and forming an enclosure, which is almost a second
26 court, is the restored cemetery and garden where Süleyman and Haseki Hürrem
are buried in separate türbes.[154] Because of their eminence the two domes stand
clearly against the skyline below the great cupola of the mosque. Just beyond the
kıble wall are the east and west gates into the enclosure, joined by a path which
runs between two stone sofas full of the graves and headstones of lesser men. At
the centre it opens onto a courtyard with the tomb of Roxelane directly facing
one and that of Süleyman, larger and grander, to the right. Gyllius[155] reports that
the Sultan was at work on a mosque, a tomb, and a han and it is assumed that the
tomb was his own. Roxelane predeceased him in April 1558,[156] and this is the date
of her türbe. Süleyman's türbe bears the date 974/1566, the year of his death,
but an order of Selim II's in 1567 implies that it was still unfinished.[157] One may
conclude that both tombs were begun by Sinan while he was still engaged in
building the complex, which is usually stated to have been finished in 965/1557;[158]

it was only the portico of Süleyman's which was not finished until later. In Ottoman, as in other societies, it was often the fashion to erect one's tomb before one's death.

Roxelane's classical octagonal türbe is today plainly whitewashed inside, and her tomb is set inside a rail under the lofty dome. All that has survived of the original decoration are the sparkling panels of Iznik tiles depicting blossoming fruit trees, leaves, highly stylized flowers and incisive inscriptions like those over the windows of the son cemaat yeri. They appear to be exactly from the period of her death and that of Rüstem Pasha. Hidden by the doors, when they are open, are earlier tiles in meadow green, blue and white which are kin to those in the türbe of Şehzade Mehmet. Windows, cupboards and stalactite niches are of excellent workmanship and one can only suppose that the ceiling was once brilliantly painted in red and blue and white.

The türbe of Süleyman faces east instead of north and is a far larger octagon built of the best stones from St Euphemia of Chalcedon. It is preceded by a peristyle with its roof supported by four beautiful verd-antique columns. This is now glassed in to protect the two sumptuous Iznik flower panels of matching design in the grandest manner, the stylized leaves and blooms displayed on a pure white ground. A fine colonnade encloses a verandah which encircles the tomb, each of its facets having three arches borne by four slender columns. The doors into the chamber have been recently restored and varnished and open inwards into the flanking walls to confront the visitor immediately with the massive symbolical sarcophagus of the padişah, foot to head with his immense turban looming over all.[159] The effect is dramatic and it is clear that it was carefully planned, for there is no such drama on entering the tomb of Haseki Hürrem whose sarcophagus lies sideways to the door. It was traditional, or almost so, by then because the tombs of Selim I and Fatih are entered from the east, as are those of Süleyman's immediate successors: Selim II, Murat III, Mehmet III and Ahmet I. At the beginning of the eighteenth century, Thévenot[160] reported that the catafalque of Süleyman lay beneath a finely embroidered cloth from Mecca on which was a picture of the Holy City. Grelot reports[161] that a great silver candlestick stood at its foot; such a candlestick stands there before the inlaid railing in need of much repair to this day. The türbe has been cluttered with other tombs and a candle is also placed before that of Ahmet II. Modest in size but at her father's right hand, is the sarcophagus of Mihrimah Sultan. When Süleyman's stood alone as those of Selim I and Fatih still do, the effect must have been overwhelming and the culmination of the feeling of space in the dome have been serene.

Like several of Sinan's türbes, that of Süleyman has a false dome within the outer shell. The narrow stairway inset in the wall on the left of the entry leads to a dusty passage which circumvents the inner dome. The outer dome is supported by the thick wall into which, in addition to the door, fourteen windows are set at ground level, while twenty-four more of stained glass, restored originals or copies,[162] are set in the tympana under the eight arches which rise from eight columns, some of porphyry, which sustain the inner dome. This has been restored with an elaborate arabesque pattern of black and white and terracotta over engraved three-dimensional plaster reliefs. While the brown, rather than red, tone of the terracotta may have dubious authenticity, the overall restoration is praiseworthy; the whole ceiling is set with sparkling ceramic stars, and in the centre of many of the star designs are small pieces of rock crystal engraved with roses in the heart of which are, allegedly, emeralds. The dome is very much the starlit heaven that Sinan first intended. The pendentives are filled with tile for the first time in Ottoman architecture, and the lower panels between the casements are later and richer than those of Haseki Hürrem's türbe but less feminine and fresh. The great frieze of inscriptive panels above was never excelled.

It is all the more shocking, therefore, to find that the revetments between these tiles and the string-course below the upper windows are of the cheapest fake marbling, which one would like to blame on the Fossatis if not some more

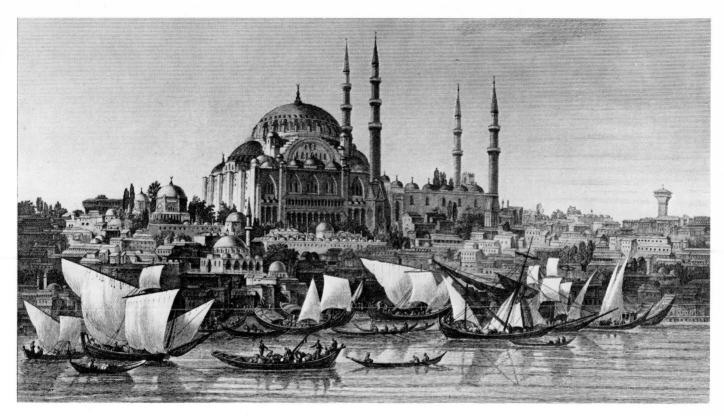

227 Detail from an engraving made for the Comte de Choiseul-Gouffier, showing the türbe and mosque of Süleyman I, with Rüstem Pasha Cami below and, on the right, a now demolished fire-tower.

recent restorer. As with all the false marbling, here red and there green, found in mosques, more particularly in the voussoirs of high arches, and türbes like that of Cem, one would like to know if it was the accepted canon. Almost certain proof that it was can be obtained from miniatures, including one in the Top-kapısaray library of Selim II in the Divan or Kübbe Altı[163] where a fake arch and revetment is clearly shown. In high voussoirs, as has already been discussed,[164] it was necessary; but it is difficult to believe that Sinan, whose work on this complex was so manifestly austere, in sympathy with the retrogressive outlook of his sultan in his later years, and whose aesthetic sense reduced ornament to that minimum at which it appears most striking and articulate, should have made use of a crudity which might have pleased a Mussolini in his office at the Palazzo Venezia or helped let an apartment in a cheap block at Centocelli in the meaner purlieus of Rome. Total disbelief is arrested, however, by the recollection of the crude imitation of marble produced by Iznik in its greatest period to form the skirting under such great ceramic masterpieces as the kıble wall of the mosque of Sokollu Mehmet Pasha at Kadırga. Fake marble was used in the palaces of early Islamic emirs such as that at Ukhaydir. Moreover, coloured marble panels would have been difficult to find by the middle of the sixteenth century and a set of forty may have been impossible. The only marble quarried in Turkey at that time appears to have been from Marmara Island and the limestone workings of the Bosphorus. Apart from this, and the loss of the lamps besides, here is the most beautiful imperial tomb of the Ottoman house, which even that of Selim II was not to excel, except in size. Equally, it is the most beautiful of all the buildings of the complex, sombre though this beauty be.

'The sixth hill hathe the marvailouse church and sepullcer of the trioumphant and invinsible Sultan Solimen; a buildinge worthy of sutch a monarke, in the best and most frequented place of the citie, which passeth in greatnes, wourke-manshipp, marble pillars, and riches more than kinglie, all the other churches of the empirors his predecessors; a wourke which meriteth to be matched with the 7 Wonders of the World.'[165]

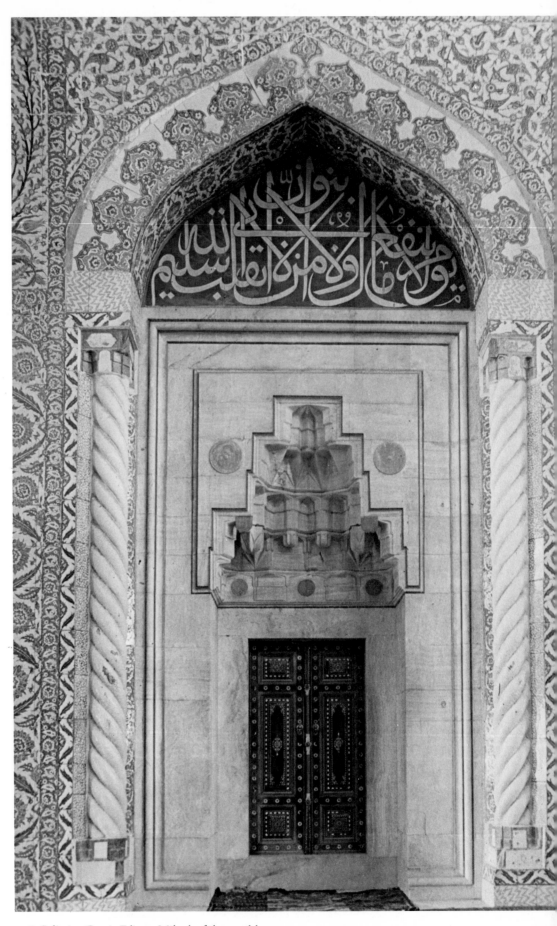

228 *Selimiye Cami, Edirne. Mihrab of the royal loge.*

7

Sinan – the master

THROUGHOUT THE PERIOD that he was building the Süleymaniye, Sinan was busy with other tasks all over the empire. While he may have drawn up the plans and issued definitive instructions, the erection of a mosque or han or bridge was carried out under the supervision of subordinates unless built in the capital or at Edirne where the court was often in residence. His work in the provinces was less inventive than that of the two capitals and it is for this reason that the development of his genius is little to be seen there.

29 As early as 951/1544–958/1550,[1] Sinan had built a han for Rüstem Pasha in Galata near Fatih's bedesten which had to fit a lopsided and narrow site in that crowded district by the quays where land values were high and vacant lots hard to find. He economized in space by sending the stone stairway up from the middle of the lean court; the two staircases rise along the axis of the yard so that they can be approached from either of the gates situated at each end: in the centre they branch left and right to reach the galleries and bridge the court below. It was probably some ten years later that he built another han for the
30 Grand Vezir at Edirne where it stands south-west of the Eski Cami. It has undergone hard use and now is reconstructed as a hotel. It was built in two parts with a secondary court added to the great rectangular court of the main block with its fine basin in the centre. The spaciousness of this quadrangle with the shade and shelter of its trees reflects the ample dimensions of the whole han as do the broad galleries which offered splendid vistas to the traveller seeking the seclusion of his cell. The lower range of circular arches are broad in span as are the pointed arches above, between each of which is a sandstone balustrade carved with bold and simple, varying traditional motifs. The walls are built of alternating courses of stone and brick and the coffee rooms in the corners of the han and the cells for sleeping in are all domed and lofty. The upper galleries are reached by rebuilt, broad stairways which rise through the middle of them. Passages lead to the second court above, which is a terrace over the forepart of the stables, and to the closets. The arrangement is no different from that of a host of Ottoman hans in Bursa and elsewhere but there is a sense of harmony and space which comes from an assured hand. The main façade turns slightly back where the sections join and this gives an added sense of size. Seen from the suburbs at the back, the huge bulk is monumental, for the land drops and there is a vast expanse of bare wall rising from the valley below, before the two tiers of windows and the crowning batteries of domes and chimneys are reached. Here, in its ordered monotony, is something of the grandeur of a nineteenth-century warehouse by Telford.

Somewhere between 1544 and 1561,[2] Rüstem Pasha ordered the building of
31 the now heavily restored Taş Han at Erzerum which is severely constructed of large blocks of ashlar. The ground-floor cells have one window each and plain

229 Rüstem Pasha Han, Galata, Istanbul. The courtyard with the central staircase.

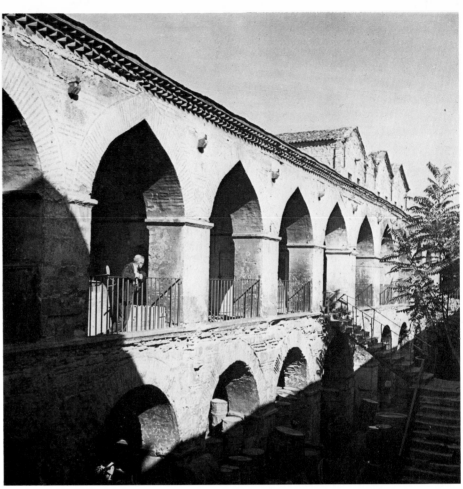

230 Rüstem Pasha Han, Edirne. The courtyard during reconstruction, 1968.

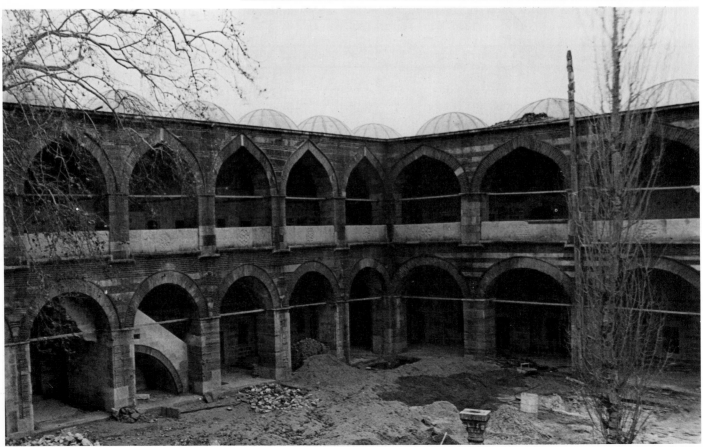

ocaks while the upper, which because of the fall of the land can be reached from the street on one side, is now a great barrel-vaulted çarşı with domes at each of the four corners. There are also small central cupolas and all the domes have lanterns because this upper storey is without windows. The alcoves on each side of the broad passages are clumsy and it could be that these were originally dormitory areas put to a new use. The range of chimneys is striking and must have been more so when the second court of the han still stood. The remaining principal court had revaks behind broad low arches and it was paved beyond the low vaulted passage in the centre of the left revak leading to the low demolished stables. It was formerly possible to step out of the dormitory onto the flat stable roof to sleep in the open in summer for the door on that side survives. Another door opened onto the roofs of the second court in which there was a pool and probably trees. The large corner domes are set over squat towers and the responding arches of the square piers of the courtyard colonnade. Their interstices are filled with brick. Although it is basically a square design, this is a complex if sombre building.

It is certainly complex when it is compared with the barn of a kervansaray which Sinan also designed for Rüstem at Eregli near Ulukışlar; it is improbable that he supervised any part of the construction of this or any other provincial han. It consists of four interior piers which help support the five traverse barrel-vaults. These are made of brick but the rest of the building is stone and it has a very grand and high central doorway. Inside, there are ten ocaks along the south wall with slit windows above and there are also groups of three windows in the tympana of the vaults; nonetheless, the interior is exceedingly gloomy.[5]

In Istanbul, Sinan built an octagonal medrese for Rüstem Pasha which is related to the Kapıağa Medrese at Amasya. The latter was truly octagonal, whereas Sinan squared the external corners of his medrese and incorporated the washrooms and other offices in the triangular areas which he thus created. It is a single-storey college with a small şadırvan among flowers and saplings which hide the dishevelled state of the courtyard without cluttering this spacious haven. There are twenty-two cells, each with its dome, and a large dershane which extrudes to the south and could act as an oratory since the medrese is not attached to a mosque. The baklava capitals are mixed with simple lozenge forms and in some a rose is inset. Above the arch of the entrance is a single tulip which is said to have been Sinan's own device.[4] The octagonal form makes for an attractive central garden and gives lively circular movement to the revaks; but it is to be noted that Sinan never used this plan again. The triangular areas are clumsy and wasteful of material and space, although they are partly squared off and a rectangular alcove, cut into the thickness of the angles, gives additional room to the cells; this is neither integrated nor lit, nor does an extra recess compensate for the area lost by cutting passages through to the offices. The only satisfactory solution to this problem would have required a baroque architect like Borromini and the supple ingenuity which designed San Carlo alle Quattro Fontane.

Rüstem Pasha was not yet sadrazam when Sinan built his medrese in 958/1550.[5] The office was still held by Hadım, or Eunuch, Ibrahim Pasha who was no relation to Süleyman's strangled Greek favourite. For Ibrahim, Sinan built a mosque at Silivrikapı in 959/1551[6] which is set among the market gardens of the less populous quarters of the capital and is really a country mosque with a little park around its şadırvan. The eunuch was a modest builder: his türbe to the west of the portico is an open rectangle and he has acquired the attributes of a holy man, so that ribbons are stuck on his tomb in the hope of finding husbands or of bringing children to forlorn girls. The mosque is the usual domed unit with a five-domed portico with ogee arches which are not the common form.[7] The central cupola is raised on a high drum with squinches at the corners. The north door has handsome stalactites in the vault above it and there are Iznik tiles in the lunettes above the casements which predate those of the Süleymaniye and are related to those of the türbe at the Şehzade.

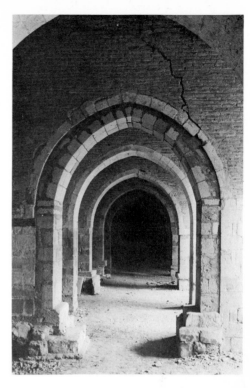

231 *Taş Han, Erzerum. Revak of the courtyard.*

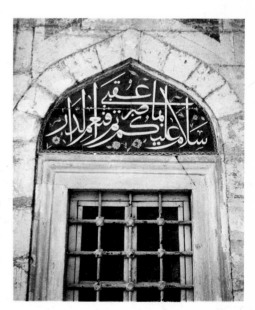

232 *Hadım Ibrahim Pasha Cami, Istanbul. Inscriptive tile over a portico window.*

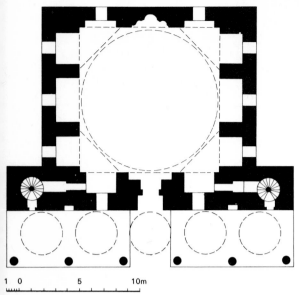

233 *Ibrahim Pasha Cami, Istanbul.*
Plan, scale 1 : 300.

The prayer hall is grand because of its loftiness, without the distortion found in the tomb chambers of the Cairene mosques and medreses such as those of Hasan and Barkuk. There is a closer kinship with the Bahri Mamluk period and the mosque of Khaibak. It was to serve as a very elegant model for other vezirs' mosques; its own plan is based on that of Bali Pasha's built in 1505, with its three deep recesses between the piers of the side galleries, the two recesses each side of the door, and two shallower recesses each side of the mihrab. The frequent attribution of Bali Pasha to Sinan may be due to his acceptance of this plan as the classical norm, a stock design which reappears at Kayseri and Tokat and elsewhere. Earlier examples of the shell squinches are to be found at the Mustafa Pasha mosque at Gebze. Passages from the north recesses extend inside the wall behind the mihrabs of the portico to the stairs to the minaret and to the gallery. Both mihrab and minber are of very fine workmanship; the latter has axle rosettes inset into the interlocking polygonal wheels of its balustrade. The minaret is set conventionally at the north-west corner and is balanced, as far as its base is concerned, by the stair to the gallery on the north-east. These bases extend the width of the portico onto which they open but there are the additional entries from inside which have been noted above. The multifaceted minaret is tall and has one şerefe. It was rebuilt in 1177/1763[8] when the mosque was restored and so it is baroque in style.

Between 1553 and 1555,[9] Sinan built, for the Grand Admiral Sinan Pasha, a smaller version of Üç Şerefeli Cami at Beşiktaş on the shores of the Bosphorus facing the Barbarossa sepulchre. It has been mutilated by the incorporation of the son cemaat yeri into the mosque in order to cope with a growing population. The second revak, which is probably original, remains under its shed roof and now acts as the portico. The court was always modest and rustic in appearance because of its narrowness and its long, clumsy şadırvan. With no domes but only a shed roof over the revaks, it resembles an Orthodox monastery, even more now that it has been painted brown and white.[10] The alterations have been too drastic for it to be possible to determine how much this avlu has been altered, but it is likely to have been less than at first appears. The mosque is important because it shows how thoroughly Sinan studied the Üç Şerefeli, just as he did the works of other architects; and, indeed, he had to because he was responsible for the repair and upkeep of their buildings. He was unable to solve the problem of the triangles at the meeting of the central dome with the pairs of lateral domes, but his two free-standing piers are less clumsy and the main dome proportionally more lofty. The little plaster lanterns in the triangles are expressed externally as pretty turrets with segmented whorl caps. They go well with the somewhat garish appearance outside, due to the vividness of the alternating courses of brick and stone in proportions of three to one. While Sinan Pasha is an acknowledgement of Sinan's debt to Üç Şerefeli Cami and his interest in the potentialities of that plan, it also shows him experimenting with the requirements of a rectangular plot, facing southwards, more successfully than at Mihrimah across the water. He was to use the form of Sinan Pasha, but resolve the problems, with the building of his first hexagonal mosque in 962/1554.[11] It was at Topkapı and was for the Grand Vezir Kara Ahmet Pasha. Kara Ahmet took over office from Rüstem Pasha until the anger of the Janissaries with that great minister over the execution of Sultan Mustafa died away. When it did, Kara Ahmet was executed.[12]

The dome of his mosque is supported on six antique columns while two half-domes open obliquely over each wing towards the north and south walls and the arches behind, which support the east and west galleries. These galleries are divided by powerful rectangular buttresses through which their stairs ascend and which take the thrust of the central columns. By reducing the side domes to half-domes set at an angle of forty-five degrees, the rigid compartmentalization of the Üç Şerefeli is eliminated and the wings become an integral part of the whole mosque.[13] This opens up the interior space and so gives scope to the creative power of the architect to mould and modulate. Sinan was clearly pleased with this hexagonal form and returned to it with such mosques as that of Sokollu

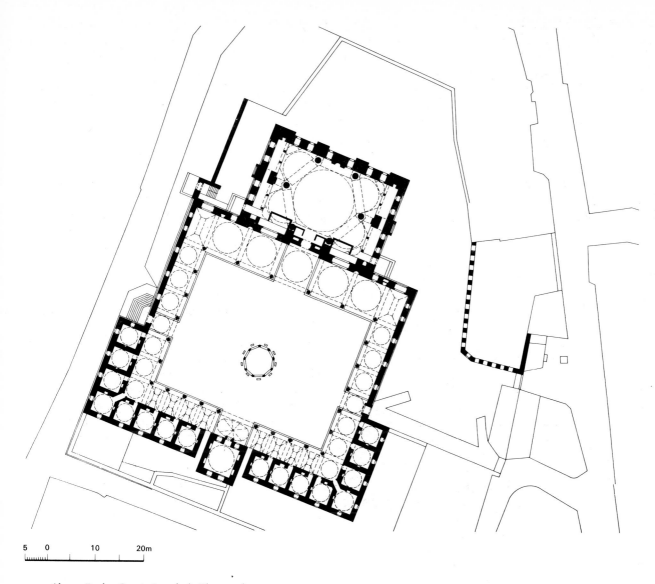

5 0   10   20m

234 Ahmet Pasha Cami, Istanbul. Plan, scale 1 : 750.

72 Mehmet at Kadırga and the Atık Valide at Üsküdar. The two columns against
the south and north walls transmit the pressure of the central dome to buttresses
inset into the wall. Each column is crowned by a large and richly carved stalac-
35 tite capital which bears an additional base from which the pendentives spring.
At the corners formed by the north and south walls and the galleries, and again
between the central buttresses of the east and west walls and the galleries, small
shell-shaped exedras help support the half-domes. The result is a high dome
(12 metres in diameter) in a relatively cramped space counteracted by the opening up of the wing areas and a sense of depth due to the lateral arches and the
galleries which they bear. The six columns stand free of the walls and plainly
express their function[14] and the six tie beams call attention to the hexagonal form.
The only discomfort arises from the unavoidable dominance of the minber over
the column on the right of a mihrab which is surprisingly modest. It is crowned
by two windows, one over the other, while a tier of three windows stands on
either flank. The minber is finely carved, its balustrades and triangular flanks
becoming a lattice of geometric patterns. The two tribunes flanking the entrance
are lower than the galleries[15] on the east and west and are intended for the müezzins. They are carried on marble columns and their floors become the ceilings of
the bays beneath; these retain early paintwork of great richness.[16] Deep red

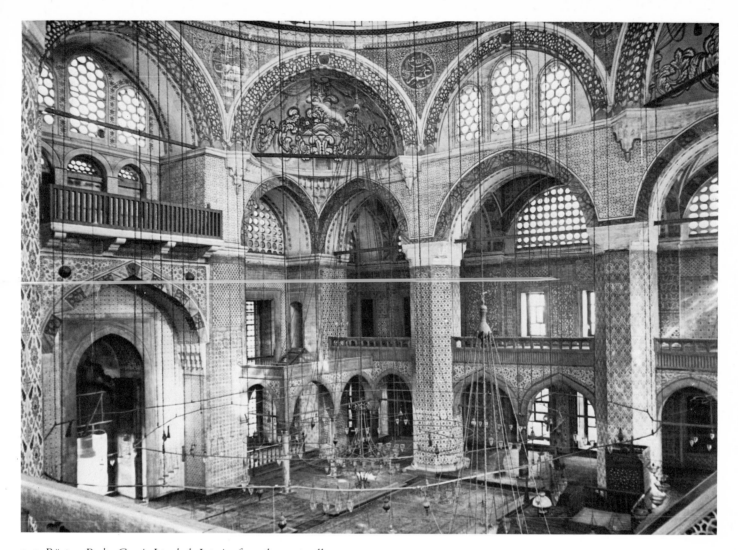

241 Rüstem Pasha Cami, Istanbul. Interior from the west gallery.

supported by three vaults and three pairs of arches under their balustrades. The span of the central arch on each side is greater than those on the flanks and this gives the little arcade the appearance of a façade and so adds to the detachment of the areas under the galleries. The four recesses between the buttresses of the north wall have been recently glassed in because the mosque is now a Koran school. This emphasizes their functionalism but masks the grandeur of the great casements each side of the door. These were already hooded by a pair of tribunes which cut across them. The east gallery is reached by a broad staircase from the outer terrace while the west gallery is reached by the staircase of the minaret. This has had to be rebuilt because of the weakening of its foundations due to the unwarranted alterations to the shop in the vault below. Arches in the north buttresses give access to the tribunes at lower level. High above these, across the vast ogee arch of the portal, a balcony projects on four prominent marble consoles in line with the string-course and the squat capitals of the piers. The only access is by ladders; its importance is that it gives access to the roof.

The arches under the exedras are set at right-angles so that the centres of the squinches are borne on stalactite pendentives and the sides on stalactite corbels set in the octagonal piers and the engaged buttresses supporting the central dome. The doorway is unexpectedly monumental because of the span of the deeply recessed arch above it, its own size, and the canopy formed by the high balcony. The minber is finely carved and has a tall hood supported by an elaborate alem; the kürsü is an excellent example of sixteenth-century inlay: but the modern red fitted carpet divided by white ribbing is incongruous. The mosque was painted in the nineteenth century wherever there was room to paint and the arches have been coated with ugly false marbling. This savagely detracts from the splendour of the tiles, which cover a great area of the walls and piers with an extravagance that only a sultan or sadrazam could afford. While those of the kıble wall are the richest and have the deepest red, there is exceptional elegance in the wild tulip patterns, with their nostalgia for the steppes, on the right and left of the door. There is every type of tulip and geometric pattern[28] that the palace artists and the kilns of Iznik could conjure up at that period, and it takes time to appreciate each separate panel without being overwhelmed by the profusion. The gallery tiles also have variations on a common theme of flowers in which the tulip is always predominant. At the top of the minber is a panel of blossom which is a miniature replica of those in the türbe of Haseki Hürrem. In the mihrab niche, with a thick black line firmly depicting the vases and the medallions of stylized flowers and buds, are four interrelated panels which appear to derive from a Persian design.[29] Above is a fine panel of calligraphic tiles. The vigorous script is set on a white ground; and the white of this collection is very clean indeed as are all the pigments which run only sufficiently to cast the faint shadow which gives them the three-dimensional force that brings the Iznik tile to life. Red is the dominant colour and the emerald green of the 1570s has yet to be obtained, but the varying shades of blue are exquisite.

Because the market hemmed in the mosque, its only dependencies are the hans and the mahkeme which is now a sacking warehouse. The latter stood across a small court at the back of the mosque and faced an L-shaped gallery. The central area under the mosque was designed as a warehouse. It is reached through a large coach door in the middle of the north side.

In the year of his death, 1561,[30] Rüstem Pasha's türbe was built by Sinan in the garden of the Şehzade mosque, and there Mihrimah installed panels of tile as splendid as any produced at Iznik. Outside, the tomb is a plain octagon with a porch and a dome. This rises straight from the wall without the recession of the türbes of Barbarossa or Hüsrev Pasha, but like that of the princes of Süleyman I *19* at the Selim Cami it has a shallow relief inscriptive band instead. This was to recur with later türbes at Hagia Sophia and Eyüp. Defined by the sharply cut corners, the eight facets are framed by ribbing and incisions in the stone which are outlined with a thin shadow as if they were calligraphy. All that remains of the flamboyance due to Persian influence lurking in the mosque to the north or the sepulchre of Şehzade Mehmet to the east is the rippling cresting at the edge *20* of the dome. It is because the exterior is so boldly puritanical that the rich tiles within have so majestic an effect. Only the Ramazanoğlu Cami at Adana, where panels of tile were added after 961/1552, can rival the tiles of the mosque and türbe of Rüstem Pasha. At Adana the panels are of uniform design except in the mihrab niche and subsidiary areas, unlike those of the Rüstem mosque. It is a matter of opinion whether this monotony is more dignified than the diffusion caused by a multiplicity of designs.

The death of her husband did not diminish Mihrimah's love of building, and *II* her own wealth was redoubled by that of the dead minister. Soon after his death, Sinan built the great mosque at Edirnekapı for her. There is no inscription *24* but a formidable welter of learned speculation concerning the date. Until recently, the mosque was generally supposed to have been built between 1540 and 1550, but Eyice[31] cites documents from Konyalı which show it to have been built between 1562 and 1565 for Süleyman in memory of his daughter. Since he predeceased her, this is incorrect.

Once more, Sinan was faced with an awkward site on the crown of a hill. *p* Here on the sixth hill once stood the monastery of St George and, although it is the most far-flung of the great mosques in the city, he raised it high on a platform set on vaults and gave it a tall and slender minaret so that it could be seen from afar both from within the walls and by the traveller from Edirne, in much the same way as, in England, Gothic spires such as Salisbury were signposts for the weary. Its height also served as a foil to the dome. A single minaret is always less

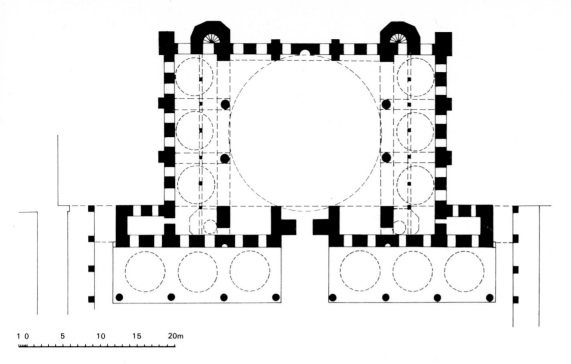

242 Mihrimah Cami, Istanbul. Plan, scale 1 : 500.

satisfactory than two, and one of normal dimensions would have looked weak beside so large a cupola. The mosque and its dependencies have twice suffered from severe earthquakes. The Hadika reports that some of the stairs in the minaret were damaged in the first quake of 1719 and had to be replaced by a ladder. The mosque and the medrese also suffered.[32] The much more severe quake of 1894 brought the all too slender minaret crashing down athwart the north-west corner of the mosque and its portico. A result has been the disfiguring of the interior by twentieth-century stencilling.

The double hamam is in ruins and used as a depot, and the imaret has been reduced to rubble, but the medrese has returned to its original function and is now a school for future imams. The main stair from the highway leads under the gatehouse to a fine platform which once had views over all the city, but these have been diminished by the increasing height of the blocks of apartments in the vicinity. The vantage point was also designed to receive the coffins at funerals. A postern leads to the paddock behind the kible wall from which a view of the grandiose buttresses exposed along that wall is obtained. There is a second entrance from the lane which runs between the mosque and the city wall, and a third from the track on the east side of the complex. Through extensions of the mosque façade on the north-east and the north-west, arches admit to the courtyard, which is an exceptionally large and long garden set with trees and stone paths which radiate from the şadırvan. This is large and its canopy is carried on two sets of arches, those of the outer ring on free-standing columns, and those of the inner ring on arches springing from columns incorporated into the cage over the water tank thus creating a new form of şadırvan, the forerunner of those of the later sixteenth century.

Each of the entry arches is double because there is the tall gateway wing of the mosque and a brick arch which forms part of the revak of the medrese. Entering the north gateway from the lane against the city wall, the visitor ascends a flight of stairs and passes under a large stone portal of great dignity which offers a fine vista through, to, and beyond the north-east entry. The double medrese,[33] built of alternating courses of brick and stone and heavily restored, lies behind revaks arched in ashlar. It is irregular in shape because of the restrictions of the site, and it has suffered from alterations. The rank of cells on the east begins under the north-east arch and stretches down the passage to the north-east gate.

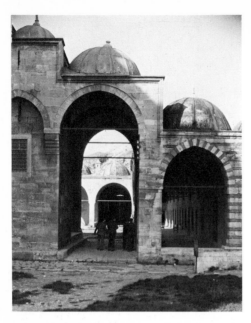

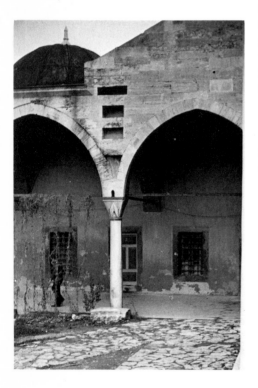

243 *Mihrimah Complex, Istanbul. Above: the south-west entry to the courtyard. Below: medrese wall onto the courtyard, showing the slots in the masonry which were sockets for the support of the roof of a second portico now demolished.*

Remains of ocaks can be seen on the exterior wall on the opposite side of this passage and suggest that there were once at least two or three more cells facing the city wall. But there could not have been cells along the whole length of the north wall, because the lane narrows so much that even the revak is distorted just before the north-west corner, where an arch admits to the present latrines. Because the platform on the south-east was part of the ceremonial entry, there was no extension of the medrese there, but on the west the cells continue beyond the minaret and the arch which unites mosque and medrese as far as the gateway onto the west lane. A colonnade along this flank of the mosque has fallen, but a flagstone path leads between two grass sofas to the restored double dershane which is triple-domed. It served the two medreses which shared the court. The scattered graves and washing in this little garden make this battered corner picturesque. On both the east and west sides of the medrese vestigial eyvans remain but are mere lobbies to the cells that flank them; obviously, for summer study, the double revak would have been as shaded and more airy.

The wide span of the arches of the revaks and of the loftier ones of the portico of the mosque add to the spaciousness of this complex. As has been noted in relation to the Kara Ahmet Cami on the next hill, the façade has been extended beyond the limits of the mosque by the addition of two rectangular stair halls, approximately one and a half times the size of a cell. Each has two casements onto the portico and two corresponding windows on the other side looking south towards the paddock. They are faint echoes of the vast tabhane wings of Beyazit II Cami. The stairs lead up to the lateral galleries inside the mosque, from which they can also be reached. Their architectural function is of first importance, for Sinan was concerned with grandeur when building Mihrimah, both inside and out. Originally, there was a second portico with a sloping roof. There are still traces of where the columns stood and of the lower sofa, while the holes in the medrese walls on the south-east and south-west of the court were once sockets for the support of the roof. This second portico would have made the court even narrower, but the added shade was important because it was at this mosque that the sultan and his officers prayed before leaving for campaigns in Europe.

The great dome rises from a formidable square base which completely dominates the three cupolas over each lateral gallery. At the four corners stand gargantuan polygonal turrets between which thrust immense arches which rise in giant steps to their flat crowns. The tympana of these arches are as near to sheets of glass as sixteenth-century building methods could allow, and carry the concept of the mosque as rib and fenestration in the Gothic manner as far as Ottoman structure permits. The Ottoman love for the open air is inescapably present and one is only surprised that the glass world of the International Style did not originate in Turkey.

Each tympanum has fifteen large windows and four circular ones within the movement of the curve of the arch. Below, in the wall area, are three more tiers of windows to which must be added those in the dome itself.[34] So striking is the effect of this fenestration that Sinan felt it necessary to reassure the beholder; hence the strength of his turrets and his addition of stepped buttresses carried on corner piers at the south-east and south-west. The effect is an illusion. The turrets have little more purpose than the more modest ones at the corners of normal Ottoman domes. Only the heavy upper parts serve the structural function of loading. Two-thirds of the structure of the northern pair does not even reach the ground. Seen from the interior, the structure is found to be based, as always, on the four piers at the corner of the square on which the dome is set. These merge with the turrets but form their support as much as they are their dependencies. The south tympanum is carried on the thickness of the wall, which explains the need for battered buttresses which protrude impressively into the paddock. The north tympanum is carried on the corner piers and two engaged piers in the usual manner. The lateral tympana are visibly supported by the corner piers and by large twin granite columns, perhaps from the monastery of St George.

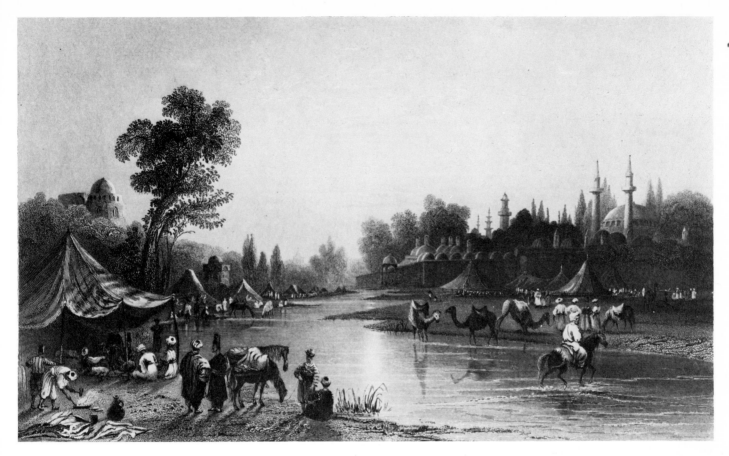

244 The Tekkiye, Damascus, from the Baraka river. Nineteenth-century engraving.

The dome is thirty-seven metres high[35] and twenty metres wide but it appears to be even higher, partly because the broad side galleries over six wide-span, semicircular arches are relatively low. There is a small mihrab in the south wall of the east gallery where a loge is latticed off for royal use. The supporting arches are skilfully painted green and white and there is the recurrent problem of historical justification for this use of fake marbling. Here, it would appear authentic. The three upper arches supporting the tympana add to the impression of space because of the grandeur of their scale. The greatest single contributing force to the sense of the limitless is the multiplicity of windows of which only those above the mihrab attempt to copy sixteenth-century coloured glass: the rest are platitudinous baroque. Whether there were ever tiles round the mihrab cannot be proved because of the earthquake damage, but since there is no trace at all it may be assumed that there were not. The white marble minber excels that of Süleymaniye in its grace, although it lacks a crown of sparkling stars in a dark night. It is not a popular mosque, yet it is one of Sinan's most imaginative works in Istanbul. At the time of its construction it was a revolutionary building.

A number of saints and holy men are buried within the precincts, including one whose grave is under a tree in the court on the western side; more intriguing is the grave behind the damaged stretch of north wall, recessed out of sight and out of reach unless one climbs up onto the window ledge. South-west of the mosque is the private cemetery and türbe of Ahmet Pasha[36] which has lost the double domes which once covered it.[37] There is authority for rectangular two-roomed türbes with twin domes in the one Sinan later constructed for Pertev Pasha who died in 1572[38] and whose complex at Izmit he also planned. This family tomb at Eyüp once possessed two gilded and painted wooden domes.[39] Such a türbe was rare in Ottoman times and makes that at Mirimah all the more noteworthy. It was the family tomb of the Rüstem Pasha family.

One other major work completed Sinan's services to Süleyman I whose reign was drawing to a close. He planned a great complex at Damascus beside the Baraka river known as the Tekkiye to serve as an imaret for the pilgrimage or Hajj. Selim II was to add a convent round a square courtyard with a large pool in the spacious Syrian manner. It is now in a sadly neglected state. West of it, Sinan enclosed an area more than twice its size in the meadow by the river which acted as a boundary to the tented encampment of the pilgrims.[40] Across the north side of Selim II's extension is a broad walk between two plain gates, each side of which he built rows of vaulted shops from which the necessities of life could be purchased by the travellers. In the middle of the north parade and opposite the gate into the tekke, he built a third portal, but the complex in the rectangular area between the shops and the river has been destroyed. The gate is of interest because of the elaborate decoration of alternating dark and light courses in the voussoirs and the remarkably rich carving. This presents a shock, because the white marble turns out to be plaster filling of exceptionally good quality, for it has endured for four hundred years.[41] Nothing comparable can be found in Istanbul and it must be assumed that it is local workmanship, as are the fine tiles in the lunettes of the windows of the complex. They never match those of Iznik in the intensity of their colours and only offer pale mauve instead of the brilliant reds of the Anatolian kilns.[42] It need not be assumed, because the work was carried out by local contractors, that Sinan may not have inspected it in person at least once, although for the greater part of the time his task must have been delegated to a subordinate. The success of his plan indicates that he had some knowledge of the site.

On the opposite side to the street of shops is the elaborate main entry to the complex. The site was cut out of the flank of a low hill and this has been used to mass trees above the buildings as a backdrop. Through the east gate one steps down into the great court with its splendid pavement. It had to be large because of the crowds for which it had to cater. How large, is indicated by the fact that the vanguard of the caravan had pitched its tents and slept before the rearguard had arrived, and meals must have been served in shifts continuously throughout the day. It is not the space that is wonderful but its control and the relationship of the buildings, which never lose contact with each other and which, although only one storey high, are never crushed by the fine trees inside and round the yard. Before one, on entering, is the rectangular central pool which lies in front of the mosque and its tall double porticoes. These are unusual because both have central cradle vaults with twin flanking domes; two more domes retreat down the side of the mosque behind the son cemaat yeri. At the end, great grille windows right and left of the mosque complete the outer portico. They are united to the revak of cells on each side of the court by a stone wall. The mosque extends into the cemetery garden behind. The broad porticoes cover an area as great as the mosque interior itself and form a summer mescit, but when the pilgrims gathered for prayer they filled the whole avlu and were reflected in the waters of the pool beneath the clouds and the blue sky. Inside, the mosque is not large; indeed, it is no more important a domed square than many a vezir's mosque in spite of the twin minarets which announce that it was a royal foundation.[43] The vivid use of alternating courses of black and white marble in the local tradition, which is so sympathetically controlled outside, is here manifested by a vigorous marble dado dominated by ranks of large black circles.

Even the pavement in front of the mosque is striped black and white,[44] except where strips of garden lie between it and two lines of six cells along the east and west walls, facing each other across the mosque. Their porticoes consist of twelve domes carried on columns which must have been in short supply because the alternation of light and dark shafts is not consistent. It may also be that the window

III Selimiye Cami, Edirne.

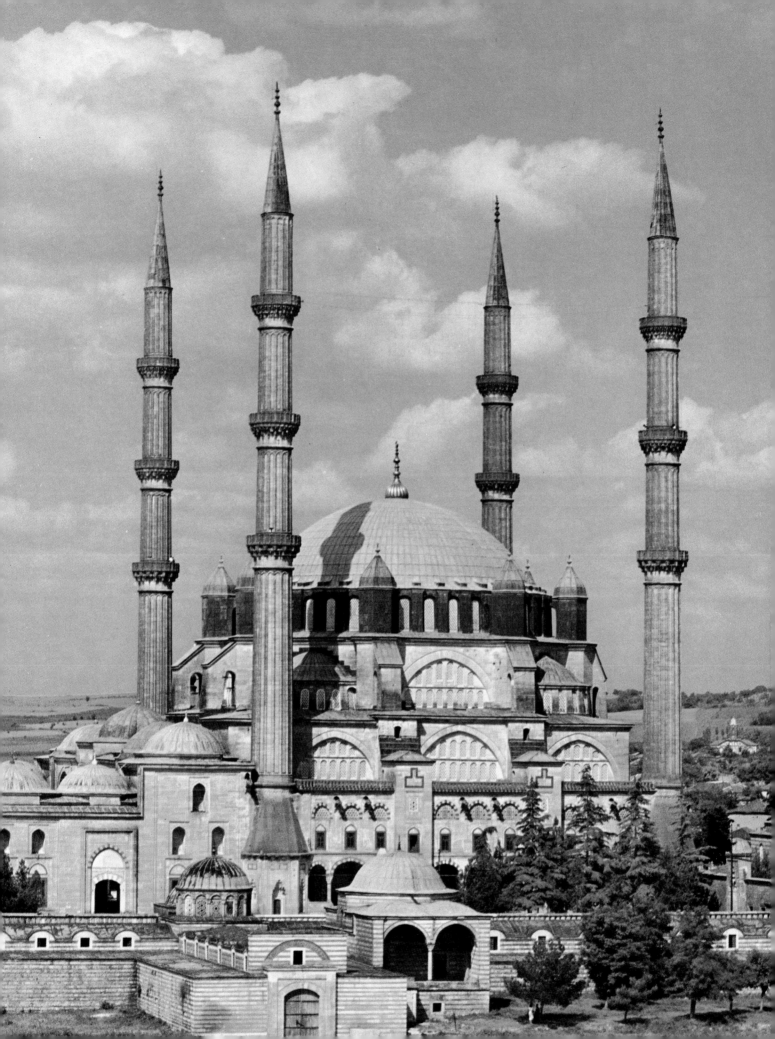

frames and lintels were obtained ready-cut, for the attempt to alternate basalt with orange composite stone is not successful. Opposite the mosque and the cells – doubtless for important travellers – is the imaret which forms a C round a wide stretch of lawn and trees. Two long refectories reach down the east and west walls to the north, each with fourteen domes divided into two ranks by five piers. In the middle is the large kitchen, once under two big ventilator domes with cradle vaults also capped by ventilators.[45] They have been remodelled and it is impossible to be sure of the original plan. Two small doors give access to the long yard behind this wide lean building, and there is a major door in the centre opposite the gate to the precinct in the middle of the north wall. This gate is preceded by a domed porch, while the wall on each side is lightened by three windows. The door was clearly intended for the delivery of supplies. On each side of the central kitchen are two twin-domed lesser rooms, each with a very large ocak or range at the far end. These could have been stores or served as dining chambers for the leaders of the Hajj. Each is divided by a pier. These rooms have doors in the middle, between the two windows, onto the portico, while the kitchen door is set to the east but its position may have been altered at a later date. The kitchen block is preceded by a portico which could have given shade to the pilgrims queueing for food, but which also gives it a certain splendour with its ten domes, its tiles, and the liveliness of its black and white arches over the windows as well as those of the colonnade. The side doors from the kitchen are almost opposite doors at the north end of each refectory, but the main entry to these long halls with their fine vistas is near the east and west central gates. That the back door was for servitors and not for pilgrims is suggested by the gates in the walls which join the kitchen portico to the refectories, six domes back from the gates.

However much may be due to local workmanship and Sinan's respect for local traditions this, like other buildings of the period or later in Damascus and Aleppo, is an Ottoman complex in every respect. It was a royal foundation, and Sinan is likely to have sent his best trained student to supervise the work.[46] Elsewhere, his plans were either less successful or less intelligently carried out. The very standardization that made remote control possible led to slipshod mistakes and ugly improvisation. These occur in the mosque of Ali Pasha at Babaeski[47] where the clumsy work in the galleries is matched by the ugly workmanship at the mosque of Mehmet Ağa at Çarşamba, an early work of Davut Ağa. At Babaeski, it is probable that Sinan's subordinates and local contractors were unskilled and missed the guidance of their master. This was not the case with whoever carried out his modest plan for the mosque of Lala Mustafa Pasha at Ilgin[48] nor that of Bosnalı Mehmet Pasha at Sofia, the headquarters of the Viceroy of Europe; but these were simpler designs than that of the elaborate mosque at Babaeski and it was Sinan's own fault if he misjudged the capacity of his deputies. A mosque which he certainly supervised and which was an astonishing experiment was that built for the bully who strangled Şehzade Mahmut at Amasya, Zal Mahmut Pasha, on the hillside beyond Ayvansaray just before entering Eyüp.[49]

Eyice, with his usual sensitivity, dates the mosque between 1560 and 1566[50] but has little to say about this fine complex. Gabriel misdates it as 1551[51] and so does Öz.[52] Boyd offers the definitive explanation[53] and copes with the misleading date on the çeşme due to a profusion of Ottoman aunts. He shows that Zal Mahmut was in no position to build such an expensive complex prior to the 1560s. The medreses are not listed in the Tezkere and, with the upper one, the break in the stone and brick courses at the beginning of the cells beyond the stairs to the lower complex is plain to see. It is likely that Sinan conceived the plan of the mosque and left the building of the lesser areas to subordinates. The plan of the upper court is muddled, so that half-arches are necessary in order to complete the north revak, while ungainly vaulted cells on the west and roadway side make any revak there impossible. The dershane is pushed into the north-east corner. The lower medrese, which may be earlier in date, also has recessed cells requiring

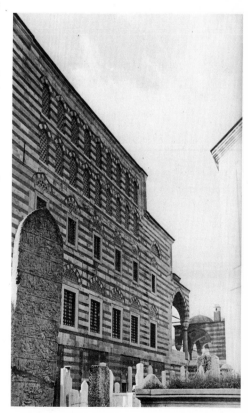

245 *Zal Mahmut Pasha Complex, Istanbul. The east flank of the mosque with, behind the gravestones, the basement cells.*

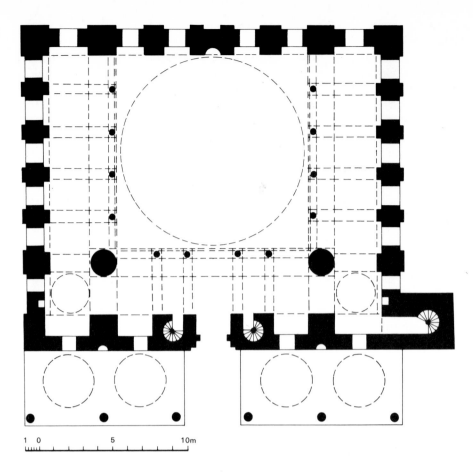

1   0   5   10m

246 Zal Mahmut Pasha Cami, Istanbul. Plan, scale 1 : 250.

passages and a dershane which fails to unite its college about it. The terrain was difficult, but a more satisfactory solution might have been found by Sinan who would have enjoyed the challenge just as he did that presented by the mosque itself. It may indicate an interruption to his work, possibly the all-important order to raise the great mosque of Selim II on the height above Edirne. If so, it is no wonder that the completion of the work for the objectionable Zal Mahmut was thrust into less than competent hands, since his best assistants would be needed to help with the masterpiece of his life. Howsoever this may be, the building is not an early one, for too much experience has gone into it and the first half or middle of the 1560s is the likely date.

One either enters the complex by the gate off the upper road opposite the little mosque of Silahşor Mehmet Bey[54] or by the plain and solid, but handsome, gate off the lower highway beside the Horn. This admits to a large garden with the lower medrese on the right and the very large türbe of the pasha on the left; this is an austere octagonal building but grandly proportioned. Beyond it is a small cemetery on a grass sofa some two feet high with a retaining wall on each side of it. Behind it are cells set back into vaults under the mosque itself in the same way that shops are installed in mosque foundations, but this is the only sixteenth-century use of vaults as cells that I have discovered. The result is highly dramatic because the mosque rises to a seemingly great height with its tiers of windows transforming it into a palace or even a block of apartments. This escarpment of stone and brick courses is united by the stone coping of the wall east of the mosque portico, above which it connects with the flight of stairs from the upper court down to the parterre and becomes part of the arched doorway at their foot. It also unites the first cell of the east range of the upper medrese which, as we have seen, becomes plaster where Sinan's work breaks off. The east wall of the mosque is pierced by as many as four tiers of windows, including six casements with honeycomb semicircular fanlights above them,

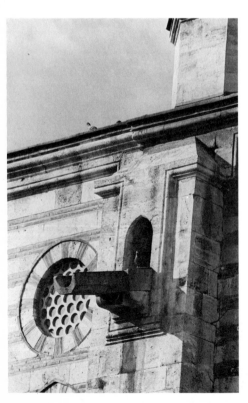

247 Zal Mahmut Pasha Cami, Istanbul. A drainspout in the south wall.

and two rows of nine double windows over yet another, but smaller row of casements below them. There are also the doors and windows of the basement cells.
Four turrets stand at each corner of the mosque roof[55] and on the south, where two
formidable buttresses project, are two immense drain-spouts. The portico,
reached by the flight of stairs between the medreses, has four low domes and a
rectangular roof. The domes ride on shallow octagonal brick drums coated in
terracotta plaster, which was also used to clad the rubble walls of the medreses.
The spandrels of the arches are of alternating brick and stone courses supported
by handsome stalactite capitals of six columns of Marmara marble and granite.
A screen wall rises behind the domes and behind this, on the east and west, are
two low corner domes. Between these rises the main wall of the mosque. This is
divided into two sections of two windows each by hexagonal turrets which do
not reach the height of the main four. They contain stairways to the roof. The
minaret projects beyond the west wall of the mosque and is reached by an unexpected passage inside the mosque itself. It was rebuilt after the earthquake of
1894[56] but is probably approximately its original height.

Inside the mosque there is a fresh surprise, because the north end forms a
narthex which is cut off from the harem by four columns which carry the five
arches of an arcade between two thick and stumpy piers.[57] These, together
with the buttresses of the south wall, support powerful arches of considerable
and exposed thickness from which rise the pendentives which carry the dome.
Behind the arches on all but the south side are large galleries covered by gently
sloping roofs. These galleries make the interior look unusually compact and the
dome unexpectedly lofty. Each side of the narthex, as might be expected, the
corner areas are cut off and dark. Between the humpy piers and the south wall,
on each side is an arcade formed by four columns with baklava capitals carrying
arches, each with a rosette at its tip and a disc in its spandrel. The balustrades
of the galleries are pierced by miniature arches like those associated with a
papuçluk. The galleries are so broad that they seem to look down into a pit,
like some *avant garde* theatre, rather than up to the dome. They also look as if
they were a preliminary essay for the great galleries of the Selimiye at Edirne.
The heaviness of the structure that hems it in gives height to the dome from
ground level, but also brings one immediately face to face with the kible wall
where the mihrab and minber also emphasize the height. The mihrab has a frame
of exceedingly pretty tiles decorated with wild flowers and discs on a white
ground, and there are tile inscriptions over the windows although nothing to
justify Evliya's enthusiastic description. He also says that there are 366 windows
which is about twice the actual number.

The strong use of contrasting courses emphasizes the length of the building
as opposed to the height outside, and it is a pity that they were not extended
the length of the east flank of the upper medrese. Sinan solved the problems of Zal
Mahmut Cami with inventiveness and accomplishment. The Syrian love of
stripes occurs throughout his work, but sometimes he modified the effect with
stone or plaster.

The mosque of Kadıasker İvaz Efendi built in 1585, possibly under Sinan's
aegis,[58] amid the few remains of the Blachernae Palace hard against the Byzantine
walls may usefully be discussed in connection with Zal Mahmut Cami because
both can be seen, and their relationship appreciated, from the Horn. İvaz Efendi
is a relatively small and intimate mosque with exceptionally large and fine panels
of Iznik tiles in the mihrab apse. There is a familar use of vivid alternating courses
of stone and brick, and the north façade also has four tiers of windows which
include a set at attic level rising above the subsidiary corner domes on the north-
east and north-west. It is this feature which most imitates the Zal Mahmut
mosque with its spectacular scheme of fenestration. In addition, in accordance
with a growing tradition, the lead which covers the dome of İvaz Efendi Cami
covers the buttresses at the corners and descends to roof level, an aspect of the
roofing of the late sixteenth-century mosques which gives them a certain serious-
ness and heaviness and is most marked in the mosque of Kılıç Ali Pasha at

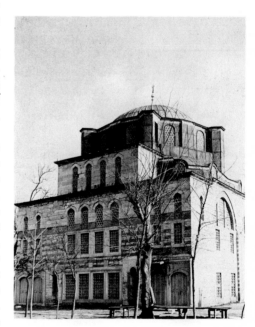

*248 Hacı İvaz Efendi Cami, Istanbul, seen
from the north-west.*

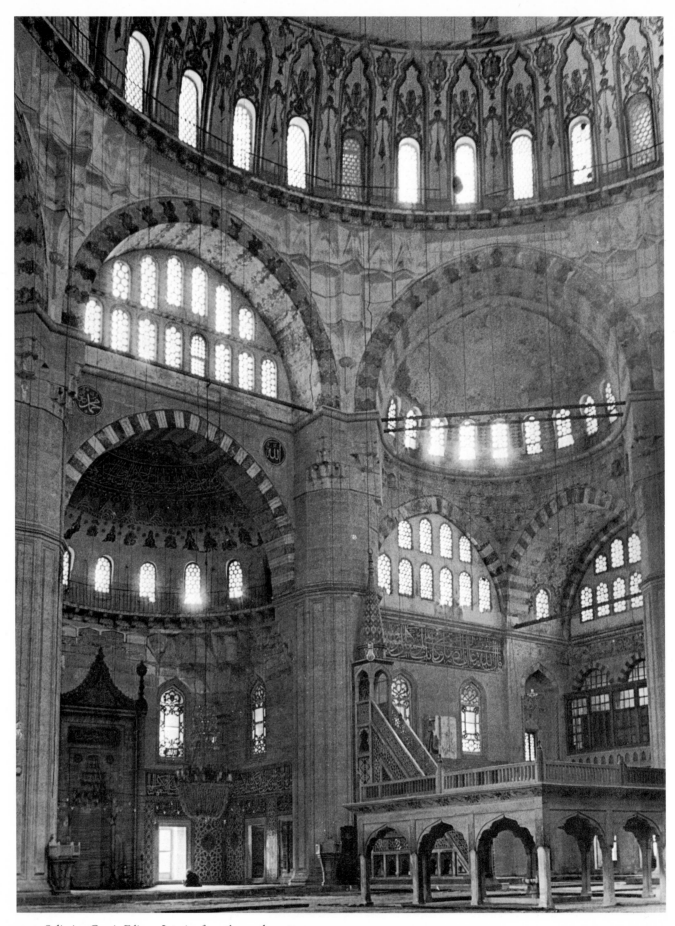

249 *Selimiye Cami, Edirne. Interior from the north-east.*

Tophane, one of the last works of Sinan.[59] İvaz Efendi Cami has its main entry in the north-west corner side by side with a twin door to the stairs up to the gallery and a secondary door across the four casements at ground level, which are only divided by their stone frames, on the north-east. It is related by the placing of its doors to Piyale Pasha Cami at Kasımpasha.[60] There was once a portico on a low sofa on all three sides at İvaz Efendi Cami but not along the mihrab wall. This forced the minaret back to the south-west and it is the only example of a minaret in this position in Istanbul. The very high base of this minaret is due to the need for it to clear the roof level of the missing portico which it once helped to support.

At Zal Mahmut Pasha Cami, Sinan was still working as much within the restrictions of standardization as are modern architects who are forced to economize by using prefabricated units of standard measurement. Forms of window and door, turret and buttress, chimney and arch recur, although on occasion they are modified. There are only two types of capital, with some deviation in details, the chevron and the stalactite. The buildings of Istanbul are unified by the use of limestone which grows grey with age. Marmara marble was frequently employed because more exotic columns had been exhausted. There could be no escape from the domination of the dome. But all the time, after 1556, Sinan was striving to excel the limitations of mediaeval obstinacy. He toiled hard and had he died in 1560 he would have left a good name behind him if no more; but he then had twenty-seven more years in which to work.

The highway to Edirne from Istanbul is still indifferently paved here and there, but the journey takes less than half a day: it could take a week in the sixteenth century. Visually, the best approach to the city is from Greece, where the road runs along the opposite shore of the Maritza or Meriç river. Edirne can be seen above the trees, standing on its hillside with all the domes and minarets lined against the sky above the white mosques. The Selimiye with its minarets reaching over seventy metres into the sky dominates the scene.[61] It is the climax of the work of Sinan and therefore of all Ottoman architecture. No successor, not even Mehmet Ağa, his senior assistant and the builder of the mosque of Ahmet I, was gifted with either his imagination or his courage with which to develop the form of the mosque any further. With Sinan's death, invention withered away. So little was the master's work understood that his students retreated to the plan of the Şehzade. Here at the Selimiye, Sinan built such a space that has rarely been excelled under a dome, which in width equalled that of Hagia Sophia,[62] and freed his work of any trace of the regimentation of a military past. The four minarets at the corners of the mosque boast of his success. In the years that Selimiye was being built, 1569-75,[63] Sinan could do no wrong.

The genius of this mosque lies in the organization of interior space. There is the bold size of the apse recess which sets back the mihrab in a highly theatrical manner. Because of this withdrawal, it is possible to light it from three sides and this, together with the brilliant colours of the concentrated panels of tile, floods the area with its own glowing light. Thus set apart like a sanctuary, the mihrab area leaves the central space free to express a counter mystery largely lit from the circle of windows in the dome above. There is an elation in the way the dome rides on eight huge, independent supports, fluted at first but plain at their summit, without capitals but with squinches or consoles instead, so that the arches appear to grow integrally out of the piers. The result is that triumph of space which dominates the interior. It absorbs all interest, and the lateral galleries seem far away. The manipulation of these galleries and their arcades beneath, so that interior and exterior are used as the reversals of each other, gives that deep satisfaction that the perfect solution of an intractable equation offers. The lateral arcades of the Şehzade and Süleymaniye mosques are here articulate inside as well as out and have a real function. At ground-floor level they serve to bring the interior walls in nearly to the side piers and thus give an almost square form to the central area while, above, the galleries are recessed over the exterior arcades to create handsome porches. Thus valuable extra space is created at upper level which both has a functional purpose and adds aesthetically to the

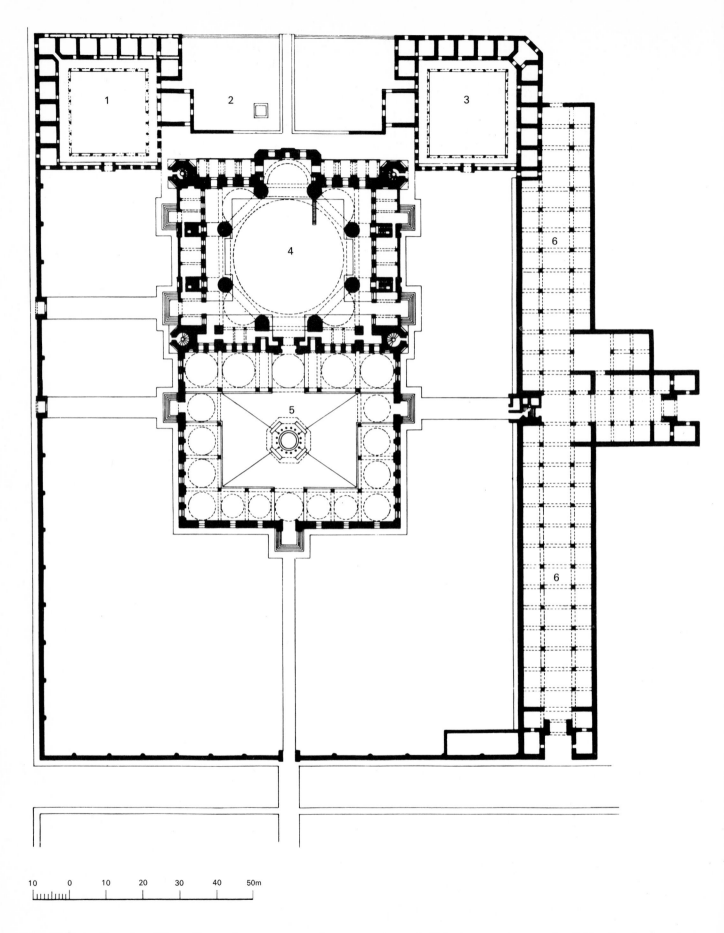

250 Selimiye Complex, Edirne. Plan, scale 1 : 1,000. 1 medrese; 2 cemetry; 3 darül-kurra; 4 mosque; 5 avlu; 6 Kavaflar Arasta.

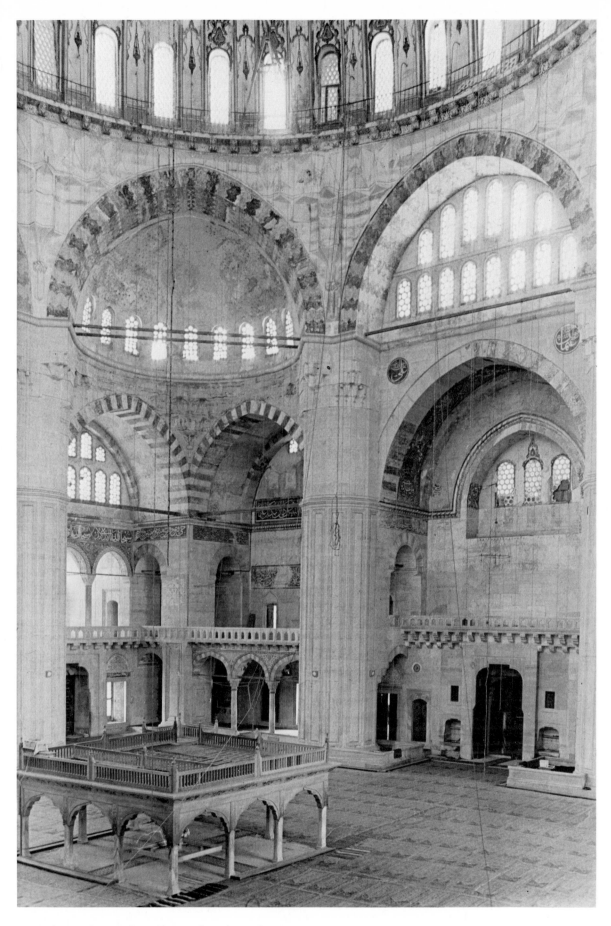

251 Selimiye Cami, Edirne. Interior from the south-east.

feeling of freedom which this interior breathes. Equally assured is the placing of the tribune under the centre of the dome: a distracting piece of furniture is   25 made to punctuate the central space. Thus the infinite volume of space under the dome is beautifully balanced, just as the sphere of heaven must be, yet with that definition which all space requires. And the square singing gallery, by anchoring the centralized force of Sinan's plan, defines what would otherwise be diffused.[64]

The tribune is of marble and set on twelve low arches of elaborate foliate design. It roofs a marble patio in which is set a water basin which is highly cusped and curved.[65] This can be seen as the vestigial remnant of the old central court of the Bursa-type mosque. At the north-west corner of this mahfil is the stump of a pier with panelled facets like those of the eight main piers. Into this the stairway to the platform for the chanters is cut as well as niches for jugs. The tribune is deliberately kept low but it is not so unobtrusive that it does not mark the navel of the mosque.

The traditional furniture of the mosque is as elegant and finely worked as it   25 could be in the sixteenth century. The mihrab is of Marmara marble and is tall and narrow, culminating in arabesques. These sweep up to the apex of a triangle between two alems set on shafts like miniature minarets. The lofty marble minber has claim to be the finest in the country simply because of the quality of the carving. The design is taut within the equilateral triangle which holds the big fretted sun disc. The balustrade and borders of interlocking polygons are traditional in form, and so are the multifoliate arches of the papuçluk. It is the fine workmanship which makes this minber outstanding, that and its splendid hood of tile; but when stone is turned to lace a certain femininity develops. There is a fine kürsü still to be seen but Koran desks and other furnishings have all gone. Round the edge of the floor runs a ledge of opus sectile marble which also paves the deep recesses of the casements.

A white on blue ceramic inscription runs round all three sides of the apse above the casements. A lower inscription is set above each window in addition. There are other much larger painted inscriptions, some on a terracotta ground, under the first tier of the tympana, and they also extend along the south wall of the mosque.[66] Above the hünkâr mahfil they are on Iznik tile again. Over the lower windows of the south wall, the inscriptions are inset into the movement of the arch above. The panels between the casements which form a great dado round the apse

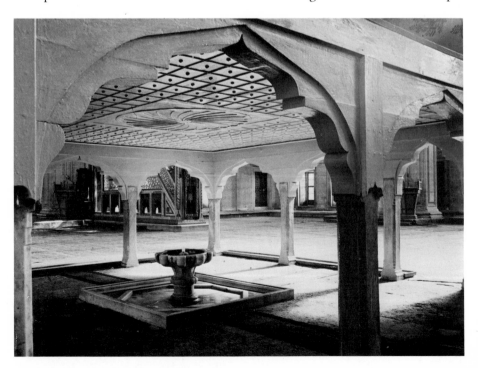

252 Selimiye Cami, Edirne. The central fountain below the müezzins' tribune.

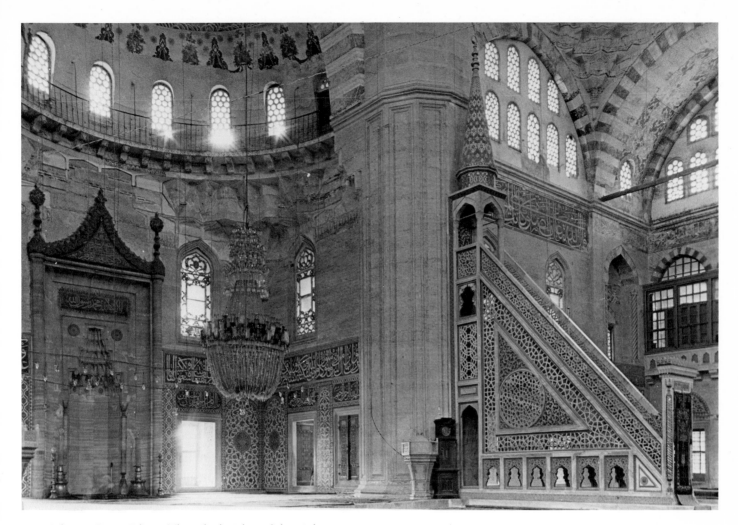

253 *Selimiye Cami, Edirne. The mihrab niche and the minber.*

are of those rich-hued floral designs that are the most spectacular of all the panels
249 produced at Iznik. The dome and the semi-domes are defaced by florid Italianate
paintwork, but it has flaked and faded and is less obtrusive than it is elsewhere.
251 The floor is partly carpeted by sets of united prayer rugs from Hagia Sophia in
panels of six in two rows. Others of this eighteenth-century type can be found at
Üç Şerefeli and also among the mosques of Üsküdar.

The imperial loge is in the traditional north-west corner. In the spandrels of
254 its four arches are delicate floral tiles which are also inset in the spandrels of arches
supporting other tribunes over recesses elsewhere in the mosque. The royal
balustrade is a continuation of that of the east gallery and supports a seventeenth-
century lattice added by Ibrahim I. The loge projects beyond balcony level to
incorporate the first windows on the south side so it forms a spacious room.
228 The inlaid doors are without peer, those which prove to be the shutters of the
window of the south wall being of particular quality. Inscriptive panels are set
above the doors and windows and above these are bold friezes. Between are set
234 the finest panels in the mosque which are not excelled by the famous trio which
used to be in the hamam at Topkapısaray[67] and which were, until recently, on
the wall of the Altın yolu, the Golden Road, of the harem.[68] Such panels are
great set-pieces of multifoliate flower and leaf.[69] Above the doorways are crestings
in tile which are more elaborate and bold than any I have seen elsewhere. Most
exceptionally, the south window with its matchless shutters forms the mihrab of
the loge within an elaborate, orthodox frame. To kneel before this casement when
it and the shutters are open and look out towards the cloudy sky is an intensely
poetic experience. The staircase up to the loge is set into the thickness of the
wall but is much wider and the stairs less exactly high than usual.

There is a little modern stained glass in the building, which may replace older examples. However, it would have detracted from the warmth of the sandstone if the light, which is already softened by the traditional double glazing, had been yet more obscured, and there is always a serious clash if any but the best coloured glass is set anywhere near tiles. It is impossible to tell what the original dominant colour in the dome was,[70] but terracotta appears likely because it reflects the brick and plaster out of which the stalactites are carved. If the dome had been mainly terracotta the harmony achieved would have been most satisfactory. Two details may be mentioned. There is a marble çeşme with a hipped arch *251* under the double consoles of the north gallery and set between the buttress and the door to the stairs. Above this door is a large spoked wheel ventilator recalling those of the Şehzade and the Ulu Cami at Bursa.

Outside, the dome is massed logically without the weakening of the central *III* force through semi-domes at the flanks. Instead, the mass is held tensely between the four great minarets at its corners. The courtyard, although grand, is strictly subordinated to the dictatorship of the great dome and its massive supports. Continual variation in the proportions and the delineation of the details in red stone also contribute to Sinan's achievement, but the decoration is always restrained and integral with the structure. No other Ottoman architect was to have this knowledge of the handling of mass of masonry, of structure, or of the behaviour of materials, or his experience in the control of men so that they may produce their best work. This mosque and its dome have the right to rank with the first monuments of architecture, for they break free of the handicaps of tradition while expressing the sum of Islamic idealism. In bringing the classical period to its climax, Sinan destroyed it. There was nothing left to do save change.

Selimiye is built of red and honey-coloured stone. Red sandstone is used to outline the windows and courses and form geometric patterns in the lower buttresses in particular. The voussoirs of the exterior arches are made of alternating stone and marble to attain a brilliant red and white effect. Both the mosque and its courtyard are rectangular over all, but the mosque is square apart from its flanking coulisses and the deep apse of the mihrab.[71] The areas between the minarets on the east and west are deeply recessed and are divided into three porches by stair towers which also act as buttresses. Between tower and minaret on each side, and tower and tower in the centre, are three arches which carry the galleries above. These have polychrome voussoirs and honeycomb fan windows in their tympana and tall rectangular windows below, which are framed in red by a line which also etches a pointed arch above each of them. Between the upper arches are set powerful gutters[72] which with their shadows make a strong three-dimensional accent out-thrust from the building in contrast to the deep recesses of the porch. The lower arches are supported on antique marble columns of verd-antique with stalactite capitals.[73] The centre arch from which the steps fan out is wider than the two at either side under which are stone balustrades. The central arcades have a lower and more pointed middle arch between two which are larger and almost semicircular. By contrast, the wide arcades above the steps have the larger arch in their centre.

The roofline acts as a string-course which is contiguous with that of the top of the octagonal bases of the minarets which on the south-east and south-west are three-quarters independent of the building. They project nearly as far on the south side as the apse itself and form two deep recesses in that wall. These form sofas under an arcade and echo the rhythm of the son cemaat yeri, but there is only room for one arch on the apsidal side and not a pair. Inside the mosque, the string-course is reflected in the top of the panels which form the lower and major section of each of the eight great piers that carry the dome. It is from this level that the lower range of tympana arches spring. They are clearly defined outside as three on the east and west and two on each side of the half-dome crowning the apse. The two arches on the south in this range carry rows of six and four windows, while the lateral ones are larger and have seven and five; the centre tympana are exceptional because they are broadest of all and carry eight and six

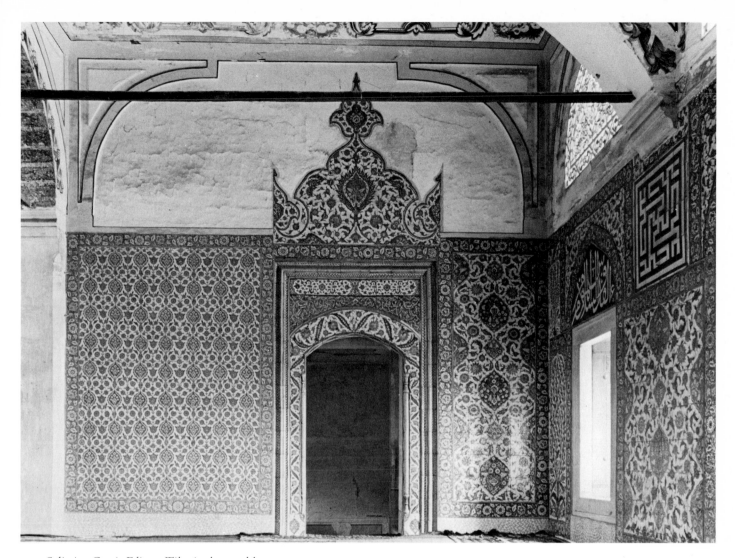

254 Selimiye Cami, Edirne. Tiles in the royal loge.

windows each. The piers inside are recessed into the south wall so that the arch over the apse springs from a large console which is, in effect, a stalactite squinch. Two narrow arches spring from the lateral piers to join the rectangular piers behind which are also buttresses. These divide the galleries into three sections, but archways pierced through them give access from one part to the other.

The success of this plan, as has been shown, comes from the impression of all-envelopment which is given by the broad and lofty dome rising from its eight clearly distinguished piers, and which is not diminished by the depth of the galleries; for it is only at their level, and then under a relatively low ceiling, that the interior of the mosque is extended laterally over the exterior porches. Because the walls below are drawn in close to the piers, the whole movement upwards is unimpeded, and when one eventually notices the depth of the galleries it is to gain a sense of release rather than of diffusion. Above those arches whose tympana ride on the colonnade of the galleries, soar the eight major arches whose bold honeycomb squinches of mortar and brick carry the dome. In each corner, the four half-domes set at angles of forty-five degrees are supported by irregular stalactite squinches.

Outside, the four large upper tympana are set between two thick flying buttresses of the utmost simplicity which form slightly pigeon-toed pairs on each of the four sides. Above each of these eight buttresses, hexagonal turrets mark the tops of the eight interior piers and take the major thrusts of the dome at the level of its belt of windows. They are equidistant from each other, there being three buttressing ribs and four tall windows between each turret. Behind the domes of the son cemaat yeri at tympana level, there are two stair turrets at the north-east and north-west corners with small onion domes which were only repeated by Sinan with the minaret of the mescit at Büyükçekmece. Finally, the dome itself appears, seeming from without to be only one third of a circle whereas, inside, it is revealed as a full half sphere. This is because its lower sweep is concealed outside by ribs which serve as a series of twenty-four clamps of stone. These and the eight turrets act as a drum in accordance with Ottoman practice. It is at the level of the lead caps of the stabilizing turrets of the dome that the first balcony of the minarets is set.

The minarets are fluted and have three şerefes, each of which has fine stalactite corbelling supporting it. The pair on the north side have three independent and intertwining stairs by which to reach each şerefe. They are all equal in size and may represent the four corners of the universe but, because the mosque is not square but rectangular, they are not equidistant: indeed, their interval at the flanks is only two-thirds that across the front and mihrab walls: they appear to be four-square until subjected to scrutiny. They add immensely to the power of the upward thrust of the building. Had two more minarets been added at the corners of the courtyard, in the manner of Mehmet Ağa's Ahmediye, some of *189* this force would have been diminished and their symbolism lost. The courtyard flows outward from the static mass of the mosque and down through the heights of the son cemaat yeri, the domes of which reach the level of the first tympana. The flanks of the son cemaat yeri are walled and have tiered windows which from outside makes them a continuation of the main building. The lateral doors into the courtyard are set between the son cemaat yeri and the revaks and are traditionally double-arched in a frame which is boldly expressed as are all the roof courses of the courtyard. The three pairs of double windows are equally sharply framed along the east and west walls, but the three each side of the main gate in the north wall are smaller and set independently. The double-arched main gate is remarkably modest, especially in comparison with the stately build-up of that of Süleymaniye. Perhaps Sinan wished to avoid trouble over the north revak, and he certainly wanted nothing to detract from the single, momentous presence of the great dome. The north gate into Selim's court has no stalactite recess, but an arabesque pattern which is flanked by slender pilasters crowns the larger arch. Above the inner arch over the door is the traditional inscription in gold relief on a green ground.

On entering the courtyard there is an immediate impact of splendour. The *255* façade of the son cemaat yeri and the pavement are of Marmara marble. Spaciousness flows from the great span of the five main arches of the portico which are all of the same width; but the central arch is flanked by two small ones which add to its grandeur. Its cantaloup dome, which is the most heavily fluted of all the domes, is set on a higher base than the others and is masked on the courtyard side by a rectilinear apron inset with two inscriptive panels. Above the small arches, ogee unlike the rest, which are semicircular, are set two bold marble discs inscribed with quotations from the Koran in the manner of Karahisari. The three arches on the east and west and the four domes which they and the walls bear are slightly smaller, but they are still impressive. The arch and dome before the north door have the same proportions, but the pairs on each side of those on the north are smaller in order to fit into a space which is irregular as a result of the insetting of the two small arches of the son cemaat yeri opposite. It is the constant adjustment of proportion which is a continuing source of interest when studying Selimiye.

The great door into the mosque is said to have been taken from the Ulu Cami *p 2* at Birgi; it is surmounted by a fine stalactite vault with two lovely whorled bosses right and left as if the sun were in motion and is embellished with small gilt rosettes like lesser stars; it is flanked by plain niches. The narrow arches on each side of the door have to have lower pairs of cross-arches between them and the mosque wall. Between these, and against the wall under an inset ogee arch, are two more modest niches above single windows. Two tiers of windows with

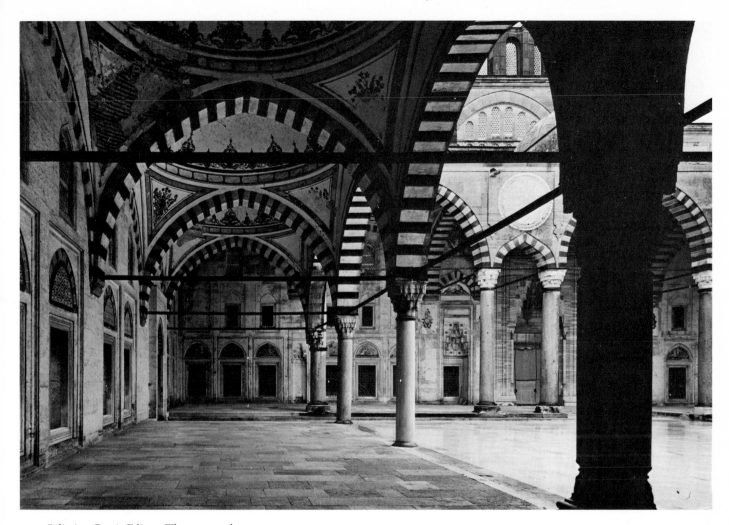

255 Selimiye Cami, Edirne. The courtyard.

Iznik tiles between them and their relieving arches complete the organization of the wall. The upper and lower windows on the east and west are blind because they are against the bases of the minarets. In the height of each of the four arches a further window is set. The columns are a mixture of Byzantine marble and granite, each with a complex stalactite capital. The centre pair before the north door of the court are rectangular and of an unusually shallow design faintly reminiscent of Byzantine types but which is closely related to examples in the Alhambra at Granada. The polygonal şadırvan has no canopy, and this has kept the court open and free.

The mosque and its court stand in a walled enclosure for the caravans and booths, and its dependencies are surprisingly small. There is a medrese and a darül-kurra south-east and south-west of the kıble wall, with high grassed sofas of some size each side of the path which leads to the south postern on the mihrab axis. These sofas are gardens planted with cypress trees and scattered with graves. The buildings and their courts, now stuffed with trees and shrubs, are the traditional C shape, with a fenestrated north wall on the entry side, but the dershane is set on the inward flank towards the grass sofas and not opposite the gate. There are two cells and a passage on their north sides, but these are missing on the south because of the close proximity of the mosque that towers above them. Indeed, the angle of the north wall in each case is so close to the minarets at the corners of the kıble wall that there is only a narrow path between them; thus the cemetery area is cut off from the main precinct. This arrangement required vaulting and terracing on the townward slope to the west which is now masked by the 255 metre-long market for cobblers, the Kavaflar arasta, built by Sinan's student and successor, Davut Ağa, in the 1580s.[74] This runs the length of the west side of the terrace and, besides a vista of 124 shops, it has a fine entrance hall and handsome stairs up to the complex. The arasta was built to bring revenue to the mosque but also, probably, to attract worshippers there from the town below, for the Selimiye is relatively far from the old town and may almost be thought suburban. The higher central dome before the stairs has a latticed drum made up of columns and arches like an arcade; this acts as a lantern for the central hallway of the arasta beneath, and is designed to eliminate the need for costly glazing. Handsome as it is, the arasta, like all the other buildings of the complex, which include the two-storey sibyan mekteb beside it, is kept low or set beneath the mosque in order not to mask it. The school is large and has a handsome loggia.

This mosque, inevitably, has been repaired at various periods; the first time was unexpectedly early because it was struck by lightning in 1584 when Yörüks were conscripted from Vize:[75] but it has suffered less than most and its total conception has not suffered at all. It can be seen, therefore, to be a great intellectual and emotional achievement of mathematics and religion, of reason and the Faith.[76]

The ideas underlying the design of the Selimiye were not entirely without descendants. The concept of the recessed gallery was employed by the unknown architect of the mosque near Fatih built for Mesih Mehmet Pasha,[77] Viceroy of Egypt and Grand Vezir under Murat III, in 994/1585,[78] three years before the death of that unattractive potentate. The mosque is set on the edge of a hill, and full advantage has been taken of the broken site in the manner of Sinan but it cannot be attributed to him. It has been suggested that it is by Davut Ağa[79] but it could just as easily be by Mehmet or some other subordinate of the master. It contains fine tiles and very good carving on the mihrab and minber. The tiles which flank the mihrab are a unique design of white circles with red and blue flowers set on a meadow-green ground and recall mahjong pieces. Each side of the north door which has a fine stalactite entry are deep eyvans. The lateral galleries are also large. Although nothing detracts from the volume of space under the central dome and, indeed, the spaciousness of the eyvans and galleries adds to it, yet it is a mosque of nooks and corners for intimate gatherings and personal meditation; this also adds to its unique character.

The main entrance to the precinct is up stairs under a domed gatehouse into a garden, rather than a court, before the high son cemaat yeri.[80] This west wall is a domed revak while that opposite, against the hillside, contains a row of latrines. The north wall has a domed arcade over a row of ablution spigots because, where the şadırvan ought to be, is the open türbe of the sadrazam in an octagonal grilled wall. I know of no other example of such a setting for a tomb, for even that of the seventeenth-century Köprülü complex at Çembelitaş is in the centre of the north flank of a medrese, not of a mosque.

From the Meydan below it, the mosque rises up very handsomely on an arched platform with two floors of big windows. Their tympana are completely fenestrated along the exposed west flank. The east side is so close to the hillside that it is hard to glimpse. The south wall is broken by the apsidal extrusion of the mihrab. Eight turrets are set hard against the dome with three windows and two buttresses between them. The squinch and other lesser domes are shallow and unobtrusive. The mosque has a double revak so that the tall, fluted minaret is set well back. The columns of the porticoes are of mixed dimensions and frequently jointed, while piers have been used as much as possible. Some of the inner stalactite capitals are unusually large.

Because Mesih Pasha was only entitled to one minaret, there is only a base on the north-east corner. It contains the stair to the gallery and between it and what was once a retaining wall against the hillside is an arch which admits from the garden court to the terrace alongside. This terrace and the corresponding one on the open west side of the mosque have doors into unique oratories which are set under the galleries where at the Selimiye there are three porches. At Mesih Pasha the three large arches are equal in size. The two towards the south, each

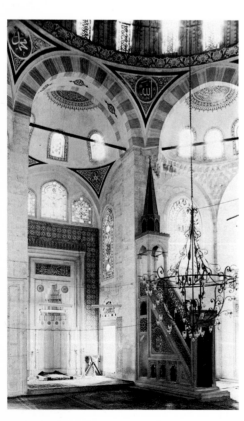

256 Mesih Pasha Cami, Istanbul.
The mihrab and the minber.

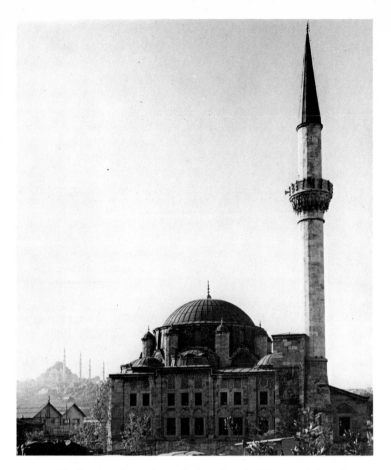
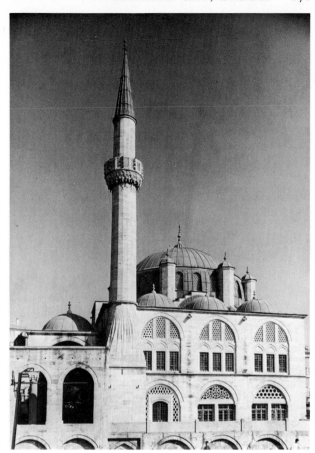

*257, 258 Left: Azapkapı Cami, Galata, Istanbul (see p. 285) – a late mosque of Sinan,
seen from the east. Right: Mesih Pasha Cami, Istanbul, seen from the west. The two mosques
are similar in size and date, but Sinan's domes are more sophisticated with stronger forms.*

of which must have been open originally, today have a pair of glazed casements,
while the windows in the tympana above have a grid of interlocking polygonal
wheels of stone or the more usual oval form. The single window opening onto
the south side is in each case identical in form. The third arch nearest the courtyard has a framed door set in a stone-diamond-patterned grid. All these grilles
have bold designs and before the glass was fitted the chambers must have been
very cool and airy. Their inner walls are, of course, the walls of the mosque and
this makes it clear that they are arbours and not rooms; for the mosque walls
have windows in the normal way as if they opened onto the outside world
directly. Similarly, the doors from these oratories into the mosque are not internal
communicating doors but designed as external doors and so much stronger than
would otherwise be necessary. These spaces under the balconies today serve for
private prayer, and this may have been their original function. Since this development of the concept of the lateral arcade was not copied later, it cannot have been
found satisfactory.

Before the first prayer was chanted in the mosque of Selim, Sinan completed
the most important of the mosques built by him for Sokollu Mehmet Pasha,
then sadrazam, and his wife, Esmahan Sultan. Born in the castle of Sokol in
Bosnia in about 1505, Mehmet Pasha was of royal blood. He came to the Enderun
College to graduate as Falconer Royal. This was the commencement of a long
career which brought him to be Grand Admiral in 1546, Viceroy of Europe in
1552, and then successively third and second vezir until he became Chancellor of
the Empire in 1565. He retained this office throughout the reign of Selim II and
into that of Murat III when, after months of fading favour, he was assassinated by
a madman in the Divan itself on 12th October 1579. Sokollu Mehmet had
served for thirty-three years as a cabinet minister.[81] He was a man of imposing
stature and commanding presence, with a black beard and hawk nose, and his
courage was commensurate with his intellect.[82] He gave to the office of Grand

Vezir an importance which it had not possessed before. It was to be months after his death before his successor, Şemşi Ahmet Pasha, was appointed in his place. His wife, Esmahan Gevher Sultan,[83] the daughter of Selim II, whom he married in 1562 when she was seventeen years old, appears to have been a cultivated and intelligent, if very ugly woman. Both of them must have commanded the respect and affection of Sinan for, padişahs apart, it was for them that he built his three most exquisite buildings.

Among the lesser buildings which Sinan built for Sokollu Mehmet is his hamam at Edirne which has recently been restored, although not to its original grandeur. The camekân with its stone sofas under a handsome dome is of fine proportions and the decorative plasterwork of good craftsmanship. The marbles remain but the tiles have all been lost and they must once have added sumptuousness to grace.

The mosque below the Atmeydan at Kadırga, near where Sokollu Mehmet Pasha had a palace, was the masterpiece among vezir foundations. Sinan completed it in 979/1571.[84] Once again the site on the steep slope of the hill offered him that challenge which he knew best how to exploit. The door is set back deeply into the body of the mosque to avoid the need for a vestibule and so admits one at once into the area under the dome. Stairs left and right lead up to the galleries under the recesses on the north between door and buttresses and then on up to the higher gallery over the entrance. This incorporates the two powerful piers which with the two weaker ones either side of the mihrab and the much stronger single lateral piers support the pendentives that carry the dome. The south piers only appear to be weaker: as usual, they are expressed at buttresses externally. Inasmuch as Sokollu Mehmet has hexagonal support for its dome, it is a descendant of Kara Ahmet Cami at Topkapı. The striking thing about this mosque is the height of these piers and the consequent loftiness of the dome, a loftiness which does not reach the distorted proportions of the Cairene tomb halls, however.[85] This loftiness is partly due to the need to incorporate the finest single wall of tile ever created by Iznik. It carries the eye upwards and subdues the space. On the east and west, broad lateral galleries ride on five polychrome arches arranged as pairs of broader span each side of a smaller arch in front of the side pier. The gallery balustrades are formed of the traditional interlocking wheels. At the level of these galleries, the east and west piers are ribbed to the height of the string-course under the upper windows with pointed arches containing small rosettes – the sculptural motif of this building – to produce a Gothic effect. Above string-course level the piers are fluted. The half-domes behind the free-springing pendentives have fine stalactite squinches at their angles. Their powerful tie-beams make a prominent accent. The pendentives themselves are remarkable because they are inset with tiles. There are also panels of inscriptive tile over both the lower range of casements and that at gallery level. The stained-glass windows of the north and south wall, the gift of Cevdet Pasha,[86] are excellent replicas while the others have the sinuous character of baroque but are also replacements.

Recently, the mosque has been restored and the stencilling is more sensitive than usual while the ceilings under the galleries have been copied from the tatterdemalion ceiling of the porch under the dershane. The remains of original paintwork on the wall above the door shows vividly what has been lost, for the mosque must have been painted as lavishly as it was tiled. Even finer paintwork is to be found on the wooden interlocking ceiling of the müezzins' tribune which is set below gallery level in the north-west corner of the harem. The triangular crested crown of the mihrab is also painted in orange and gilt. It is of Marmara marble with its richly carved stalactite niche set with gilded rosettes on each side and flanked by two revolving verd-antique colonnettes. This mihrab is matched

IV Alay Kiosk, Istanbul.

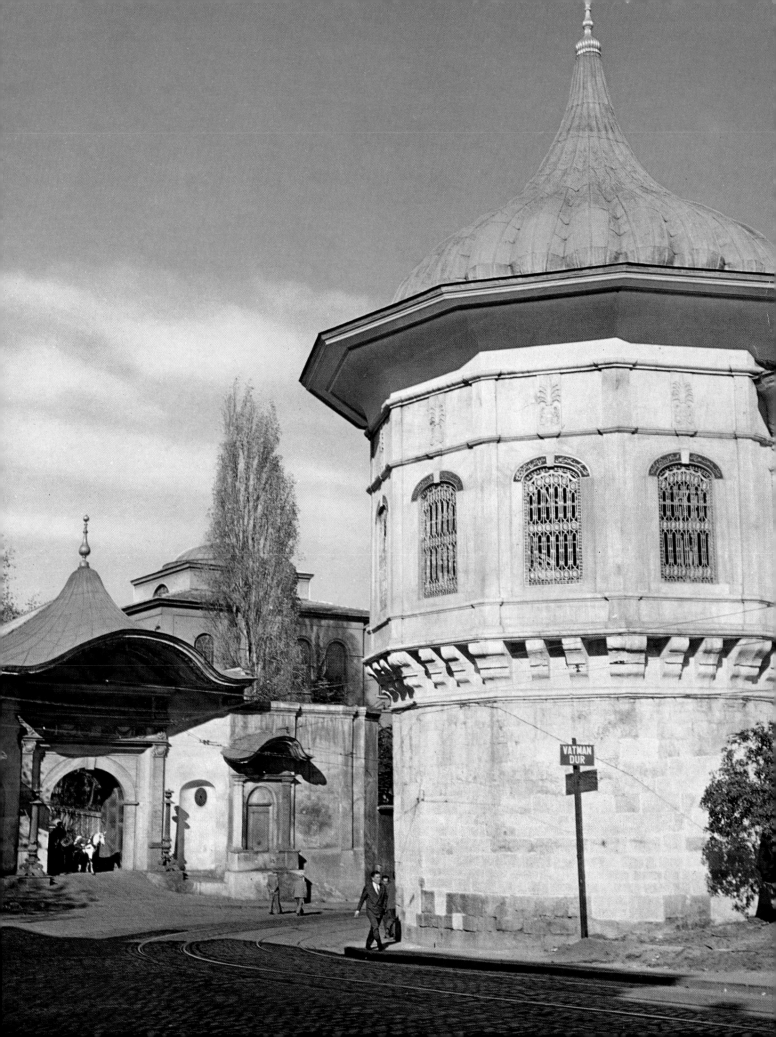

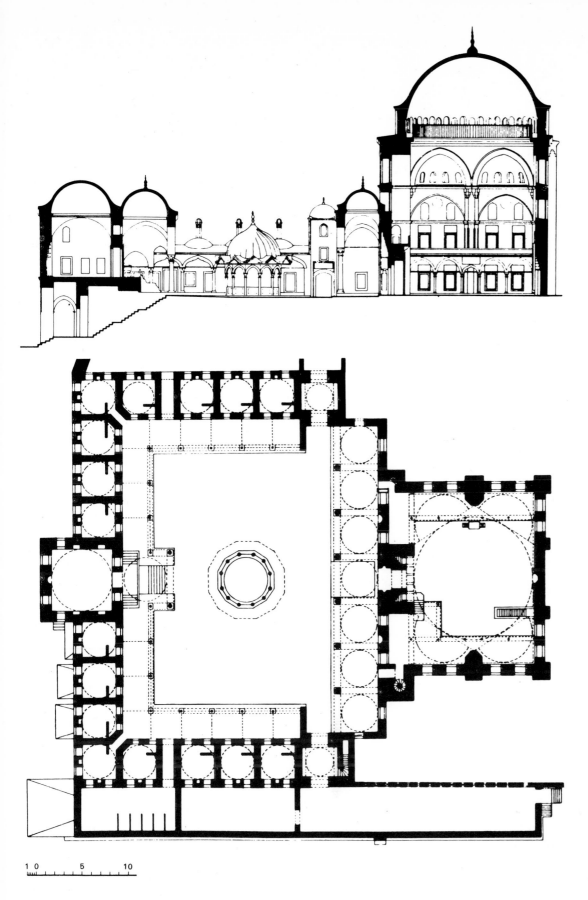

259, 260 Sokollu Mehmet Pasha Cami, Istanbul. Elevation and plan, scale 1 : 400.

by the minber which has traditional carving and fine marble arches and voussoirs supporting its hood. The conical hood and its drum are not only tiled but the tiles are of bold design and of the deepest tones of red and blue on spotless white. Inset into the canopy and the gate of the minber, and above the mihrab niche and the central doorway, are four pieces of the Ka'ba stone at Mecca framed in brass. They were given to Sokollu Mehmet Pasha after he had ordered extensive restorations at the sanctuary. These would have been carried out with the overall supervision of Sinan, who may have made the pilgrimage to the sacred city.[87] He is not likely to have worked there at all and another member of the team under him would carry the real responsibility. Much of the sanctuary area is clearly Ottoman, particularly some of the revaks and minarets.

The tiles of Sokollu Mehmet Pasha Cami are of three main types. There are the white inscriptions on a blue ground with a red floral border over doors and windows, already mentioned; there are the semicircular inscriptions on the walls under the arches below the semi-domes, in the pendentives, and in the south wall – and these include the two huge discs which flank the crest of the mihrab and resemble in style the painted inscriptions in the Süleymaniye attributed to Karahisarı; and there are the purely ornamental panels which surround the discs in the pendentives, stand between the windows in the south wall, and attain their apotheosis in two great compositions on either side of the mihrab. The emerald green is so vivid that it requires a great amount of red to subdue it. The flowers are on the grand scale. The foliage, of jungle dimensions, proliferates with a sinuous vitality which is at its most lively above the mihrab where it blooms into giant tulips. At skirting level is a border of mock marble which was in vogue at this time but which is not attractive. It is for its tiles that this mosque is justly famous but, overwhelming as they are, the architecture is

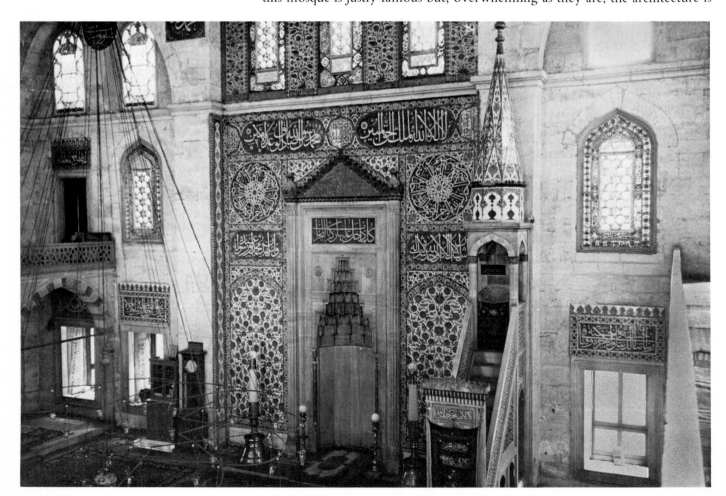

261 Sokollu Mehmet Pasha Cami, Istanbul. Interior from the north-west.

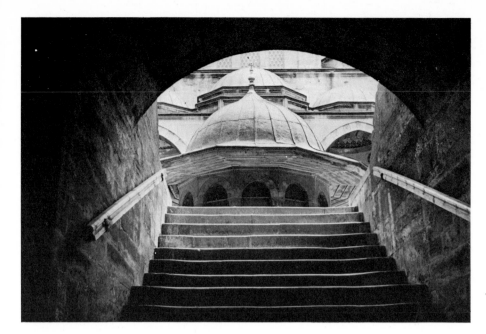

262 Sokollu Mehmet Pasha Cami, Istanbul. The şadırvan seen from the north stairway into the courtyard.

strong enough to bear them and bear with them whilst not losing its own identity. They are incorporated into the structure.[88]

The mosque and its courtyard are raised on a platform and the cemetery is dug back into the hillside below an earlier double tekke to the south. The medrese is built round the courtyard with considerable effect, for the main entry on the north side is from the street level below, where the foundations of the north range of cells are arched and vaulted to create caverns for shops on each side of the porch. Here a broad stone arch juts out above steps into the little meydan, and its powerful piers carry the back half of the dershane above, so that this hall is set flush with the cells on the courtyard side. This big room with its pairs of casements and upper lights is thus lit both from the east and from the west. The back of the medrese is built of one course of ashlar limestone to three of brick and mortar. Rising from the great stone arch of the entry with its dome on an octagonal drum, the dershane adds to the importance of the approach from the lower street. It is flanked by four cells on each side with two windows apiece. There is a broad stairway[89] which sweeps up under the dershane and through a narrower and lower arch to the court itself, bringing one face to face with the şadırvan and the mosque beyond. Left and right are stairs which lead to a raised and domed porch from which the dershane is entered. The complexity of levels has been exploited to solve the problem of the united mosque and medrese court, where the dershane should normally occupy the centre of the north side; and so, also, should the principal entry to the avlu of a mosque. Sinan has been able here to combine them with monumental effect.

The medrese of sixteen cells has revaks of bold and attractive ogee arches that move with vigour from marble column to marble column. Of these, Sokollu commanded a fine supply, unlike Mesih Pasha fifteen years later. The şadırvan is commodious with an elegant twist to the flow of its dome which is low enough not to crowd the courtyard area. The revaks are joined to the portico by two lateral gatehouses with a room for a müezzin over each. That on the east connects by a winding path with an outer gate to the hillside street. On its north side is a rectangular garden between the cells of the medrese and the street wall. The west gate admits to a lane which runs down the side of the cemetery wall to the thoroughfare. The cells on this side back onto a yard off which are the latrines. The east garden and the west latrines are each reached through slypes in the north corners.

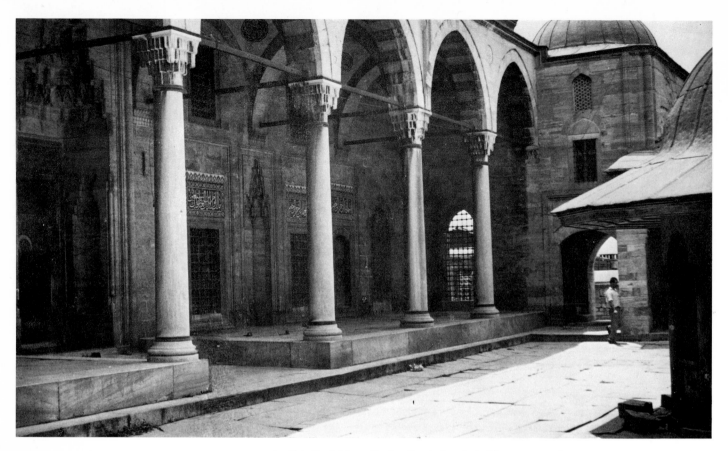

263 Sokollu Mehmet Pasha Cami, Istanbul. The portico and west gate.

Considering the moderate size of the mosque, the main portico is noble. The lofty arches carry seven domes and themselves stand on six handsome Marmara marble columns. Over the large windows and the two doors at the extremities are blue panels with white inscriptions framed in floral borders. These tiles are of the best period of Iznik pottery, for the white is pure and the red intense.[90] As has been discussed before,[91] this mosque is too narrow to fill the south side of the court, so a hall with a stairway to the gallery is added to the east side to mask the gap, and a library was added behind at a later date. It has since been gutted. On the west is set a large grilled window onto the cemetery so that Sinan has been content with only half a solution; but this is only apparent after scrutiny, because the clifflike foundations of the tekke behind act as a mask and there is no view of the sky and the town as there is at the mosque of Kara Ahmet Pasha. Moreover, the façade is sufficiently strong for the extra dimension created by the vista to enhance and not dissipate the sense of controlled space. What could have been an ugly transition from the relatively slender columns to the broad springing of the polychrome voussoirs of the portico arches is concealed by the flowering of the stalactite capitals, which are sharply carved as are those of the niches over the main door and those on each of its flanks. Handsome rosettes are carved in the spandrels of the portico.

At the north-east corner is the minaret which is no less excellent in its proportions and decoration than the rest of the building. The ribbing of its trunk ends in pointed arches into which are set rosettes, thus echoing the decoration of the piers inside. The stalactite corbels and the balustrade of the balcony are also of fine workmanship. From it one looks down on a small complex which, in its way, is as final a statement of the ideal vezir's mosque as Selimiye is that of a royal foundation.

While Sinan was at work on his two greatest achievements, the last expression of the great conservative ulu cami form was constructed by some other member 264 of the Office of Architects, since Sinan was far too busy at that period to work

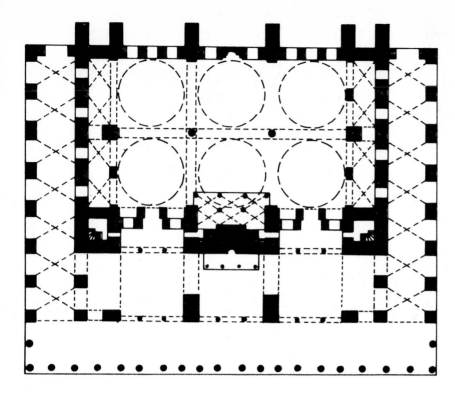

1 0   5   10m

264 Piyale Pasha Cami, Istanbul. Plan, scale 1 : 500.

for even so remarkable a man as Piyale Pasha.[92] He was the Grand Admiral and had added sixty-nine islands, including Chios, to the empire.[93] Moreover, Piyale was a favourite of Selim II, partly because of his renown which had won him a triumphal entry into Constantinople, partly because of his upbringing,[94] and certainly because of his prudent bestowal of lavish gifts on his sultan. The mosque was completed in *981/1573*[95] by which time the Kaptan Pasha had become Third Vezir. Seven years before, he had married Hace Guheri Mülük Sultan, daughter of Selim and sister-in-law of the Sadrazam Sokollu Mehmet Pasha and Zal Mahmut among others, when she was twenty-two years old.[96] She, like Esmahan her sister, may have been consulted over the details of this mosque, but the large structure has a masculine appearance. It was built in the fields behind Kasım Pasha and the Tershane, or dockyard, which contained the barracks of the sailors, the pavilion of the Grand Admiral, and the dreaded Bagno[97] where the galley-slaves were penned. Piyale Pasha dug a canal, because of the poor roads, from the Horn to the village where his mosque stands, but it was neglected after his death in January, 1578. Evliya speaks of it as neglected and unnavigable,[98] an appearance which it contrived to retain into the twentieth century, although a long stretch of this public drain has now been concreted over and so no further ignominy can be thrust upon it nor into it. Once, it must have been an attractive approach to the mosque in the meadows among the trees.

264   The mosque inside is roofed with six domes (approximately 9 metres in diameter) with two very large granite columns indeed to support them. These columns may have inspired the plan for they would have been difficult to incorporate into any other building. They do not block the view of the mihrab and no other ulu cami expresses such free-flowing space which could contain a multitude. On each side of the rectangular building, two piers take part of the thrust of the lateral domes which is then carried by an arch to the walls. The three north-side domes are borne on powerful supports incorporated into the lateral walls of the

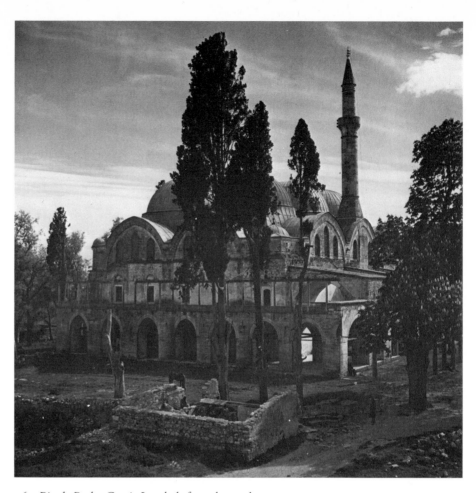

265 *Piyale Pasha Cami, Istanbul, from the north-west.*

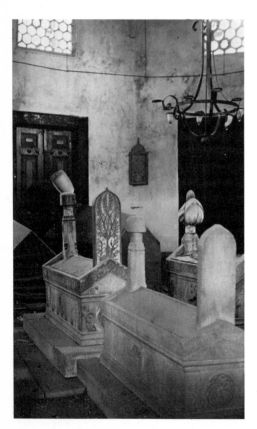

266 *Piyale Pasha Cami. Interior of the türbe.*

central tribune and the square towers at either corner. On the south side, four mighty external buttresses lean their shoulders to the wall and they are reinforced by one more at each corner to help support the three southward domes. The doors into the mosque are recessed east and west of the north front under large porches between these buttress walls. The porches are carried on two marble columns and through them one enters immediately without further vestibule or narthex.[99]

Inside, on the east and west, are lateral galleries carried on four wide-spanned arches which are supported by the central piers and the walls, with two smaller piers set between. These galleries belong historically to the sixteenth century and not the ulu cami period. Two great arches span each gallery and an arch in the central pier from which they spring permits passage from one half of each tribune to the other. The mihrab niche and its stalactite vault are faced with Iznik tiles of unique design and excellent craftsmanship, while a large white inscription on a brilliant deep blue ground runs as a frieze across the south wall and those flanking the mosque.[100] The stained-glass windows each side of the mihrab are nineteenth-century and clash painfully with the tiles. There are traces of terracotta paint in places which may be original, and it would have been impressive if the whole mosque had once been this colour. It has now been whitewashed which enhances the grandeur of this spacious interior. Opposite the mihrab, the müezzins' mahfil, supported on six columns, is set back into the central eyvan which lies between the recessed north-east and north-west doors. From the mahfil, stairs lead up the single minaret which is set in the middle of the north flank in a most unconventional manner.[101]

If the interior of Piyale Pasha is unusual, the exterior is equally revolutionary, 265 quite apart from the siting of the minaret. In the middle of its heavy base is set a prayer niche preceded by a small canopy on four columns. Unfortunately, the

mosque has been gravely damaged by earthquake and neglect, for the neighbourhood suffers from considerable poverty. It was last restored, roughly, in 1890 and
has long needed new restoration. Columns have fallen, roofs caved in. Before
the north façade is a great porch with two large central piers and smaller ones
paired at the wings. The three main bays are divided by a screen of three arches
carried on two columns each. Down the east and west sides, partly supported by
the walls and partly by a line of eight powerful piers, are two narrower terraces
down which a spectacular vista is obtained. This is due to their length and the
span of the brick responding arches between the cut-stone piers and the walls.
They end with broad arris arches which are infrequently used in Istanbul.[102] These
exceptionally strong constructions are strictly functional because they carry
the broad open gallery which once ran round three sides of this mosque. It is
all too open now because the columns which supported its lean-to tile roof have
fallen. They once had curiously carved capitals in a Corinthian style. Before the
north front, spanning the whole width of the mosque and its galleries, is a fine
colonnade of twenty antique columns with two lateral ones in addition and
these once supported the sloping roof of the outer revak of this country-style
building. It is to be noted that not only are the lateral arches brick and mortar[103]
but so is part of the side walls up to tympana level, an economy likely to have
arisen from a shortage of stone.

266   In the graveyard on the south side is a traditional türbe which was once
surrounded by a gallery of twenty-two columns, all of which have fallen. There
are many finely carved headstones, many belonging to dervishes, and the
Hadika[104] states that there was a convent of Halveti dervishes on one side of the
mosque and an orthodox medrese on the other; but both these foundations have
268 disappeared. From the cemetery, the full power of the buttresses of the south
wall can be appreciated. Rising from heavy bases, they taper gradually to be
capped with octagonal turrets at the level of the drums which support the domes.
The drums are blind and the lead roofs of the domes cover them also and give an
impression of hoods on their exposed sides while, when viewed from the minaret,
they are seen to flow and undulate between each other.

It is to be hoped that this slightly ungainly but handsome mosque, idiosyncratic but never quaint, may be restored with respect for the surrealist spirit
lurking in the long grass of the cemetery with its crowds of lively urchins.
Sinan was to copy the architect of Piyale Pasha when he built a mosque for
Kasap Hacı Evhat[105] in 993/1585[106] which was heavily restored in 1945[107] after
years of neglect following a fire in 1920.[108] The only present interest in this
mosque is that its minaret stands over the doorway which is in the centre of the
north façade. It would be interesting to know the function of the great galleries
of Piyale Pasha which the Hadika weakly states were used to make the call to
prayer[109] but which certainly had another purpose. They would offer splendid
cloisters in which dervishes might pace and meditate.

Since this mosque had no comparable descendants, the development of Ottoman architecture must again be sought in the works of Sinan. He returned from
Edirne to be called in at the request of his subordinate, Mehmet Ağa, to inspect
270 the structure of Hagia Sophia which was giving cause for concern. He was also
ordered to build two minarets at the corners of the west front; or else he himself
suggested it. His repairs included the addition of the large north buttress, but a
detailed analysis of his work is not yet available.[110] The first minaret at Hagia
Sophia had been built of wood on top of the small southern turret of the west
façade immediately after the conquest, and Fatih had added the brick minaret on
the south-west overlooking Topkapısaray later. Beyazit II had added the stone
minaret on the south-east to make a pair. Now the old wooden structure above
the turret was rotten and, moreover, squatters had built their hearths along the
south wall, thinking nothing of burrowing into the stonework. It took the
combined authority of the sultan and the mimarbaşı and a fetva of the Şeyhül-
İslâm to eject them before work could begin.[111] A detailed firman was issued by
Selim II on 22 June 1573, ordering the building of one minaret only, on the

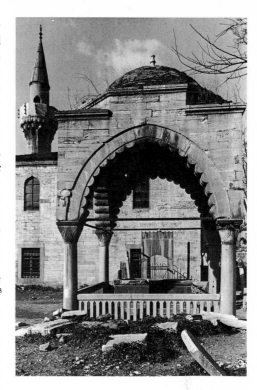

*267 Defterdar Cami, Istanbul. (See note 103.)
The open türbe with examples of an arch
form rarely used by the Ottomans.*

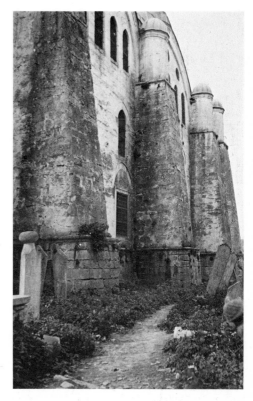

*268 Piyale Pasha Cami, Istanbul. Buttresses
along the south wall.*

south-west, but when Murat III succeeded on 12 December 1574, Sinan seems to have prevailed on him to add the one on the north-west for symmetry, and the minarets were dedicated to the two respective monarchs. The old wooden structure on the turret was cleared away and both the turrets of the west façade were restored and capped with lead.[112] The stage reached by Selim's minaret on the day he died is problematical, for it would look as if Murat's was the first to be completed. This is because it is odd, for it has a main stairway and a subsidiary one which would appear to have been meant to reach a second şerefe which does not exist. The second stair is difficult of access at the bottom and blocked at the top. Moreover, the series of triangles at the base were too difficult to plan intelligibly in the sixteenth century and so were worked out on the spot just as the marble soffits of the exedra inside were worked out *in situ* in the sixth century. The minarets are very thick and powerful, set on massed limestone bases which taper at gallery roof level making a transition to twenty-sided shafts. Sinan took great care to see that their height was uniform with that of the earlier two to the south, which makes it odd that second galleries were ever contemplated. It may be that he intended that their bulk should relate to the mass of the building and its buttresses, feeling that the minarets already built were disproportionately slender, or he may have deliberately imitated the thickness of Selçuk minarets since Hagia Sophia was an ulu cami.

The death of Selim II necessitated the erection of his türbe, and a plot in the south courtyard of Hagia Sophia was chosen by his son. He was the first Ottoman sultan to be buried there, possibly because work was already going on at the building. The türbe was begun in 1574 and not completed until 1577 which was a long time to take. The elaborate three-domed porch has a fine Iznik panel and a

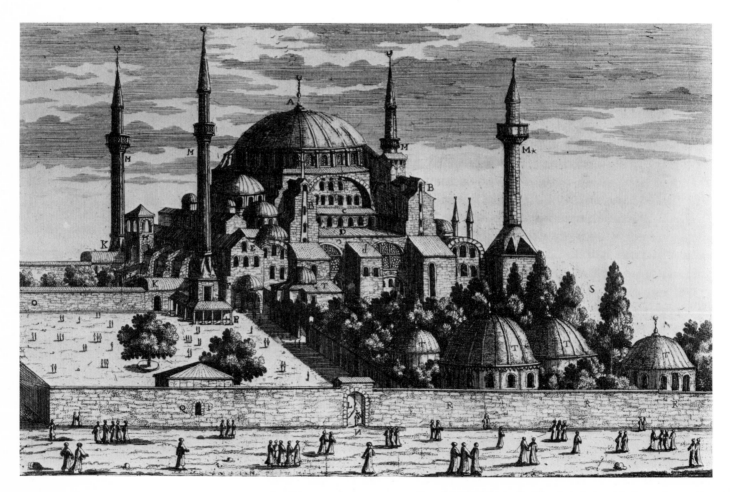

269 Seventeenth-century engraving showing Hagia Sophia, Istanbul, with the garden of royal tombs.

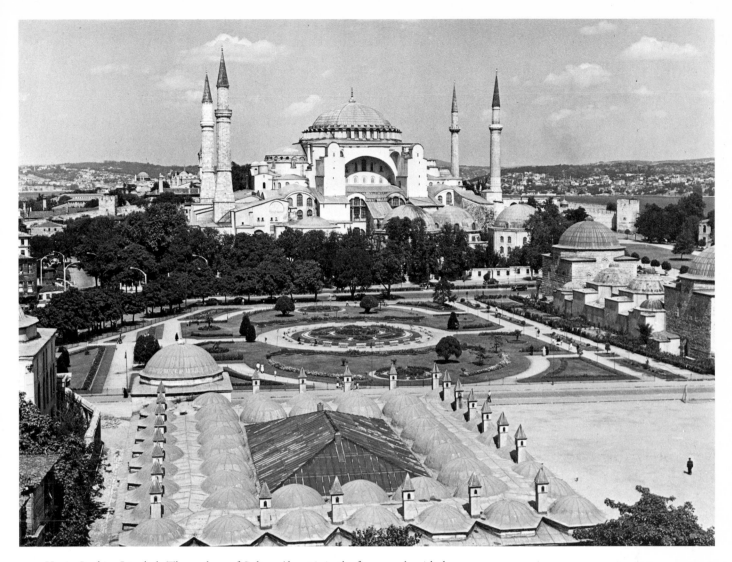

270 Hagia Sophia, Istanbul. The medrese of Sultan Ahmet is in the foreground, with the hamam of Haseki Hürrem on the right. The gardens are on the site of a once populous neighbourhood.

fair copy flanking the richly inlaid door. The domes are concealed under the lean-to roof which extends a wide eave in front of the large central arch and the two smaller arches of the portico which has escaped glazing, doubtless because the tiles are protected even against driving rain. The marble of the portico and fineness of the ceramic are foretastes of the splendour within. The sixteen metre square funerary chamber has a great dome (11·50 metres) borne on eight free-standing columns from whose stalactite caps supporting arches return to the walls across a perambulatory. The sarcophagi are therefore set in a large central trough beneath the dome while the visitor, like a spectator, is balustraded off, with the varied panels of deep-toned tiles ranked between the casements behind him. The central area is lit from the windows in the dome and filled with soft light. As at the Süleymaniye, the inner dome is false and the walls carry the larger one which looks so grand from outside even when, as now, it is partially masked by trees. The restored inner dome, like that of Süleyman's türbe, is covered in an elaborate interlacing pattern of black and cream and terracotta. There are miniature exedras at the corners. The overwhelming impression is of space and loftiness and this must rank as one of the finest examples of the Ottoman türbe and among the biggest.

In the year 1574, Sinan built a more modest tomb for Sokollu Mehmet Pasha at Eyüp.[113] It is plainly designed, but the proportions of the stone octagonal tra-ditional türbe are good and the interior spacious and light, partly due to the

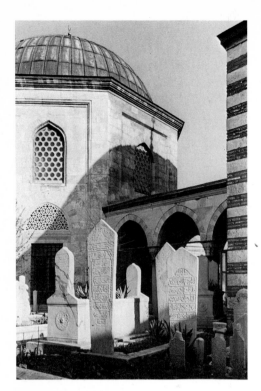

*271 Sokollu Mehmet Pasha Complex, Eyüp.
The arcade linking the dershane, left, to the
türbe.*

fretwork of marble in the tympana above the casements. There is a handsome tile inscription, and the stained-glass windows have been restored. The türbe is connected to the dershane, which is a similar octagon, by a roofed and arcaded passage which makes a charming loggia. The complex is entered by stepping down from the highway which runs past the türbe. The arcade is reached across a small open court and entered through a central arch. The tomb is then on the right, the college on the left. Behind, beyond a garden of graves with the grand headstones of the descendants of the vezir, is a third octagonal building. This is the independent darül-hadis with its own portico. The balustrading of the loggia is of the traditional interlocking wheels cut to emphasize the pattern of hexagonal concave lozenges. Over the door of the türbe, the interlocking voussoirs are of good verd-antique and Marmara marbles, contrasting with a similar door and arch to the dershane, where the voussoirs alternate red with white instead of green. On each side of the walk there are three polychrome arches carried on stalactite capitals on columns of Marmara marble. The interior of the dershane hall is light and spacious like that of the tomb. The medrese revaks and court-yard are reached by a door opposite the entry. From beneath the domes of the east revak one is presented with a vista down the long narrow lawn of a medrese of exceptional grace and elegance. The revaks have three arches at each end and seven along each side. In the middle of the lawn is a cistern resembling a sarco-phagus on a low plinth one third of the way down the length of the enclosure. The arcades of the revaks have been glazed in because the medrese is now a clinic, but the sober white paint used everywhere is inoffensive. The arches are wide so that there is no feeling of confinement resulting from the narrowness of the court. Once more, Sinan had been faced with a difficult site and triumphed over its narrowness. He had also seen that the details, such as the plasterwork, were good and so achieved a small and sympathetic masterpiece.

The türbe of Siyavus Pasha opposite is unlikely to be Sinan's work but it is also in the classical manner and the two together make a worthy pair. Both are strikingly restrained compared with that of Ferhat Pasha farther down the street with its polychrome stone and columns, stalactite cresting and many facets. Beside a lane which leads behind the royal mosque of Eyüp is the türbe Sinan built for Pertev Mehmet Pasha in *980/*1572[114] which has now lost its wooden domes. It is unusual in that it consists of two rooms, which are now open to the sky.

Şemşi Ahmet Pasha[115] had plotted against Sokollu Mehmet Pasha for some months before the assassination.[116] He had to wait for some time before Murat III gave him the seal of the Grand Vezir. The appointment was noteworthy for he was the first sadrazam since the fifteenth century who was of noble, indeed royal, Ottoman descent and not the child of a devşirme. He was the head of the İsfendi-yaroğlu family and a descendant of the Candarlı house which had been stripped of its immense powers by Beyazit II and Selim the Grim. He was not to hold office for long, and when he commanded Sinan to build him a mosque in 1580 there was little time to spare.[117] The little complex – among the smallest erected by a Chancellor – is set against the water along the point of Üsküdar. Its garden is charmingly open towards the sea from which it is cut off by a wall with grilled windows and a modest gate. It is clear that this was meant to be the approach because the backs of the medrese cells on this side are faced in stone and not in mixed courses. A large land gate from the town lies to the south-west behind the small square mosque with its minaret short in proportion. Entering by this gate, the visitor has the L-shaped medrese to his left and the mosque to his right. The dershane is set in the middle of the trunk of the L opposite the mosque, from which it is divided by a large lawn. The medrese recalls that of Süleyman Pasha at Iznik because large, circular windows surmount the casements, symbols of the sun in the Pasha's poetic name. While the arches of the medrese portico are simply pointed, those of the mosque are depressed ogee and broad in shape. One is surprised that so small a mosque has five arches to its son cemaat yeri; this is due to the continuation of the façade by the türbe of the pasha which is not only

27[?]

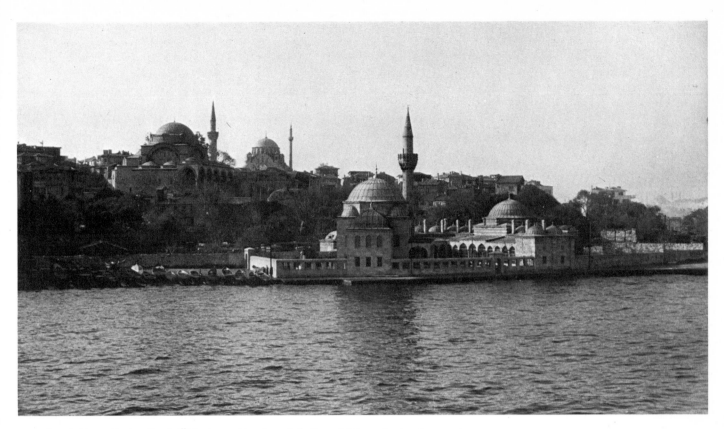

272 Şemşi Ahmet Pasha Cami, Üsküdar, with, above left, Rum Mehmet Pasha Cami and, on the skyline, the Ayasma Cami.

set against the side of the mosque, of which it is half the size, but is entered from within as if it were an eyvan opening out of the prayer hall. However, it is cut off from the harem by an elegant bronze grille of considerable size. The mosque and türbe are of cut stone and the dershane and medrese cells behind of courses of stone and brick in the traditional manner. It is the miniature size of the complex and its setting by the sea which make it exceptional. The dershane revak and the façade of the mosque are set at angles to each other so that the garden opens like a cone towards the water.[118] It is the forerunner of the small sadrazam complexes of the next century which were built along the Divan yolu in particular.

The greatest praise that may be offered Sinan is that the years of his greatness were the great years of Ottoman architecture. When his powers declined, this decline was reflected in all the work which followed on the 1570s. Fine buildings were still to be erected but the old man's inventive powers, although not dead, became forced, and some among the more ingenious effects are not satisfactory. The Selimiye mosque, by very reason of its excellence, exhausted Sinan and condemned the classical period to a lingering death.

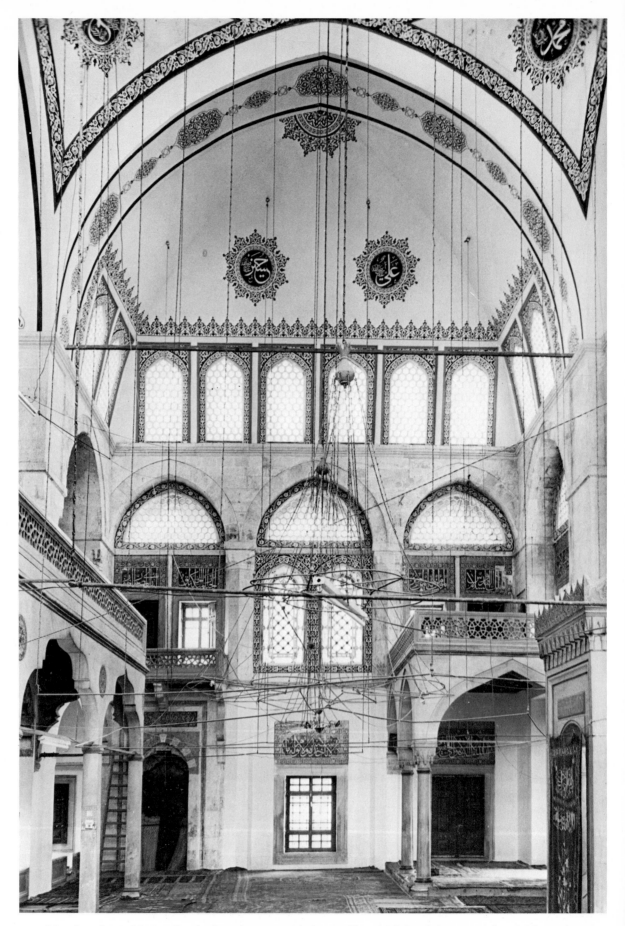

273 *Muradiye Cami, Manisa. Interior from the west, with the royal loge (right) and sloping windows in the vault.*

8

The powers decline

IN THE LAST QUARTER of the sixteenth century, Sinan must have seemed immortal to his contemporaries and the quantity of work handled by his office did not diminish. It takes time for a strong engine to run down or the heat of a furnace to fade, and his declining power was hardly perceptible. But signs can be detected with yet another mosque built for Sokollu Mehmet Pasha in 985/1577,[1] the year of his murder, on the shore of the Horn beside the Tershane or Dockyard. It was in ruins after 1914 in spite of a nineteenth-century restoration when the minaret was rebuilt. It was restored again in 1942 and has recently been refurbished and the floor relaid.

The Azapkapı Cami has a number of unique and inventive features. It is raised above a stone basement, in some of the arches of which were shops that have been walled across. In this, it is like any other market mosque but another reason here is likely to have been fear of flood. Two stairways east and west of the north front are set where a pair of minarets might be expected. They lead up to the narthex in which there is a complete son cemaat yeri with tile sofas and stone kerbs each side of the two entrances which have replaced the central door and two stalactite niches. The roof area round the dome, which is given the appearance of having a drum by the formation of a lip over its buttresses, is almost baroque; for the lead curves over the five windows of the semi-domes which are prominent between turrets which are the outward expression of the interior piers. The shallow exedra cannot be seen from outside, unless from above, because they are masked by a stepped arch; this recedes and so gives a concave response to the convex movement of the semi-domes. The narthex is covered by a lean-to lead roof. The minaret, which stands independently on the north-east, is joined to the narthex by a broad stone passage reached by a flight of newel stairs in what appears to have been the base for the first minaret. This passage is carried across a lofty pointed arch which is a striking feature of the mosque but which may be due to restoration and not Sinan's original concept; but this is not certain.[2] Beside the two entries at court level at each end of the north façade are deep niches, and there are pilasters set in the corners. Washing spigots lie between them and there is a çeşme at the end of the narrow precinct, now half under the Atatürk Bridge, facing down the vista to the sea.

In plan, the interior is like a small Zal Mahmut mosque with the addition of an apse, and there are echoes of the Selimiye. The walls are largely windows with fine inscriptive plaques in relief, gold on green, over the apse casements. There is much renewed coloured glass but the stately minber is original. The recessing of the apse and its large mihrab gives the mosque considerable southward axial force. The dome is supported on six free-standing polygonal piers which are fluted above gallery level, and there are two which are engaged each side of the apsidal arch which have fine stalactite consoles. The trim cutting of the capitals

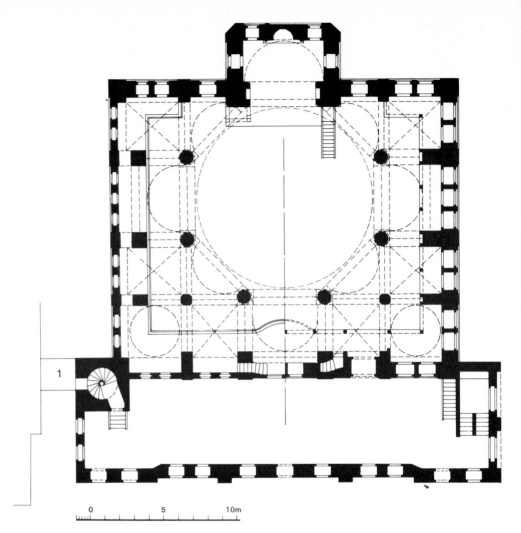

274 Azapkapı Cami, Istanbul. Plan before restoration, scale 1 : 250. 1 minaret bridge.

which are rectangular, and slightly angled where the arches of the two faces of the octagon meet, are related to those at Edirne. There were once tiles in the eight shallow spandrels between the arches. The four arches of the small semidomes, abutted by the four exedra vaults set at forty-five degrees in the corners, form a strong semicircle under the dome. Their movement is not arrested by the engaged piers because the consoles strongly express the thrust of the apse arch. The relatively narrow lateral galleries not only extend along all three sides but turn inward along the south wall for half the span of the relieving arch. They are reached by stairs in the buttresses east and west of the central window where the door was likely to have been originally.

An inevitable weakness of this plan is that, on the north-west and north-east, there have to be secondary columns in order that the exedra should be supported from behind and also to effect the return to the square from the circle. This results in clutter in the north corners, which is not improved by the restorations along the west flank. In addition, the galleries are supported on piers which develop into simple braces to produce a familiar Islamic pattern dating from the days when mosques were built of timber. The three lateral piers, which respond to the thrusts of the dome, the half-domes at the four quarters and the exedras, are conveniently inset with shelves. The overall effect is a busy one except in the central area of the hall, while from outside the quantity of windows gives the impression that they were inserted everywhere possible just as at Zal Mahmut Pasha Cami.

The area round the mosque has been completely cleared and no dependencies survive. The twentieth-century bridge now looms over the building and

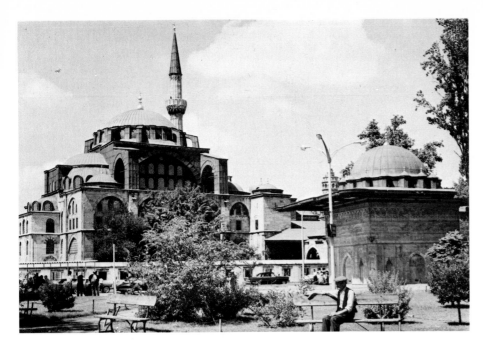

275 Kılıç Ali Pasha Cami and Tophane Fountain, Istanbul, from the south-east.

destroys its former eminence over the lost neighbourhood of bustling alleys beside a ferry landing-stage. At one time,[3] there was a frail white wooden bridge – straight out of a Chinese landscape – which could not last long. The mosque has, therefore, suffered from exposure, since the basement was never meant to be seen so plainly as much as from the shadow of the bridge. It was very much the expression of a desire for more and more light that is a feature of Ottoman architecture in the later sixteenth century. Over-zealously refurbished though it be, the result is an interior which is light and gay: too light, for shadows would have obscured the crowded corners or the inevitable problem of arches at two stages under the exedras. But these problems did not concern Ottoman architects, who all believed that structure should express its functional purpose truthfully.

A larger mosque built by Sinan in 1580[4] at the same time as Sokollu Mehmet Pasha, is the Tophane Cami of the Kaptan Pasha, Kılıç Ali.[5] It stands between the gun foundry on the hillside and the beach where the barrels were rolled down to be shipped to the dockyard and fitted to the galleys refitting or building in the safety of the Golden Horn. This mosque is in no way as large as Hagia Sophia but bears a striking resemblance to that monument:[6] it would look as if Sinan, within the strict limits of the requirements of religion and engineering, deliberately produced a modified copy of the interior of the church across the water. The repairs which he had carried out there had resulted in his making an extensive study of that building, and it was natural that some aspects of it interested him enough for him to want to incorporate them in his new mosque. It is not the semi-dome over the apse which is new but the arcades along the upper galleries which stretch the length of the mosque. The result is not altogether a success from the viewpoint of Moslem as opposed to Christian ritual, because Kılıç Ali has something of the character of a processional way.

The mosque – which was near the water, appropriately for an admiral – was built in a busy quarter just outside the gate of Galata, and the courtyard has a double revak like a suburban mosque. The inner portico is grilled but the outer covers a broad sofa which was the haunt of apothecaries until recent times. Its broad eaves overshadow those of the şadırvan which is hemmed in by the arcades of the courtyard wall on its northern side.[7] The entries are on the east and west; that on the east has a sebil beside it which forms the north corner of the complex. The buttresses at each corner of the dome take the form of large arches clad in lead. These are a logical development but ugly, nonetheless, and they were to be copied at the Şerefettin Cami at Konya when it was restored in the seventeenth century. The dark lead draws attention to them and they are ungainly rather than grand. The whole roof area, including the flanks of the smaller domes and the great tympana, is covered in lead, so that for the last third of its height the building is mainly black. The result is oppressive and is related to the increased use of lead at İvaz Efendi and Zal Mahmut mosques; and it is typical of the last period of Sinan's work. The sombre effect is increased by the all-enveloping size of the big sloping roof, also covered in lead, over the double portico and its sturdy, marble columns. The doorway is remarkable for the upper inscription which is a reversal pattern of considerable elaboration set inside a triangle of vertical chevrons instead of the usual stalactite semi-dome. There are two doors from the second revak at the east and west corners between the ends of the portico and the base of the minaret and the corresponding base, for symmetry, which contains the gallery stairs. Both stairs are reached from inside the mosque, and thus the area under the north gallery becomes a narthex. The repaired minaret is slim and tall and, like that of Mihrimah Cami at Edirnekapı, its height acts as a foil to the bulk of the building and its domes.

The mosque possesses a remarkable range of stained-glass windows of flamboyant colour and arabesque designs which have no historical antecedents but are at least cheerful. The original paintwork under the müezzins' tribune is preserved and the tones are now deep and mellow; there is a handsome kürsü still; but the hailstorm of mosque lamps and votive offerings, resplendent with tassels, has diminished since Gurlitt's day. The present paintwork on the walls is appalling, but there are fine tiles in the apse and also large inscriptive panels in relief above the casements which are interestingly grouped in pairs. The panel with a circular inscription over the crest of the mihrab in the manner of Karahisarı at the Süleymaniye is perfect. Above it is a late stained-glass window. Both the mihrab and the minber are small but of good workmanship, while the minber's hood is tall and tapering. Two of the lanterns from the pasha's galley are set each side of the mihrab. There were as many windows as ever at this period and the lunettes are glazed for the full range of lower arches beneath the galleries; yet the overwhelming impression is not of light but of masses of detail. This is partly due to the depth of the galleries, their arcades, and the bulk of the masonry piers which support the four arches under the dome. The lamplighter's gallery at dome and semi-dome level meandering along the string-course, the clumsy jointure of the stalactite squinches under the exedra where they meet the great round piers – although themselves of excellent workmanship – and the darkness beyond the four supporting piers of the wide gallery at the main entry make for clutter and formlessness.

In the small garden behind the mosque, there is the classical octagonal türbe of Kılıç Ali Pasha;[8] behind this, again, but reached by the lane which runs down the west side of the mosque, is the medrese which is now a clinic. On the other side of the lane is the hamam which has a nobly proportioned camekân now filled with nineteenth-century modifications. The soğukluk is merely a lobby, but the hot rooms are of marble and their design is less cramped by the restricted site.

The last major work attributed to Sinan is the complex built at Toptaşı, on the heights above Üsküdar, for Nur Banu, then the Valide Sultan or Queen Mother. She was the mistress of the court and said to have had great influence on her son, Murat III.[9] Her foundation included an imaret, a darül-kurra, a darül-hadis, a large han which is now demolished, a şifahane, and a double hamam a mile away down the hill near the mosque of Mihrimah. This hamam is now a department store but is at least preserved in part. It contains some fine verd-antique columns. There is also a large medrese, or possibly a tekke, which forms a second, lower court. The Hadika records[10] that there was only one şadırvan at upper level, perhaps because there was only one spring on the site. Lack of water might also explain why the hamam was built so inconveniently far away, for there was no shortage of land and the complex is spaciously laid out; the

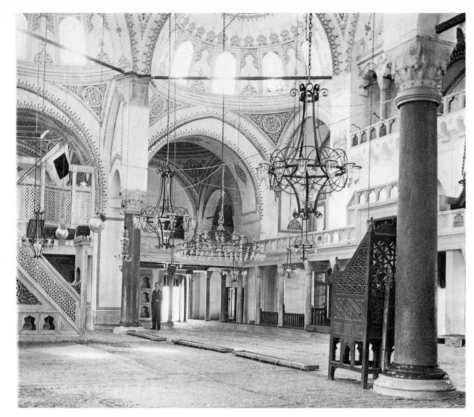

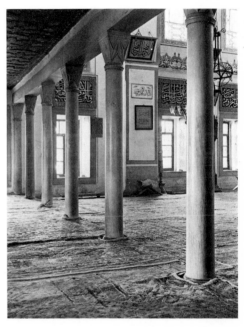

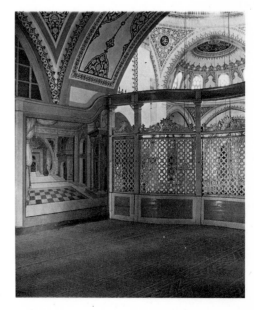

276, 277, 278 Atık Valide Cami, Üsküdar. Left: interior from the south-east showing the hoca's chair and the flags. Below: the north-east arcade showing the ceiling under the gallery. Bottom: the royal loge with its baroque grille and fresco. The 'trompe l'œil' fresco was added during the reign of Osman III.

burial ground on the south side has never yet been filled. There are precedents for scattering individual elements of a complex and for them to be built at varying periods, but it is unusual.

The Atık or Eski Valide was simply called the Valide Cami until the building of the Yeni Valide Cami at the landing stage early in the eighteenth century. There is no inscription but the darül-kurra is dated 1577 and may have been the first completed building of the group since it is a simple domed room. This would make the accepted date of 1583 for the completion of the complex probably correct.[11] It is not likely to have been later because Nur Banu died at this time and was buried beside her husband, Selim II, in his türbe at Hagia Sophia.

There is a double portico to the mosque, the second of which is an addition dating from the following century when the mosque was enlarged. Originally, the two lateral porches in the revaks were on the axis of the son cemaat yeri, to which they were joined by direct flagstone paths. The Hadika records that Pir Ali, the administrator and dean of the dervishes, added two domes to the mosque when, in fact, he added four: two on each side. Because of these later additions, the interior is impressively broad but, although it is brilliantly lit by many windows, there is a feeling of crowding due to the size of the galleries on all but the south side; the galleries also vary in level. The eighteenth-century hünkâr mahfil contributes to this impression. The apse is large and splendidly tiled with panels of vases and flowers and double rows of inscriptions. Two flags, black with yellow borders, hang each side of the hood of the minber. They may be symbolic of the dervish orders or laid up by some unit of the Janissaries. A bow also hangs on the beam under the western arch which connects the pier to the wall.[12] The symbolic meaning of this bow has been forgotten but it reminds one that archery was always a sacred sport. There is rich paintwork under the tribunes along the north wall and fine encrustation on the doors. There is also a large amount of false marbling.

The mosque has two minarets, which were probably restored in the nineteenth century, because it is a royal foundation and the plan is a sophisticated reversion to that of Sinan Pasha with the dome carried on six supports. This has

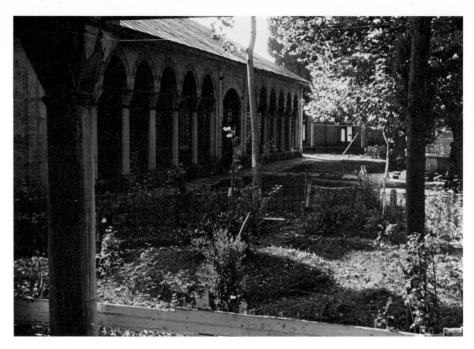

279   *Atık Valide Cami, Üsküdar. Courtyard and second revak from the north-west.*

made some reluctant to accept this mosque as the work of Sinan, but there seems no reason to doubt that the conception was his originally. The minarets can be reached from the portico and from inside, which is exceptional at this period. The stalactite capitals of the son cemaat yeri, the multifoliate rosettes in the spandrels which are more elaborate than the usual Kadir rose, and the boldly carved niche over the north door are all of fine craftsmanship. This is true also of the superb Iznik inscriptive tiles, decorated with flowers and leaves, above the casements.

Two side doors admit to the courtyard, but the main gate is reached from a lane to the south by an avenue which leads past the cemetery to the south-west corner of the precinct. This is a spacious garden, agreeably countrified with grass and ancient trees. The large open şadırvan was damaged when one of the cypresses fell. The two planes are believed to date from 1583. The court is nobly enclosed by open revaks and handsome gatehouses. That on the east leads down to the hospital and that on the west to the imaret which is now a jail. The gate in the middle of the north revak admits to a flight of stairs which lead down from the upper garden to the parterre of the three-sided medrese. None of the eighteen cells has an ocak, and this increases the suspicion that it may have been a tekke. At the end of each wing are open porticoes in place of cells, which give access to the latrines on the east side and the street on the west. The medrese is set askew because of the lane behind it, over which the dershane rides on arches like a bridge. On the court side it is central and reached by twin stairs recessed in a small portico.

The forty cells of the şifahane are now restored. It was a very large asylum and was in use well into this century when its inmates were transferred to the modern hospital at Bakırköy. It may also have been the residence of the dervishes who, like monks, tended the sick.[13] Only the two cells opening off the open hall in the middle of the east wall have ocaks. Patients and hardy dervishes alike must have shivered through the winter; the former, perhaps, because they were accounted too foolish to be allowed near glowing charcoal. The large court is also like a garden and the revaks with their ogee arches are graceful. The entry is at the south-west corner, and the door opens into what at the other corners is a large cell which can only be reached through a smaller neighbouring one. At the entry this cell becomes a vestibule to the hospital and ensures that strangers cannot peer into the court until they have been admitted by the porter. The court

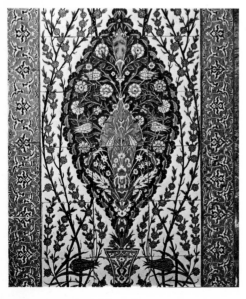

280   *Atık Valide Cami, Üsküdar. Panel of tiles.*

is trapezoid in shape due to the awkward shape of Nur Banu's plot of land. The hall, however, is able to extend into the field behind. There are thirty-eight cells of normal proportions, three larger ones, and two tunnel-vaulted closets which are half the size of a normal cell and, possibly, were once latrines.

The Atık Valide is a handsome complex and worthy to mark the end of Sinan's long reign over the architecture of the Ottoman Empire. A great number of other works in Istanbul have not been discussed, since they made no important contribution to Sinan's development. A mosque such as that at Fındıklı, built for Molla Çelebi[14] late in his career, is a good example of a neighbourhood mosque. It has a handsome dome on squinches, a tall minaret, and a portico with five cupolas and a sebil added by Koca Yusuf Pasha in 1787. The plan is related to that of the Kadırga mosque, but without lateral galleries and with the addition of a large mihrab apse roofed by a semi-dome and small exedras. The recessed walls of the entry, which usually create north eyvans, are reduced to octagonal piers with two small rectangular piers between, thus opening up the area of the north wall. The mosque has been renovated and repaired, but the courtyard was shorn off when the highway was driven along the coast. The building is neat and of ashlar limestone with its roof area completely covered in lead in Sinan's later manner. A feature which was to be much used in palace architecture, such as the Revan or Baghdad Kiosks, is the insetting of windows into the curve of the semi-domes by opening stunted tunnel vaults. The graveyard forms a small walled paddock between the mihrab wall and the sea.

As late as 994/1586, Sinan built the modest mosque of Ramazan Efendi towards Yediküle for Hacı Hüsrev Ağa and one wonders why the royal architect was bothered with so small a commission. Yet the inscription over the door is by his friend and chronicler, the poet Sâi Çelebi,[15] and the little mescit is sheathed in panels of Iznik tile as splendid as those of quite different designs at Takkeci Ibrahim Ağa on the road to Bakırköy,[16] built a few years later. Ramazan Efendi probably had an inset wooden dome like Ibrahim Ağa originally. It is a rectangular room with a gallery which is set over the porch of the north wall with a small baroque bow front towards the mihrab. The proportions are simple but good, but the columns of the portico are gone and the area walled in.[17] The cells of the dervishes by the gatehouse have disappeared also, but the rectangular şadırvan survives with its pleasant floral reliefs on stone panels. The garden, rather than a court for it is full of flowers and trees, is a retreat from the mud of the streets of the quarter beyond the precinct wall. The minaret is fluted and tall in order to top the trees.

When discussing Ottoman work farther afield, reference was made to the Tekkiye of Süleyman at Damascus and the greater authority of the sultan which enabled him to erect monuments close to the traditions of his capital. Yet it has now been shown that, although Süleyman has been credited with the repair of the Dome of the Rock at Jerusalem, the work was never properly completed, even in the reign of Murat III.[18] So it is that the attribution of mosques to Sinan, even when they are listed on the Tezkere, if built outside Istanbul must be accepted with reservations. Since many of them were a long distance from the capital, it was impossible for him to supervise their building himself, and he either sent a subordinate – as he did to Manisa even for the royal mosque of Murat III – or else he enlisted the local city architect or master builder. His job would be to execute Sinan's plan, but he would be allowed more or less free rein as far as local techniques and materials were concerned; this has been demonstrated in connection with the Tekkiye at Damascus where there was an important architects' department. In some cases, Sinan may have visited the site before drawing up the plan or he may have recalled its main features from memories of earlier journeys, but often he can never have been to the place at all. Some of the provincial buildings are clearly a variation on a standard plan, just as if the founder had ordered a mosque with a dome of such and such dimensions, one or two porticoes, this decoration or that, according to taste and fortune.

82

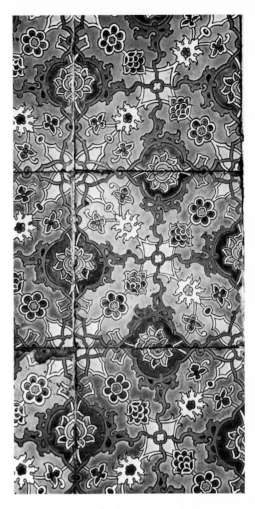

281 *Ramazan Efendi Cami, Istanbul. Tiles.*

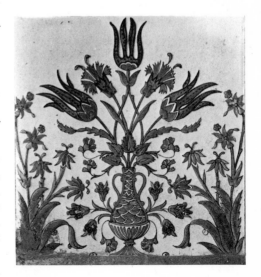

282 *Ramazan Efendi Cami, Istanbul. Skirting tile.*

The office of the Royal Architect had many skilled men who were able to execute good work from a ground plan especially if there was at least a rudimentary model of the building.[19] Ground plans do exist; in the miniature painted by Osman for his Surname, a large model, resembling a theatrical flat, is to be seen carried by the architects guild in the procession for the festival which Murat III held on the occasion of the circumcision of his heir.[20] Moreover, small models decorated the mosques after their completion. There appear to have been no elevations, and this accounts for the variation in proportion apart from clumsiness of detail; and so the presence of a master architect was essential all the time if a worthy building was to be achieved. With the porticoes of the Kurşunlu Cami, for example, which Sinan built at Kayseri, the height of the columns controlled the span of the arches, just as it did in Renaissance Europe where more detailed models were employed, and the lower outer portico of Rüstem Pasha at Tekirdağ, which is like the colonnade of a cloister, provides supporting evidence. Sinan, therefore, could at least be sure of the success of the main, north front of a mosque even if, when seen from the south, it might be less satisfactory.

31

20

He could visit certain work easily, for example the complex of Sokollu at Lüleburgaz on the road to Edirne which Sinan must have known very well; yet Semiz Ali Pasha's mosque at Babaeski is on the same road and there the workmanship is not good.[21] Izmit could be reached by road or sea and is on the main highway into the hinterland, and Sinan may have inspected his work for Pertev Mehmet Pasha there at least once. But work at Erzerum or Payas was quite a different matter. In the end, the only proof that Sinan did more than sketch the plans of mosques outside the two capitals is in the quality of the workmanship and the nature of such defects as the building may reveal. It would be interesting to find evidence which might help attribute a particular work to a certain deputy, but it is dangerous to speculate far about minor similarities between,

p

p

p

p

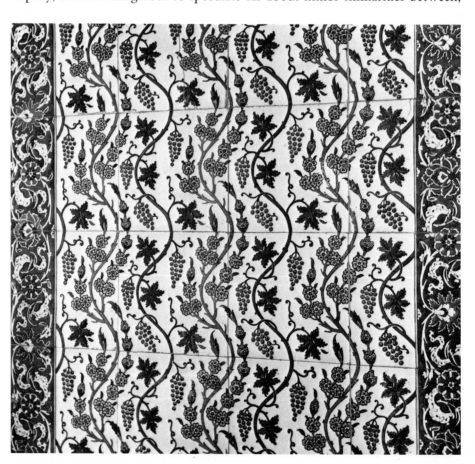

283 Takkeci Ibrahim Ağa Cami, Istanbul. Vine panel.

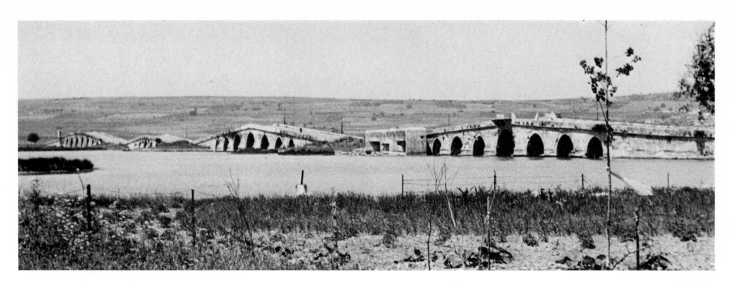

284 The bridge at Büyükçekmice.

say, the handling of the gallery doors at Babaeski and the Mehmet Ağa Cami
317 at Çarşamba by Davut Ağa. The records of the architects working at Manisa on
the Muradiye, however, have been found by Ahmet Refik, and these support
the obvious supposition that Sinan had no time to travel all over the country in
one year. He sat in his office and received reports and gave out instructions
except when a major work, such as the Selimiye at Edirne, required his presence,
and then a specific deputy, in this case Mehmet Ağa, was appointed in Istanbul.
Moreover, the architecture was impersonal so that a change of men on the spot,
such as occurred at Manisa, does not appear to have held up the work. All this
does not mean that provincial work is uninteresting or even second rate nor that
there is no definite work by Sinan outside Istanbul or Edirne. Of his work at
Büyükçekmice, there can be no doubt.

While hunting over the marshy land near the Marmara coast close to Silivri
on 20 September 1563, Sultan Süleyman Khan was nearly drowned in a flood
due to a cloudburst although he took refuge on the roof of a pavilion. He had
good reason, therefore, to command the building of a new bridge across the
284 estuary. The bridge at Büyükçekmice[22] is near a very long and low bridge at
Silivri which is also by Sinan, who repaired and built bridges frequently both
when he was a soldier and after he became the Architect of the Empire. The
Saray Bridge at Edirne is a good example. Ottoman bridges were nearer to
Roman models than Selçuk and usually lacked the pronounced hump of the
earlier Turkish period. They are handsome, plainly built works of engineering
which are demonstrably strong because many are still in use. The bridge at
Çekmice, however, is not only distinguished by its size but because it is really
three large and one smaller hump-back bridges which meet on artificial islands
in the midst of the lagoon. These islands are the key to a problem which Sinan
was immensely proud to have solved. The three main bridges rise to pronounced
peaks where there were once bowers extended on consoles over the water, and
sentry boxes of stone. These bridges are broad enough for two caravans to pass
each other with ease and were still used as the main highway to Edirne and
Tekirdağ until the middle of this century. Sinan was pleased with their strength
but he was also delighted with their grace; and, indeed, the rhythm of their rise
and fall is very fine. Sâi, as we have seen, on Sinan's tombstone resorted to an
old Moslem compliment and called the bridge the Straw Way or Samanyolu,
the Milky Way of the West. The return to the donkey back is strikingly archaic
nonetheless.

At the head of the bridge on the Istanbul bank, he built a small complex for
285 Sokollu Mehmet Pasha which consisted of a modest, square mescit which has
been heavily restored and a great rectangular barn of a kervansaray under a shed
roof.[23] The windows at the gable end on the east are alternately tall or round,

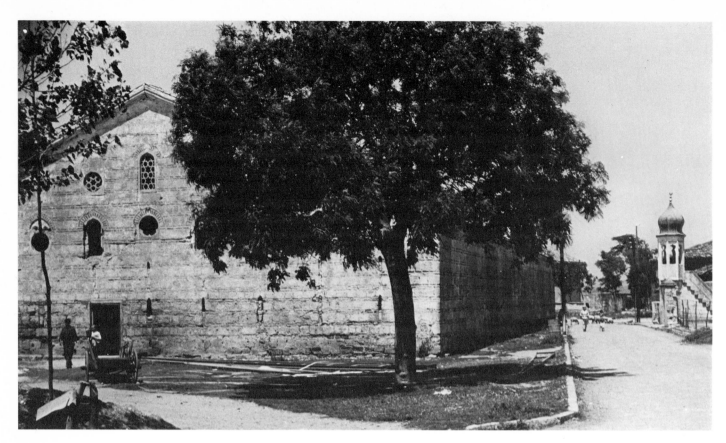

285 Sokollu Mehmet Pasha Kervansaray, Büyükçekmice. The combined mihrab and minber are on the right of the picture.

except for the lower tier in the middle where a wheel window reappears, after quiescence since the Sungur Bey period at Niğde. They were unglazed but inset with grilles of stone as an economy measure, and this form occurs frequently in the seventeenth century; an example is the Ekmekçioğlu Ahmet Pasha Kervansaray, dated *1018*/1609, at Edirne. The high roof at Çekmice is sustained on wooden rafters which are themselves supported on a central line of ten stone piers and two lateral arcades at the edge of the sofas which run the length of the hall on either side. These have huge impost capitals, once of wood but restored in concrete, which created hipped arches. Between the piers, along the walls of the high sofas, are twelve ocaks with deep niches for belongings on each side of them both sides of the hall.[24] The west end wall has tall slits below the grilled windows already discussed. The door, which still possesses its great chain, would have been closed at night against draughts and cold and thieves. A small stone annexe with a pair of two-tier windows may have been the lodging for important guests where the Marquis de Nointel escaped the hurly-burly in the hall in the late seventeenth century.

There is a fine triple-arched çeşme which forms the end of a compact complex, and a remarkable minaret of stone beside the gate to the small avlu. This minaret has a straight flight of twelve stairs leading up to its octagonal platform which has six foliate arches set between fluted ribs and a fine fretted balustrade. It could also serve as a minber when, with the coming of a large caravan, prayers were held out-of-doors. The little dome swells up like an onion and for this reason it has been suggested that it is a later addition or an alteration but, as has been pointed out, the form occurs above the portico at Selimiye at Edirne. The Çekmice mosque is square in plan and the pent roof extends over the portico of the son cemaat yeri to be supported by wooden posts. It has been restored out of recognition inside and it is impossible to tell if it had an inset wooden dome or not. The walls are of good quality ashlar with a course of brick between each course of stone. A feature which is a throwback to the Beyazit II period, and which Sinan must have intended for he must have used this kervansaray often, is the use of the peaked relieving arches as the sills of the upper windows; the expression of a point in these sills is new.

287   One of the finest hostels on the road to Edirne, also built by Sinan, is the Sokollu Mehmet Pasha complex at Lüleburgaz. The original nucleus, constructed in 956/1549,[25] included the mosque and its medrese round the large court, some thirty by forty metres in extent, and the darül-kurra behind. A kervansaray must have existed at this important staging post from ancient times and it is possibly because this became dilapidated twenty years later, in 977/1569, that the market, hamam and large new kervansaray were added to achieve a considerable social centre. It is significant that Sinan was already at work on Selim II's mosque at Edirne and passed frequently through Lüleburgaz. An especially good quality limestone is quarried there. Because of the vaulted street of the market between the medrese and the kervansaray, now demolished, there is a large gate in the middle of the north side of the court where the dershane should be found The dershane is placed at the end of the west arm of cells. These are twenty, or twenty-two, in number and none of them has an ocak. The cells across the north side of the avlu are matched by the shops which back onto them along the main street of the market; thus their only windows look southwards onto the court. The wing cells, in addition, look out onto narrow yards in the

208 same manner as those of the medreses of the Süleymaniye. At the end of these yards are the privies which can only be reached through the first cell which is really a vestibule, not only to the latrines but also to the corner cells which had windows on their north side until the çarşı was built and they became storage space for the shop built against them. The dershane is four times the area of a cell and not well lit, for it has only one window on its east side and one onto the yard on the north with a third onto the long and unusual hallway of the side entry from the lane which bounds the complex. This entry, like that opposite facing the hamam, has a fine gatehouse over the arch into the courtyard with a small ogee-shaped dome. These gatehouses close the lateral revaks of the medrese and unite them structurally to the side walls of the mosque portico. There is a şadırvan set centrally to the medrese area and not in relation to the whole court, which would indicate that mosque and medrese were still considered distinct units. This fountain has a romantic undulating baroque canopy, added in the eighteenth century. It may be noted that, if the double portico is taken into account, the court is then forty metres square. These porticoes consist of the traditional first rank of columns with chevron capitals and a second with stalactite capitals; each has eight marble or granite shafts and nine arches to its straight arcade. There is a low step up onto the paving of the outer portico and a double step onto the much higher sofa of the son cemaat yeri. A puzzling feature is a single granite column, set in front of the entry on the court side of the stone path which extends in front of the revaks between the gatehouses because the court is sanded but not paved.

   The façade of the mosque extends exactly half the width of its porticoes with slight additions due to the minaret and dummy bases on each side. It is set centrally and the added width is filled east and west by a curtain wall the span of two arches of the portico. Consequently, each wall has two large grilled windows looking out on the garden beyond. At each end, the same length of wall, set at a right angle, joins the gatehouse to form the flanks; there is a third window and also a door into the garden. The great door of the mosque is set back under a fine stalactite half-dome with narrow niches on each side. It is flanked by two casements with floral tiles in the tympana, and there are two more rectangular windows above these. On the west is the very broad and strong base of the lofty minaret which is balanced by the false base on the east which contains a stair to the gallery inside. The façade is low and broad, proceeding from the shed roof of the outer portico to the four domes each side of a slightly elevated cradle vault before the doorway. The main dome lies low behind a gradually stepped gable above the tympanum. It is lipped and gives the illusion that it rests on a

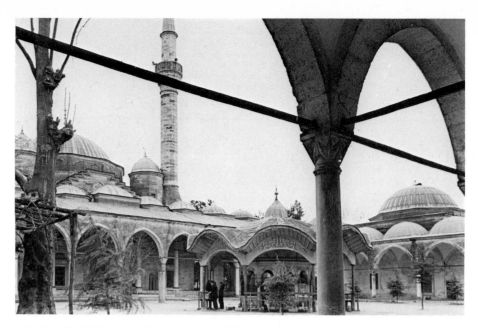

286 *Sokollu Mehmet Pasha Complex, Lüleburgaz. Mosque and medrese courtyard, showing the baroque canopy to the şadırvan and the dome of the dershane.*

true drum. Flanking it are thick and prominent decagonal stabilizing turrets with lead caps. The minaret rises immediately beside the north-west turret and its şerefe is high above the alem of the major dome. The height of the minaret helps it unify the extensive range of domes, vaults and open spaces beneath it. The four corner turrets are equally imposing when seen from the garden; the stepped tympana between them are related to those of Mihrimah at Edirnekapı *II* except that here they are soundly anchored and highly functional. Because of them, the main dome appears grander than its twelve and a half metres in width.

Inside, the deeply inset doorway creates a large recess between its flank and that of the base of the minaret – a recess which is more than usually cut off from the central area. There are large internal buttresses at the south corners, and along each side of the mosque are three columns and four arches to mask these lateral areas and their four casements in the outer wall. Thus the area under the dome is kept independent of these subordinate spaces, but only below gallery level.

The mosque garden, including the area of the mosque and its porticoes and the darül-kurra, is nearly square (60 × 70 metres). It is handsomely walled with small gates in the centre of its west and east sides, each of which also has three grilled windows. There are only two such windows in the southward wall. There, the darül-kurra, built of alternating courses of stone and brick, is on the axis of the mihrab and has a dome set on an octagonal drum. Between it and the mosque is a garden full of trees and a rectangular pool which must have been a pleasant retreat where weary travellers could sit and gossip about their journey. The darül-kurra is reached from outside the garden by flights of steps each side of its square platform under a dome which forms a handsome porch. It has as many windows as safety permits and so is bright and cheerful inside.

The kervansaray was large and complex without being complicated.[26] The gate from the street of shops on its south side and from the camping ground to the north admitted to a central court some thirty-five by forty metres in dimension with a pool in its centre and a number of large rooms along the north and south walls. Each side of the court to the south were two large halls, twenty by forty metres, with windows on their far sides only; these were set closely in order to obtain a range of ten casements in a narrow space. The halls also had one window beside the door into the court. These halls were for animals and servants. On their north side, and of equal overall dimensions, were two porticoed inner courts, fifteen by twenty-five metres, with chambers forming an L along their two outward walls. The east court had two big dormitories for lesser

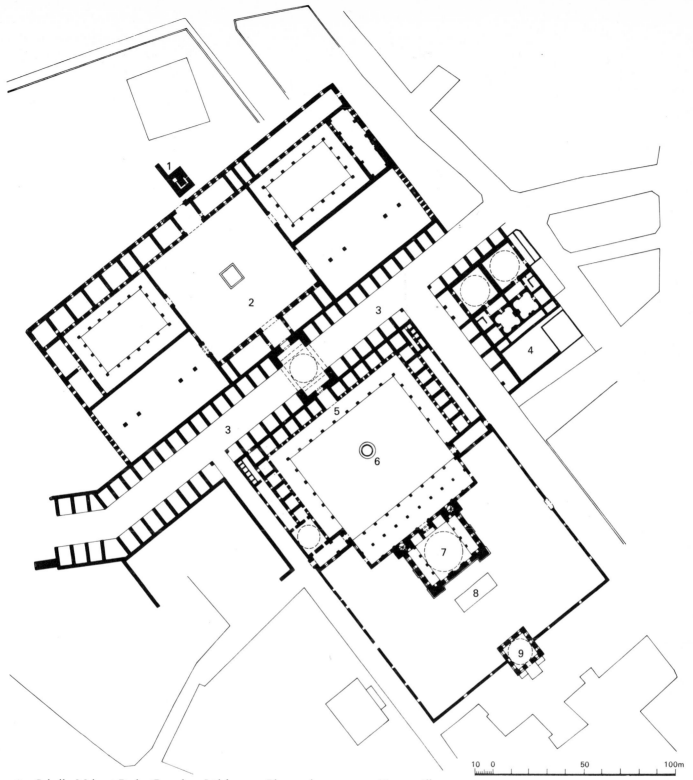

287 Sokollu Mehmet Pasha Complex, Lüleburgaz. Plan, scale 1:2,000. 1 Tower still standing; 2 kervansaray; 3 market; 4 hamam; 5 medrese; 6 şadırvan; 7 cami; 8 pool; 9 sıbyan mekteb.

merchants but that on the west had five large cells, thirty-six metres square as opposed to the sixteen metres square of the cells of the medrese; in addition, the west court had two intercommunicating double cells. It would look as if this court was reserved for the sultan and other notables.[27] Nothing of this kervansaray remains, but beside the site of its north gate is a square tower built of alternating courses of brick and stone with a shallow dome on a round drum. Inside, this relic consists largely of stairways and it has been used until recently as a jail; it may claim to have been the entrance to the outer compound.

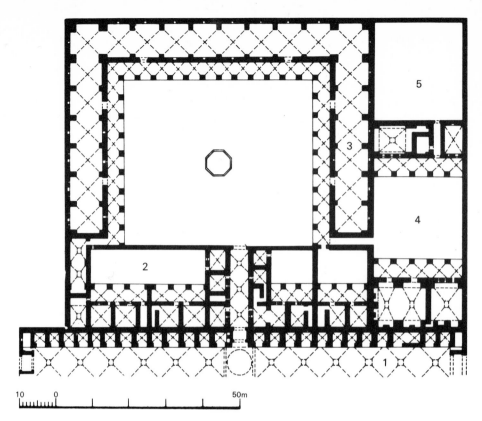

*288 Selim II Kervansaray, Payas. Plan, scale 1:1,000. 1 market; 2 private apartments;
3 dormitories; 4 kitchen court; 5 garden.*

The double hamam has been repaired and much mutilated including the
building of a blind concrete dome over the east camekân. The west camekân
was approached through a three-domed portico set between shops, and that on
the east may have had its own porch with a shed-roof. Shut in on all sides by shops
as they were, these halls must have depended on lanterns for light. The hamams
are not unusual except that their hot rooms have alcoves at each of the four angles
but only one halvet which is too large for the purpose and so likely to be a
private bathing place for potentates. Behind the stokehole is a suitably large
woodyard.

The Sokollu Mehmet complex at Lüleburgaz is handsome and its mosque is
more important than that at Payas but the plan of the latter kervansaray is
grander, especially so now that it is more intact. It was built for Selim II in
982/1574[28] and almost certainly Sinan never saw it but only drew up the plans.
Payas was a vital port for Aleppo at the start of the caravan route across the
Amanus range. Beside the village is a large castle in the Ottoman tradition of
towers and curtain walls, but the wooden barracks, at one point rebuilt with
rubble, are roofless and there is only a market garden inside. Nearer the water is
a second castle built by Christians with the help of masons trained in the Moslem
tradition to judge by the localized architectural detail. Sinan's deputy when he
came to build this important trading station would have employed local foremen
and workmen also.

The mosque is cruciform with a central dome and small wing rooms on the
north each side of the door. It has been often repaired and is being repaired again.
The stumpy, coarse minaret is an excellent vantage point from which to survey
the whole complex. The porticoes of the mosque and those over the now grassy
sofas in front of the cells have all fallen; the cells, themselves, are sadly battered:
there are twenty or twenty-one of them and, in all, the astonishing number of
thirty-seven small portico domes. The court is an irregular rectangle full of old
trees and flowers. Along its east side was driven the long, straight street of the
covered market with some twenty-five shops on each side. This forms the main

north-south axis of the complex, just as the similar market at Burgaz forms the east-west axis of its complex. The arched entries at Payas are broad and pointed and in the centre is a domed carfax. Here the east-west axis of the lane to the main gate of the castle crosses into the main court of the kervansaray. Behind the shops on the south-west side is the avlu of the mosque, which is reached through a fine gate under a segmental arch beneath a pointed relieving arch in grey, white and red stone. The north-west side is occupied by a ruined double hamam with camekân domes of nine and ten metres, whereas the crossing dome is only six metres and the mosque dome little more (7.50 metres). The changing rooms are lofty and lit by large windows on the outer walls. The men's hall has deep sofas recessed each side of the door, pretty papuçluk under the sofas round all the walls, and a fountain in the middle. A passage leads to the hot room which has four corner halvets with four eyvans between, but the circle of eight arches which once supported the dome disguises the simplicity of this cross plan and the halvet entries are set at an angle. Above each of them is a splendidly bold foliate design in relief.

There is a fine vista down the length of the market which is punctuated by six square light wells each side of the central dome. From there there is the passage into the kervansaray off which were latrines and rooms for the porters. The open court is cobbled and measures some 42·50 by 50·00 metres. It is bound on all but the west side by revaks for those who preferred to sleep out of doors in summer when it is hot in the vicinity of Iskenderun. Travellers could also sleep on the roofs. Inside, there is a continuous hall forming a C behind the revaks. There are windows only on the court sides and there are two doors on each front so that the dormitories are not well lit but kept cool in summer and warm in winter. Including those engaged at the end walls, there are seven great arches springing from square piers along each of the north and south sections of the hall, and eight along the central section. Between these, on the outward walls, are sofas for grooms and lesser travellers well above the stable floor; and there are twenty-two handsome ocaks. The vistas down these halls and down the revaks, which have broad pointed arched arcades carried on thick piers, are exceptionally grand. On the north side of the entry passage is a small, long court partitioned across its arcade so as to form two separate sets of large cells. This can only be reached by a narrow alley, past the north end of the public dormitories, which also leads to a small, twin-vaulted hall. This could have served for an oratory or the guardroom of the more illustrious travellers who enjoyed such privacy, or even as a stable and store. There are two similar sections south of the entry where the court is completely divided by a wall to form a suite of three or four apartments with a three-arched portico and a small court area each. Between the second of these and the south dormitory is a narrow passage leading to a court some 21 by 22·50 metres and so approximately square. On the west is a large vaulted double kitchen with four ranges; beside this is a second single kitchen with only one range. These open onto a portico, as do the storerooms opposite between which is a slype to the kitchen garden and orchard. These are bound along the south and east by a high ashlar wall with handsome cresting running along its top.

The Payas complex was built on flat terrain and the plan has mathematical and logical neatness which must have given great satisfaction to the architects who built it. The use of valuable cut stone of three main colours shows it to have been a major work and much money must have been spent on it. Nonetheless, there is no likelihood that Sinan ever strolled down his market or slept in the calm of one of the courts reserved for ministers or potentates.

Near Payas, on the pilgrimage route, is one of a number of fortified kervansarays[29] on the road to Mecca. These are of varying dates, but many built in the sixteenth and seventeenth centuries are distinctly Ottoman in appearance, partly because of their mutual northern ancestry in cold Selçuk Anatolia. The one near Payas is at Beylen on the Iskenderun to Antakya (Alexandretta to Antioch) road and is a rectangular hall some seventy by thirty-one metres with two small domed chambers each side of the door. It is in a bad state of repair and was never of outstanding workmanship, but in its humble way it is more typical than Burgaz or Payas. For although close in date, 957/1560,[30] it has none of their grandeur.[31] The little mosque across the way served as the oratory and was built in the reign of Selim II. The Hasiye kervansaray is reached soon after Homs after passing several seventeenth-century examples. Here Süleyman I added a large second court to the existing humble han built round a court beside a fort. The new great hall has two rows of ten columns on the west with colonnades outside for summer rest. There is a square mescit with a two-column porch in the centre of the court and a rectangular pool to the east of it. Its similarities to Selçuk-style hans are immediately apparent.

On the last stage before reaching Damascus is the most impressive of these kervansarays, that of el-Ktaifé which dates from 1000/1591.[32] It was built for Yemeni Fatih Sinan Pasha who also built the mosque at Damascus at the same time when he was Viceroy there. It is the most Ottoman of them all and very large indeed. Its vast walled enclosure measures one hundred and forty metres by a hundred but has only two small gates. The main one is flanked by a hamam and a bakehouse followed by a vaulted hall with nine shops on each side, most of which are in ruins. Set beside the hall, on the south, is the square mosque which has two small tabhane rooms flanking it and a five-vaulted portico facing onto its own small walled court. This has a rectangular pool in the middle. On the east lies the nearly square, commodious kervansaray with an echo of the four-eyvan medrese plan, for the centre of each side is marked by passages. The main entry has a room and a stair to the roof on one side and two rooms on the other. Opposite, on the east, is the passage to the latrines with seven well-appointed cabinets whence the waste water escapes to fertilize the small garden behind. On the north is a square apartment divided into a foyer with two eyvans and an oda or room, each occupying a quarter of the total area; this would appear to be an apartment for a potentate. Opposite, on the south, are the four rectangular rooms of the kitchen department enclosing a small court with a triple-vaulted portico. The kervansaray court of flagstones has trees to shade its rectangular pool and there are tall colonnades to shade the revaks all round. Each of the four L-shaped halls has the usual high sofas, and nine alcoves with ocaks. Each side of the passage to the kitchen block are two small private rooms and there is a long chamber each side of the passage to the viceregal suite. The workmanship is good and the kervansaray is built of ashlar.

One other which may be mentioned is Er-Resten, between Homa and Homs for it, more than any of the others, owes much to the Anatolian Selçuk tradition. This is partly due to the watch towers[33] on the southern corners of the long, rectangular building, some ninety-five by forty-five metres in size. Like the Selçuk hans, it has only one entry, for defensive reasons; there are two rooms on one side and a room and a staircase to the roof on the other. The court is enclosed by a dormitory which occupies all sides of the building except for the entry. There is no revak, but there are sixteen large archways onto the court. The walls are of basalt relieved by limestone decoration and voussoirs. In the centre of the court, its dome in ruins, is the fine ashlar limestone mescit which is octagonal in plan[34] and, after Bursa, one of the few of this type to appear in an Ottoman foundation prior to a revival in the seventeenth century. Except for the sides containing the door and the mihrab, there is a large rectangular casement window on each side, and much play is made with courses of basalt and limestone. Sauvaget dates this kervansaray about 1600[35] although its characteristics are so much earlier in date.

In Anatolia itself, the Bitlis road is also remarkable for its kervansarays of the period although many are only aisled halls with a room each side of the entry like the Babşın which was built in the town itself in 1001/1593,[36] but the Hüsrev Pasha kervansaray in sight of Lake Van is comparable with the great Syrian hostels and those of Payas and Lüleburgaz.

South of Bitlis, the Hasan Pasha Han at Diyarbakır, dated 980/1573-983/1575,[37] is a fine example of provincial work of the period. It has a deep central gate with

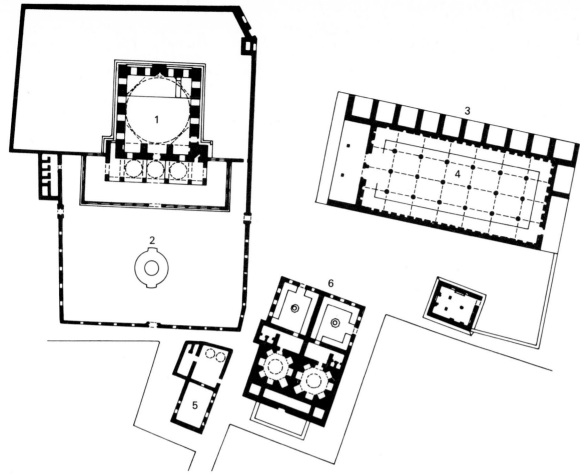

289 Pertev Pasha Complex, Izmit. Sketch plan. 1 mosque; 2 şadırvan; 3 shops; 4 kervansaray; 5 sıbyan mekteb; 6 double hamam.

windows in the Syrian manner with stalactite decoration above them sharply cut to form the frame each side of a tamgâh. Such windows are common to the great hans of Aleppo and Damascus. There are six cell windows at first-floor level above the shops on the street front on each side of the entry, and the han is faced with alternating courses of basalt and limestone in the local manner (which grew up due to the southern influence and the lavish supply of basalt in the region). The fine galleries of the inner court with their broad arch span look down on an octagonal şadırvan with a lead-covered dome carried on stone arches above marble columns. It is interesting to compare this very Ottoman han with its many domes and the Deliller Han of fifty years before[38] at the far end of the same thoroughfare. This han with its shed roofs and severe black façade has much smaller windows partly relieved by white stone in their frames. There are alternating white and black stone voussoirs in the arcade of the shops below and this severe aspect is partly relieved by the striped gateway which has low sofas in its deep cool entry passage. The han has a large court with wide arches and a very grand hall for beasts with five rows of seven piers behind. In the keys of the cradle vaults are skylights. There are stairs each side of the entry and of the small but deep eyvan across the court. The niches in the thirty-six lower cells, as well as those of the upper floor, suggest that at court level they were used as lodgings and not just as the usual storerooms.

These are city hans, and not kervansarays which were based on the concept of the large stable and dormitory combined, like that at Büyükçekmice or of the complex of Pertev Mehmet Pasha at Izmit. There, the imaret and han appear to have been built of wood on stone foundations. There was also a stone double hamam which is now in ruins. Here, the mosque and perhaps the çeşme outside the west gate can be partly attributed to Sinan. The mekteb in the north-west corner of the large garden which serves for a court has been completely rebuilt.

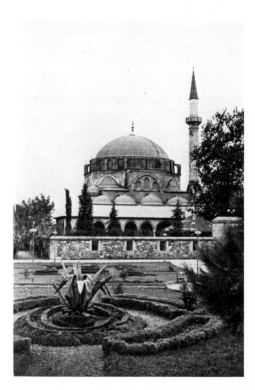

290 Pertev Pasha Complex. Mosque and court from the north.

The complex was probably complete in 987/1579 which is the date on the plaque over the west gate. The court was once surrounded by a high wall with a şadırvan in the centre which is still in use. The mosque rises in three clearly defined stages. There is the square basic block with the base and foot of the minaret against its north-east corner behind the son cemaat yeri. Above this is the high octagonal base on which the drum stands with the small lead domes of the squinches at the four angles and three windows on the sides. The dome with its small flying buttresses at each corner forms the third leaded area. The silhouette is bold and puritanical and related to the Edirne mosques of one hundred years before, such as that of Ayşe Kadın,[39] but it is much larger. The fluted minaret still has its short *10* sixteenth-century cap and its balcony is set above the crest of the dome. The son cemaat yeri has three central domes and a flattened cradle-vault at each end and is preceded by a second portico of eleven pointed arches with chevron capitals on good columns of Marmara marble except at the corners where piers are employed. This double portico is the most handsome feature of the mosque and with its three lateral arches completely embraces the sofa of the son cemaat yeri; it is covered with a lean-to lead roof. This frontage is a grander version of that of Rüstem Pasha at Tekirdağ.[40] The north wall of the mosque has suffered *20* from restoration; on the right of the door the mihrab niche of the son cemaat yeri is set against the casement and shares its frame on their common side: this is a novel design but looks cramped. The great door has no niche and looks like a replacement.

The interior of the Pertev Mehmet is boldly square under its dome and corner squinches on well-cut stalactite corbels. The casements are large and their lunettes glazed, and the windows above the inscriptive frieze of tile are large also, although some have later, coloured glass in them; the third tier is smaller and there are twenty-four windows in the dome: yet the overall impression is not of an overwhelming number of windows because they are spaced well apart. Both the mihrab and minber are handsome and of marble but the latter has suffered from painting and gilding. The other strong features of the interior are the two buttresses right and left of the entry which create the usual three recessed areas across the north wall. It is a fine lofty hall, commodious and light, but it is simple in form and adds nothing to the stature of Sinan.

Even plainer than Pertev Pasha's mosque at Izmit, is the small mosque completed for Selim II in 977/1569[41] at Karapınar; but it is an example of good work- *29* manship and trim organization of elements. The complex, which included a stone kervansaray and arasta besides the still working hamam and a medrese round the court, does not appear on the Tezkere, only the mosque. This was heavily restored in 1223/1808[42] when the original main door was replaced and the niche became a ribbed fan or shell under an elegant nineteenth-century inscription. Since it was built for the sultan, Sinan must indeed have been responsible for the plan. The twin royal minarets are set neatly behind the five-domed portico, and the flanking wall is buttressed in the centre on each side and at the corners. Further buttresses occur each side of the mihrab niche. The dome is relatively low and has only one window on each side and single flying buttresses at each angle. On each side there are only two casements with two small light windows above and a very small circular window over each central buttress. The mihrab wall is no better lit, and there is nothing on the north side except one casement right and left of the door. This is surely due to the need to exclude the strong hot sun of the Konya plain and accounts for the small windows of the Kurşunlu Cami at Kayseri and the Cenabı Ahmet Pasha Cami at Ankara, inscribed 973/1565 and attributed to Sinan; other examples could be cited. There is no proof that Sinan travelled to Konya to build this mosque at Karapınar which depends entirely on exactitude of proportion for effect and also the grace of the portico and the minarets. Its sharp lines and right angles contrasting with the circular elements have some of the abstract quality of a Quattrocento work.

The interior could not be simpler. The mosque is a domed square without recesses or gallery. The stalactite mihrab contrasts with the plain minber and

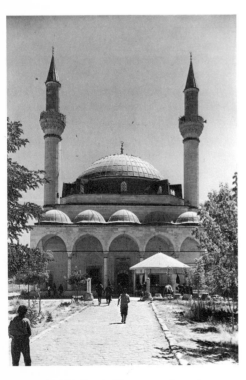

291 Selim II Cami, Karapınar, from the north.

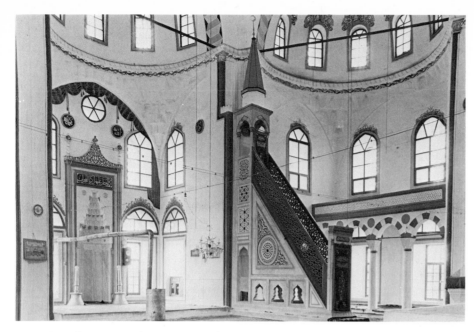

292 Ali Pasha Cami, Babaeski. Interior from the north-east.

there is a small platform in the north-west corner for the müezzin. The dome is supported on pendentives which spring from only twelve feet above floor level. There is no shell squinch as at the Cenabı Ahmet mosque and this total austerity, accentuated by the lack of fussy paintwork, is a complete success.

Even in its present ruined state, the approach is very fine even if Sinan can claim no credit for it. The lofty archway into the kervansaray is opposite a large çeşme on the highway. The L-shaped medrese is in decay and its garden neglected but the forecourt of the mosque is paved and the building well-maintained.

Far away in Thrace, the mosque of Semiz, or the Fat, Ali Pasha at Babaeski[43] was also built in the 1560s.[44] The best view is from the bridge, on the approach from Istanbul, from which it looks a handsome if complex pile. On close inspection, it will be seen that the exterior of the mosque is square with two large arches over two tiers of paired windows on the south wall which are set off-centre each side of the rectangular mihrab apse. The single tier of windows each side of the door on the north side are also off-centre, due to the base of the minaret. The concern with inward, as opposed to outward, appearance also accounts for the lopsided organization of the windows of the Kurşunlu at Kayseri, and this clumsiness indicates that Sinan had little if anything to do with the actual construction of the mosque. The lateral arches at Ali Pasha are divided by battered buttresses with arched buttresses above between the semi-domes; and these are connected by three lead-capped steps to the projection of yet another buttress which is the external exposure of the hexagonal interior organization in the manner of Kara Ahmet Pasha at Topkapı.[45] In addition there are turrets at each corner. Those on the south-west and south-east are set awkwardly close to the drums of the southerly semi-domes and are out of alignment with the battered buttresses; these latter might more nearly be described as battered exterior thickenings of the corner of the mosque. Turrets which had become weak independent elements at roof level were a feature of seventeenth- and eighteenth-century mosque architecture. The north-west turret is even more unhappily placed because it is caught between the semi-dome and the foot of the minaret; this is lofty and multi-faceted and has fine stalactite corbelling under its single şerefe which is set well above the crown of the dome. The corners of the exposed square base of the dome are extended to act as yet another pair of buttresses on the south side, but on the north they are incorporated into the great arch across the façade and its rect-angular crested apron above. The four angle buttresses of the dome itself are set on these extensions of the base, and two more pairs are set above the buttresses arising from the inward piers on the east and west. The crown of the dome is lipped and the stonework between the windows is not leaded so that there is the impression of a drum. This occurs with other country mosques, like the Sokollu Mehmet Cami at nearby Lüleburgaz, but there the independent turrets have a strength that the mosque at Babaeski cannot match and they are not set against a complicated and cluttered backdrop.

The court of Ali Pasha is a walled garden in front of a double revak which extends beyond the mosque. The lateral gates to the garden are handsome and here, as with the north gate, there was much rebuilding due to earthquake damage.[46] The very high base of the minaret behind the portico wall and against the mosque on the traditional north-west exposes two handsome panelled faces west and south. The foot is so high that its multifaceted unification of the base and trunk can be seen above the domes of the son cemaat yeri. The double portico is akin to that at Burgaz but less well ordered, and the columns of the outer revak are a poor collection of varying heights and thicknesses with a squat and dumpy pair in the centre which, moreover, have been gnawed away with a chisel at the top in order to make them fit their capitals and not the capitals fit them. This is unashamedly bad workmanship. The ordering of the doors and windows under the domed son cemaat yeri is undistinguished.

The interior has been whitewashed, but colourful rococo decoration has been retained over the windows and elsewhere. There are many large windows and casements with glazed tympana, and large panes of modern glass flood the mosque with light. In the apse the corner windows are set so close together that they look like a half-open book, and there is a distinct sense of weakness at the springing of the great arch over the mihrab which also crowds upon the upper lights over the casements. The round window over the mihrab which appears satisfactory externally is disproportionately mean and set too high above the triangular cresting of the niche. The handsome müezzins' tribune west of the door is set on hipped arches and has escaped the garish painting of the gallery balustrades and the fine marble minber. The dome and semi-domes are carried on subdued plaster stalactite squinches which are of good workmanship, but their springing brings them uncomfortably close to the windows. There is considerable use of thick plaster in the mosque and the doors are cut crudely into the mahfil; the comparison with the work of Davut Ağa at the Mehmet Ağa mosque at Çarşamba has already been made.[47]

The interior today is that of a light and cheerful country mosque with some good appointments and no serious attempt to solve the problems of relationship between structure and aesthetic excellence. Externally, the elaborate build-up of the roof and the plethora of buttresses of all kinds is confusing, achieving a clutter which was intentional in French Renaissance work such as Chambord but not here. Sinan had resolved some of the interior problems in the past and had never let his structure become so needlessly complicated before. He left the major work of construction to a subordinate, and Davut Ağa whose known work has a tendency towards complication and clutter could have been the man.

There are a number of provincial mosques by Sinan which, like that of Mehmet Pasha in Sofia, once the seat of the Viceroy of Europe, or of Lala Mustafa Pasha at Erzerum, or Ali Pasha at Ereğli, are built of local stone; that of Mehmet Pasha at Sofia is a sombre red. They represent prototypes of similar mosques of medium size where often large ulu camis dating from Selçuk or Beylik times already existed. From time to time, one comes upon one which has not been attributed to Sinan, such as that of Mehmet Bey at Sivas, dated 988/1580; this may have been built by Mehmet Bey's father, the vezir Mahmut Pasha, and is known as the Kale Cami.[48] It is the work of an architect well-trained in the manner of the times and, so, likely to be a product of the royal office at Istanbul. The portico has been lost and replaced by a forehall of no interest.

Inside, it forms the usual domed hall but it has been prettily repainted recently by one of the decorators of the splendid local arabas, or carts, and is as gay as a fairground. There is a good mihrab of the traditional form. The mosque is built

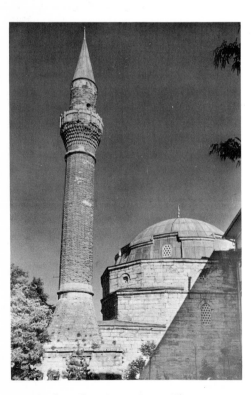

293 Mehmet Bey Cami, Sivas. The minaret.

293 of cut stone but the thick and stumpy minaret is of brick. There are four consoles set at unequal heights about nine feet from the ground on the east side but their function is impossible to determine. The interest of this mosque lies in the complex build-up of the dome as if the master builder were afraid to use a pendentive. From a distance the walls appear to rise steeply to the dome, but above the casements the square block is translated into a duodecagon by cutting away the corners at angles of 22·5 degrees. There are pairs of windows on each of the sides. Inside, and above these windows, and inset with four arches to form four squinches in the corners, are sixteen small arches with a circular window in each alternate one, thus creating an interlocking movement from arch to arch. Seen from outside, a sixteen-faceted base has been created for the dome. This carries eight pointed windows which alternate with eight round windows in the base below. The leaded window area of the dome is joined to the crown by a lip which is stepped above each window. The dome is slightly concave at this point.

294 The mosque of the redoubtable Lala Mustafa Pasha, conqueror of Cyprus, was completed in 971/1563[49] at Erzerum. The details of the plan derive from those of Istanbul mosques but its conception belongs to a form familiar in Anatolia. It is related to Elbistan and Çankırı, with its central dome supported on octagonal piers and with four corner cupolas and lateral cradle vaults on all but the north side. There is a good stone mihrab with recessive columns, and capitals with small hexagonal windows set right and left above it. The vaults are clumsily constructed but this may be due to repair: this absence of semi-domes is the hallmark of provincial workmanship, for where no models existed and the tradition of the vault was strong a hereditary craftsman could not adventure into new forms. The central dome appears small and low from inside and out where the pairs of buttresses at the angles, although strongly expressed, can only be seen from above the mosque on the south side. The mosque furniture is nineteenth-century and unappealing.[50]

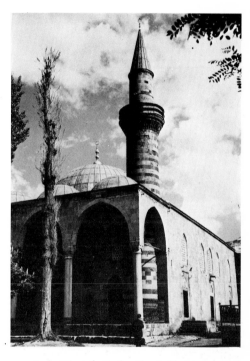

294 Lala Mustafa Pasha Cami, Erzerum, from the north-west.

The son cemaat yeri is the same height as the mosque and supported by coarse stone columns with inferior capitals. The organization of the façade is distorted by the minaret, which is as local in design as it is in execution with its bands of grey and red stone, the shallow honeycomb corbelling under the şerefe and its small lead cap. It is disproportionately thick and short[51] and is half engaged in the north-west corner of the portico.[52] The side walls are trimly organized with three wide-spaced casements, one of which is actually a door, and large upper windows over those at the ends but – significant of eastern Anatolia – three grouped over that in the middle. The mosque has tiles inset in the casement lunettes inside and some have survived externally as well. They are remarkable for the thin elegance of their lettering, partly due to the length of some of the quotations, and the correspondingly miniature quality of the floral and arabesque decoration which recalls certain rugs from Isfahan. The whole design is intricate to the point of fussiness.

The attribution of such a mosque to Sinan, unless his plans were mutilated in the building, is impossible because of the clumsy minaret, the disorder of the north façade, and the vaults instead of semi-domes of the roof. It is true that the Constantinopolitan parade of cupolas round a central dome is unsuited to snowbound winters, but the vaults create a series of independent units of space utterly alien to Sinan's precepts. Whatever contribution Istanbul may have made to the design of the mosque of Lala Mustafa Pasha, the execution was in local hands. It is related to the less elegant Kuyucu Murat Pasha Cami dated 981/1573,[53] also in Erzerum of which Murat Pasha was then Governor-General. Like the Lala Mustafa mosque, it has a low dome with four windows, but otherwise it has squinches the same span and height as the lateral arches, a form which is related to that of the mosques of Van.

Eastern Anatolia had maintained independence and ties with Iran into the sixteenth century. The old ulu cami at Van was eccentrically modelled on the south dome of the Friday mosque at Isfahan, and the ulu cami at Eski Malatya also shows Iranian influence, which can also be traced in the inset casement

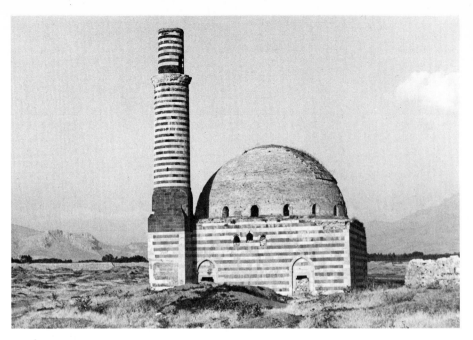

295 Kaya Çelebi Cami, Van, from the west.

windows and the size of the minaret in the two sixteenth-century Ottoman mosques of the old city of Van which were abandoned after the destruction of April 1921. Syrian influence is also strong and both mosques are striking for their alternating courses of black and white stone which also appear in their minarets. They look as though they are the work of the same architect and also follow a pattern which recurs in the region and can be said to be based on a standard design for a mosque of some size; it could be turned out wherever needed and the same model and ground plan used over and over again.

The Hüsrev Pasha Cami is dated 975/1567 by the decorative inscription over the door and the Kaya Çelebi Cami, a hundred metres east of it, must have been built very little earlier. The workmanship of this is slightly better than that of Hüsrev Pasha and so are the interior proportions. Both mosques have simple brick squinches creating the octagonal support on which their domes rest and both are low buildings with their domes little higher than their diameters. The flanks of the Kaya Çelebi Cami have only two wide-set lower casements with three small upper lights between and above them. The Hüsrev Cami has the more usual, and better balanced, set of three casements. The trefoil mihrabs in nearly square frames differ because that of Hüsrev extrudes and the brick dome of this mosque, which retains none of its stone tiling, unlike Kaya Çelebi, has only eight and not twelve windows and these are bound in a collar of stone. Neither mosque exposes its squinches externally; they are formed within the supporting arches which are of the same dimension as the four engaged in the walls so that an unbroken movement is created round the octagon: but Hüsrev Cami has a north gallery which cuts across the rhythm and diminishes the sense of space which is so powerful in the Kaya Cami. This is important because the low domes are always visible in both mosques.

The square bases of the minarets become octagons at roof level by means of small triangular buttresses at the corners. The round frames of the facets of the feet of the minarets reflect the movement of the eight arches inside the mosques. The trunks are thick and look all the more so because of their rings of black and white masonry and there is little honeycomb corbelling where the şerefes are formed out of the thickness of the trunks. The top of each minaret is necessarily thinner than the shaft and presumably once supported a lead cap. The minaret of the Hüsrev Cami is the more elaborate but it is also less bold because of this. Inside, there are some traces of tile; some were octagonal but those in the mihrab were square and may have come from Iznik or from Damascus. There is also the

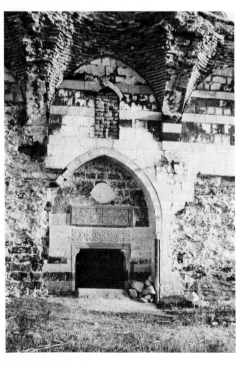

296 Hüsrev Pasha Cami, Van. The north door. The level of the portico has risen due to fallen masonry.

open türbe of Hüsrev Pasha inscribed *989/1581*. It has interesting dervish symbols engraved on it and is set against the south-east corner of the mosque. The five-domed portico has brick pendentives whereas those of the Kaya Çelebi were of stone. The north door, in both cases, was the only entry and was framed beneath a recessed arch without a stalactite semi-dome.

A forerunner of these mosques was the one which was probably built by Selim I across the ravine from the palace of İshak Pasha at Doğubayezit. This mosque is raised on a huge platform which is higher than itself at its deepest point and faced with ashlar. The mosque is plainer than those of Van and there are only rectangular casement windows except for one small light in each of the eight facets of the low drum supporting the dome of stone over brick. The base of the minaret springs from below the mosque and the giant foot reaches drum level and so seems exceedingly high while the trunk is disproportionately stumpy. The effect is less awkward than might be expected because it is clearly explained by the steep fall of the mountainside. The cap of the minaret is of stone. İnside, the plan closely resembles that of the Van mosques on a smaller scale; the eight arches are the same size and the quarter-circular squinches are not expressed at roof level. The plain stone mihrab survives at Doğubayezit, but there is no trace of a minber in any of these three derelict mosques and it is possible that they were of wood.

The two mosques of the old town of Ahlat within the walls of the spacious citadel, completed by Selim II in *976/1568*,[54] belong to the same type. That of İskender Pasha dates from *972/1564* according to the inscription over the north door, but the minaret was not completed until *978/1570*, the date given by an inscription below the cap. This provides evidence in support of the theory that mosques were completed first, then the portico and, finally, the minaret. The angled squinches are made of brick and there are ten windows in the dome, but otherwise it closely relates to the later mosque of Kadı Mahmut, dated *992/1584*.[55] This is in even worse repair but the resemblance to the Van mosques (but without a gallery), is very clear. Like Hüsrev Cami, it has three casements on the east and west and one each side of the mihrab on the south. There is also a light over the mihrab and a casement on each side of the north door. The sofas of the portico are high and each has its own small mihrab niche; the façade is decorated with

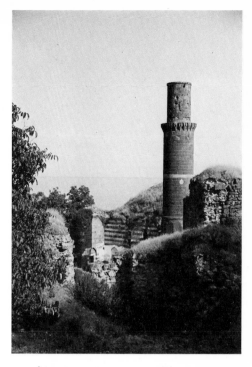

297 İskender Pasha Cami, Ahlat. The minaret and the ruined portico.

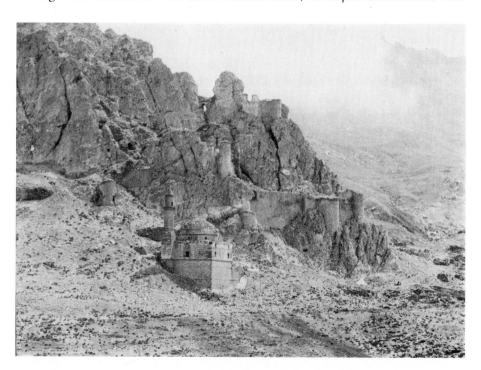

298 Selim Cami, Doğubayezit, seen from the İshak Pasha Saray. Note the lofty podium on which it is set.

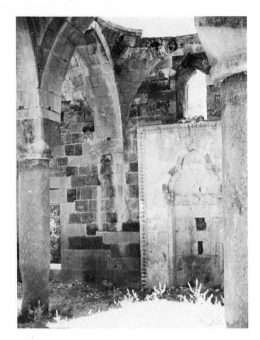

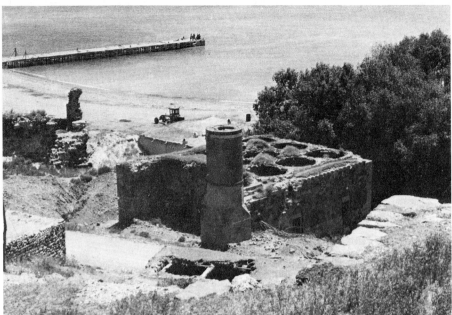

299, 300 Ulu Cami, Adılcevaz, Lake Van. Left: the mihrab. Right: view from the north-west.

patterns, like those of the other mosques, which are influenced by the mass of Selçuk monuments to be seen around. Unlike the mosque of İskender, however, the Kadı Mahmut has no true dome but a high octagonal drum and a very large pitched roof into which the interior dome is set. The mihrab niche protrudes like that of Hüsrev Pasha but unlike İskender. Both the latter and Kadı Mahmut have, or had, triple-domed porticoes, and the minaret of İskender still stands except for its cap. It has only one band of white stone decorating the middle of its trunk but, like the striped façade of the portico, is otherwise so closely akin to those of the mosques of Van as to suggest the same builder. It is not, however, set at the north-west corner of the mosque, like them, but at the end of the flanking wall of the portico which is closed on either side except for casement windows. The recurrence of random-coloured ashlar with the Kadı Mahmut Cami arrests attention and is added evidence that the plans of these mosques were carried out by an Armenian master builder.

Nearby, at Adılcevaz, on the same shore of the lake, is a ruined nine-domed *299* ulu cami with four supporting columns which is a small version of the Eski Cami at Edirne. The trefoil arched version of the mihrab recurs and the minaret relates to that of İskender Pasha and is reached across the top of the west flanking wall of the portico from a gallery inside the mosque. The capitals on the columns are plain and their arches simple and pointed, as are all the relieving arches over the casements and upper lights. The pendentives are of stone inside and out, and there are two windows and two niches in the façade under the three domes of the son cemaat yeri. The windows are set above the casements to make a pair and there are no zebra effects, yet this mosque, for all its unexpected reversion to the past, is clearly of the same period and replaces the Selçuk ulu cami on the hill- *30.* side above.[56] This is long and narrow with a narthex at its east end.

A much earlier example of the type of minaret common to this group of mosques is that of the Şerefiye Cami, or Birinci Şeref Cami built of the local *30.* reddish brown rock and dated 935/1528,[57] at Bitlis. The movement from base to foot to trunk is the same but there is no use of coloured stone; instead, there is an inscriptive band round the base and the middle of the trunk with an inscriptive lozenge between: this suggests the link between the Ottoman and the Selçuk minarets in the province. The mosque has an unusual approach by a bridge and a path beside the stream which cuts through Bitlis. A gatehouse to the east of the portico faces southwards and there is a fine polychrome trefoil arch supported

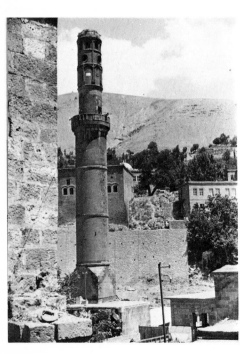

301 Ulu Cami, Bitlis. The Selçuk minaret.

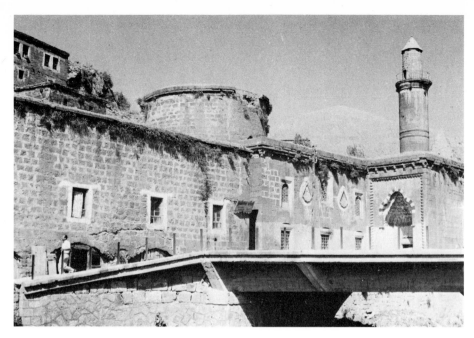

302 Serefiye Cami, Bitlis. East flank with the gatehouse, from across the bridge.

on engaged pilasters over a ten-tier honeycomb semi-dome. There are three casements along the east wall with windows above them inset with marble screens, the central window being slightly higher than those flanking it. Between the windows are two leaf or flame forms decorated, like the frame set in dog-toothing round the door, with shallow carving in the Selçuk manner. This shape has some connection with that each side of the entry to the Selimiye at Istanbul and also appears elsewhere in the Bitlis region – on the minaret of İskender Pasha at Ahlat, for example, where it acts as a frame for the date. The fragments of tile decoration found in the grounds of this mosque suggest that it held true to the ancient Selçuk traditions of Anatolia.

The great door admits to a square-domed vestibule with a door on the left leading into the five-domed portico. Immediately on the left again is the door into the mosque, this corner being more convenient than a central setting. Behind the vestibule and facing the garden court is the octagonal türbe of the Bey. On the far side of the court is a çeşme and, in the Selçuk manner or as with earlier Umayyad examples, the minaret[58] stands in the centre of the north wall of the court where there are now latrines but which was once a dependency of the foundation. The interior reverts to the plan of the Blue Mosque at Tabriz, for there is a central dome – but supported on pendentives – before the mihrab and five piers with three aisles roofed by a mixture of barrel vaults and domes on squinches. The mihrab projects into the lane behind. The work is in cut stone, including the tall exterior drum supporting a dome so shallow that it cannot be seen from the court. This is so far removed from the Ottoman canon as to make it almost certain that the builder was an Armenian.

The Van form occurs all over Anatolia, and the Sungur Bey and the Çelebi Ali mosques at Eski Pertek are sixteenth-century examples of small versions. Overseas, the mosque of Recep Pasha on Rhodes, which has an inscription dated 996/1588, is remarkable for its fine workmanship and tiles. Architecturally, the square hall with its dome (12 × 17·50 metres) supported on squinches is related to the Van type. Like that of Ibrahim Pasha Cami, the second portico may well be a later addition.

The Van style was itself partly inspired by that of Diyarbakır and, self-evidently from the striping of the stone, from Syria and Damascus. The mosque of Melek Ahmet Pasha was built in 999/1591[59] when he was governor of the city and is set at first-floor level. The trefoil arch appears in the gateway which leads

303

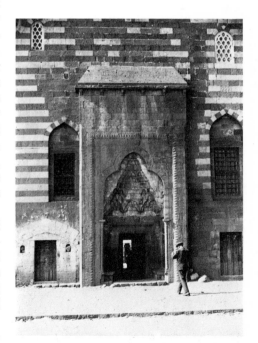

303 Melek Ahmet Pasha Cami, Diyarbakır. The south gateway to the passage leading under the mosque to the courtyard.

to a vaulted passage. This passes under the mosque and opens into a garden court where there is a flight of stairs to the entry on the west side. The dome is carried on an octagonal drum with four windows and the casements, and the small windows high above them, taken together with the zebra courses and the externally hidden squinches, show affinities with the Van type. The exceedingly lofty minaret belongs to the tradition of the town. Melek Ahmet contrasts with the nearby, low-lying İskender Pasha Cami with its handsome portico and superior proportions dating from 959/1551.[60]

The most important Ottoman mosque in Diyarbakır is that of Bayram Pasha built in 980/1572[61] with the greatest care for detail. It is, indeed, the prince of provincial mosques as splendid in its decoration as it is in its proportions within the limits of the severe local style. In the courtyard there is a şadırvan with bundled and interlacing columns supporting its roof. The same, unusual type of column is repeated on a grander scale with the central columns of the outer of the two porticoes where an interlacing section is set between bands of black and white. The nine-domed outer portico is set in a rectangular zebra frame and the façade behind the inner portico is equally uncompromisingly striped. There are also trefoil relieving arches and fine stalactites over the door before which a star in a wheel is inset in marble in the pavement. The affinity between Bayram Pasha's second portico and that of the Adliye at Aleppo is tenuous and the inspiration would appear to come from Sinan's examples. The use of striping is superficial: the core of the architecture is Ottoman in feeling.

The interior is a splendid domed hall with three deep casement recesses down the east and west sides each with its own mihrab niche. The north wall also has three recesses under the gallery which is reached by stairs inset in the piers each side of the central entry. These eyvans are roofed in stone, the blocks lying flat without visible support like small paving stones suspended. In the north-east corner there is a small retiring room for the imam, to balance the minaret on the opposite side. Passages lead from the north gallery to those on the east and west above the casement recesses which give form to the interior and also add move-ment. The mihrab niche repeats the stalactiting of the vaulting over the entrance and there is a noble marble minber with carved doors. The whole room is en-riched by a series of tile panels which form revetments right round the walls. They fit so exactly into recesses, areas between engaged piers, and other corners, that they can only have been made to precise specifications. They represent the only example of meticulous panelling for a mosque where the pattern does not vary, so that the tiles unify the chamber. The consistant quality of these tiles represents a *tour de force*. They are executed in varying shades of blue on a white ground and with a restrained use of tomato red. Compared with this mosque, the interiors of the Kurşunlu at Kayseri or Ali Pasha mosque at Tokat are dull and even ungainly. The tiles of Bayram Pasha Cami are rivalled by those of the Ramazanoğlu mosque at Adana with its superlative panels in and above the mihrab, and also by the octagonal examples in the türbe of Halil and Piri Pasha there; but that mosque belongs to a less sophisticated period and the tiles were added afterwards so that the complete effect is less satisfactory than at Diyar-bakır, where the mosque and its tiles were conceived as one unit. Nonetheless, at Adana they appear in the side of the minber as they do at Bozüyük and have a panache that the Bayram Pasha Cami with its deliberate monotony appears to avoid. Both these mosques are well maintained.

So is the Yeni Cami at Tosya between Ankara and Kastamonu, which was 304 built by Abdurrahman Pasha and severely damaged by an earthquake so that it had to be heavily restored. It is large and spacious but it must always have been a second-class mosque. The casements of the portico are off-centre and the setting of the east mihrab is awkward. There is a central north door with an inscription dated 982/1574[62] over it. Inside, it is unique in plan because the very large mihrab apse has been created by the removal of the south-east and south-west corner units from what was the basic plan of Şehzade, so that only the north pair of piers is free-standing and those on the south are engaged at the corner of the apse.

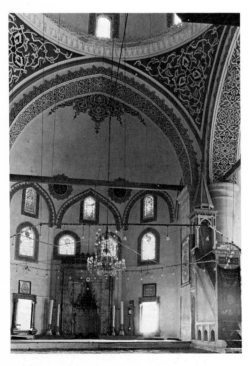

304 Yeni Cami, Tosya. Interior from the north door.

305 *Sağmanbahçe Cami. The türbe and mosque from the south.*

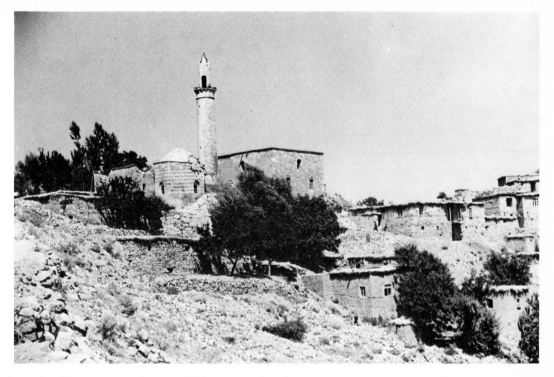

As a result the space before the mihrab seems very large and the apses of such works of Sinan as the Atık Valide mosque or the Selimiye at Edirne seem small by contrast. The plan also gets rid of the sense of useless corner space felt at İskele Cami; but it only does this by reverting in part of the form of Early Christian and Byzantine churches. The apse is five-sided but its semi-dome matches those on the other three sides; the mihrab itself is broad in proportion. The minber is a replacement. The Tosya mosque is large and there is a side door on the west behind the minaret. The semi-domes are supported on squinches and there is a plaster frieze round the lip of the central dome. The windows are framed in marble. It is a successful variation of the normal centralized plan and it would be interesting to discover the name of the architect. It was not Sinan but could have been one of his better followers like Mehmet Ağa. The interior is full of good, framed calligraphy dating from the beginning of this century. It is one of the few mosques which still uses kilims for windshields over the doors.

305   Not well-maintained, but interesting, is the little mosque in the village of Sağman near Elazığ which was once on a caravan route but is now reached with difficulty. It was originally a Selçuk foundation which included a tekke but was rebuilt in the reign of Murat III when it was panelled in tile; but little of this

306 remains. The tiles were not of the superlative quality of those of Adana and the designs were small, although this would not be out of place in a small mosque. There is a north gallery partly inset into the wall and partly carried on two columns each side of the entry. There is now a wooden ceiling, but in the sixteenth century the mosque was domed. The triple-domed portico is damaged, but the façade of polished rose and white composite stone remains, as does the large türbe which is reached by an extension of the portico and a vestibule beside a large zaviye chamber against the west side of the mosque and the minaret. The türbe is octagonal and built of alternating courses of brick and stone and has a cupola under a conical roof in the Selçuk manner. A balancing extension of the portico on the east side leads to a square of four intercommunicating rooms and eyvans which make up the rest of the tekke or zaviye which was last used as a medrese. The sofa before the mosque is high because it is built on a ridge above the gorge and the village. Below it there is a double çeşme and a pool which also appear to be sixteenth-century in date. The mosque was severely damaged by earthquake forty years ago and the village is far too poor to cope with its proper restoration.

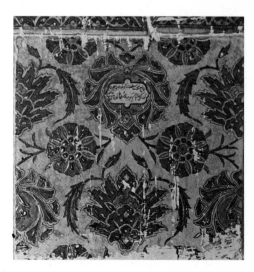

306 *Sağmanbahçe Cami. A tile.*

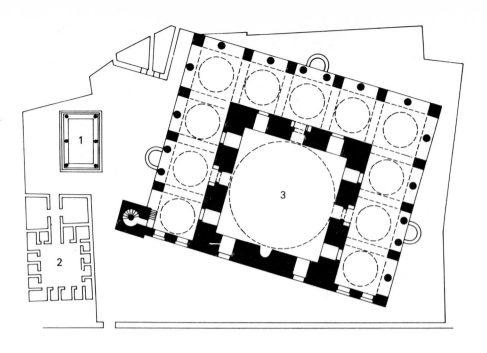

307 Sinan Pasha Cami, Cairo. Plan, scale 1 : 500. 1 cistern; 2 tekke; 3 mosque.

Ottoman influence extended all over the empire. In Egypt, the mosque of Süleyman Pasha in the citadel at Cairo has been mentioned,[63] and with this early mosque we have a typical example of mixed forms and decoration. The court conforms to Ottoman tradition and the interior is a true T in the manner of the mosque of Firuz Bey at Milas but without any dividing walls. The unification of the three subsidiary areas with the central dome by means of their three semi-domes is strikingly effective. The mihrab is traditional Cairene work in marble. In the much later period that we are discussing, two major works were built at Cairo of which Sinan Pasha Cami, near the Nile at Bulaq, is the more satisfactory. *307* It dates from 979/1571[64] and sets an example which was followed by the eighteenth-century mosque of Abu Dahab. The dome is set on two tiers. The lower is octagonal with paired windows between octagonal buttresses which are united to it by only one facet and may more correctly be called turrets. The upper tier is more truly a drum which is hard to recognize as a mere collar although this is what it is, with sixteen turrets and sixteen windows in the shape of trefoil crests.[65] Inside, the octagon is seen to derive from trefoil squinches set across the four corners to create triangular bays. Above this, the twin windows, which are seen outside to be deep set in pointed arches, prove to be rings of six circular windows round a ninth which is much larger. The mihrab and the heavily striped horizontal emphasis of the walls makes this interior very un-Ottoman in feeling and although the hall is square it is made to feel circular.

The mosque has a broad portico which extends along all sides save that of the kible wall which faces onto an avlu. The arcades are made up of three pointed arches on marble columns between thick buttresses for the length of two large bays on each side with plainly cut ribbed bases and capitals. The heavily ribbed cornice is stepped over each doorway and a circular, fretted window inset below. Cresting runs the length of the porticoes. The stalactite work over the windows is in the Egyptian style and the minaret is thick and short. The tekke or imaret adjacent is even less Ottoman in style.

The mosque of Malika Safiye dates from the late sixteenth century. The court is entered by a semicircular grand staircase under a trefoil arch. It is stone and plain and grand and the minaret above it is panelled and short but less squat than that of the Sinan Cami. The prayer hall is a rectangle with the two corners each side of the mihrab cut off to create a wide apse – partly, but not exactly, like the Yeni Cami at Tosya – in which the minber as well as the mihrab is set. The central dome is carried on a circle of six arches springing from six free-standing columns. It is clear that the architect was unaware of the tradition of such mosques as Kara Ahmet Pasha or the Selimiye. To one third of its height the Malika Safiye is almost all window, for there are twenty-four large ones and it is further pierced with small circular ports like a hamam dome. There is a plethora of casements and tiers of corresponding lights above them, but these are double-glazed and the light that filters through is soft so that when the casement shutters are closed the diffusion of light from the central dome and from that over the mihrab is very successful. There is also a certain spaciousness in this mosque but otherwise it is of no particular style but, rather, a painful marriage of two which in many ways were disparate.

Two important mosques were built at Damascus in the Sinan era: that of Dervish Pasha in 979/1571 and of Sinan Pasha in 994/1585.[66] The latter is famous for its tiles which are Damascene although the pounces may have been sent from Istanbul. The trunk of its minaret is clad in meadow green of moderate quality. Both mosques are by local architects although that of Sinan Pasha is the more heavily influenced by the concepts of Istanbul. In Aleppo are some more definitively Ottoman buildings among which the Osmaniye Medrese is an interesting example. The dome and the minaret are distinctly the work of an architect influenced by the saray school; the minaret is exceptionally tall and graceful,[67] its şerefe supported on stalactites under which is a pattern of reverse crestings. The summit of the minaret above the şerefe has been girdled with blind arcading in an unexpectedly archaic manner. The mosque dershane is fronted by a spacious triple-domed portico and divided from the thick square base of the minaret by a large open eyvan now glassed in. The minaret, exceptionally, has no true foot and its base ends at the roof level of the eyvan into which it is incorporated. A very large medrese indeed forms the revaks round the broad court with its handsome rectangular pool and trees in the Syrian manner. There are forty-two cells with ocaks against the cold of Aleppo winters.

Influence from Syria and Egypt in the later sixteenth century increased the height of the mosque and reduced the width; and this was to be an important aspect of the baroque period. In Diyarbakır, this was not a successful development and can be seen as the poorly assimilated influence of the lofty mosques of pre-Ottoman Aleppo and Damascus, not to mention the tendency in Cairo to turn domed chambers into near towers such as the mausoleum of Hasan or most of the major erections in the City of the Dead. The fine black basalt of Diyarbakır also palls after a time, for the strong contrasting courses shout in the southern light. The Akkoyunlu princes and the Selçuks before them were aware of the dazzle and the weariness resulting from the repetition of a loud motif and so they used the black stone effectively by widening the courses or reducing them or by facing whole areas with it.[68]

The Balkan mosques of the sixteenth century contributed little to the development of the Ottoman style. Some were exceedingly large such as that of Gazi Kasım Pasha at Peç in Hungary which has been converted into a church. The tiers of rectangular windows with voussoirs over blind lunettes above them are orderly but meanly proportioned compared with the square hulk of the mosque; it needed to be powerful in order to carry a dome twenty-two metres in diameter,[69] among the largest in the Balkans. The octagonal masonry collar, which is so heavy that it looks like a drum, has a window in each facet. The building has the appearance of a fortress and this may have been intentional in a frontier city. The most beautiful monument of the period is the single-span bridge at Mostar in Yugoslavia.[70] A much grander eleven-arch bridge was built over the swift Dvina at Visegrad (Vişgrad) in 985/1577[71] for Sokollu Mehmet Pasha; it is 179 metres long and 4·30 metres wide. It makes a remarkable right-angle turn and so echoes a Selçuk tradition of adjusting the span to the fall of the land. An inscription refers to its beauty being such that the beholder sees a pearl upon the

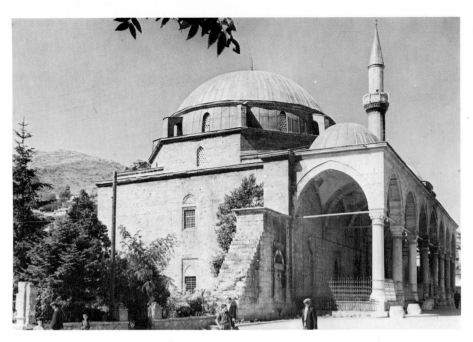

308   *Ali Pasha Cami, Tokat, from the east.*

waters with the firmament for its shell. The eulogy, taken together with the pride of place given to the bridge at Büyükçekmice in Sinan's epitaph, confirms the basic respect for engineering underlying the Ottoman appreciation of architecture. There was a great amount of building of minor mosques and tekkes throughout the province including the very trim Karagöz Mehmet Bey Cami at Mostar, dated 964/1554[72] with ogee portico arches and a bold octagonal drum to the dome. But the standard Ottoman mosque of the period is found mainly in Thrace or Anatolia. If the Balkans contributed anything to its development in the second half of the sixteenth century, it was the loftiness of the minarets.

In Anatolia, a mosque of some importance which is a tougher version of the Sinan mosque at Kayseri is that of Ali Pasha at Tokat.[73] It is not attributed to Sinan, even locally, and dates from 980/1573. Inside, the buttresses each side of the entry are extended so far that the stairs to the galleries inserted in them rise straight up with only one turn instead of forming a spiral. The south-east and south-west corners of the building are so thick that they form disguised buttresses, while the lateral window recesses are deep enough for there to be prayer niches in each of the three south walls on either side of the mosque. The three upper windows above the kıble are tall and narrow in the Byzantine manner and recall the mosque of Ayşe Kadın in Edirne of the previous century. The seventeen-metre dome is carried on an octagon over sixteen juxtaposed arcades above squinches. Loftiness is a feature of the Ali Pasha Cami and, as has been pointed out, an underlying trend of the sixteenth century. On all sides except the south there are galleries over very deep recesses; and there are shallow recesses on the south side also just as at Ibrahim Pasha Cami at Silivrikapı or at Bali Pasha Cami. They are so deep on the north side that the north-east and north-west windows of the east and west flanks are cut off by walls and turned into small rooms so that the first window on these sides does not look into the mosque at all but into these closets. On the north-east this compartment is used to store brooms, but on the north-west it is the unlit vestibule to a hallway to the minaret and this hall extends far enough westwards to have a south window. The minaret is set on a remarkably thick base. Vestibule, hall and base combine to extend the wall of the son cemaat yeri by a dome and a half of its portico; this is an expensive solution, therefore, to the perennial problem of the portico and mosque not corresponding in breadth. On the east side, a similar wall is extended for symmetry, but it is a screen with nothing behind it. The result is a handsome and lofty seven-domed portico which was railed in, unfortunately, in the last century. It is high enough

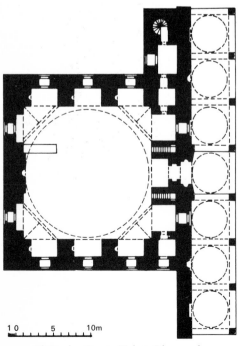

1 0   5   10m

309   *Ali Pasha Cami, Tokat. Plan, scale 1:500.*

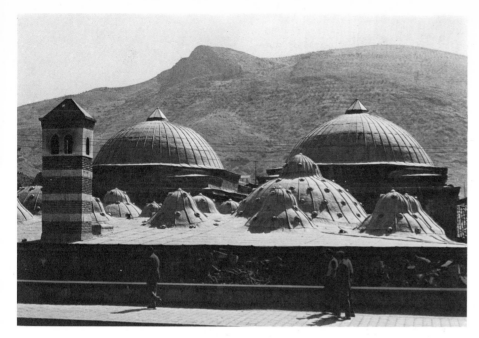

310   Ali Pasha Hamam, Tokat, with the chimney of the furnace in the foreground. The women's section is on the right, the men's on the left.

to have windows above its casements each side of the stalactite porch in a frame of striped stone over the entry. The façade is not otherwise distinguished and blind recesses have had to be added beyond the casements and mihrab niches right and left of the door in order to break the monotony and to give some meaning to the first and seventh archways. There is a fine pavement of variegated marble before the main door, and the columns, which are a mixture of Marmara marble and stone, are set on handsomely carved bases which, like the capitals, appear to be copies of the originals.

Raised on an octagonal base, the dome has eight flying buttresses set equidistantly which is idiosyncratic. The full curve of the dome is expressed and leaded but an artificial lip is formed for effect above the buttresses. The mosque is again aggressively square like the Valide at Manisa and this reduces the exterior effect of the dome so that the mosque relies entirely on its courtyard façade for its aesthetic appeal. It is interesting to note that the architect deviated from the canon and created a building which is sufficiently memorable to be distinguished from the many others of its type.

The türbe of Ali Pasha on the east side of the open courtyard is square and plain; the inscription above the door of this tomb is the only indication of the date of the foundation of the complex because there is none on the mosque. The double hamam has been heavily restored and is used again. The two sections are divided by an arch in the east wall, and the entry to the women's section is protected from prying eyes by a masking wall, which was the tradition. The rebuilt smoke stack of the furnace is in courses of brick and stone. Like a stumpy minaret it is a foil to the twin domes between which the smaller domes, with large nipples, rise and fall over the cool and hot rooms out of a broad expanse of lead roof. The men's camekân has fine ribbed squinches and there are good starlights in the soğukluk and the sıcaklık which has a marble göbektaş.

The double portico of the Kurşunlu Cami at Kayseri is symbolic of its connection with Sinan. It is an exceptionally fine example with its thirteen arches across the façade and four down each flank with two more behind to open up vistas and create a fascinating play of light. It is the gross proportions of the main block and the clumsy decorative insetting of geometric dark stone framing above casements, the meanness of the upper lights and the steep pitch of the dome which show that the execution of the plan was either by a local man or one of Sinan's students. The plan itself is surely his because of the fine portico and also because Kayseri was his home town with which he never severed his connection.

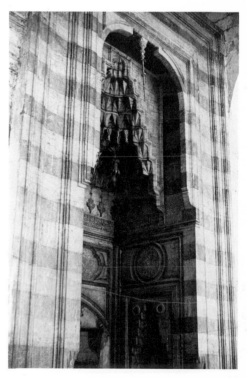

311   Ali Pasha Cami, Tokat. Stalactite vaulting over the north door.

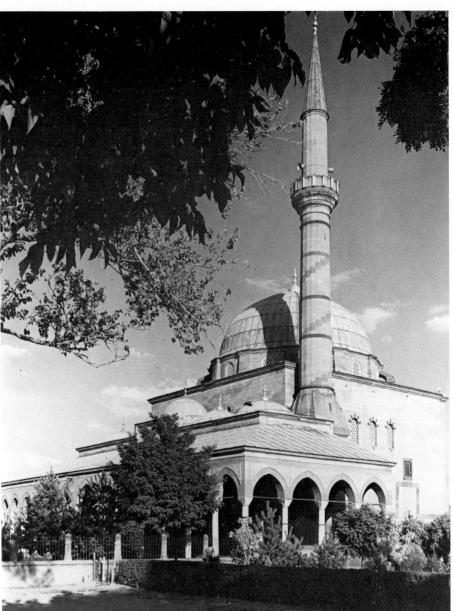

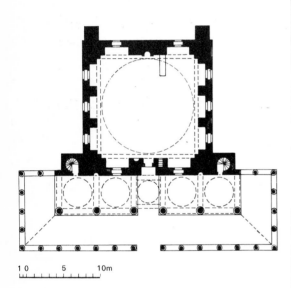

1 0   5   10m

312, 313 Kurşunlu Cami, Kayseri. Plan, scale 1:500. Right: view from the north-west showing the double portico and the pattern on the minaret.

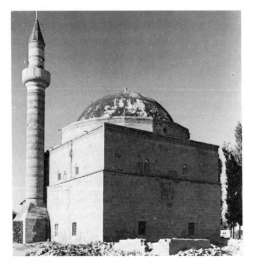

314 Diş Cami, Niğde, showing the minaret. (See note 74.)

The masonry is good and stonework is bolted with lead while the stone pendentives have the traditional pots as infill. There is an extravagant waste of masonry at the corners which incorporate their own buttresses, yet on the south side an extra pair of buttresses was cautiously added. It is clear that the solid and uncompromising cube on which the saucer of a dome sits outside was meant to be emphasized just as it was at Ali Pasha Cami.

Inside, the corners are explained: by their arches and their stepping diagonally. The first thickness is that of the wall; the second is the broad arch over the casement recesses; the third is that of the main lateral arches between the pendentives which support the dome. On the portico side the corners are extended by the base of the minaret – which is patterned both by bands and by its stair treads[74] – and the false base containing the gallery stair on the east corner. The three lateral casement recesses belong to the standard plan of the period as do those each side of the entry. Less usual, but like Ali Pasha Cami, is the depth of the corresponding recesses each side of the mihrab. At Bali Pasha Cami, these are shallow and elsewhere the wall is flat and the mihrab forms a small apse externally. The Kurşunlu Cami is too late in date, 994/1585,[75] to have been supervised by Sinan, but it might have been superintended by the architect of the mosques of Bayram Pasha

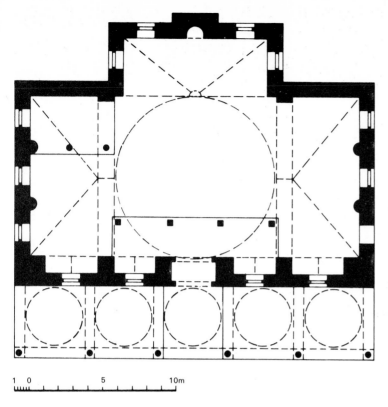

315 Muradiye Cami, Manisa. Plan, scale 1:250.

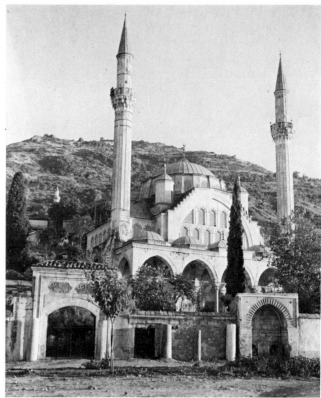

316 Muradiye Complex, Manisa. The mosque and court from the north-east.

or of Ali Pasha, although there is no evidence at all to support this suggestion. It was certainly the work of a man who had been trained at the saray offices of the imperial architect.

When Murat III came to the throne at the age of twenty-nine, Istanbul and Edirne were filled with royal mosques so it was at Manisa in a beautiful meadow beyond the Valide Cami,[76] below the wooded hillside, that his külliye was built. Murat was of a melancholic disposition and needed dwarfs and fools to cheer him, but he also preferred the company of intellectuals like Şemşi Ahmet Pasha to that of soldiers. If he is accused of indolence and taking pleasure in trivial things, he had also a truly Italian love of splendour and spectacle which reached its apogee with the festival in the Atmeydan for the circumcision of his son. He would have demanded excellence of craftsmanship in his mosque and fine appointments and furnishings, and these are to be found. Since he had leanings towards mysticism, which for so many intellectuals made the puritanical faith of Islam tolerable, it was appropriate that he chose to build his memorial in Manisa with its Sufi traditions.[77]

Ahmet Refik says that Sinan visited Manisa in 991/1583 on his return from the Hajj[78] and that he designed the mosque only. He must have known that he would never see the completed building and so would have chosen the best among his subordinates to carry out the most important commission of the time, both because it was a royal task and because he had new ideas to express in this his last great work. It is of interest, therefore, that he chose an architect named Mahmut for the task, but all we know about him is that he died and had to be replaced by Mehmet Ağa, the future builder of Sultan Ahmet Cami.[79] In spite of this change of overseer, the work was completed on time in 994/1586[80] in three years, but the whole complex took far longer to achieve, for an order as late as 1592 refers to an usta or foreman who had been jailed in Manisa and who was to be released in order to lay the pavements of the külliye: one detects impatience in an order which upsets the established course of justice. After nine years, Murat, who was to die in 1595, might well have felt that he had waited long enough.

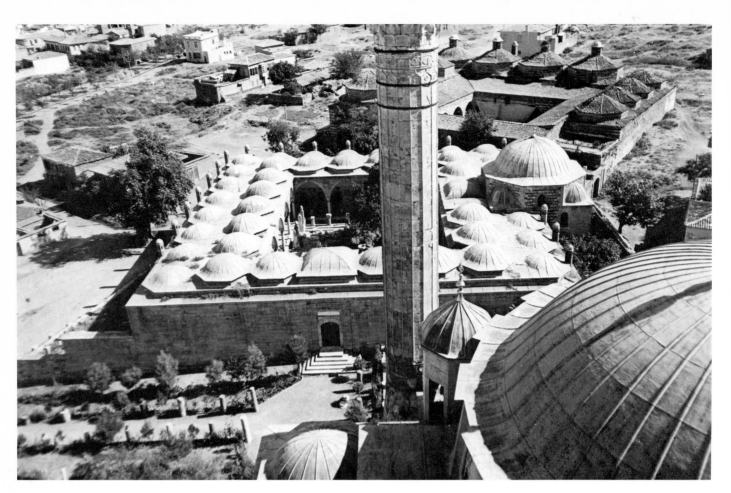

317 Muradiye Complex, Manisa. The medrese and imaret seen from the north-west minaret.

The mosque is at the west end of a parade of buildings. Originally, a medrese shared its fine garden and marble şadırvan under a hemispherical dome carried on slender columns, but it has been demolished. To the east is a library[81] which may once have been a sibyan mekteb but is not of the same date as the rest of the complex. Past it is the still-standing second medrese, now fitted out as a museum. It is built of alternating courses of brick and stone and lies low under the hillside. It is both large and handsome and the court is splendidly spacious and the porticoes graceful. The entry is set asymmetrically on the west side, and the very large dershane is set equally asymmetrically on the south. This is not apparent when one looks down on it from the road above, for there are five windows on each side of it. It has a small portico with the dome raised over the large central cradle vault and with two arches half the span each side; there are pretty cartouches in red frames above them. There is a mihrab niche in the south wall of the dershane. In the arcades there are some Byzantine capitals and the court is handsomely paved in marble, presumably by the usta when he was released from jail. Meyer-Riefstahl suggests[82] that a third medrese or tekke once stood between this college and the imaret but it is impossible. The imaret is large and must have dispensed food to a very large community including, one might suppose, travellers on the road to Izmir from the capital. It has been heavily restored and altered but the yard door remains grand.

The mosque is not large but this is not the impression one gains from it. Moreover, it is distinguished by its twin minarets which rise from the midst of beautiful trees; it is quite unforgettably poetic in the early morning light. The minarets are tall and fluted on bases as high as the portico behind which they stand. Their doors terminate the north wall of the mosque. The two Marmara marble and four granite columns which carry the five domes are tall but slender and – although this gives an air of almost rococo grace as do those of the canopy of the şadırvan in front – this is because of the difficulty of finding Byzantine and Hellenistic columns left among the ruins of Magnesia at the end of the sixteenth century and not by design. As a result, the stalactite capitals had to be deeply cut and taller than usual in order to expand from a small base to a broad head fit to support the almost semicircular arches. Thus what could have been a handicap was turned to advantage. Inset in the cornice is a corded frieze of red and white under the lead lip of the roof, and this motif continues as a string-course at first-floor level round the mosque. The voussoirs of the windows alternate between sandstone and rose as do the major relieving arches up to roof level. This pretty effect is enhanced along the ground floor by use of the same rose-coloured stone in the spandrels which are inset with white multifoliate rosettes in relief, except in the façade where there are fine tiles over the casements. These are cartouches of white inscriptions on a blue ground bordered by flowers and serrated leaves on a rich orange field. The north door is traditionally set under a stalactite half-dome with a marble mask and is flanked by niches; it has inter-locking voussoirs making a reversal pattern of crestings. The elaborate door of this mosque is superb late sixteenth-century work and the fine knockers are ring-shaped in the form of a dragon's head.[83] Twin oval medallions hold an inscription in Persian which reads, 'Be it blessed; be it joyful: be it happy'. When the doors are open, they fit exactly into recesses in the walls between the outer and the inner arches. This and the gilded bronze bosses, rosettes and other ornamentation are traditional, but the door of the Muradiye is a good example of the co-ordina-tion needed between the work of the masons, the carpenters and the coppersmiths.

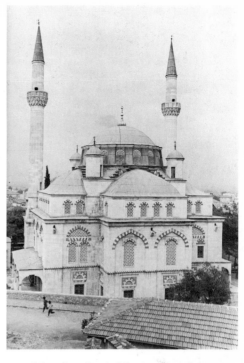

318 *Muradiye Cami, Manisa, from the south-west.*

On each side of the mosque is a deep arcade with a shed roof carried on four square marble piers with long consoles on each side to create strongly hipped arches. Their marble balustrades of interlocking polygons, recurrent throughout the mosque, are nicely in keeping with the elegance to be found on all sides. On the west, steps behind the minaret lead up to the portico and to a door into the mosque; southwards, beside two casement windows, the area is free for relaxation and meditation. But on the east there is a second door on the south and only a single casement in the middle and so the arcade more closely resembles the porches of the Selimiye at Edirne in function. But these lateral galleries are not connected with any washing facility in the way that they were at the Süleymaniye and were to be again at the Yeni Valide and Ahmediye. In the tympana over the casements at the Muradiye interlocking wheels occur like those of the balus-trades.[84] Above the lead roofs of these porticoes stand three fine arches in which

27

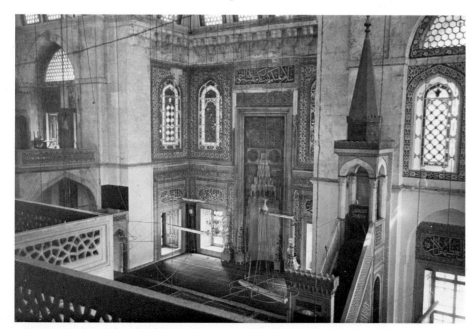

319 *Muradiye Cami, Manisa. Interior from the north-west.*

pairs of tall windows share an all-openwork tympanum to fill the whole space with window. Here the lattice of marble is made up of a simple grid of small circles.

A strong eave cuts off this level, which corresponds to that of the inside gallery level, from a rank of six small marble grilled windows under a lead-covered vault. The mihrab apse on the south wall projects in a similar way, but there are only four windows along the south side of the vault and a single window in each arch right and left of the mihrab niche, perfectly central in each case; this, together with the partial buttressing of the corners of the apse and the south wall, underlines the lack of mastery shown in such mosques as that at Babaeski. Below the vaults, the corners of the dome base are revealed and capped by neat but well-proportioned turrets between which on the south and north, are the great arches which are pointed and have steps on each side culminating in the suggestion of a pent roof. The south arch is concealed by the vault of the apse but the north arch has an exposed tympanum which repeats the six windows of the lateral vaults and has five above, of which those at the side are cut to follow the curve of the arch. Above these is the dome with its large windows set between buttresses which express its curve and are also covered in lead and so cannot be mistaken for a drum. Their mouldings at the top echo those of early Ottoman buildings and also look forward to the eventual elaboration of Turkish baroque. Examples of excellent workmanship in the exterior are the fine stalactite corbels of the şerefes, the stepped concept re-expressed below the apse vault, and the neat petaled corbels beneath the familiar giant drainspouts at the corners of the south wall.

The interior of the mosque takes one by surprise by whichever door one enters because the inner windows of the three outward sides of all three vaults lean inward and downward at a marked angle. This reflects the structural movement and can either alarm, and so displease, or become acceptable. Outside, the movement is concealed because the outer of the double windows is vertical. The vaults inside bend in three curved planes which meet in unusually formed groins. I cannot accept that these windows are a success and they were not repeated later.

The mosque is splendidly lit and, because the windows are large, the reduction of the walls to the skeleton of the structure is neither chaotic nor irritatingly fussy. The north gallery projects from a deep recess over exceptional multifoliate archways carried on square marble piers. In their spandrels are richly coloured stone rosettes. The stairs are reached through the casements and are concealed in the thickness of the walls. There is a fine hünkâr mahfil above a shallow sofa. The loge rests on three sweeping ogee arches set on two marble columns and the walls. It is on the south-east side of the mosque and out of sight of the main mihrab. Beside it is a high marble kürsü on pretty marble colonnettes set against the wall at the corner of the apse. The ceiling under the royal loge is one of the finest of the period and forms a complex but familiar design based on a twelve-pointed star and a cross.[85] The gilding and the colours, red and black predominating, are mellowed, and this ceiling is only rivalled by the dome of the Kafes at Topkapısaray which is later in date.[86] The casements are deeply recessed under dentillated arches and have small marble railings to their low sofas. Over each is an inscriptive panel of the same quality as those of the son cemaat yeri and these recur over the windows above the side doors at gallery level and in the south wall. There are small galleries, in addition to those over the north door, across the north-east and north-west doors in from the loggias. The additional door on the south-east opens under the hünkâr mahfil; and since there is no corresponding mahfil beyond the minber on the south-west there is no need for an extra door in this corner. The gilded and painted marble of the minber is of excellent craftsmanship and its hood is richly adorned with stylized flowers. The first climax of any mosque interior should be its dome and then the mihrab niche but, although the repainting in this mosque excels any elsewhere, the splendour of the apse dominates all else; this is partly because, when stepping from under the north gallery, the dome is too high to see unless one cranes one's neck. The four

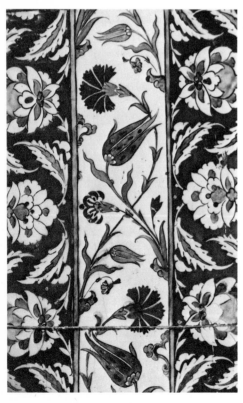

320 Muradiye Cami, Manisa. Tiles.

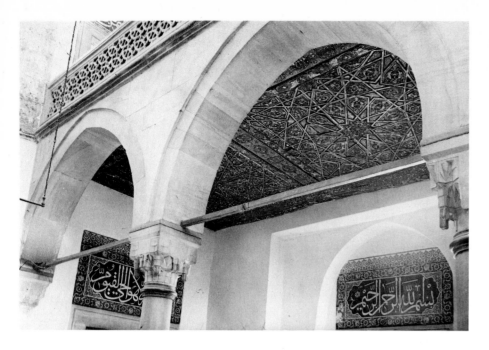

321 Muradiye Cami, Manisa. Ceiling under the royal loge.

piers which carry its supporting arches do not accent the central area either. As with other late sixteenth-century examples, the dome tapers very slightly and is not a hemisphere.

The stalactite work in the mihrab niche, foreshadowed by that above the door, has remarkable finials into which a vandal of genius has inserted light sockets. The barbaric red and green ground recalls the Mevlana türbe at Konya and is set with inscriptions and symbols in gilded bronze which are superb. So is the re-painting of the cresting above the mihrab frame and the brick-red tinting of the plasterwork of the stalactite skirting of the vaults above. On the other hand, the minber in the royal loge is plain but is flanked by gilded rosettes. Each casement in the apse has its own inscriptive panel of tile like the rest, but above them is a narrower one which extends along all three sides of the recess except where the mihrab stands; there the panel is elevated above the cresting of the frame. Between each casement is a band of floral tiles set in orange borders among the finest that Iznik ever supplied; the upper windows are also framed in tiles of varying design. Below, the twist of the leaves has that zigzag movement which imparts such vitality to the motifs of the period. Above, the effect is lighter and the flowers and leaves smaller and they appear to float. Serrated vivid green leaves are full of movement and sprays of rosebuds and almond blossom are particularly beautiful, although the individual carnations have claim to be the summation of Iznik's art. The coloured glass is restored and is less satisfactory than the rest of the decoration. The carpets, some of which are united prayer mats, are older and finer than those in most mosques today, and the new one in the mihrab area is, sensibly, plain red. No other mosque has been restored to quite this degree of excellence[87] and it serves as a fitting farewell to all those which, in some degree or another are the work of Koca Sinan.

In April or May of 1574, a fire started in the kitchen of Topkapısaray where the cooks were preparing the kebabs.[88] The cause was the ignition of the soot in the upper part of the chimney and it could have been brought under control speedily if it had not been for the wind. The fire spread rapidly, fed on the grease of many banquets, and the servants' wooden rooms above their stone basements were soon ablaze and so was the Helvahane, or *confiserie*. The Commander-in-Chief and the ministers at the saray were alarmed enough to send a message instantly to Murat III who was relaxing in the royal garden at Beykoz far up the Bosphorus. The harem was damaged, but not as severely as was once believed, although the furnishings suffered, and it was soon rebuilt to the old plan. The opportunity was taken to enlarge the kitchen quarters at the expense of the second court, and it was then that the great phalanx of chimneys and ventilators were built under the orders of Sinan. These are still the most striking feature of the palace when seen from the Marmara. Behind the colonnade along the south side of the great Divan court which was rebuilt at that time, a veritable village was reconstructed along the street which led from the waterworks outside the palace wall to the coffee chamber which terminates the kitchen court and backs onto the dormitories of the Enderun College.

The new kitchens, modelled on the old, consist of ten great halls, each with a chimney for its ranges and a ventilator over the working area set in a dome. The chimneys, like the stacks of ships, were designed to carry the smoke and fumes as high as possible and, doubtless, the kitchens were originally sited where they are in order to exploit the prevailing wind and get rid of the stench except when the humid south wind blew. These kitchens have been extensively repaired and rebuilt and they do not represent a revolution in design for they are similar to those already built at Edirne; but they are the largest in the Ottoman Empire and they had to be: as many as six thousand meals might have to be prepared there. The piers are of ashlar or of alternating courses of stone and brick, but the arches are all brick with very thick layers of mortar; so are the domes and cones of the chimneys which are supported on small squinches. Rubble was used in the spandrels and one has the impression that the building was made as fireproof as could be by the minimal use of wood and by the long court or firebreak between the kitchens and the portico of the second court.

Because the harem and selâmlık area is very restricted and is carefully divided into a logical sequence of departments and private suites issuing off the Altınyolu or Golden Road, which runs in two sections from the carriage gate past the Divan Tower to the court of the Valide and then on to the door to the Pavilion of the Robe of the Prophet, the rebuilding which Sinan carried out after the fire must have followed the old plan. The only possible expansion was on the open side towards the city by means of lofty vaults and terraces.

Immediately beside the carriage gate to the harem, and backing onto the paddock of the lower stables, is the barrack of the Halberdiers of the Long Tresses who were responsible, blinkered and used only at fixed hours, for carrying logs and heavy loads to the private quarters; they were also a royal guard. This must have been one of the worst burnt buildings, for it appears to have been completely rebuilt by Murat III and with some panache, for the long narrow central court was faced with splendid tiles and even in ruins retains the aspect of a fairy-tale village street: the more so because the different barrack rooms, officers' apartments, mosques and so on each have projecting eaves and gables which at the far end nearly touch. The main barrack hall is related to the pages' dormitory which is now the Miniature and Portrait Gallery, and is the only one to survive in something of its original state; but the Halberdier's dormitory is unaltered except for the removal of the lockers at gallery level. It is a long lofty hall with a wooden gallery on all four sides and a separate long gallery onto the court. On the stable side tiers of large windows look out onto the paddock. The tall wooden piers, which are roughly painted to suit the Halberdiers themselves, give this grand hall the look of an early Beylik forest mosque but on a much larger scale. It is also easy to see how the ground-floor sofa was divided into compartments between pairs of columns to be assigned to each picquet on the basis of the small field tents of the Ottoman army. This chamber has a large outer stairway leading up to the long gallery and to the inside galleries and which rises over a very fine çeşme inscribed and dated 998/1590, so that it is clear that alterations and improvements were constantly going on. Beyond the dormitory is a second hall as lofty as the first but much smaller, for it is only as long as the former is wide, and without a gallery. It is, notwithstanding, a handsome hall and served as the armoury, for all along the walls are the tall narrow closets in which the halberds were stored. Opposite is a small hamam with room for ten or fifteen

322 Topkapısaray, Istanbul. Hall of the Halberdiers.

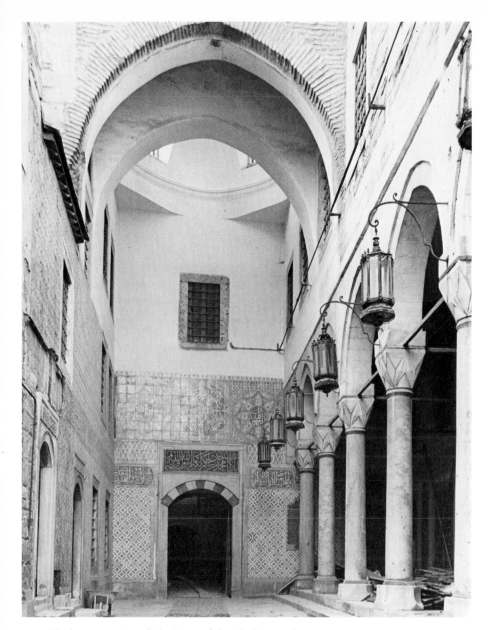

323 Topkapısaray, Istanbul. Court of the Black Eunuchs.

bathers at the most, and the mescit which is unique because it is built on two
floors like a house, the upper having a narrow slit cut in the south wall so that a
glimpse can be got of the mihrab on the floor below. This second floor appears to
have been an addition at a date when either the Halberdiers were increased in
number in the eighteenth century, to judge by the broad staircase, or other
members of the palace staff were admitted to share the mosque.

    It is likely that the Court of the Black Eunuchs beyond the Divan Tower and
before the inner door to the harem was refurbished at this time, along with their
barracks which are long and narrow with two stone galleries and spacious
washing facilities behind. However, the major work here was to follow a second
great fire on 24 July 1665.[89] This was started by a malicious servant, and all
the Harem is said to have been burnt together with the Kübbe alti or Divan Hall,
the Treasury of Mehmet II and the Secretariat behind it (where skeletons have
recently been dug up), the Darül-Saadet Gate to the third court, the Valide
apartments and also the kitchens.[90] Such reports often mean only that a building
was gutted or damaged to some degree and it is unlikely that the fabric of the
palace was destroyed by this fire, but any wooden structure is likely to have been
destroyed in those areas. In the private apartments, the core of the harem must

have been ravaged and, on inspection, the Valide Court which opens off a vestibule past the eunuchs' entry is seen to date from several periods. Since the tiles in the eunuchs' quarters are all of the period following the seventeenth-century fire, and those of the Valide Court even later or imported from Vienna or Italy, these would seem to have been the centre of the conflagration. The Eunuchs' Court tiles are of splendid bold designs indifferently executed in watery greens and sad blues on muddy grounds. It is the tragedy of the tiles of the period of Mehmet IV that the designs remain excellent but the execution poor, the range of colours sadly limited.

The Valide apartments were rebuilt after the second fire in about 1667[91] and other royal rooms were added to this section in the eighteenth century including the small music room beyond the charmingly tiled oratory off the bedchamber. The equivalent of the Enderun College, the girls' quarters must have been badly damaged and wooden dormitories destroyed. A number of rooms for the senior women of the Court have been restored and these, being built of stone appear to date from the sixteenth century. They formed well-designed, compact apartments with a lofty chamber complete with ocak beyond the foyer; there was also an upper gallery in which to stow bedding and a broad closet or wardrobe with a window beside it. At this upper level there is a second chamber behind a handsome landing with windows onto the courtyard. The superior ground-floor room has fine views over the Horn. Both were enriched with good second-quality tiles, and a great quantity of broken Iznik porcelain, covering the full range of designs of the sixteenth century, has been recovered from the courtyard drain. The hospital court at lower level is reached by a broad flight of stairs under a tunnel vault. The stone structure has survived as have the kitchen and washing facilities. It is overlooked by a very intimate pavilion built for Ahmet I which was once full of late but splendid tiles.

There is no record of damage to the selâmlik, the Imperial chambers and kiosks between the Valide Court and the Room of the Robe with its splendid colonnades and terrace of the Pool beyond which the Baghdad Kiosk was later to be built together with the Revan Kiosk by Murat IV. It is likely that the two great chambers which Sinan built for Murat III were untouched except by decorators who reflected the changing fashions of the years. The great salon was clad in lath and plaster and, when they were out of fashion, the tiles were painted over. The present restoration of this hall, the Throne Room Within or Hall of Diversions,[92] has revealed that its dome, the largest in the palace, was carried on stone arches. Whether the gallery on the north side was only added in the eighteenth century or whether there was an earlier version is uncertain; its stairs are trimly hidden behind cupboards in the wall. The salon opens off a passage to the Valide's apartments and so to those of the women whom she controlled. Another door admitted to the sultan's hamam which was reconstructed in the eighteenth century. Opposite are doors to the small dining chamber rebuilt by Ahmet III[93] and to the great bedchamber;[93] another admits to the series of ante-chambers and halls, including those of the Ocak and the Fountain,[94] which were all re- 324 decorated and retiled in the seventeenth century.

The bedchamber has a dome only slightly smaller than that of the salon.[95] It has its own hall, with one of the finest doors of the saray, opening from the open corridor leading past the Kafes, or princes' kiosk, to the Room of the Robe through which the sultan must usually have come and gone and at the door of which was the royal mounting block. The bedchamber has been completely restored and the large arabesque patterns of the dome have been regilded as well as repainted in red and black. The gilded bronze ocak is tall and majestic and its tapering hood suggests that this may have been the period when the caps of minarets grew taller too. There is a superb two-tiered çeşme on the inner wall under a fine hipped arch. This room was also partly redecorated in the period of Ahmet III and later refurbished, but it has suffered less than any other room. Water was very much present in the palace and here and there are spigots in the windows supplying hot and cold water; the sills served as water troughs.

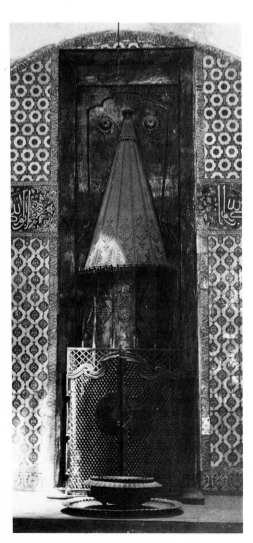

324 *Topkapısaray, Istanbul. Hall of the Hearth.*

Handsome stone shelving recurs on every wall, with tiles set back into the niches; these are the same as those which cover the wall. They are Iznik floral designs of superlative beauty, richly framed in the thick orange borders of the 1570s. These also frame the çeşme, the shelves, and the doors, together with the band of inscriptive tile which runs right round the room above shelf and door level. The walls of tile reach to pendentive level and because – like those of the mosques of Ramazanoğlu at Adana and Bayram Pasha at Diyarbakır – the intense red and blue pattern is repeated, the effect comes curiously close to that of polished wallpaper. In the pendentives there are splendid medallions in which a twelve-pointed star radiates to six half-stars at the rim. The windows in each wall – and it is to be noted that those on the salon side are blind – are also framed in orange borders. The finest tiles are reserved for the ocak which is framed in an orchard of dazzling pear blossom, matchless among the products of Iznik and among its most popular designs. The quality of these tiles was not excelled because the white ground is sparkling and reds and blues not only brilliant but deep. This chamber is the finest surviving private room of the sixteenth century. The extra tiles not used in this room were taken for the mosque of Ramazan Efendi.

The Kafes or Cage, where the princes were confined, is likely to date from the reign of Murat III or, far more probably, of Ahmet I[96] and its proximity to the bedchamber suggests that it would have been added afterwards. It is an independent pavilion off the corridor which links the bedchamber to the Golden Road, and it looks out across the high terrace and the garden of the pool below. Together with the Revan Kiosk, it retains its tiling although it has almost all been replaced by modern copies. The pavilion has been completely restored and quantities of baroque woodwork removed. The paintwork needed little attention, and it is therefore a most important example of the rich and intricate designs of the late sixteenth or early seventeenth centuries. The second room has a very fine ocak which has been cleaned to its original splendour. At some period its floor was raised, perhaps due to damp. It has been retiled with modern copies of the original panels where the design could be reconstructed from fragments of the original work. The tiles revealed at the old skirting level belong to the same period as those of the bedchamber but are not exactly the same design. The richness of the paintwork of the ceiling of this inner room is due to restoration; but that of the dome of the main chamber has hardly been retouched. This was not necessary because it had been hidden by a false ceiling; it was a momentous day when a hole was first pierced in this and a glimpse caught of the dome above. As in the bedchamber, spigots are set in the windows, and the red and black and gold decorative designs that surround them have been handsomely restored; the casement grilles have also been regilded. Nonetheless, this splendid pleasure dome was indeed a cage until the late eighteenth century.

Erkins states[97] that Murat III was responsible for the cupolas as well as the tiles of the Hırkai-Saadet section, the sacred chambers of the Prophet[98] including the Room of the Robe. It is possible that some repairs were carried out but unlikely that the rooms were not already domed from the first. It would be pleasing to attribute the false minaret to Sinan and it would not have been out of character. Recently, another false minaret has also been built at Özdemiş but previously that at the saray was unique. What is more important is the date of the great colonnade of splendid columns before the north and west sides of the apartments and it would look as if they may have originated at this period, although the addition of the Revan and Circumcision pavilions would have necessitated alterations. However, there is no doubt that Çoban Mustafa Pasha added the marble revetments from the Divani-kebir in Cairo at the beginning of the reign of Süleyman I[99] and it would be more consistent to suppose that this noble portico was added at this time. The ugly fenestration is now happily removed but that there were screens there before can be seen from the Surname Vehbi. The tile revetments inside the Hırkai-Saadet section, including panels of false marble and a rich peacock design, date mainly from the late sixteenth-century renovations of Murat III; and so do the superb inlaid doors and shutters.[100]

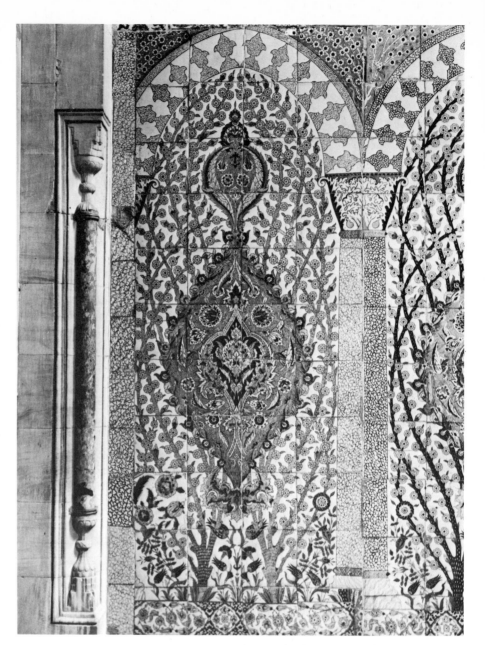

325 Topkapısaray, Istanbul. Antechamber to the Royal Saloon. Panels of tiles representing a garden seen through a portico.

326

The selâmlık and all the Istanbul side of the inner palace are supported on a series of immense stone piers and vaults. The concept of terracing was traditional in Constantinople,[101] but here is a township carried on a bridge or series of bridges. Dalgıç Ahmet won preferment to the office of Imperial Architect because he was able to build the foundations of the Yeni Valide Cami at Eminönü which again follow the principles of a bridge. In the sixteenth century, there was pride and delight in the feat of engineering involved in such foundations which truly underlay the aesthetics of the monuments on top. It was not confined to royal work; the bridge at Urfa is remarkable for the height and power of its arches which carry a street across the gulley. The main criticism is of the extravagance of some of the stonework due to over-caution. It is possible that the stone undercroft of the great rooms that Sinan built for Murat III already existed but, if so, he certainly refaced them; between the broad outward arches are large medallions incised in the stone identical to those painted in the pendentives of the bedchamber above. The capacious basements are at several levels and were put to many uses; wooden floors were added so that they could be used as dormitories as well as stores. The recent work at the saray has cleared away several levels of accumulated rubbish and shrubs to dig down to the original sixteenth-century gardens, revealing the terraces below the Kafes and bedchamber and also exposing their vaults which were intended to be seen as architecture. Below the bedchamber and its anteroom is a large indoor swimming pool[102] fitted in among the lofty vaults and arches with a stone walk all round and a projecting platform at the end on which the sultan might be enthroned below stairs leading to a private disrobing chamber. There are taps for hot water as well as cold and a charming fountain. It is said that the sultan watched naked maidens of the harem disport in the shallow water and that he threw gold to those who pleased him most. This is as it may be,[103] but what is certain is that the pages of the Enderun College came weekly to enjoy an afternoon bathing here where, presumably, even in winter one could ignore the cold. The whole of the outer terrace at this level forms a large outdoor pool with a miniature dock for the sultan's boat. It is worth comparing the quality of the sixteenth-century piers and arches with those added in the eighteenth century to support the terrace and pavilion added by Osman III. The later work is still tough but it is crude workmanship compared with that of Sinan, and although the shelving land makes the arches tall and handsome they are utilitarian and lack any fine finish.

Listed in the Tezkere are a number of vezirs' sarays, and these must have been large and their gardens have had many kiosks because the great officers of state had households running into hundreds and some even maintained smaller versions of the Enderun College. Many had several palaces, some so close to one another that one suspects that it was due to dilapidation, for it is an Eastern habit to build anew rather than to repair. This was one reason why so much of the construction was in wood. A house was no more expected to endure than a tent could, nor was a father's house inherited; only his clothes. The direction of religious affairs now occupies the site of the palace of the Ağa of the Janissaries. This was a series of buildings standing shoulder to shoulder round a large court on a promontory below the Süleymaniye commanding splendid views over the Horn. It can be seen quite distinctly in Lorichs' engraving and it was obviously built as a series of apartments at various periods in the same way as the royal palaces. The Ibrahim Pasha Saray has already been discussed. That of the Grand Vezir opposite the Alay Kiosk at the corner of the palace park below the Çinili Kiosk was burnt and reburnt so frequently, particularly in the eighteenth and nineteenth centuries, that one is astonished that a seventeenth-century sibyan mekteb has survived at all. The palace occupied a large site which now contains the Vilayet and Record Office of Istanbul. It began as a new saray of Sokollu Mehmet Pasha[104] and the little postern in the park wall beside the Alay Kiosk is known as his gate. It had to be large since much of the business of state and the general administration of the city was conducted within its halls.[105]

The then Valide erected the vast han above the Mısır Çarşı on the site of a ruined palace of a vezir, and this again gives some indication of the manner in which these palaces sprawled from court to court from one intimate unit to the next. The Ottomans did not envy the west its grand and cold mansions but kept their homes private and snug. All these lesser palaces have gone but, because it was built of stone, one vezir's hunting lodge does survive with its garden and park off the road to Yeşilköy and it has been restored. This house is not the work of Sinan because it dates from *1000*/1592.[106] It was built for Siyavuş Pasha and was clearly intended as a 'pleasure dome' where one could rest and feast after the hunt. There is a plain but handsome çeşme at the new gate. Beyond is an avenue of cypresses leading to the little pavilion which is reached up a flight of stairs across a bridge because it is set on broad arches above a pool. Round the pool is a paved walk with a bower or belvedere at one corner from which to admire the rolling country beyond the garden and the park. The terraces can still be made out as can some of the waterworks, including a large stone cistern and a second pool at the end of what was once a little glade. The pavilion is modest. There is a fine domed chamber with an ocak and a second one which is rectangular and small off a hall with a lavatory. All the cooking must have been

329

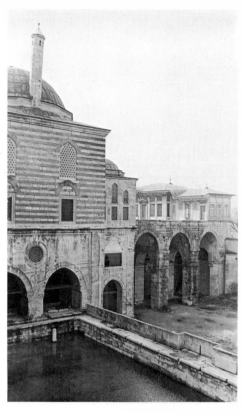

326 Topkapısaray, Istanbul. Vaults supporting the Murat III Bedchamber, the Ahmet I Library and (left) the terrace and pavilion of Osman III with the pool in the foreground.

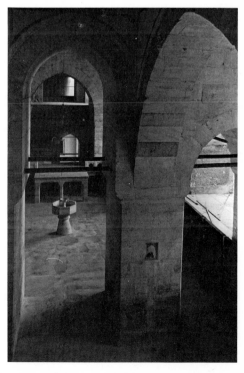

327 Topkapısaray, Istanbul. The indoor bathing pool in the vaults below the Murat III Bedchamber.

328 *Topkapısaray. Plan.*

1 *The Ortakapı or Middle Gate.*
2 *Palace water works.*
3 *Kitchens and cooks' quarters.*
4 *Mosque of Beşir Ağa.*
5 *Stables and harness rooms.*
6 *Barrack of the Halberdiers.*
7 *Hall of the Divan.*
8 *Offices of the Divan.*
9 *Inner Treasury.*
10 *Gate of Felicity.*
11 *Quarters of the White Eunuchs.*
12 *Throne room.*
13 *Ahmet III library.*
14 *Privy kitchen.*
15 *Cook's house.*
16 *Mosque of the school, now the library.*
17 *Harem mosque.*
18 *Quarters of the senior students and officers of the household.*
19 *Court of the Room of the Robe.*
20 *Room of the Robe of the Prophet.*
21 *Rooms of the Relics of the Prophet.*
22 *Hall of the Treasury.*
23 *Hall of the Pantry.*
24 *Pavilion of Mehmet II, now the Treasury.*
25 *Disrobing chamber of Selim II hamam.*
26 *Site of Selim II hamam.*
27 *Site of Selim II hamam boilers.*
28 *Hall of the Expeditionary Force.*
29 *Forehall of the Room of the Robe.*
30 *Circumcision Kiosk.*
31 *Terrace and bower.*
32 *Pool.*
33 *Baghdad Kiosk.*
34 *Pool.*
35 *Revan Kiosk.*
36 *Tulip garden.*
37 *Mustafa Pasha Kiosk.*
38 *Physician's tower.*
39 *Abdül Mecid Kiosk.*
40 *The Third Gate.*
41 *Entry to residential area (a) Shawl Gate (b) Carriage Gate.*
42 *Mosque of the Black Eunuchs.*
43 *Court of the Black Eunuchs.*
44 *Barrack of the Black Eunuchs.*
45 *Princes' school.*
46 *Quarters of the Chief Black Eunuch.*
47 *Quarters of the Treasurer.*
48 *Quarters of the Chamberlain.*
49 *Aviary Gate.*
50 *Main Harem gate.*
51 *Courtyard of the women of the Harem.*
52 *Kitchen of the women.*
53 *Hamam of the women.*
54 *Stairs to bedrooms.*
55 *Commissariat.*
56 *Laundry.*
57 *Women's dormitory.*
58 *Apartments of senior women.*
59 *Stairs to Harem garden.*
60 *Court of women's hospital.*
61 *Hospital hamam.*
62 *Hospital kitchen quarters.*
63 *Sultan Ahmet Kiosk.*
64 *Harem garden.*

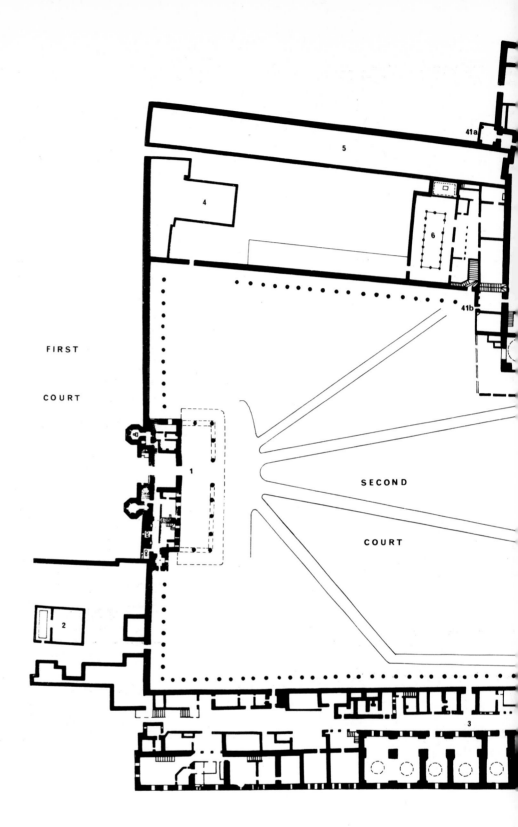

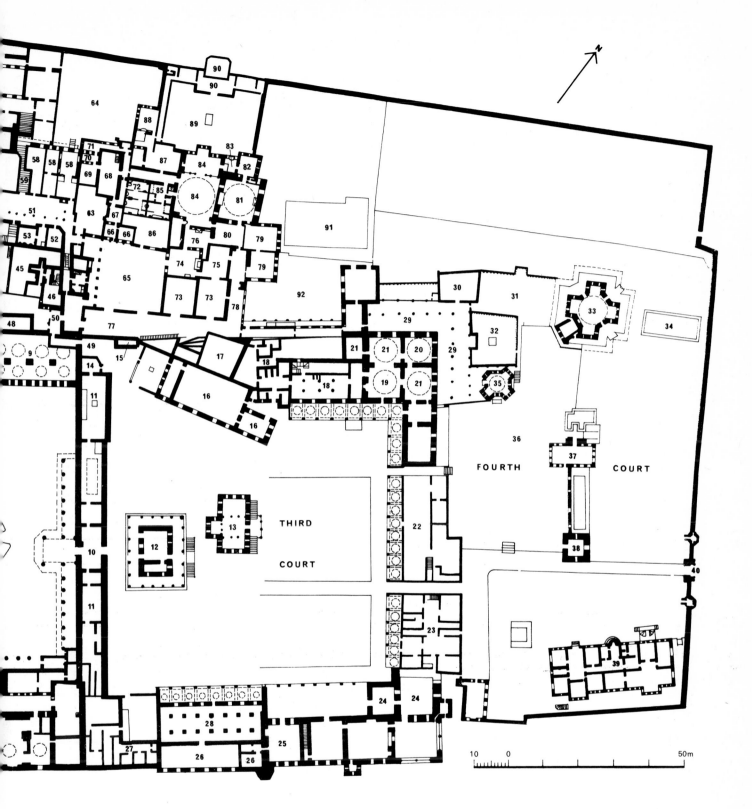

- 65 Valide court.
  66 Valide's salon.
  67 Valide's antechamber.
  68 Valide's dining-room.
  69 Valide's bedroom.
  70 Valide's oratory.
  71 Music room of Selim III.
  72 The Valide's hamam.
  73 Kadın's quarters.
  74 Hall of the Hearth.

  75 Harem Treasury.
  76 Hall of the Fountain.
- 77 The Golden Road.
  78 The Jinn's consultation hall.
  79 The Cage.
  80 Ante-room of Murat III.
- 81 Murat III bedchamber.
- 82 Ahmet I library.
- 83 Ahmet III dining-room.
- 84 The Throne Room Within.

  85 The Sultan's hamam.
  86 Boiler-room.
- 87 Bedchamber of Abdül-
       hamit I.
- 88 Salon of Selim III.
- 89 Osman III Terrace.
- 90 Osman III Kiosk.
  91 Boating pool.
- 92 Terrace of Selâmlık
       Garden.

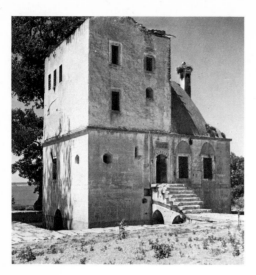

329 Hunting lodge of Siyavuş Pasha, near Istanbul.

done in the open and doubtless there were wooden shelters and stables for the servants and horses, perhaps outside the gate. A stairway leads to the roof over the second chamber where a later room was clumsily added at an uncertain date. The walk round the pool under the kiosk stands on a retaining wall on the garden side where the land drops away rapidly and the belvedere was supported on four fine triple consoles and recalls that of the pavilion of Mehmet II which is now the Treasury at Topkapısaray. The windows of the kiosk on the side with the view are large casements set in arches and the pavilion was built with the view foremost in the pasha's mind. If Siyavuş Pasha could build a house of stone in the country, then one wonders why others were not built or did not survive if they were. Royal work and the building of mosques must have used up the output from the local quarries to such an extent that little was left for private purposes.[107] The sense of the transitoriness of all but God's affairs undoubtedly accounted for the Ottoman tolerance of gimcrack housing built for a term only.

During the reign of Süleyman Kanuni there were four vezirs because four is a number sacred alike to Moslem and Turk.[108] Like the other first officers of the realm, they had large slave households and devşirme recruits might also be housed by them and by provincial governors.[109] Moreover, the emphasis on charity and hospitality meant that their palaces needed several guest chambers and large stables.[110] The Persian custom of facing pavilions with tile had spread all over the city and is illustrated in the miniatures showing the Ibrahim Pasha Saray during the festival of Murat III. The fashion may account for the number of orders sent from the Divan to restrict the sale of tiles to anyone but the palace in the later sixteenth and early seventeenth centuries.[111] The Ottoman love of flowers presupposes that, within the limitations of a crowded city, there were some gardens, and there is a rescript extant issued in *1001*/1592[112] ordering the supply of roses from the gardens at Edirne for Topkapısaray where there were several small gardens and the park. Such an establishment as Ibrahim Pasha maintained also had space for orchards and gardens which we have found[113] specifically mentioned in relation to the fifteenth-century establishment of Mahmut Pasha. Gyllius[114] praises the garden of Süleyman at Chalcedon (Kadiköy) and the sovereigns from the sixteenth century on had gardens along the shores of the Bosphorus for their delight.

The vezirs were not the only dignitaries to maintain their state. The office of the royal architect at Vefa is referred to as a saray and a large establishment of students, foremen and assistants was installed there. Since Sinan appears to have had his home below the Süleymaniye and next to the lower medreses, this may merely have been a government building and not a residence, but household and office were so mixed up in the sixteenth century that it could well have been both. Sinan was not only exceptional as a personality, he must also have been rich from many sources as a reward for his work, and his wills indicate that he expected to leave a handsome fortune behind him. If the chief architect had a large palace so must many others, like the senior officials of the city and even the kadıs and principal members of the Ulema on occasion; the Şeyhül-İslam, however, frequently complained of the lack of an official residence for entertaining and had, indeed, to hire an apartment for this purpose until 1826. We certainly need not believe Evliya when he says that there were 6,890 vezirs' palaces, or even a hundredth of that number.[115]

The two exceptional houses attached to the medreses at the Süleymaniye are *208* likely to be the work of Sinan. They are very pleasant residences because of their proportions and because they are easy to keep cool in summer and warm in winter. The door opens into a lobby with a stone staircase on the left and a double chamber on the right which was originally divided into two smaller rooms. Beyond, is a lobby now used as a kitchen opening into a long and narrow paved court or garden running across the back of the medrese. The stairs lead to a spacious landing with an alcove large enough to make a study today under the centre dome and a comfortable bedroom under the third dome beyond. From the small window of the low loft, there is a memorable view of the mosque

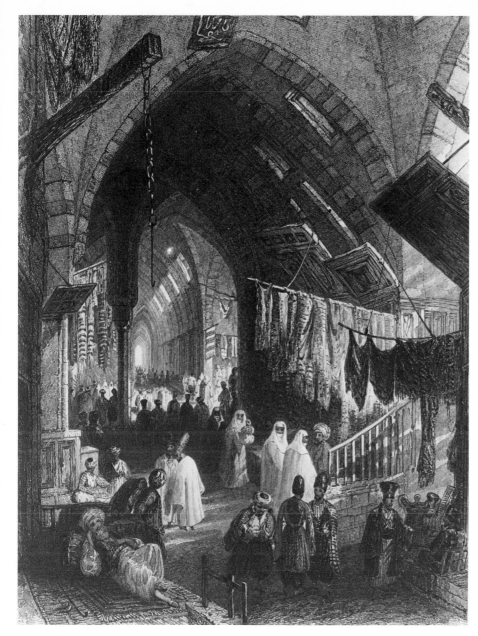

330 The Kapalı Çarşı or Covered Bazaar, Istanbul. Nineteenth-century engraving.

across the domes of the medrese. But the rest of the city bore no resemblance to dwellings like these. It was a sprawling mass of narrow lanes with stone public buildings at the heart of each neighbourhood just as it had been in Byzantine times.

In the market area, the core of the commercial life of an Ottoman town was the bedesten, like those at Bursa and Edirne which have already been discussed. Just as a town could have only one ulu cami so it could have but one bedesten; and here Istanbul, with two, is exceptional. The bedesten built by Mehmet II across the water belongs to the separate town of Galata; but to the old bedesten at Beyazit a second, the Sandal Bedesten,[116] had to be added in order to cope with the quantity of trade in fine fabrics that the capital attracted in the sixteenth century.

Bedestens everywhere more or less followed the same pattern according to their importance. There is the very grand hall at Ankara with ten vaults and eight piers which is completely surrounded by a double arcade of shops on all four sides. It was built in *869/1464*[117] by Mahmut Pasha and has been considerably altered by its conversion into a museum. There is the very modest bedesten at Gelibolu

(Gallipoli) with six domes and two piers. There are others which modify the formula, like that at Tokat which had three rows of three domes each divided by three narrow vaults and the roofing supported by four pairs of piers. Moreover the streets of shops are placed on the east and west sides and by extending beyond the hall at both ends act as antechambers to it. The Eski or İç Bedesten was the first erected at Istanbul and, although claims have been made that it was built before the conquest, the only Byzantine feature is the eagle over one of the doors borrowed from some ruin or other. It is a fine example of an Ottoman hall for precious goods, which is locked up and guarded at night. It is surrounded by shops with porticoes in front in the manner of the Kapalı Çarşı or Covered Bazaar; the corner shops are mere stalls for the square space is diagonally cut in two by a party wall. This also happens with the shops each side of the entries on all four sides. Inside, there are shops or strong-rooms, totalling thirty-six in all, all along the walls. Again the corner cells are cut diagonally but they are added to those beside them and do not form independent units. The fifteen domes in five rows of three are supported by massive piers round which the merchants built their booths. The domes are nearly seven metres in diameter and the overall area some forty-five by twenty-eight metres.[118] This bedesten may well have been built by Fatih. The Sandal Bedesten was built later and is even larger for it has twenty domes in four rows of five and twelve piers. Writing of the disastrous fire of 1546, Gyllius[119] says that these basilicas were the only buildings to survive the conflagration. The Sandal Bedesten is attributed to the reign of Süleyman.[120]

The bedestens were the foremost civil buildings of the Empire after the fortresses and citadels of the provincial towns. Waterworks, which were sacred, were rarely as spectacular but always more graceful and often exquisite. The Master of the Waterways was a senior official under the Imperial Architect in Sinan's time, but the Superintendent of Works more usually was the supreme authority. It was an act of outstanding charity to build and endow a çeşme or sebil.[121] The Byzantines had already established a splendid water system which included great open cisterns such as those of Mocius, Aspar or Aeteus which fell into disuse before the fall of the city; there were also such majestic underground halls as the Yerebatansaray which has 420 columns and still fills up with water due to seepage after rain. There were also many humbler cisterns in the basements of private palaces and houses: over two hundred have been listed at various periods although many are now completely inaccessible. The Ottomans often chose to build mosques above cisterns, as with Nuruosmaniye, Hekimoğlu or Nişancı Mehmet, just as churches had been built over their own water supply like the Pammacaristos or St Saviour Pentepoptes. The main sources of water were the reservoirs or bends fed by the springs and streams of the Belgrade Forest. These waters were conducted to the city by aqueducts of which by far the grandest, built by Justinian, is two-tiered. This, among others, carried water to the taksim or distribution point at Eğrikapı whence the main flow reached the Aqueduct of Valens[122] in the middle of the old city between the mosques of Fatih and Şehzade. These aqueducts were repaired by the Ottomans and properly maintained. The Valens Aqueduct was considerably rebuilt by Sinan during the reign of Süleyman Kanuni.[123] When this work was completed in the 1560s, an increase in the number of fountains was possible. It is easy to distinguish the Turkish stonework but less easy to make out the date of some sections of the work since Mustafa II also ordered extensive repairs to the same aqueduct. The Uzun or Long Aqueduct in the Belgrade Forest follows the Byzantine pattern of tiers of tall arches, pointed not rounded however, and may be to Sinan's plan, but the short Kavas Aqueduct of only eleven arches in all is likely to date from soon after the conquest.[124]

An alternative method of getting water to Istanbul was by su terazi which also occur in Spain[125] and it is not clear if they were a Roman or an Islamic invention. They consist of water towers about two hundred metres apart. Water descends in underground conduits until enough pressure is built up to send it up the tower to fill a tank which, when brimming, sends its contents down with enough force to travel underground to the next tower where it is again forced to the top. The cost of these conduits and syphons was less than half that of an aqueduct. All this water served the mosques and the mansions of the vezirs and also the public fountains. In the sixteenth century these were plain, usually being ashlar storage tanks faced with a pointed or ogee arch over the spigot. The decrees of the Divan show that the populace was quick to tap a water supply and pipe it to their own homes; Sinan was no less guilty than the rest.[126] Sinan, however, was an experienced hydraulics engineer, or saw that his subordinates were; this is made clear from the flow of orders addressed to him not simply about the supply of water but also its drainage: but drains remained rudimentary in the great city and, in many areas are still primitive. In the Divan yolu the Byzantine drain is still used.

An historical loss to Ottoman architecture was the destruction of the Observatory built at Cihangir by Sinan for Murat III. In 1571, at the instigation of Sokollu, Takaldin Mehmet al-Raşid bin Marūf was appointed head astronomer. The observatory was completed above Tophane in 985/1577, but no sooner was it open than the famous ill-omened comet appeared which led the Şeyhül-İslam to determine that it should be abolished and a mob was incited to wreck it in 1580. It had been an elaborate building with dwellings and offices for the astronomers and administrative officers; its most important feature was the observation well which was twenty-five metres deep and to which access was obtained by a ladder. In comparison with the great observatory of Ulu Bey at Samarkand or of many in India, this was a small establishment with fifteen doctors of science and five learned men for each instrument together with two or three observers and an assistant for miscellaneous work, so necessary for Turkish life.[127] The set-back to Ottoman science was lasting. In 1705, the then Şeyhül-İslam Feyzullah Efendi planned to convert Galata Tower into an observatory, but without success.

13   Sinan built his tomb at the corner of the street at the bottom of his garden above that çeşme of his which was the subject of an official investigation.[128] He died, it is said, as the result of an accident, but there is no order to him dated later than some months before his death. The tomb[129] is an oblong open türbe with six ribbed ogee arches and a magnificent headstone carved in the form of a voluminous turban of state, in honour of his high rank. Relatives are buried in the little terrace behind, and all is enclosed by a handsome wall with wheel grilled windows and pretty cresting. The tombs of the Selçuks tended to be symbolic, long, narrow stone coffins but those of the Ottomans were a flat stone or marble slab with a turbaned headstone and a less ornate secondary pillar at the foot. Suitable verses from the Koran, a brief eulogy, and usually the date of death were inscribed. The sixteenth-century inscriptions are less bold than those of the preceding centuries but still stronger in form than those which came later. There was little room for more than a leaf or bud by way of decoration, even on the graves of women which had not yet developed the richly carved floral framing and cresting of the baroque period. It is probable that the stones were painted, as is still the case with those of certain popular holy men, at least to the extent that the script stands out on a green ground.[130] In the sixteenth century it would have been important to use paint in order to differentiate the orders of dervishes first and foremost and also the rank or office of various officials where the shape of the turban was alike. The headstones of the rich had the inscription silvered or gilded. The headdress is interesting because it echoes the pre-Islamic Central Asian gravestones of the sixth century, in the museum at Tashkent for example, which have faces carved on them in shallow relief.

The death of Sinan in 1588 was not the end of Ottoman architecture – he had taught his students too well for that; but no single architect was ever to be as creative again because none was to match his experience with his genius. Nor did they enjoy the fortunate patronage of his wealthy age. None ever achieved the authority which established his individuality although he used traditional forms and obeyed the tenets of his faith.

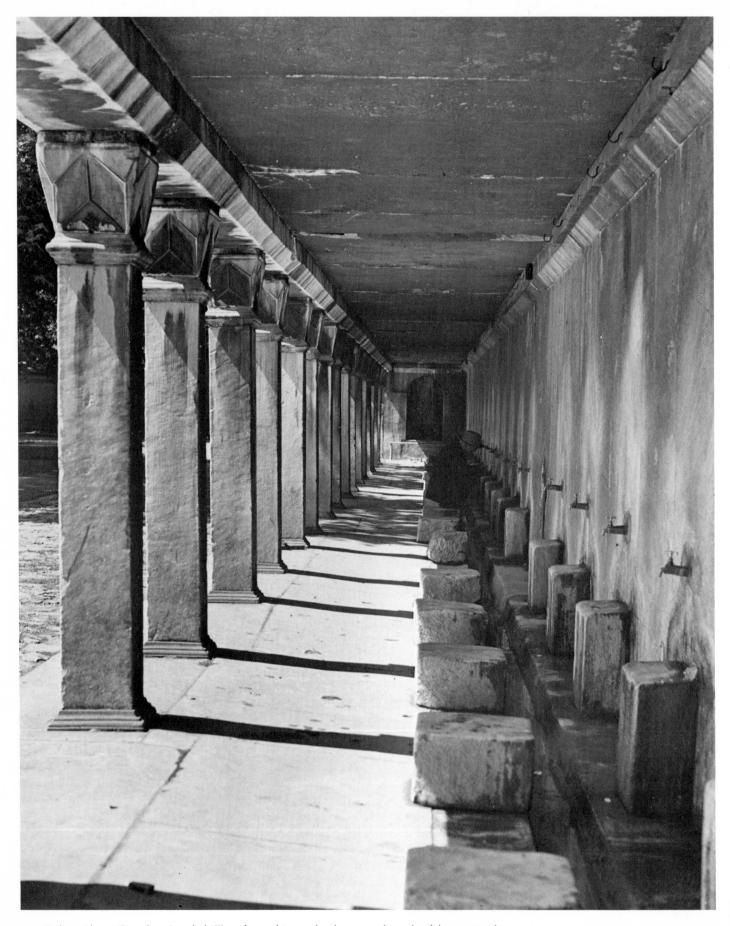

331 *Sultan Ahmet Complex, Istanbul. Taps for washing under the external arcade of the courtyard.*

9

Prelude to change

SINAN DIED ON 17 JULY 1588 and it might have been supposed that Mehmet Ağa who had supervised the work on the royal mosque at Manisa would have been appointed the Architect of the Empire, but instead the choice fell on the senior officer of the department, the Master of the Waterways, Davut Ağa. The appointment would depend on the then sadrazam, Siyavuş Pasha,[1] and would be of particular interest to the sultan who may have made the final selection. It is likely, therefore, that both had seen buildings by the new royal architect: the problem is simply which. Although the orders to the Master of the Waterways during 1585 show him to have been fully occupied, the mosque at Çarşamba of the Kızlarağa Mehmet (the Chief Eunuch) is attributed to him by Eyice[2] although Erdoğan[3] claims that the building was under the direction of Sinan. Important as the Chief Eunuch was in the hierarchy of the saray, Sinan indeed delegated the work because there is a reference to Davut Ağa in the verses of an inscription by Asarı over a courtyard gate.

The plan is not inspired and the execution of the details is poor in places, although this may be due partly to restoration. It is a square mosque with an eleven-metre dome and a large mihrab apse. The five-domed portico is conventional and faced with stone but the rest of the building is of alternating courses of stone and brick. The dome is supported on squinches carried on engaged piers and columns expressed as turrets externally. The columns of the portico are a motley collection of Marmara marble made up of three or four drums bound in bronze, a sure sign that the Byzantine ruins were nearly exhausted by the last quarter of the sixteenth century. What could not help but be splendid at this period are the tiles in the lunettes of the casements and the gorgeous panels of the apse, although these have been carelessly reset. The capitals of the portico columns are well-cut stalactites but an interesting detail is the use of painted wooden capitals in the interior. The doors of the north gallery are set into plaster shoulders which are made uglier by being outlined in red paint. There are fewer windows than in any Sinan mosque at this period and the base of the minaret only reaches to the springing of the portico pendentives, sharing the same string-course, unlike the major country mosques. On the north-east is the usual stair hall, to balance the minaret base behind the ultimate dome, and this collides with the frame and voussoirs of the window and casement in the north-east flank of the mosque. The stair casement is also placed without concern for symmetry. At the south-east corner of the mosque stands the crumbling türbe of the eunuch which was a large square ashlar building with a dome. Of his palace nearby, there is now no trace in the mud, but the double hamam is of good traditional workmanship and still in use. The attribution of this mosque to Davut Ağa seems to be justified but the mosque of Nişancı Mehmet Pasha, the Lord Privy Seal, represents a greater problem.[4]

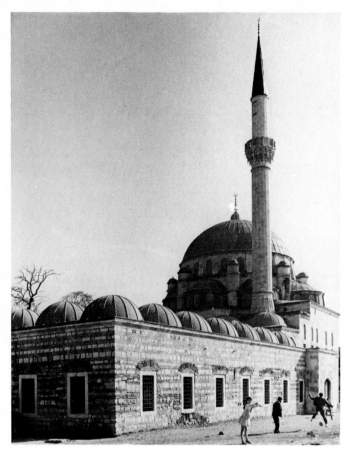

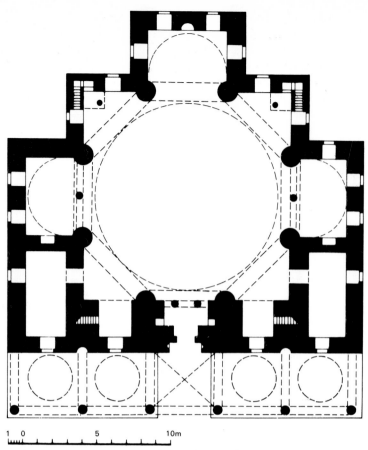

*332, 333 Nişancı Mehmet Pasha Complex, Istanbul. Left, view from the north-west.
Right: plan of the mosque, scale 1:250.*

The mosque is not listed on the authoritative Tezkere compiled by Ahmet
Refik although it does appear on other lists. Sinan's age makes it likely that it
was the work of a leading assistant; Erdoğan[5] suggests that this could have been
either Mehmet Ağa or Davut Ağa while Eyice is silent.[6] It is a magnificent monument and there is a tendency to group it with the Mesih Pasha and Cerrah Pasha
mosques although these buildings are only alike in date. Nişancı Mehmet is
fine enough to be a sadrazam's mosque for it is built of stone and has a fine
arcaded garden. Whether it, or the nearby Mesih Pasha Cami, was the first to
establish the garden court tradition in Istanbul[7] can be disputed, but the court
of Nişancı is much the larger and more attractive.[8] It is not quite a rectangle because of the exigencies of the lanes that bound it and because of the insetting of a
çeşme onto the street at the north-east corner. The revaks of ogee arches are
elegant and lit by grilled casements. Those of the loftier son cemaat yeri have
stalactite as opposed to chevron capitals and are pointed and broad, being one
and a half times as high as they are wide. All the columns are of Bosphorus or
Marmara marble and their shafts unjointed. In the centre of the garden towards
the north door is a simple şadırvan under a polygonal hood. There is also a well
to the east of the north door.

The larger central arch of the portico carries a slightly raised cradle vault.
There are two domes on each side of it. The casements and the doors to the
minaret and gallery stairs on west and east have fine bronze inscriptive lunettes
fitting exactly into the relieving arch, their ground painted green and the
letters gilded. Above the two casements on each side are two more, properly
ordered in the centre of each arch, while the mihrab niches, set exactly under the
springing of the traverse arches between the casements, are excellently carved as
is the stalactite semi-dome over the door. The minaret base is arranged so as to
appear to be part of the structure of the building and the windows are set in
relation to the flanking windows of the harem. The minaret, and the corre-

sponding stairway to the gallery on the east, rise above the level of the domes where the shaft appears to dispense with a foot. Plain but handsome gateways divide the mosque of ashlar from the revaks which externally are built of alternating courses of brick and stone. Outside, the mosque appears splendidly high because of the tall stabilizing turrets which hug the octagonal base of the dome. The external expression of the squinches forms eight semi-domes and exedras outside; these are covered in lead and their three or five windows give a flowing upward motion which is enhanced by the lofty elegance of the multifaceted minaret. The use of stone buttresses for the first third of the dome between the windows which follow the curve is sufficiently baroque to consider alterations in the eighteenth century when the mosque was repaired[9] were it not so clearly a logical part of the design.

The interior plan is unique. In the centre is the square from which the squinches rise to carry the dome, themselves borne on lofty engaged columns. On the south is a rectangular mihrab apse and on the east and west are eyvans of equal dimensions. In the north-east and north-west corners, two long tabhane rooms unexpectedly appear. They have doors onto the portico at each end but are not staircase halls, for the stairs to the minaret and to the gallery are set in thick buttresses at the north corners of the harem and reached from small square eyvans created by the equally heavy buttresses each side of the entry. This in itself is unusual, because beyond the door is a small vestibule with a niche on each side and two colonnettes which act as a second portal to the harem. Like the tabhane rooms, this harks back to the style of the fifteenth-century royal zaviye-mosques of Bursa and could be deliberate revivalism. The kürsü takes the form of two small tribunes in the south corners projecting from the walls and supported by a single column. Access is obtained by stairs in the wall which are entered from the casements on each flank. This is traditional, else the similarity to the stairs at the Muradiye at Manisa might suggest a connection between Nişancı and Mehmet Ağa. The idiosyncrasies in the plan would not be important were it not that the interior of this mosque is particularly fine, partly because of the puritanical restoration which has exposed the fine stone and reduced the quantity of the insensitive stencilling, but mainly because of the proportions which create a mosque of great height and lightness due to many windows. There is not, however, an excess of them as in some later works of Sinan.

Of the three mosques often grouped together, that of Cerrah Mehmet Pasha is less finely proportioned than the Nişancı and less interesting than Mesih Pasha Cami. It suffered very severely from the earthquake of 1894 and its broad domed portico has not been rebuilt. It was built in 1593 for the doctor who circumcised the future Mehmet III and who was, for a short term, sadrazam. As at Ali Pasha at Tokat, the width of the portico required the insetting of a purposeless niche between the second casement and the doors to the stairs to the gallery and the minaret in order to break the monotony. Further stairs are set in the square buttresses each side of the north door. Because of its size, the mosque has lateral doors. There is a large apsidal mihrab area and the dome is carried on four free and two engaged columns. The architect had to project a pier at each corner of the apse in order to accommodate the latter. The squinches are turned at a right angle to form pairs of half-domes over the lateral galleries. These are carried on arcades as is the equally deep north gallery which, as at Zal Mahmut Cami, creates a broad narthex instead of the usual eyvans of the north wall. This is accentuated by the lack of depth to the buttresses each side of the door. The mosque is heavily buttressed externally at each corner and twice along its flanks, while the bases of the minaret and the north-east stairway are very heavy indeed; the reason for this is the large number of windows which weaken the side walls. These external buttresses are also revealed inside. The mosque is large and light and less cluttered than its plan suggests; it makes a handsome pile when seen from the Marmara but it lacks the proportions of a masterpiece.

In 1593, the same year that the mosque of Cerrah Pasha was completed, the Sadrazam Yemen Fatihi Sinan Pasha built his türbe on the Divan yolu near

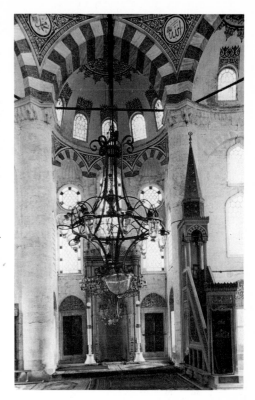

334 Nişancı Mehmet Pasha Complex, Istanbul. Mosque interior.

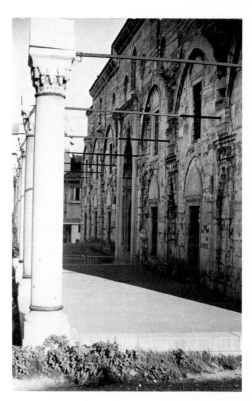

335 Cerrah Mehmet Pasha Cami, Istanbul. The damaged portico.

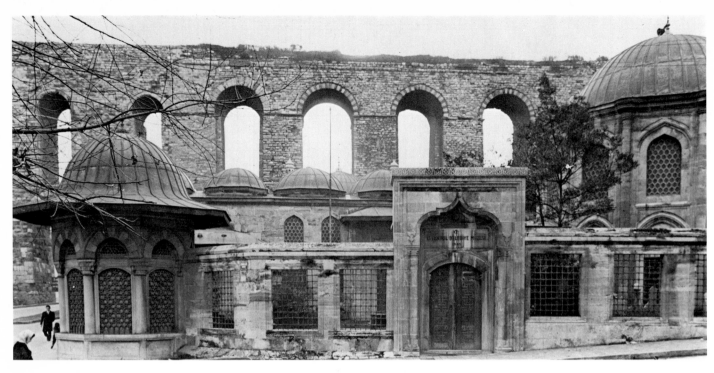

336 Gazanfer Ağa Complex, Istanbul. The türbe is on the right, the sebil on the left, with the medrese under the Valens Aqueduct behind.

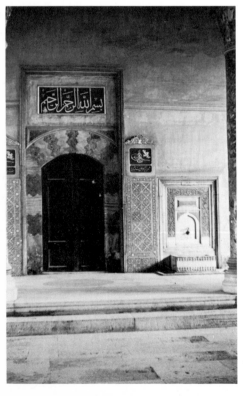

337 Topkapısaray, Istanbul. Door to the Throne Room and the çeşme set in its sixteenth-century tile frame. (See also ill. 382)

Beyazit, together with a small medrese, the dershane of which is at the courtyard gate and served as a mescit.[10] There is a handsome sebil with five grilles separated by marble columns with lunettes of marbles above them, in the manner of the latter half of the sixteenth century. Sinan Pasha died two years later.[11] This complex is attributed with assurance to Davut Ağa[12] and shows some of the characteristics of the few other works that are likely to be his. There is a richness in the decorative detail which seems lavish after the relatively puritanical restraint of Sinan. The türbe is polygonal with polychrome voussoirs to the double tier of windows set between pilasters in each facet. There is a large square porch set on four piers and a column with hipped arches which continue in relief as foliate crests on the architraves. The roof is leaded. The small graveyard with a tree or two crowds around it, and the porch to the dershane serves as the entry to its court through a dentillated archway. The medrese is very plain and has been much restored but the ogee arcades are elegant. The small size of the complex is due to lack of space in the heart of the city: Sinan Pasha, as has already been noted, built extravagantly when Viceroy in Syria.

The medrese, türbe and sebil of Gazanfer Ağa[13] beneath the aqueduct are less certainly attributable to Davut but the complex is similar to that of Sinan Pasha in its compactness and the form of its sebil. The medrese is much more elaborately built but the court is equally small. The alterations converting it into a museum have reduced its importance historically. The work was completed in 1599 when Davut died, three years before Gazanfer Ağa, the Chief Eunuch.

The earliest building attributed to Davut is the Has Oda or Throne Room and a hamam, presumably that of the school, at Topkapisaray built in 993/1585;[14] the former is a splendid hall with a fine colonnade supporting eaves so broad that they unite with those of the Gate of Felicity. He also built the Incili (or Pearl) Kiosk[15] in 1593[16] of which nothing now remains except fragments of its superb tile revetments, and its basements and çeşme over the undercroft of the church of St Saviour Philantropos set in the sea walls. These are in the grand tradition of stone foundations already discussed in connection with the bedchamber of Murat III.

What other work was done under Sinan for the sultan after the fire of 1574 is not known, but it is likely to have pleased Murat III and been the reason for

37

Davut's appointment as royal architect and he was to build the mausoleum of this sovereign when he died in 1595. It was set beside that of Selim II in the garden at Hagia Sophia and took four years to build.[17] The türbe is also associated with Dalgıç Ahmet Ağa[18] who may have completed it after Davut's death. Interestingly, one learns that upon his death, Murat III was brought head first to the site of his tomb and there left in his otak or magnificent military tent:[19] if the relationship between tent and türbe has been much disputed, it would seem that in the sixteenth century the Ottomans had no doubt of its significance. Murat III's türbe is a vast hexagonal hall with a double dome and portico and fine tile revetments. Sanderson[20] records how the sons of Murat and half-brothers of the new sultan were decently strangled – because royal blood may not be shed – on 7 January,[21] ten days before Mehmet III arrived from Manisa. Their funeral procession was conducted with due decorum and the seven vezirs present were robed in black, the sombre black of execution not the purple or white of mourning.[22]

Royal orders concerning buildings for the palace, especially for the Incili Kiosk, for the cleanliness of streets, for waterworks and the work of the new master, Hassa Mimar İsmael, for sending architects to the war of 1595[23] all flooded into Davut's office as steadily as they had under Sinan. It is clear that the post was in no way diminished in importance by his successor. The problems seem always to have been the same; either shortages of workmen or materials. In 1592, it was ordained that all faience made in Iznik was to go to Constantinople, and Davut requested the Chief Justice of the city to see that wood for the brick kilns was not sold to anyone else. Masons had to be called from as far off as Gelibolu in order to expedite work on the Incili Kiosk and they were said to be good – so good that their names are listed, a team of eleven under an usta – and

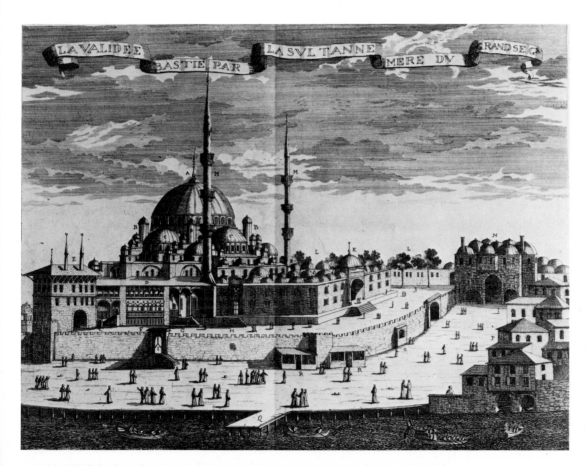

338 Yeni Valide Complex, Istanbul. Seventeenth-century engraving showing, from left to right, the royal-pavilion, the mosque and courtyard and the entry to the Egyptian Bazaar.

all Greek. Mehmet III was pleased enough with Davut's reputation to retain him as a royal architect, or possibly his re-appointment was due to the Valide Sultan who knew his palace work well and who was to give him his major task, *339* the Yeni Valide Cami at Eminönü.

The city was full of mosques but this was not likely to deter Sâfiye Sultan. *356* A Valide mosque was no revolution yet it is significant that there is no sultan's mosque for Mehmet III's reign. She selected a most unsatisfactory site by the water beyond the walls of the summer saray at a point which later became the hub of the old city. It was a slum neighbourhood inhabited by a strange sect called the Karai[24] who were not true Jews. Indeed, they were considered damned by the orthodox and said to be Tartars, but this is a malicious fabrication. They were ordered to go down the Horn to Hasköy but were to be paid compensation. However, the treasurer, Kara Mehmet Ağa, was replaced within a year, probably because he embezzled so much of the funds designed to compensate for the demolition of a synagogue and also a church. This suggests that others than the Karai lived in the neighbourhood. The precincts were to be walled, but the exact complement of dependencies is not easy to determine since they were never built. It can be assumed that there would have been many, for the area allocated was large. The work met with difficulties from the start because there was constant seepage from the sea, and it is Ahmet Ağa who receives the credit for building foundations which have withstood four hundred years of use. They are stone reinforced with iron and effectively a series of bridges, possibly on the principle of islets like that at Büyükçekmece. It was this work which gave him *284* the honorific of Dalgıç or diver. These foundations represent the most daring aspect of the Valide Cami for the plan is sadly conservative, foreshadowing the end of the golden age of the Ottoman Empire. It was drawn up but never completed by Davut because he was executed at Vefa for advanced thinking or heresy in 1599,[25] a different plague from that which Eyice politely suggests.[26] Moreover, this plan was pursued by Dalgıç Ahmet until the death of Mehmet III in 1603 and his mother's banishment to the Eski saray until her own death in 1605. Ahmet I ordered the work to stop when it had reached the level of the lower casements and the Karai rejoiced and returned to camp in the uncompleted building.

The plan which Davut had submitted and which the Valide had accepted was none other than that of the Şehzade with modifications. The mosque is forty-one metres square and the dome is seventeen and a half by thirty-six metres instead of nineteen by thirty-seven metres and is therefore fractionally more than twice as high as broad whereas the Şehzade is fractionally less. The lateral doors are set at each end, like the Süleymaniye and Şehzade, and an arcade above spigots fills the interval. It is two-tiered. Unlike the Şehzade, the court is not square but rectangular and there are seven domes to the Valide's son cemaat yeri, not five, and seventeen smaller revak domes, not eleven. There is no true sadırvan but only a tall and slender octagonal water tank richly carved, which is likely to date from the seventeenth century. Inside, the müezzin's tribune is in the same position as at the Şehzade and the quatrefoil plan, modified by exedras, is the same, and so is the problem of the stalactites bleeding into the voussoirs. There is, however, a gallery on three sides with pretty, alternating large and small arches and with a fine continual marble balustrade. Although the dome and semi-domes and squinches are set above a ring of windows and buttresses, there is less fenestration than in the later work of Sinan. The four great piers are expressed outside as tall octagonal turrets with cantaloup lead caps. Small turrets rise in steps each side of the semi-domes to meet them and create a handsome build-up towards the alem; the corner domes remain cut off from the main movement both inside and out, if less so than at the Şehzade. The stepped turrets completely overshadow them. There are two minarets which are reached from inside. They stand at each end of the portico and are multifaceted and have three şerefes with superb stalactite carving. Although executed sixty years later, there seems no reason to suppose that this work is not faithful to Davut's plans. The

339 Yeni Valide Complex, Istanbul. The mosque and the courtyard from the north-east.

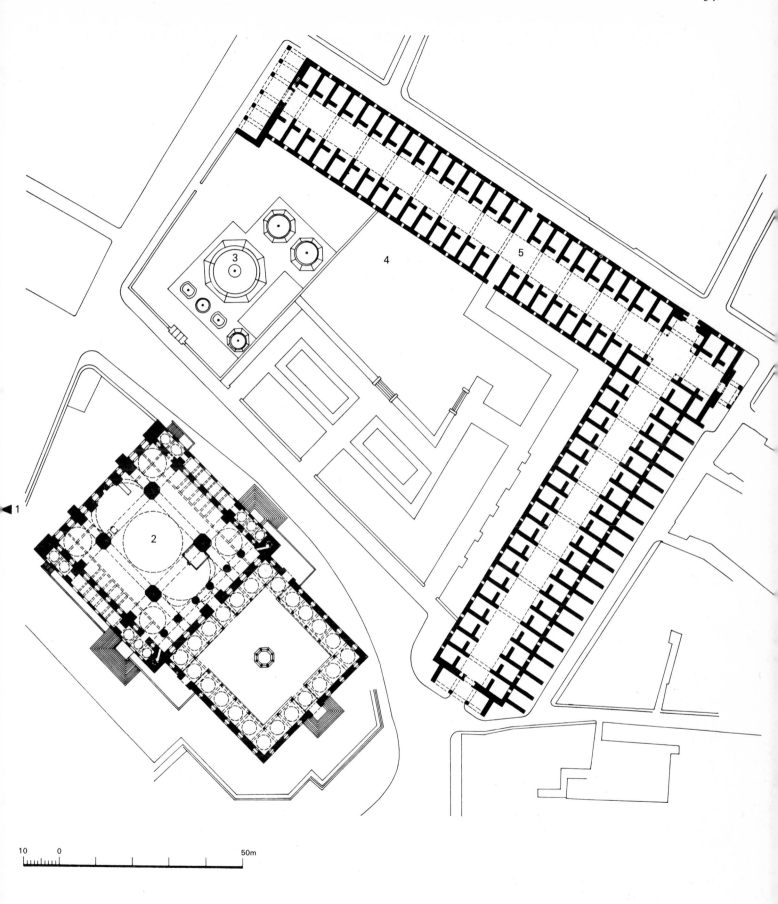

10   0   50m

*340 Yeni Valide Complex, Istanbul. Plan, scale 1:1,000. 1 Passage to royal pavilion;
2 mosque; 3 türbe; 4 garden; 5 Egyptian Bazaar.*

projection of heavy eaves over the side washing area is clumsy, but much of the gloom of this unfortunate building is due to the soot of the steamers that ply to and from the Galata Bridge.[27]

Dalgıç Ahmet Ağa was not dismissed on the accession of Ahmet I, then a boy of thirteen, and few royal architects were ever deprived of office except by execution. It is not clear when he gave up his post, but the last order appears to have been issued in *1013*/1604 when Ünsal says that he was succeeded by Mustafa as Hassa Mimarbaşı; he died or lost his office in *1015*/1605.[28] Dalgıç Ahmet probably died in 1607, perhaps forced to retire owing to ill-health or because Ahmet I or his sadrazam had already decided that Mehmet Ağa, now the Master of the Waterways, was a fitter man to be entrusted with the projected royal mosque. Mustafa has been credited with nothing and the exact proof of his ever being royal architect has not been published. Dalgıç Ahmet, however, had one important commission proven to be his work and that was the large türbe for Mehmet III added to those already existing in the garden at Hagia Sophia. Ahmet I was impatient and within a year he was complaining about the slow progress of the building of the tomb to which the architect replied that the marble was not yet come from Marmara. The sultan immediately ordered three more ships with better oarsmen to be sent to the island.[29] Mehmet III's tomb follows the plans of the preceding ones but is in no way as fine either in proportion or in the execution of its details. Dalgıç Ahmet was a good engineer but not a gifted architect.

Mehmet Ağa had already been entrusted with the building of a throne for Ahmet I, which can be seen in the saray, when in *1016*/1606[30] he at last succeeded to the office of Imperial Architect. The throne is not ostentatious but made of walnut, mother-of-pearl, and tortoise shell with a green zircon hanging from its vault to symbolize the world, and a pearl tassel symbolizing the ruling of it. Like the Koran case of Dalgıç Ahmet it appears to have been proof of the architect's abilities. According to Cafer Efendi, who was his friend and wrote a brief account of his career, Mehmet Ağa had been born a Christian in Europe about 1540 and came to Istanbul as late as 1563, whether to join the Janissary corps or as a result of his training in the provinces is not clear. After six years as an acemi-oğlan, he became a musician and after that he was for twenty years a worker in mother-of-pearl and so known as Sedefiâr Mehmet, but he appears to have been an architect as well for he was left in charge of the office when Sinan was away. It is said that on Sinan's advice he gave Murat III a Koran box in 1589 and so was given the post of Kapıcı or Gate Keeper, and in 1591 he gave the sultan a quiver which won him promotion to muhzirbaşı, or Chief Bailiff. Later, he was for a time Mütesellin of Diyarbakır, lieutenant-governor or revenue officer. These offices are remote from the work of an architect and were surely sinecures symbolic of the decline in Ottoman standards. He was also made Inspector of Works in 1591 and visited Arabia, Egypt and Macedonia before his appointment as Master of the Waterways in 1597.[31] Ahmediye was to occupy all his time from 1609 to 1617 when he died at about the same time as his master.

The year 1606 was one of misfortune. The young sultan spent so much time with his women that it caused a scandal and during August there were disturbances.[32] In October, the Sadrazam Dervish Pasha ordered the assassination of the Jewess La Quira who had cured the youth of smallpox and had become Procuress Royal as well as one of the wealthiest women of the times through royal favours.[33] Like all his ancestors, Ahmet loved the chase and would escape along the Black Sea coast or towards Edirne with his panthers and his greyhounds. He would hunt his way along the tedious road to Edirne, and Naima reports a royal bag of eighteen deer, one hundred and fifty hare and forty foxes and also a great many pheasant brought down by his falcons. The grimmest blow to the prestige of the throne was the humiliating treaty of Sitvatorog which presaged the failure of Ottoman power. The unhappy prince decided to build a great mosque in order to placate God, and from that moment he devoted his life to that task, but without abandoning his pleasures.[34] Unfortunately for him,

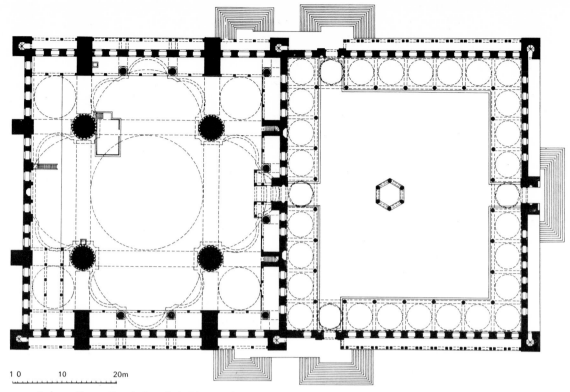

341 Sultan Ahmet Cami, Istanbul. Plan, scale 1 :750.

the Ulema did not receive his decision with pleasure. He must have made extensive preparations including the assembly of quantities of materials long before 1609 when he came in person to break the first sod. To begin with, several palaces had to be pulled down including those of Sokollu and Güzel Ahmet Pasha in order to free the whole of the south side of the Atmeydan and the ancient Sphendone as well.[35] The palaces were costly to buy but much revenue was diverted to the mosque and perhaps the Ulema were right to protest that mosques should be built out of the wealth of conquest and not the straitened circumstances of political defeat. The legend that there were only six minarets at Mecca and that to exceed four was therefore sacrilege is false but may have been used as an argument by unscrupulous doctors of the law. There were seven minarets for the great mosque at Basra[36] and in Asraki's *Chronicles of Mecca*, before the last version of 1429, Kut-al-din reports seven minarets there. This is not to count the eight minaret-cum-stabilizing turrets of the tomb of Olcaytu at Sultaniye.

The Şeyhül-İslam in his hostility provoked a revolt, but Ahmet was determined to achieve his ambition and building began in August 1609, even though the citizens were forbidden to pray there; in October, he was reported to be continuing the work with might and main.[37] He was certainly the victor in this struggle, for the Ahmediye was to become the first mosque of the Empire and the favourite of the general public until this day. The organization of the work required great experience and the architects' department had had long training. Eight volumes in the saray record the work of construction and the supply of materials, in particular marble[38] and stone. Stone was the major portion of the material used and it was given to batches of workmen with special marks such as bow, fork, drill, flag, key or balance.[39] Monthly accounts were signed by the sultan and the proof that the complex as opposed to the mosque was not completed when Ahmet died is that the later accounts are signed by Mustafa I. The foundations of the mosque were laid in *1018*/1609[40] and the work finished in *1026*/1617 when the opening ceremony was held, although *1025*/1616 is recorded on the targets of the gate and mahfil. The accounts were so meticulously kept that even the cost of snow for the sebil is recorded.[41]

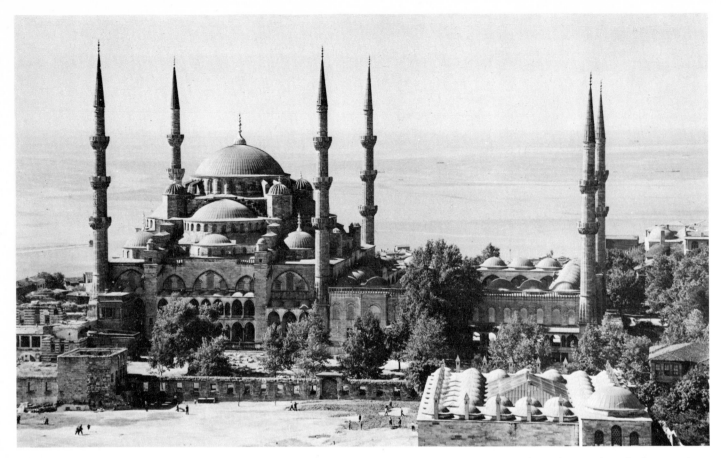

342 Sultan Ahmet Complex, Istanbul. Mosque with the medrese in the right foreground.

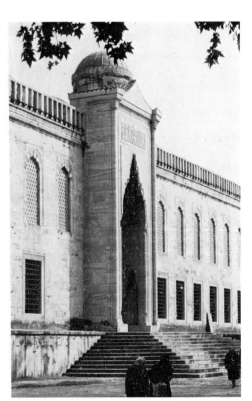

343 Sultan Ahmet Complex, Istanbul.
Gateway to the courtyard.

It is stated that before he drew up the plans, Mehmet Ağa inspected all the major monuments of the Empire, and although this is poetic licence it is the key to his approach. The mosque is a marriage of other men's ideas in most but not all particulars, and where it is not inspired by previous masterpieces it is often ungainly or monotonous since the dominant ideals were size and splendour. It is the exterior which approaches total success. From the Marmara it is seen to dominate its quarter, and from the gate of the saray its most noble aspect is seen in alignment in order to delight the sultan. From the Hippodrome it has a weak aspect and appears to sprawl and lie low behind its trees. The reason is that it is only elevated on the south side where it is founded on the vaults and undercrofts of the Great Palace of the Emperors; on the north it is level with the meydan. The two extra minarets at the north corners of the court draw attention to its great size but weaken the tension, for the distance between these and the minarets flanking the portico is greater than between the latter and the minarets each end of the kible wall. Thus the building relaxes visually along its south–north axis and only when framed in the courtyard gates does tension mount from the fountain of the avlu to the climax of the central dome.

The court façade is built up in the same manner as that of the Süleymaniye except for the addition of two round turrets beside the corner domes. Also, the dome itself is lower and smaller and where, immediately above the higher central dome of the portico, the Süleymaniye has a flat rectangular face with four round windows which reflects the rectangular fountain in the court below, at Sultan Ahmet the fountain is hexagonal. Moreover, above the middle arches of the façade, the curve of the central exedra is expressed and the rectangular form subdued. The build-up of the mosque, therefore, is logical and graceful and predominantly curvular, whereas the tensions between curve and rectangle at the Süleymaniye were stronger and so the dome was a dramatic climax and not merely the top of a pile.

344 The spaciousness of the court of the mosque of Ahmet is one of its virtues. Like the Şehzade, it covers the same area as the mosque, but here again the relaxation of tension is such that monotony ensues. Mehmet Ağa solved the problem of the encounter of the revak and the portico by widening the span of the arches of the latter and also lowering them until they are only fractionally higher than those of the revaks; there is, therefore, no conflict with the capital level of the corner columns. Moreover, there were no gatehouses; and although the gates on the south-east and south-west remain, they are kept low. They are set in stone frames with handsome niches on each side. The central fountain which is so effective when seen through the north entry to the court as the first step up towards the dome, its pent roof echoed in the slight triangulation of the inscriptive base to the central cupola of the portico, is found to be too small and insignificant when seen from the revaks of the court, in spite of its elaborate foliate decoration in low relief.[42] Mehmet Ağa also avoided the monumental size of Sinan's great entry to the court at the Süleymaniye. The lofty gate at the Ahmediye is impressively deep and has a fine stalactite semi-dome but it is detached from the revaks architecturally. If the problem of joining arches of disparate heights is avoided once again, the ribbed dome on a tall drum above the gateway is too small. The weakness of Mehmet Ağa is revealed where his work is most admired. The problems which harassed Sinan were not solved but avoided. And other weaknesses occur. The Yeni Valide court also united portico and revak by keeping the arches at the same level, but the arch before the main door is the largest whereas at Sultan Ahmet it is the narrowest of the portico. Moreover, the cost of keeping the portico low and subdued was to expose the wall behind and above, not as a drop against which the cupolas are defined but as a blind expanse. The ordering of the north wall is also unsatisfactory because the two tiers of casements are grouped in pairs to make sets of four between the three arches on each side of the door except where a mihrab niche has to be inserted to the right of the central arch, an asymmetry which does nothing to relieve the monotony but disturbs because of the break in progression; nor is this feature bold enough to dominate its area.

The mosque and its court are set in a larger enclosure in accordance with tradition. The four minarets at the corners of the mosque have three şerefes and the north pair have two, making sixteen in all and this follows the correct example of Süleymaniye where it was plainly necessary to progress from a lower to a higher level at the apex of the triangle of the dome and semi-domes. Nonetheless, Naima states[43] with uncertain arithmetic that this number of şerefes was

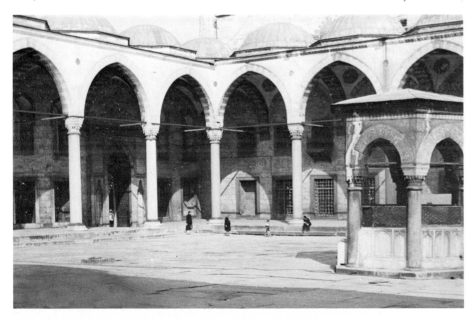

344 *Sultan Ahmet Complex, Istanbul. Mosque courtyard and cistern.*

chosen because Ahmet was the fourteenth sultan. The minarets are fluted and the şerefes have stalactite corbels. They have often been repaired but the caps may well be original in form although they taper. The exterior wall of the court has a balustrade which tends to conceal the domes. A new concept is the setting of spigots under an outer gallery which extends beyond the flanking gates the whole length of the court. The need for a shed roof is therefore eliminated. The upper gallery consists of twelve ogee arches between small round ones. These are carried on columns but, below, the walk is carried on piers[44] which are monotonous. The steps to the side doors of the court are noble and the arcading is carried on down the flanks of the mosque but on a grander scale.

At the south-east corner is the royal kiosk which has been recently rebuilt after a fire. A ramp leads up to a platform and a fine loggia which look out across the sea. From this, access is obtained to two small but handsome retiring rooms, while on the other side is the upper gallery of the mosque admitting to the royal loge.[45] This is the first appearance in Ottoman architecture of a ramp to the royal kiosk and has been considered a baroque development. These retiring rooms were to become famous as the headquarters of the Grand Vezir in 1826 when the rebellious Janissary corps was annihilated at the orders of Mahmut II.[46] The outer court can be reached by another ramp below the south wall through a gate on the south-west side, while on the north-west and north-east corners[47] there are big gatehouses onto the meydan with chambers above. Beside that on the east were once cells, probably over market rooms, and at the end the very large marble türbe of the sultan. This is set in its own dwarf garden and has a triple-domed portico and an annexe but is in bad repair. It is strikingly larger, with its three-tiered side windows in ranks of five, than the dershane of the medrese beside it. This dershane is set at the north-east corner of the medrese court and the entry to the college is on the north-west down the lane between it and the funerary garden. The medrese has no east windows where buildings may once have stood.

In the middle of the east wall of the outer precinct of the mosque is a postern and the elevated sibyan mekteb[48] which has now been restored. All the other buildings of the complex were set above the Sphendone on the west where there is a large cistern. The most important was the tımarhane[49] which was demolished in the nineteenth century and which was second only to that of the Süleymaniye in importance. The tabhane has also been destroyed, but the large imaret has been incorporated into the buildings of the trade school which stands on the site of the lost buildings of the complex. Other minor buildings have also been destroyed but traces of foundations and walls can be found between the western precinct wall and the imaret area.

The interior of Sultan Ahmet Cami is based on the quatrefoil plan and its monotony is only diminished by the use of galleries on all sides but the south and the resulting abruptness of the kıble wall, where there are no recesses corresponding to the completely externalized buttresses. The three exedras on the other sides, are consequently reduced to two on the south by the necessary elimination of the one in the centre. The four elephant feet[51] make the greatest impression, for they are oppressively big although their marble bases have multiple convex facets and there is inscriptive banding dividing them from the painted upper half of the shaft. Their size is particularly damaging to the proportions of the dome which is relatively modest for it is only twenty-three and a half metres in diameter and forty-three metres high. These dimensions in part reflect the inadequacy of Mehmet Ağa as an engineer and his wasteful use of an inflated margin of safety. The whole hall is forty-seven metres square.[52] The mosque is, therefore, little bigger than the Şehzade and less extensive than the Süleymaniye. The problem of stalactite corbelling bleeding into the voussoirs is worse here than at any other imperial mosque. The müezzins' platform has come to rest behind the south-west pier and obstructs the view of the mihrab in the western area. The hünkâr mahfil fills the whole of the area under the south-east dome but otherwise the corner areas are as detached as they always are.

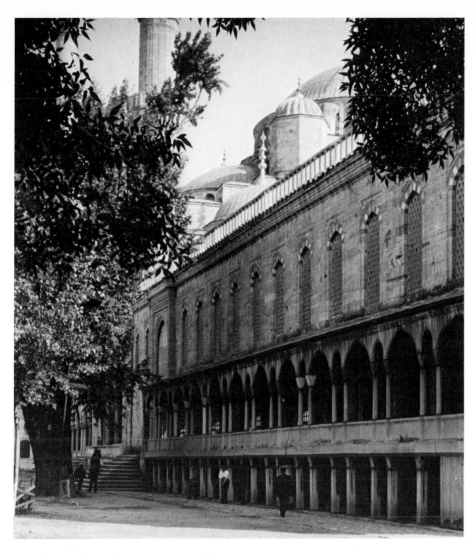

345 Sultan Ahmet Complex, Istanbul. East arcade.

The unkindest praise a mosque can receive is that its beauty lies in its decoration[53] and not in its structure; but this is not true of the Sultan Ahmet mosque, partly because the predominantly blue paintwork covering seventy-five per cent of the wall area and the arch surfaces is poor quality stencilling, and partly because the mosque is spacious due to the exploitation of many tiers of large windows. There are deep lower casements at floor level with fine opus sectile surrounds, and a second tier at gallery level with windows ranked above. Each exedra has five windows although two among those of the flanking exedras are blind; above these are the fourteen windows of each semi-dome and the twenty-eight of the main dome, four of which are blind. In the April of 1610, Ahmet I approached the Bailio of Venice concerning glass for these windows, for his obsession with his mosque increased with his girth rather than diminished[54] and the Signoria, who never lost a chance to keep in the sultan's favour, agreed to make him a present.[55] Bottle glass for outer windows was made in Istanbul but all other glass was imported, especially if coloured.[56] Dalloway remarks on this coloured glass in 1795 and says that it was made of small pieces, clearly in the traditional manner. It is this which led Lechevalier in 1800 to say that the mosque was ill-lit, and in 1836 Cotton makes the same observation.[57] By the present century, this fine glass had been lost but has now to some extent been replaced by coarsely designed modern coloured windows of no merit.[58] The result is that, while the mosque is no longer as bright as the market place as it was some years ago, it still lacks all mystery. Evliya states that all the windows were coloured; and he knew a great amount about this mosque.[59]

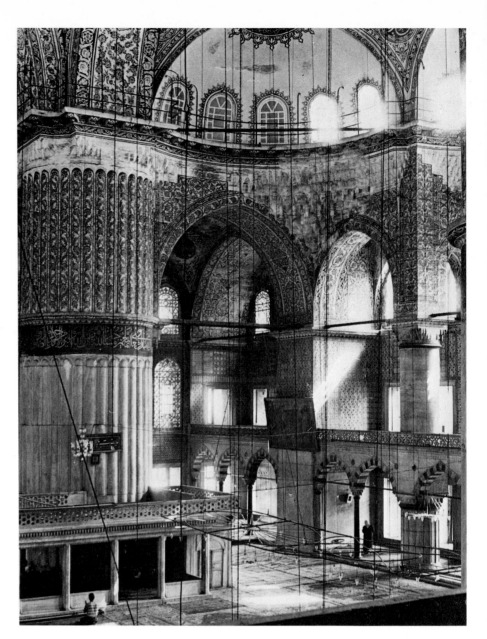

346 Sultan Ahmet Cami, Istanbul. Interior looking towards the south-west.

His father was responsible for the fine courtyard door[60] and, indeed, all the inlaid woodwork that survives is very good. He also remarks on the lavish furnishings of the mosque, and some of what he claimed is substantiated by later travellers. The lofty minber is traditional in form but is of exceedingly richly carved marble with an exceptional design of artichokes in the flanking circles and it is crowned by a golden alem. Evliya draws attention to the fountains in the two north elephant feet which copy those at Süleymaniye. Lechevalier also noted the fine carving and open marble of the balustrades. The mihrab caught his attention and it has a many-tiered stalactite niche with a double inscriptive panel above it; but its grandeur is diminished by the quantity of window all about it.

The hünkâr mahfil is carried on ten columns of precious marbles and has a richly adorned mihrab niche of its own in the pier of the south-east arch. Evliya speaks of emeralds and gold in its decoration which Lechevalier correctly reduces to jade and gilt.[61] Evliya says that there were one hundred Korans on inlaid and gilded desks and Dalloway also says there were a great many inscribed placards hanging.[62] In Evliya's day there was a well-stocked library. Thévenot, writing in the second half of the century, comments on the number of lamps and on the curiosities in glass bowls: one contained a little galley, well-rigged, another a model of the mosque in wood, and the rest 'a great many knacks of that nature'.[63] The galley and the model of the mosque were noticed by the Marquis de Tournefort in 1700 but he calls the model a bas-relief. He also comments on the ostrich eggs, lustres and crystal balls among the lamps – lamps which Naima[64] declared to be covered with gold and ornamented with gems. Such splendours have been pawned or pillaged for museums. In 1800, Lechevalier is already stating that the only decoration is the great tablets with the names of the caliphs and verses from the Koran. These were originally the work of Ametli Kasım Gubarı who could write on a grain of rice[65] but they have been restored so often that only their distance from the viewer conceals their present remoteness from the refined hand of the famous seventeenth-century calligrapher.

Arcades carried on columns and piers, both at ground and gallery level, subdue the light where the tiles, which are the boast of the mosque, are massed in panel after panel of more than fifty different designs. The finest are reserved for the north wall which is the worst lit of the three and they are rarely clean and sparkling so that they have become difficult to see. Dwight makes the cogent point that Sinan was wise after Rüstem Pasha not to attempt to smother a huge interior with tiles again.[66] The Yeni Valide and the Sultan Ahmet mosques have panel after panel at gallery level, and at the former yet more clad every pier. The result is a diffusion which detracts from the individual work. Ahmet I had a passion for tiles, and orders concerning them flowed from the Divan from 1607 onwards. Clay was sent from Kütahya and Afyon to Iznik[67] and no more tiles were allowed to be sold until the work in hand at the saray was finished.[68] In 1609 an order states that the tiles had not arrived for his kiosk and that they were to be re-ordered and sent as soon as possible, in four or five days and no excuses were to be accepted.[69] In 1613 the edict went out that no more Iznik tiles were to be made without orders from the saray, not even for the vezirs, because ordinary people were buying them against the sultan's express wishes.[70] The result was an accumulation of 21,043 tiles with 350,958 akçes worth in the gallery over the main door alone.[71] Some fit their areas exactly and it is clear that their designers inspected the mosque carefully before sending the pounces to Iznik and, just possibly, Kütahya but others form a polyglot collection from other buildings. The individual tiles at lower level are traditional as are those set in the southeast porch to the royal loge which, in addition, are of poor quality. At gallery level, the panel designs represent a *tour-de-force* including cypresses, flowers and fruit with blue, green, red, black and turquoise colours predominating. The designs are flamboyant to the point of being fairly described as baroque, while the more abstract panels of the lateral walls are crowded with repetitive motifs to the pitch where decadence, presaged in the upper walls of the Muradiye at Manisa, has set in. It was the last cry of Iznik, for the reds were about to turn brown and the greens blue, the whites become mottled and dirty, the glazes pitted like the face of the moon. Sultan Ahmet, man and mosque, exhausted the potters, and the kilns closed down one by one until by 1620 probably little more than twenty were still at work. The master potter responsible for the superintendence of the more than 20,000 tiles of the mosque was Kaşıcı Hasan.[72]

The year 1617 was no more auspicious than any other during Ahmet I's reign for it was marked by a rebellion and the sack of Bursa, but in this, the last year of his life, he was able to see his mosque completed and to pray in the hünkâr mahfil. Since the Yeni Valide was completed to the original plans of Davut Ağa, or so far as was possible, Sultan Ahmet Cami is the last great mosque of the classical age. It aspires to majesty and to some extent achieves it; it cannot sustain it. The whole complex has noble dimensions, particularly externally, but inside the space is squandered and lacks Sinan's economy of purpose born of creative thinking. A long pause in the impulse to renewal with regard to architecture had set in, although the flimsy but charming summer pavilions, at Kağıthane and in the meadows at the far end of the Horn, which grew up at this period prior to the coming of the yalıs along the Bosphorus, were a prelude to the next Ottoman development. One change which occurred at this date was in the old standard measure: from the concept that from shoulder to fingers equalled sixty fingers width to a new measure equalling twenty-four fingers widths; this suggests an increase in accuracy of workmanship and a concern with more detailed planning.

Just outside the city on the old Edirne road are the barracks of Davut Pasha which ever since the conquest had been the parade ground and assembly point of armies destined to invade Europe. Here, Davut Pasha built a pavilion which was severely damaged in the sixteenth century, perhaps by earthquake. It was repaired for Ahmet I by Mehmet Ağa,[73] or possibly Dalgıç Ahmet.[74] It was a ceremonial pavilion for the review of the army and therefore related to the Alay Kiosk opposite the Porte and rebuilt by Mahmut II in the early nineteenth century on its original sixteenth-century foundations. The Davut Pasha or Sancak Kiosk, the Pavilion of the Standard, was used as a hunting lodge by Mehmet IV and in 1848 Abdülmecit watched the last military parade there before it became a training centre for auxiliary reserves. Architecturally, it is important because it is one of the few buildings of its type remaining. The plan is T-form, but the two rooms forming the cross are not important at ground or upper floor levels. The entry porch has been restored with a dome but at one time was used as a balcony. It admits to a central hall which runs the width of the building. Off it, to the south, is a large chamber and to the north is the staircase which divides the two minor rooms. The stairs lead up to the grand landing of the piano nobile which forms the ceiling of the entry hall. Two corner doors admit to the royal chamber which is a lofty room with a ten-metre dome and a fine ocak. On the south side is a broad rectangular vaulted bay with a sofa. It is very much a pavilion for reviews, for the room is full of large casements with grilled windows above them. The upper and lower chambers have five such pairs along their side walls and three across the south bay. Mehmet Ağa was responsible for the repair of the water system[75] and there is a çeşme in the lower half added by Rabia Sultan, but the fine trees and the pool in the once walled court have disappeared. The upper floor is supported on quite unnecessarily powerful vaults which cut across the corner windows of the upper tier so that they are, therefore, only there for symmetry. The whole basic structure is closely allied to the more modest and more poetic Siyavuş Pasha hunting lodge a few kilometres away.[76]

The first quarter of the century had been dominated by the building of Ahmet I's mosque which, by the monopoly of supplies of stone, marble and tiles, frustrated other important works. Early in the century, Bayram Pasha added a small complex beside that of Haseki Hürrem. The small, plain medrese with ogee arches is akin to that of Yemen Fatihi Sinan Pasha on the Divan yolu and is reached down a lane past a single-storey stone chamber, polygonal in shape, under a tile roof which was a mekteb. Across the road is a sebil with three grilled windows between columns in the style of the period. The last years of the sixteenth century can be seen as those when this form of water architecture truly developed and the embryo of the great fountains of the seventeenth century was formed. A gate beyond the sebil leads to a long court with a cemetery and a plain şadırvan and the large türbe of Bayram Pasha on the street side. This is remarkable for its grandeur and for the remains of paintwork inside. Such large tombs have been seen at Eyüp, though of a different style, including those of Siyavuş Pasha, or the vast, richly crested, mausoleum of Ferhat Pasha built of polychrome marbles. It was a time when the vezirs vied with each other in the building of grand türbes, and that of Bayram Pasha with its three chevets is more elaborate than most. Beyond it is the L-formed court of cells of a tekke with an octagonal semahane in the centre. The irregular vista from the gate to these cells contrasts strongly with the rigid planning of the classical Ottoman era. It is another example of the happy effect of a difficult site on traditional forms and must have been a beautiful haven before it became a picturesque slum.

At this period, the benevolent and the proud were forced to make use of awkward sites simply because the centre of the city was heavily built over. The

IV

34?

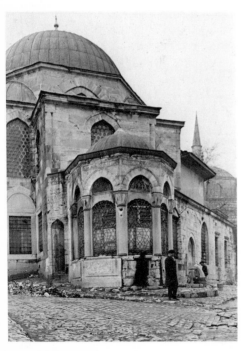

347 Bayram Pasha Complex, Istanbul. Sebil and türbe, with the mosque of Haseki Hürrem behind.

small complex of Kuyucu Murat Pasha built in *1015/1606*[77] is an example. The site is triangular and somewhat long and the solution was to make a strong accent at the apex of the triangle by setting the sebil in it. On the street flank towards the Şehzade is a restored line of shops. Inside, the cells of the medrese flank a triangular court including the tiny mosque-cum-dershane and the tomb of the founder. The length of the court and its fan shape help reduce the feeling of constriction. The smallness of this complex compared with those of the sixteenth century was part of a trend towards reducing the emphasis on the mosque in the capital, where there were now so many, and instead supplying educational centres and waterworks alongside the tomb of the potentate who endowed the foundation, such as Sinan Pasha,[78] Gazanfer Ağa[79] or Bayram Pasha just discussed. It is also a reflection of the reduced wealth of the vezirs compared with such men as Ibrahim Pasha and Piyale Pasha but this did not mean that some magnates did not build liberally and spaciously in the hinterland.

An example of the reduced scale of royal building in the mid-century and also of the elegant use of an awkward site is the Çinili complex on the hill above Üsküdar begun by Mahpeyker Kösem Sultan, the widow of Ahmet I and valide of Murat IV. The mosque has the charm of all miniature buildings and contrasts strongly with the size of its şadırvan under a flamboyant hood roof. As has been seen, the roofing of şadırvans was a mark of Murat IV's reign. The mosque is famous for its tiles which are of good design but reduced to blues and greys and so seem impoverished after those of the sixteenth century elsewhere. It has a portico on all three sides like the Sinan Pasha Cami in Cairo dated 1571. The court is irregular in shape, and advantage has been taken of the fall of the land to raise the mosque on a platform. To the south-east is an awkward triangular corner where the medrese has been ingeniously placed on a terrace which extends to the cistern behind the kible wall. The mosque itself served as the dershane. It was not essential to set the medrese in this spearhead corner, and the architect[80] has taken pleasure in overcoming his difficulties rather than resorting to the easy solution which was to build to the north-west facing the mosque. All the features remain strictly traditional, even the triangulation of wall thicknesses at awkward corners, but under this conformity there is a certain restlessness and a weariness with the constraint of accepted rules.

Even a rectangular site might produce unusual plans. The medrese of the notoriously corrupt administrator, Ekmekcioğlu Ahmet Pasha,[81] at Vefa has a large but normal court with a gate in the centre of its flank but at the south end the dershane and the türbe are set side by side; the latter has a sebil set into its corner on the street side. The twin rooms are domed and the students studying in the hall would have been reminded constantly of the presence of their founder. Ahmet Pasha also built a kervansaray at Edirne opposite the Ayşe Kadın Cami[82] to whom it is sometimes attributed. This kervansaray has a shed roof and lattice windows of stone like those at Sinan's inn at Büyükçekmece[83] but it was representative of a development in the design of kervansarays which set the two main halls each side of a large recessed court and arcade. It was also proof that Ahmet I had not absorbed all the architectural energies of the empire in *1018/1609*.[84]

However, the period was fundamentally conservative and this is illustrated by the restoration and partial rebuilding of the Şerefettin Cami at Konya in 1636 on much older foundations.[85] This mosque is remarkable for the re-appearance of the four large arches, rather than buttresses, at the corners of the domes in the manner of Kılıç Ali Pasha and also for the height of the base and trunk of its minaret which is set well back along the flank of the building on the east. Externally, partly helped by the large archways, the segments of the building are handsomely built up into a unity which is all the more surprising because of the amount of restoration and repair at various dates; these are revealed by patches of brick and stone courses amid the prevailing ashlar and even little fragments of ceramic in the mortar. The interior has suffered from formidably vulgar nineteenth-century repainting, the vitality of which submerges the forms. The plan is a late sixteenth-century exercise with a domed square cramped by heavy galleries on

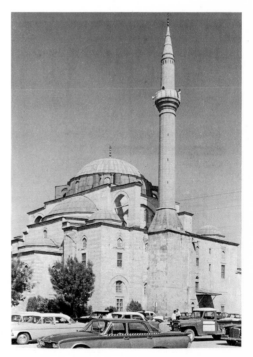

348 Şerefettin Cami, Konya, from the south-west. The arched buttresses can be compared with those of Kılıç Ali Pasha Cami (ill. 275).

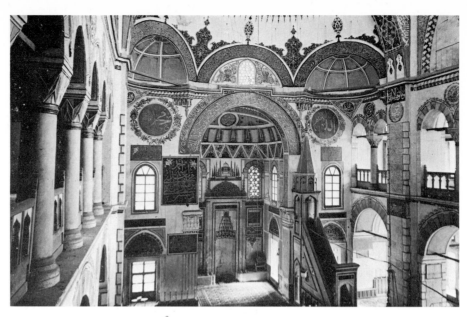

349 *Şerefettin Cami, Konya. Interior from the north.*

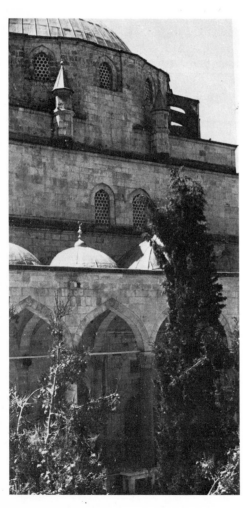

350 *Ömer Pasha Cami, Elmalı. North front.*

three sides and on the south a large apsidal recess for the mihrab. Nothing about this building indicates a development in architectural thought.

This is less true of the much earlier mosque built by Ömer Pasha at Elmalı in south-west Anatolia in *1019/1610*.[86] This lofty mosque dominates the town when seen from the plateau beneath it. It has been heavily restored as have its court, or garden, and the medrese facing it. The medrese forms a C-plan, without a der-shane but, in its place, an arch through the north range of cells up which steps lead into the market. It shares its şadırvan with the mosque. The plan of Ömer Pasha is the normal square chamber with a portico but with a number of unusual features both inside and out. The enhanced height is expressed externally by the recessing of a second square base above that formed by the four main walls of the chamber. These have elegant buttresses at the corners and in the centre of each flank, the latter possessing unusual circular windows at the top. Above the second square is the octagon on which the dome rests with its eight corners marked by small elegant turrets with pretty caps. The four corner areas over the internal squinches are filled to half the height of this level with extensions of the wall so that yet another recessed square is created; out of it the semi-domes of the squinches emerge between pairs of flying buttresses set at an angle. The minaret stands orthodoxly at the north-west corner but its base is short and the foot begins at the springing of the portico arches and the trunk at the level of the portico roof. This results in a long polygonal trunk although the height of the minaret is not exceptional for its period. There is a small lobby in the false base at the north-east corner. The care taken over details is shown by the con-tinuance of the string-course of the third level of wall round the trunks of the turrets, thus binding them to the body of the building, and the symmetrical grouping and spacing of the upper lights which are relatively few and small. The fine ashlar limestone portico is nicely ordered, the pair of wing arches over the high sofas being one course lower than the central arch. All five are ogee and set on modified stalactite capitals and granite columns matching in height. Pairs of domes on each side flank the central vault where the width precluded the use of a cupola. The door under a relieving arch has a handsome hour-glass motif engraved above it at a later date. The responding arches are carried on six stone segmental columns engaged in the north wall and half-engaged ogee arches are expressed across the façade. The relieving arches above the four casements at sofa level are inset with plaques of tiles, remarkable for the quantity of inscrip-tive and floral work and their brilliancy as, indeed, are those inside. While each plaque is unique, there is an overall unity of design. The calligraphy is thin and lacks the boldness of the sixteenth-century inscriptions but it has elegance, and the floral and abstract decorative motifs are exceedingly rich. They are related to those in the mosque of Lala Mustafa at Erzerum and, in part at least, have been restored.

The ogee form of arch is repeated throughout the interior of Ömer Pasha where the emphasis on height recalls Nişancı Mehmet Cami.[87] The minber is plain, but good paintwork remains on the mihrab. One is struck by the Hellenistic form of the consoles on each side of it. But the most unusual feature are the four squinches. An arch spans each corner from wall to wall forming a roofed area covered by the half-segment of a circle. At the level where the arch springs, the octagon is framed within this segment by a squinch made up of four rows of honeycomb vaults reaching to the string-course. Above this, a miniature dome is recessed on a base which is made up of five sides of an octagon. The remaining three sides would, if they could be built, have to be suspended in space. The elaboration of this squinch is to be associated with early Islamic monuments such as the Friday Mosque at Isfahan. It is at once striking but clumsy. In Ottoman terms it is related to the squinches of the Muradiye at Bursa and the Hamza Hamam at Iznik of the fifteenth century, but only slightly. The mihrab is recessed in a small apse and in the south-east corner is the remarkable, modest domed square room which is the türbe of the pasha. This mosque, in spite of certain weaknesses, is the most handsome built in the provinces at this period.

The reigns of Mustafa I and Osman II were brief and sordid and Arseven lists three architects who succeeded to the office of Chief Architect after Mehmet Ağa, one simply known as Turnacıbaşı Yetim (Orphan) Ali Baba and another as Kücük Sinan. Whether these men, if they existed, were architects or not, there is no building attributed to them.[88] In 1620, Mimar Koca Kasım or Koca Kasım Ağa was appointed and held the office until 1660,[89] nearly as long as Sinan, but he seems to have been incompetent. Indeed, he was dismissed in 1642 but regained his office in 1643 only to be dismissed a second time in 1651.[90] Mayer says that he died in 1660 while Arseven says that he was dismissed again and died immediately afterwards. The story is complicated by the likelihood that Hasan Ağa, who built the Revan and Baghdad pavilions for Murat IV, was royal architect in fact if not in name in 1638–9. However, all these changes could be due to the whims of this unamiable despot.

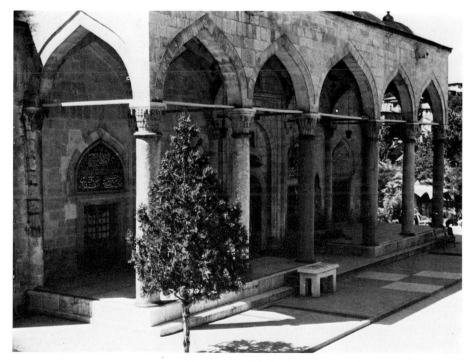

351 Ömer Pasha Cami, Elmalı. Portico with inscriptive tiles.

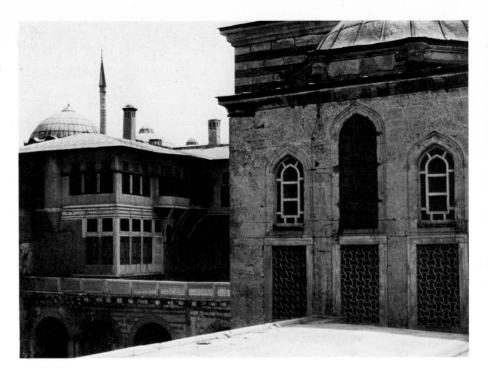

Ahmet I had built little at Topkapısaray except the small pavilion overlooking the women's quarters, and the private library between the bedchamber of Murat III and what became Ahmet III's dining-room. The library is clad in second-class tiles but possesses an elaborate and beautiful çeşme. As has been discussed, the Kafes may well date from his reign. Of Murat IV's two major additions, the Revan Kiosk was the first. It was to serve as a çilehane, or religious retreat of forty days, and stands above the tulip garden in front of the Hırkai-Saadet. The small pavilion consists of a central dome and three apses for sofas while the fourth wall has the door and a fine ocak set in it. It is faced with marble on the colonnade side, but the walls onto the garden are clad in mediocre blue and white tiles. The windows at dome level, like many at the saray, do not slant as they did at the Muradiye at Manisa[91] but are inset upright in primitive tunnel vaults. The

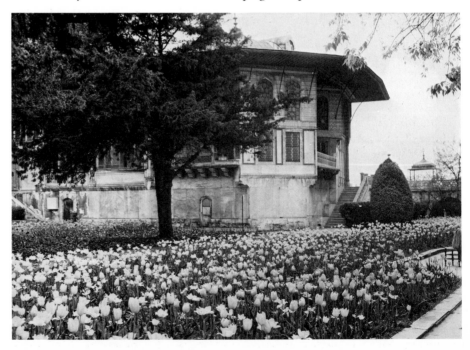

353 *Topkapısaray, Istanbul. Revan Kiosk and Ibrahim I bower.*

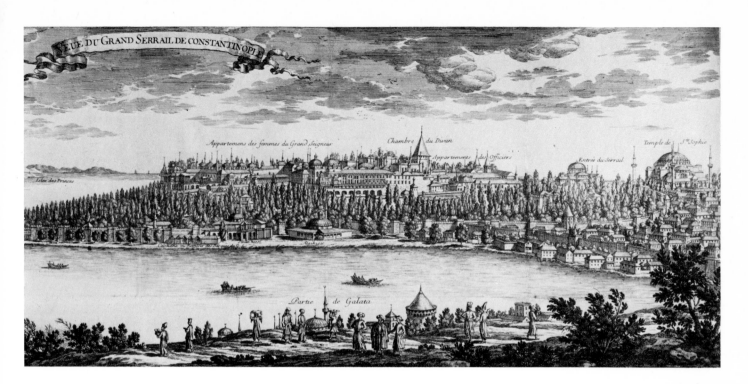

interior has lost its original paintwork, a disaster which the Baghdad Kiosk has partly escaped. The Revan Kiosk had been built in 1635 in honour of the capture of Erivan and the second celebrated the conquest of Baghdad and was built in 1638.[92] This is still the most splendid of all the pavilions and commands superb views of the Bosphorus and the Horn.

The Baghdad Kiosk is the ideal Ottoman room. The plan is based on the four-eyvan plan with a central dome and sofas filling the four rectangular bays. Between the sofas are the three doors to the porch, which rides on columns on all sides, and the huge bronze ocak. The façade has a two-metre high wainscot of antique marbles including strips of porphyry and verd-antique which are not well organized. The interior is faultless. The red dome with its golden stars needs restoration but the elaborate gilded and painted ceilings over the sofas are in good repair. The shelves and cupboards are backed with early sixteenth-century tiles in meadow green, yellow and blue while fine panels of blue and white tile in the walls are either copies of the panels of the mid-sixteenth century on the outer wall of the Sünnet Oda across the terrace or, less certainly, originals of that date.[93] The inlaid doors and closets match the finest in the palace and have been meticulously restored. While it is grand and lofty, it remains an intimate pavilion.

Ibrahim I added the Sünnet Oda,[94] a handsome room with a very mixed collection of tiles inside and out of varying periods which came from the royal stores. They include the matchless chi'lins or Kylins panels referred to above and a frieze of stars of indigo with inset patterns of blue on white. Otherwise, the well-proportioned room is spacious but not remarkable. Ibrahim I also organized the upper terrace between the Sünnet Oda and the Baghdad Kiosk and erected the gilded bower[95] from which is obtained the noblest view of the city. It introduces the ridged cradle vault which became a more and more common feature of Ottoman architecture with its charming echo of China and India.

Kasım Ağa erected a pavilion for the summer palace,[96] the Serpetciler Kiosk; this was an important saloon raised on the monumentally high vaults of the sea wall and possessing a splendid terrace. The summer palace was destroyed by the coming of the railway in the nineteenth century.

The greatest builder at the saray after Murat III was to be Mehmet IV because of the extensive damage to the harem, in particular by the fire of 1665.[97] Once again, limitations of space forbade the alteration of the plan. The Eunuchs'

354 Topkapısaray, Istanbul. Seventeenth-century engraving showing the summer saray along the shore with, above from left to right, the Baghdad Kiosk, selâmlık, harem, Divan tower, Halberdiers' Barrack, Hagia Irene (the armoury) and Hagia Sophia. In the foreground the cap of the Galata Tower can be seen.

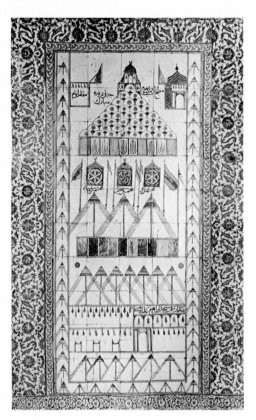

355   Topkapısaray, Istanbul. Tile panel of a camp near the Kafes.

Court, together with their mosque, was refaced in tile but although the designs are interesting, the execution in dirty whites and muddy greens is depressingly bad. Shortly after, imported tiles appear. The panels representing Mecca or Medina in the mosque of the Eunuchs and the Valide's oratory, or the tented camp in the corridor near the Kafes represent a fascinating innovation at Iznik at this time; some are signed by Osman Iznikli Mehmetoğlu who may have claims to be the creator of this style. Oddly, there appear to be no examples of the Tekfursaray period tiles in the saray.[98] The sultans were less and less inclined to live at Topkapısaray at all, and the flimsy pavilions and waterworks at Kağı- thane were now matched by the extension of the royal residences down the Bosphorus. Ahmet I built a pavilion in the royal garden at Istavros[99] which was much used by Murat IV who added others at Kandilli and Üsküdar[100] and, from his reign onwards, the straits became more and more of a pleasure resort. But Murat was a soldier and concerned for the defence of his capital against the grow- ing menace of Russia; he built fortresses at the entry to the Bosphorus as well as elsewhere in the Empire and strengthened the citadel at Kars. His military architecture retains its international style.

Although the impulse to build mosques diminished in Istanbul during the seventeenth century, more were founded or enlarged in the provinces, although few are noteworthy. It is not significant that neither Mustafa I nor Osman II built royal mosques since both reigns were brief, but it is interesting that Murat IV erected no mosque of his own and was content to embellish Hagia Sofia. Evliya[101] records his delight in this temple where he added a throne on four columns for the preacher and arranged an enclosure for singing birds near the south door. Ahmet I had organized a humble royal box under the north-east arch of the apse and endowed it with fine tiles; nothing else was done to improve this cold pew until Fossati built the present gilded cage in the mid-nineteenth century.

In keeping with his militant outlook, one of the few religious endowments which can be attributed to Murat IV is the namazgâh of the Okmeydan or archery ground above Kasımpasha.[102] It is a platform with a carpet of grass and a stone border and an ashlar minber which is a simple flight of stairs. The fallen mihrab has been mutilated beyond recognition by the local children in the last few years. The art of archery was a sacred pastime with a long and severe period of training. Most of the sultans were adept at it, more especially Murat IV.[103] The namazgâh of the archers was typical of the military type and was as much associated with the army as with the brotherhood of archers to whom the whole area was dedicated. It was also used for the annual rain festival.[104] The earlier namazgâh at Anadolu Hisar is similar in form but overgrown by weeds and p 1 enclosed by a wall to make a field of prayer. The mihrab still stands against the castle wall and must date from after the conquest to be in so exposed a position. A third namazgâh at Bursa, below the Yeşil Cami, is complete with wall and gate and comprises a platform (12 metres square) and a handsome plain minber and a mihrab with a rich stalactite half-dome over its niche; the re-use of Byzan- tine material makes it difficult to date, which is not true of the handsome fifteenth- century example above the water at Gelibolu because there is an inscription 132 showing it to have been built in 810/1407: there the marble facets have been inset like the pieces of a jigsaw. These mosques have roots in the concept of the original Mosque of the Two Kıbles founded by the Prophet at Medina. The army when on the march must often have enclosed such an area for its mescit and set up portable wooden minbers and mihrabs carried in the baggage train. Namaz- gâhs were also set up along the highways and are sufficiently difficult to find these days for even the most modest to be interesting, like that at the Valide Bend in the Belgrade Forest. They were to be erected as platforms over çeşme cisterns in the eighteenth century.

Mehmet IV endowed no royal mosque but was content to let his mother complete the abandoned Yeni Valide Cami at Eminönü. When she vowed that 338 she would build a mosque, the sadrazam, Mehmet Köprülü, persuaded her to 357

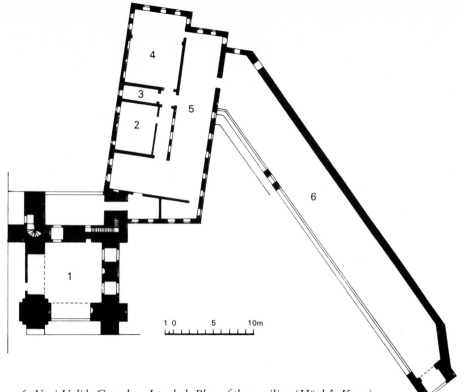

356 Yeni Valide Complex, Istanbul. Plan of the pavilion (Hünkâr Kasrı).
1 Royal box; 2 bedchamber; 3 water closet; 4 salon; 5 hallway with kitchens beneath;
6 covered passage from the precinct.

finish the work of her lively predecessor, Sâfiye Sultan, rather than embark on a
completely new and yet more costly project. The foundations were there and
the lower walls partly achieved and it was already a Valide's mosque. The Valide
Hatice Turhan Sultan was as able and as noted for her humour as Sâfiye, and it
would seem that the plans were filed in the archives so that the new architect,
Mustafa Ağa, could start work at once.[105] It must have been a sad assignment for
a creative man, if such he were.

The Valide was determined to survey the work in progress, so the first task
of the new architect was to erect a kasır or large pavilion. This apartment is
approached by a magnificent covered ramp which is a development from the
open ramp of Sultan Ahmet. It rises across the south end of the mosque to reach
a grand door which admits to the hallway or sofa which stretches from end to
end of the kasır.[106] Below are low but large kitchens. At the south-east end of the
hall is the salon with panels of late tiles from Iznik except where a marble plaque
was inserted a century later. The stained-glass windows are of larger design than
those of the sixteenth century and there is a fine painted ceiling – although not
to be compared with that of the Kafes – with a small inset dome where the paintwork conceals rough workmanship. There are shuttered casements looking out
towards the Horn, and a handsome ocak. A small vestibule admits to a water-
closet and to a second chamber or, more exactly, into an ante-room created by
a prettily painted wooden screen some eight foot high beyond which is the
retiring room. The hall is L-shaped and at the south-west end turns to the north
to open into a triangular lobby. This is because the kasır is set over the great
arched gate which admitted to the dependencies of the mosque. When work
began on the complex, and the kasır was, in my opinion, the first building completed, this end which is set at an angle of about forty-five degrees to the mosque
would have been sealed. After the mosque was completed, this passage was
joined to the broad upper storey porch leading to the Imperial Loge inside.[107]
This is spacious and has a gilded lattice. Access was also possible by a stairway
in the wall from the porch at ground level below, just as at Sultan Ahmet. At the
Valide, the pavilion is more spacious and it is much more enclosed compared to
the open galleries and loggias of the earlier monument.

Because the court is smaller, the ornate central cistern of the Yeni Valide is a more satisfactory accent than that at Sultan Ahmet. The twenty-four domes of the revaks and the portico are of equal dimensions and there is a central gate[108] to the north under an oddly shaped lead roof preceded by a grand stairway. There are the usual lateral doorways between the revaks and the portico, and these also are approached by stairs because the mosque stands on a high base. The lateral galleries are set between porches, that on the south having two domes and that over the side doors into the building on the north having three. These side doors are important because the ritual washing had been banished from the courtyard in the manner Sinan had established. As with the Süleymaniye, monotony is avoided by the variation in height of the arches of the arcades. The use of *218* polygonal and engaged columns and poor quality colonnettes suggests that an easy supply of antique columns was almost exhausted. Inside, the stumpy brown columns under the galleries were said by Tournefort to come from Troy but Mantran[109] implies that Bandırma was meant and this is the mainland port for Marmara Island.[110] The courtyard was a refuge for beggars and Edhem Pasha[111] reports that it was only cleared for Ramazan. In his day, Circassian refugees camped there. The inscription over the courtyard door reads, 'Health be with you; should you be worthy, enter in for eternity!'. The thought is reinforced by the half-light of the interior due partly to the use of coloured glass but mainly because of the filthiness of the windows thick with soot from the ferryboats. The tiles which should have been a dazzling display are the usual sombre blues and greens and tired whites of the later seventeenth century; nor are the brown columns cheerful.

The plan is more interesting than that of the Şehzade, its model, or indeed of *196* the Ahmediye because it is trim where the latter is obese. The dome is only *341* seventeen and a half by thirty-six metres and the total floor area forty-one metres, yet the interior is grander and the dome feels loftier than that of Sultan Ahmet Cami. This is partly due to the cladding of the piers with tile, which reduces their thickness more successfully than fluting, and partly because they are not as gross as the elephant feet of Mehmet Ağa. The gallery arches vary from ogee to pointed to round. The windows are ordered in patterns and the mihrab[112] and minber are of good workmanship. The sombre stencilling may be based on the original designs. The mosque has lost in splendour since the days when Lady Mary Wortley-Montagu thought it to be the finest in the city[113] and Bobovio[114] wrote about the infinite number of lamps and the red, green and yellow glass from Danzig and Venice. It was completed in 1663[115] and the opening ceremonies were of exceptional splendour. It was to have an unexpected descendant in the mosque of Sidi Mahrez at Tunis[116] besides the Citadel mosque of Mehmet Ali at Cairo.

The mosque was set in a larger outer precinct once filled with pines, cypresses and planes[117] where now there is tarmac and traffic. The wall ran the length of the east side from a Byzantine tower to where the ferry jetty used to extend until the building of the Galata bridge. Thence it ran north to the Mısır Çarşı or Egyptian Bazaar.[118] The name is significant because the mosque was endowed with the Cairo imposts.[119] The L-shaped market has six gates and eighty-six shops with chambers over the major end gateways. Its north flank once supported the stalls of the coffee grinders but these are now given over to fruiterers and such. The market is exceptionally lofty and handsome and the smell of spice still lingers there. It was damaged by fire on several occasions and by the earthquake of 1894[120] and was last restored in 1944. In the mid-nineteenth century, shops spilled over into the Valide precincts and the outer walls were gradually destroyed. Now the Osmanlı Bank has replaced the Great Gate, the Vakıflar Bank the hamam, and the İş Bank the library.[121] The tımarhane and the sıbyan mekteb are also gone while the medrese was never built. However, the very large türbe[122] with its many different tiles still stands and so does the large bow-windowed sebil which has its own su terazi. It also has the finest deep blue and red tiles to be found in the complex and it still functions. Opposite, is the

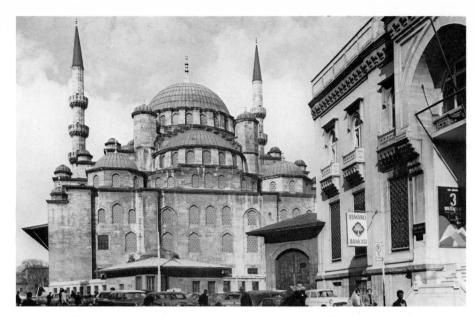

357 Yeni Valide Complex, Istanbul. Mosque and muvakkithane from the south with the gate to the ramp leading to the pavilion on the right.

remodelled muvvakithane with a low dome which was once the most important in the city. Kasım Ağa is said to have begun the Egyptian Bazaar, which was completed earlier than the mosque in 1660,[123] and may also have worked with Mustafa Ağa on these other buildings.

Mustafa Efendi, as he then was, had been appointed Chief Architect in *1052/ 1642*,[124] when Kasım was dismissed after nineteen years[125] on his completion of the Serpetciler pavilion which cannot have pleased the sultan. Mustafa was promoted Ağa in that year but lost office when Kasım was recalled from exile and reinstated so he, too, cannot have been an impressive architect. Mehmet IV probably dismissed Koca Kasım in *1060/*1650, and again Mustafa succeeded his chief and it is uncertain whether he had to give the office up again when Kasım returned to work. Between 1660 and 1665, Mustafa Ağa held office undisputedly because Kasım was dead. He was known as Mustafa Meremetci, or The Mender, because under Kasım he had been responsible for the repair of monuments, and it is to be noted that between 1658 and 1660, when he himself was certainly Chief Architect, he repaired the two Bosphorus fortresses. The term Meremetci is not particularly polite since it also means tinker or cobbler and implies a patching up rather than durable workmanship. The completion of the Yeni Valide Cami and its complex was his only major task, although at the time of his death he is reported to have been working on a palace for Davut Pasha.[126]

The commercial side of city life continued to ebb and flow and the Valide Mahıpeyker Kösem was responsible for the largest han in Istanbul shortly before her death in 1650.[127] The Valide Han occupies the site of the decayed palace of Cerrah Pasha and consists of a great gate with the best room above it admitting to a narrow, lopsided court caused by the lie of the land. Beyond this is the main court surrounded by a double tier of cells, stores and workshops. The upper storey has long, broad corridors wider than the common alley of the time. Today, they are as ill-lit as the han is dilapidated but the impressive vistas give some inkling of the original grandeur. The court is spacious, but the central mescit has been replaced by an ugly clutch of shacks following on a fire. A vaulted tunnel leads to a third court which, because of the fall of the land, is set considerably below the others. It faces the mosque of Sinan Pasha and at its corner is a square Byzantine tower much reduced in height but still large. It has a mescit in its top storey which can only be reached by a ladder. It must also have formed part of Cerrah Pasha's palace.

Very grand kervansarays were built all over the empire during the seventeenth century with plans based mainly on the concepts of the preceding century

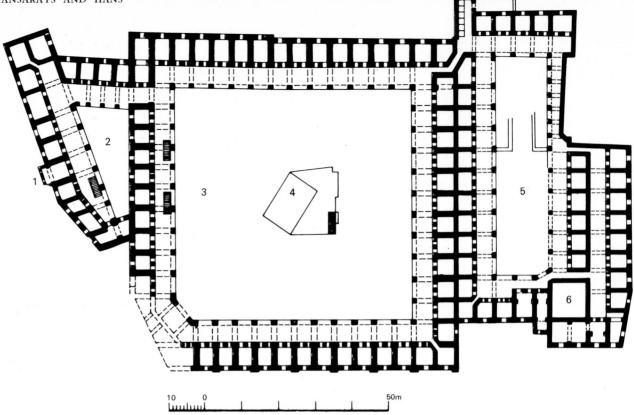

358 *Valide Han, Istanbul. Plan, scale 1 : 1,000. 1 Main gate; 2 first court; 3 second court; 4 mescit (destroyed); 5 third court; 6 Byzantine tower.*

which worked well. One of the largest of these kervansarays is at Eski Malatya 359 and related to the Büyükçekmece type. It once covered the enormous area of sixty-eight by seventy-five metres.[128] The rebuilt, groin-vaulted great hall has two rows of ten columns with one central door, a small central octagonal oculus and two smaller rectangular ones in the middle of each wing. All round, at sofa level, there are as many as twenty-seven hooded ocaks with large niches for possessions on each side and two windows above. These have the sloping sills already noted at the Çinili Kiosk in Istanbul. In the northern Anatolian provinces at Erzerum or Kars or Doğubayezit these sills are common and, indeed, the window may open inwards like a trumpet, so dramatic is the splaying. This magnifies the amount of light admitted while reducing the quantity of cold air blown in through the unglazed apertures. The twenty-seven ocaks are some six metres apart and there are thirty-three vaults, some of which have had to be rebuilt. This great dormitory was reached across a large courtyard to which entrance was gained by a vaulted gate with two unusual small porters' rooms on each side. Externally, the three sides of the court facing the street were lined with thirty-eight shops. Backing onto the hall on the south-west side of the court, twelve private cells with their niches and ocaks survive. The portico across this wall ends in two small eyvans which, if reversed, would have brought the total number of shops to forty. Here is an example of the simple flexibility of much Ottoman planning. The other three walls of the court, each backed by shops, have all been destroyed; the gateway survives. Gabriel in his plan[129] shows a series of twenty-eight ocaks between niches which are the only example of fireplaces under the portico of a courtyard that I know and quite exceptionally interesting as a concept.[130] That it was not followed elsewhere would indicate that it was not altogether a successful experiment.

Unfortunately, the once spacious han at Yildizeli is a total ruin. It was built each side of a street of shops to a plan modified, in essence, from that of Payas.[131] That at Edirnepazar, built in 1651,[132] is nothing more than a long barn built of roughcast stone. It still survives because of the wasteful and clumsy sets of four triangular buttresses on one side and the same number of circular buttresses on

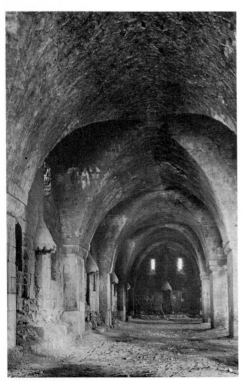

359 *Kervansaray at Eski Malatya. Fireplaces and vaults in the great hall.*

the other. The hall is thirty-seven metres by sixteen and a half and divided into three aisles by two rows of seven rectangular piers. There are high sofas along the walls with sixteen ocaks in all and the usual niches for belongings. There is only one door and the windows are small so that it must have been both gloomy and foetid in summer. Gabriel suggests that it replaces an earlier Selçuk construction[133] and this is assuredly the case.

A much better example of this type of construction is the Yeni Han at Sivas which was, fortunately, extensively photographed at the end of the nineteenth century. Gabriel[134] argues that it is a seventeenth-century building because of the formation of the arches, and the concentrated plan would support this theory; but he also suggests that there was a Selçuk han there before, and this is now less easy to verify because it is so badly mutilated. Two great gates with porches are set each end of the street which has eighteen shops on each side and central doors into the two major halls. That on the north side has four aisles divided by three rows of ten square piers to which animals could be tethered. A sofa for men runs round the rectangular hall on all four sides. On the south side there is no such sofa and only twenty-one instead of thirty piers because the mescit was set in the east corner, with a separate exterior entry, besides other offices of the establishment. It would look, therefore, as if this smaller hall were used only as a stable and a store. A feature of this han is the primitive beam construction of the roof with its beaten mud interstices forming a flat terrace for summer use. Such kervansarays as the Yeni Han would be near or in a town in order to justify the maintenance of thirty-six shops, which form too considerable a bazaar for a village or country hostel.

The second half of the century saw the rise of the great foundations of the Köprülü family and of Kara Mustafa Pasha, who was related to them. The Köprülü Han at Gümüşhacıköy was similar in plan to that at Edirnepazar and has also been destroyed. But the central street with its gate at each end is partially preserved and the town clock tower was later built over one gate. In Istanbul, he built a considerable complex at Çembelitaş set on both sides of the Divan yolu. Beyond the hamam, to which it has a passage for use by travellers, the Vezir Han[135] is built round a rectangular court on the most spacious possible scale. It has fine arcades with shops upstairs and down[136] but it has suffered from constant use although it retains some of its grandeur and all of its exterior monumentality and austerity. Across the street to the south is the small domed square library approached through a porch with tall chevron capitals.[137] Next to this is the mutilated medrese with the open türbe of the sadrazam, while the dershane has become one of the few mosques to be octagonal in shape, except for the mescits of hans such as that mentioned at Er-Restem in Syria.[138] Its capitals are debased, being mere cushions with pendants, and presage a decline in craftsmanship. The Köprülü complex was founded by Mehmet Pasha in the year of his death, 1661; he had also been responsible for building the Köprülü Cami at Safranbolu. Its courtyard is disordered and pleasantly informal and shaded by fine old plane trees. The mosque is set in the centre of the town so that there was no place for a medrese. It is large and coarsely built with a tiled roof common to this area which gives it an archaic appearance. Inside, it could never have been more than a great barn, and the clumsy arrangement of the windows on the kıble wall under the springing of the main arch is distracting; but it is not as distracting as the hideous early twentieth- or late nineteenth-century *trompe-l'œil* dome decoration common to the region.

A feature of the Köprülü endowments is the continuation of the tradition of small complexes in the capital and the increase in the size of building in the provinces during a period which is often dismissed as if no architecture occurred at all after 1617. A sadrazam of evil repute in his lifetime[139] and since, who followed after the great Mehmet Köprülü, was Kara Mustafa Pasha of Merzifon who commanded the Ottoman army at the second siege of Vienna in 1683 and whose failure to take the city cost him his head. He, too, commenced a small complex in the Divan yolu at the Beyazıt end – which was piously completed

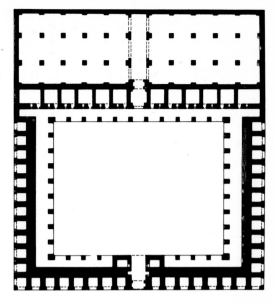

360 Kervansaray at Eski Malatya. Plan, scale 1:500.

1 0   5   10m

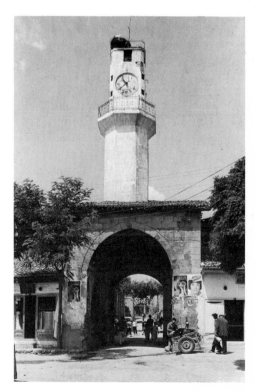

361 Köprülü Han, Gümüşhacıköy. Gate surmounted by nineteenth-century clock tower.

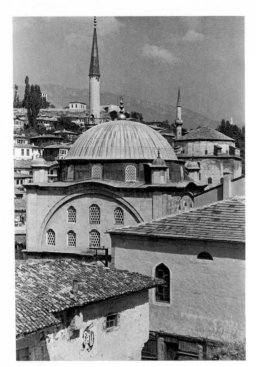

362 *İzzet Pasha Cami with Köprülü Cami, Safranbolu.*

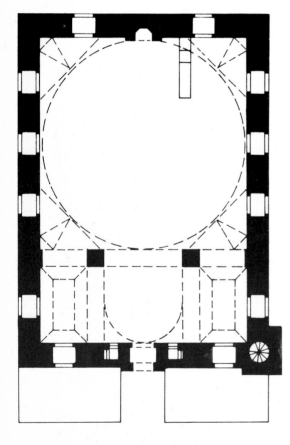

363 *Kara Mustafa Pasha Cami, Merzifon. Plan, scale 1:250.*

by his son, Ali Bey – to the plans of an architect named Hamdi.[140] Like that of his predecessor, the complex was mutilated by the widening of the street. His türbe was also open and the court was enclosed by a school. Once again, there was an octagonal mescit which appears always to have served this purpose. The most remarkable part of the complex is the sebil which is very large and has a handsome bronze grille. Kara Mustafa also built a magnificent kervansaray at İncesu and another at Vezirhan but the most interesting, if smaller, han of this vezir forms part of his complex at Merzifon. This also includes a large medrese and a mosque higher up. The mosque has another fine courtyard with noble trees, including two of the largest plane trees in Anatolia, and a very large şadırvan under a steep conical roof.[141] The mosque is simple in plan, consisting of a restored son cemaat yeri above a grand staircase, the platform glazed in and faced with hideous modern tiles.[142] Inside, it is a straightforward rectangular mosque with a deep gallery across the north wall and the dome supported on squinches. The casements are carefully placed to avoid cramping or distortion and it is a far finer building than the Köprülü Cami at Safranbolu. But although certain details are significant, such as the large windows which presaged future changes of form, it is the han which is the most interesting building of the complex.

The han is reached from the north-east gate of the mosque courtyard down a flight of stairs which leads directly into the bazaar. The arched gateway of the han opens into a rectangular court which is flanked by the ground-floor rooms with open arched galleries above, off which are the cells for travellers. At either end the central portion is closed and only the flanking arches are open. The formal and by now monotonous han form is broken up and a new interest aroused. Moreover, at the far end, the levels are varied to permit the siting of the stables underneath, in a basement down to which a ramp on the right and steps on the left lead; there, eight huge piers support the upper storeys. The first-floor gallery above it is therefore higher than the other three and a fine battery of corbels helps support it. Moreover, the closing of the arches here, and those over the doorway opposite, is due to the addition of extra cells since the galleries are very broad and would be wastefully so were it not that they were used as dormitories in warm weather. Stone dovecotes, which were later to be a feature of eighteenth-century buildings in Istanbul, make one of their first appearances at this han. The Taş Han is a good example of an architect striving towards change and also of excellent masonry.

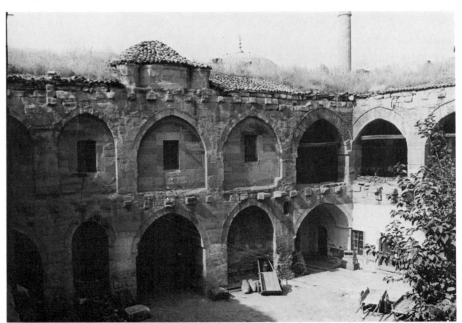

364 *Taş Han, Merzifon. Courtyard.*

Its influence was to develop at Amasya where the Taş Han of *1110/1698*,[143] wantonly destroyed by a timber merchant, had such close affinities as to suggest the work of the same architect. Its court at first-floor level once consisted of three pairs of arches with two cells projecting in between them with two windows apiece. The space between these cells was left as an open verandah. Only one cell projected at the ends, and over the gate this was carried on columns to form a portico. The cells at lower level were set behind an arcade which had larger, higher arches. The result was an energetic interplay between extruding and receding planes with additional interest and contrast due to the hollow court and the minaret of the mosque which rose immediately behind.

One other major seventeenth-century kervansaray remains to be noted: the very large foundation of Okuz Mehmet Ali Pasha at Ulukışlar, dated *1098/ 1685*.[144] It is in bad condition but it is monumental enough for its great hall to be impressive. This and the stables at right angles to it are covered by a series of pitch roofs with lipped, large and square stone tiles which are slightly concave in form. The hall is long and lofty and there are deeply recessed rooms for dormitory use all along the north side, and partly along the south. In the south-east corner is a large hamam with a domed camekân and cruciform sıcaklik with four domed corner closets and a larger dome above the göbektaş. A central door on the south side of the hall admits to the long stable with its six central piers. Further along still is the door which leads to the mosque. On the north-west corner is the extensive communal kitchen which explains the absence of ocaks elsewhere, for where they occur at hans and kervansarays they are primarily for cooking, animal and human warmth being considered sufficient to keep temperatures adequate. In the centre of the north side is the great door into the large courtyard which has one entry to the road on the east. The west flank is made up of open arcades, and along the north side is the summer dormitory behind a series of wide, arched openings; but considerable alterations have been made to this part of the inn. The design of this kervansaray returns to a formality from which architects had shown signs of breaking free; nonetheless, the setting of the stables at a right-angle and the breaking down of the great hall into compartments was new. The masonry is good and the tiling exceptional.

Provincial work of the early eighteenth century is not of major importance, but an exception is to be found at Urfa where, beside the canals of Abraham, there is the elegant medrese of Abdurrahman.[145] The entry is in the south-east corner beside the stair to the roof. The cells make a long C-plan facing a broad triple-domed mosque with a tall minaret on the north-east which is reached from the sill of the end window of the portico. The mosque is preceded by a three-domed son cemaat yeri with unusual recesses under semi-domes at each end and two early eighteenth-century capitals. The very beautifully inlaid and carved door is set back under a marble arch of black and white diamond-shaped voussoirs beneath a typically eighteenth-century inscription painted black and set in a series of small cartouches. Above all this is a larger black and white marble frame with a pronounced ogee arch. All three mosque domes are steeply pitched. Either side of the mosque, uniting it to the belvederes and the ends of the east and west medrese porticoes, are elegant arcades with pronounced cresting. They have wide arches with keystones in the form of curvular brackets and lissom columns like those of the porticoes. The thirty-two cell medrese has a dershane opposite the mosque and a summer eyvan beside it. The vista down the north portico is very fine, as is the sizeable garden with its central pool in the Syrian manner. Gabriel describes this foundation as one of the last in a pure Ottoman style,[146] but it seems more Syrian than Ottoman in style.

In the year 1700,[147] the Sadrazam Hüseyin Köprülü Pasha, known as Amcazade because he was the cousin of Fazıl Ahmet Pasha, built his large complex at Şehzadebaşı which included his türbe and other graves, a mosque and medrese, library, shops, a sebil and a çeşme, together with the very fine tabyrinth trees in the garden court. The organization is in keeping with those of the later complexes of the Divan yolu and the architectural details are mainly traditional.

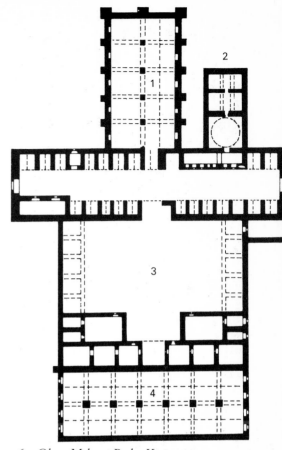

365 *Okuz Mehmet Pasha Kervansaray, Ulukışlar. Sketch plan. 1 Dormitory and stables; 2 hamam; 3 yard; 4 dormitory and stables.*

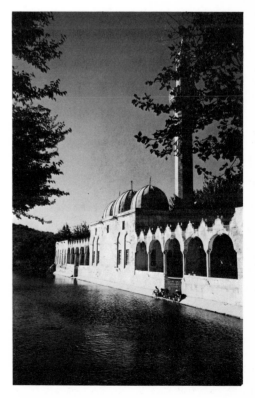

366 *Abdurrahman Medrese, Urfa.*

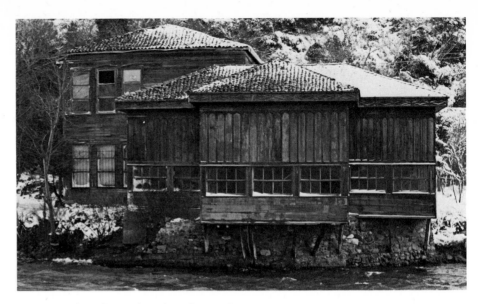

367 Köprülü Yalı, Kanlıca, from the Bosphorus.

Once again, the mosque is octagonal, but it has a portico which is not the normal three-domed porch because it has to recede in conformity with the angles of the octagon; this recession is happily used to link the mosque with the cemetery in the north-east corner onto the highway; to the north-west, it joins the mosque to the revaks of the medrese; the medrese, in turn, is linked to the library building which connects with the highway wall and the gate and so completes the square. The library is on the first floor and so sets a precedent for the city. Beneath it, facing onto the street, are the shops in its supporting vaults. The plan is compact, but the courtyard is spacious and thus the relatively small complex is given a feeling of size. A significant feature is the dominant rectangular block of the library because it is the one unit unmasked by arcade or grille. Another feature is that, like others of the later seventeenth century, the buildings are welded into a group rather than suitably arranged, which is what would have been done in the sixteenth century or before. This is important, for without some sense of flow developing in the architecture no transition to baroque could occur. The immediate heir of the Amcazade foundation was that of Çorlulu Ali Pasha built eight years later,[148] but this clearly belongs to the new period which served as the entr'acte between the dying classical and the coming baroque, the Tulip Period of Ahmet III, so-called because of the sultan's love for these flowers. In 1708 he instituted the Festival of the Spring when at night the tulip gardens were lit by coloured lights.[149] He also appointed Şeyh Mehmet Lalezari the first Master of the Flowers.[150]

The most famous yalı, or waterside mansion, on the Bosphorus was also built by Hüseyin Pasha. It was completed about 1698[151] between Anadoluhisar and Kanlıca. It is now in a deplorable condition and has lost its wide eaves which projected above the water. The plan consists of an anteroom in which servants waited and a wooden-domed central hall with a marble basin and fountain; from this hall open three chevets or bays for sofas with coffered ceilings: a plan related to that of the Baghdad Kiosk. The external use of wood and the large and low-set windows of the sofas contrive to give a Japanese effect which would have been stronger when the building was freshly painted red. The interior has been used by fishermen as a place in which to dry their nets and the decoration is sadly decayed. It is among the first examples of the new order which was to become fashionable under the leadership of Ahmet III, but the plan is as old as that of the Çinili Kiosk in its antecedents and endowed with some of the same symbolism. A series of panels above the windows is brightly painted with stylized flowers in vases; the panels are related to certain tile panels in the mosque of Sultan Ahmet, and richness of colour is matched by the primitive execution

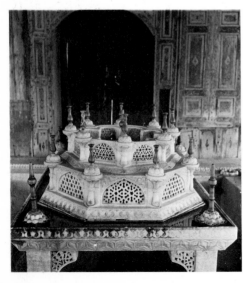

368 Köprülü Yalı, Kanlıca. Fountain in the salon.

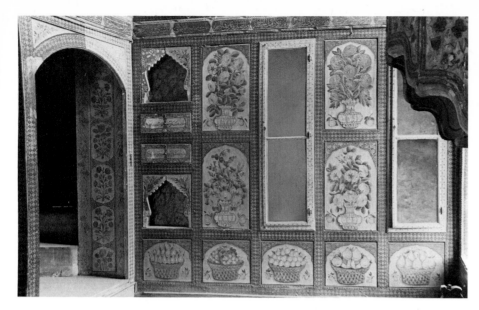

369 *Topkapısaray, Istanbul. Dining-room of Ahmet III.*

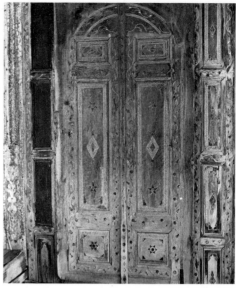

370 *Köprülü Yalı, Kanlıca. A painted door.*

to create an air of innocence. This is also marked, for example, in the little dining-room of Ahmet III in the selâmlık of the saray which was redecorated with panels of flowers and bowls of fruit for that monarch. The Köprülü yalı is also important because it represents the first serious urban development of the shores of the Bosphorus and the consequent relaxing of the strain of life in the capital.

At first sight, the Yeni Valide Cami at Üsküdar, built by Ahmet III in honour of his mother – Gülmüş Emetullah – between 1708 and 1710,[152] is in the old tradition although it lies lower than similar earlier mosques. There is also a flattening of the recesses of the doors and windows which indicates a weakening in the style. The plan is based on that of Rüstem Pasha Cami and the interior suffers from noisy paintwork and the mediocre quality of the tiles round the mihrab.[153] It has undergone a major repair lately. The mosque is set in a spacious and shady precinct entered through a high archway, above which is the sıbyan mekteb built of one course of brick followed by a course of ashlar and brick headers alternating. If the interior is overdecorated, the mihrab and minber are handsome and so is the mihrab of the hunkâr mahfil. The türbe of the Valide and the courtyard are also noteworthy. The tomb is large and open and consists of an octagon of shallow multifoil arches set beneath broad ogee arches supported on engaged columns with stalactite capitals. On the crested drum a fine mesh cage is set with the aim, as always, of admitting the rain to the garden tomb beneath and keeping out the birds. The bronze grillework in the windows is of fine workmanship. Next to the türbe is a sebil with, over the cistern, a shallow dome expressed in its pent roof, in a form seen in engravings of the lost Incili Kiosk and elsewhere. An additional semi-dome projects over the grilled windows from which the water was issued. The neat ogee arches above these windows share their capitals and thus create a strong movement. The sebil arches have a narrow span and thus a greater sense of flow than the static, digni-fied arches of the tomb, light though this is for its size. Beyond the sebil is a pretty çeşme with a scallop shell for a half-dome in a dentillated frame but with bold cresting above. Beyond this, again, is the east gateway into the precinct which seems suddenly sober after so much that hints at baroque. The courtyard contains an octagonal şadırvan related to the sebil and the türbe and deriving from the cisterns of the Sultan Ahmet and the Yeni Valide at Eminönü. The grilles be-tween the arches are highly elaborate and although forming a distinct pattern have the effect of entangled thorns or torn leaves. Again, the ogee arches share the same stalactite capitals and the keystones have rosettes set in them. Their stonework surrounds are carved to match the grilles as is the cresting above the cornice. The lead dome curves gracefully to carry a tall and elaborate alem. The

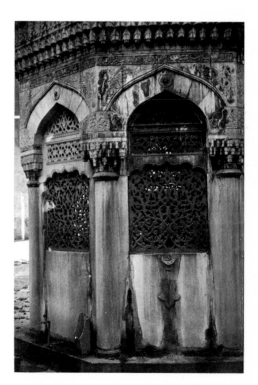

371 *Yeni Valide Cami, Üsküdar. Detail of cistern.*

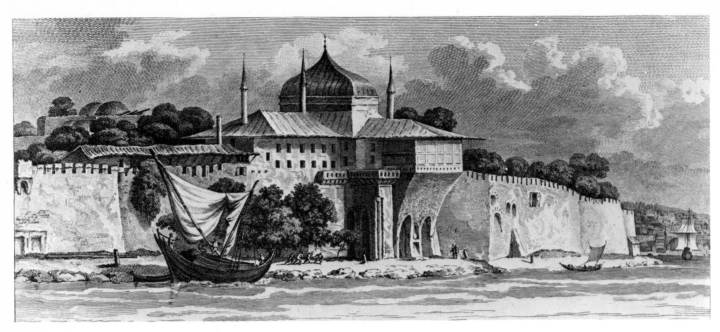

372 Incili Kiosk, Istanbul (see pages 338 and 365). Eighteenth-century engraving. The pavilion was built over the vaults of the church of St Saviour Philantropos.

revaks round the court are shallow and the small domes are carried on pointed arches; significant of the rising value of metal, perhaps, the finials are of stone. The portico lies behind three large arches, deep-set under three vaults and two domes, presenting an almost flat façade, with the door in a dogtooth frame dominated by an elaborate gilded and painted inscription in that small and thin calligraphy which had gradually replaced the bold strokes of the great period. The stalactite semi-dome over the main door has gone and with it a sense of the mediaeval.

This was to be Ahmet III's imperial mosque just as the Yeni Valide Cami at the Galata Bridge was Mehmet IV's. He also rebuilt the minarets at Eyüp, slender and fluted in the new style and with double şerefes. His domestic architecture or waterworks were to be more significant. The more interesting mosques of his reign were built by his ministers. His sadrazam, Ali Pasha of Çorlu, nephew of Mustafa II, continued the tradition of the small complex on the Divan yolu, completing his mosque in 1708.[154] It is very small with a miniature portico which is balustraded in and with capitals which mark the new style; this is no more than the decline of the stalactite, for they are round with one lonely pendant at each corner. The mosque is set at the end of a long and narrow garden which contains the şadırvan, and all along the north side is the first medrese with its colonnade. Along the south are the back windows of a second medrese, and to reach its portico and its dershane opposite this one must either enter by a second street gate or walk right round the mosque. In the south-east corner of the complex is a stone sıbyan mekteb set above a postern gate. The parallel arrangement of cells is unusual and partly accounted for by the probability that the first medrese was originally a tekke, the pır of which had a set of small chambers at the gate. The street wall consists of an arcade of columns and arches and grillework which has a new openness and lightness compared with that of Atık Ali Pasha nearby. It is related to the sebil windows of the period.

A unique mosque is that of İsmail Efendi, Şeyhül-İslam, who died in 1725. It was completed the year before his death[155] in the Çarşamba quarter of the city. It is built to the dimensions of the Ka'ba at Mecca which explains its odd plan. There is a sibyan mekteb over the gateway on the street side to the west and a postern gate through the small burial plots on the south where the mosque itself protrudes into the court; this has a şadırvan. On the east there is a small darül-hadis. The mosque is built high above vaulted shops and reached by a stair. It was rebuilt rather than restored in 1952[156] – except for its five-dome portico – and the interior is bright and fresh but retains the old proportions, including those of the wooden gallery which runs round its three sides.

The tombstones of the founder and his relations are large and tall and form an important part of the complex. Whether the architect took them into account when drawing up the plans is debatable, not, I think, because architects were unaware of the importance of clusters of erect elements within a given group of buildings, but simply because tradition and the exigencies of the terrain dominated the organization of the complexes. Nonetheless, these stone thickets and copses skirting the foundations along the Divan yolu or, in particular, at the Amcazade complex are highly important foils to masses of masonry, and form a transition between natural growth, above all trees, to man-made structures. In earlier Ottoman architecture, within the türbe the tall pier, with its turban of stone facing a corresponding symbol across the length of the gravestone, was used with dramatic effect; this was the case at the Candarlı türbe at Iznik and that of Pertev Pasha at Eyüp. It could be used poignantly, for example, at the türbe built by Dalgıç Ahmet at the Şehzade for the Sadrazam Ibrahim Pasha in 1603[157] where the tomb of the minister lies amid the splendour of the finest faience but where, a little to one side, are the two miniature cenotaphs of his son and daughter in the shadow of his greatness. With the türbe of Süleyman I, the crowding in of princes and lesser sultans has destroyed the intention that the sultan should lie – just as his father, Selim I, does yet – in solitary grandeur. Although the placing of the small coffin of his beloved Mihrimah was emotionally apposite, such nonentities as Ahmet II should have been deposited elsewhere. In these examples, and always because he was organizing an interior space, the architect could exert control over the effect that he hoped to achieve. But when it came to open courtyards and grave plots, then time and chance would multiply the memorials, new ones would be erected, the old would lean, eventually to fall and be left on the ground in accordance with tradition. Nonetheless, the architect could imagine a cluster of miniature towers in a certain area of a complex, even if he could not organize a dramatic effect. In the precinct west of the İskele Cami, for example, at the north-west corner of the portico there is a tomb with a grandiose stone turban under a canopy; this is particularly important because it closes the southward vista through the colonnade with a magical silhouette and because its elaboration projects from a bare expanse of wall. This was not a contrived effect but due to exigencies of space, although it must not be overlooked that good work sits happily beside good work and whoever chose this position for the tomb had a poetic eye.

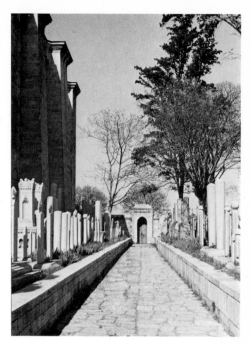

373 Süleymaniye, Istanbul. Tombstones.

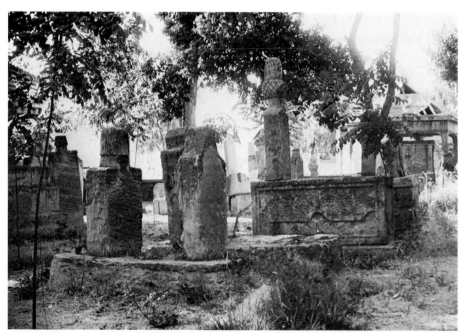

374 Karaman. Mevlevi dervish graves.

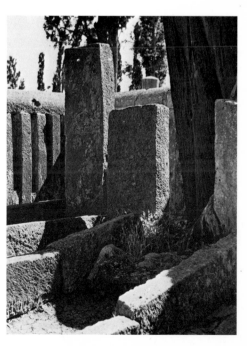

375 Topkapı, Istanbul. Graves.

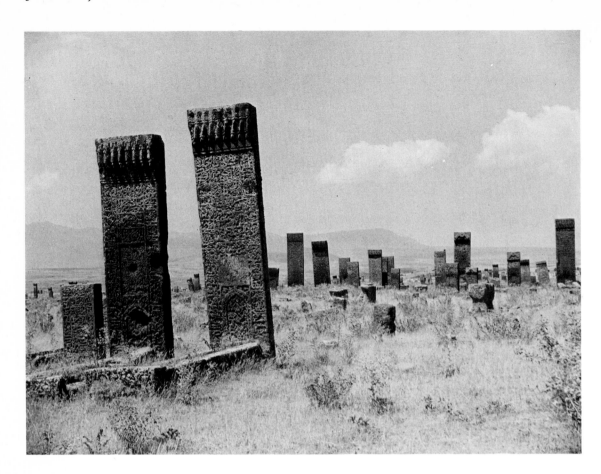

*376 Ahlat, Lake Van.
Traditional tombstones.*

The İsmail Cami is an oddity, although it conforms to the break-up of the traditional organization of the complex, and it had no heirs; the buildings of Damat Nevşehirli Ibrahim Pasha are the forerunners of the new era. The son-in-law and sadrazam of Ahmet III was a man of intellect who was in advance of his time. Apart from civilizing his master, he attempted to establish an Ottoman printing-press and revive the art of tile-making. His judicial murder spared him assassination, and the lynching of his corpse was the popular expression of hatred for a tax-gatherer grown immensely rich; that his fate may have been deserved, does not detract from his achievement nor diminish the setback to Ottoman progress. The tiles produced at Tekfursaray[158] are too thick and clotted in quality 35 to reach the clear excellence of the best Iznik examples, although rich colours, including red, were revived. But revivalism ran against the trend towards paint and plaster which grew stronger and stronger. Tiles are permanent. The sultans took the old ones down and put them up again, sometimes re-arranging them and mixing their periods as Ibrahim I did inside and out of the Sünnet oda or Murat did at the Baghdad Kiosk, but they were a conservative art form like mosaic and inflexible. The Tekfursaray potteries were always an economic liability and could not survive the death of their patron. Excellent examples from them are to be found in the mihrab of Cezeri Kasım Pasha Cami at Eyüp, dated *1138*/1726 and signed by Osman Iznikli Mehmetoğlu. The custom of dating is helpful. They include a series of panels depicting Mecca which are the most delightful products of this kiln. The largest collection of all was assembled for the Hekimoğlu Ali Pasha Cami at Samatya to which reference will be made later. There is also the sumptuous ocak from a pasha's saray in the Victoria and Albert Museum, London.

In *1133*/1720.[159] Ibrahim Pasha built the darül-hadis opposite the Şehzade 37 cemetery, which was among the richest and most heavily staffed of all.[160] The handsome but small door into the spacious court is richly inscribed. It is set between the square mosque and matching library-dershane each of which has

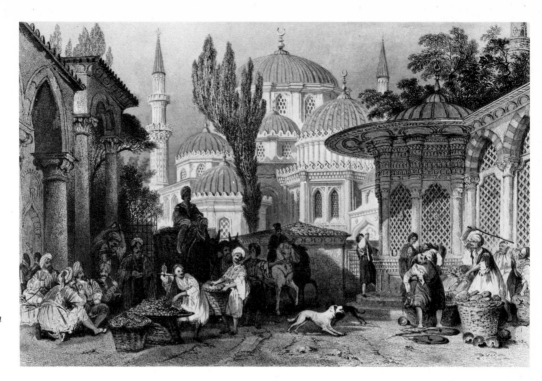

377 Nevşehirli Ibrahim Pasha Sebil, Istanbul. Nineteenth-century engraving. Behind are the mosque and türbe of Şehzade, with the türbe of Ibrahim Pasha on the left and that of Rüstem Pasha, partially obscured, right. (See page 252.)

arcaded galleries on its two court sides. They are entered through their east and west flanks respectively and their porticoes are united by triple arches that stand before the street door. These serve to join the roofs of the two porticoes and unify the north side of the court. To complete this unity, the steps up to the balustraded sofas of the mosque and library ascend to low landings under the slightly narrower arches of the entry which face the grilled casements flanking the gate. The portico arches are very broad but slightly pointed and rest on baklava capitals. The two buildings stand on foundations of alternating courses of stone and brick but are faced with plaster at portico level. The change of surface and of arch form is definitive but not yet baroque. The lintels of the doors are carved with stylized flowers and leaves in pots and jars, some on little tables in a very Chinese style, and they are related to the painted wooden panels of the Tulip period of which Ibrahim Pasha has claims to have been the greatest patron.

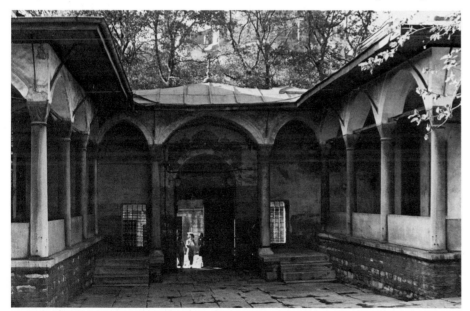

378 Nevşehirli Ibrahim Pasha Darül-hadis, Istanbul. Main door to the enclave, with dershane and library porticoes. The mosque of Şehzade rises behind.

A broad court opens before the mosque and library with the şadırvan and cells of the post-graduate college behind. These form an orthodox C-plan, with porticoes, on baklava capitals which are traditional, save for the highway side where the same problems of space that deformed the Zal Mahmut Pasha mosque make them impossible; there, vaulted cells with an eyvan in their centre destroy the symmetry. The narrow graveyard which runs beside the street has an arcaded wall of columns and bronze grills under flowing arches behind which the lofty tombstones stand in ordered ranks. At the corner of the street is a sebil which has claim to be the most beautiful of its time because of its elegant proportions. It is related to the sebil and şadırvan of Ahmet III at the Yeni Valide mosque at Üsküdar but has a single dome with eaves which extend above the five grilled windows under multifoliate arches. The eave continues over the doorway in the side street and the pretty çeşme beyond. The unifying flow of the roof is logical but the extension of the eaves, along with the lead awning over the entry to the complex, presages a growth into the chinoiserie extravagance of later doorways of the century when baroque was established. The sebil is covered in a fantasia of carved flowers and leaves and abstract designs in shallow relief which creates a surface texture which combines happily with the richness of the convex forms of the five windows that dominate the plan. Against the plain external wall of the mosque and the openwork arcade of the cemetery, the sebil is rich but modest in size. Sebils were to be the ideal medium for Turkish baroque well into the nineteenth century for water in itself is the essence of baroque, as the great fountains of Rome demonstrate. But the concave elements and the arabesques curvetting under the grilles are all forms which had been part of the Ottoman and Islamic tradition. What has happened is that the curves are boldly used and the decoration has spread over the whole surface less from *horror vacui*, which is nothing new to the Orient, than exuberance, and that the parts are bound into a whole which, if small, is notwithstanding perfect. There is movement, and the curves order that movement; in this sense, this is the first baroque building in Istanbul. The complete circle of the şadırvan of the Valide at Üsküdar is too complete and ordered to be baroque. It is, moreover, an octagon, and the interior çeşme is also made up of the greater part of an octagon so that the flow is not complete. With the sebil of Nevşehirli Ibrahim Pasha it is; and because, of necessity, a sebil cannot be completely round it encounters the tension of the straight wall in which its door and the çeşme are set.

In Anatolia, Ibrahim Pasha built the model town of Nevşehir with ordered streets and a long, broad piazza between the market and his mosque. It was a new conception and the town is still unlike any other in Anatolia. The religious need for a square hall was to frustrate the development of a truly baroque plan, and the square-domed mosque with its large mihrab apse is not new in conception. It dates from 1139/1726.[161] Set on the side of the citadel hill with its medrese and library above it, together with the narrow lanes of the residential quarter, it is enclosed in a large precinct and commands fine views. The north and main gateway stands at an angle and the şadırvan is placed off-centre in order that the diagonal path to the north door should not be obstructed.[162] The gateway is impressive and so is the lesser gate to the south-west above a flight of stairs. The workmanship in this mosque is excellent but orthodox. However, the windows of the son cemaart yeri are cramped against the responds of the arches of the three domes and so is the window beside the minaret. Only certain details point to coming change. The corner turrets above the buttresses are thin and stand out alone at roof level while the eight turrets of the octagon each with a tall alem are even more slender and their outward expression begins with the flat octagonal masonry collar round the base of the dome which comes close to being a drum. The buttresses carefully correspond to the turrets, while horizontal steps reflect the springing of the semi-domes at the corners (which internally are carried on squinches) and of the main dome. Their recession is very strongly marked. The pleasant yellow stone is undecorated and the casements and lights with their egg-latticed grilles are traditional; so are the chevron capitals

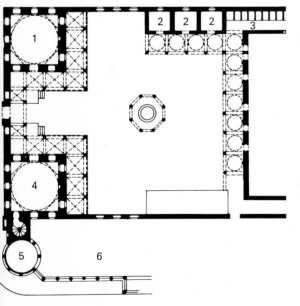

379 Nevşehirli Ibrahim Pasha Darül-hadis, Istanbul. Sketch plan. 1 Library; 2 cells; 3 latrines; 4 mosque; 5 sebil; 6 cemetery.

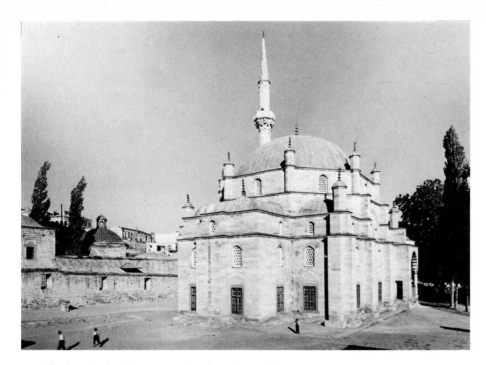

380 Ibrahim Pasha Cami, Nevşehir, from the south-east.

of the şadırvan which is large and grand. The portico has stalactite capitals, and rosettes appear in the bosses of the central pair which are preceded by a flight of C-shaped steps. The rich paintwork around the casements internally is very good indeed and this is one of the elements in the mosque which plainly show it to have been endowed by Ibrahim Pasha. It is difficult to define why the building is of its own period and not classical, and the answer appears to lie in the angle at which it is set towards the town, its high triple-domed portico above the spreading stair, and the slenderness of its turrets which recall those of Ömer Pasha at Elmalı. The minaret with its tall hood and its şerefe riding on an imitation Hellenistic capital was surely rebuilt in the early nineteenth century.

Nevşehirli Ibrahim Pasha's greatest contribution to Ottoman architecture was the interest in it which he stimulated in Ahmet III while diverting him from his more cruel pleasures. The reign saw a considerable amount of building for which it is famous, and there was an awakening of historical perception which led to the repair of existing monuments. In 1722, for example, the first major restoration of the Byzantine walls since the earthquake of 1509 was undertaken, and it is probable that the city never looked so spick and span again until after 1960 and the vast programme of restoration of recent years.

The most characteristic addition to the apartments at Topkapısaray by Ahmet III was his dining-room with its flowers and intricate tiled ocak; but the most important was the library beyond the throne-room in the third court which served as the quadrangle of the Enderun College. This replaced the Havuzlu Kiosk, the colonnade of which, with new capitals, is probably the one standing before the present Treasury.[163] In plan it consists of a domed central hall with three rectangular bays set behind twin columns with the fourth arm of the cross represented by the porch which is approached by flights of stairs from either side because the building, which is of marble, is set on a low basement. The three bays are balustraded off to form large sofas and the books were, in part, stored in cupboards in the walls which provide fine examples of inlaid woods. Above casement level are panels of seventeenth-century tiles of varying designs and some distinction said to have been brought from the yalı of the Sadrazam Kara Mustafa Pasha on the Bosphorus. This is an example at once of the re-use of tiles, the rapid decay of private dwellings, and the total nature of death duties in the Ottoman state.[164] The rectangular bays have painted vaults and the central dome is also painted, the triple honeycomb console from which it springs having

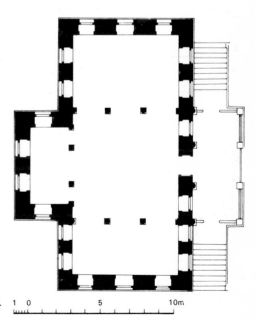

381 Topkapısaray, Istanbul. Ahmet III Library. Plan, scale 1:250.

its contours picked out in paint. Some of the marble columns are round and some are polygonal, and the stalactite capitals have long corner finials and narrow necks banded with rosettes. There is an elaborate çeşme with niches each side and a large crest beneath the central arch of the portico which, with its dome, is slightly larger than those flanking it. The inner of the two windows on the south side of this portico is cramped against the engaged column at the end and so draws attention to the main asymmetry of this pavilion, which is splendidly faced in marble. Its lopsidedness arises because the south bay is only 3·78 metres deep whereas the north bay is 4·88 metres.[165] The north bay was the model, for there the windows are decently spaced whereas in the south bay they are cramped. Once again one is driven to suppose that the Ottomans ignored such faults when they resulted from necessity, and the only reason that can be suggested in this case is that the foundations of the Havuzlu Kiosk were re-used and Mimar Beşir Ağa could not make his plan fit.[166]

Inside there is a second surprise because the normally slightly pointed central arch of the west bay is flanked by two rectangles, as if door frames had been hoisted onto capitals. Finally, the transition from the square to the octagon is made without resort to pendentives or squinches, the vacuum being filled with triangles of ceiling covered with floral decoration. What is significant in this is the return to a primitive use of timber to span the gaps, as if either of the more sophisticated forms had not yet been invented. It is a form which developed with the construction of inset wooden domes, yet here the dome is over seven metres in diameter and covered in lead.

The windows are excellent examples of their period and belong to the type which had already appeared at the Yeni Valide Cami at Eminönü and which was used constantly from then on. The change was partly due to the importation of large panes of glass and partly to a love of light. Colour was reduced to decorative borders inset in clear panes of glass. In the library there is a central arched pane with a clear rectangle in the middle and small pieces used in the inscriptive plaque below; a third of the area at the top is filled with a lively ornamental design. The deep frame is of clear glass over which a sinuous line snakes, ancestor of Art Nouveau. Where there is colour, it is used boldly if less richly than before and it is limited to two or three hues such as red, blue and yellow. This is the only detail of Ahmet's library which directly heralds baroque. The building was completed in *1132/1719*,[167] the year before Yirmisekiz Çelebi Mehmet Efendi

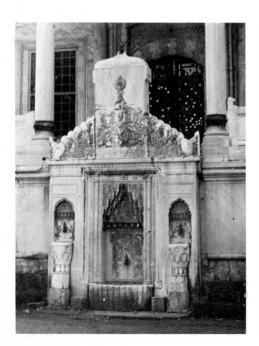

382 Topkapısaray, Istanbul. Ahmet III Library portico and çeşme.

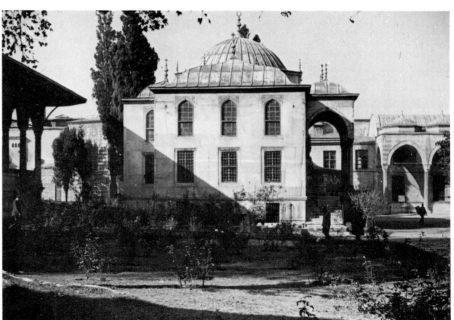

383 Topkapısaray, Istanbul. Ahmet III Library in the third court, with the throne room on the left.

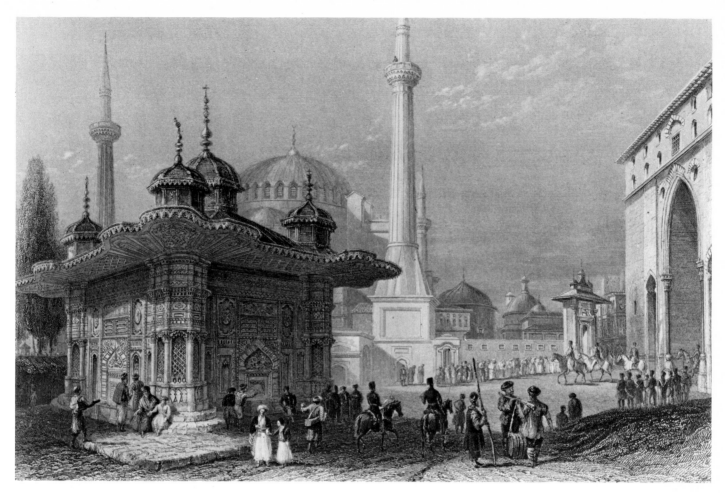

384 Nineteenth-century engraving showing the Ahmet Fountain, Istanbul. The Gate of Majesty with the saloon above intact can be seen on the right. Behind are the royal gate to Hagia Sophia and the imaret.

went as Ambassador to France which, with his immediate delight with the style of Louis XV, was to have a profound influence on Ottoman architecture. Eventually, a train of French and German architects like Préault and Melling among other foreigners sought their fortunes in Turkey culminating in the Fossati brothers and Montani in the nineteenth century and d'Aronco in the twentieth. What is important with the library is that there was awareness that the old order had ceased to inspire; this resulted in a willingness to accept new forms which, when they came, were to grow out of existing decoration and accepted religious planning.

Yirmisekiz brought back the plans of many details of Versailles and Marley-le-Roi which led to the clumsy imitation of only partially understood ideas. For the delight of the Court, a fantasy world of pavilions was erected beside the marble quays at Kağıthane. It was really no more than a field of 173 tents since the kiosks were built of lathe and plaster, their frailty adding to their delight. Nothing was farther from the ideas of permanence and overwhelming pomp that created Versailles, even if much of the workmanship of that palace has been found to be shoddy. Ahmet III's pavilions and pleasure domes are all lost because they were wantonly destroyed upon his overthrow.[168] From accounts like that of the French Ambassador, the Marquis de Villeneuve, who presented forty orange trees in tubs to the frivolous enterprise, the pavilions were Ottoman pomaded *à la française*. Yet the desire to copy Western ways and emerge from the restraints of a mediaeval past was genuine. Nevşehirli Ibrahim Pasha's printing press was matched by the founding of more and more libraries. In the grounds of the present Vefa school, for example, all that remains of the large palace of the sadrazam, Damat or Sayit Ali Pasha, who preceded Ibrahim, is his fine library built

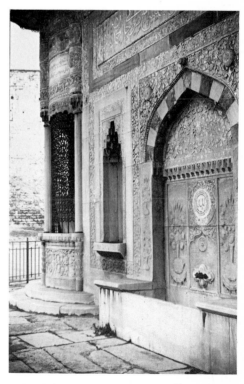

385 Ahmet III Fountain, Istanbul. Detail of a çeşme and a sebil.

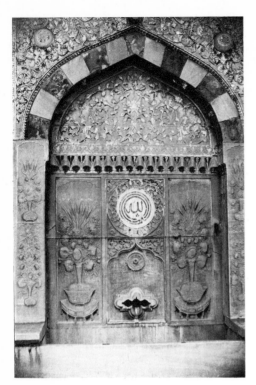

386 Ahmet III Fountain, Istanbul. Detail of a çeşme.

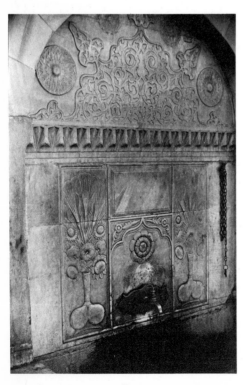

387 İskele Fountain, Üsküdar. Detail of a çeşme.

above a very high basement in *1127/1715*.[169] A stair with the remains of a balustrade and flanked by two arches leads up to a landing and thence to a small lobby projected on corbels. This opens into a passage which runs parallel to the upper flight of stairs and opens into the rectangular chamber where once the books were stored. There is good workmanship in the shutters, marblework, and remarkable tiles but the room is now used as a depot and it is impossible to inspect it properly. Below the stairs is a small but elegant çeşme.

The great fountains built between 1728 and 1732 are the climax and the end of the Tulip period. Of the seven most grand, only two were built by Ahmet III; the others belong to the reign of his successor, Mahmut I. The most famous of these fountains is the sebil and çeşme at the palace gate because it was the first *384* and because it could never be surpassed. It was built in *1141/1728*[170] and consists of a central cistern with a çeşme flanked by niches in each of the four façades and triple-grilled sebils on each corner. There is, therefore, a contrast between the curvular and the straight but not the flow essential to truly baroque monuments. There is a long poem in honour of water which contains the chronogram of Ahmet III set in the frieze among a great many foliate and floral designs in low relief. The calligraphy is framed in bands and is as elegant as it is small. Yet only one[171] of the patterns is new to Ottoman architecture: it is the quantity which contrasts with the sober lack of ornament of the sixteenth-century ideal. The polychrome voussoirs of the four pointed arches in the centre of each façade are intensely conservative; and the Bursa Yeşil Cami has flanking niches with sculpture in low relief not unlike those beside each çeşme. What is striking is the central dome on an octagonal drum which emerges from the middle of the roof, the four slightly smaller turrets over the corner sebils and the roof itself; this extends to form a deep eave under which is harboured an elaborate panelled ceiling; its triple projection over the three convex facets of each sebil is very close to baroque. The use of a band of tile and paintwork and gilding, now faded or lost, in rich profusion is also new. The painting of the fountains in order to pick out details seems to have been an eighteenth-century practice,[172] just as was the whitewashing of mosques and also of city walls when celebrating a victory.[173] The Sultan Ahmet fountain served as a gathering place and social centre and it was also remarkable because its cups were made of bronze.

In the same year,[174] the fountain below the İskele Cami was built at Üsküdar *387* by Ibrahim Pasha and his sultan. The sebils at the corners were replaced by extra spigots while the çeşmes on the four flanks are set in what can only be described as mihrab niches. The foliation has decidedly baroque features but traditional elements still predominate. The small marble Bereketzade fountain which, although much restored, is a good example of the Tulip period, was built in *1145/1732*[175] by the Defterdar Mehmet Efendi. This shows no Western influence on its patterns, but mounts a fine display of vases of fruit carved on a marble façade which is conservative enough to have a frieze of stalactites. The mosque to which it belonged was demolished, so that it had to be moved to its present site in the walls of Galata; this explains the appearance of a heavy eave above it.

More flamboyant in its decoration is the Tophane fountain built by Mahmut *275* I. Like that of Ahmet III, it was the centre of life in its neighbourhood below the Arsenal and beside Kılıç Ali Pasha Cami.[176] Whole orchards of fruit trees are paraded in panels under the stalactite frieze below the restored dome and broad eaves, which served a useful protective purpose in a wet city. Below these, which must have been splendid if they were brightly painted, is a double band of inscriptions, which once were gilded, and a broad foliate frieze. At the corners, further stalactites are bunched above spigots set in the angle below small inscriptive plaques and a strongly ribbed shell. The lipped basins under the spigots – the elaborate scroll elements of which are coils clipped off arabesques – are a truly baroque element, unlike the flower panels below in their rigid ranks. The sides are occupied by large ogee, engaged arches flanked by tall niches with stalactite half-domes. There are panels of potted fruit trees again but in the spandrels the foliate decoration shows Western influence.

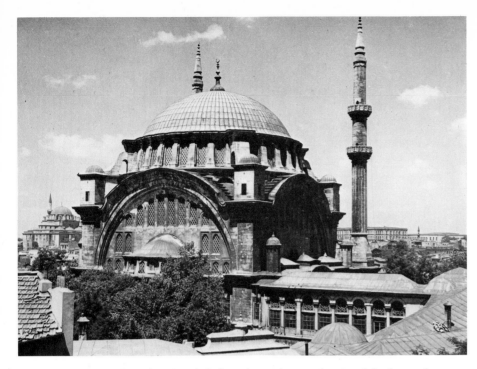

397 Nuruosmaniye Complex, Istanbul, from the south-east, showing, left, the royal gallery and Sultan Beyazit Cami with, behind right, the Law Faculty on the site of the Old Saray.

central shell. The composition of the çeşme is rich but shallow and reticent, whereas that of the sebil – three concave bays between pilasters – is strongly articulated and ends in prominent capitals in sets of three, one projecting before the other. The short rectangular pilasters which support them and divide the three inscriptive cartouches are overlaid with thick sagging straps of stone which swell towards the base of the pilasters, each with its cartouche and each an extrusion of the architrave borne by the slender columns which divide the grilles. The convoluted arches above the three windows, composed of shells and foliage, excel in fantasy and three-dimensional force those of any of the sebils yet discussed.

The window grilles of bronze, which were originally gilded, are particularily elaborate and intertwined, but follow a definite pattern partly defined by rows of small bosses. Grillework of the eighteenth century is an outstanding example of the change of rhythm during the reigns of Ahmet III and Mahmut I. Apart from their bow and their cresting, the grilles of Mehmet Emin Ağa are very traditional, that is to say they are grids of small squares knotted together like nets. Those of the earlier fountain of Ahmet III are more elaborately looped while those of Beşir Ağa sebil make a mesh of circles and small diamonds. After the Nuruosmaniye, the elaboration of grilles continued and a number of patterns and combinations of patterns was achieved including leaf designs at the Nusretiye. The love of rich detail inherent in the Islamic tradition was well suited to rococo style buildings.

The principal gate to the precinct of Nuruosmaniye was suitably grandiose and the mosque and its complex are the first considerable baroque achievement in Istanbul. The mosque has been severely criticized and the buildings of the complex ignored until very recently, but it is a work of considerable interest and by an architect with inventive and assimilative powers. The Sultan Mahmut I when he commissioned it was said to have wanted a building in the Western manner but was dissuaded from such a folly by the Ulema. The prayer hall had to be square and although this was inescapable, considerable ingenuity was used to add flow to the outward appearance below the springing of the tympana arches. Moreover, a complete break was made with the traditional rectangular avlu which here was shaped like a horseshoe. Nor are the mosque and its court mounted on a plain platform but, insofar as the terrain permits, there is a play of levels, and radiating stairways of varying form descending from an irregular terrace. This is concentrated at the courtyard end. The principal entries are the two major wing doors and, although the central north door remains the most grand, the court is more of a sanctuary within the precinct than a means of access. There is a third entry reached by an independent set of stairs through a lobby with a concave external south wall and, on the east, a small loggia of four vaults. The lobby admits to a salient wing area and there is a corresponding rectangular bay on the west side. On the north there is an extension of the mosque wall, so that between bay and wall is a spacious gallery – deriving from the lateral galleries of the Süleymaniye – with an eight-arch arcade in each case. 217 These arcades serve as porches to the two most frequented portals. Beneath that on the western side are set the handsome range of ablutions complete with stone stools for the faithful to sit on. On this side the platform is carried over vaulted shops where the hill slopes downward, and is also supported by a restored colonnade of stumpy columns with gross cushion capitals. To the south are a medrese and an imaret, the latter crushed into the western corner to create an interesting huddle of vents and chimneys when seen from the outside, and the former more traditional in form but not in decoration. There is a second large gate on the eastern side facing Cağaloğlu with upper rooms including the mekteb connecting it to the medrese. Here is a pleasant area, full of fine trees, which swells out again under the gallery. This is approached by a ramp up which the sultan rode to his loge. The second precinct contains the türbe of Şehsuvar Sultan, the mother of Osman III, in the style of the mosque and with a claim to be the first baroque türbe, and a very fine library which has been recently renovated. It is a domed cruciform chamber with free-standing columns and a broad terrace approached by sweeping stairs.

The marble courtyard consists of a tall five-domed portico and a revak of nine 39 domes, all on low drums except for those over the north doors into the court and into the mosque. Flanking the five domes on the curve of the horseshoe are six triangular vaults of varying widths. The capitals are plain with bosses at the corners while the arches spring from consoles and have shallow keystones. The voussoirs alternate in colour and there is a simple trefoil device in the spandrels. These are divided by small engaged piers. Both the high drums of the north doors are unusual in that they have windows and buttresses. These are curved beneath engaged capitals as if they were distorted pilasters. This horseshoe court is a bold but isolated attempt to introduce baroque form, and not just decoration, into Ottoman architecture. But intellectual acceptance of the baroque could not be complete in a society where superstition remained paramount. The royal interest in European culture came from curiosity about the ideas of the victorious, and not from any desire to achieve intellectual equality. Sundials, not clocks, were designed for Hekimoğlu Ali Pasha Cami and for Laleli Cami. The hour of Nuruosmaniye's foundation was still determined by the royal astronomer and the Şeyhül-İslâm scattered gold in the trench in the old style.

The concept of an external approach to the royal loge reached its apotheosis in the mosque of Nuruosmaniye. A large south gateway admits to a spacious ramp, under a barrel vault. The ramp is blind to the street but has a series of seven tall piers bearing round arches open on the mosque side. It reaches a grand gallery which is carried across the precinct on lofty arches. There is no pavilion attached, as there is at the Ahmediye, because the gallery is as big as a saloon and for this reason it is impressive. There is a fine baroque ocak.

The external build-up of the mosque can only be appreciated fully from the Divan yolu above, or from the Horn below. This build-up depends on the powerful span of the four great lateral arches (which are very slightly pointed), the emphasis of the four square stabilizing turrets, and the curvular form of the battery of tall buttresses with spreading capitals around the dome, of which there are six between each of the large flying buttresses at the four angles. A continual sense of stress, height and slenderness, is achieved by the arcade of the

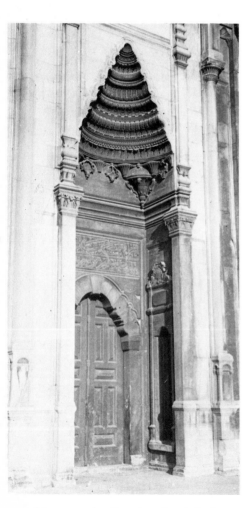

398 Nuruosmaniye Complex, Istanbul. A doorway in the new style.

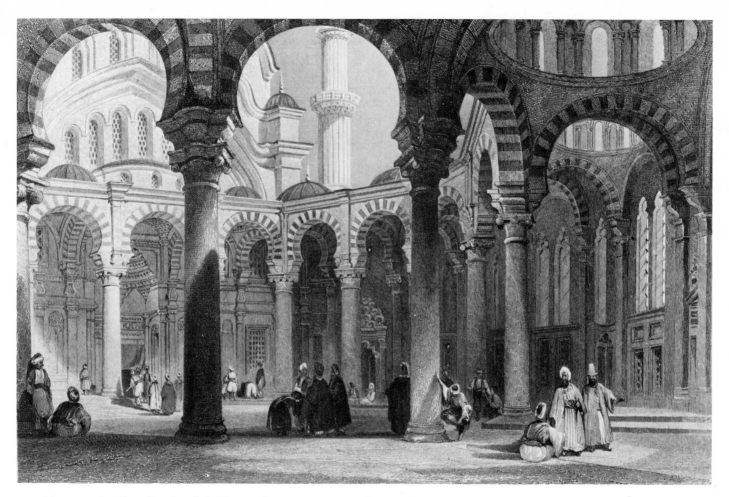

399 *Nuruosmaniye Complex, Istanbul. Nineteenth-century engraving showing the mosque courtyard without a fountain.*

royal ramp, and the upper range of windows which share each others' frames in the tympana. The minarets are fluted and their pairs of şerefes are supported on continuous circular consoles; they were no longer capped in lead but have tapering stone finials and this was a complete break with the past. A feature of the external decoration of this mosque is the extension of engaged pilasters and piers in tiers from string-course to string-course, and multiple cornices which encompass their capitals fan out along the skyline. The extremities of the curve of the great arches sweep up towards the turrets. These little turrets express the engaged pier and spreading capital again; corners are curved and the row of arches may be multifoil but the voussoir always has a keystone. The doorways take the same form but still have lateral niches, although they are made as tall and as elegant as possible. The great stalactite semi-domes set on squinches like bulbous vases have been shaved clean and converted into a series of diminishing semicircles ending in a scallop with stylized fronds as the principal decoration. They are handsome and, though forming a complete break with a dead tradition too long repeated, they still have the old flat-faced and sliced-off appearance although a shallow frame is etched round the multifoil contours. The windows are either rounded or cinquefoil at the top with some exceptions, including wheel windows with splayed terminals and triple struts between each spoke to create the effect of a rising or a setting sun.

The interior of the mosque modifies the boredom of the domed square, partly because of the size of its semicircular mihrab apse, just as many sixteenth-century mosques employed rectangular or polygonal apses; partly, also because of the grandeur of the inscription in relief which runs the whole way round the cornice below the semi-dome of the apse and the springing of the tympanum arches; and also by the insetting in the walls of galleries extended over arcades

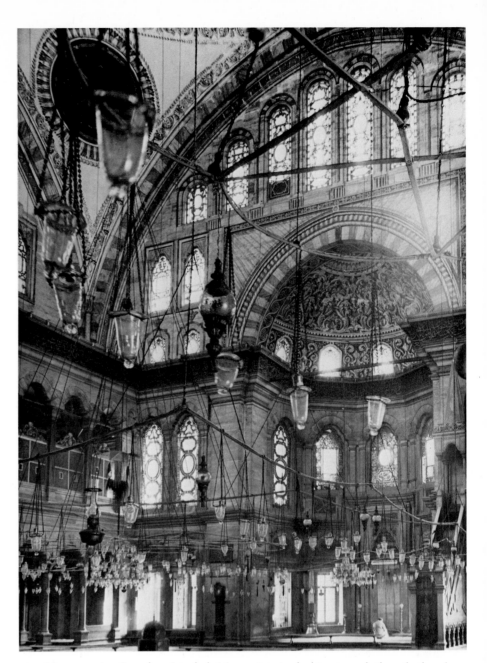

400 Nuruosmaniye Complex, Istanbul. Mosque interior looking towards the mihrab and the royal loge.

before the north door and the two bays already described on the south of the east and west flanks, like grand tier boxes at the opera. Thus below the frieze there is a continuous arcade which lightens the general effect and at three salient points breaks the uniformity of the floor plan. The glass is coloured, except in the casements, and is in need of a clean, while the paintwork has long lost its lustre. Thus this very fine hall has become musty and lacks light – though the multiplicity of windows shows that the architect planned for it to be light and airy. The heavy paintwork with its arabesques and foliation, particularly in the apse, also needs refurbishing. Nuruosmaniye's contradictions were irreconcilable, but within these limits it was a *tour de force*.

Eyice does not attribute this mosque to anybody at all, which is discreet, and Öz attributes it to Mustafa Ağa assisted by Simon Kalfa, and he is also supported by Mayer who calls him Çelebi Mustafa; but Doğan Kuban states that the architect was Simon or Simeon and, apart from his superior authority, there can be no doubt that the revolution in decoration and design could not have been the work of someone brought up on the saray or Vefa offices of the royal architect.

It is not clear whether foreign advice, French in particular, was sought but some elements of the complex remain traditional, or a possible logical development from the past; other elements in its design are alien although assimilated to an extent which makes it most improbable that it was the work of a man inexperienced in Western baroque and rococo. Whoever was the architect, Nuruosmaniye introduced a new style to the Empire which was instantly adopted as the fashion and retained its vitality into the next century. If it shocked the conservative in 1755, today the controversies are dead. Writing in 1765, Grenville, who was then Ambassador to the Porte, states that at that date the Mimar Ağa was always a favourite and creature of the Grand Vezir, ignorant of the first principles of architecture whether civil or military.[5] The Turks spared neither promises nor money in order to have the services of renegade experts in military architecture, for there were no engineers although there was a school under the Mimar Ağa where young men learnt to make plans.[6]

The passion for building continued, and Mustafa III began his reign by founding the Ayazma Cami in honour of his mother, Mihrişah Emine Sultan, in 1171/1757,[7] completing it in 1174/1760,[8] on the heights above Üsküdar. Outwardly, it is a small version of the Nuruosmaniye, but there is a greater sense of height especially when seen from the sea, because there are no subsidiary buildings or courtyard skirting the central hall. Its design is simplified and the gateways, although solid and grand and vaulted, are not embellished with shell or foliation. The south wall rises impressively above the burial ground.[9] Two tiers of engaged piers divide the windows of the tympana and end in engaged three-tier finials. There is also a fine cluster of stone dovecotes which become common on buildings of this period. The gate is handsome with a large fan-shaped canopy over the combined round steps and mounting-block. It admits to a square stair hall with two tiers of galleries with open arcades, the lower leading to the public prayer area and the upper to the royal loge. The square vaulted roof curves upward to a lofty alem and is a variation on the somewhat Jacobean silhouette of the roofs of the cemetery gateways and recalls Chinese roof forms.

The interior of the Ayazma Cami is crowded both because of the detailed ornament and coarse paintwork which covers the walls and dome, pierced by sixteen large windows, and because of the gallery supported on many pillars and recessed under a wide vault and two small domes over an open narthex. Marble, or plaster disguised as marble, replaces tiling as interior decoration, and in the gallery is a fine example of an inlaid mosaic of marble possibly imported from Italy.[10] The mihrab and minber represent the new style begun at the Nuruosmaniye but are necessarily traditional in form. Details of window framing, the capitals of the slender columns and the slightly pointed large arches over the tympana with their turrets and dome buttresses so closely follow the style of the Nuruosmaniye that it would seem either that the architect was the same man or that he had worked extensively on the former building.[11] The Ayazma also represents the Ottoman habit of standardization of parts. On the east, behind the royal gallery, is the cistern of alternating courses which gave its name to the mosque. It is worth noting that the mosque of Hekimoğlu Ali Pasha and the Çinili Cami each have a large cistern behind the kıble wall while the Nuruosmaniye is built over one. The most interesting development at the Ayazma Cami is the very high son cemaat yeri approached by a circular grand stair. The high sofas, under domes, set on pairs of round arches each side of the vaulted forehall, are belvederes over the Marmara and the European shore. This portico represents the final development of the portico from the high sofas noted at Erzerum and elsewhere; it was to be the model for the Imperial mosques of the early half of the nineteenth century.

There is an immediate predecessor to this portico at Aydın in the Cihanzade Cami, completed in 1170/1756,[12] where the portico is orthodox but is approached by an even grander stair. The mosque is set obliquely on an artificial platform raised above low arcades with pointed arches. These arches give it a falsely

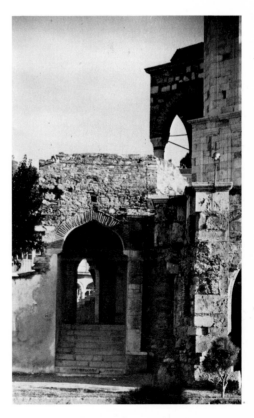

401 Cihanzade Complex, Aydın. Entry to the mosque precinct.

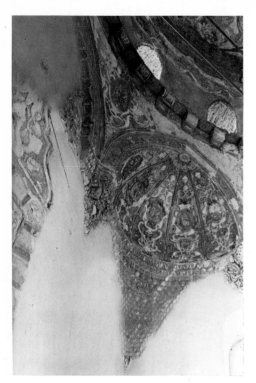

402 *Cihanzade Cami, Aydın. Above, the interior before repair.*

archaic air but the concept of exposing the undercroft was traditional and paralleled by the exploitation of foundations, as with the lofty arasta of the Laleli Cami in Istanbul.[13] The court of the Cihanzade is contained by arcades of brick on stumpy stone columns with simple eighteenth-century capitals and Tulip period floral designs in the spandrels. The şadırvan is decagonal with pretty baroque devices in the ten panels of the basin under a small dome, while the surrounding canopy is carried on mixed spiral and fluted colonnettes which are matched by smaller ones which divide the damaged grilles above the basin. The four-centred arches again give it a falsely archaic air for it is quite different in feeling from the şadırvans of earlier periods.

The interior of the mosque is a domed square room with squinches, but this commonplace plan is overwhelmed by stucco decoration with vegetal convolutions and arabesques all over the area of dome and arches and framing the windows. The squinch arches spring from consoles which are encrusted bouquets of leaves and entwining coils and achieve a hyperbole of rococo, while the corners are changed to the semicircle of the squinches by tier on tier of very small shaved honeycombs somewhat akin to the doorway vaults of the Nuruosmaniye. The minber has a tall tapering conical crown made up of circular elements like an elongated pawn from a chess set, and even the tiebeams across the squinches are entwined and embellished. The new style not only spread immediately in the provinces but some of the finest work was to be done there.

Mustafa III's imperial mosque was Laleli Cami built between Beyazit and Aksaray in *1173/1759–1177/1763*[14] and not finally restored until *1197/1783*.[15] Both Öz[16] and Kuban[17] attribute this mosque to Mehmet Tahir and Kuban states that Seyit Mustafa Ağa was responsible for its repair. The street side of its terrace has been altered by the widening of the highway. The mosque has many details common to those of the Nuruosmaniye and the Ayazma Cami including the now established debased Ionic form of capital which appeared at the beginning of the century, the form of the windows, the buttressing of the dome, and the şerefes of the twin minarets. There is also the irregular setting of the stairs which are grander than any before, and the use of engaged piers in tiers surmounted by spreading capitals which are extensions of the cornice of the court wall. The approach to the north-west door into the court is particularly splendid because a balustrade emphasizes the spreading of the stairs. The south-east corner is cut by the royal gate which admits to a broad ramp leading to the artificial precinct on which the mosque rides and, by the door to the ramp, to the short gallery

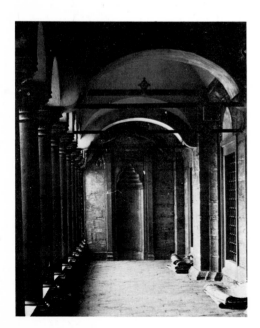

403 *Laleli Complex, Istanbul. Arcade along the east side of the mosque.*

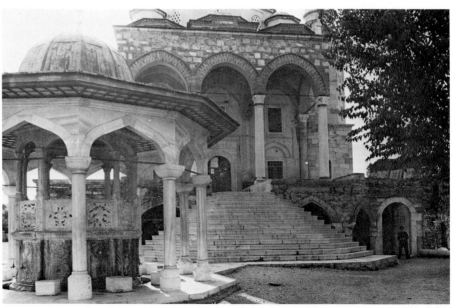

404 *Cihanzade Cami. Exterior view. The fountain and mosque are raised on a second tier of vaults behind the sweeping stair.*

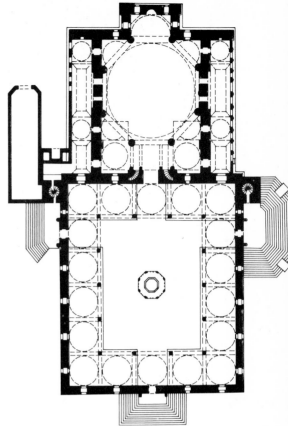

1 0   5   10m

406 Laleli Cami, Istanbul. Plan, scale 1:500.

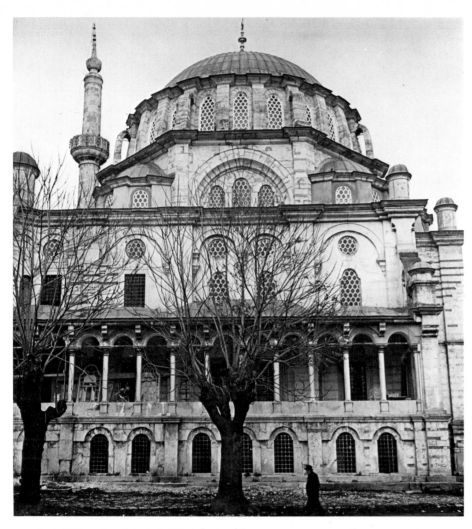

405 Laleli Complex, Istanbul. West flank of the mosque seen across the upper precinct. The lowest windows light the central hall of the market.

leading to the Imperial loge. This loge has an open arcade on both sides and so is lighter than that of the Nuruosmaniye and, because of the vistas seen through the open arches, more interesting if less powerful. The plan of the mosque is akin to that of the Ayazma Cami enlarged by lateral arcades with a monotonous range of twelve arches with consoles supporting the roof of shallow domes and low vaults. The basic rectangular plan is also emphasized by the apse.

Inside, the domed square of the prayer hall is enlarged by a domed and vaulted narthex over which is set the gallery which projects right and left of the free-standing pair of columns supporting the major dome on its north side, to form the royal loge and a mahfil. The other six columns which support the dome are engaged in the walls and the corners of the apse. Corner squinches diminish the size of the four lateral arches below the dome and the stabilizing turrets are banished to the corners of the roof where they appear as independent units. This latter feature is typical of mosques in the second half of the eighteenth century, and breaks the unity of form at roof level which was so strikingly successful with the great mosques of the sixteenth century. Inside, the eight columns supporting the faintly pointed arches carrying the dome help the sense of loftiness, while the angled squinches with the small semi-domes over the north gallery and the south apse give movement and break down the deadness of the square plan. But the mosque is cluttered by pillars supporting the galleries and by the familiar coarse paintwork. There is a return to the circular window below the springing of the arches at roof level, and the twenty-four large windows in the dome create a cordon of light considerably more arresting than at the Nuruosmaniye. Marble is extensively used in the mosque and some of the panels

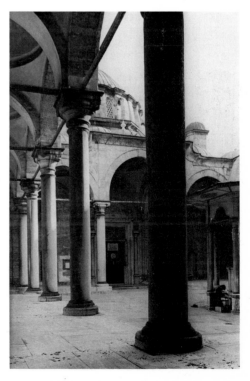

407 Laleli Complex, Istanbul. Mosque court from the north-east.

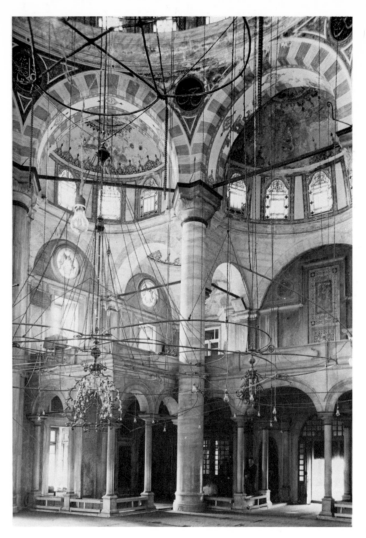

408 Laleli Cami, Istanbul. Interior from the south-east.

are very rich indeed.[18] The mosque and dome are small, the latter only 12·50 metres in diameter and 24·50 metres high whereas the Nuruosmaniye achieves 25 by 43·50 metres.[19]

The courtyard is twice the area of the prayer hall and built externally of alternating courses of brick and stone. The minarets are placed outside as an extension of the north wall and in no way interfere with the organization of the mosque façade. The fountain is only a reservoir and is set back from the centre of the court towards the north entry. There are five large cupolas over the son cemaat yeri which is divided by domed entries from the eleven cupolas of the revaks. There is a central door into the court from the north, on the axis of the principal entry to the mosque, which is not set in a semi-domed recess but is flanked by two columns and surmounted by two finials each side of a cartouche surmounted by a large baroque device. The overall effect is disjointed.

For all its details and its grand staircases, the Laleli mosque is closer to the old tradition than are the other larger mosques of its time. Its subsidiary buildings, however, are freer and the organization of its precinct, its levels, and its approaches are very much in the new manner. The principal public entry leads up a second ramp with glimpses through grilled windows down into the cemetery at road level. Beyond the mosque in the north-west corner is the imaret with a cluster of chimneys and two vents, and the two-storey medrese which shares its small court, thus completing the move to unity expressed by the close-knit group of medrese and imaret at the Nuruosmaniye. But at the Laleli Cami both are smaller and the effect is curious rather than architecturally important. At street level, west of the second ramp, is the sebil divided by three windows of the cemetery wall from the türbe of Mustafa III in which Selim III was later to be

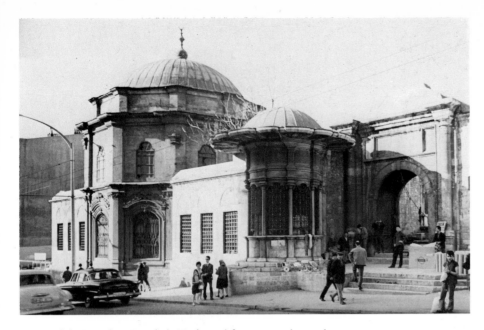

409 Laleli Complex, Istanbul. Türbe and fountain at the south-east gate.

buried after his assassination by the Janissaries. It is large and well-ordered with boldly designed window grilles within heavy frames between pilasters, and with the engaged piers of the period at each corner of the octagon and strong cornices that swell into capitals. The sebil is not remarkable for its time, although nicely set above three stairs which merge with its base and form a semicircle round its five convex windows, for it is very much in the style of Beşir Ağa; but the projecting eave makes a magnificent segmented canopy with encrusted decoration opening like the petals of a lotus above the steps. It is to be noted that the gates of this complex are vaulted and roofed in the manner of those of the Ayazma Cami and are also relatively simply decorated while expressing strength and having excellent proportions. The precinct is raised on high vaults which form a noble basement transformed into a large arasta. This has a central underground piazza with a fountain in a pool lit by high windows which appear under the lateral galleries of the mosque and add a third lower tier to the windows of the courtyard.

Beyond the precinct to the north of two ruined halls is the Çukurçeşme Han, built as an endowment for the foundation. It has several unusual features due to the irregular nature of the plot of ground available in the crowded centre of the city. The design is relatively conservative insofar as gateway and window forms are concerned, but the brick arches are plastered and the square piers of the arcade and gallery at first floor level are plain. The long rectangular court is also a trend which recurs with the Büyük Yeni Han which is of approximately the same date. The Çukurçeşme Han has a long vaulted entry passage with cells down the north side, for there is only room for latrines on the south. Apart from the five cells forming an east wing, all the others are more or less distorted, some cramped into angular spaces in order to fit round the main court. A passage leads to a smaller inner court and then to a corner room with a central pier while the south-west corner of the main court opens into a second court which again has a passage off to an extra room. The building has been mutilated by time and heavy use.

The Büyük Yeni Han is much grander and exploits the angling of its façade to set its upper rooms in a series of six projections which are impressive when seen from lower down the street. The alleys on each side also present exciting vistas because of their length. The han is three storeys high so that the court has two tiers of galleries over the long arcades of shops and stores. Its original great length has been divided by a later building in rough stone, but some idea of its old immensity can be gained from the vaulted passage under this extension.

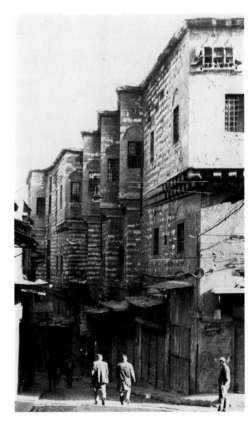

410 Büyük Yeni Han, Istanbul. Façade on to the street.

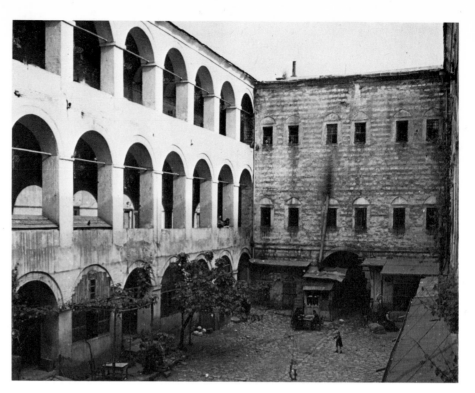

411 *Büyük Yeni Han, Istanbul. Courtyard with its nineteenth-century addition.*

The plan was imposed on the architect by the site, but he used its limitations creatively. The court was once over eighty-five metres long by fifteen metres at the widest and twelve and a half at the narrowest end. The han was one of the foremost commercial centres and possessed over one hundred and fifty cells, exclusive of porters' rooms and the shops built down one flank to utilize the irregularity of the lane on that side. There is now no trace of a mescit associated with this building, and it is possible that one of the larger rooms may have served this purpose. Farther up the street occupying the next site is the Küçük Yeni Han, also built by Mustafa III, where there is a handsome mescit on the first floor with a dome which flows up and down over the windows to create a wave like that of the dome of Rüstem Pasha and which must be counted a p 2 piece of revivalism; this could have served as the mescit of the Yeni Han as well since access is obtained from the street.

The new fashion for the baroque led to the redecoration of old apartments at Topkapısaray and the building of new ones by Mahmut I and Osman III. It was probably at this period that first the hamam and then the School of the Princes 41 were redecorated or built.[20] It is interesting to compare the bath, which has echoes of the earlier Tulip period and some formal weaknesses, with the elegant ocak of the schoolroom. The latter is an ideal rococo conceit, and the over-mantle forms four flowing tiers over which the shallow linear decoration of arabesque and scallop and flowers is gracefully carved, as are the border and shelving on either side. It is gaily painted in whites and pinks and yellows and blues, and is a pretty foil to the heavier gilded motifs of the niches and cup-board doors. The hearth is particularly elaborate and has a confidence that the work in the hamam lacks. It is surprising that fine panels of seventeenth-century tiles have been installed above the level of the cupboards, for although there are baroque elements latent in the traditional sinuous portrayal of the branches of fruit trees they belong too much to the old order and the two styles clash. The anteroom and common room are heavier and the use of tile there is less incongruous. The school is situated above the rooms of the Kızlar Ağa and approached by a Western-style stair making a complete break with the old stone tradition which, like that of early Renaissance Europe, preferred to hide rather than exploit the drama of the stairway. The treads are also of that light

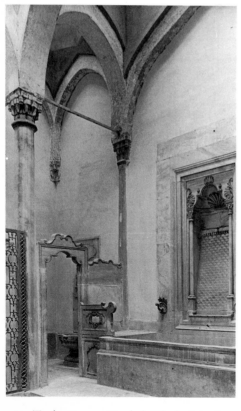

412 *Topkapısaray, Istanbul. The bath in the sultan's hamam.*

construction which is an important attribute of Ottoman baroque. The buildings were not meant to last but were settings intended to be used for a generation and then replaced. Just as Ottoman society looked on mansions and possessions as transitory so it thought the masterpieces of the past hindered new creation. It is this concern with the present moment which is important in the understanding of the baroque, its shoddy decoration and gimcrack construction. It has been preserved fortuitously through the years and patched up to its disadvantage. This, of course, is true of some aspects of Western baroque where the materials also were plaster and the workmanship rough.[21] Both in Europe and in Turkey the style has a relationship with stage scenery against which grandees could act out their lives.

The ocak of the Princes' School, an apartment which was revolutionary in concept and presaged a new freedom for the brothers of a sultan, is clearly contemporary with the even more successful ocak of the apartments of Osman III because, while its general concept is similar, this ocak is set admirably in a lofty niche crowned by a handsome shell and it is also more three-dimensional than the school fireplace. The hearth is much the same as are the niches for pokers and vases, but the relief decor is free and asymmetrical where the Princes' ocak and that of Abdülhamit I is ordered. The Abdülhamit I ocak, built a generation later, places niches and shelves flat against the wall and its crown is set in a puny frame with the gauche paintwork of the upper walls all about it. It is handsome enough but lacks the elegance of that of Osman III. The suite of apartments of this prince are built upon an extension of the vaults which carry the hünkâr oda, the dining room of Ahmet III and the bedchamber of Murat III. On the east side, which can be seen from the old orchard and gardens, the new vaults are faced with stone, but behind they are much rougher workmanship than those of the sixteenth century. The kiosk runs along the north side to enjoy that splendid view over the city which can also be obtained from the belvedere of Ibrahim I. Between the old apartments and the new is a fine paved terrace with a basin. A corridor leads from the chamber – which was later remodelled as the bedroom of Abdülhamit I – to close the west end of the terrace. It is a simple wooden passage with large latticed casements divided externally by engaged wooden pilasters painted red. A hall with a closet leads to an anteroom and then to the central room. A large and a small anteroom are on the east side for symmetry. The sofa of the main salon forms a bower which projects in order to enjoy views to the east and west as well as north, while the windows and door of the south wall look out onto the court. The gilded ceilings are rich and embossed and decorated in gold paint on a blue ground. Between the second tier of windows, the frames of which are baroque in the Western sense, are fronds which are related to those above the dome windows in the Laleli Cami and to others which appear later at Fatih Cami. The tiles used are imported and there is such a great amount of *trompe-l'œil* in paint and plaster that it is difficult to believe that this pavilion is not largely of Western design and workmanship, although details like the ceiling ornament are Turkish.

In the latter half of the seventeenth century Kara Mustafa Pasha built a pavilion in the fourth court between the Baghdad Kiosk and the Physicians' Tower which projects over the lower garden. Only a sadrazam would be permitted to build in this court and the attribution of this to Mustafa Pasha can therefore be accepted as correct. The pavilion continued to be used by successive sadrazams and was restored by Ahmet III in 1704 and by Mahmut I in 1752.[22] The second date is useful, for it shows that by then an urbane rococo decor had been achieved. The plan is rectilinear in conformity with original foundations, but the kiosk is transformed into a frail summer house. There is a large sofa at either end completely surrounded by rectangular casements each with six of the new large panes of clear glass which had been introduced at the end of the seventeenth century. The upper lights carry baroque framed cartouches in elegant outline. The ceiling is richly ornamental and heavy in contrast to the glass walls, except in the central, principal foyer area between the two asymmetrically placed doors on the north above the steps to the lower garden. This pavilion is a belvedere full of light and

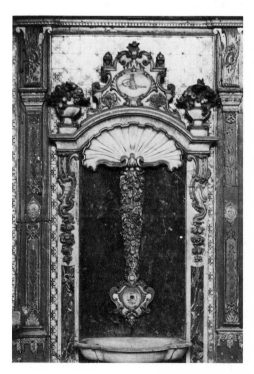

413 Topkapısaray, Istanbul. Fountain in the royal saloon (hünkâr oda).

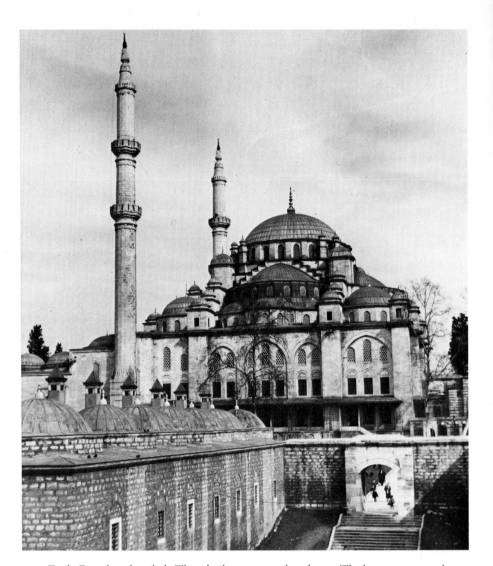

414 Fatih Complex, Istanbul. The rebuilt mosque and medreses. The baroque caps to the minarets have been replaced by others of lead in the late classical style.

air, and offers the least possible barrier between interior and outside world thus presaging the picture windows of the twentieth century.

The reign of Mustafa III saw the devastation of a great area of the city by an earthquake in the early morning of 22 May 1766, which left many minarets and domes damaged or in ruins. The two worst-shaken major mosques were the brand new Laleli Cami and the Fatih Cami of which only the court and north door and probably the mihrab survived. The work of rebuilding the mosque of the Conqueror began in *1180/1767*.[23] The old foundations were re-employed but the plan was based on that of the Şehzade and it was a conscious piece of revivalism in the grand manner, although much of the detail, such as the heavy cornice and the plant paintings, was in the new style. But the many windows are simply rounded as are the arches carried on plain columns with debased Ionic capitals. The white tiles of the dados and the clumsy paintwork in blacks and greys are unfortunate because it is a splendidly spacious building and the architect has struggled to add interest to its uncompromisingly square design by the use of a recessed balcony over the north door and lateral galleries. The exterior build-up of the roof and the lateral arcading are traditional enough to be deceptive, but the hünkâr mahfil in the south is approached by a typical eighteenth-century Imperial ramp running from south to north with a fine landing as large as a saloon before the loge itself. The paintwork in the dome above this spacious gallery is much more delicate than that found elsewhere but has the air of a box at the opera. The minarets were largely rebuilt with baroque caps. One of these was struck by lightning and both were demolished and replaced with tall conical lead caps in 1967. The undamaged baroque cap was reassembled and is to be found at the Amcazade Hüseyin Köprülü complex which became a museum in the same year.

The mosque is a partial success as a work of revivalism marred by poor if bold decoration. Öz[24] attributes it to Mehmet Tahir Ağa, while Mayer[25] says that he restored it along with Kör Yani Kalfa and Hacı Ahmet Dayazade. Cezar[26] refers to both Haşim Ali Bey and Sarım Ibrahim Efendi. Eyice again avoids any attribution. Mehmet Tahir was chief architect at the time and the amount of rebuilding must have strained his department to capacity so that he may have been the overall supervisor of other architects' work. To him, Kuban attributes only the rebuilding of the türbe of Sultan Fatih Mehmet, the octagon of which is divided by the usual engaged piers and heavy cornices in the style of the Nuruosmaniye, the Ayazma, and Laleli mosques. The windows are simply rounded and this links the building with the mosque, but the grillework enclosing the sarcophagus is very rich as might be expected in so important a tomb. The inscription over the richly carved door honours Abdülhamit I and is dated 1199/1784, and the vast flowing canopy over the porch may be assigned to this year. Behind the türbe in the shadow of the south-west corner of the mosque is the library built by Mahmut I in 1169/1756[27] of familiar alternating courses of brick and stone and with traditional rectangular casements and pointed lights above. It appears to have survived the earthquake better than the other monuments of the complex. Its plan is interesting for it is tall and cruciform with lesser domes in the crook of each arm.

This is one of several libraries in the city of which a good example is that of Atıf Efendi below the Süleymaniye which was built in 1154/1741, by the Defterdar Mustafa Atıf Efendi[28] to house over nine thousand books and manuscripts. The apartments of the librarians are in a large building of brick and stone courses with the upper rooms projecting over the street. A vaulted passage leads into a small garden. On the left is the loggia by which the reading room is entered with a depot for books preceding it. The main room has rectangular vaulted bays and a large polygonal apse together with marble columns and a central dome. There is no baroque exuberance but the plan is original and makes for a well-lit and airy room ideal for study. This room is built over a large basement which has recently been excavated and will become a second reading room.

416 *Atıf Efendi Library, Istanbul.*
Apartments projecting over the street.

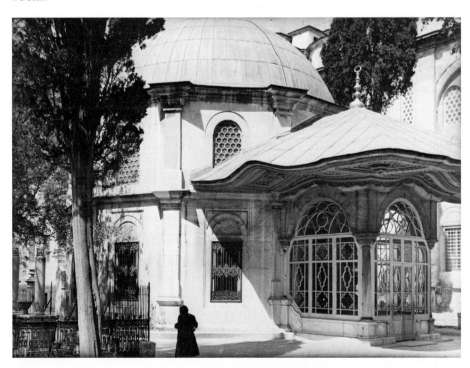

415 *Fatih Complex, Istanbul. The rebuilt türbe of Mehmet II.*

Mayer[29] says that the library of the sadrazam and poet Ragıp Pasha near 417 Beyazit was built in *1176/1762*[30] by Mehmet Tahir, but this attribution is ignored by Kuban. The library is reached by a vaulted passage under the large mekteb which projects over five arches carried on columns. It is situated in the middle of a paved court and there is a garden behind. There is a burial ground beneath the high wall to the east with the modest open tomb of the chief minister behind the sebil onto the street. The sebil has çeşmes flanking its central grille. The library building takes the form of a miniature mosque with a central dome flanked by four cradle vaults and with small cupolas in each corner. The walls are faced in tile and the central dome, which is supported by a column at each of the four corners, is over the square deposit for books behind an ornamental grille usual at this period. The area for study surrounds this and is remarkable for carved wooden chandeliers based on inscriptions and embellished with tassels. The casements and windows are plain and there is no extravagant paintwork to detract from the lofty eminence of the room. It is preceded by a high vaulted porch with polychrome voussoirs in the round arches carried on the usual capitals of Ionic derivation. This is reached by twin flights of stairs rising on the left and right. The door is set under a traditional arch of interlocking voussoirs forming reversal patterns. It admits to a foyer beneath a cradle vault with a small domed room on either side. Although this library could only have been built in the baroque period, aspects of the plan and execution are sufficiently traditional to be revivalist and so for it to be possible to associate it with the spirit of the Fatih Cami.

The more modest library of Murat Molla at Çarşamba which is set in a garden is approached by a path, off which is the small lodging of the librarian. Steps lead up to the porch beneath honeysuckle, and the door admits immediately to the reading room which is similar in plan to that of Ragıp Pasha except that the books are stored in large glass-fronted bookcases[31] endowed by Abdülhamit I and the central area under the main dome is therefore free from encumbrance. It was founded in *1189/1775* by the Kadasker Damatzade Murat Efendi, who died in 1778,[32] and it once had a tekke attached to it but this was destroyed by fire in 1927. There is no proof that this too is the work of Mehmet Tahir but there are close resemblances in the style.

However, the mosque of Zeynep Sultan, daughter of Ahmet III, below Hagia Sophia is attributed to him by Kuban[33] and by Öz.[34] It was built in *1183/1769*.[35] It is a simple domed square with a rectangular, vaulted mihrab apse preceded by a modest son cemaat yeri of five arches and built of alternating courses of brick and stone. Only the undulation of the lead over the tall windows of the dome is baroque and that, too, can be seen to be influenced by the Rüstem Pasha Cami and Byzantine roofs before the Conquest. The minaret has a simple pointed cap and an eighteenth-century form of şerefe, but the trunk revives the archaic patterning due to the treads being built spirally into the outer walls. The mekteb on the west is reached from a side lane and faces a shady garden plot. On the east of the mosque, which lies below it, is a small cemetery.

The reign of Abdülhamit I (1774-89) saw the consolidation of the baroque style and the arrival of increasing numbers of foreigners in all the creative fields, often men of indifferent calibre who could find no lucrative appointments at home. It is this which accounts for the shoddy paintwork in the handsome dining room of the Valide at Topkapısaray but the vulgar work in the bed-chamber of the sultan and in the Hünkâr Sofa is twentieth-century.[36] The transformation of the great chamber designed by Sinan had already begun in the reign of Mahmut I when a flimsy musicians' gallery was installed across the north alcove with access stairs in the traditional style set behind cupboard doors in the walls. The fine sixteenth-century inscriptive tiles were painted over and inscribed in gilt, and a çeşme with those weaknesses of design which have been discussed in 413 relation to the Maçka sebil of Mahmut I was installed, probably by the same sultan.

The türbe of Abdülhamit I was built between Sirkeci and Eminönü together with a successful and pretty çeşme – now moved to the corner of the Zeynep

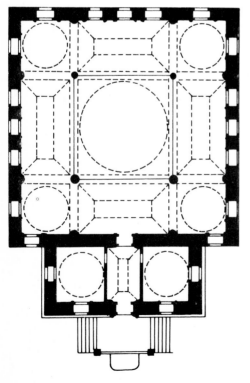

417 Ragıp Library, Istanbul. Sketch plan.

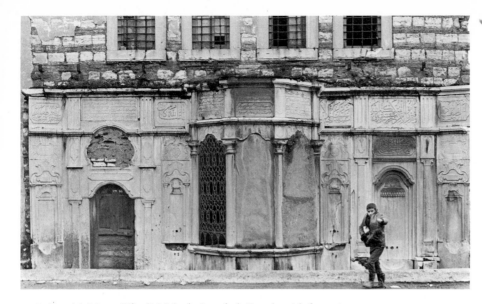

418 Recai Mehmet Efendi Mekteb, Istanbul. Façade with fountains.

Sultan cemetery – and other components of a complex which was broken up when the road was widened. The mausoleum is square with inset rounded windows at the corners and with a large dome on an octagonal drum and diminutive squinches. There are baroque details here and there and the form is an attempt to modify the traditional octagon or square, but it is a relatively sober building which foreshadows the more ponderous works of the first half of the nineteenth century such as the türbe of Mahmut II.

This heavy character is not characteristic of the period and the lower floor of the Defterdar Recai Mehmet Efendi Mekteb east of the Şehzade, dated *1189*/1775[37] and founded by a minister of Abdülhamit, is particularly elegant. The triple grille of its sebil is flanked on the south by a door between two small çeşmes. A window in a baroque frame above the door balances the outward movement of the sebil with its recession. On the north side between two more çeşmes is a third sunk in a frame. Inscriptions are set in the nine panels which run along the top of this composition. The stone and brick courses of the upper floor contrast rudely with the marble of the lower floor and the four windows of the schoolroom in plain stone rectangular frames, grouped together centrally, also seem alien to the fountain on which the mekteb stands.

The mosque at Beylerbey, built for Abdülhamit in *1192*/1778, and again attributed to Mehmet Tahir by Öz[38] is quite different from other work executed for this sultan and it is the first large mosque of the baroque era to be designed to front the water. This was because it was built to be the sultan's place of prayer when he was residing at one of the many palaces along the Bosphorus.[39] The court therefore faces the sea and is little more than a stretch of foreshore enclosed by walls with large windows and three doors of handsome proportions.[40] Mosques had been built beside the Bosphorus or the Marmara Sea before, but their courts were not made part of the landscape but kept confined and independent. Even Mihrimah at Üsküdar has no true court but only a walled plot on its west side; it does have a double portico towards the water and then, in the canopied area of its şadırvan, a belvedere. The little mosque of Şemsi Ahmet nearby hugs its court between the son cemaat yeri and the medrese opposite and walls it off from the sea. Other mosques along the Asian shore of the Bosphorus where the court might be expected to be onto the sea are built back from the water, like that at Kanlıca where the court is the village piazza. On the European shore, contemporaneous with Beylerbey, is the mosque of Emirgan where the court is hidden from the sea by the mosque; here the fountain was built under a famous tree on the east side of the mosque, and in the shade of its immense branches a meeting place grew up which became the best known coffee house on the

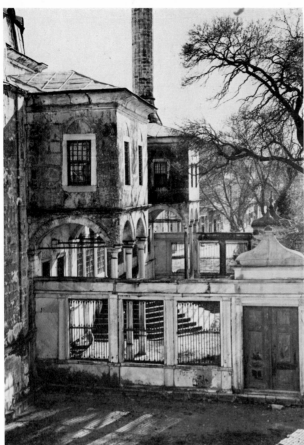
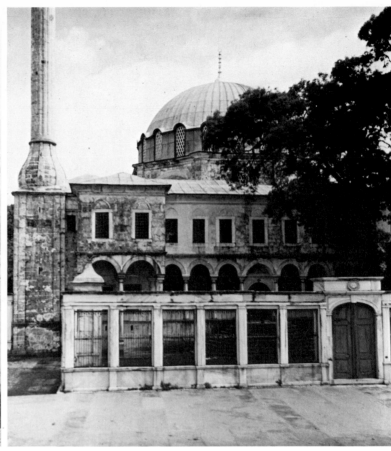

419, 420 Beylerbey Complex, Istanbul. Bosphorus façade of the mosque from the east (left) and the view from the quayside.

Bosphorus. The mosque of Sinan Pasha at Beşiktaş ignores the water and so does the court of Kılıç Ali, although the mosque was built upon the shore.[41] After the example of Beylerbey, the nineteenth-century royal mosques on the European shore had their courtyards set beside them in order that the Bosphorus should be present in the complex and, in contrast to the search for confinement in the courts of Beşiktas or Kılıç Ali, or the now destroyed Fındıklı, there was an exploitation of the open, and therefore infinite, quality of the sea. But this development applied, essentially, only to royal mosques like the Nusretiye or Dolmabahçe and, in particular, the spectacular rebuilt Ortaköy Cami on its promontory.

The court at Beylerbey is only an apron stage before the flight of grand stairs which lead to a hall and a suite of royal apartments, ranged across the north face of the mosque for the first time since the royal mosques of Bursa. This is a feature that the Balian family, who were the successive royal architects of the nineteenth century, were to repeat with the bigger mosques they constructed, like the Nusretiye and Dolmabahçe,[42] where these rooms were light and gaily painted but have been much damaged, partly because of the dismantling of the minarets which are to be re-erected; the minarets' foundations go down fourteen metres and their base blocks with modulated corners reach roof level. Here for the first time appears the bulbous foot, rather like a fat-bottomed jar, which in various forms became the hallmark of the late eighteenth- and early nineteenth-century minaret. At Beylerbey these bases are short, only the height of the exposed octagon supporting the dome, and they taper elegantly and organically into the fluted trunk. There is a single şerefe and a bulbous stone crown with a tall horned alem.[43] The royal apartments and the lateral galleries are carried on a fine range of arches, which are glazed in, and the rectangular range of casements of the upper floor gives the mosque more the appearance of a palace than a place for prayer because only the dome expresses any religious significance. The north range of apartments continues to be a cause of architectural disequilibrium as it is with the Balian mosques; although the religious purpose at the Nusretiye or Dolmabahçe is not obscured, the rooms form a rectangular pavilion which is a detached unit fixed onto the face of the mosque. They do ride over the portico – and at the Nusretiye there is an elaborate exploitation of stairways – but a true fusion of parts is not achieved. This tendency towards segmentation had been the earliest weakness of Ottoman architecture.

The mosque at Beylerbey is the usual domed square with a rectangular mihrab apse, at the corners of which are coupled columns with a tier of engaged piers above. Like the mihrab, the capitals are topped with finials, but the white paint of the walls saves the interior from fussiness and wearisome ornateness. The casements are traditional while the large windows above are rococo-crested, with pleasant red and gold paint for frames and with their glass only moderately decorated. The apse is filled with a surprising mixture of tiles from the royal store[44] ranging from sixteenth- to eighteenth-century examples and including some imported from Europe. The mihrab has the shaven niche which originated at the Nuruosmaniye and is set in a deep rectangular frame between piers crested with alems on bulbous bases. The minber is also typical of its period with a very tall gilded hood set on a canopy carried by four slender colonnettes. The flanks are still triangular and the papuçluk still incorporated but there is a play of coloured marbles, and the motifs are baroque insofar as the rigid triangular design permits.

The minber at Emirgan is more modest but has an equally tapering hood which becomes almost a spire and the flanks, although still rectangular, are encrusted with gilded foliage which is freer than the more ponderous decoration at Beylerbey. This is true also of the mihrab which is surmounted by an elegant gold inscription on a panel of green[45] and has no fussy finials. The kürsü, unlike the traditional form of that of Beylerbey, opens like a marble lotus and has an elegant balustrade. It is an early example of a type which would become common. The whole interior of this mosque is refreshingly light and elegant. It is a rectangular hall with a flat ceiling which has a fine central baroque device from which the gilded chandelier hangs. The north gallery is supported on the columns of the portico but its ceiling is held up by a range of four free-standing and two engaged columns. There is a bow in the centre projecting over a semicircular console, a common feature of mosques of this period. The gallery has a pretty balustrade of circles inset with petals and their hearts form a second miniature version of themselves. The gallery extends down the east wall only and is carried on a handsome row of columns. At the south end the last three openings between the upper range of columns have delicate gilded grilles to form a royal loge. The lower range of capitals are Doric and the upper composite and it is a feature of this mosque that the details are good. The upper range of windows are also rectangular like the casements. There is no lower range of columns inset into the walls but an upper tier carried on a recessed ledge. The overall white together with the light marble and the gilding of the capitals is so Western in atmosphere that it is difficult not to believe that the architect was a foreigner. It was completed in *1196*/1781[46] for Abdülhamit I when Hafiz Ibrahim Ağa was chief architect. The east side of the mosque is given over to the royal apartments and has the aspect of a yalı with a projecting room carried on columns over the royal porch beyond the grand gateway facing the sea. The minaret is particularly slender.

The çeşme was added in *1197*/1783.[47] It is an octagon with engaged piers cladding the corners and is more severe in design than earlier examples, although the four spigots have elegant rococo frames. The dome on its octagon emerges above the leaded eaves, which are shallower than other examples of the time, extending over the basins of the çeşme. A typical double-roof form of the period is thus created. There is a mekteb and a muvakkithane across the courtyard at Emirgan and this interest in time is paralleled by the importation of clocks from the West; a fine example can be found at Beylerbey. The Beylerbey complex is also modest and, apart from the muvakkithane added by Mahmut II, there is only a pretty triangular mekteb with a rounded apex which has four grilled windows onto the small and narrow piazza south-west of the mosque, where there is a small walled court by the lateral door used by the general public.

Provincial architecture continued to flourish in the second half of the eighteenth century. The charming library of Bağdati Necip Efendi at Tire[48] is preceded by an elegant porch with a simple roof with wide eaves above trefoil arches supported on slender wooden columns. The paintwork of the ceiling, above the windows, and round the inscription over the door is lightly handled and the flight of circular steps which spreads before the porch is handsome. The books are stored on shelves inside the central case under the high octagonal drum on which the dome rides. A much more ambitious room is that of the library of Yusuf Ağa which, according to the inscription, was built as a west annexe to the Selim Cami at Konya in 1210/1795. The dome is very grand but the squinches are weak and the four turrets at the roof corners unconvincing. By contrast, the library of Hafiz Ahmet Ağa on Rhodes dating from 1208/1793[49] is interesting because, though expressing the spirit of new learning in the provinces, its double domes supported on shell squinches are so archaic architecturally.

Two outstandingly important mosques were built at Gülşehir on the road through Haci Bektaş to Nevşehir, and at Yozgat where there is the double mosque of the Çobanoğlu potentates. The mosque at Gülşehir is dated 1193/1779[50] and is situated on the outskirts of the town. This is relatively small to be endowed with so large a mosque and rises along the terraces of the hillside above. The mosque was founded by Sayit Kara Mehmet Vezir but is commonly called the Kurşunlu Cami. It is built of pink and yellow sandstone and is a square-domed chamber with a rectangular apse and a graceful gallery supported on marble columns. The slender minaret beside the north-west corner of the mosque is preceded by a vaulted extension of the three-domed portico which is the width of half a dome and supported by an extra column. Three of the four stabilizing turrets are large; the fourth, beside the minaret, is thinner but taller. There are additional small turrets at a higher level above the four flying buttresses. The dome is not a hemisphere but develops from the swollen curve at its base to a pointed crown, a form kept in the past for turrets and minor domes or vaults in particular. The south-east and south-west corners of the building are strongly buttressed. Both outside and in there is elegance, pretty paintwork and good workmanship. The interior is light and has a mihrab and minber in the baroque manner.

The court is walled on the east side beside the highway but is hemmed in by the hillside on the north and west where there is the elegant, hooded şadırvan and a range of spigots for ablutions under a canopy, a form which is frequent with lesser mosques. Across the street towards the river, forming the north and east walls of a rectangular court, are the cells of the medrese which was completed a year later than the mosque. The L-shaped plan is sealed at the south end by the square dershane which extends over the portico before the twelve cells. The seven cells on the north side descend the now gradual slope of the hill and, from the lane which runs behind it, the roof levels can be seen to be stepped in groups of two and three and two; but from the court this is masked because by heightening the drums the domes were kept level. It is not a baroque response to the possibilities of the site but a traditional search for geometric order but without the inspiration with which Sinan dealt with the medreses at the Süleymaniye.[51] The complex has handsome gates and it is much enhanced by its setting among old trees above the river and its bridge. The mosque is one of the best of the smaller mosques of its period. Fortunately, unlike the mosques of Istanbul, it has not been soiled and darkened by the soot and dust of a city but retains in its freshness much of the spirit of its time.

The first of the marble[52] Çobanoğlu[53] mosques at Yozgat was large and lofty with a dome with a lamplighter's gallery supported by squinches and another gallery over the narthex, the wall of which is divided by three large arches.

421 Ulu Cami, Yozgat. The north door, now incorporated in the mosque extension.

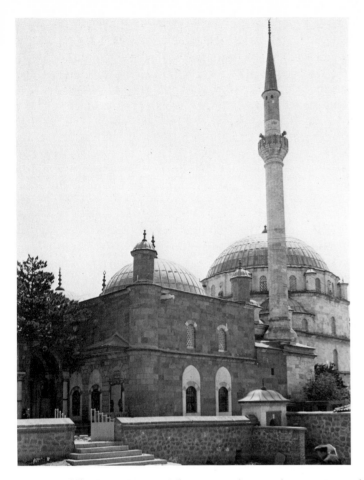

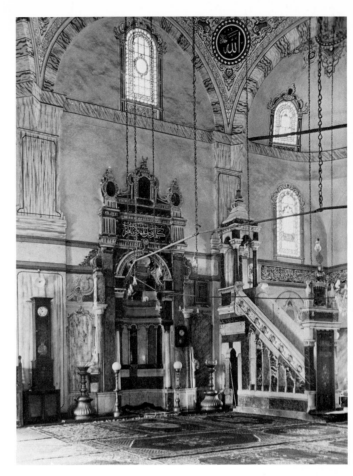

422, 423 Ulu Cami, Yozgat. The exterior showing the extension to the original mosque and (right) the mihrab and minber in the original mosque.

A müezzins' mahfil extends to the right of the central arch and there is a kürsü inset before the wall east of the mihrab; both mihrab and minber are spirited examples of eighteenth-century baroque. The stairs leading from the west side of the narthex up to the north gallery are lightly built of wood and exposed to view. When this mosque was built by Mustafa Pasha in *1192/1778*[54] to be the Ulu Cami of Yozgat, it was preceded by a three-domed portico supported by marble columns. This was closed on the east by a square türbe containing the tombs of the Çobanoğlu chieftains and on the west by a balancing subsidiary room now used as a store. The minaret rises at the north-west corner of the narthex behind this annexe.

By *1210/1795*[55] the mosque had become too small to hold the growing number of townsfolk and, rather than build a second, Süleyman Bey decided to extend the mosque of his father. There had been additions to existing mosques often enough in the early days of Islam, notably at Baghdad and Cordova and also, latterly, in Selçuk times at Konya to the Alaettin Cami. But Ottoman mosques were always planned as complete entities and so were not easily enlarged without being completely rebuilt. Süleyman Bey removed the north door of the first mosque, leaving the inscription behind, and opened arches through the flanking window walls of what was now no longer the son cemaat yeri. Four extra columns were coupled with those of the portico to help carry the weight of the roof of the second chamber. This is rectangular with a central section the width of the middle arch of the portico only and so, because the area had to be rectangular, cradle vaulted. The two flanking areas stretched the width of the arch on each side and of the annexe on the west and the türbe on the east. The türbe retained its window which now looked out onto the room. These square areas were domed, and determined the proportions of the new extension. It is broad and lofty with large exposed arches dividing it into its three sections at roof level. It

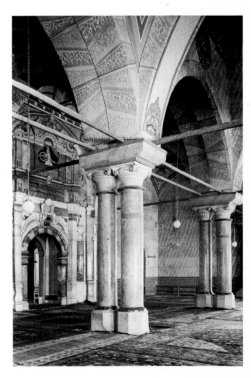

424 Ulu Cami, Yozgat. The original portico.

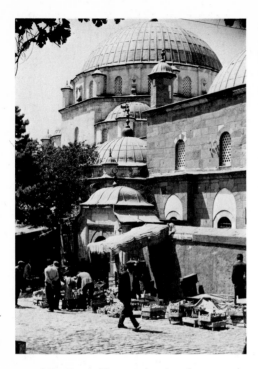

425 *Ulu Cami, Yozgat, showing the collision of the mosque with its extension, from the north-east.*

is cut off from the main mosque but there are fine vistas through the archways of the former portico and the narthex, particularly that of mihrab from the new north doorway. It was not entirely successful as an operation but influenced the enclosing of other porticoes in the region when it was necessary to increase the area of the hall.[56] The new or outer mosque was built with some fine marbles and much scagliola, and the lavish paintwork has panache while the *trompe l'œil* work in the domes, similar to that at the Köprülü mosque at Safranbolu, is p more successful in a baroque setting. The inner and the outer mosques are lavishly carpeted including the deep casement areas, and the effect in the outer mosque is opulent to the extent that it has something of the atmosphere of an Edwardian Grand Hotel.

Only a small portico consisting of a central dome between cradle vaults was added to the extension. The platform has a railing and is simply a porch and not a son cemaat yeri. The whole new hall is in effect just a porch. There are no arcades forming a diminished court but a wall with handsome gates and a commodious şadırvan. From the front, apart from the turrets at the four corners of the roof of the later mosque, the union of the two buildings is less incongruous than might have been expected. The trough caused by the vault between two domes is a weakness, but it is only from the side that the five domes of the annexe, türbe, and original portico can be seen and then the impression of two buildings 42 colliding, which is the real weakness of the design, is marked. The squinches are also visible from the sides but they are obscured from the north so that from there the build-up of the şadırvan dome, the two domes of the extension, and finally the original main dome is effective. The contrast between the small and slender turrets of the major dome and the larger and stouter ones of the addition is also noticeable, while the polygonal minaret is made disproportionately slender by the bulk of the double building.

Other eighteenth-century provincial mosques are less interesting nor are they as large. The urge to build continued in Erzerum where the Şeyhler Cami was built in *1185/1771*[57] with a large vaulted portico; but it shows no development in style, nor does the Ayazpaşa Cami of the same period nor the Mehdi Efendi Cami of *1210/1795*.[58] This is true of provincial mosques elsewhere such as the Ali Pasha Cami at Kütahya built in *1212/1797*.[59]

The period also saw extensive repair or rebuilding of older foundations. A spirit of revivalism which was already latent at Adana, for example, where the Yeni Cami, built in *1124/1712*,[60] has a twisted minaret, led to such plans as that of Nur Mehmet Pasha Cami in the same town, dated *1205/1790*,[61] which has nine cross-vaults and a cupola over the mihrab together with four stone piers. But usually rebuilding was ruthless and without respect for the past as with the Demirtaş Pasha Cami at Kütahya.

Yet good provincial mosques continued to be built until the end of the century and an example is the İzzet Pasha Cami at Safranbolu dated *1211/1796*.[62] It is 36 built on the side of a hill on a platform and has an irregular court plan with the entrance gate set at an angle to the mosque. The spigots are ranged under an arcade on the north side. On the south side, twin flights of stairs sweep up to a domed porch which is set before the central cupola of the son cemaat yeri. This is flanked by a wide cradle-vaulted sofa with balustrades on each side. Inside there is a narthex the width of the north wall, with a triple-domed gallery above it, which is nicely baroque in its movement. The hall beyond is square with a dome fourteen metres in width. The walls are painted with frippery and false pillars, but interest is awakened by the gay and elaborate candelabra which gleams with lamps and ostrich eggs. The mihrab and minber are also good examples of baroque and there is a silvered model of the mosque suspended in the traditional manner. An example of the pursuit of height in the baroque period is provided by the mosque of Mustafa Sultan on Rhodes dating, according to the inscription, from *1174/1764*. The dome is only eight metres wide but eighteen high. It is flanked by three vaults and two small corner cupolas which reduce the dramatic effect. Like so many mosques on the island it has a double portico.

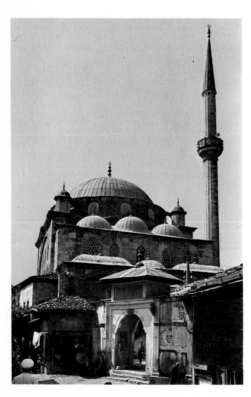

426 *İzzet Pasha Cami, Safranbolu, from the north-east.*

Civil buildings dating from the end of the eighteenth century are, apart from konaks and houses, less important, but the large Taş Han built by Armenian merchants at Sivas is a solid stone building which from outside is seen to be built of five sections framed by engaged pilasters and a string-course. A window is set in the middle of each section at upper level and each has a triangular gable and shed roof. This is a style which was commonly used for markets in the nineteenth century and there are examples in Sivas itself as well as at Kayseri. The interior of the han lies along the axis of a rectangular court which has a large upper vault at each end and a gallery all round. There are two tiers of heavy columns with clumsy capitals, but a certain grandeur is achieved. The upper arches are set into the gables of the roofs. Nearby is the Şehit Orhan Tunçöz Çeşme, dated 1204/1789[63] which is a good example of a fountain inset in a wall with baroque decoration in relief. But the most flamboyant çeşme of the period stands beside the mosque at Yozgat; it is an oval marble cistern surmounted by an ogee gable on colonnettes and flanked by big free-standing petalled sun discs and it has a large basin. This monumental çeşme has little baroque decoration but is most successfully baroque in form. In this it resembles the Beyhan Sultan Çeşme at Arnavutköy dating from 1219/1804[64] which is a solid rectangular cistern faced with an undulating spigot wall with triple tiers of engaged pilasters and a strong frieze, and with inscriptive panels framed in undulations which reflect the movement of the frontage. Here, however, there are no sun discs or other architectural hyperboles. The tuğra of the Sultan[65] rides over the inscriptions, and there is a restrained use of foliate decoration which in no way breaks into the movement of the building but rather enhances it. After this the large fountains with cisterns standing independently in public spaces became formalized and followed a European tradition; examples are that of Mahmut II dating from 1254/1839[66] at Boyacıköy and that of Bezmialem Valide Sultan near Maçka built in the following year.[67] Both are strictly rectilinear in form with engaged pilasters rising the full height of the façade and with all decoration kept to the central spigot area and the inscription above.

Beyhan Sultan was the sister of Selim III who ascended the throne in 1789. He and his generation of the Osmanlı family were considerable builders and his apartments are the most ornate in the Saray. He had had European tutors and his sister employed Melling at Ortaköy, and Kauffer, who succeeded him, planned rebuilding the Saray in the French style. The first of Selim III's salons dates from the year of his accession,[68] and from the start these rooms and those of Mihrişah Valide Sultan present a relatively plain exterior of wide windows between

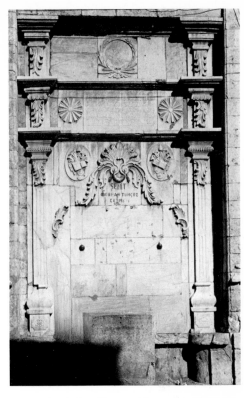

427 Şehit Orhan Tunçöz Fountain, Sivas.

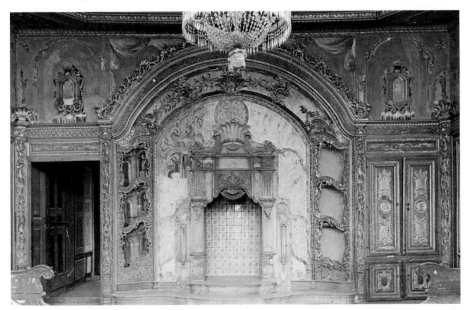

428 Topkapısaray, Istanbul. Salon of Selim III.

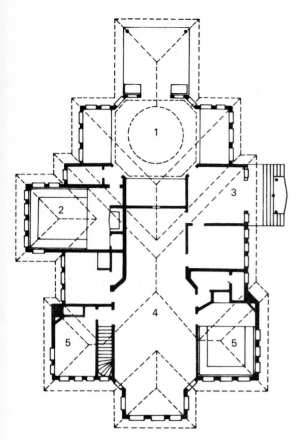

429 *Aynalı Kavak, Istanbul. Sketch plan.*
1 Salon; 2 dining-room; 3 entry; 4 hall;
5 odas.

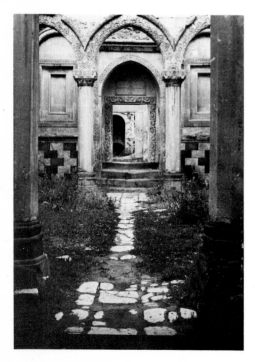

430 *İshak Pasha Saray, Doğubayezit.*
Dining-hall with the door to the harem.

pilasters under deep highly embellished eaves and much cantilevering. The interiors have varied carved and gilded ceilings, with windows and mirrors much ornamented with baroque motifs; and cupboards, shelves, and walls lavishly enriched by gilded foliate reliefs, ribands and flowers, none of which is Turkish in style. There is also much painted plasterwork, some in relief, besides imported tiles to back shelves and ocaks. These, submerged as they are in rococo abundance, retain some of their earlier Ottoman form and are still the focal points of the rooms, rivalling the views. Melling and Allom's engravings clearly 50(show how the princesses embellished their palaces along the Bosphorus with similarly fantastically fretted frames and pilasters, using equally fragile and sometimes gimcrack materials. They also were fond of lavish gilding and paintwork, while crude landscape paintings were frescoed above the wainscots and even appeared as embellishments of the rebuilt Gate of Felicity. The structure was frail but suited the mood of the moment and some pavilions and retreats have survived remarkably well.

A good example is the Aynalı Kavak Kasır at Hasköy. This is much more 42 sober in decoration, even severe after the apartments in the Saray, partly because it has lost all its brocade and silk furnishings, crystal chandeliers and mirrors. It is a series of rooms lit by large rectangular casements and lights embellished with ornament above, and is built on one floor over a basement. The walls are as close to being all glass as early nineteenth-century construction would allow. Between the casements and the upper lights, verses by Selim III were written in gilt on a green band. The kasır is entered up stairs under a porch, and on the right of the square hall is the salon which has a domed central area with sofas on either side and French windows leading to a terrace with a fountain under a canopy. A corner door through a lobby leads to a more intimate room with fine views and an ocak. At the rear of the salon is a third recess which acts as an anteroom to the long central hall which ends in a large sofa projecting towards the gardens and the park. The salon dome is segmental and the eaves are broad, and from the outside the kasır has the appearance of a spacious villa. It is no longer one room like the Baghdad Kiosk but a retreat with kitchens and service rooms. The idea of a single room serving all purposes is breaking down and separate rooms for sleeping and eating are now regarded as essential, at least in a royal pavilion. Aynalı Kavak has survived where the palace at Edirne has perished, and it is therefore important as a guide to the form and function of such buildings as the Kum Kasır there.[69]

The greatest private palaces outside the suburbs of the capital were built by the Al Azam family in Damascus and Hama mainly in the 1740s, but these are essentially Syrian in style and plan and wholly Damascene in decor and craftsmanship. However, in common with the Ottoman traditions, the Al Azam palace at Damascus is not only built round a harem and a selâmlık court but is a series of pavilions. These are so big that they are mansions in their own right. Emphasis is also placed on the eyvans for summer relaxation, the marble pavement of the courts, trees for shade and beauty including palms and orange trees, and the cool pool. Whereas Topkapısaray has a plan but was nonetheless expanded at hazard and whim, the Al Azam palace is a strictly co-ordinated concept. It is also much more ornate, from the varied coloured marbling to the lustres and the gilding. The lesser palace at Hama has the distinction of an upper court for the harem and a splendid view over the river, but it is earlier and more modest in scale.[70] No saray in Anatolia can compare with these two treasure houses save one and that, too, is not at all in the Ottoman tradition. This is the palace of İshak Pasha[71] at Doğubayezit on the Silk Road near the present Iranian 430 frontier. The highway now runs across the plain below and no longer climbs up the gorge above the present town. There the old town lies in ruins on the steep slopes although one or two homes have been built afresh due to the growth of the population. On the steeper side of the gorge are the formidable remains of a fortress with antecedents before Assyrian times. Its strategic position made sure that whoever ruled the territory maintained this fortress, and so the Selçuks and later Selim I restored the building. The mosque has already been discussed.[72]

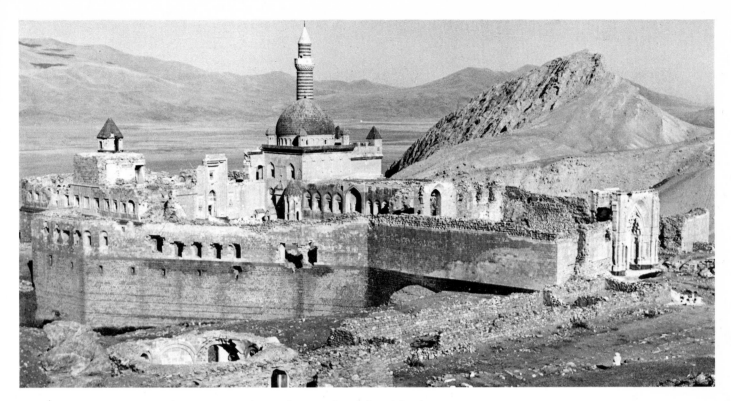

431 *İshak Pasha Saray, Doğubayezit. General view showing, from left to right, the kitchen, the great door to the dining-hall, the mosque, türbe, selâmlık and service court.*

Across the gorge is the palace, probably largely completed by 1784,[73] attributed to İshak Pasha but commenced by his father Behlül Pasha and actually completed by Mahmut Pasha his son.[74] İshak Pasha's power made him almost independent of the Padişah. If he was something of a robber baron, he seems also to have been an effective emir and a man of considerable culture to match his wealth. The building is unique for several reasons although the plan is logical, if large, and traditional in conception. The architect is not yet known but could have been the prince himself with the assistance of trained architects and masons. The imprint of a unique personality is strong, but the mixture of styles is stronger. It is important not to see this palace as a personal possession. It was the seat of government for a turbulent province, that of Mount Ararat with which the building stands face to face. When power passed out of the hands of his descendants, the building naturally became the Vilayet, or government house, until after the Second World War, when it was moved to Karaköşe now renamed Ağrı, the Turkish name for Ararat. It had been built of government money for a semi-hereditary Lord Lieutenant and was not to be regarded as his property. But government was despotic and absolute in Kurdistan and İshak Pasha built to suit himself.

The result is the appearance in Anatolia of a true piece of revivalism in the sense that the Gothic revival of Pope and Wyatt was an attempt to bring the past to life again. There are straightforward baroque elements in the palace, particularly the stone cartouches of the pillared dining hall, but the dominating styles are Selçuk or Georgian although with modern conveniences. In a region where the winter is bitterly cold and snow can lie for five months, every room has an ocak and no room except the council chamber, the mosque and the dining hall is very large. Moreover there was a hot air central heating system piped through earthenware in the wall cavities with ducts which could act as passages if a repair were needed.[75] The plan was based on a rectangle divided into three separate sections in accordance with the requirements of the site which is a long spur thrusting towards the broad plateau which is the apron stage of Mount Ararat. The first court is reached through a grand stalactite portal decorated with Selçuk motifs interpreted in eighteenth-century terms, and, because no plaster

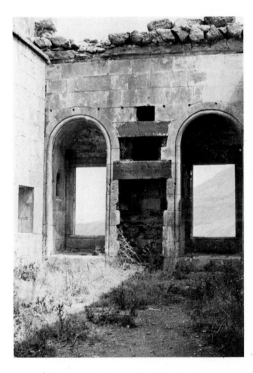

432 *İshak Pasha Saray, Doğubayezit. Room with a ruined ocak in the selâmlık.*

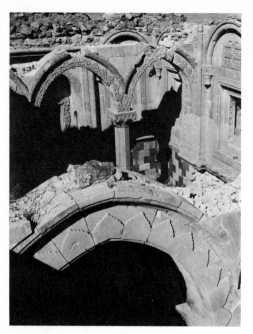

433 İshak Pasha Saray, Doğubayezit.
Detail of an arch.

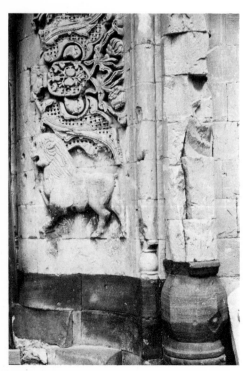

434 İshak Pasha Saray, Doğubayezit.
Detail of decoration.

is used, with stone buds rather than stalactites in the semi-dome. This court was a service area which included the furnace for the central heating system. A much more modest gate admitted to the second court which was the selâmlık. On the south side, above lofty vaults which reach over twenty-five metres in height where the land level falls, was a suite of rectangular apartments each side of a corridor. These rooms are of like dimensions and contain two windows, one on each side of the ocak on the outward wall. In the sides of the deep casements are niches for lamps or flowers, and niches appear in profusion in all the walls of the building. On the north side there is a large hall of some thirty by twenty metres – which presumably was the divan of the pasha – as well as an entry hall and a passage with rooms similar to those on the south side, one of which is said to have been the library for the imams and probably other less orthodox holy men, since Kurdish practices have always been heterodox.[76] The passage leads to the mosque which is very high and has a gallery for women supported by columns. The minber is unusual in that it is approached by stairs in the wall beside the mihrab which lead to an arch and a balcony on a solid semicircular console projecting from the wall. The stone decoration here is florid and cut in deep relief. Behind the mosque and divided from it is a pillared hall, which may have served as an extension on Fridays, as well as a dershane. The windows here are small to keep out the cold, but their arches open like trumpets while the sills splay in conformity with the arch to diffuse the maximum of light. This is a theme throughout the palace and is expressed also in the formation of the squinches when they occur. Externally, the mosque has a high dome on a drum and an orthodox stone minaret set on the north-west above the precipice to which the only possible access is by a continuation of the gallery stairs which are set in the wall and reached from inside the mosque. They, like the other stairways of the palace, are narrow and steep in the Selçuk and classical Ottoman tradition and show none of that baroque influence which had led to the grand staircases of the yalıs of the Bosphorus. Two stairways lead to the roof but where they emerge they do not form true turrets because half their sides are cut away.

Beside the mosque, in the courtyard, is what appears to be a thin ornate Selçuk türbe made up of a series of cusps surmounted by a conical roof. Its fifteen stairs   436
do not go up but down five metres. Beside it are what seem to be two stone dog-kennels. In fact, the türbe is false and but a tower, and the real tomb is a rectangular vault below ground level; the kennels prove to be two windows or ventilators whose sills at an angle of forty-five degrees look like shoots. The roof is a cradle vault cut into somewhat clumsily where there is need for headroom at the foot of the stairs. The graves of the Pasha and his wife are set side by side towards the west end.

The same architect may have been responsible for a large rectangular kümbet at Hamur near Ağrı built of ashlar stone with basalt bands for decoration. This is above ground level and the door admits to a small hall which leads into a similar funerary chamber. Because it is built above ground the windows are normal rectangles although set high up the wall.

All the floral decoration at Doğubayezit is flamboyant, and most flamboyant is the very tall doorway into the harem. This is further enriched by lions in the Selçuk and Persian manner, a feature which appears in the wooden consoles of a vanished wooden bower in the north wall of the selâmlık. These are strikingly   434
Iranian in style, whereas much of the floral work would tempt one to think of India, were it not for the relationship of all this three-dimensional flamboyance to the mosque and maristan at Divrik dating from the early thirteenth century.   44,
What has happened at İshak Pasha's palace is precisely what happened at Divrik: 438
an Iranian plaster style has been translated into stone by local masons.

Through the great arch a passage leads past the kitchens to an antehall, really a continuation of the passage which turns sharply to the right in order to reach the dining hall. Beyond this hall, with its pillars and walls of sandstone and basalt making formal patterns, are the rooms of the once two-storey harem similar to those of the selâmlık but commanding the incomparable view of Ararat and the

and the placing of the minarets is particularly happy. They are far enough apart to add grandeur to a relatively small mosque without reaching the absurdity of those at Beyazit, and they are slender enough for their height not to dwarf the dome. A parallel search for far greater height in Europe resulted in Antonelli's tiered dome at Novara but the nineteenth century could not sustain such ambitions in Turkey. There was no tradition of a drum in Ottoman architecture no more than of expanding volume in the Western manner. But there was a marked change of style. The mosque silhouette ceased to fit into a triangle, and the rigid angles of the past were made to curve and flow. The stylized floral decoration of the Tulip era grew more natural, but the colours lost some of their intensity. Shells and fronds, exaggerated cornices and more organic capitals, together with festoons and swags which made a late appearance, replaced geometric decoration and rosettes. An increased use of vaults and stairways achieved stately effects. Wooden staircases replaced stone. All this represented radical changes requiring the learning of new techniques and skills, and it is not surprising that many foreign architects were employed including Melling. What is surprising is how Ottoman the baroque period remained in feeling: and it was this period, not the classic, which made a strong romantic impact on Europe.[119]

After the Nusretiye, most major buildings erected for the sovereign were to be the work of the Balian family or their Armenian assistants. The ministerial form of the office of Architect of Empire had disappeared and the heirs of Kirkor Balian were royal architects but the appointment was no longer a national one. There is no proof that either Kirkor nor his son Karabet studied abroad, but three grandsons, Nikogos, Sarkis and Agop went to St Barbe College in Paris and Nikogos came under the influence of Henri Labrouste. The dynasty introduced European fashions and a flamboyance which has been popular ever since. Allom[120] speaks approvingly of this influence in relation to the Nusretiye with particular regard to the clock tower between the mosque and the parade ground. His engraving shows the original tower[121] as a three-storey pagoda in wood and without a timepiece. He hoped that it would eventually have bells which would replace the call to prayer. In this he has been disappointed, but Nikogos Balian rebuilt the tower in stone and there is now a clock. It was socially important to dissociate time from religion and the erection of clock towers throughout the Empire was a symbol of progress. Eventually, all towns of any size achieved one and they are a curious collection. The stone towers at Tophane and Dolmabahçe by Bali Balian are built in sections and so is the more modest but lofty tower in the citadel of Bursa or those at Tokat and Yozgat. These are pagodas without eaves. The Adana tower is severe brick recalling Italian mediaeval watch-towers like those at San Gimignano; but the one at Niğde is less severe and shorter because it rises from the citadel and not the plain. It is crowned by an open belvedere. Another simple tower which is less severe than that at Adana is to be found at Kastamonu. At Gümüşhacıköy the tower was added to the gate of the Köprülü han, while at Merzifon a monstrously fat tower was brutally set on top of entry to the fifteenth-century medrese. Inevitably, some towers took the form of enormous minarets; examples occur at Bayburt and at Çorum where the tower stands at the end of the main avenue with a bulbous foot on a square base and has a şerefe. At Kocaeli, the tower is built above a pretty pavilion and the clock faces are framed in the third storey. The belvedere on top has a concave conical roof which is as slender as a spire. Exotic erections such as the mauresque bibelot at Izmir are later in date.

There had always been fire towers, especially in Istanbul, and Kirkor's brother Senekerim Balian[122] built the present Beyazit fire tower in 1828[123] to replace one of wood erected by his brother. The original wooden top of Senekerim's tower was rebuilt in stone later and the tower is now fifty metres high. The bulbous base and the trunk containing the broad wooden staircase resemble a minaret, but above the observation room the triple crown of additional floors diminishing in height and circumference looks as if it had been screwed on to the original. The building of this tower marks the end of the Old Saray and its occupation by

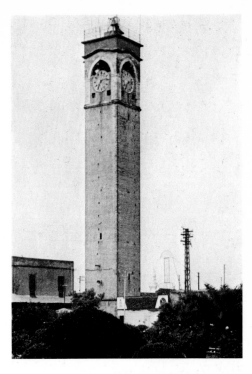

460 *Clock tower at Adana.*

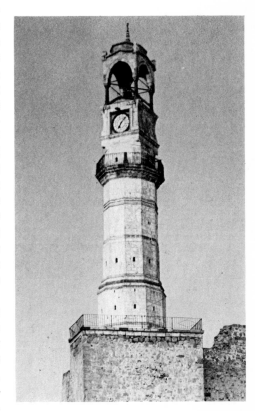

461 *Clock tower at Niğde.*

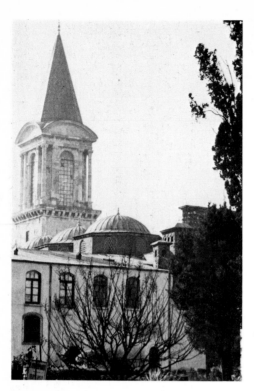

462 *Topkapısaray, Istanbul. Divan Tower.*

the Ministry of War and finally the Law Faculty of the University. Mahmut II in *1241/1825*[124] rebuilt the lantern of the tower of the Divan while retaining the mediaeval base attributed to Mehmet II. The greater height added dignity, but the tall windows between engaged columns and the niches filling the other four flanks of the octagon carry segmental Renaissance pediments under the lead spire. The result is so Palladian as to be out of place in Topkapısaray.

The vast new barracks which were built after the massacre of the Janissaries and the destruction of their ocaks[125] dominated the suburbs of Istanbul. At Haydarpaşa, the wooden barrack of Selim III was rebuilt in stone by Mahmut II in *1244/1828*. Three more sides were added by Abdülmecit between *1258/1842* and *1270/1853*.[126] It was to be used as a British military hospital during the Crimean War. The size of these enormous barracks is grand and at each corner is a fine tower rising to five storeys with a lantern on top. The barracks are raised on a basement where the cliff shelves to the sea and thus stand boldly above the Marmara. The windows are grouped in threes and divided by engaged piers which reach to the tiled roof. There are over eleven hundred exterior windows. The long flanks are faced with white plaster and escape the ponderousness which came later in the century. Only the tuğra and the royal arms over the great door are essentially Ottoman. Kirkor Balian built the original barrack but it is not clear who it was who completed it for Abdülmecit.[127] Sarkis Balian built the stone barracks at Gümüşsuyu and Maçka, now part of the Technical University, and the headquarters at Harbiye.

The octagonal türbe of Mahmut II on the Divan yolu, complete with sebil and fenestrated wall, has already been mentioned. It was the work of Kirkor's son and successor, Karabet Balian (1800–86) and dates from *1256/1840*,[128] the year after Mahmut's death. In the same year[129] the Alay Kıosk, opposite the sadrazam's palace gate, was rebuilt on its sixteenth-century foundations. It is a large wooden room reached by a broad ramp from the park below the saray. Parades and Guild processions were watched from its battery of gilded grilles under a ribbed onion dome and it was set on consoles at the corner in order to improve the view.

Gateways continued to have huge eaves and handsome vaults in a style thought to be typically Ottoman by the West but which developed late in the eighteenth century. A good example is the gate to the royal court at Hagia Sophia opposite the Bâbı-Hümâyun. It is high and the structure of columns, cornices and baroque niches is clearly expressed. The eaves stretch out on all four sides under a typical two-tier vault which is flanked by uneasily perched small turrets. It is of stone whereas the surviving gate to the palace of the sadrazam is largely of wood. It has eaves as vast as canopies and dates from *1259/1843*.[130]

Such magnificence contrasts with the sobriety of much early nineteenth-century work such as the western classical façade of the Cevri Kalfa Mekteb built in *1235/1819*[131] opposite the Atmeydan where the main block is built up

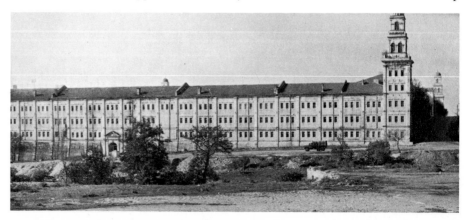

463 *Selimiye Barrack, Haydarpaşa.*

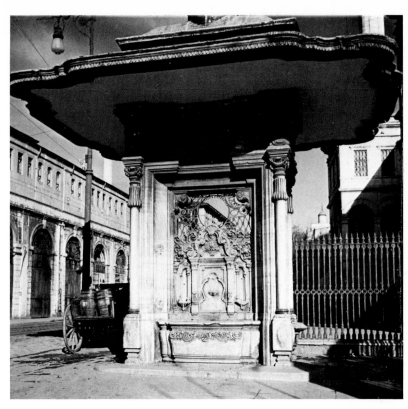

464 Abdülhamit II Fountain, Istanbul.

in three tiers with simple, engaged pilasters. The façade is divided into two blocks by gates and the subsidiary unit houses a saloon under a version of a gatehouse vault. At street level the grilles of a sebil are incorporated into the line of large windows. The fountains of the period have been mentioned. They became plainer and plainer like that of Ali Bey at Beşiktaş dating from *1252*/1836.[132] It is a stone block relieved at the corners by pilasters. These support a rectangular pediment above the spigot and an equally rectangular basin. The fountain of Mehmet Hüsrev Pasha built seven years later[133] in the same district is even more severe. The only decoration is the cartouche with the tuğra of the sultan and a repetition of dead baroque forms, as with the Kethuda Halit Efendi Çeşme, erected at Aksaray in *1269*/1852[134] or the Abdülhamit II Çeşme at Kağithane dated *1310*/1892.[135]

The mid-century produced no Ottoman work of value. Yet more foreigners arrived and local talent was eclipsed, apart from the Balian family. The Fossati brothers restored Hagia Sophia and built the Imperial pew in a mixture of the Ottoman and Byzantine styles. They also built the Russian Embassy among other secular commissions and repainted the interior dome of the Süleymaniye in an incongruous fake rococo style. Karabet Balian built the first of his notorious palaces at Dolmabahçe in 1853 together with the mosque of the Valide Bezmialem in a very bombastic style.[136] The mosque is unremarkable save for the slimness of the twin minarets which take the form of Corinthian columns. The royal suite cuts straight across the north front. The court of the mosque is set beside it as an extension of the palace garden where the clock tower stands. The palace itself is designed to face the water, from which it is protected by a long marble terrace behind a wall divided by tall pillars bearing lanterns and linked by curvular, crested railings. Behind lie a series of buildings in a style that may be called Classical Western. The first section, which might not be out of place in Regent's Park, is the selâmlık. It is followed by the huge concourse or throne room which is double the height of the rest of the palace, and which inside is like an opera house, and then by the harem. Beyond this, identical in appearance, is the apartment of the heir to the throne which is now the Beşiktaş art gallery. The palace is narrow in relation to its great length. Thus the saloons of the selâmlık and the harem are grandiose corridors broken by the imperial stairway

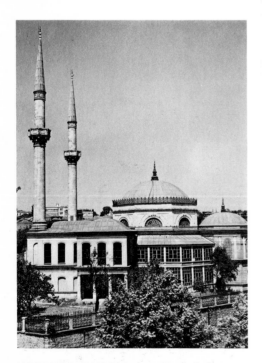

465 *Ortaköy Cami, Bosphorus, from the north-west.*

466 *Hırkai Serif Complex, Istanbul, from the west, showing the galleries encircling the prayer chamber.*

and the throne room. Each section is based on the Çinili Kiosk plan. They are cruciform with a room in each of the four corners. To the north there is a pink aviary supported on pretty fluted columns above the pavement of the present highway which runs between the high walls of Dolmabahçe and Yildiz. This pretty glass room is reached by a long corridor behind which was once the royal menagerie. The grand staircase consists of a double flight leading up to an oval *469* gallery with fake marble columns and is European in style. The throne room or muayede salonu[137] was built by Karabet's son, Nikogos (1826-58), who was a talented engineer and decorator.

The gateways to the gardens of the palace are of unparalleled ornateness and size, and incorporate all manner of styles and complexities of decoration; they are built of stone, marble and plaster. The metal gates themselves are built up of voluted foliage ending in flowers that presage Art Nouveau, and circular medallions inset with flowers in borders of stylized leaf forms. Further wheels of vegetation grow on the gates and the piers are topped with finials springing from volutes. Nothing is allowed to rest uncarved and this excess continues on the west façade above the grand entry, where star discs and leaves fill spandrels, and windows are divided by fluted columns. The relief is shallow and the columns are free-standing, so each element of the structure is distinct and its task of supporting a cornice or balustrade is defined. Thus the façade does not become flabby or meaningless. It has the exuberance of Garnier's Paris Opera House but lacks the unity and force of that masterpiece.

Dolmabahçe was built at a speed which is a tribute to the Balian organizing ability, and within a year of its completion Karabet Balian, assisted by Nikogos, went on to build the new mosque at Ortaköy.[138] The family worked as a team, *465* otherwise they could never have built so much. The Ortaköy mosque occupies a fine site jutting out into the straits and can be seen from afar when the coarse details are hidden and a lively ornateness can be enjoyed. Like Nusretiye, the royal apartments are divided by the entry. The minarets are closer set, have stone finials and only one şerefe. There are corner piers with large turrets and three big windows in each of the two storeys of the tympana. The interior is brightly lit and rich in marble. The minber has baroque panels in foliate frames, yet the canopy of trefoil arches with the triangulations recalls Gothic revivalism. The tapering hood is studded with gilt stars.

The little kiosk by Nikogos[139] at Küçüksu replaced a wooden one in *1273/ 1856.*[140] The exterior is thick with carving but the twin flights of stairs curving up from the water to the terrace are charming. A garden lobby leads to the main hall; off this are a pair of rooms onto the garden at each corner and a second pair identical in plan look onto the water. A similar monotony occurs at first-floor level, for this is the Çinili Kiosk concept once more. To reach this floor, the stairs double back from the half-landing to reach a central gallery. On entering from the garden, one steps under the flight of stairs rising from the hall beyond. The stairs have no apparent support and one feels uneasily that they could snap down on one like a trap. But they are regal when approached from the water and, in fact, the stairs are always the delight of a Balian palace. There is a tradition that they were designed by specialized architects.[141] They are outstanding at Beylerbey, *468* the most sympathetic of the palaces, which was built by Sarkis Balian (1835-1899)[142] assisted by his brother Agop (1838-1875).[143] There the wooden flights are made to turn and twist and divide and join as if to the measures of a dance. Like Dolmabahçe, but smaller in size, the palace lies along the Bosphorus. It is divided into harem and selâmlık by a grand saloon in which is a marble basin filled with fountains which glitter under the coloured chandeliers imported from Vienna. The grounds are full of pavilions and retreats where great use is made of porcelain appointments and bright paint. The palace is full of marble and mahogany yet is not overwhelmingly ornate. At each end of the terrace by the race where the Bosphorus currents clash, there is a small octagonal pavilion with a ribbed conical roof. The slender-columned porticoes have roofs which sag as if they were made of canvas between poles.

Besides innumerable kiosks, the Balian family built the gutted Çirağan palace, also by the water. It was planned by Nikogos and built by Sarkis who was responsible for Galatasaray Lycée and for adding the last kiosk at Topkapısaray. Karabet erected factories which included the royal carpet mill at Hereke; also various Armenian and Gregorian churches were built by Balians. Their style grew less and less Ottoman while growing more and more flamboyant to reach a climax with the giant vases which formed the bases of the gates at Galatasaray. Such a style could not survive the end of the Empire.

466   The most accomplished mosque of the period was the Hirkai Şerif built by Abdülmecit to house the second robe of the Prophet. The sultan was a calligrapher and the mosque is a museum of his and Mustafa İzzet Efendi's inscriptions.[144] The detail of the architecture suggests that it is also the work of a Balian. A carriage drive sweeps up to the broad, low façade.[145] There is a colonnade at ground-floor level and a plain central door surmounted by a round window. The minarets, in the form of Corinthian columns like those at Dolmabahçe, are wide apart at each end of the building. A vestibule leads into a spacious foyer off which are halls and ante-rooms. A saloon on the upper floor opens into the royal box as if in a theatre. The octagonal prayer hall is lit by immense, two-tier windows designed as single units and guarded by richly wrought inner grilles. The walls are panelled in brown marble encrusted with gilt leaves and framed in white. The red carpets enhance the effect of opulence. The two loges are bow-fronted each side of the high arch of the vestibule. The composite marble kürsü is a low marble basin akin to a font, set on a pedestal and richly carved. The ornate mihrab has traditional stalactites in its niche but these are nineteenth-century in detail. There are five star discs above the inscription over the niche which is framed by pilasters. The outer frame has a spiral frond design and there is three-dimensional cresting. The mihrab is of grey polished marble and so is most of the minber. The triangular flanks are plain and as with other minbers of the time there is no place for slippers. Under a white marble handrail, flowers in small medallions cover the balustrade and the elaborate gate is of brown and white marble. There is a touch of chinoiserie about the support and vault of the hood which is thin and tapering, raised on fretted arches, and set in a grid. It resembles a Gothic *flèche* in the manner of Viollet-le-Duc. Because space is well defined, there is grace as well as splendour in this room. This definition, inherited from the classical period, was never lost either in the baroque or Empire periods and no structure is ever awash with plaster hyperbole in the manner of Vierzenheiligen. This is due in part to the rejection of human representation and to a limited repertoire of decorative forms.

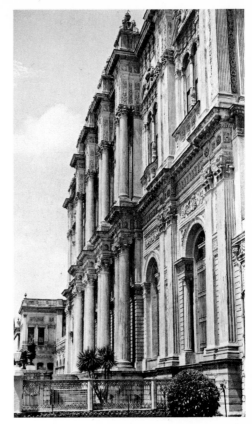

467, 469 Dolmabahçe Saray, Istanbul. Part of the Bosphorus façade and (below) the great staircase.

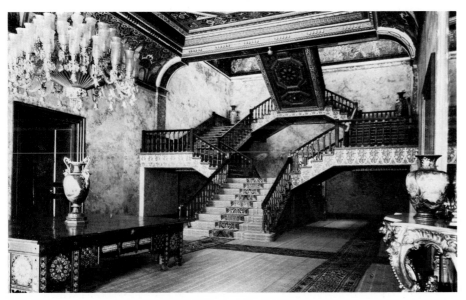

468 Beylerbey Saray, Bosphorus. A staircase.

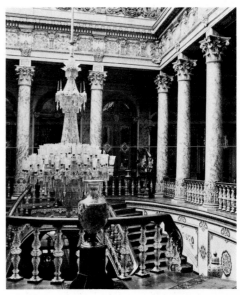

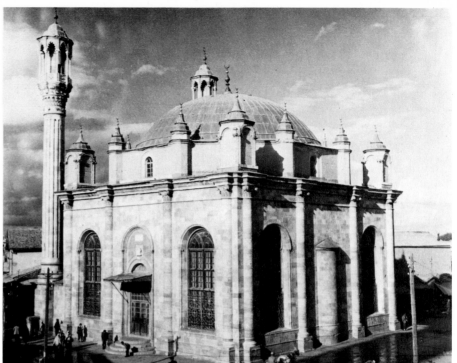

470 *Abdülâziz Cami, Konya, from the south-west.*

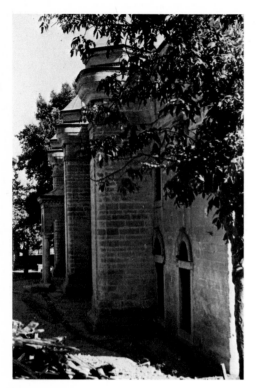

471, 472 *Ulu Cami, Kütahya. The west flank and buttresses and, below, the kilim which acts as a windshield to the north door.*

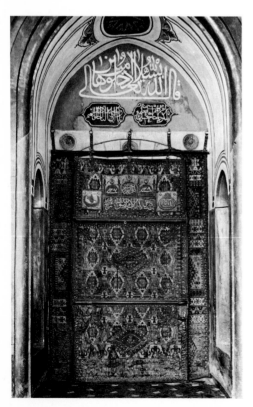

The mosque of Abdülâziz at Konya, built in *1289/1872*,[146] attempts to achieve similar magnificence on a larger scale. There is the same rank of vast windows rising to the height of the chamber. There is a bow in the middle of the gallery and the mihrab has a double tier of colonnettes carrying an arch that foliates over an inset radiance. The portico is very lofty and its columns spindly. The twin minarets have elaborate corbels which mount band upon band to support the şerefes. These are hooded by their caps in the Egyptian manner.[147] The caps are carried on toothed arches set on eight slender colonnettes. Like the Hırkai Şerif Cami, the Aziziye belongs to the Balian era.[148] There are other less richly appointed mosques in the same style for it was a period which saw much building and re-building. It also fostered a romantic appeal to the Ottoman past in an effort to bolster the dynasty. The türbe and the mescit of Ertuğrul at Söğüt[149] were rebuilt, and Abdülhamit II restored the Çelebi mosque there in the old Ulu Cami manner with four piers and nine domes.

The vast Ulu Cami at Kütahya was completely rebuilt by Sultan Mustafa who only reigned a few months in *1222/1807*. According to the inscription the marble columns and sculpture were added by Abdülmecit and the dome was repaired by Abdülhamit II in *1309/1893*, the year in which the then vali, Celal Pasha, composed the verses. The first mosque built by Beyazit, son of the Germiyan Bey Süleyman, has disappeared. The inscription attributes the plan to the architect of the then vali, Çelebi Mustafa Pasha. The vali was acting for Sultan Mustafa but the mosque belongs in appearance to the 1850s and the reign of Abdülmecit. The deep porch has a large dome and there were once cradle vaults over the sofas on each side: but that to the north-west is converted into a room. The independent base of the minaret is set at the north-east corner of the high portico. In the middle of each flank of the mosque are side entries preceded by porches, and a small polygonal mihrab apse projects from the south wall. Large buttresses are a feature of the exterior. The interior is so large that it is softly lit even in summer, although there are two tiers of ten windows along each flank. Across the north end are five eyvans and beyond this vestibule are large twin domes on the mihrab axis. The first has a lantern but the second is sealed as if they represented the court and mescit of the Bursa period. The domes are supported by six free-standing marble columns which are faceted and not round. This is an indication that they are likely to belong to the time of Abdülmecit and quarried freshly. Under the first dome is an octagonal marble mahfil carried by columns. If two İskele mosques were turned face to face without a dividing wall, this would be the plan. Had there been no semi-domes and corner cupolas at each end of the mosque and four cupolas down each side it would have been related to the Bursa style more closely, but the immediate impression is of openness and the size of the interior dwarfs the mihrab and the minber. The mosque measures approximately twenty-five and a half by forty metres.

The Ulu Cami at Çorum was either rebuilt on an older foundation or else extended and extensively renovated in 1909.[150] It is early nineteenth-century style and is a large square room with a broad but shallow central dome borne by twelve green plaster columns grouped in threes at each corner. The early nineteenth-century *trompe l'œil* shell decoration of the dome is like that at Yozgat and the Köprülü Cami at Safranbolu. The son cemaat yeri was made into an extension of the mosque with a gallery over it and a porch has had to be added. The capitals are like those at Yozgat which suggests a late eighteenth- or early nineteenth-century date for the major alterations.

There is an excellent tradition of carpentry and plastering at Çorum. The galleries of the eighteenth-century Sulu Han are an example while the Veli Pasha Han is a fine nineteenth-century kervansaray on the grand scale. It has a large rectangular court and wooden galleries reached by elegant staircases. A patrician central block of apartments rises to three storeys above the lane and the carriage gate on its right. The ground floor is masonry but the others are timber framed. Hans were still being built in the old manner in market towns, but in Istanbul these buildings were no longer Ottoman except for their courtyards and sometimes a mescit or a room for prayer. By the end of the century, their galleries were built of iron like Western warehouses and department stores.

The eclecticism of this period and the European appearance of the new neighbourhoods of the capital, for which mostly foreign or Armenian architects were responsible, provoked a reaction. This was first inspired by such visitors as Montani who prepared numerous plans and drawings of monuments such as Süleymaniye or the Yeşil Cami at Bursa for the Turkish section of the exhibition in Vienna in 1873. The Pertevniyal Valide Cami, built by the mother of Abdülâziz at Aksaray in Istanbul in *1288/1871*[151] is attributed to him by Eyice and to Agop Balian by Pamukciyan.[152] The scholarly details could be by Montani while the mass might be by Agop.[153] The widening of the streets has cut down the courtyard size and dismantled the elaborate gates. A large foyer with a broad wooden staircase leads to an upper landing and the royal gallery. The hall of prayer is a domed square painted all over with that love of massed rich colour which disfigures Sinan Pasha Cami at Beşiktaş. At Beylerbey, the salons are as brilliant with reds, blues and greens as a gypsy caravan. It is a success here for bargee art may be fit for a palace but it is not necessarily ideal for a mosque.

A second foreigner to inspire the revivalist movement was Valori, or Valloury, who built the present Yüksek Ticaret Okul or Commercial College and the Office of the Ottoman Debt, now the Istanbul Erkek Lise or Boys' High School. The latter is the most impressive of his buildings and still a landmark above Eminönü. The garden is bounded by a sober wall with plain, rectangular grilled windows, and the lofty gates have pointed arches in unembellished stone frames. Their undulating eaves are, however, baroque. The entry into the central hall is carried to the height of two storeys and surmounted by an upper chamber under equally broad eaves. A mezzanine floor is but one sign that the building is essentially nineteenth-century in design and built for use as offices even if the ogee or other medieval arches are genuine attempts to mask the present with the image of the past. The windows are grouped together in a manner unrelated to the style of the sixteenth century. Light was better achieved by the bold new windows of the Tulip period at the kiosk of Kara Mustafa Pasha or later at Aynalı Kavak. Valori's offices have dignity because of their height and commanding site and because their bulk is boldly handled, but they revive nothing: remove the roof

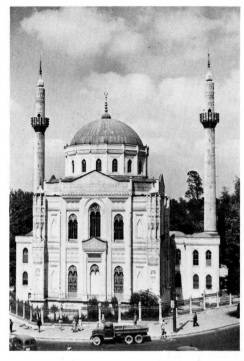

473 Valide Complex, Aksaray, from the south.

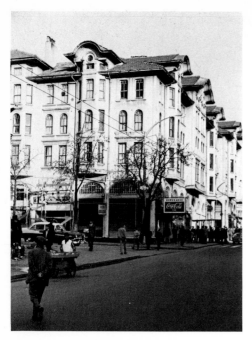

474   *Apartments built by Kemalettin at Aksaray, Istanbul.*

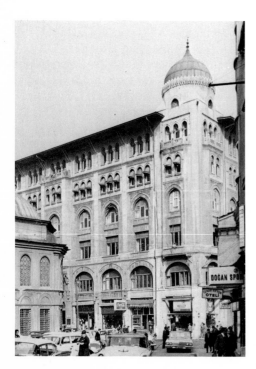

475   *Vakif Han, Istanbul, with the Abdülhamit I Türbe in the left foreground.*

and eaves and substitute castellations and they are as Gothic as they are Ottoman.

The architect of Sirkeci Station, Jasmond, taught the first consciously Ottoman architect to be seen for many years and who became a leader of a revivalism that petered out after his death in 1927. Kemalettin was firstly an able engineer. His buildings are impressive and expensive architectural failures. His massive use of stone was improvident and unrelated to the building techniques of his time. He was born in 1870 and rapidly rose to the first rank. He has a long list of works to his credit including the three small mosques at Bebek, Bostancı and Bakırköy which are modest essays in the sixteenth-century manner, nicely executed, but lacking vitality and warmth. His own inventions, such as the framing of the segments of the octagon between the eight turrets below the drum of the dome at Bebek, further compartmentalize the traditional structure and weaken the effect. When revivalism is so painstaking, any deviation from the historical form is disturbing. The triangulated tops of the buttresses which sheer up the stabilizing turrets at the corner of the roof of the mosque at Bostancı are an example. Kemalettin's creativeness overwhelmed his historical decorum and uppermost at his open türbe of Mahmut Şevket Pasha at Şişli is an unattractive Germanic love of the ponderous.

The türbe of Mehmet V Reşat, the last sultan to be buried in Turkey and the only one buried at Eyüp, may be considered the last monument of the dynasty. It is more than usually faithful to the past yet it is a composition of dead elements and some of Kemalettin's own inventive idiosyncracies.

Kemalettin experimented with baroque when building an apartment block at Laleli, but apart from curvular decoration above the windows which is reflected in the eaves, the design is rectilinear. His masterpiece is the large office block of the Vakıf Han between the Yeni Valide Cami and Sirkeci Station. It was begun in 1914. He was responsible for the plan and the façade. The han encloses a high and narrow central court which has become gloomy because of the grime and his use of yellow glass, but it has spacious galleries and corridors. The corner cupolas were designed to conceal the lift machinery, an idea as ingenious as it is historically absurd. The roof of cement and iron is incongruous but it is the façade that determines the extent of Kemalettin's failure. It is based on a series of fifteen tall rounded arches over the shops and the mezzanine floor. Those at the ends protrude while the fourth from each end acts as a portal. Another series of pointed arches encloses the windows of the next two floors. Above these are triple windows, except at the ends where there is only a pair, and the top floor has a further series of triple windows which are divided by short round columns. Each tower has a half-onion cupola. In imitation of a pishtak entry, a section is projected on consoles above the two doorways. Above this is a small open balcony and this projection recurs with the corner towers. Kemalettin liked balconies and he used them to divide windows or recess façades but never in the Ottoman manner. The strong framing of the windows of the han and the divisions – for they are not engaged piers – make for a firm contrast between the vertical and the horizontal movements of his façade in a nineteenth-century way related to the neo-Romanesque of a Richardson or the earlier works of Sullivan. The shallow protrusion of the towers and entries is too weak and so are the eaves at roof level which are purposeless, unlike those over baroque sebils and portals which could shelter people from Istanbul's rain or sun.

Kemalettin's colleague, Vedat Bey, was born in 1873, trained in Paris, and died in 1942. He achieved a particularly happy relationship with his artisans. The Istanbul Central Post Office is his major work and it is easy to compare it with that of Kemalettin, Jasmond, and Valori, examples of which are near at hand. The Post Office was completed in 1909 and decades of grime darken the glazed court. The grand marble staircase has lost its lustre. Here revivalism is boldly handled in a search for grandeur. Stars and consoles obtrude while the back windows are grouped to admit the maximum light Vedat Bey is said to have designed his own tiles. But for all his care, the Post Office is a monument without a future.[154]

Attempts at classical Ottoman revivalism continue. The most distinguished is the Şişli mosque completed between 1945 and 1949[155] by Vasfi Egeli. In plan it recalls the Süleyman Pasha Cami at Cairo or an İskele Cami deprived of its corner cupolas. There is care over such details as the stalactite squinches and the raised mekteb yet the building is architecturally dead. Ankara, too, has cut stone mosques built since the Second World War, and there has been much religious building all over Anatolia. The work is bad and lacks any feeling for true Ottoman forms.[156] This is often due to the use of concrete or of concrete framing with brick interstices, a hideous example of which is the large Söğütlüçeşme Cami at Kadiköy, completed in 1965. It is almost a caricature. A modest impulse to revivalism among municipal buildings in the provinces produced plain office blocks faced with good ashlar stone such as the Belediye or Town Hall at Sivas which has the advantage of being set in ample surroundings. Only the entry is accented while the eaves and tiled roof make no serious allusion to the past. Attempts have been made to adapt commercial buildings to a historic setting. An example is the İş Bank at Konya which seeks to be a worthy companion for the Mevlana Museum and the Selimiye Mosque at the end of the street. The Ottoman mannerisms such as the bays projected on piers across the street are restrained by a modern formal straight-jacket but the ashlar facing is excellent and this makes this particular anachronism inoffensive. It is not a corpse like the cumbersome ministerial buildings of Holzmeister in Ankara built when a determination to smother the past blighted the new capital with neo-Nazi architecture and statuary.

A revivalism with its own dynamism which produced spectacular results in Istanbul and along the Bosphorus was Art Nouveau which, from its conception, had owed much to Islamic inspiration. Flowering wrought iron is still abundant although many houses in the style have been pulled down. The Egyptian Embassy at Bebek has survived with its magnificent staircases and some of its frescoes, but the palace of Nazime Sultan at Ortaköy, built in 1905, has been wantonly demolished to make way for a lignite dump. It was the work of Raimondo Aronco, court architect from 1896 to 1909, who was influenced by the Austrian school of Olbrich. It had horseshoe-form windows under deep eaves, strapping and sun discs. But Art Nouveau was an imported style executed by foreigners or members of the minorities with a foreign education. It was very popular but has no place in the history of Ottoman architecture.

When it appeared in Istanbul, Ottoman architecture was already in its death agonies. It flourished under an absolute, theocratic monarchy with a lavish supply of stone: neither of these is to be found in Turkey today. Its monuments may still inspire echoes but it can have no living future within the Republic nor anywhere else any more.

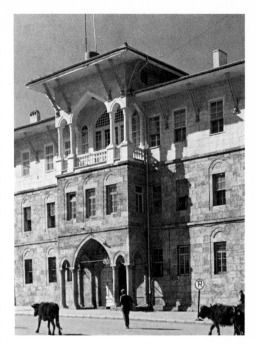

476 *Town Hall, Sivas.*

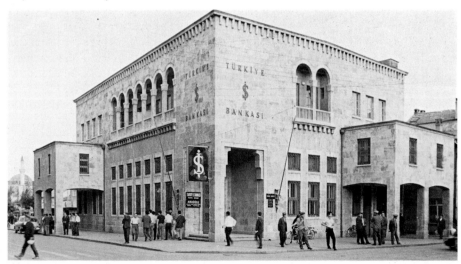

477 *İş Bank, Konya.*

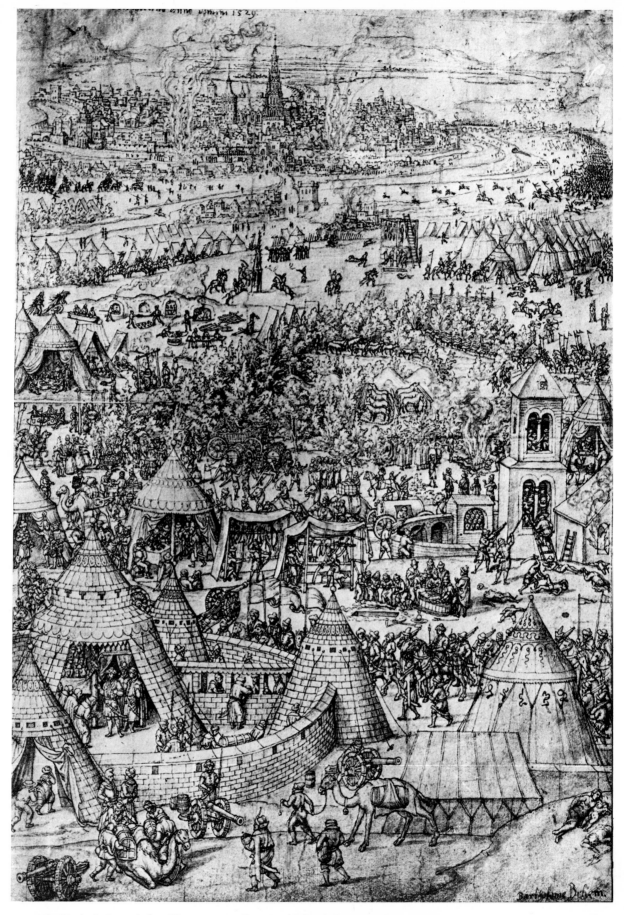

478 The Turkish Camp before Vienna, 1529. Drawing by Bartholomäus Behen.

II

The Ottoman house

PRIVATE PROPERTY AND THE sense of a home were not greatly sought after by
the Ottomans or the Selçuks before them. There are no sure and certain remains
of a Selçuk house[1] although there are some vestiges of palaces or their foundations – on an island on the lake at Beyşehir, for example, and a belvedere belonging to the saray at Konya. The first Ottomans left even less behind and it may be
concluded that even at Bursa their royal mansions were built of wood on stone
foundations. The real home of the sultan was his tent; that is to say a series of day
and night tents corralled in a wall of cloth.[2] And this was also true of his vezirs and
lesser men. The miniatures of the period show this very well[3] for the sultan is
constantly portrayed sitting before his tent or under a canopy in the open. This
was very much an Asian delight, and the Jengiz Khan miniatures for the court of
Akbar the Great reveal the same love of the field as do the various collections in
Istanbul or Teheran.

The royal tent was often of cloth of gold inside and the Altın Oda[4] was a symbol
of power just as was the parasol;[5] this is still the case in Ethiopia, for example,
even today. The Ottoman throne, like that of the Selçuks, was more of a dais than
a chair and it was made to be taken apart and packed up when the army was on the
march, while mats and bedding were simply rolled. Cooking was done out of
doors wherever possible. The saray was built for open-air ceremonial and even
the Kübbe Altı, or the Divan, was a grand loggia rather than a hall. In the
morning the sultan would leave his selâmlık for a kiosk in which to pass the day,
and this pavilion was nothing more than a tent in stone or wood, later walled
with glass. Travellers report that the Ottoman camp was clean and orderly[6] and
the citizens of Vienna were astonished to discover that, when the Grand Vezir
Kara Mustafa Pasha raised his siege in 1683, he left behind a garden and an
orchard and that the camp had been laid out in rows of streets like a Roman
town. The very display of the Ottoman court – the trumpets and the drums, the
banners and horsetails and feathers, the love of colour which was so important a
means of identification amid an army – were splendours of the tented field.
It was not, of course, merely an Ottoman idiosyncrasy, as the Field of the Cloth
of Gold bears out, nor were the Ottoman sultans any more or less infected with
the love of the chase than the Byzantine emperors before them. Royal sports
tend to be alike. But the Ottoman love of the open air, even when the empire had
sunk into decay and the sultan no longer ventured his life in battle, remained until
the twentieth century.

The humbler soldiery were so used to the concept of the tent that, in their
barracks, they were divided into groups by means of screens. These corresponded
to the sections who shared a tent when in the field. This love for camp life is
reflected in village life to this day, where the croft is mainly a refuge from rain
and, whenever possible, all the household activities take place in the open air.

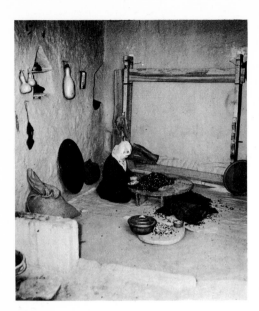

479   *Interior of a peasant house, Göreme.*

Nowhere in Anatolia can be called typical, but the central region from Amasya to Kayseri may serve as an example: the village and town houses alike were based, and many still are, on the concept of one all-purpose room where beds were spread on the floor at night and kept in a chest or cupboard in the wall by day. The mattresses served as sofas and the pillows or yastık for arm rests. A niche for utensils and another for a lamp, with all its symbolism, completed the essential furniture. The poor had very few possessions at any time and the rich were not acquisitive but content with splendid objects meant for daily use. A vase and a flower, therefore, completed the furniture together with a pitcher of water. The croft also had a threshold over which all who entered had to step and this was a symbol shared with the chambers of the king. Busbecq[7] in 1554 found the houses at Amasya 'as they are in Spain' built of loam and clay with a flat roof. On it was kept an old piece of column or roller which was rolled up and down to close any chink or crevice made by the rain.[8] The houses, Busbecq remarks, were not pretty. They were, however, functional for, including the roller, there are still many like them all over Anatolia today.

The village houses in the Kayseri region are related in style to those of the town but they are more modest and are rarely more than one storey high. Ten kilometres north of Kayseri is Erkalat, for example, on a hillside covered with loose rocks above a valley green with trees and vineyards. Here the houses are built of stone – which lies at hand without need for quarrying – but there are few window frames that have been geometrically carved like those at Kayseri itself. In spite of the whitewashing of door and window frames, the village merges with the landscape out of which it is built. The better houses have arched eyvans or loggias but the humbler ones are simply crofts. The humble single-storey village architecture, based on a flat-roofed room and a barn with a walled yard, is transformed in summer when the hay is stacked high on the roofs and gradually fades from green to dun.[9]

Such homes are more commonly built of mud and straw than of stone and the sandy earth gives them the colour of crystallized honey and the same febrile texture. Sometimes they are painted white. Necessarily, the walls are thick and the windows deep in order to keep the rooms cool in summer and warm in winter. They have prehistoric origins, but since they were the housing of the majority of the countryfolk of Anatolia and many of the townsmen, their structure is worthy of consideration. Their function was, and is, to meet the basic human needs with the cheapest possible local materials. Apart from foundations of stones from mountains or river beds and some timber supports for roofs and lintels, the cheapest and best Anatolian building material is a mixture of peat,

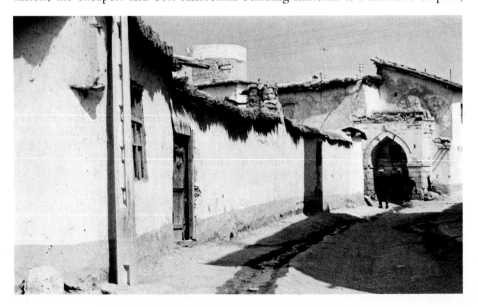

480   *Street below the citadel, Karaman.*

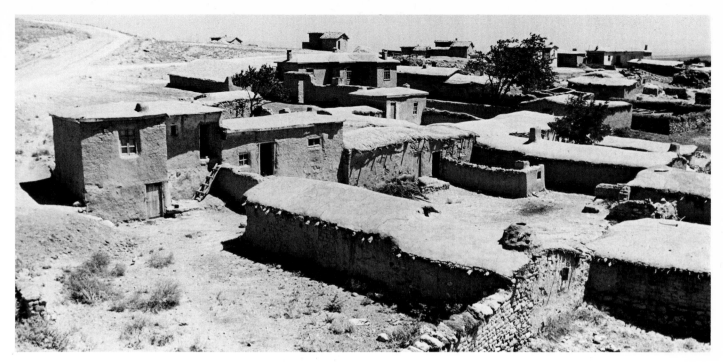

481   Village houses, Dokuz, Central Anatolia.

mud and straw which is left to mature. If some timber framing is employed, its connection with the walls is weak and they are quick to collapse in an earthquake. Moreover, timber is costly so, if possible, not more than one tree is used to make the roof beams, lintels and window frames. The roof beams or poles are covered with a layer of thatch and then a mixture of clay and salt to keep the roof water-tight. The gutters are clay drain-spouts which keep the water away from walls and windows. The floors are of beaten earth and there is a hole in the roof: if there is a chimney it is often made of a pitcher without a bottom. The daub and straw are insulators, but a further economy is achieved by connecting the stable with the family room to take advantage of the heat given off by the animals which also need protection from the cold. The storage room is made a part of the house in order to guard against theft. The winter living-room is heated by dried dung with sand banked round it which gets very hot. The beehive heaps of these bricks of dung are a characteristic sight in more primitive villages and, when large enough, can be architectonic. The court is the summer living-room and it and the roof of the house may be used for sleeping. In the court is a shelter of woven branches with poles for piers which makes a cool bower. Sometimes when the son marries, rooms are added to the parental croft but this is not the rule. Mats are the chief decoration and are either woven or of beaten felt but are less and less made at home. The villages of immigrants and of Circassians have scattered houses and are less tightly knit family and social units than those of the long-established inhabitants of the plain whose houses traditionally crowd together – partly as protection against bandits – and whose lanes are labyrinthine.

Such a village is related to those of Central Asia insofar as the idea of a house or fixed dwelling has gained a footing among the peoples of that region. Vambéry[10] gives a clear description of the building of a house by the Özbeks which could well apply to many Anatolian villages. The walls were either of clay or slate[11] or of wooden lathes laid crossways and the interstices filled up with clay and unbaked tiles.[12] Small holes served as windows; they were left open in summer and in winter were pasted over with oiled paper. The roof was like a terrace.[13] Regular bricklayers were seldom met with and every man was his own architect, convinced of possessing sufficient knowledge to build himself a house sufficient for his wants: since a plumbline was still unknown, it is not to be wondered at that the walls were cracked and uneven, bulging either in or out, and soon became dilapidated.

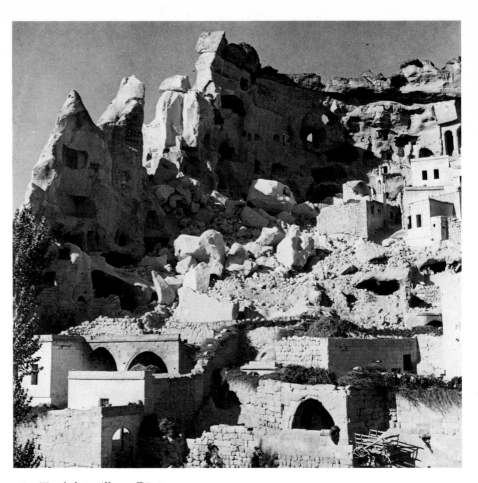

482   Troglodyte village, Göreme.

There are many variations of the humbler Anatolian house and some have good woodwork and sound floorboards. They are spread all over the Konya plain where two-storey dwellings occur in the more prosperous villages. There, the upper floor is often reached by ladders, while the doors are sometimes low and recall those of Selçuk times at the hospital at Divrik and the Kiosk Medrese – or Köşe Kiosk – outside Kayseri. In some eastern areas where stone and some timber are available, the villages consist of large low dwellings which when built on the hillside become camouflaged as terracing. They may be dirty but they can be unexpectedly spacious inside and in some villages are prosperous enough to have some wainscoting, which at Çatakköy,[14] for example, on the Kars-Erzerum highway is decorated with good carving. Since no Kurd is a carpenter, these are likely to have been Armenian homes originally. One house at Çatakköy consists of a large room divided from a long living-room with sofas along three walls by a roofed eyvan with a very large beam supported on poles. Behind is a stable and the kitchen which is also the harem. In front of the larger, unused room is a second extension of the roof which forms a shallow portico. The deep windows are splayed and neatly panelled.

Unlike Çatakköy, the truly Kurdish village is so primitive that even elementary carpentry is not understood. Timber framing is extensively used in all forest regions such as the Black Sea provinces, and there the transition from croft to farmhouse to konak is difficult to define. But even there, purely wooden buildings are rare except for sheds and barns although they do occur in the region of Kastamonu and also in the Taurus and other mountain areas. In western Anatolia there are both mud, brick and timber-frame houses and there, particularly in the more prosperous Greek littoral of Ottoman times, the houses of the poor tend to be humbler versions of the mansions of the notables. It is to the grander house that it is now proper to turn.

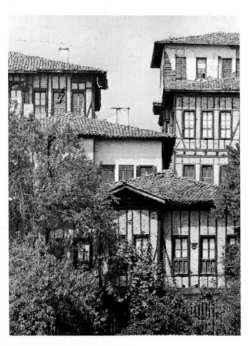

483   Houses in Safranbolu.

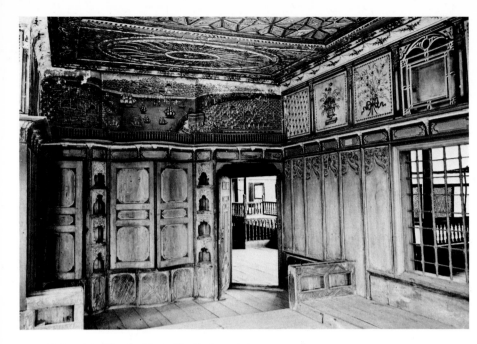

484 Çakır Ağa Konak, Birgi. Vestibule to the summer salon.

28   The Ottoman konak derives its plan from that of the Çinili Kiosk. The symbolic meaning of the plan, which gathered more and more mystical associations, is retained to the extent that on occasion not only is there a dome over the central area but it is painted a celestial blue. The four corner areas in the crook of the arms of the cross become withdrawing-rooms while the four eyvans become chevets or foyers or, sometimes, are divided into additional rooms. In smaller konaks sufficient likeness survives to suggest that even with these the symbolism retained its vitality. And such houses are found in the Balkans and Greece just as much as in Anatolia, which suggests that the plan was ideally suited for the way of life of the period.

       The largest room in such a house was the mabeyin or salon which was common
84   to the harem and the selâmlık. It was preceded by a vestibule from which one stepped up onto the carpeted wooden floor of the chamber. Sometimes this fore-hall was large enough for several servants to stand in, but in more modest houses it was no more than a corner with space in which to kick off a pair of slippers. The entry wall was usually made up of cupboards and niches. Beyond the low rail which divided the vestibule from the salon, the room itself would have a high and ornamental ceiling sometimes with a shallow dome in the centre. One wall would have an ocak in the middle with niches for lamps and water-jugs or a vase with a single flower set in it; the other two were likely to be filled with windows, especially if the room was the highest in the house which was often the case with medium-sized mansions;[15] or one of these might have built-in cupboards running the whole length. The low sofas or divans ran along at least two if not
68   three walls. Pleasure houses like the great room of the Amcazade Köprülü yalı at Kanlıca had windows on all three sides and might be further extended by the projection of three eyvans; but more than one bay or eyvan was rarely added to a country konak: instead, the room itself was often extended over the street or garden on consoles or corbels.

       The development of the larger house in the provinces began in the seventeenth century and spread rapidly in the eighteenth. A simple example is the Kavasun
87   Aptullahın Ev near the citadel at Karaman. It is preceded by a large yard and is only one storey high although built in the latter half of the eighteenth century. It was designed for Hacı Ömer Ağa who died in *1295/1778*.[16] A large door admits to a central lobby off which on the left and right are the two principal odas or chambers. Each is preceded by an ample foyer from which the main room is railed off, and each has a range of windows onto the yard and a brick and plaster

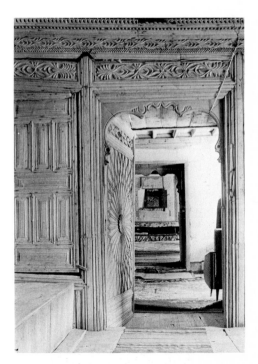

485 Kavasun Aptullah House, Karaman. Interior.

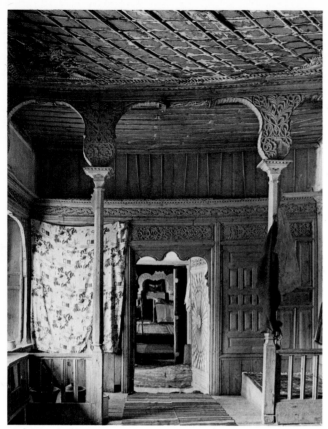

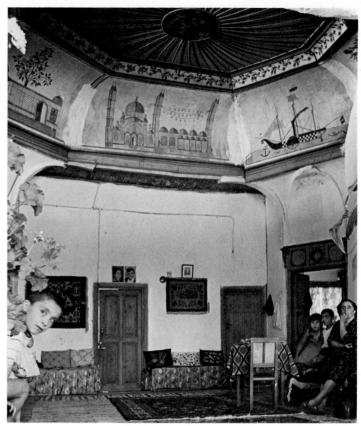

486, 487 *Kavasun Aptullah House, Karaman.*
Interior and, below, detail of a door.

488 *Hasam House, Karaman. The central landing.*

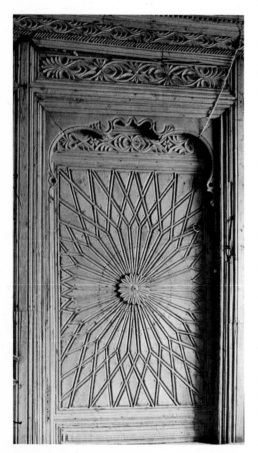

ocak at the far end with shelves and cupboards on either side. Divans run down the sides of the room and they are still used for sitting on by day and as beds by night. The quilts and blankets are stored in a large and handsome cupboard when not in use. Behind these rooms, which form a harem and selâmlık with the hall as neutral ground, are the kitchen quarters and storerooms. The odas are large, but what makes them remarkable is the magnificent eighteenth-century woodwork which covers doors and ceilings, railings and pillars with a mixture of traditional and baroque designs. The crisp plaster carving has been thickened by whitewash.

A grander mansion, also in Karaman, is the Hasamı Ev which is more typically a konak although it lacks the splendid woodwork.[17] The house opens onto the street on both sides and has a separate garden beyond the town centre. This is important because, had it been set in its garden, it might have been built at ground level like the house of Ömer Ağa. It has lost its main entry to the basement hall, in the centre of which a grand wooden stairway ascends to the living area. This stair forms the fourth eyvan at first-floor level and opens onto a large central saloon with a dome on a drum which is charmingly painted with a paddle steamer and other nineteenth-century scenes of the Bosphorus. Three other eyvans once opened off this. The two main corner salons have their doors cut across the angle of their walls, which was the usual custom, and a modest version of the Çinili Kiosk is thus obtained. Wherever possible, tall sash windows are set in rows to obtain the maximum amount of light and air. The konak is timber-framed with the wattle and daub interstices plastered over, the most common form of structure in Anatolia and the Balkans until recent times. It results in charming white and black streets with upper rooms jutting out under wide eaves to create shade, and rows of windows projecting as if hungry for the view and for fresh air. Like those of most larger houses, the salons have ocaks, but portable charcoal braziers or mangals were also used. The kitchen was in the yard downstairs, as was common with most private dwellings because, wherever possible, cooking was done in the open.

In the nineteenth century, variation in the plans of houses was increased by the growth in the number of the retiring rooms. One of the most splendid mansions, that of Çakır Ağa at Birgi, probably dates in its present form from the reign of Abdülhamit I or even Selim III[18] and is one of the few which approach a Western country house in size, for homes on such a scale seemed impersonal and comfortless to the Ottomans. The Birgi konak is, however, very much a town house fronting a lane and has only a small garden behind it. The farm and its buildings were outside the town boundaries. The open sofa of the third floor or piano nobile has a projecting bower besides two large and two small salons at each corner. Beyond one of these, the water closet opens onto its own extension of a wing verandah. There are three eyvans between the chambers; one without a window wall acts as a service corner complete with sink; but the central eyvan, looking onto the street between the state rooms, is a fine open chamber. The main saloon is entered by a door which is cut across the corner to create an oblique approach to the room under a receding eave. This setting of the door, as we have seen, was a common feature of the better houses. The salon has windows opening onto its lateral eyvan as well as along the outside walls which project over the street and towards the ravine and the town. Undulating across the wall in the forehall there is a row of cupboards and niches. The chamber proper is panelled, and each frame is topped with an asymmetrical baroque foliate relief. Between the casements and the square, glazed upper lights are further panels painted with flowers in ribboned bunches or in ornate urns. Across the entry wall is a crowded panorama of Istanbul and its mosques, with sailing ships on the roads. There is a similar painting of Izmir in the winter salon and both are charmingly naïve. The ceiling over the forehall has an oval central panel but a complex traditional Islamic design in relief covers that of the main room which is rectangular.

This is a summer room. The corresponding salon on the other side has an ocak as have the two smaller rooms: indeed, the oda with windows onto the garden beyond the pantry-eyvan has a very elaborate baroque example. The smaller room between the summer salon and the lavatory only has windows onto the verandah. The middle floor is a more modest and lower version of the top, but the ground floor, which was reserved for servants, is really a courtyard with rooms cut out of it. The many wooden piers at this level give the impression that the upper floors are raised on pilotis. The konak has stone foundations but is otherwise built of timber, lathe and plaster.

The garden side is made highly elaborate by the two tiers of open sofas with their lattices, the cantilevered bowers, the recessions and projections of rooms and eyvans, and the stair rails which add diagonals to the play of the horizontals

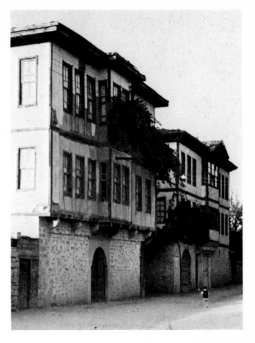

489 Safranbolu. Two konaks.

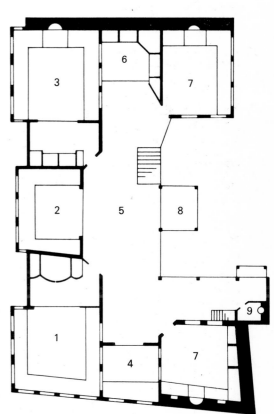

491 Çakır Ağa Konak, Birgi. Sketch plan. 1 Summer salon; 2 open divan; 3 winter salon; 4 eyvan; 5 living area; 6 service eyvan; 7 chambers; 8 belvedere; 9 water closet.

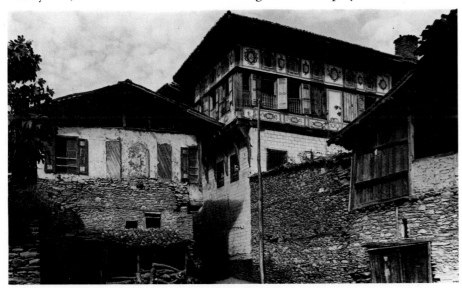

490 Çakır Ağa Konak, Birgi. A corner from the street.

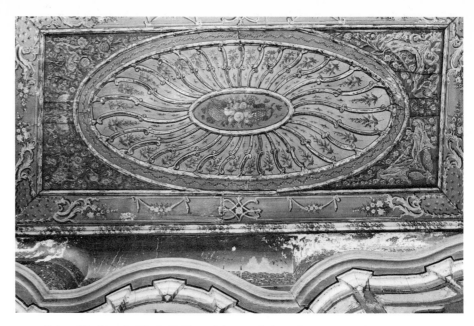

492 *Çakır Ağa Konak, Birgi. Ceiling of the vestibule to the summer salon.*

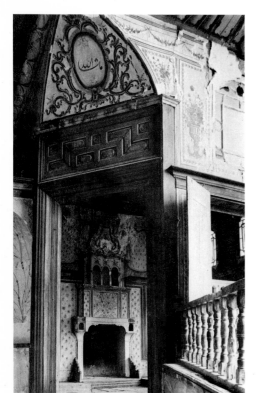

and verticals of piers and banisters with beams and eaves. These eaves are up-turned at an angle of thirty degrees and plastered over. Such full, often curved, white eaves are found in particular, but not exclusively, in the Balkans. The tiled roof of the konak is only slightly inclined. The capitals are carved out of the heads of the columns and carry flat imposts shaped like the wings of moths. Both columns and imposts were plastered originally and were as gaily painted as the rest of the building where so much of the original decoration has survived in the rich, now faded, colours and crowded designs of the late eighteenth century. This decoration was also applied to the outside lane façade where the two salons and the central eyvan project at upper floor level to create a certain grandeur. The garden front is like an open doll's house or, still more, a triple-tiered stage in which daily life was acted out in public; this is the heart of the matter, for the centre of the mansion and its administration is here since, were the garden wings united and the verandah and its bower enclosed, the plan of the Çinili *128* Kiosk would emerge again and reveal the bower as the hub of the plan.

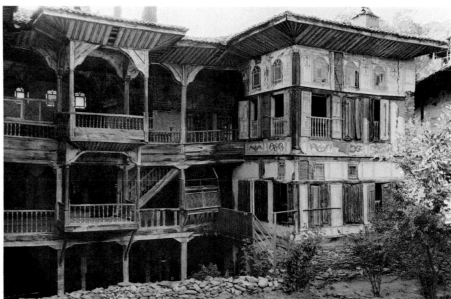

493, 494 *Çakır Ağa Konak, Birgi. The baroque hearth from the gallery and, above, part of the garden front.*

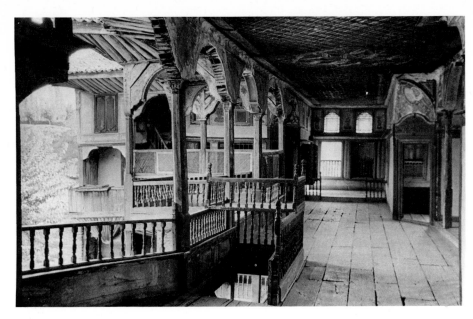

495 Çakır Ağa Konak, Birgi. View down the great gallery from the room with the baroque hearth. The door to the summer salon is on the right.

Few konaks can rival the Çakır Ağa, but the same play of extension and regression, closed wall and open gallery, of diagonals linking verticals and horizontals is achieved on the garden side of the so-called House of Murat at Bursa which is not likely to date from earlier than the eighteenth century.[19] Here the imposts are modest in size and the six arches of the upper veranda are hipped. Like most of the houses discussed, which are prior to the nineteenth century in date, only the upper windows of the salon were glazed. All the rest were open grilled casements, with wooden shutters to protect them from the wind because imported glass was too costly. The veranda has a deep eyvan between the two winter rooms and a second only open onto the verandah side. This has two tiers of three windows in its garden wall and of two windows onto the lane, to make a summer salon approximately ten by eighteen feet which is halfway between the open sofa and the closed extra room of the nineteenth century.

The streets in the Muradiye district of Bursa still retain many nineteenth-century houses in the wooden-frame tradition, some with gables and a few with bow fronts. The colour-washes used on the plaster include a pale blue and varying shades of green in addition to the ochres and deep reds, blues and, above all, white which are so common in Anatolia. This type of house if in disrepair, which it frequently is, with its plaster flaking to reveal the timber and the wattle and daub beneath, can achieve a great variety of texture and colour. There is that of the smooth plaster itself and of the red porous tiles, the darker and lighter browns of the fibrous exposed or varnished wood and the softer browns and surfaces of the wicker or the clay. All these go well with the cobbles or the gravel of the street and with the surrounding trees.

The fluid plan of the Bursa houses is caused by the size and importance of the town and the high land values compared with other towns of the central plateau. This plasticity of form creates ideal streets which have unity of material and, to a great extent, of roof levels, but which are filled with individual homes striving with each other to give their upper rooms a view of the life of the street and the landscape beyond. This true elsewhere, for example in the older parts of Tokat which Jackson in 1797 said was the size of Sivas but had a much better appearance than any town he had before seen 'in Turkey's dominions' and where he found the houses were all tiled and chiefly built with wood. He had the same respect for Amasya which has a fine array of konaks along the north shore of the Yeşil Irmak.[20] But in these less compact towns there was more regularity in the plans than in crowded Bursa, and the rooms all tend to be rectangular. One of the most interesting konaks at Amasya is built above a stone basement and

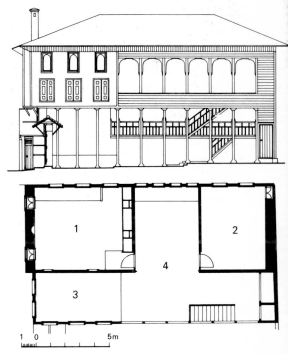

496 Ethnographical Museum, Bursa, known as the House of Murat. Elevation from the garden side and plan of the upper floor, scale 1:250. 1 Winter salon; 2 bedchamber; 3 summer salon; 4 gallery.

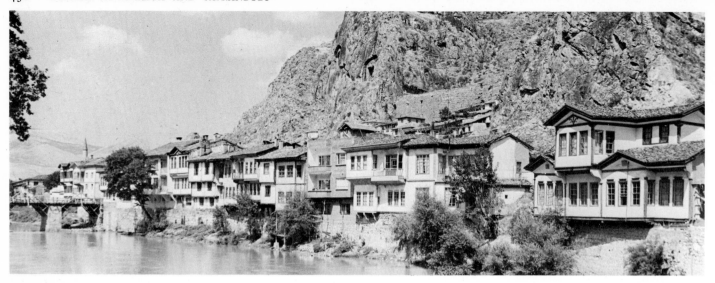

497 *Houses on the shore of the Yeşil Irmak at Amasya below the citadel and the tombs of the Mithridates family.*

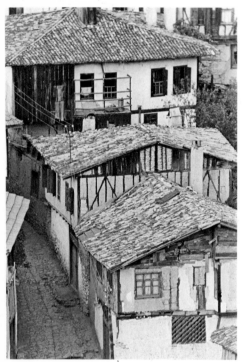

498 *Houses in Safranbolu.*

projects over the river. A triangle of gabled rooms, the central one above a recessed eyvan forming the apex, look out onto the water. Other gables project eastwards from the upper room and the end room on the first floor, while on the west further bays survey the lane from above the wall and gate into the courtyard. Like most of the nineteenth-century houses of Amasya, the plaster is white in sharp contrast to the black of the exposed stained beams. The humble bentwood props and struts of Bursa become elegant consoles, and the eaves are uplifted like those of the Çakır Ağa mansion; but the windows are standard sizes and akin to those of the humbler houses.

Amasya, unlike Bursa, still has some little-altered streets, particularly those west of the mosque of Beyazit II where, although the houses are of modest size, the busy casements projecting and receding at varying angles and heights create a lively play of light and shade. The builders took delight in exaggeration but only if it was functional and created new space. Tokat has a good example of the habit of setting a room across the triangle caused by the fork of two lanes. There is another characteristic example, sadly repaired with tin, between the Babı-Ali and Zeynep Sultan Cami in Istanbul. Another example is a remarkable konak, and one of many, at Safranbolu, which has claim to be the most beautiful timber-frame town in Anatolia because it is unmauled by modernization and because of the beauty of its setting. Originally, Safranbolu was two towns combined, with the Greeks living on one side of a gully and the Turks on the other where the mosques and markets are centred. The architecture of both quarters

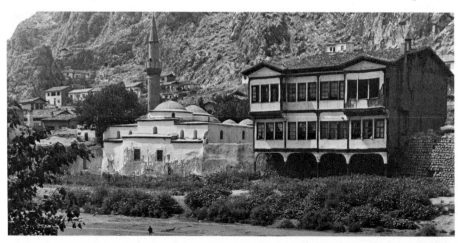

499 *Konak and Bülbül Hatun Cami, Amasya. The mosque dates from about 1500 and is related to Zincirlikuyu Cami, Istanbul.*

is similar and thus would seem to provide evidence against the assertion that the handsomest houses of Anatolia were all Greek or Armenian homes. Some were, but others were built by Moslem families who still live in them in many instances. Safranbolu is full of large burghers' and farmers' homes built on stone basements and with the main rooms protruding in moderation over the broad lanes and the gardens around them. Because these houses follow the movement of the narrow valleys, they are continually turning and achieving vistas down the street. There is none of the multiple shouldering of one another like with the houses of Amasya; due to their size and the space, many of them are spaced apart, but there is still a true sense of a street and also of windows watching and so of life behind the large, closed gates to their courtyards.

A handsome example of a konak of this period and of wooden-frame construction is the Ali Pasha Ev at 20 Kemeraltı sokak, at Kütahya. The date on the çeşme in the wall behind the entrance reads *1151/1738* and this is acceptable as the date of the house. The doorway admits to a covered court with the hay loft in an eyvan on the right and then a stable and a store. Entering the open court before the garden, there is a lavatory on the right and the stairs up to the entresol on the left. This floor consists of a sofa or living area open on two sides to the garden and the court. Behind the sofa, a large chamber with a small washroom and a cabinet or retiring room off it is the winter room of the harem. The closets for washing are a common feature of houses of this size and importance. There is an eyvan projecting over the street but with fewer windows than is usual. The stairs continue to the principal floor where the veranda is open to the garden. Behind it, with a range of windows onto the street, is the principal saloon complete with ocak and sofa and cupboards and niches. Beside this room is another small cabinet little bigger than the one off the salon on the floor below. There is a fine ceiling which is related to those of the Ömer Ağa house at Karaman. The plan of each floor is alike for each has in effect only two living areas, the one closed, for use in winter, and the other open for the summer. The courtyard is reserved for the kitchen and the stables, the middle floor for family life, and the upper is the mabeyin. This was the house of a pasha but only the reception room has any pretensions to grandeur and it measures just over twenty-five by sixteen feet including cupboard space. Through the use of sofas along the walls and built-in cupboards and shelves, all these Ottoman rooms gain considerably in grandeur, yet they are deliberately kept small enough to allow

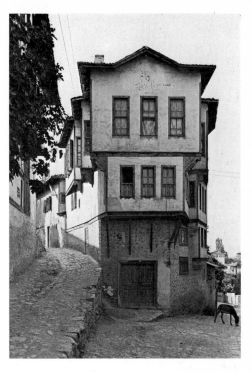

500 Konak in Safranbolu. This is a striking example of the Ottoman exploitation of an awkward site to erect a comfortable home with views in all directions.

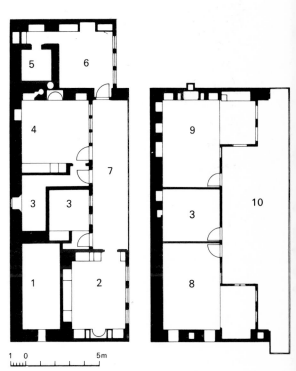

502 Cihanzade Nuri Bey Konak, Kütahya. Plans of the ground floor (left) and of the upper floor. Scale 1:250. 1 Store; 2 salon; 3 service rooms; 4 bedroom; 5 hamam; 6 vestibule; 7 gallery; 8 summer salon; 9 winter salon; 10 gallery.

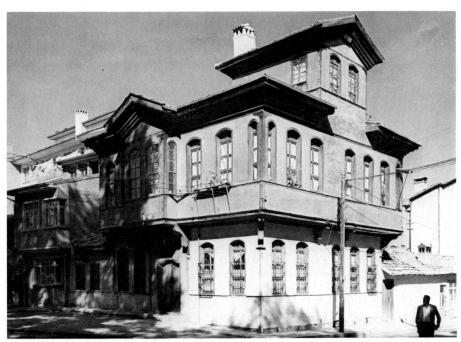

501 Konak in Kütahya. A late nineteenth-century example of a provincial town house.

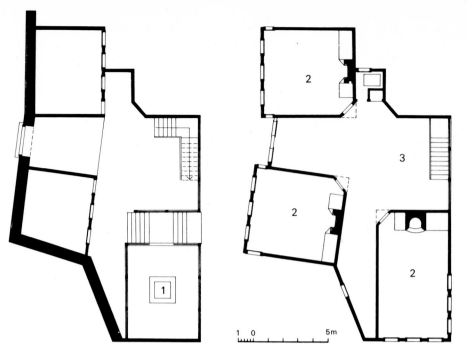

503 *House at 33, Reyhan Pasha Caddesi, Bursa. Plans of the ground floor (left) and of the upper floor. Scale 1:250. 1 Pool; 2 chambers; 3 living area.*

general conversation; and eyvans were common so that people might withdraw to converse intimately while admiring the view on all sides.

The variations on such a plan are innumerable, and if the open area may some- *502* times be little more than a veranda it is also on occasion a state apartment, as is the case with many yalıs on the Bosphorus. In the effort to make the rooms of town houses rational in shape, besides the resort to cantilevering over the street, these halls could take distorted shapes which were and are exploited to advantage. An example is at 33 Reyhan Pasha Caddesi at Bursa,[21] where two long eyvans *503* are created forming intimate corners for gossip, or the piano, or for the children to study their homework in. This is a nineteenth-century house and has three rooms more or less identical in size on its upper floor. Two jut out over the street and the third looks onto the small garden behind. The usual form of this living space or open sofa is a broad veranda with the main rooms opening off it and an eyvan between them: a modest and truncated form of the Çinili Kiosk.

The nineteenth century brought everywhere an increased interest in the definition of space and function in domestic architecture and a new regard for privacy even within age groups of a family. The result in Ottoman houses was for an extra room to encroach on the area of the open sofa, and at the Hacı Çakır Ev at Kütahya, dated *1196/1782*,[22] it is reduced at harem level to a large landing with a small tahta serving as a belvedere. All the houses of the period have the same fine doors, a tradition which was still alive at the end of the nineteenth *504* century. In many houses, the wooden lattices which could be raised up and *507* down on the courtyard and garden sides have disappeared. Where they remain, the seemingly random levels at which they are left, half open or closed, adds an interest to the façade which is consciously sought by the use of blinds in certain modern glass offices and apartments.

The houses of Kütahya have survived better than those of Ankara which are rapidly decaying together with their equally fine ceilings and woodwork. There, considerable use is made of receding ranks of corbels, often diminishing into the wall at a sharp angle, because there is emphasis on rectangular rooms and even rectangular yards and open sofas in spite of the rugged contours of the hillsides. An example is the Kasap Mustafa Ağa Konak, now in decay. There the salon stretches the width of the garden front with two tiers of eight windows, and measures over nineteen by thirty-seven feet.[23] The outer sofa is only a landing and its function is taken over by a secondary chamber with a wall of windows

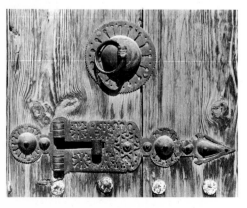

504 *Detail of a door, Safranbolu.*

onto the court and another inwards on to the landing. In the Ankara region, the interstices of the timber framing are filled with bricks often set in herring-bone designs which, when not plastered over, preserve a living tradition which is strikingly Tudor in appearance.

This type of house is to be found all over the Balkans and is well preserved in Bulgaria because of the severe laws protecting monuments. At Plovdiv, the Ethnographical Museum is installed in a remarkable early nineteenth-century example. It is in the middle of a large garden with a pool and a fountain and pleasant trees. Because it is only two storeys high, its size is not at first evident. There is a large bow front with five standard sash windows carried on four wooden piers projected over the porch which leads through a foyer into a great hall which has four corner rooms with doors cut across their angles and four eyvans, one of which serves as the vestibule to the harem wing; the other contains the grand wooden staircase. It is typical of buildings related to the Çinili Kiosk in plan, except that the central area is rectangular and on the upper floor forms a vast saloon under an oval ceiling which forms a shallow dome.

128 The rivals of these provincial residences were the yalıs of the Bosphorus. These, like the konaks of Plovdiv, closely follow the plan of the quasi-religious Çinili Kiosk. The old palace at Beşiktaş, demolished by Mahmut II, was described by Allom[24] as the pavilion (otak) of the sultan with those of his officers pitched around as if in an encampment. The meaning of the old symbolism was not, therefore, dead and the design of some yalıs was clearly related to the concept of a central dome which could be painted blue, like that of the Koca Yusuf Pasha Yalı at Cengilköy where the four corner rooms are all the same shape and dimensions but each is painted a different colour.[25] The concept of a central court suited sophisticated Ottoman life where each member of the family required his or her own room, the corner rooms with projecting bays being reserved for the senior members; but the climate turned the concept outside in so that the court became a hall and the rooms now looked outwards through ranks of windows. The yalı of Sarfat Pasha at Kanlıca is much closer to a Venetian palace in atmosphere than that of a sacred pavilion on which its plan is based, for it has a central hall with a grand staircase at the back and the water entrance at the front, and rooms down either flank. Only at first-floor level does the familiar form become apparent.

The Sarfat Pasha Yalı has been half demolished and has lost its harem and stone hamam, but the remaining wing is spacious and typical. The ground-floor hall is marble and approached from the sea and there is also a garden door under the landing where the two arms of the ascending stairway meet. There is a pretty çeşme in the hall, but the yalı does not possess the fountain found in certain *505* grand saloons beside the water.[26] Other such mansions had selsebils, usually in their gardens; these were marble panels with small cups distributed over them: water trickled down from one to the other and played a tune.[27] Other great houses even had grottoes in their halls or saloons – like the Şakır Pasha Konak on Prinkipo, or Büyükada – as well as in their gardens; there is an elaborate example in the park at Emirgân. Off the hall of the Sarfat Pasha Yalı are two, long subsidiary rooms facing onto the side garden, the kitchen and service rooms, and a passage off which are chambers onto the Bosphorus. It leads to a subsidiary hall and stair beside the main garden which replaces the demolished harem and hamam. The great landing of the piano nobile forms a grand saloon, off which are rooms each side overlooking the garden, now divided from the house by the road, and a fine salon on the corner projecting towards the sea. Other rooms give off the corridor corresponding to that at garden level. It is the spaciousness of the rooms rather than their number which makes this house palatial. The basement is masonry, but all the upper structure is of wood with standard sash windows and a tile roof. There are examples of Edirne work, that is painted wooden cupboards and niches with baroque borders and leaf designs.

The yalıs of the eighteenth century varied in size and ornateness but it is not until the beginning of the nineteenth century that great changes occurred, due

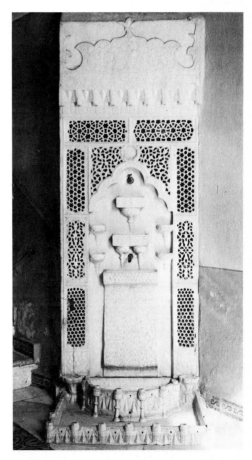

505 *Yılanlı Yalı Bebek, Istanbul, now destoyed. The musical fountain or selsebil.*

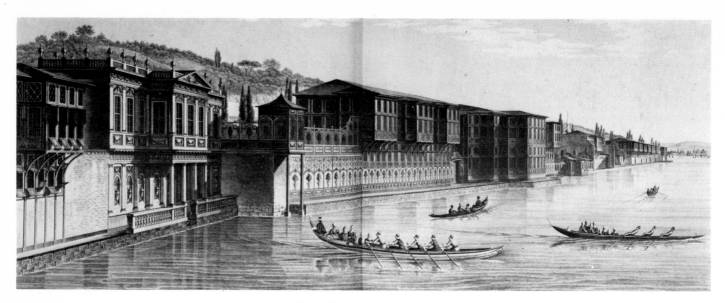

506 *Palace of Hatice Sultan, Bosphorus, now destroyed. Nineteenth-century engraving.*

to the increasing employment of foreign architects like Melling. The Divana- 50(
Kıbrızlı Yalı at Kandilli, which once had a fine park and still has a pretty garden,
was built at the start of this new era right alongside, indeed, projecting over,
the bay at Küçüksu whereas the Sarfat Pasha Yalı has a broad quay which serves
as a terrace. Life at a yalı was lived as much as possible outside and the more
important, like the Divana, had rambling gardens and woods on the hillsides
behind, as well as a privy garden by the water. These gardens were divided into
harem and selâmlık by high walls. They were made up of flowering shrubs and
trees including magnolia, and lilac and, above all, the Judas tree which, if the
winds are kind in spring, turns the Bosphorus pink. There were also fruit trees
and patches of herbs and vegetables besides clusters of flowers rather than
orderly beds. A green shade was what was prized and also gay coloured lights
at night.

The Divana Yalı lies long and low with a series of recessions and bays defining
the units of its structure. It is this definition which is the key to Ottoman
domestic architecture and which, with its use of wooden pilotis as well as cantilevering, fascinated Le Corbusier: each room is a part of a structure which must
express how it is built up, and the number of rooms in a house, together with

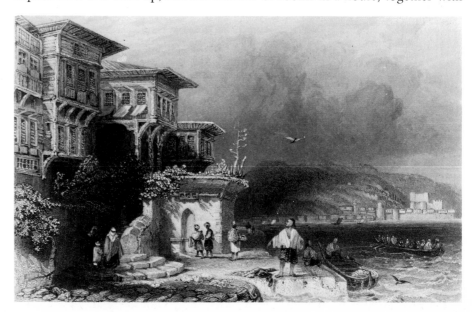

507 *Yalı opposite Anadoluhisar, Bosphorus, now destroyed. Nineteenth-century engraving.*

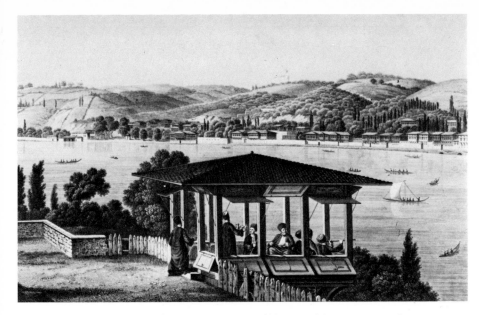

508 *Kandilli, Bosphorus. A belvedere opposite Bebek. Detail from a nineteenth-century engraving.*

their probable size and purpose, can be read from the façades and flanks; there could be no passages pretending to be saloons as with the Horse Guards in London. Yet the rooms are bonded and organized into a complete statement and never become a series of independent boxes.

Sometimes the harem and the selâmlık of a yalı were two separate buildings with a courtyard or a garden in between. All had either a small private creek or dock or else a kayıkhane (boathouse) running under them into their basements. A great many have been burnt or pulled down and one of the greatest misfortunes was the destruction of the Sayit Pasha palace above the race at Akıntaburnu where, on a double tier of curved consoles, two storeys with five saloons each projected over the quay. They were set one above the other, three gabled and two with hipped roofs.[28] The terraced gardens rising up the hill behind were divided with the customary high walls and reached by a bridge across the lane into Bebek, as was done at the end of the century with the Art Nouveau palace which became the Egyptian Embassy where the gardens were reached from the first floor dining-room.

Some yalıs were no more than summer houses, like the Cebeciler Kiosk which had a dome and broad eaves supported on many piers, or the grand pavilion at Bebek which was used for conferences and had an attractive wall and fence along its waterfront. Here, half of each shutter lifted to form eaves and the other opened downwards in a manner common to coffee house kiosks and the pavilions of the saray. The little belvedere[29] opposite Bebek on the cliff at Kandilli was nothing more than twelve piers sustaining similar shutters between them. Such windows could be taken away completely and an example of this was the Kum Kasır, at Edirne. In some nineteenth-century konaks the party walls of the main floor could be removed to open up the whole area for a great reception. But lightness of touch was gradually lost when stone and brick replaced wood as a building material and stucco as a finish. There are remarkable examples of various European fashions but none that need be discussed here except one of the first, since demolished, built by Mahmut II to replace the old-fashioned palace at Beşiktaş with its associations with camp life. It was Greek Revivalism executed in the best manner of the German school and must have looked alien in its virgin whiteness when it was completed.[30] It was the first of many royal palaces to be rebuilt and set a fashion in destruction, only to succumb itself in due course.

However, the demolition of a building at least reveals interesting details in its construction, and the loss of the Koca Reşit Pasha Yalı is compensated for by the revelation of the skill with which its floors were designed in order to combat damp, fire hazard and noise. Between the floorboards and a subsidiary

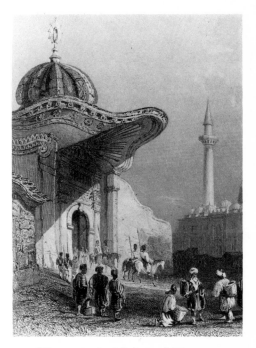

509 *The gate to the Ministry of War (formerly the Eski Saray). The University Gate now stands in its place. The Sultan Beyazit Cami is opposite. Nineteenth-century engraving.*

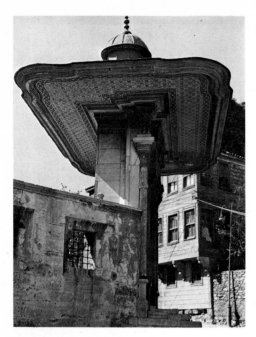

510 Sultan's Gate to Hagia Sophia, Istanbul. See page 420.

layer of planking was a five-centimetre stratum of sawdust and this was true of the ceiling of the room below, while between these two layers there was a ten-centimetre layer of charcoal. Good, seasoned timbers, often from Roumanian forests, were used in these buildings and the main structure, if cared for, is durable; the weatherboarding is relatively easily renewed and so are the tiles, and standard windows were once easily replaced if blown in by a gale. The two inescapable major expenses are the quays which are attacked by frost and the equinoctial gales, and the great expanse of timber needing paint; this accounts for most wooden houses now being left a natural grey when once they were painted red or white[31] or displayed panels of flowers in bright colours along the water's edge. Inside, the woodwork is still ornate and the ceilings painted and even gilded.

Chinese influence has always been important in Ottoman art and affected certain architectural elements. The dragon clouds and foliate and floral patterns on Chinese porcelain are reflected in the designs of Iznik tiles, and their presence as restless and lop-sided elements in design eased the transition from classical formalism to the baroque although the movement was fertilized from the West. The konaks of Anatolia and the yalıs of the Bosphorus in the upward-slanting of some eaves show a relationship to Chinese architectural forms as well as to Chinoiserie. Most striking is the use of large eaves above gateways; and from early Ottoman times the use of broad impost capitals making for hipped arches is particularly Far Eastern in feeling. Allowance as always, must be made for parallel development or the natural forms imposed by such materials as wood.

The materials readily available are, indeed, a determining factor in architecture along with wealth or poverty and climate and its ordering of a local way of life. This was tempered in the case of the Ottomans by their hardiness, for they seem to have taken small note of Istanbul damp or Anatolia's winter cold. Wood and plaster and brick were the three main materials of western and central Anatolia and relate the houses of Kastamonu or Ankara to those of Bolu or Tire or Elmalı. The stone of Kayseri was to produce a series of magnificent nineteenth-century konaks and many more modest houses in that city, often Armenian built. Among the earliest appears to be the Zennecioğulları mansion, built as two single-storey houses sharing the same basement. The selâmlık is reached by a flight of stairs and has a loggia with a large hall behind, off which give four corner rooms with their doors across the corners and with three smaller rooms, replacing the eyvan concept, between them. A door in the south-east chamber leads to the landing of the stairs in the harem section and thence to the only upper oda, a grand saloon with windows on three sides. On the west the windows are divided by an elegant rococo ocak, and the pillars separating it from the forehall have multifoliate, flat imposts painted with flowers. In the centre of the main floor of the harem is a large sitting-room with the kitchen on one side and an inner boudoir on the other. Beyond the kitchen is the hamam and an open hearth for summer cooking, while on the far side of the living-rooms is a guest room opening onto the stairs beyond the foot of which is an open kiosk. The arrangement has all the interest of split-level planning and all the rooms face north in order to escape the heat and enjoy the views of the garden.

The Mollaoğullar Konak, in much the same style, has the date *1198/1784* painted over the door to the sofa of the harem.[32] Here, the harem and selâmlık are detached buildings each facing its own garden from opposite directions. The street gate opens into the selâmlık court where there is a kiosk on the right recessed into the harem area for protection from sun and wind. It is preceded by a portico above a small fountain in a miniature basin from which a narrow, short canal fills a larger octagonal pond. This kiosk is an open coffee-room with cupboards in the wall for cups and pots. A passage leads down between the house and the harem to the stable behind. The selâmlık has a porch leading to a hall which has an oval apse at the back, round which the wings of the stairs ascend to meet at a landing above the door to the service room. On the right of the entry is a foyer to the hamam and on the left a reception room. Behind this is the stable.

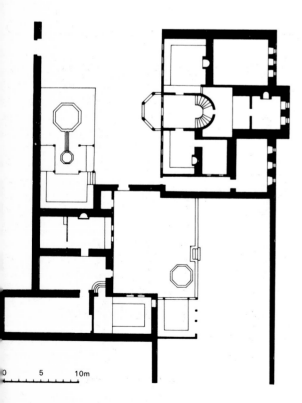

511 Mollaoğullar Konak, Kayseri. Plan, scale 1:500.

0   5   10m

The harem court also has a pool and a fountain, set on a low terrace with its own pavilion on the corner. A very richly carved portal with twin windows in ornamental frames above it admits from the court to the lofty salon of the harem. There are a pair of subsidiary or guest rooms on the right and a reception room looking out onto the courtyard approached up three steps to the left. At the back of this room are closets and washrooms. Most Kayseri houses, however, are much more modest than this and have only one upper room; their life is concentrated in the courtyard. Some have private rooms serving as mescits with stairs to a platform on the roof under a stone hood supported by four columns for a minaret. But they are all built of the same quality ashlar and have the same grilled, rectangular casements and square-cut façades with handsome stone corbelling. They are also all disappearing rapidly to be replaced by monotonous apartment blocks.

In the suburbs there are a number of large houses, including that of Akif Ağa at Talas built by an Armenian master mason in 1883.[33] This is a very grand konak built on the side of a hill with an upper floor, a mezzanine which becomes semi-basement at the rear, and a ground floor which extends back into the hill. The main floor is approached by double stairs which meet at a landing from which a single flight forms a bridge to the pillared portico.

Another stone region is that round Diyarbakır and Mardin which stretches as far as Urfa and Antep in the west. There is considerable Syrian influence and at Diyarbakır the stone mansions are mostly nineteenth-century in date. Some of the konaks of that city are palatial and they are related to those of Kayseri in that harem and selâmlık often stand side by side with an upper saloon raised between to serve as the mabeyin. The severe heat is countered by large airy casements and lofty arched eyvans. Some of the more lavish houses have winter quarters across the courtyard with its pool, opposite the summer apartments. The courts are paved and have low-walled flowerbeds and mature trees.

A good example is the Park Hotel, the former Gevraniler Konak dating from 1235/1819.[34] The harem court was built round a walled garden and a hexagonal pool. The ground floor consisted of considerable semi-basement cellarage on the south side, and a cistern with two rooms in front of the stables on the west each side of the changing room to the private hamam behind. On each side, also, were stairs to the upper floor. On the north side there was a corner stair and then another pair of storerooms followed by a room and an eyvan in front of further stables. On the south side, two flights of stairs led to a landing and to a fine stone terrace, facing north for the sake of coolness, with a long apartment with a central pool and a line of ten windows on to the terrace. From this room the kitchens were reached and at the end of the terrace was a recess in which there were stairs leading to the selâmlık and a mabeyin which divided it from the harem. This chamber was exceptionally grand. On the west side, clearly defined as a separate kiosk – recalling those individually ranged sets of apartments in the Al Azam Palace at Damascus – the double flight of stairs led up to a large eyvan with an east outlook through two arches onto the flower garden heavily shaded by trees. The two rooms in front on either side were broad and shallow and walled with windows on the garden and eyvan sides.[35] Behind, two similar rooms looked out into the street. The third pavilion, on the north, was for winter use and so faced directly south and here the eyvan became the porch to an inner room with a hearth. This opened onto a heavily protected balcony leading to a windowless private chamber and, on the garden side, to a large salon with six windows which could also be reached by a balcony from the eyvan beside it but onto which it had no windows. The balcony was carried on consoles, unlike the other rooms. Even the winter salon had large casements with small pairs of lights above, typical of the town. Long and narrow rooms occur frequently at Diyarbakır and they are modulated by the spacing of their supporting beams. There is use of alternating courses of basalt and limestone in the voussoirs and the spandrels where arches occur and there is much good nineteenth-century wrought-iron.

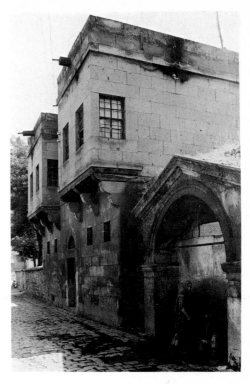

512 Kayseri konak dating from the nineteenth century and due for demolition.

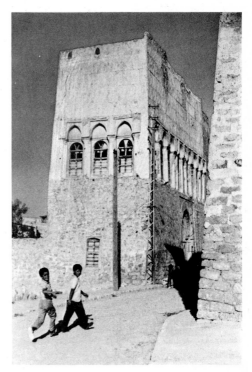

513 Konak at Siirt.

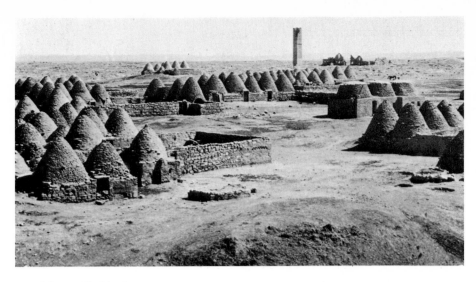

514 Harran. Beehive houses.

Houses built for hot climates are inward-looking in order to find shade and shelter from the sun; thus Diyarbakır is still largely a web of alleyways with high blank walls and closed doors.[36] It belongs to the Kurdish and Arab provinces within the Ottoman dominions where some leading buildings reflect the culture of the ruling élite but where the domestic way of life is unchanged. This is equally true of southern towns which were built in adobe, such as Siirt or Urfa. Harran, now a village, is an example of a community which has strayed over the 514 artificial Syrian frontier. Its homesteads are made up of a series of standard-sized cubes with flat-topped domes like childhood bricks, some with only two sections and some with several. These houses are ideal for a near desert area, for they are lofty enough to be cool in summer but have walls thick enough to be warm in winter, while the windows are few and small and light comes in through the door. Their height, moreover, gives them a certain dignity, which in konaks is expressed in the basic concept of the noble chamber, the principal oda, placed if possible at the top of the house in order to command a view and high enough to have two tiers of windows. Some konaks of this order survive at Siirt, for 513 example. The concept of the sofa is also common to the two worlds but, whereas the Ottoman was raised eighteen inches or more from the ground, that of the Arab houses is often lower.

The towns of Anatolia and other Ottoman dominions inherited the dispositions of the Byzantines, and the alleys of the citadel at Bursa meander now as they did in the days of the emperors. But there was a clear concept underlying the organization of an Ottoman town however chaotic it may appear on first sight. The concept of the administrative, commercial and religious centre and the residential neighbourhoods spread around is a common one in Moslem towns: it is not European because there the citizens crowded within the walls for security. It was a measure of Ottoman self-confidence that their towns spread over the plateau and were defenceless, unless they were frontier cities. The result was a natural growth of the garden city without self-consciousness. The early houses of the towns were no better than those of the villages and, indeed, the mahalle or suburb was no more than a substitute village which was the satellite of a major centre with ulu cami and bazaar and the konaks of the governor and the senior citizens. Even in Istanbul, in the Byzantine manner, the walls enclosed a number of villages sprawled among market gardens and there are still a few country walks left within the urban boundaries.

A capital city is never typical and Istanbul for long periods was not even a capital, although always the centre of trade. It gave way to Edirne which was the preferred residence of the sultans, and there the likeness to a garden city must have been marked when it was four or five times its present diminished size. None the less, the City, Constantinople, not only excelled all other cities of the

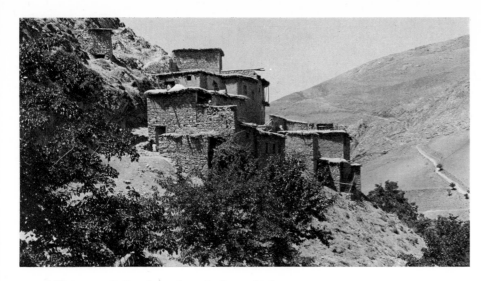

515 Village near Sağmanbahçe from the former highway.

empire in size, but was also the source of ideas and fashion in architecture as with other arts. The provincial governors, homesick for the incomparable City, diffused the Ottoman way of life wherever they were posted. At no time was this more noticeable than during the growth of the baroque period when the new forms were rapidly spread across the country. Before considering the provincial towns, therefore, Istanbul may be briefly surveyed.

The great majority of the houses outside the central neighbourhoods must have resembled the gecekondu of the present day. These are humble dwellings based on a primitive law of squatters' rights which enables anyone who can put up a roof in one night to hold the ground that he has taken. This is usually part of unguarded state or vakıf lands outside the town centres. Made of any available material in great haste, over the months they are often improved until eventually a decent two- or even three-room cottage matures. Where the migrants are very primitive, the worst aspects of a shanty town without sewage systems prevail, but where the villagers have come from a better skilled environment a relatively clean neighbourhood develops, although the mud can no more be subdued in Istanbul than it can in Anatolia. When Mehmet II brought citizens from Aksaray or Karaman to populate his empty capital, the neighbourhoods must have taken on their individual character in just the same manner. It was not until the eighteenth and nineteenth centuries that wooden houses of two or three storeys spread beyond the wealthier areas round the seat of government and the markets. The absence of stone mansions has already been discussed in relation to the sarays of the vezirs in the great days of the empire, and the imperial palace bears witness to the frailty of much domestic construction. However, stone houses were built and some of them survive in a deplorable condition although more and more are demolished every year.

They once formed a street of mansions belonging to the Phanariot nobility outside the sea wall beside the wharfs of Phanar on the Golden Horn. These men were the remnants of the Byzantine ruling class who chose to grow rich as traders under Ottoman rule – the Cantacuzene, Dukas and other famous families. It has been suggested that their houses date from as early as the sixteenth century but this is improbable. At first, after the conquest, the city walls were carefully maintained, and it is improbable that anyone was allowed to build outside them for a long time nor would anyone wish to live outside their protection. The salon of the former legation of the Monasteries of Mount Sinai to the Patriarchate, itself founded on the slope of the hill above the same stretch of wall, has eighteenth-century fitments. Here the piano nobile is reached by a broad wooden staircase leading to a landing, off which are a number of small rooms. All this section of the house is of wood. On the left is the grand salon of stone above a mezzanine and a basement. It runs the length of the house but

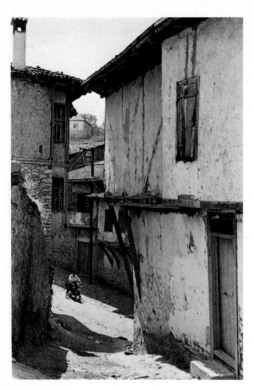

516 Amasya. Houses with elementary bracket supports.

is blind on the Horn side, presumably because the back of the house always served as a warehouse, the present employ of most of these mansions, and also because the owner did not wish to look out upon the wharf or suffer the stench of the polluted water. There is a stone foyer divided from the main part of the room by a step onto the wooden floor and a frail balustrade. In the walls are capacious niches and cupboards, and over the street a great bow window projects on bold corbels. Such a shape would be unlikely to occur before the eighteenth century. Other houses in the street are similar in plan and also of stone or of alternating courses of brick and stone. This type of structure recurs in the eighteenth-century hans of Galata, as well as in those of the great period in the old city which produced the Hasan Pasha Han and the Büyük Yeni Han.[37] The earlier Galata houses dating from the sixteenth century, such as that of the Podesta which must have been the grandest, have no corbelling and such as occurs in the early seventeenth century is usually restricted to the support of the room over the gate, as at the Valide Han which has ranks of seven rising in four tiers.

This form of cantilevering had much older origins[38] and was often employed by the Byzantines; but they were rarely employed in domestic architecture prior to the seventeenth century and the vaults of Topkapısaray are evidence of this. Bracket supports were used with wooden houses and, until the later seventeenth century, were unadorned although they became more and more curvular as the building projected more boldly. Later, they were not only decorated with fretted strips or actually carved but stucco was used to link the foundations with the first floor. These supports were important if the upper rooms were to be a reasonable rectangular shape and also to increase the floor area to a maximum where sites were often irregular because land became more and more valuable. Projecting rooms catch the sunlight and enable the women behind the jalousies to watch the life of the street below; in this sense they were the open eyes of the house and its link with the world around. For these reasons even suburban houses, where land values were less of a consideration, had projecting upper storeys. Although the Phanariot mansions are more recent than has been suggested, they are likely to have been modelled on Byzantine houses of old. They do not relate to the standard form derived from the plan of the Çinili Kiosk which has been traced with Ottoman houses. Their affinities with the domestic houses of the conquerors are in details rather than in substance. Indeed, while Byzantine forms of structure were willingly assimilated by Ottoman builders of homes, just as they had been when it came to erecting major monuments, the konak of a Çakır Ağa was not a copy of a mansion of a Dukas.

Until recent times when so many of the older houses have been torn down to make room for small blocks of petit bourgeois apartments, the majority of the dwellings of Istanbul were of wood, and few date from earlier than the eighteenth century. They are probably bigger and certainly more ornate than the houses that they replaced, but the reports of the travellers echo each other when they describe Constantinople. Busbecq speaks of the very narrow streets and also of the old relics, by which he means the Byzantine ruins,[39] and Ramberti writing at much the same time, 1543, reports that there were not many good houses; most were built of wood and clay with only a few of stone; he also says that the city was full of 'wild and uninhabited groves'.[40] The narrowness of the streets is a theme which all the travellers repeat and Lord Henry Howard's secretary, in the second half of the seventeenth century, speaks of only one main street – and that not large – which is the old Byzantine Mese running from Hagia Sophia to the Adrianople Gate:[41] all the other streets were lanes and the city ill-built. Pococke in the 1730s found that the houses of Constantinople were for the most part built with wooden frames, mostly filled up with unburnt brick and that a great number were made only of such frames covered with boards; and many examples of this can still be seen now. 'They had notwithstanding very good room in them.' The streets were tolerable with a raised footway on each side.[42] Lechevalier,[43] in 1800, found straight but dirty roads with no plan or regularity

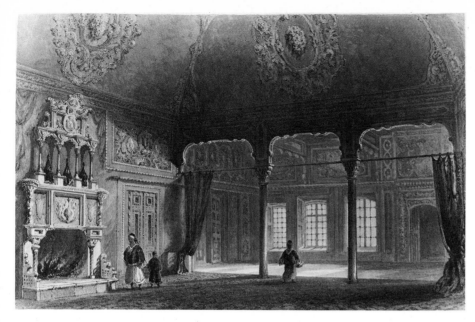

517 Fenar, Istanbul. Nineteenth-century engraving of a house interior.

and poor wooden houses with upper storeys jutting out. He also saw open spaces with the ruins due to fires, the scourge of Istanbul as they had been of medieval towns in the West. Levinge says in 1839[44] that the houses were in general frail tottering tenements of wooden framework, the interstices filled up with sun-dried bricks pasted over. None of them had chimneys or glazed windows;[45] a projecting wooden shutter which admitted light and concealed the females made up for the latter. Few dwellings exceeded two storeys, the upper of which frequently obtruded over the street and heightened the gloomy appearance. This was further increased by the sombre red with which the majority were painted, but occasionally the various devices and lively colours which adorned a few relieved the monotony of the scene. The best houses stood singly within an enclosure which was sometimes spacious enough to form a garden. None of them presented an architectural front to the street and they were nearly concealed by the trees which surrounded them. Houses of individuals were never built of stone, as that scarce material was reserved for public edifices whose inspiring grandeur formed a striking contrast to the simplicity of the unpretentious habitations of the citizens. To this Southgate[46] adds that although the plague was frequent in Constantinople, it was a 'more cleanly city than New York'.

The Romantic Movement was to quell criticism, and soon the visitors were to see the city with something of the sympathy felt for it by its inhabitants. It was picturesque and full of trees and all the more charming because its architecture was hidden by leaves or embellished by quaint gardens. But the narrowness of the lanes, which were meant for pedestrians and pack animals, continued to displease.[47] In his list of guilds, Evliya Çelebi reports only five hundred makers of baked bricks as opposed to the fifteen hundred who made them of mud and straw. The cleanliness of the streets depended partly on packs of scavenging dogs, partly on the season, but also on the control of the Divan. An order of 1585 complains to the kadı of the city that the Atmeydan used to be cleaned once a year and Beyazit square twice a month but that this had been neglected recently.[48] A further order in 1595 requires the cleaning of pavements and roads and reports the stealing of paving stones and the destruction of pavements by dirty water flung into the street.[49] What is missing from the accounts of the travellers is the palaces belonging to the grandees listed so proudly by Evliya. The reason is that most of them were concealed behind high walls similar to those of the royal palaces;[50] and they were also transitory like the houses of the poor, and frequently devastated by fire. Even the palace of the Grand Vezir, which was an official residence from the reign of Murat IV onwards, was burnt down time and time again.[51] This transitoriness was due to the Moslem respect only for the permanence of God, which had inbred habits of building afresh instead of maintenance. Therefore, kiosks were belvederes from which to observe the universe and admire the beauty of the world, but were in themselves ephemeral and built as flimsily as that of Kara Mustafa Pasha at the saray. Lamartine called them tents of gilded wood, and this description must have seemed apt when they were hung with rustling silks. Moreover, the otak of the sovereign and the marquees of the vezirs had painted domes and ceilings as well as tent flaps which, when lifted on poles, became their porticoes.[52] Reference has been made to Ahmet I being better lodged on occasion in his tent than in any available house on the Edirne road, and Mehmet IV is reported as finding it more convenient to stay in his tent when hunting.[53] Hunting was a passion with the Ottomans but only the Siyavuş Pasha lodge has survived and this is surely significant.[54] Even there, his huntsmen and cooks must have camped round about.

It may be wondered why, when fires were monotonously frequent and devastated large areas, the city was not built in stone or brick in spite of the traditional indifference for property, if only to spare human life. Edicts were frequently issued. In *1114/1702*[55] the kaymakam was ordered to see that houses were built of stone and brick and tiles from Bakırköy, Yalova and Iznik. And sixteen years later in *1131/1718*[56] the Kadı of Istanbul and the Chief Architect were told that nobody could build except of stone, brick and tile, and the width of the eaves was to be controlled because in some streets thieves were jumping from one roof to the other. Christian and Jewish houses were not to exceed two storeys. In *1137/1724*[57] the subject of house heights and tiled eaves was brought up again with the Chief Architect, Mehmet. It is clear that the laws were neither obeyed nor upheld for two good reasons; firstly, the populace could not afford any but the cheapest materials, and secondly the number of craftsmen such as carpenters, stonemasons and brickmakers available, even if not exaggerated by Evliya, indicates the limits to building capacity in the city.[58]

In discussing the principles of Ottoman town-planning, I am concerned with the towns west of the former Armenian and Kurdish provinces where they are strictly Ottoman however much they may owe to the influence of conquered peoples. Where possible, the Ottomans built their towns on a hillside or slope so that each house might enjoy a view. This was bound up with a canon which went further than the common law of Ancient Lights in Britain; you might build what you liked, how you liked and where you liked: but you might not block your neighbour's view. This law has disappeared in present-day Turkey with monstrous results which emphasize the degree of civilization, now lost, of the towns of the past.

Moreover, not only was the siting and the height of new buildings controlled by a simple social obligation, but you could not, in fact, build how you liked – unless you were as extravagant as the nineteenth-century sultans and their more opulent subjects – because so many architectural elements, such as timber lengths, were standardized. The result of this standardization was that the architecture of a town, small or large, from Kula to Sivas or Mut, was unified in style if diverse in detail. There was no mistaking your street for that of someone else, any more than the house of your neighbour was the image of your own. This was not the eighteenth-century discipline of a Georgian terrace where only the fanlight over the door might differ from dwelling to dwelling, but it was close to the romantic ideals of Ebenezer Howard and the Garden City. The resemblance is all the closer because the Ottoman town was full of trees. Villages, indeed, might have two centres; the mosque and the great tree under which the men still meet to discuss local affairs: indeed, the great tree at Emirgân now shelters an enormous coffee house.

Towns were divided into two centres. There was the külliye round the major mosque, and the commercial area round the bedesten. These were compact and largely built of brick and stone. The homes spread in neighbourhoods or mahalle

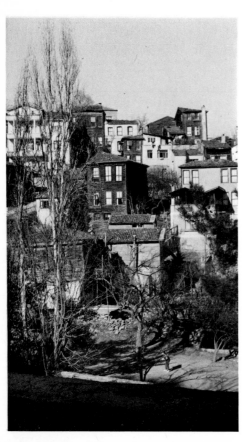

518 Houses at Rumelihisar. Each has a view of the Bosphorus.

all around in the manner described, and there the streets are so low that the trees in those parallel may be seen over the roofs and give the walker a sense of continuity and of being a part of a community.[59] The towns were intimate and rejected the idea of the tall block; each neighbourhood retained its identity in the way that London is often said to be a collection of villages. The towns were divided into religious communities – the Millet – a system which has not yet entirely ended, but there was no conception of a ghetto even if size and colour were regulated theoretically. There was no deliberate division by class, and the konak and garden of an ağa might be surrounded by crofts and, as has been noted,[60] a minister such as Mahmut Pasha opened his orchards to the populace. The result was a local intimacy which was an antedote to the extreme inward family orientation in towns where shutters and doors were bolted at sundown and where there was no public lighting because no one except dogs and thieves was out after dark. Thus towns like Kastamonu or Karaman were pleasant to frequent and abundantly green, less because of deliberate planning – except of the commercial and religious centres – than because of civilized habits it was found unnecessary to change.

In Istanbul, there were sultans and vezirs who were interested in beautifying the capital. The Sadrazam Boylu Mehmet Pasha in 1656 whitewashed the walls and also demolished the old houses between Ahırkapı and Yediküle.[61] Formerly the whitewashing of the walls only celebrated the return of the monarch after a victory. Mosques and other public buildings were also whitewashed until recent years, and it would appear that for the Ottomans the beauty of cut stone lay not in its texture or colour but in the smoothness of its surface.[62] The setting of monuments on hilltops is a frequent resort in architecture, but this does not lessen the magnificent achievement which is represented by the great Ottoman skylines at Istanbul and Edirne or lesser provincial cities from Bursa to Siirt. At Bursa the effect is particularly felicitous because each sultan in turn built his complex on one after another of the spurs of Uludağ or Olympus about the market and the citadel while time filled the slopes and the gulleys with ordinary homes among the woods. In Istanbul, while the saray occupied the ancient acropolis the silhouette of major mosque after major mosque filled the famous skyline, marking each neighbourhood and co-ordinating the seven hills.

It is not correct to say that Ottoman towns sprawled but rather that they were sketchily planned; when a new centre was endowed, the builder was aware of what would follow: aware, too, that the new neighbourhood would be one of wandering lanes governed by rigid laws of property. The meandering by-ways serve to mark the monumentality of the mosque and its dependencies: each is complementary to the other. Such freedom for the individual builder was possible without disaster because the traditions were stronger than his whims, whereas now similar laxity within the urban grids of a Brasilia, although economic conditions are no worse than in medieval Constantinople, has resulted in physical and spiritual slums because of the lack of the social unity found within a shared culture. This is not to suggest that the ideal society existed in the Ottoman capital in the sixteenth century or at any other period.

A second co-ordinating factor inherited from before recorded history was the bazaar. This took two forms which made a single whole, the covered and the open market. In a city as big as Istanbul, the covered area is immense, but between it and the Horn there is an even larger open market which unites Beyazit to the Yeni Cami. The covered market, originally, was not free of traffic because it was supplied by pack animals, and the better customers came on horseback, but it now forms a shopping centre free of any vehicle. The open bazaar is not so fortunate but, when it was planned, it conformed to the laws enforced by the guilds in order to reduce competition between traders. Each shop was a single unit with its owner and his apprentice and no one else. Nor could a successful merchant or craftsman expand his trade. The shops, therefore, were small and the supplies that they needed could be brought on the back of a mule without the need for carts, whereas now the lanes are made hazardous by trucks. The principles of the bazaars of other towns like Kayseri, Sivas or Samsun are identical to those of Istanbul.

Western influence in the eighteenth century had led to the baroque and rococo invasion. It had already interested such men as Ibrahim Pasha in the creation of model towns – although model towns had been built in the Balkans as early as the sixteenth century – and the idea of broad boulevards. Between 1718 and 1730, Ibrahim took the little town of Muşkare and created a new city, Nevşehir, divided by grand avenues, too grand for the modest buildings that line them, and with a long, narrow piazza between the market place and his mosque. Selim III was to lay out a model district, including factories, round his mosque and barrack at Haydarpaşa, and after the disastrous earthquake at Harput, Abdülâziz built a model town of his own on the plain below which has become Elaziğ and lost much of its original elegance. In the 1860s, Mithat Pasha aggrandized Damascus with magnificent arteries and designed Sofia's handsome avenues[63] with yellow cobblestones that shine like gold in the rain and which have survived recent mutilation because of a public outcry. But these were largely second-hand ideas with roots in the Ottoman tradition of a civilian town although appealing to the military caste used to well-regulated camps.

A Western concept which was slow to be accepted is that of the square or place either grand or small. The renaissance piazzas of Italy or the Grande Place of Brussels or Antwerp were not copied. The tradition of the meydan remained an untidy one and was either meant as an encampment for caravans or as a sports field like the Atmeydan. A Western square is architectural like the Piazza Navona, converted like the Atmeydan from a circus or hippodrome,[64] or the Place des Vosges; and the criticism of the Place de la Concorde is that the space is so great that it is meaningless; but Taksim in Istanbul has neither form nor dignity nor freedom and Eminönü is worse. In the late nineteenth century, the square did develop timidly in Anatolia, but often unsuccessfully in architectural terms because the buildings were low and the lavish amount of space disproportionate, as it is at Yozgat and to a lesser extent at Kastamonu where the modern square is saved from vapidity by the hillside and the river. At Tosya, however, the square is long and narrow and set on the slope of a hill and it is pleasant in its proportions and its relationship to the provincial houses which bound it and its gardens. At Aksaray there is a true municipal square which, although spacious, has buildings tall enough to make that space expressive; but the architecture is undistinguished. It is a shock to come across a form so alien to Turkish life even if it is an agreeable change from the thronged market streets and the sense of vitality which characterizes the Ottoman public place.

The Ottoman love of crowds extended to the graveyards and cemeteries also. These gardens of the dead were public parks without morbid connotations, and the acres of Eyüp and Üsküdar are still places in which to stroll. Thus the dead encircle Istanbul with tall tombstones among the cypresses and other trees and shrubs. They were also buried at vantage points down the Bosphorus. These tombstones are architectural and the baroque revolution altered their design as radically as did the substitution of the fez for the turban. The baroque gravestones developed a trend towards concave and convex sides, more elaborate and much longer inscriptions, and, most notably, the floral headpieces on the stones for women. A stone sarcophagus with westernized floral and leaf motifs also developed during the eighteenth century, but the designation of rank by means of the turban continued until its abolition. The fez could never attain the splendour nor the sometimes surrealist effect of the more noble turbans of the higher officers of state. The pashas compensated for their loss by elaboration. An example of this is the naval tomb in the cemetery at the Süleymaniye complete with compasses, telescope, and maps among other paraphernalia. Türbes continued to be built, but their decoration became more and more eclectic, in the manner of the Valide Cami at Aksaray, or the türbe of Fuat Pasha at Beyazit.

On the Okmeydan, or archery ground, a notable flight had long been recorded by a mark of honour in carved stone where the arrow fell. During the seventeenth

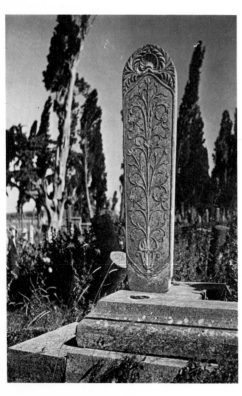

519 Gravestone at Topkapı, Istanbul. The flower is symbolic of a woman.

and eighteenth centuries and well into the nineteenth these became taller and
taller posts more and more richly ornamented. These marks like the gravestones
feel far more like an actual extension of the living city than do the walled
cemeteries of the Orthodox or the Armenians. In the provinces there are stones
so humble that they may be mistaken for the boundary stones of peasant plots;
and the village graveyard is usually far enough out of the living centre to be
detached in the Western manner. Among the broken stones all sense of architecture peters out. It peters out no less among the ramshackle concrete apartment
blocks of the present uncontrolled expansion of the cities. The present and future
problems are no longer Ottoman or Turkish in particular but universal ones of
low-cost housing and amenities deemed necessities in the present century.
Something of the Ottoman spirit does survive in the vivid window displays and
the flowers among the fruit and vegetables at a greengrocer's shop. Even the
use of brightly coloured mosaics on the façades of tenements including lemons
and mauves and pink represents a will to survive. But not to revive. The architects
of Turkey coming to the fore today are adamantly concerned with facing the
second half of the twentieth century in universal terms, however much they may
revere the achievements of another age which seems no less strange to them than
it would to any stranger from anywhere who contrived to journey back into the
imperial past.

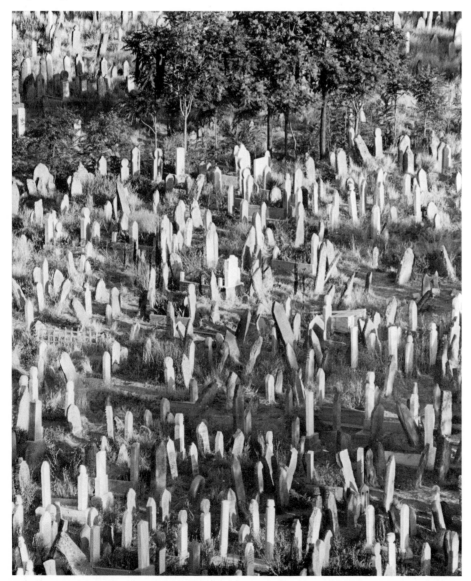

520 Cemetery, Konya. Nineteenth-century graves from the Selimiye Cami.

Appendix I   The Janissaries

THE JANISSARY CORPS supplied so many architects that a brief summary of its formation may help to give some idea of who these men were and what their training had been. The concept of a slave guard was old in Asia, and Turks had formed the bodyguard of Ismail the Samanid[1] as they had, later, of the Abbasids whose power these guards usurped and who produced Ibn Tulun builder of the great mosque in Cairo. Such a guard and the palace school which was essential for its training, therefore, was not a new concept.

It is not known when the first Janissary unit was formed, but the first Western reference to the corps occurs in 1438.[2] It may have been recruited initially by haphazard raids on Christian villages but after the conquest of the Balkans in the late fourteenth and fifteenth centuries it was organized on the basis of a levy from Christian families at intervals of seven or so years. No Jew could be admitted to the corps and Arabs were exempt and so, at first, were Armenians.[3] The earliest levy in Anatolia did not occur until 1512[4] when Sinan was recruited from Kayseri at the age of twenty. This seems to have been in excess of the age limit which is believed normally to have been between eight and eighteen years of age.[5] The reason for the increase in the number of recruits was the coming campaign against the Persians and also, perhaps, the unrest in Anatolia following the Sufi rebellion of 1511.[6]

The Bektaşi dervishes' affiliations with the Janissaries grew rapidly and by the end of the fifteenth century had been cemented, but the legend of Hacı Bektaş is a fabrication.[7] The order was a liberal one which taught music to the populace,[8] held a form of communion and drank wine so that Esad[9] accuses them of making their tekkes into taverns and roistering with young girls and boys. Their mystical practices had affinities with those of Christianity and with popular religions which were somewhat similar to the beliefs of the Bogomils, who were strong in the Balkans, and through them to various heretical movements which were suppressed in Europe, including the Albigensians. It is easy to see why such a sect would be popular with young men recruited from the European provinces.

The recruiting officer or sürücü[10] – the literal meaning of which is drover – had the best youths and children of a district brought to him for inspection at the konak of the Sancak Bey of the region, and little by little a brigade of these boys was collected and marched to Edirne where they were lodged in barracks and hans.[11] Some, but not all, went on to Istanbul. There they were circumcised and then registered in their father's name, which is no guide to any individual's identity because it was either recorded simply as Abdullah, meaning the slave of God, or an equivalent name like Abdülmenan.[12] The Yeniçeri Ağa then came to inspect the recruits who were stripped naked and presented to him one by one.[13] The best in looks and wits were sent to the palace school and the rest distributed among the secondary establishments at the Ibrahim Pasha Saray, or Galata, or the provincial schools at Edirne and at Gelibolu where they were apprenticed to a trade.[14] There was an early distinction between the Men of the Sword and Men of the Pen, but this was blurred in practice because civil servants were also soldiers on occasion and all had to learn archery which was a sacred ritual as well as a sport. The recruits who could not speak Turkish – doubtless most of them until the levy of 1512 – were sent to work in the country for Turkish tenant farmers and landowners particularly in the region round Ankara, Kütahya and Karahisar; the work was also intended to build up their strength and toughen the future shock troops.[15] After five years, they were sent back to their units[16] but must also have spent some years of training in the barracks.

The main barrack was on the Etmeydanı which was to be destroyed during the overthrow of the corps in 1826,[17] but there were subsidiary odas including, at least for a time, those at the Ibrahim Pasha Saray.[18] The barracks were known as ocaks due to the association of the corps with food and cooking, hence their habit of overturning their kettles, or huge bronze tureens, when mutinying. The sleeve which formed their headgear, however, came from the Ahis whom they displaced as the power behind the throne.[19] The ocak was divided into ortas and odas; the latter in wartime meant a large round tent,[20] and clearly the files of men who shared such a tent were assigned the same fenced-off section of the barrack hall.

Süleyman I raised the number of ortas from 165 to 196[21] but at the start of his reign there were probably only 12,000 men in the corps.[22] Due to its dilution by children of Janissaries and Turkish recruits, the corps had swollen to 48,000 by the reign of Murat III[23] when it was losing its reputation as a corps d'élite. Murat IV was to abolish the devşirme system altogether[24] and so destroy the character of the corps. The crack ortas were the Hasekis or privileged units, in other words the household brigade, and were the 14th, 49th, 65th and 67th according to Cevat.[25] The commander of the 55th Orta was head of the Janissary school.[26] Each orta had its own emblem, such as keys or an anchor or massed weapons, which was tattooed on the arms of recruits.[27] The standard of the Corps was the sword of Ali on a half red and half yellow field.[28] Since the records of the Corps were systematically destroyed after their suppression and massacre by Mahmut II, who handed over the palace of their commander to the Şeyhül-Islam, there is much conflicting evidence, and clearly practices which were normal in the fifteenth century had greatly altered by the end of the sixteenth. What is important is that recruits, or acemioğlans, worked on buildings such as the mosque of Haseki Hürrem and there is reference to Janissary units helping build the mosque of Beyazit II.[29] They were taught many trades including carpentry, and the recruiting of masons and architects to accompany military campaigns seems to indicate some sort of reserve system after a man left the corps, if he could.

Finally, the position of kul or slave should not be taken as one of undue humility. It did not imply inferiority[30] but obedience due from a junior member of the Imperial family to its head. Nonetheless, the absolute submission to authority and the life-long bondage imposed on the Janissary recruit is inescapably slavery. As slaves they were exempt from taxation, but even the Grand Vezir on occasion was not permitted to bear witness in court because he was not a free-born Moslem. The Ottoman aristocracy lived only at the will of the ruler.[31]

Appendix II   The Vakfiye and Imaret System

ANY CHARITABLE FOUNDATION serves its purpose only if it is suitably endowed; and the pious who, for the good of their souls and future life, built a fountain, mescit, or a great külliye, also gave lands or other goods for the maintenance of the property and the payment of its workers. This endowment was administered by a mütevelli or nazir and, although religious lands were given mainly out of the motives of genuine piety, the fact remains that the mütevelli was often the heir in perpetuity of the founder of the charity or holy place.[1] By this means, a rich man's estate when he died devolved on his chosen heirs and could not be alienated as death duties by the sultan or any other officer of the government who might otherwise dispose of everything that the dead man left behind, especially if he were a high officer of the state who had graduated as a kul from the Enderun College. In the vakfiye drawn up by Kara Ahmet Pasha prior to his execution, when his foundation was not complete, he orders that the post of mütevelli be given to his children when he dies and, if he leaves none, then to his nearest kin; and if there be no relative either, then the decision is to be made by the kadı.

The principal units of the largest complexes were the mosque – which was a meeting place as much as a place of worship and also a lecture hall – and the medrese or college of religious law where any acceptable student lived free of charge and got a small daily allowance; some of them were day students. The professor and assistant teachers might live in on occasion. There was also the tabhane or guesthouse where the traveller could stay free and be fed for three days. There might also be a tımarhane or asylum, or a darüşşifa or hospital for the sick with an out-patients department as well and sometimes these were combined.[3] The Fatih hospital was exceptionally well endowed as was the Süleymaniye which was the leading medical centre of the capital.

Since many people were fed each day, the kitchen department was of first importance and the vakfiye was not only precise about the number of people to be employed but also about the food to be served. The vakfiye of Kara Ahmet lists the menus to be served on ordinary days and holidays including the cost, exact weight of rice, butter and honey and the type of soup. Cooks and bakers, inspectors and buyers are listed along with the woodcutter and the kitchen doorkeeper who also looked after the stable door.

The caravans often numbered well over a thousand beasts,[4] and large stables were needed for foundations as large as that of Fatih. The smallest building was usually the mekteb where young children learnt the Koran by heart. The first in Istanbul was opened at Fatih[5] and burnt down in 1918 and is now a coffee house. The first library was also included in the Fatih foundation and began with a collection of eight hundred books given by the sultan. These were intended for the use of the students of the eight medreses. Finally, there was the all-important muvakkithane where time was kept and the auspicious hour for great events determined. To the extent that all astrology involves astronomy, some science and mathematics developed in these offices up to the end of the sixteenth century, but since the premises were medieval there was a rapid degeneration in the intellectual standing of the personnel who became little more than sophisticated time-keepers, tenders of water-clocks, constructors of sundials[6] and surveyors of astrolobes. A royal foundation which had all of these institutions to maintain needed vast revenues for there might be as many as 366 people on the pay-roll, excluding the students; and this was the case at Fatih.[7] The vakfiye had to be a thorough legal document in order to protect the revenues and the conduct of religious affairs; that of Fatih, for example, ordains that the marble paving of the court shall be kept so clean and shining that anyone who looks shall see his face as if in a mirror.[8]

The workers at the mosque were lodged and fed, and a hereditary system grew up with the apprenticing of the children to their fathers.[9] The Yeni Valide at Eminönü, which was endowed with the Cairo imposts, had two katips or clerks who were responsible for the repairs. They had a stonemason, a stone-dresser, a guardian of the shutters and a lead-roof worker permanently at their command. The vakfiye reflects a natural fear of men's dishonesty and so, as a control, the value of the land with which Fatih endowed his university was estimated by the Vezir Faik Pasha and Davut Bey of Mytilene, Kadı of Istanbul.[10] Strict accounts for every detail of daily work on the Ahmediye and Süleymaniye have survived in quantities of notebooks, and the department of the imperial architect must have had a large secretariat in order to prepare detailed and exact estimates of costs and to order the correct quantities of the various materials, particularly shipments of marble from Marmara Island. In Selçuk times, when the vakfiye system was introduced to Anatolia in place of similar Byzantine endowments, the fear of dishonesty was strong enough for a curse on any man who misappropriated the funds of the Karatay Kervansaray at Bunyan to be written into the deed.[11] However, mosques were considered sufficiently safe for the public to use them as deposits for valuables and furniture.[12]

Since the list of those employed by a royal foundation is a key to the kind of state kept there, it is worth scrutinizing the complete list of the men attached to the Fatih külliye.[13] There were eight müderris or professors and ushers, ten to fifteen danişmend or tutors, eight porters and eight cleaners. The auxiliary schools had a librarian and a clerk each, besides the porter. The hospital staff of twelve included an overseer and two cooks for the special kitchen, two washerwomen, two handymen, a porter, a keeper, and a majordomo or steward, besides doctors, an oculist and a surgeon. The imaret was staffed by a clerk and a steward, a cellarman, six cooks and six bakers, two sweepers, two caretakers or watchmen, two lampmen, four porters, two doorkeepers, a meat porter, two wheat cleaners, and two potboys. There were also two stablemen, a storeman, a wood porter, and a handyman. In all, there were thirty-seven employees which indicated a large and busy establishment. The list of those entitled to be fed mentions four sets of forty sofas for guests[14] suggesting an average of 160 guests each night who lodged in the tabhane and something like 1,100 meals were served twice a day including those for 600 students.

The mosque itself had the hatip, two imams, müezzins, reciters, a sentry, a cleaner, a doorkeeper, lamplighters, caretakers, a timekeeper, seven security officers and some thirty other minor holy men. The meal roster also included Janissary sentries, windowmen, three primary-school teachers, a wardrobe master, the controller of the waterworks, the manager of the hamam, and an imam and a müezzin for both the tabhane and the hospital each of which had its own mescit, two drug grinders, the keeper of the honey, two dispensers of charity, the washer of corpses at the hospital, and a leadworker for the roofs.

The establishment listed in the vakfiye of Kara Ahmet Pasha[15] could not rival this but there are a number of interesting notes and appointments, including the building of a sixteen-cell zaviye with a man in each cell to pray for the pasha's soul. There was to be a man to keep the fountains filled.

The vakıf was endowed with three million silver dirhems, a very large palace near Topkapı with two courtyards and considerable stables producing a yearly rent of 140 dirhems and a rich garden which made 400 dirhems a year for the vakıf of Beyazıt Sultan. A number of small towns are listed, and the properties set aside for the benefit of the külliye included a hundred shops in one of them; among several others listed were over twenty mills and watermills, three complete villages with all their slaves and animals, various gardens, a bakery and a soap factory at Antakya, small houses and kervansarays and nine thousand sheep. What is striking is the immense wealth that a sadrazam could acquire.

The system continued until the end of the sultanate, and the vakfiye of Princess Fatima, daughter of Ahmet III, issued on the foundation of the darül-hadis of the Sadrazam Damat Nevşehirli Ibrahim Pasha is typical.[16] It also reveals problems common to the present day. Books were not to be taken outside the library to which readers were to be admitted three times a week. There had to be guard for the nearby aqueduct also. The foundation was heavily staffed. The senior professor must have been among the best paid in the empire at one hundred dirhems a day. His two senior assistants were instructed to teach Sufi'ism free from vices of superficiality. There was also a reader of Celâlettin Rumi's poem, indicating that the establishment was indeed connected with the dervish movement. The library had a staff of five, and a bookbinder, plus doorkeepers, water-servers, a burner of incense during lessons (which indicates a new luxury), a man to look after the fountain, a keeper of the drinking cup, a conduit cleaner, a lavatory man and a cleaner of the sewers, and the already mentioned guardian of the Süleyman canal (Valens Aqueduct), a sweeper, the doorkeeper of the garden, a scavenger, a mason, a plumber and a stonecutter. The complex was not large and the staff of thirty-five appears to have been considerable.

The striking thing about the vakfiyes, apart from the pious belief that nothing would be left behind by a man except good children and good works, is the intense conservatism of the meticulous detail. The philanthropist is determined that the trust shall be administered exactly as he would wish, and in listing wages and stipends down to the last dirhem along with the exact tasks to be performed, no thought is given to inflation and rising prices nor is any form of development possible, whatever may be discovered after the founder is dead. The vakıf of Ibrahim Pasha included an endowment of two villages in the Aydın province, and two more in the Epirus besides land at Monastir in the province of Pasha Liman, probably the village of that name on Marmara Island, eighty shops in Constantinople and various properties on Naxos.[17] These endowments financed charities unconnected with the darül-hadis, including payment of Koran readers at Mecca and Medina, eight nurses for the asylum of Haseki Hurrem, the cost of illuminating the minarets at Eyüp during Ramazan, grants to the Halberdiers to celebrate the Prophet's birthday, and grants to the staff of several mosques including those of Fatih and Kılıç Ali Pasha. By such means the revenues of major or popular mosques could be maintained in face of inflation.

Glossary

ACEMIOĞLAN   Cadet.

ALEM   Crescent and star, bull's horns, etc., sometimes of gilded bronze, which is the standard, talisman or symbolic finial on top of a mosque dome, minaret cap, etc.

ARASTA   Covered market associated with a mosque.

ARCH   The common Ottoman arches are variations of the two-centred type, sometimes so slightly pointed as to appear round. The Iranian keel form and the ogee occur. Other types are rare and include stilted, hipped, segmental and multi-foil arches. The horseshoe is almost unknown but the gate to the Arap Cami, Istanbul, is a fine example.

AVLU (Harim)   Courtyard forming a summer extension of a mosque.

BAKLAVA   Chevron pattern.

BEDESTEN   Domed building usually in the centre of a market area where luxury goods were sold and stored.

BEND   Dam.

BEYLİK   A small domain, vassal or free, in the period which followed the disintegration of the Selçuk state in Anatolia.

BİMARHANE   A hospital, which could be combined with a tımarhane or lunatic asylum.

CAMEKÂN   Disrobing room of a haman.

CAMİ   A Friday (Cuma) mosque with a minber from which the Hatib may preach the weekly sermon or hutbe. Most mescits are now used as camis.

ÇARŞI   Market.

ÇEŞME   A drinking fountain whether a tap alone or a monument.

CHRONOGRAM   An acrostic inscription from which the date can be deciphered.

DARÜL-HADİS   College of advanced studies in the religious law (Şeriat).

DARÜL-KURRA   House for the readers of the Koran.

DARUŞŞIFA   See bimarhane.

DERGÂH   Hanıkâh, tekke, or dervish convent.

DERSHANE   Study or lecture hall or both at various times.

DIVAN   Council of State and Justice. The royal divan met under the high cupola, Kubbe Altı, in the second court of the saray. The Grand Vezir held a lesser divan at his house.

ELİF   First letter of the Arabic alphabet and of Allah's name.

EYVAN   A vaulted or domed recess open on one side.

GÖBEKTAŞ   Navel stone. The marble platform in the middle of the hot room of a haman.

HALVET   Cubicle or cell.

HAMAM   Ritual warm bath usually attached to a mosque.

HAN   Inn, usually in towns. Title of prince or ruler.

HANIKÂH   See dergâh.

HARARA   Hot room of a hamam.

HAREM   Place of privacy, especially for women, in a home.

HAREMLİK   The family rooms of a house.

HASSA   Royal.

HOCA   Teacher.

HÜCRE   A cell.

HÜNKÂR MAHFİL   Royal box in a mosque.

HUTBE   See cami.

İLWAN   Portal rising above level of the roof.

İMARET   A soup kitchen for students, the poor, etc.

KADI   District judge.

KADIASKER   Chief Military Justice – Judge Advocate.

KAPLICA   A hot spring with the bath built above it. It has a pool for swimming in, unlike a hamam.

KAYMAKAM   Chief Constable.

KERVANSARAY   Hostelry, usually beside the highway.

KIBLE   See mihrab.

KİLİM   Tapestry weave mat.

KİTABE Inscriptive plaque usually found over mosque doors.

KİOSK Pavilion.

KONAK Mansion.

KÜLLIYE Educational and charitable dependencies of a mosque.

KÜMBET Mausoleum.

KÜRSÜ High chair for the imam when teaching.

KÜTÜPHANE Library.

MABEYIN Reception room dividing harem from public rooms.

MAHFİL Tribune for müezzins or the royal loge.

MAHKEME Court of summary jurisprudence or magistrate's court.

MARİSTAN Hospital.

MEDRESE College for the teaching of the orthodox law (Sunni).

MEKTEB See sibyan mekteb.

MESCIT A prayer hall without a minber; not used for the noon prayer on Friday.

MEYDAN Open space.

MİHRAB Originally a spear (kıble) then a plain niche which was elaborated into an ornate portal. It indicates the direction of Mecca and therefore of prayer.

MİMAR Architect, hence Mimarbaşı, Chief Architect.

MİNBER The hooded dais reached by long stairs from which the hutbe is declaimed at noon on Fridays.

MİSAFİRHANE Guest house.

MÜDERRİS Professor and director of a college, member of the Ulema.

MÜEZZİN Mosque officer responsible for the call to prayer.

MÜFTÜLİK Headquarters of the Grand Mufti or Şeyhül-Islam.

MUMHANE Candle factory.

MUVAKKİTHANE Timekeepers' room also used by astrologers.

NAMAZGÂH Open air mescit or cami, especially for the army.

OCAK Fireplace with tall hood of plaster or bronze. Unit of the Janissaries deriving from the concept of a camp fire.

ODA Room.

OGEE See arch. Used here to describe the typical pointed Ottoman arch which has two slightly pointed arcs at its peak. The pronounced ogee form is rare but notable examples occur.

OTAK The royal tent which might take a decade to embroider.

PADİŞAH Sultan.

PAPUÇLUK Cubby-hole for slippers.

PİR The doyen and administrator of a dervish community.

PİSHTAK Grand gateway rising above the walls or buildings on each side of it.

REVAK A domed or vaulted colonnade enclosing a court.

SADRAZAM The Grand Vezir or Chancellor of the Empire.

ŞADIRVAN The fountain for ritual ablutions before prayer.

SARAY Palace.

SEBİL Tank from which an attendant issues cups of water, sherbet, etc., from behind a grille.

SELÂMLIK Men's apartments.

SELÂTİN CAMİ An imperial mosque; with two or more minarets.

SEMAHANE Hall of a dervish convent used for ritual dances.

ŞEREFE Gallery of a minaret from which call to prayer is made.

ŞEYH Head of a religious order; elder. Hence Seyhül-Islam, the Grand Mufti of Istanbul, who was president of the Ulema and senior minister after the Sadrazam with the power to depose a sultan on canonical grounds.

SİBYAN MEKTEB Koran school for small boys.

SICAKLUK Hot room of a hamam.

ŞİFAHANE Hospital.

SOĞUKLUK Cool room of a hamam.

SON CEMAAT YERİ The portico of a mosque where latecomers could pray before external mihrabs. It is an extension of the mosque area in a way that the revaks are not.

SU TERAZİ Tower syphoning water, as opposed to an aqueduct.

TABHANE Hospice where travellers might lodge free for three days forming part of the külliye of a mosque.

TAHTA Wooden platform, throne.

TAKSİM The building where the water supply is divided into various channels for different districts.

TAMGÂH Seal, emblem or talisman.

TEKKE See dergâh.

TEZKERE Official record.

TİMARHANE Asylum. See bimarhane.

TUĞRA Seal of the Sultan.

TÜRBE Tomb or mausoleum.

ULEMA Doctors of the law (Şeriat), senior officers of the Faith.

VAKFIYE Endowment.

VEZİR A minister of state. The four vezirs of the Cupola were of cabinet rank.

VEZİRAZAM Chief Vezir. The office grew in importance during the sixteenth century; see sadrazam.

YALI Mansion on the shores of the Bosphorus.

YOL Street. Hence Divan Yolu, the Street of the Divan.

YURT Home, native land, camping ground.

ZAVİYE The cell of a recluse, but in this context the hostel of the Ahi sect, the Brotherhood of Virtue, which was connected with the guilds and the Janissaries. The word came to be applied to lodgings for itinerant dervishes and later the imaret system of the major mosques.

Notes on the Text

1 BEFORE THE CAPTURE OF BURSA

pages 14-33

1 The former Miletus.

2 Wittek, *The Rise of the Ottoman Empire*, p.39, says that the Mevlevi order of dervishes designated the emir of this family Sultan of the Gazis and presented him with his war club. The girding on of the sword of Osman – the accession rite of the Ottomans – relates to this practice. The receiving of a weapon refers to the Futuwwa. The Cup is also important symbolically.

3 The traditional date for the founding of the Ottoman state is 1299. Two monuments of Osman's reign, which are now lost, were the mosque at Karacahisar and a zaviye near Inegöl; see Ayverdi, 'Le premier siècle de l'architecture ottomane' in *1st I.C.T.A.*, p.49. Edib, in *The Conflict of East and West in Turkey*, p.13, says that Osman's grandfather was a shaman who had been converted to Islam in the north-east and who came west full of Central Asian traditions and lore.

4 Lybyer, *The Government of the Ottoman Empire in the time of Suleiman the Magnificent*, p.12, says that the Ottomans had no race problems nor racial pride. Anyone could attain the rank which he deserved. Thus they were a mixture of many peoples. Edib, *The Conflict of East and West in Turkey*, pp.10-15, says that they were of any race, like the Romans, and because they judged only by capacity they were glad to convert young Greeks like Evrenos. This must have been a drain on the best Byzantine warriors. Gibbons, *The Foundation of the Ottoman Empire*, pp.81-3, says that the troops of Ertuğrul and Osman were all volunteer horse (Akıncı), but Orhan recruited irregular infantry (Azabs) and a paid royal guard.

5 His symbol was a bird derived from the Shaman concept of the animal form of the soul or double. Hence the totem names of Turkish tribes such as the Oğuz (ox), Akkoyunlu (white sheep), etc. An alternative rendering of Orhan's name is Okhan which means the Lord of the Bow. On the importance of the symbolism of the bow see Chap.9, p.356.

6 The Futuwwa.

7 Gibb, *The Travels of Ibn Battuta*, II, p.416.

8 Barkan, 'Les fondations pieuses comme méthode de peuplement et de colonisation' in *V.D.*, II, Supp., p.59 et seq.

9 Gibb, *The Travels of Ibn Battuta*, II, p.433.

10 See Appendix I.

11 This room had none of the sacred symbolism of a church; the whole world is a mosque.

12 Aytöre, 'Turkish Water Architecture' in *1st I.C.T.A.*, pp.40-4, says Sokollu Mehmet Pasha was to attempt to dig a canal from the Volga to the Don and so link the White Sea with the Black.

13 Diez, 'L'Emblème dans le Palais byzantin et la grande Mosquée turque' in *1st I.C.T.A.*, pp. 90-1, says that the dome was sacred in Roman and Byzantine times, and Byzantine law forbade the use of a dome in civil buildings. The five domes of the Chalké hall of the Great Palace of Constantinople were emblematic. The pharaohs of Egypt had sat under a baldaquin or celestial vault and this, in the form of a ciborium, was adopted by Augustus as the cosmic symbol of the celestial vault and of the emperor, a step perpetuated by Nero and brought back east by Constantine. (It may be added that a mihrab has a miniature cupola as well as being the gate of paradise.) Palen, *Mission to Turkestan*, p.3, describes the yurts, or willow-framed tents, of Central Asia, which are circular and shallow-domed.

14 Kuran, *İlk Devir Osmanlı mimarisinde cami*, p.16, *inter alia*.

15 It had been the Selçuk capital under Süleyman Shah, regent for his cousin, Melih Shah Kutulmuşoğlu, to whom it had been surrendered by a mercenary Turkish garrison in 1080. The First Crusade under Godefroi de Bouillon drove the Selçuks to Konya in 1097. Sacked by Timur in 1402, it was retaken by Murat II. See Yetkin, *Turkish Architecture*, p.5; Runciman, *A History of the Crusades*, I, p.180; Fıratlı, *İznik*.

16 Among other churches converted early in the Ottoman period and still standing are those of Gazi Süleyman Pasha at Vize and Filibe (Plovdiv) now in Bulgaria. The latter building is a precursor of the form of centralized mosque which reached its apogee with Şehzade Cami, Istanbul. The mosque of Murat I Hudavendigar, also at Filibe and, probably, his mosque at Behremkale (Assos) are also converted churches. Yıldırım Beyazit converted two important churches – now the Ulu Camis at Bergama and at Balikesir – but both were heavily rebuilt.

17 7·92 metres.

18 The interior proportion of the wall is roughly four to two to four, since the wall is 3·9 metres high, the triangle frieze 1·9 metres, and the dome to its crown is 3·8 metres. The wall and frieze together, therefore, are in the proportion of three to two in relation to the height of the dome.

19 Pier Luigi Nervi's Turin Exhibition Hall revives the concept of these triangles in modern form.

20 Otto-Dorn, *Das Islamische Iznik*, p.14, says that traditionally the mihrab was roughly identified with the south direction and this resulted in errors of up to forty-five degrees. See also Sayılı, *The Observatory in Islam and its Place in the General History of the Observatory*, p.25.

21 Casements of wooden shutters. It is probable that the lower windows of Ottoman mosques were unglazed until the late eighteenth century.

22 The son cemaat yeri, or place of prayer for latecomers, existed in Central Asia where some early domed mosques had a large arch open to the court on the north side. People outside could follow the prayers as they do at such Iranian Selçuk monuments as the Friday mosque at Isfahan. See Yaralov, 'Architectural monuments of Middle Asia of the 8th and 12th centuries' in *1st I.C.T.A.*, p.365.

23 Of a type which would appear to be Syrian in origin.

24 Kuran, *İlk Devir Osmanlı mimarisinde cami*, p.8. Kızıltan, *Anadolu Beyliklerinde cami ve mescitler*, p.104.

25 Palen, *Mission to Turkestan*, p.33.

26 Although the Turks use them when sitting on threshing boards driving mules or oxen at harvest time.

27 Pardoe, *The City of the Sultan*, I, p.40, mentions nail heads as large as shillings on the floor of the tekke at Tünel in order to spare the feet of the dancers.

28 Fitzgerald, *Barbarian Beds. The origins of the chair in China*, London, 1965, p.3 et seq. It may be noted that the decorative edges of wooden Chinese sofas from as early as the thirteenth century took forms related to the multifoliate arches in universal use in Islam.

29 I am indebted for these facts to Mr Robert Van Nice.

30 See Bell, *The Thousand and one churches*, p.441 et seq. A brick pendentive discovered in 1967 at Sardis would appear to be the earliest known. Marçais, 'Binā', in *E.I.*, I, p.1228, says that plain and shell squinches originated in Iran. The niche form occurs in the Great Mosque at Damascus.

31 The first Ottoman vezir or minister. Gibbons, *The Foundation of the Ottoman Empire*, p.71, says that the post of Chief Vezir or Vezirazam, developed out of this appointment and may be thought of as that of Lord President of the Council. The appointment of Sadrazam or Grand Vezir had the importance of a Chancellor of the Empire in the German sense, but this post did not develop until the sixteenth century.

32 Kuran, *İlk Devir Osmanlı mimarisinde cami*, p.6, n.1. Ayverdi, 'Orhan Gazi devrinde mi'mari' in *Y.A.D.*, I, p.124. Kızıltan, *Anadolu Beyliklerinde cami ve mescitler*, p.110, gives 1326 as the date of the Alaettin.

33 Kuran, *İlk Devir Osmanlı mimarisinde cami*, p.6, gives 8·20 metres.

34 Ibid., p.7, gives 1·05 metres.

35 Ibid., p.7.

36 Gabriel, *Une Capitale turque, Brousse (Bursa)*, p.50. Kızıltan, *Anadolu Beyliklerinde cami ve mescitler*, p.110.

37 Kuran, *İlk Devir Osmanlı mimarisinde cami*, p.18. Diehl, in Pope, *A Survey of Persian Art*, III, pp.928-9, says that in east Islam a minaret is a monument but in west Islam it is a structure devised in terms of interior space. He traces the origin of the round Ottoman minaret through Selçuk Iran to its beginnings in Indian-Buddhist art as a tree pillar. Its translation into stone took place in the Asoka period (272-232 BC). The Persian minaret was the first to be crowned with a balcony like a pavilion.

38 Kuran, *İlk Devir Osmanlı mimarisinde cami*, p.18. Ayverdi, 'Le premier siècle de l'architecture ottomane' in *1st I.C.T.A.*, p. 52, states that the mosque of Orhan at Izmit, although rebuilt, follows the old foundation and was twenty metres square. This is hypothetical.

39 Godard, *L'Art de l'Iran*, p.338. This form is a direct descendant of such mosques or converted fire temples as that at Yazdikhvast discussed there.

40 Ayverdi, *Osmanlı mi'mârîsinin ilk devri*, pp.31-2, gives exact measurements down to centimetres. I respect his figures but think that they can mislead because (a) there is a great variation along the surface of any given wall; (b) cumulative layers of plaster alter proportions; (c) restorations have certainly made changes. Therefore I give all measurements, as a rule, to the nearest major fraction of a metre and seek to avoid centimetres entirely.

41 Possibly a deliberate return to the early tradition.

42 Kuran, *İlk Devir Osmanlı mimarisinde cami*, p.18.

43 Ayverdi, 'Le premier siècle de l'architecture ottomane', p.51.

44 Perhaps the organization of the streets may owe something to the period of Orhan. The mosque of Orhan Gazi at Yarhisar is also rebuilt but possesses a beautiful minaret of an early date. The pediment shows Byzantine influence. The minaret is placed inside the mosque at the north-east corner. See Ayverdi, 'Le premier siècle de l'architecture ottomane', p.52.

45 Ayverdi, ibid., pp.37-8.

46 An inscription still extant on the tomb of Hacı Hamza at Iznik gives the architect as Hacı Ali who probably built the mosque, too, in 1345. It was demolished in 1930. See Fıratlı, *İznik*.

47 He could also be the architect of the İlyas Bey Cami at Balat. See Otto-Dorn, *Das Islamische Iznik*, p.21.

48 By stalactite is meant a concave surface covered by tiers of small quarter domes or cells set at varying angles. Each tier projects forward from the tier below. Between each concave quarter-dome is a convex bracket which supports the springing of the dome above. For a full description see Wilber, *The Art of Islamic Iran: the Il Khānid Period*, p.72. On p.33 he attributes the development of the stalactite to Selçuk Iran.

49 Similar frames were set into the windows of the Cacabey Türbe.

50 Kuran, *İlk Devir Osmanlı mimarisinde cami*, p.15.

51 Diez and Aslanapa, *Türk sanatı*, p.37.

52 Inscription.

53 Meyer-Riefstahl, *Turkish Architecture in Southwestern Anatolia*, p.26, says that the capitals are fourth-century. Note may be taken of the Ahi Elvan Cami at Ankara dating from the end of the fourteenth century – the fine mihrab is inscribed with the date 816/1413 – which has twelve columns in three rows of four. This creates four aisles resulting in the placing of the mihrab off-centre to the east facing the second aisle and the mihrab to the west facing the third. Because the mosque is built on a hillside the north door beside the minaret leads to the large C-shaped gallery and that on the east to the lower floor.

54 A forest mosque is one with an interior full of piers. Note the likeness to the Hittite audience hall at Hattusas, Büyükkale, reconstructed by Akurgal in *The Art of the Hittites*.

55 See pp.108, 165.

56 Sungur means a bicephalus bird, the gerfaunt of Western heraldry.

57 A new and vast restoration is under way.

58 They do appear in Burgundy, significantly at the twelfth-century church at Montréal (Yonne), in cusped form. There the twin west doors are multifoliate and the convex central and other consoles supporting the tribune strikingly resemble those of the north tribune of the Sungur Bey Cami.

59 Hammer-Purgstall, *Histoire de l'Empire Ottomane*, I, p.143. Otto-Dorn, *Das Islamische Iznik*, p.69, dates it 732/1331.

60 Gabriel, *Les monuments turcs d'Anatolie*, I, p.134.

61 Kızıltan, *Anadolu Beylikerinde cami ve mescitler*, p.52.

62 Ibid., p.48.

63 Ülgen, 'Le Décor intérieur de l'Architecture turque au XVIe siècle' in *1st I.C.T.A.*, p.350 et seq. says that the decor is original and he may be correct.

64 Kızıltan, *Anadolu Beylikerinde cami ve mescitler*, p.89. Wittek, *Menteşe Beyliği*, p.127, gives 1375.

65 In its original form the Ahmet Gazi mosque must have been the last of the Kayseri type of ulu cami.

66 Kızıltan, *Anadolu Beylikerinde cami ve mescitler*, p.89, and n.2. The year 777 was a mystical date if ever a year could be.

67 Ibid., p.51.

68 It has been extensively restored and refurbished.

69 Kızıltan, *Anadolu Beylikerinde cami ve mescitler*.

70 Ibid., p.76.

71 Ibid., p.72.

72 See p.166.

73 Kızıltan, *Anadolu Beylikerinde cami ve mescitler*, p.92. It is known as the İlyas Bey Cami but also as the Koca Cami and the Cuma Cami.

74 Ibid.

75 Chandler, *Travels in Asia Minor*, pp.329-30, reported as early as the 1760s that there was a noble and beautiful mosque of marble and that the dome, with a palm or two, towered amid the ruins. Wittek, *Menteşe Beyliği*, p.131 et seq. calls these rooms part of an imarethane, which suggests dervish rather than orthodox use originally.

76 Staircase minarets occur with the nineteenth-century mescits of Kayseri where they lead to an open belvedere. A charming example is the free-standing minaret carved out of the rock in front of the troglodyte mosque of Taşhanköy, forty kilometres north of the city. Such minarets are frequent in Africa – see Schacht, 'Ein archaischer Minaret-Typ in Ägypten und Anatolien' in *A.I.*, V, p.46 et seq. Also Schacht, 'The Staircase Minaret' in *1st I.C.T.A.*, p.297, says that it appears to have been the earliest type of minaret to occur along the wall of the Ulu Cami at Bosra although there is a tower at the north-east corner. The simplest minaret that I have seen, apart

from a house roof, is the ladder leaning against a tree in the yard of the mosque at Monastir on Marmara Island.

77 Kızıltan, *Anadolu Beylikerinde cami ve mescitler*, p.90.

78 Diez *et al.*, *Karaman devri sanati*, p.5. Yetkin *et al.*, *Turkish Architecture*, p.28, dates the mosque 1320 and calls this portico the first narthex in Ottoman architecture.

79 Godard, *L'art de l'Iran*, p.116, fig.142, shows a house in the form common in the Teheran region.

80 Yaralov, 'Architectural monuments in Middle Asia' in *1st I.C.T.A.*, p.367.

2 BURSA – THE FIRST MOSQUES

pages 34-57

1 Gibbons, *The Foundation of the Ottoman Empire*, p.54. See p.43 re tomb of Osman.

2 Babinger, 'Nilufer Khatun' in *E.I.*, III, p.921, says that she was the daughter of the Lord of Yarhisar and was kidnapped by Osman in 1299 to be the wife of his twelve-year-old son, beside whom she is buried. There is no Byzantine reference to this, only a Turkish source. She built a bridge and a zaviye near Bursa. Bernard, *Les Bains de Brousse*, p. 70, and Lybyer, *The Government of the Ottoman Empire*, p.17, both say that she was of Greek origin. It was she who was regent in Iznik when Ibn Battuta arrived.

3 The importance attached to building mosques on hilltops was to culminate in the incomparable skyline of Istanbul.

4 At this period in Ottoman history the sultan was moderately democratic and walked in the street. The chivalrous ideal was freedom and social justice, according to Edib, *The Conflict of East and West in Turkey*, p.14.

5 Pococke, 'A Description of the East' in Pinkerton, *A general collection of the best and most interesting voyages*, X, p.717, reports that this was burnt down at the beginning of the eighteenth century.

6 This is itself a descendant of the Sırçalı Medrese, Konya, of which one of the dates given is 1242.

7 Sayılı, *The Observatory in Islam*, p.253, says that this medrese was the centre of astronomical teaching but admits that there is no reference to this in the vakfiye – see Appendix II – although he suggests that the minarets were observation towers.

8 First known at Leshker-i Bazar near Bust in Afghanistan in the eleventh century according to Yetkin *et al.*, *Turkish architecture*, p.26; but Godard, 'L'origine de la madrasa, de la mosquée et du caravansérail à quatre ivans' in *A.I.*, XV-XVI, p.1 et seq. says that the four-eyvan type medrese began in the teachers' home in Iran in the fourth century after the Hegira and gradually developed round his private court. Sunni atabeys took it to Syria in the sixth century.

9 Mantran, 'Les inscriptions arabes de Brousse' in *Bulletin d'Études Orientales*, XIV, p.90, gives the sense of the inscription as: 'The Sultan of the Warriors and Champions of the Holy War, Orhan Bey son of Osman Bey – on whom the earth lie lightly – has ordained this noble edifice in the year 740 [1339-40]. A Karamanid burnt it; subsequently, the intendant, the very great vezir Beyazit Pasha, ordered its restoration on the command of the sultan son of a sultan, Sultan Mehmet son of Beyazit Han – may his power be eternal – in the year 820 [1417-18].' The inscription is written in small neshi calligraphy in an ogival cartouche over the door of the prayer hall. Lechevalier, *Voyage de la Propontide et du Pont-Euxin*, I, pp.29-30, says that the mosque of Orhan the Victorious is an old monastery at the entry of which one is shown an enormous drum; the credulous were persuaded that this Emperor returned every Friday to his mosque to beat the drum and tell his beads.

10 Gabriel, *Une Capitale turque, Brousse (Bursa)*, p.46.

11 Former ambassador to France and translator of Molière and Shakespeare.

12 This mosque is orientated south-south-west, like all Orhan's mosques at Bursa, and not south-south-east which is approximately the true

direction of Mecca. See Gabriel, *Une Capitale turque, Brousse (Bursa)*, pp.45-7.

13 Kuran, *İlk Devir Osmanlı mimarisinde cami*, p.71.

14 This long-established division persisted into the Classical period. The mosques of Sinan and later ones also have raised areas before the mihrab, as does the Ahmediye.

15 Ergin, *Türk şehirlerinde imaret sistemi*, p.23, says that in Selçuk times tabhanes were called Darül-Rahat or Houses of Ease and he quotes Evliya Çelebi as saying that they were places for leisure and for pleasure. Tritton, *Islam, belief and practices*, p.30, speaks of a retreat as the result of a vow, when a man fasts in the mosque for several consecutive days, perhaps ten in all. Women also went into retreat.

16 Eyice, 'Un type de mosquée de style Turc-Ottomane ancien' in *1st I.C.T.A.*, pp.141-3. He also suggests that these eyvans were originally cut off from the court by partitions demolished after the decline of the Ahi brotherhood in the early part of the sixteenth century.

17 See p.78.

18 Sun discs or Aristotelian wheels of the spheres of the Zodiac.

19 Inscription.

20 The shell form existed in embryo in Damascus, and also in the Piazza d'Oro of Hadrian's Villa at Tivoli, but there it was set on a round base.

21 Gibb, *The Travels of Ibn Battuta*, p.444, says the traveller lodged in the hospice of one Ahi Mehmet, a most saintly man who (n.113) may have been the Emir Mehmet ibn Kalaman who built a mosque in Tire in 1338. It could be that it was in this zaviye that Ibn Battuta lodged.

22 The kaplica, or hamam centred on a pool of still water, was inherited from the Byzantines; but the Moslem prefers to wash under running water, in accordance with the traditions, and thus Ottoman hamams differed from the established form of bath.

23 Çetintas, *Türk Mimari anıtları Osmanlı devri; I. Bursa'da ilk eserler*, p. 25.

24 The Büyük Hamam at Iznik is built over and seriously altered. It could have been of much the same date, just as could the Hacı Hamza Hamam which is still in use and akin to the Bey Hamam in plan. The double hamam of Süleyman Pasha at Göynük may be older still.

25 Çetintas, *Türk Mimari anıtları Osmanlı devri; I. Bursa'da ilk eserler*, p. 26.

26 La Mottraye, *Travels*, I, p. 216, writing in the early eighteenth century, praises the excellent Bursa hans and (p. 189) says that their cells were unfurnished but free.

27 The first Ottoman pasha. Gibbons, *The Foundation of the Ottoman Empire*, pp. 71-2, calls Alaettin the first. The title was borne by Süleyman, Orhan's eldest son, in accordance with the tradition in Iran where it is the title of the eldest son of the ruler. It is an abbreviated form of padişah. Süleyman died before his father in 1358. Hussey, *Byzantium and its neighbours*.

28 Firatlı, *İznik*.

29 Hammer-Purgstall, *Histoire de l'Empire Ottomane*, I, p. 143. Sarton, *Introduction to the history of science*, III, part 1, p. 105, says Davut bin Mahmut al Kayseri wrote popular poetry as well.

30 See p.25.

31 Kuran, *İlk Devir Osmanlı mimarisinde cami*, p. 71.

32 Pardoe, *The City of the Sultan, and domestic manners of the Turks in 1836*, II, p. 215, stated that the stairs were decaying; this would indicate that a major reconstruction has been carried out since.

33 Kuran, *İlk Devir Osmanlı mimarisinde cami*, p. 72. I am not convinced of this.

34 Just across the Meriç river into Greece from Ipsala is the former Ferecik where Süleyman Pasha clearly converted a church into a mosque. It has a central dome and four corner domes with four barrel vaults between to form a cross. The relationship of this mosque to Murat's, which is later, is slight but pertinent; the relationship to the Şehzade or centralized type is dramatic although heavy restoration has weakened the evidence.

35 Pardoe, *The City of the Sultan, and domestic manners of the Turks in 1836*, vol. II, p. 215, was admitted to this mosque and there found a

lonely lunatic in residence. She does not say how long it had served as a tımarhane but it is easy to see that it would have been necessary to cut off the mosque from the madhouse.

36 Each cell has its niche for a lamp. See Koran, xxiv, 35, p. 357 for the significance of a lamp in a niche. It symbolizes God in a human soul according to some mystics. Any light may also be the moon or Muhammed, the Nur of the Koran. Candles were particularly significant soul symbols for the Bektaşi order of Dervishes. See Esin, *Mecca, the blessed; Madinah, the radiant*, p. 211. Coomaraswamy, 'Notes on the philosophy of Persian Art' in *A.I.* XV & XVI, p. 127, says that the niche represents the world; the light is the light of Essence; the glass through which it shines is the human soul; the tree is the self of truth: and oil is the timeless spirit.

37 The frame of such a doorway rises above the level of the façade. It was a symbolic setting for a ruler.

38 Ayverdi, 'Le premier siècle', p.55, says that the minaret existed in the 1870s but was broken off and restored in 1892.

39 *İlk Devir Osmanlı mimarisinde cami*, p. 75.

40 *Une Capitale turque, Brousse (Bursa)*, p. 55.

41 *Türk Mimarı anıtları Osmanlı devri; I. Bursa'da ilk eserler*, lehva 8.

42 When Dr Hamlin built Hamlin Hall on the Bosphorus in the 1870s he employed Bulgars on one half of his building and Armenians on the other so as to stimulate work. It may have been an old custom.

43 *The Travels of Ibn Battuta*, II, p. 450.

44 Gabriel, *Une Capitale turque, Brousse (Bursa)*, p. 170.

45 Ibid., p. 62.

46 Eyice, 'Two Byzantine pavements in Bithynia' in *D.O.P.*, no. 17, p. 374 et seq.

47 The vakfiye clearly dates this 1366.

48 *Une Capitale turque, Brousse (Bursa)*, p. 62.

49 Texier, *Asie Mineure*, II, p. 569, curiously enough does not comment on the relationship between these two buildings.

50 Ayverdi, *Le premier siècle*, p. 54 accepts that there is foreign influence in this mosque, although he does not refer to the church at Philippopolis and makes no mention of the Ak Medrese in relation to either of them.

51 Texier, *Asie Mineure*, II, p. 128, states that Hatip Çelebi and other historians of the time report that Murat I employed Christian workmen and artists on the numerous monuments which he built in his capital. It must be remembered that no church built prior to the conquest still stands in Bursa, so we have no idea what form the Christian monuments took, but they must have been remarkable since the city was a rich one. It may well have been that a church related to that at Ohrid was standing there in the fourteenth century; but this is simply speculation.

52 See p.20.

53 Ayverdi, *Osmanlı mi'mârisinin ilk devri*, p.327.

54 Gibb, *The Travels of Ibn Battuta*, p. 420.

55 Ibid., p. 416.

56 With the monstrous addition of a steel pole and four loudspeakers set up in front of it to serve as a bastard minaret.

57 Gibbons, *The Foundation of the Ottoman Empire*, pp.114 and 125.

58 Kuran, *İlk Devir Osmanlı mimarisinde cami*, p. 77.

59 Gabriel, *Une Capitale turque, Brousse (Bursa)*, p. 72 quoting Aşikpaşazade.

60 It is probable that all the roofs and domes were tiled originally.

61 See p.19. Gray, *Persian Painting*, p.38, reproduces a miniature entitled 'Kalila and Dimna' from the Yildiz Album, Istanbul University, of the Tabriz School, 1360–74, showing a brazier in the ocak, jugs and jars on a shelf. Later, logs were stood up in the ocak to create a blazing fire.

62 Gabriel, *Une Capitale turque, Brousse (Bursa)*, p.69.

63 This elaboration has some of the mood of the late Gothic.

64 The quarries of Marmara Island (Proconnessus) and their mainland port at Bandırma and Erdek were now in Ottoman hands but their output had been greatly reduced.

65 Yeşil Cami, Bursa, not to be confused with Yeşil Cami, Iznik.

66 See Cook, *Zeus, A study in ancient religion*, I, p. 125, fig. 94, and elsewhere. This is the mosque of Lightning Beyazit.

67 *Türk Mimarı anıtları Osmanlı devri; I. Bursa'da ilk eserler*, lehva 32.

68 Such as later occurs over the door of the Mescid-i-Shah at Isfahan.

69 The hipped arch is ideally designed for this purpose. An example of lamps in use appears in the Fatih Album, H.2153, sayfa 131B, Topkapısaray, depicting a monastery scene probably in Central Asia.

70 The play of light and shade in the tones of the cut stone of the flanks, like the Kiosk Medrese at Kayseri, recalls the vivid abstract patterns distinctive of the best Armenian masonry.

71 Kunter, 'Les bases appliquées dans l'administration, la conservation, l'entretien et les réparations des monuments turcs' in *1st I.C.T.A.*, p. 233 says that there is a dynasty of lead workers at Yıldırım who, to this day, continue handing on their skill in leafing domes with lead and are hereditary craftsmen under the vakfiye of this mosque. If so, this could have been the first Ottoman building to be domed in lead, but the tradition is questionable. At this period, tile or glazed brick were common in Bursa. Yıldırım did not capture the lead mines at Divrik until after the Battle of Niğbolu (Nicopolis).

72 Gabriel, *Une Capitale turque, Brousse (Bursa)*, p. 73.

73 The difference in the size and brickwork between the arch on the south side and the central and north arches indicates extensive alterations during repairs.

74 *Türk Mimarı anıtları Osmanlı devri; I. Bursa'da ilk eserler*, lehva 47.

75 The proportions are noteworthy since the dome is fourteen metres high and the apex of the triangle of three windows in the wall is seven metres high. The dome is 3·4 metres above the drum and is a quarter of the total height.

76 With room for three to five. In nineteenth-century Tsarist Russia students prepared their own meals at the open hearth in their cells, but in fifteenth-century Bursa they were fed at the imaret. Some müderris lived in, but some together with the older students might come for the day. The cells were cramped, cold, dank and damp. See Williams, 'The Traditional Muslim Schools', *Central Asian Review*, XIII, no. 4, p. 343.

77 The cells vary considerably in size from 9·5 to 11·5 square metres. The arch-spans of the revaks vary from 2·9 to 3·9 metres and the width of the cell doors from 0·9 to 1·2 metres. This would indicate hasty work or bad reconstruction.

78 Gabriel, *Une Capitale turque, Brousse (Bursa)*, p. 73.

79 Yetkin *et al.*, *Turkish architecture*, p. 21 says that this was the first Ottoman hospital. Earlier Selçuk foundations continued in use. Bolak, *Hastahanelerimiz*, p. 32 dates it 1399.

80 This ornament is universal in Islam and, due to the Arabs, appears at Hosias Lukas, Daphne and elsewhere. See Miles, 'Byzantium and Arabs: Crete and Aegean' in *D.O.P.* no. 18.

81 Sun, moon and stars. Hastings (ed.) *Encyclopaedia of Religion and Ethics*, XII, pp. 48–103. ✡—This symbol represents alcohol in alchemy and also fire and water, the eye of God, Holy Spirit, and God Himself besides the Star of David. Eisler, *The Royal Art of Astrology*, p. 196 shows it as the Babylonian hexagram with the sun in the centre and the moon in the triangle above and the others, reading clockwise, by the five known planets – Mars, Mercury, Saturn, Venus, Jupiter.

82 Gabriel, *Une Capitale turque, Brousse (Bursa)*, p. 77, quoting from Ünver. Mantran, in 'Les inscriptions arabes de Brousse', p.104 translates the neshi inscription over the door of Beyazit I's türbe. It states that 'this is the tomb of the happy Sultan, to whom one wishes the mercy and indulgence of God, Beyazit Khan son of Murat Khan. The very great Sultan, Master of the Kings of the Arabs and the Persians, Süleyman Han son of Beyazit Khan – may God perpetuate his power – built it on 1st Muharram [18 June, 1406]'.

83 Yetkin, *L'Architecture Turque*, p. 120 says that it was begun by Selim I in 1512.

84 Yıldırım also built a more modest Bursa-type mosque at Edirne set aslant the foundations of a church – if this is not the work of Murat I (see p.164, n.95).

85 It has now been completely covered in corrugated iron.

86 Gabriel, *Les monuments turcs d'Anatolie*, I, p.32 et seq.

87 Including those at Varamin and Isfahan.

88 I am indebted to Mr John H. Harvey for this observation.

89 After the 1855 earthquake all the domes fell except the one before the mihrab and another in the east corner.

90 Ayverdi, *Osmanli mi'mârısinin ilk devri*, p.404, sheet 687.

91 Hammer-Purgstall, *Histoire de l'Empire Ottomane*, II, p. 202, says that it was filled with goldfish. Pardoe, *The city of the Sultan*, II, p. 206, says that they were tench.

92 The proportions of the minarets are three-fifths base and trunk and two-fifths from şerefe to alem. But the base is half the height of the trunk and the şerefe is half that of the base, showing that the dominance of multiples of two in the Ottoman module was still virile. Yıldırım's mosque at Edirne, however, reverts to the golden mean. The central dome is 13·75 metres high over the floor which is 8 metres square. The piers to the frieze are 8·70 metres high and frieze and dome combined are 5 metres.

93 Southgate, *Narrative of a Tour*, I, p. 122 says that it was traditional to paint mosques white. See, also, nineteenth-century photographs and engravings. The Byzantines painted their churches in various colours. Palladio stated that of all colours none is more proper for churches than white, since the purity of colour, as of life, is particularly grateful to God. See A. K. Placzek (ed.), *Andrea Palladio, The Four Books of Architecture*, Fourth Book, New York, 1965, p. 82.

94 Kocu, *Evliya Çelebi, Seyahatnamesi*, II, p. 78. See also Gabriel, *Une Capitale turque, Brousse (Bursa)*, p. 37.

95 Pardoe, *The city of the Sultan*, II, p. 206 talks of deep-coloured frescoes. J. F. Lewis's *Illustrations of Constantinople*, drawn in 1835–1836, shows writing on the walls.

96 Pope, *A Survey of Persian Art*, VI, p. 2768, calls such roundels astral bodies. Tritton, *Islam, belief and practices*, p. 18, says that there was consistant communication between the upper and the lower worlds: magic is one form of it. Mantran, in 'Les inscriptions arabes de Brousse', p. 91 says the single line inscription on the right side of the minber reads that it is the work of Hacı Mehmet son of Abdülaziz son of. . . . In the same neshi script, but without points or signs, is a larger inscription stating that this is one of the objects made at the orders of the magnificent Sultan Beyazit Khan son of Murat in the year *802/*1399 or 1400.

97 At Samarkand, he cleft a great arcaded highway through his capital in a fortnight.

98 Gabriel, *Une Capitale turque, Brousse (Bursa)*, p. 35.

99 Pardoe, *The city of the Sultan*, II, p. 209 says that they were frescoed to a quarter of their height. Mantran, in 'Les inscriptions arabes de Brousse', p. 91, translates the neshi inscription in the cartouche four metres up in large letters. It states that the Sultan son of Sultan Beyazit Khan son of Murat Khan commanded the building of this minaret. It should be noted that this inscription has been restored.

100 Kuran, *İlk Devir Osmanlı mimarisinde cami*, p. 36.

101 This is the minaret which mutilated the stables of the Bey Han.

102 The stone minaret did not appear until after 1453.

103 They are akin to those of the Laleli Cami. The original caps were probably round and of glazed tiles in the manner of the period. Later, they would become lead cones. C. Hamlin, *Among the Turks*, p. 248, says that every minaret except the one highest up Olympus was decapitated. He went to Bursa immediately after the earthquake.

104 Ayverdi, 'Le premier siècle', p. 59.

105 Ayverdi, *Osmanli mi'mârısinin ilk devri*, p.366.

106 Cezar, 'Osman devrinde Istanbul yapılarında tahribat yapan yangınlar ve tabiî âfetler', *T.S.T.A.I.*, I, p.389. Gökbilgin, 'Edirne' in *E.I.*, II, p. 685 says that it was also called Cami Atık and that a stone from the Ka'ba is placed in the window right of the mihrab. On p. 684 he dates the fire *1158/*1745 and the earthquake *1174/*1751.

107 Kuran, *İlk Devir Osmanlı mimarisinde cami*, p. 39.

108 Ibid., p. 42.

109 Ibid., p.43.

110 See p.276.

111 It was in this mosque that I once found poor travellers sleeping in accordance with the old tradition.

112 Gabriel, *Une Capitale turque, Brousse (Bursa)*, pp. 146-7.

113 Kuran, *İlk Devir Osmanlı mimarisinde cami*, p. 44.

114 See p.157.

115 Gabriel, *Une Capitale turque, Brousse (Bursa)*, p. 134-5.

116 Inscription. The present paint on the mihrab and minber is cheerful popular work; there is, indeed, much folk painting in Urfa today; but the ceiling under the tribune has traces of more distinguished early work.

3   BURSA – THE GREEN MOSQUE AND AFTER

pages 58–91

1 André Gide, *Journal, 1889-1939*, Paris, 1955, p.403, called the complex a place of rest, clarity and poise.

2 Parvillée, *Architecture et décorations turques au XVe siècle*, p. 4.

3 Gabriel, *Une Capitale turque, Brousse (Bursa)*, p. 81.

4 An exception is the dome and pendentives of the Mevlana Tekke at Konya where some likeness to the sixteenth-century designs has been attempted. The central dome design is the sun in splendour.

5 There is no strict border between the secular and the spiritual and these apartments epitomize this.

6 MacNeice, *Astrology*, p. 120 reproduces a similar Venetian horoscope board, dated 1482. They are the Mansions of the astrologists. Or these boards may simply have been used for Five Stones.

7 It may always have had one. See p.81.

8 Architects were expected to be carpenters and were trained to make inlaid koran chests. An excellent sixteenth-century example, among several in the Islamic and Turkish Art Museum at Süleymaniye was the work of Dalgiç Ahmet Ağa.

9 Tritton, *Islam, belief and practices*, p. 24 says that the place where prayer is said must be clean and this is why shoes are left outside the mosque.

10 The design of such tile decoration is based on earlier plasterwork.

11 Evliya said that it was divine beyond his power to describe.

12 Gabriel, *Une Capitale turque, Brousse (Bursa)*, p. 92. The word can simply mean 'mad', and Mantran, 'Les inscriptions arabes de Brousse', simply translates the inscriptions in the plaques on each side of the loge as the work of Mehmet the Mad. See pp. 92-3.

13 Esin, 'Influences de l'art nomade et de l'architecture du Turkistan pré-Islamique sur les arts plastiques et picturaux turcs' in *1st I.C.T.A.*, pp. 104-5, states that Turkish slaves practised arts and architecture at Tabriz and occupied a whole quarter of the city. She does not elucidate her sources. Mantran, in 'Les inscriptions arabes de Brousse', p. 106, gives the inscription in the two circles as the work of Ali Hacı Ahmet of Tabriz and on pp. 92-3 gives the neshi inscription on the right-hand colonnette of the mihrab as the work of the masters of Tabriz.

14 Gabriel, *Une Capitale turque, Brousse (Bursa)*, p. 92.

15 Sarton, *Introduction to the History of Science*, III, p. 755. Abdullah ibn Ali-al-Kashani in about 1300 wrote an account of glazing technique at Tabriz. He called faience or glazed pottery an art like the philosophers' stone.

16 Ünsal, *Turkish Islamic Architecture*, p. 102. Erdmann, 'Neue Arbeiten zur türkischen Keramik' in *A.O.*, V, p.201, is of the opinion that the Yeşil Cami group were the start of a new style.

17 Gabriel, *Une Capitale turque, Brousse (Bursa)*, p. 89.

18 Lane, 'The Ottoman pottery of Iznik' in *A.O.*, II, pp. 250-1.

19 Ibid. Similar work occurs in the Al Tawrizi Türbe at Damascus, dated 1423, and in the great mosque there. I would draw attention to similar tiles at Samarkand in the Shah-i-Zinda, 1385, or the tomb of Shirin of the same date, and in the squinches of the Emirzade Türbe of the following year. It is from the glazed domes of such monuments that one can get an idea of the roofing of the Yeşil Cami. The Bibi Hatun Cami, 1399–1404, the Ulu Bey Medrese of 1420, and the Gür Emir Türbe of 1404, all at Samarkand, and the Ulu Bey Medrese at Bokhara of 1417 can also be mentioned.

20 Ibid., p. 152, the author believes that the blue and white hexagonal tiles were the work of Syrian potters working with the Masters of Tabriz.

21 Mantran, in 'Les inscriptions arabes de Brousse', p. 92 quotes the inscription under the loge of the sultan as, 'The decoration of this noble building was completely executed by the hand of the most humble of men, Ali bin Ilyas Ali, in the last days of the blessed month of Ramazan of the year 827 [middle-end August, 1424]'. According to Erdmann in 'Neue Arbeiten zur türkischen Keramik', pp.201-2, he was taken to Samarkand by Timur from whom he learnt the Timurid style of faience – and he brought the Tabriz masters with him; perhaps he was accompanied by Ivaz Pasha, who came from Tokat, of whom it is told that he had taken his masters to Rum from other countries.

22 Gabriel, *Une Capitale turque, Brousse (Bursa)*, p. 86. Such a dome was a beacon for travellers. The thirteenth-century geographer Yakut saw the sky-blue outer dome of the Sancar mausoleum at Merv – now lost – while still two days' journey away. The remaining inner dome is thirty-six metres high and seventeen in diameter. See *Historical Monuments of Islam in the U.S.S.R.*, published by the Department of Foreign Affairs, Tashkent, n.d., p. 26.

23 Texier, *Asie Mineure*, II, p. 129 states that three years were spent sculpting this door but quotes no authority. Parvillée, *Architecture et décorations turques au XVe siècle*, p.7 echoes him.

24 Cubbyholes for slippers.

25 Yetkin *et al.*, in *Turkish Architecture*, p.50, states that the inscriptive bands round these windows are sometimes incomplete where the work was interrupted.

26 This form of frame appeared in Anatolia as early as the Mama Hatun Türbe in the thirteenth century.

27 Gabriel, *Une Capitale turque, Brousse (Bursa)*, pp. 90-1. Mantran, 'Les inscriptions arabes de Brousse', p.92 gives the translations of the following inscriptions. In two parts, over niches right and left of entry in neshi: 'He who designed (this mosque), commanded it, and fixed its proportions is the humblest of the servants of its founder, Hacı İvad son of Ahi Beyazit – may he be pardoned.' Pp. 105-6, on a series of inscriptions in neshi in cartouches, he reads: 'In the name of the Sultan who asks pardon of God, Mehmet son of Beyazit son of Murat son of Orhan son of Osman on the orders of the Vezir, head of the government, Hacı Ivad son of Ahi Beyazit.' Ibid., p.108, also gives the inscription on Ivaz Pasha's tomb as: 'He who has sought the compassion and pardon of God, the happy is dead bearing witness to his faith, the great Emir, the master and generous chief, the model of vezirs in the world, the master of the sword and pen, who was open-handed in his charity, Hacı Ivad Pasha son of the great Vezir Beyazit son of Ivad – may God make the earth lie quietly on them and give them Paradise for a dwelling – is dead the ninth day of the month of Dhual-Qa'da 831 [20 August, 1428].'

28 See p.257.

29 Gabriel, *Une Capitale turque, Brousse (Bursa)*, p.139.

30 The same thing happened when the Yakup Çelebi Zaviye at Iznik was converted in 1965. See p.44.

31 This would apply just as well to a private as to a royal mosque. At the Yeşil Cami the trace of an old base with fragments of the tiles used shows that Parvillée had historic precedents for placing his restored minarets where he did.

32 It also occurs in some mihrabs, notably at Sungur Bey Cami, Niğde, and stars are also inset in the threshold to the pavilion of Mehmet II which, is now the Treasury of Topkapısaray.

33 See p.48.

34 See p.46 for the connection with Yıldırım Beyazit. Cook, *Zeus. A Study in Ancient Religion*, III, p. 1040, fig. 836 shows a winged thunderbolt from a crater now in the Naples museum. Similar decorative devices are seen at the Masjid-i-Haydena in Iran.

35 Ben Yahia, 'Science in the Muslim World', pp. 573-4 says that the Moslem world was as versed in astronomy as the West, and Timur made Samarkand a cultural centre with a scientific academy. The Ulu Bey Observatory had a staff of one hundred, and a new star catalogue and planetary tables were prepared there; the first since Ptolemy, they were used by Western scholars. This school of astronomy and mathematics had been built in the fifteenth century with a fine cupola which represented the navel of the world. There the chief astronomer discussed decimal fractions. Towards the end of the fourteenth century, Kadızade al Rumi (b. 1337) left Bursa to become principal of the Ulu Bey College. His successor, Ali Küşı, was to be called to Istanbul by Fatih to become the first professor of mathematics and astronomy at the new medrese built at Hagia Sophia. Ulu Bey had been executed in 1449 and the importance of his observatory was declining. Levy, in his translation, *A mirror for princes. The Qabus nama*, p.177, n., quotes Diez as saying that astronomy was merely the prelude to astrology, the real breadwinner. The book devotes sections to astrology, the Zodiac and the stars. It was translated for Murat II. See n.57 below.

36 Parvillée, *Architecture et décorations turques au XVe siècle*, p. 14. It was so ruinous in 1862 that the Turks decided to demolish it. There were cracks in the dome wide enough for a man to pass through and it had become a refuge for wild dogs. Fortunately, Ritter, a French engineer, advised the vali to call in Parvillée to restore it.

37 This form of decoration which grew out of stylized vegetation is very baroque and has affinities with Chinese motifs.

38 Coomaraswamy, in 'Notes on the philosophy of Persian Art', p. 127, quotes Celâlettin Rumi as saying that the outward garden is a reflection of the spiritual garden in order that you may with purer vision see the garden and cypress plot of the invisible world.

39 Braun, *The Darvishes; or Oriental Spiritualism*, p. 106 says that counting ultramarine and turquoise as blue, here at last are the seven colours of the seven names of God. Mantran, 'Les inscriptions arabes de Brousse', p.106 gives the inscription on the tomb as 'This lighted sepulchre, this couch impregnated with perfumes, is the tomb of the very great Sultan and very honoured sovereign, pride of the sultans of the universe, auxiliary of the servants of God, he who has made prosperous the land, who has fought against injustice and corruption, the warrior for the Faith, champion of the Holy War, the Sultan Mehmet son of the sultan who hopes for the compassion of God, Beyazit son of Murat Khan – whom may God cover with his contentment and accord him sojourn in the gardens of Paradise – died in the month of Cumada 824 [May, 1421].'

40 The tomb lies east to west because the dead rest on their right side facing Mecca. The problem of people idolatrously praying in türbes arose early in Islam. At one time it was forbidden to have a mihrab niche in one for fear that someone praying with the coffin in front of him might worship the holy man inside. Since any prayer to the dead would be made by someone kneeling at his feet, the faithful are orientated eastwards, not towards the south. See Diez, 'Masdjid', in *E.I.*, III, p. 323. This was not always so in Anatolia where Sunni rules appear laxer because of dervish influence. Pilgrims to the Mevlana's tomb at Konya pray across his catafalque. In the Mehmet türbe they do tend to pray at his feet, an act made impossible at Konya by the museum railing.

41 Gibb, *The Travels of Ibn Battuta*, p. 447.

42 Ibid., n. 130.

43 At the türbe of Selim I in Istanbul, his vest was displayed until recently, and all the heads of the imperial sarcophagi are crowned with replicas of the turban of state of the monarch. Tritton, in *Islam, belief and practices*, p.135, writes that a pious man will often have his grave clothes ready and, if he has made the pilgrimage, will have brought them from Mecca.

44 Nicomedia.

45 Parvillée, *Architecture et décorations turques au XVe siècle*, p. 8.

46 In Iran brick patterns were produced in moulds like stencilling and this appears to have been the Ottoman technique.

47 Inscription. See also p.166.

48 Ayverdi, 'Dimetoka' da Çelebi Sultan Mehmet Camii' in *V.D.*, III, p.15, n.5. See also p.78.

49 Else the entry would not have been central.

50 Gabriel, *Une Capitale turque, Brousse (Bursa)*, p. 118. Alderson, in *The structure of the Ottoman dynasty*, table XXVI, gives 8 February as the date.

51 The rebuilt türbe of Mehmet II and that of Selim I in Istanbul also have only the one tomb, as do the türbes of some later monarchs.

52 Tritton, in *Islam, belief and practice*, p. 136, says that the hole left in

the grave slab is, according to popular Turkish belief, for the soul to breathe through, but may also be connected with the old custom of sprinkling water on a grave.

53 Ahmet died in 1441 and Alaettin in 1443. Alderson, *The structure of the Ottoman dynasty*, table XXV, gives May 1437 and June 1443 for Alaettin and Ali. Babinger, *Mehmet II, le Conquérant, et son temps*, p. 36, says that he was killed by Kara Haydar Pasha on the orders of Murat II but he gives no reasons.

54 Alderson, *The structure of the Ottoman dynasty*, pp. 55-6. Mantran, 'Les inscriptions arabes de Brousse', pp. 109-10 gives the inscription on the tomb of Murat II as 'In the name of God . . . Glory be to God for his presence exempt from decay or term, and that [the blessing of God] be on him whom He instructed in the way of true religion, him, his family and his illustrious companions. As for him, he has emigrated from the ephemeral and vain world towards an eternal and happy world, from the dwelling place of pain and troubles towards the region of plenty and joy. The Sultan of the sultans of the time, the sovereign of the kingdoms of the land and of the sea, the captain of the warriors and the champions of the Holy War, refuge of the feeble and the poor, pride of the sultans of the line of Osman, he has had fully the solicitude of God, the sultan son of a sultan son of a sultan, the Sultan Murat son of Sultan Mehmet son of Sultan Beyazit Han – whom the Most High lead to the fresh, limpid region of Paradise and shed on him the [dews] of forgiveness – at the hour of sunrise on the Wednesday of the New Moon in the month of Muharrem the Sacred in the year 855 [3 February, 1451].'

55 Alderson, *The structure of the Ottoman dynasty*, p. 58 et seq.

56 Magnesia.

57 Gibbons, *The Foundation of the Ottoman Empire*, p. 296. Levy, on p. xxi of his introduction to *A Mirror for Princes* (see n. 35) says that a version was made for Murat II. On p. 53 there is a reference to the limits of life being reached at forty, which in Western years was Murat's age when he abdicated. He was born in *807/1404* and first abdicated *848/1444*.

58 Hasluck, *Christianity and Islam under the Sultans*, p. 14.

59 It began in 1389 when the victorious Murat I was assassinated at Kossova. Yıldırım Beyazit had his brother, Yakup Khan, strangled on the spot. See Gibbons, *The Foundation of the Ottoman Empire*, p. 180. Fisher, *The foreign relations of Turkey, 1481–1512*, p. 23 says that Beyazit II, on ordering the execution of his brother Cem, said: 'Kings have no relatives'.

60 It is also the name of the large eighth- to ninth-century palace at Termez in Central Asia. Kırk in modern Turkish signifies umpteen as well as forty, which is one of the sacred numbers, partly due, perhaps, to Aristotle. E. Schuyler, *Turkestan*, p.261 recounts the legend that the Kırkız Turks derive their name from the forty daughters of a Khan who returned to find all in the camp dead except one red dog – the father of the tribe. In which case, the Iznik sepulchre may house a Kırkız chieftain and his family.

61 The Beylik türbe of Ahi Şerefettin at Ankara, dated *692/1292*, is preceded by a foyer or narrow passage. It contains one of the most ornate sarcophagi in Turkey. For the Aşık Pasha Türbe at Kırşehir see p. 45-6.

62 Otto-Dorn, *Das Islamische Iznik*, p.80. Yetkin *et al.*, in *L'Architecture turque*, p. 99, gives 1379.

63 The türbe is a poetic feature of the Anatolian landscape as are those of the Selçuks. The origin of these memorial chambers may go back to the stupas of the Oğuz tribe.

64 Gabriel, *Une Capitale turque, Brousse (Bursa)*, p. 120.

65 Mutilation excluded accession.

66 Or a year before, according to Alderson, *The Structure of the Ottoman dynasty*, table XXVI. Murat may have known that his father was dying or the government may have insisted on the precaution in order to prevent a struggle for the throne. It is more likely, however, that the mutilation of these princes could have been sanctioned only after Mehmet was dead. Yusuf and Mahmud also died of the plague in 1429.

67 Gabriel, *Une Capitale turque, Brousse (Bursa)*, p.128. But Alderson, *The Structure of the Ottoman dynasty*, tables XXVI and XXVII states

that he was the son of Huma Sultan and that he married Hatice off to İshak Pasha, Viceroy of Asia.

68 Ayverdi, *Fatih devri mimarı eserleri*, pp. 431-2.

69 The first known open Ottoman türbe was the rebuilt sepulchre of Ertuğrul at Söğüt. See p. 15.

70 Inscription.

71 Inscription.

72 Gabriel, *Une Capitale turque, Brousse (Bursa)*, p.105.

73 The emblems inset in the design of honeycomb and stalactite squinches are clear to see if picked out in paint.

74 Gabriel, *Une Capitale turque, Brousse (Bursa)*, pp. 108-9. Evliya in the *Seyahatnamesi*, ed. Kocu, II, p. 9, reports only one minaret.

75 Gabriel, *Une Capitale turque, Brousse (Bursa)*, p. 107, fig. 49.

76 Ünver, *Edirne Muradiye cami'i*, p.15.

77 P. 62.

78 Meyer-Riefstahl, 'Early Turkish Tile revetments in Edirne', in *A.I.*, IV, pp.260-1, refers to the Chinese antecedents of this design of tile.

79 Gibb, in *The Travels of Ibn Battuta*, p. 429, calls it one of the finest and most extensive cities of Rum, praising its water and gardens. He called the Ahi hospice the best of all, but then he says the same of his lodging at Konya.

80 Inscription. Locally, this mosque is called the Bülent or High.

81 Wulzinger, in *Die Pirus-Mosche zu Milas*.

82 The forehall and mescit form was presaged by such mosques as that at Ardabil long before.

83 The decay of the surrounding buildings contrasts with the harshness of the restoration, but their romantic charm has obscured their function.

84 Diez, Aslanapa and Koman, *Karaman devri sanatı*, p. 87.

85 Inscription.

86 Hammer-Purgstall, *Histoire de l'Empire Ottomane*, II, p. 259 et seq. gives an account of the life of this odious satrap.

87 Gabriel, *Les monuments turcs d'Anatolie*, II, pp. 29-31.

88 Inscription.

89 He was responsible for rebuilding the Orhaniye after it had been set on fire by the Karaman raiders.

90 See p. 70.

91 Gabriel, *Les monuments turcs d'Anatolie*, II, p. 30 gives Toğan bin Aptullah, see p.70. If so, he was not an architect but a controller of the work. His connection with Dimetoka has already been noted (p.70).

92 Ménage, 'Seven Ottoman documents from the reign of Mehemmed II', pp. 112-18 discussing patronymics states that abd-Allah means slave of God indicating non-Moslem birth.

93 I would suggest that his work also included the beautiful casement shutters, etc., for there is consistent quality in the carving. He must have had assistants, of course.

94 Gabriel, *Les monuments turcs d'Anatolie*, II, p. 25.

95 The müezzin denied any knowledge of the existence of a pool in his mosque. I am indebted to his great helpfulness during my visits there.

96 Gabriel, *Les monuments turcs d'Anatolie*, II, p. 27.

97 Ibid., p. 30, n. 4.

98 But at Pir Ilyas Tekke and the Mevlevi foundation at Manisa there were rooms with no windows at all.

99 Gabriel, *Les monuments turcs d'Anatolie*, II, p. 27.

100 But there were punishment cells or cellars; one such still exists at the Mevlevi Tekke at Pera.

101 Passages within the thickness of the wall recur in Ottoman architecture and have already been noted in connection with the Hudavendigar and Yıldırım mosques. Such a means of access is not out of the question.

102 Mayer, in *Islamic architects and their works*, p. 132, states that Yakup bin Aptullah restored the mosque in 1419. If this is true, then one wonders why it was necessary so soon.

103 Hussey, *Byzantium and its neighbours*, p. 768 says that Mehmet I defeated Musa at Samurlu in Serbia in 1413. He was in contact with the old Turkish spirit and the Gazis. Amasya is known to have been a dervish centre.

104 Architecture has reasons to be the most conservative of the arts because of the many preconditioned ideas among its patrons. Look how the column survives.

105 Which could mean a tabhane.

106 Another such column exists at the Cacabey college, while at the chapel in memory of the condottiere Colleoni at Bergamo there is another similar column in the façade.

107 Gabriel, *Les monuments turcs d'Anatolie*, II, p. 28. And the present müezzin.

108 Once again, the marble was probably quarried from the monuments around, for the city had been prosperous. It was the birthplace of Strabo. Few traces of its past remain today but two churches (according to Dernschawm, Reysebach, Babugen (ed.), quoted by Gabriel, *Les monuments turcs d'Anatolie*, p. 4, n. 4) still existed in 1554. Who cut the blocks and who was responsible for the marble inlay at Beyazit is another matter. Islamic craftsmen have always excelled at inlay and at joggled or jigsaw voussoirs, although these were incipient in Hellenistic times – an example can be seen at Ephesus – and rationalized by the Romans. Craftsmen could have been brought from near or far. The marble facing of this mosque is the traditional eight centimetres thick.

109 Ibid., p. 25, n. 3.

110 We have seen that the Muradiye had six steps up from the court to the prayer hall. Fatih's mosque in Istanbul has high sofas round its court also. They seem to have had a special significance throughout this period of Ottoman architecture, perhaps to add to the monumentality of the design.

111 Another suggestion from a Christian source is that it is the vestigial remnant of the niche each side of an Orthodox church door, where cakes are put to be eaten after mass, as still occurs on Mt Athos.

112 Tritton, *Islam, belief and practices*, pp. 99-100 states that the Halveti order, founded in Turkey in 1397, is a branch of the Indian Suhrawardi sect.

113 Gabriel, *Les monuments turcs d'Anatolie*, II, p. 53.

114 Ibid.

115 In the upper tekke two rooms corresponding to this one were added in the reign of Beyazit II as mescits for men and women.

116 This is likely to be original, since it reduced the size of the three cells beside it and was therefore integrated architecturally. Had it been added at a later date it is likely that one cell would simply have been dispensed with, thus avoiding a complex remodelling of the group.

117 Gabriel, *Les monuments turcs d'Anatolie*, II, p. 88. The only example that I have seen.

118 This is on the south-west side which is the logical position in relation to the portico.

119 Skopje.

120 Ayverdi, 'Yugoslavya'da Türk âbideleri ve vakıfları', in *V.D.*, III, p.154 et seq.

121 Ibid., p.155.

122 Hautecoeur and Weit, *Les Mosquées du Caire*, p.342.

123 No date is known but it is likely to be late fifteenth-century.

124 See p.42.

125 See p.412.

126 See p.54.

127 In the same way that they were to be constructed in the Selimiye at Edirne by Sinan. The relationship to Byzantine vandyking can be seen clearly where the plaster has fallen and revealed the bricks beneath.

128 Gabriel, *Une Capitale turque, Brousse (Bursa)*, p.173. This hamam and the han of the Tavuk Pazarı were built as endowments of the mosque of Ömer Bey, 859/1455. The vakıf inscribed over the mosque door is the first in Bursa to be written in Turkish. Shops and mills were also included in the gift. The mosque is a simple square hall with a small tabhane room adjoining it and its portico.

129 That some has been saved has been due to the energy of the town architect, Bay Emin Canpolat; but he was defeated in the end by economic pressures.

130 Ayverdi, *Fatih devri mimari eserleri*, pp.403-4.

131 Eyice, 'Les "Bedestens" dans l'architecture Turque' in *2nd I.C.T.A.*, pp.113-17, gives a list of the eighteen towns possessing bedestens which indicates the centres of Ottoman trade. Bursa was the first, followed by Edirne; each bedesten has fourteen domes. In the fifteenth century, others were built at Salonika (six domes), Galata (nine), Istanbul (fifteen), Kastamonu (nine), Trabzon (nine) and Ankara (ten). In the sixteenth century the second bedesten at Istanbul had twenty domes while Beyşehir, which was rebuilt, had only six, Sarajevo (six), and that at Vezirköprü, endowed in the seventeenth century, had only four. The dates of the following are uncertain: Plovdiv (Filibe), Gelibolu (Gallipoli), Istip, Tekirdağ (Rodosto), and Tire which are all small; also Kayseri and Tokat which have nine-domed bedestens.

132 Özdes, 'Türk çarşıları', p.13 dates it 1426.

133 See p.38.

134 The twentieth-century Haban Cami on the quay at Antalya is raised on six arches above its şadırvan and so continues this tradition.

135 Gabriel, *Une Capitale turque, Brousse (Bursa)*, p.190.

136 Inscription.

137 The modern Turkish translation of ıssız is lonely or ownerless but it was situated at a crossroads and a lake landing so this is an improbable meaning. It may be a corruption of issiz which means sootless. This is much more likely, but an alternate is Warm Han. İssık Kul in Central Asia means Warm Lake, see Schuyler, *Turkestan*, p.258. The suggestion that it had a connection with robbers is improbable, even if it gained the name Hirsiz among some later; see Scerrato, 'An early Ottoman han' in *2nd I.C.T.A.*, p.221 et seq.

138 Gabriel, *Une Capitale turque, Brousse (Bursa)*, p.195.

139 Texier, *Asie Mineure*, II, p.131, plate 41.

140 Pococke, *A description of the East and some other countries*, p.100, says that in the past it was considered the most extraordinary town because, in a country where all the roofs are in terraces, its houses were covered in tiles, giving it a European appearance.

141 Inscription.

142 *Histoire de l'Empire Ottomane*, IV, from Evliya Çelebi who clearly states that Beyazit II built a bridge of nineteen arches. See Evliya Efendi, trans. Hammer-Purgstall, *Narrative of travels in Europe, Asia, and Africa in the seventeenth century*, I, Part 1, p.70.

143 Arel, 'Muttaki Karamanoğulları devri eserleri' in *V.D.*, V, pp.242-5 states that Aslanapa misdates this mosque when he suggests a period between 1356 and 1390.

144 Ibid.

145 Rebuilt in 1925.

146 Ibid.

4 FROM EDIRNE TO ISTANBUL

pages 92-141

1 Hammer-Purgstall, *Histoire de l'Empire Ottomane*, II, p.304, says nothing remains of his palace there. Chandler, *Travels in Asia Minor*, III, p.203, saw pieces of wall and several stately cypress trees in the 1770s.

2 Yetkin, *et al.*, *Turkish Architecture*, p.28 dates it 1366 and gives the architect as Ahmet bin Abdülaziz. See also p.48.

3 This court is related to the far grander one of the Maridani mosque in Egypt, dated 1340. See Hautecoeur and Weit, *Les mosquées du Caire*, plate vi, fig.13.

4 Hammer-Purgstall, *Histoire de l'Empire Ottomane*, I, p.216 states that Üç Şerefeli was the first Ottoman mosque to have a court, but this is a fine point. Yetkin *et al.*, *Turkish Architecture*, p.48 gives the measurements of the whole unit as 32·95 × 36·55 metres and the court as 30 × 15·30 metres. In plan, there is a relationship between the Ulu Cami at Manisa and that at Harput dating from the mid-twelfth century and built by the Artukonullar and also the original mosque at Silvar (Mayafarıkın) probably slightly earlier in date. The latter has a similar organization of its dome and supporting piers and the former's court and minaret have resemblances. See in particular Kuban, *Anadolu-Türk mimarisinin kaynak ve sorunları*, pp. 123-8.

5 Gabriel, *Voyages archéologiques dans la Turquie Orientale*, p.26 shows the Abdul Latif Cami at Mardin dated *772/1371* has a domed prayer hall on squinches with two wing areas and that it is related, therefore, to the Syrian type of mosque and to İsa Bey Cami.

6 Yetkin *et al., Turkish Architecture*, gives the architect as Dimişkili Ali and the decorator as Yusuf.

7 Gibbons, *The Foundation of the Ottoman Empire*, p.185, states that İsa Bey gave up Ayasluğ to Yıldırım, retired to Tire and was then exiled to Bursa or Iznik. His sons fled to Timur for protection. Chandler, *Travels in Asia Minor*, p.117 says that the building of the mosque accounted for the nakedness of the ancient site around. The mosque was built to replace the church of St John which until then had served as the Ulu Cami. The method of raising the west flank on vaults derived from the latter building, which Timur destroyed in 1402; see Gibb, *The Travels of Ibn Battuta*, II, p.445, n.115. He remarks on the pool, marbled pavement and columned walks, together with the lead roof of the church.

8 The area served as one vast quarry.

9 In this, and in much of its fine window-frame carving and use of polychrome marble, it was a forerunner of the Balat mosque.

10 It was a forerunner of the still mainly intact frieze at Piyale Pasha Cami, Istanbul.

11 The first recorded mosque built for an Ottoman ruler with a central dome flanked by pairs of small domes a quarter of its size appears to have been the Yıldırım Cami at Alaşehir, south of the Menderes river. See p.55.

12 Yetkin *et al., Turkish architecture*, p.53. It was 28·4 metres high and may possibly be the first Ottoman dome to have been roofed in lead.

13 Kuban, 'Une analyse stylistique de l'espace dans l'architecture Ottoman' in *1st I.C.T.A.*, p.224, states that Ottoman mosques are the last stage in the development of the dome in architecture, and the great Turkish exploit was to explore all cupola schemes possible, including octagonal and also hexagonal bases which are almost exclusive to them. But the latter statement is disputable, and the first can also be contested.

14 A little higher than those of the Ulu Cami at Bursa.

15 Aslanapa, *Edirne'de Osmanlı devri abîdeleri*, p.14. Hammer-Purgstall, *Histoire de l'Empire Ottomane*, II, p.507, gives the dates as *842/1438-844/1440*. Gökbilgin, 'Edirne' in *E.I.*, II, p.685, says that it was also known as the Muradiye, Yeni Cami and Cami-i Kebir and that it was endowed with revenues from the silver mines at Karatovo until Rüstem Pasha transferred these to the Treasury.

16 Meyer-Riefstahl, *Turkish architecture in Southwestern Anatolia*, p.13.

17 The legend may have been due to the exchange of the title of ulu cami between this mosque and the present Eski Cami.

18 Aslanapa, *Edirne'de Osmanlı devri abîdeleri*, p.10. Cezar, 'Osmanlı devrinde Istanbul', p.389, says that the domes and minarets were damaged on 30 July 1752.

19 Gemelli-Careri, *Voyage du tour du monde*, p.256. He also remarks on the quality of the carpets.

20 Ayverdi, *Fatih devri*, p.97.

21 Yetkin *et al., Turkish architecture*, p.53. The interior is 24·25 × 60 metres; the court is 35·5 × 60 metres; this makes it 64·5 × 66·5 metres over all, or nearly square if the wall thickness is included.

22 As it was at İsa Bey Cami.

23 Ayverdi, *Fatih devri*, p.96. Hammer-Purgstall states that there are eight şerefes.

24 *Histoire de l'Empire Ottomane*, III, pp.354-5.

25 The huge fallen minaret and watch-tower at Ani which was built by the Selçuks has a double stair but seems to be a lonely example.

26 Eyice, *Istanbul: petit guide*, p.56, sect.74.

27 Aslanapa, *Edirne'de Osmanlı devri abîdeleri*, p.29. Yetkin *et al., Turkish Architecture*, p.53 says 67·62 metres.

28 Ayverdi, *Fatih devri*, p.96.

29 Aslanapa, *Edirne'de Osmanlı devri abîdeleri*, p.53.

30 Fıratlı, *Iznik*. Ünsal, *Turkish Islamic Architecture*, p.20 dates it 1443.

31 Aslanapa, *Edirne'de Osmanlı devri abîdeleri*, p.94.

32 Hammer-Purgstall, *Histoire de l'Empire Ottomane*, II, p.355. Gökbilgin, *Edirne*, p.685, says that it was originally a medrese built *839/1435*

33 and that it was destroyed in the siege of 1912. 'Destroyed' is an exaggeration.

33 This was added by Mimar Koç Ahmet when repairing the building in *1224/1809* according to Aslanapa, *Edirne'de osmanlı devri abîdeleri*, p.97. The interest in the building depends on the relationship of the restorations to the original, now impossible to assess.

34 Cf. Aslanapa's reproduction of Gurlitt's photograph of 1911 in *Edirne'de Osmanlı devri abîdeleri*, p.96, fig.11.

35 The mosque of Gazi Mihal, also at Edirne, built in *825/1422*, (see Aslanapa, op.cit., p.98) takes an elementary form of the Bursa type and has a portico walled in on the north and west with, originally, a revak of ten slender marble columns to which the sofa extended. These secondary revaks appear to be vulnerable. Not only has that of the Darül-hadis fallen but so have those of Hacı İvaz, built by Sinan, and Piyale Pasha in Istanbul. It will be noted that the central dome of the portico of Gazi Mihal is oval and so is likely to be baroque as is the second revak.

36 Esin, 'Influences de l'art nomade', p.119.

37 Rose, in Brown, *The dervishes*, p.103 states that the three circles in the inner rose of Baghdad symbolize: Malifat (Knowledge of God), Shariat (Law of God), Tarikat (the Path or the Chosen Faith). Pope, *A Survey of Persian Art*, VI, p.2, 691-2 says the three balls and undulating lines in Babylon symbolized the sun, moon, and Venus and, probably, the Milky Way. Sarre, *Islamic Bindings*, p.17, fig.4 calls them two fork-lightning clouds and three full moons. In the Süleymaniye museum in Istanbul there is a rug which has the clouds but no balls and clearly imitates a tiger skin.

38 Inalcık, 'The place of the Ottoman-Turkish Empire in History' in *Cultura Turcica*, 1964, p.59.

39 Ibid., p.61.

40 Birge, *The Bektashi Order of Dervishes*, p.62.

41 Talbot Rice, *The Great Palace of the Emperors*, I, p.28.

42 Hammer-Purgstall, *Histoire de l'Empire Ottoman*, I, p.343 et seq.

43 Surveyed by Robert Van Nice, Summer 1963.

44 Boğaz also means a strait and the name therefore expresses the precise function of the fortress.

45 Gabriel, *Châteaux turcs du Bosphore*, pp.72-3. Mamboury, *The tourists' Istanbul*, p.223 says that, according to Halil Ethem, the historian Ali gave Muslihettin as the name of the architect, while according to Evliya it was a Christian monk converted to Islam.

46 Kritovoulos, *History of Mehmed the Conqueror*, part I, sect. 44, p. 19.

47 Evliya, *Narrative of Travels*, I, part 2, p.67.

48 Gabriel, *Châteaux turcs du Bosphore*, p.60.

49 Ibid., p.62.

50 Ibid., p.70.

51 *Histoire de l'Empire Ottomane*, II, p.376.

52 Gabriel, *Châteaux turcs du Bosphore*, p.62.

53 Ayverdi, *Fatih devri*, pp.417-20 states that it was completed in Şaban 856 (28 August 1452) which would make the time of construction five months.

54 A tamga or seal in Kufic script is inset in the same tower. At Rumeli Hisar the two examples are the names of God and the Prophet, the Ismi-Celâl and the Ismi-Resul. They appear on Timur's buildings at Samarkand and are remarkably similar to Chinese seals, suggesting a relationship. There is also an echo of the Greek meander pattern. Porada, *The Art of Ancient Iran*, p.222 and p.246, n.45, calls tamgas the house-marks of nomadic peoples in Kufic and they frequently occur on fourteenth- and fifteenth-century buildings including the Hatuniye Medrese at Karaman. Deny, 'Tughra' in *E.I.*, IV, p.822 et seq. states that the tuğra, in some dialects Tura, is a Turkish word deriving from the Oğuz Turks and means seal or cipher. It was used by the Selçuks and its first Ottoman appearance was on a coin of the Emir Süleyman in 1414, although Murat I may have used one. It incorporates the name of the sultan and his basic titles in a highly formalized device.

55 Zaganos, Mahmut, Murat, Rum Mehmet, Gedik Ahmet and İshak Pasha, the chief ministers of Mehmet II, were of Byzantine origin. See Atabinen, *Les Turcs occidentaux et la Méditerranée*, p.158. Ibid., p.160 he states that Mehmet came before Constantinople at the head

of an army led by Turco-Byzantine nobles and soldiered, with its Serbs and Bogomils (whose mysticism was intimately associated with that of the dervishes) with at least as many Christians as there were behind the battlements.

56 Gabriel, *Châteaux turcs du Bosphore*, p.73.

57 If they were. Mehmet may have had reason to resent his mentor. Jealousy was also alleged.

58 Gabriel, *Châteaux turcs du Bosphore*, p.66.

59 Ibid., p.32.

60 And thus copied the European Galata Tower and not the Islamic tradition. The cap of Galata is restored.

61 Gabriel, *Châteaux turcs du Bosphore*, p.39, lists the dimensions. Karaküle, 28 metres high, 23·80 metres wide, has seven floors; sea tower, 23·30 metres high, 22 metres wide, has seven floors; Gülküle, 26 metres high, 21 metres wide, has five floors. This tower has a thick cylindrical pillar in the centre 3·25 to 3·80 metres thick. See Mamboury, 'L'art turque du 18e siècle', p.225.

62 Except minor decorative details.

63 Mamboury, 'L'art turque du 18e siècle', p.225.

64 Restored 1966-7.

65 The sea must have flowed on three sides of the castle in the fourteenth century.

66 Creswell, *A short account of early Muslim Architecture*, p.174 et seq.

67 One of the Ottoman guns is known as the Dardanelles gun and installed at the Tower of London.

68 Inscription.

69 Utkular, *Çanakkale boğazında Fatih Kaleleri* is the principal source at present. Parry, 'Çanak-kale Boghazi' in *E.I.*, II, pp. 11-12, says that both fortresses were restored by Süleyman and again in 1069-70/1658-60 when new forts were added by Tott. The name Çanakkale came into use c.1740 when Armenian, Jewish and Greek potters prospered there. Çanak means an earthenware vessel.

70 Kritovoulos, *History of Mehmed the Conqueror*, part ii, sect.2, p.93 reports that he ordered the repair and building of walls and of Yediküle in great haste. Ibid., sect.5, p.104 he states that the Eskisaray was brilliantly completed upon his return in 1455.

71 Sandys, *A relation of a journey begun An. Dom. 1610*, p. 26, says that Yediküle was employed like the Tower of London as a storehouse of the sultan's treasures and munitions. One hundred years later, Gemelli-Careri, *Voyage du tour du monde*, p.329, states that it was a depot for mosque revenues.

72 These qualities are to be seen in the work of engineers who built warehouses in the nineteenth century, as opposed to the architects who were more concerned with fanciful ornament than with structure. From such experience came the Marshall Field Building in Chicago and, later, the work of Sullivan, who can be compared in some ways to Sinan in his approach to the architecture of the city block.

73 Eyice in 'Atik Ali Paşa Camiinin Türk Mimârî Tarihideki Yeri' *Tarih Dergisi*, 14, 110, dates the Güzelce Hasan Bey Cami near Tekirdağ *809/1406*, which makes it a smaller precursor of the Üç Şerefeli mosque and such western Anatolian mosques as the Valide Cami at Manisa.

74 Emerson and Van Nice, 'Hagia Sophia and the first minaret erected after the conquest of Istanbul' in *American Journal of Archaeology*, LIV, no.1., Jan, 1950, p.29 states that a brick minaret was later added on the south-east which was the ideal position in relation to Topkapısaray and the quarters towards the sea.

75 Evliya, *Narrative of travels*, I, part 1, p.173, says that there were seventy-four disciples at this tekke in the seventeenth century. See also Chap. III, n.35.

76 Mantran, *La vie quotidienne à Constantinople au temps de Soliman le Magnifique et ses sucesseurs, XVIe et XVIIe siècles*, p.15, says that he first resided in the city during the winter of 1457/8.

77 Atabinen, *Les turcs occidentaux et la Méditerranée*, p.144, says that he was assisted by his close adviser, Molla Hüsrev, who was the son of a French prisoner taken at the Battle of Niğbolu in 1396.

78 Hammer-Purgstall, *Histoire de l'Empire Ottomane*, III, p. 6.

79 Kritovoulos, *History of Mehmed the Conqueror*, part ii, sect.9-12 p. 95.

80 Sanderson, *The travels of John Sanderson in the Levant*, p.72.

81 Ibid., p.73.

82 Gilles, *The Antiquities of Constantinople*, p.52.

83 Kritovoulos, *History of Mehmed the Conqueror*, part iii, sect.71, p.140.

84 Ibid., sect. 99-105, pp.147-9.

85 Ibid, part v, sect. 49-52, pp.207-8.

86 Inscription.

87 Aslanapa, *Edirne'de Osmanlı devri abîdeleri*, p.119.

88 Ibid., p.118.

89 Inscription.

90 Ayverdi, *Fatih devri*, p.245.

91 Aslanapa, *Edirne'de Osmanlı devri abîdeleri*, p.108. Ayverdi, *Fatih devri*, p.250.

92 Ibid.

93 Inscription.

94 See p.165.

95 *Fatih devri*, p.202.

96 Ibid., p.203.

97 Not unusual elsewhere but only in Istanbul and other major Turkish towns and cities.

98 Hammer-Purgstall, *Histoire de l'Empire Ottomane*, p.18. Kritovoulos, *History of Mehmed the Conqueror*, part i, sect.303, p.88 states that his grandfather was Philaninos, ruler of Hellas, with the rank of Caesar. He greatly praises the minister. Miller *Beyond the Sublime Porte, the Grand Seraglio of Stanbul*, pp.51-2 says that he was a Croat and known as the first graduate of the Palace School, referring to that founded by Mehmet II at Edirne. See also Appendix I on the Janissaries.

99 Hammer-Purgstall, *Histoire de l'Empire Ottomane*, III, p.18.

100 Kritovoulous, *History of Mehmed the Conqueror*, part iv, sect.34-5, pp.171-2.

101 Hammer-Purgstall, *Histoire de l'Empire Ottomane*, III, p.119 et seq. states that his deposition was barbarously announced by the severing of the guy-ropes of the tent in which he slept.

102 Ibid., p.144.

103 Kritovoulos, *History of Mehmed the Conqueror*, part iii, sect.74-5, p.141 states that Mahmut also built a very large and beautiful mosque at a prominent place in the City. It was built of dressed stone and gleaming marbles, with columns of outstanding beauty and size. It was also well ornamented with inscriptions and sculpture and very rich in gold and silver, and was adorned with many beautiful gifts, votive offerings and other things to be proud of. Around this Mahmut with noble ardour built food kitchens for the poor, and inns and baths well-suited in point of usefulness and beauty and size. Besides, he built grand houses for himself, rich and beautiful, and he planted gardens and trees bearing all sorts of fruit for the delectation and happiness and use of many, and gave them an abundant water supply. He did many such things, precisely according to the wish of the sultan, and thus beautified the city at his own expense and cost with buildings and monuments useful to the public.

104 Ayverdi, *Fatih devri*, p.396.

105 Gabriel, *Une Capitale turque, Brousse (Bursa)*, pp.183-5 says Mahmut Pasha also built the spacious Fidan Han at Bursa.

106 The decorative patterns of this tomb closely resemble those of that of Ulugay at Maragha, dated 1260.

107 Alderson, *The structure of the Ottoman dynasty*, table XXVII.

108 Ayverdi, *Fatih devri*, pp.183-5.

109 Inscription.

110 Gabriel, 'Les Mosquées de Constantinople' in *Syrie*, 1926, p.364.

111 Eyice, *Istanbul: petit guide*, p.24, sect.26.

112 *The Antiquities of Constantinople*, p.188-9. This mutilation could also have been carried out in the reign of Abdülhamit I in the late eighteenth century because the stonework is in the same style as that of the base of Constantine's Column.

113 Ayverdi, *Fatih devri*, p.174.

114 Gabriel, 'Les Mosquées de Constantinople', *Syrie*, p.364.

115 Eyice, *Istanbul: petit guide*, p.25, sect.26.

116 Glück, *Probleme des Wölbungsbaues: die Bäder Konstantinopels*, p.110.

117 Massage also went on on the floor. A sixteenth-century miniature in Princeton University Library (Garnett Collection, no.9) also shows

barbers at work. See also Tavernier, *Nouvelle relation de l'intérieur du Sérail du Grand Seigneur*, p.43.

118 Prescott, *Jerusalem journey*, quotes Friar Felix Fabri, who, in the fifteenth century, noted coloured glass in the hot room of a hamam at Gaza.

119 Mantran, *Istanbul dans la seconde moitié du XVIIe siècle*, p.617.

120 Hammer-Purgstall, *Histoire de l'Empire Ottomane*, III, p.161.

121 Ibid., p.162.

122 Gabriel, 'Les Mosquées de Constantinople', p.365. Öz, *Istanbul camileri*, II, p.108, gives *870–6/1465–71*.

123 Kuran, *İlk Devir Osmanlı mimarisinde cami*, p.92.

124 The mosque, its simple open türbe, and its medrese were damaged in the earthquake of June, 1648. See Cezar, 'Osmanlı devrinde', p.367.

125 Hammer-Purgstall, *Histoire de l'Empire Ottomane*, III, p.119 et seq.

126 Inscription.

127 Yet it is also in the tradition of Selçuk Iran where the south eyvans were, in effect, covered by half-domes. Ağa-oğlu, 'The Fatih Mosque at Constantinople' in *Art Bulletin*, XII, no.4, Dec.1930, p.180 quotes Tosun Bey as saying that Fatih Cami was built to resemble Hagia Sophia. But, ibid., p.186 he falls into the error of thinking that the Ottomans first used the half-dome at Fatih. Apart from Tire and hamam of Mahmut Pasha, stalactite portals are no more than concealed half-domes.

128 Hammer-Purgstall, *Histoire de l'Empire Ottomane*, IV, p.9.

129 Ibid., p.42. He was granted a handsome pension.

130 Gabriel, 'Les Mosquées de Constantinople', p.366.

131 Hammer-Purgstall, *Histoire de l'Empire Ottomane*, IV, p.9.

132 Ayverdi, *Fatih devri*, p.115.

133 Ibid., p.112, resim 29. So according to Paspati's drawing was the mihrab of the Demirciler Mescit which formed a part of the Fatih complex.

134 Thus the mihrab niche which developed out of the apse in the first century of the Hegira returned to lodge in the source of its inspiration.

135 The ruined Beylerbey Cami (or zaviye, perhaps) at Edirne, built in *832/1429* by Murat II – see Aslanapa, *Edirne'de Osmanlı devri abîdeleri*, p.91 – is something of a freak because it is shorn of its flanking tabhane rooms. Its long nave terminates in a semi-dome with a shell vault set in half an octagon.

136 Hammer-Purgstall, *Histoire de l'Empire Ottomane*, XVIII, p. 30.

137 Ibid., IV, p. 113.

138 Ayverdi, *Fatih devri*, p. 108.

139 Gabriel, 'Les Mosquées de Constantinople', p.368.

140 Evliya, *Narrative of travels*, I, part 1, p.168 comments on the commodiousness of this mosque which would confirm that there were no walls in the seventeenth century.

141 Ayverdi, *Fatih devri*, pp.261–2, for the date of the medrese. Ülgen, 'İnegöl'de İshak Paşa mimari manzumesi' in *V.D.*, IV, p.191a gives *881/1476* as the medrese date; the mosque has no inscription. The problem of the open tabhane area has already been discussed in relation to the Muradiye, Bursa. See p.73.

142 Ibid. He says that one room may have been used as a cookhouse.

143 Evliya, *Narrative of travels*, I, part 1, p.82 confirms this and says that he built additions to the Mevlana Tekke at the same time. Hammer-Purgstall, *Histoire de l'Empire Ottomane*, VI, p. 242 refers to the founding of a mosque with twin minarets at Konya.

144 Önder, *Konya*, p. 55 states that the mosque was built between 1566 and 1577 by Selim II when heir to the throne and Governor of Konya. This, in itself, would have been a preposterous span of time. Önder gives as his authority the Müreid-i Talabın Varak 19/6 (Konya müsesi yazma no. 4005) Peçevi c:1 s:426. This document should have been published in full. It could be that a confusion has arisen over orders for the repair of the mosque.

145 Meyer-Riefstahl, 'Selimiyeh in Konya' in *Art Bulletin*, XII, no. 4, p. 314 gives its diameter as 14·06 metres.

146 Ibid. He calls them elegant bundle columns facing round a core. The Jar Kugan minaret, c. 1108–9, is an example of the use of sixteen tori.

147 Its origins go back to the kümbets of Iran.

148 Recalling the original tiles of the Mevlana Türbe which were blue and not the present ugly Kütahya green tiles given by Abdülhamit. See Meyer-Riefstahl, op. cit., p. 318. The architect was obsessed with allusions to the past in a manner alien to Ottoman tradition.

149 The article in *Illustrasyonu* states that the cupola was ornamented by the architect Muzaffer and that the wall inscriptions were by Bekir Bey. The difference in quality is immediately apparent. No dates or information about these men is given and it is somewhat surprising to find Muzaffer called an architect.

150 Eldem, *Nos Mosquées de Stamboul*, p. 48. Kunter and Ülgen, 'Fatih Camii' in *V.D.*, I, p. 95 say that it took eight years to build, from *867/1462–875/1470*.

151 Quoted by Eldem, *Nos Mosquées de Stamboul*, p. 49.

152 Konyali, *Azadli Sinan (Sinan-i Atık) vakfiyeleri, eserleri, hayatı, mezarı*, p. 5 et seq.

153 Eyice, *Istanbul: petit guide*, p. 75, sect. 108.

154 Eldem, *Nos Mosquées de Stamboul*, p. 50. Hammer-Purgstall, *Histoire de l'Empire Ottomane*, III, p. 99, on the authority of Cantemir, says that he was rewarded with a whole street of the town and that this gift was recognized by Ahmet III three centuries later and thus saved their church for the Greeks in this quarter.

155 Eldem, op. cit., p. 50.

156 Cezar, 'Osmanli devrinde', p. 372, says August 1833.

157 Gilles, *The Antiquities of Constantinople*, p. 223.

158 Ibid., pp. 222–3.

159 Ibid., p. 223.

160 Painters' Gate and Muffin Gate.

161 Cezar, 'Osmanli devrinde', p. 379 says that it was destroyed by the great fire of 13 June 1918.

162 Reproduced in Ünver, *Ilim ve sanat bakımından Fatih devri albümü*, Istanbul, 1943, p. 15.

163 Ibid., p. 14. Matraki's drawing in the Istanbul University Library reproduced by Ünver shows two sofas but no cistern.

164 The wall of Fatih could be the oldest extant Ottoman windowed example.

165 *Narrative of Travels*, I, Part I, p. 174.

166 Bolak, *Hastahanelerimiz*, p. 32 dates it 1470. Menavino, *I costumi et la vita de Turchi*, p. 456 says that the sick included lepers and also lunatics. Şehsuvaroğlu, 'Bīmāristān' in *E.I.*, I, p. 1225 says that it was a teaching hospital.

167 See p.115.

168 Sanderson, *The Travels of John Sanderson in the Levant*, p. 70 states that this hospital dispensed syrup and medicine free of charge.

169 Ayverdi, *Fatih devri*, p. 165.

170 Gilles, *The Antiquities of Constantinople*, pp. 225–7.

171 Ibid., p. 223.

172 *The Travels of John Sanderson in the Levant*, p. 70 but Menavino, *I costumi et la vita de Turchi*, p. 45 says that there were only twenty-five domes and that the middle one under which the priests ate was larger. There were beds for travellers. This seems proof that this was the tabhane and that it was used as a hostel.

173 Evliya, *Narrative of Travels*, I, Part 1, p. 174. He praises the cooking at Fatih hospital where game birds appeared on the menu; and he had claims to be a gourmet.

174 Nicolay, *Navigations and voyages made into Turkey*, p. 69.

175 *Istanbul: petit guide*, p. 127.

176 Mantran, *Istanbul dans la seconde moitié du XVIIe siècle*, p. 137.

177 *The Antiquities of Constantinople*, p. 223.

178 Ayverdi, *Fatih devri*, p. 163.

179 The original dining hall of the imaret was temporarily established in the church of the Pentepoptes, the All-Seeing Christ, and the cooking done in its court. It is still used as an imaret for the boys of a hatipokul but the standards have deteriorated. The church is very small and the meals must have been served in shifts.

180 See Appendix II. Kunter, 'Les bases', p. 231 states that 366 employees were listed in the vakfiye.

181 Ergin, *Türk şehirlerinde imaret sistemi*, p. 14 states that it was rebuilt by Süleyman I. Kunter and Ülgen, 'Fatih Camii', p. 91 call it a darüzziyafe.

182 Ayverdi, *Fatih devri*, p. 156.

183 Cezar, 'Osmanli devrinde', p. 383, says that the dome fell in the earthquake of 1509. In this century it was a scrapyard for years, but has been heavily restored since 1965.

184 Ünver, *Ilim ve sanat bakımından Fatih devri albümü*, p. 14.

185 *Fatih devri*, p. 135, resim 55.

186 Ünver, *Ilim ve sanat bakımından Fatih devri albümü*, p. 14.

187 Ayverdi, *Fatih devri*, p. 129.

188 The pleasant myth that the revolving of the pilasters has the function of warning the surveyor if the foundations of the mosque have sunk or shifted after a tremor or other mishap is improbable; for such a device would obviously be inadequate and some mosques have pilasters of tile.

189 Symbol of royalty.

190 Aǧa-oǧlu, 'Note about one of "The two questions on Moslem Art"' in *A.I.*, III, part 1, p. 50, says that between 1453 and 1473 the theologians and their students together with the dervishes of the tabhane were lodged in the church of the Akanalasos (not listed in Janin) and surrounding houses.

191 Gibb and Bowen, *Islamic Society and the West*, II, p. 145.

192 Gibbons, *The Foundation of the Ottoman Empire*, p. 79. Lybyer, *The Government of the Ottoman Empire*, p. 134. Fatih organized pomp and circumstance after the conquest regulated by a law of ceremonial, Kanvaı Teşrifat. Ibid., p. 135 says that it ordained the exact place, uniform, and title of all office holders. The simple life had gone.

193 Or eighteen, plus one for a teacher, since eighteen had the numerical value of the word Hay or Living God. See Rose in Brown, *The dervishes*, p. 104. It also meant the eighteen different worlds to which the Prophet brought mercy.

194 Multiples of four were the conventional number of cells for students since four was a sacred number: the four corners of the earth, seasons, cardinal points, etc.

195 *Fatih devri*, p. 1495.

196 *Istanbul dans la seconde moitié du XVIIe siècle*, p. 136. Evliya, *Narrative of travels*, I, part 1, p. 171, says three or four.

197 Today as many as six share a cell by means of tiered bunks.

198 Evliya, *Narrative of travels*, I, p. 67.

199 Kunter and Ülgen, 'Fatih Camii', p. 92.

200 Ayverdi, *Fatih devri*, p. 128. Cezar, 'Osmanli devrinde', p. 382, says that during the devastating earthquake of 1509 this dome slipped sideways, crushing the upper parts of the supports but did not fall in.

201 Ayverdi, *Fatih devri*, p. 129, resim 46 and his reconstruction. Also pp. 134-5, resim 52 and 53.

202 See p. 254.

203 See p. 114.

204 But more surely in the floor of the mosque.

205 'Une analyse stylistique de l'espace dans l'architecture ottomane', p. 219 et seq.

206 Eyice, *Istanbul: petit guide*, p. 76, sect. 110.

207 Ayverdi says that by using polygonal facets the play of light is better expressed than over a round surface. It is an opinion which eschews subtlety in favour of the obvious.

208 This is clearly shown in Lorichs and Matraki, yet Ayverdi – *Fatih devri*, pp. 134-5, resim 52 and 53 – shows them as tall and tapering in a later manner.

209 Hammer-Purgstall, *Histoire de l'Empire Ottomane*, IV, p. 296.

210 Unfortunately they have been damaged in storms and are no longer the four guardsmen of the waters that they used to be. This is nicely Ottoman, however, in its feeling of dishevelment.

211 In this process, dark greasy pigment which withers away with the heat of the kiln is inset into the grooves to prevent one colour from mixing with another.

212 Fıratlı, *İznik*, dates the first Iznik tiles from 1495. Erdmann, 'Neue Arbeiten zur türkischen Keramik', p. 203 discusses these tiles in relation to the studies of Otto-Dorn and points out that they show underglaze painting, and it is suggested that they are copies of glaze painting faience replacing the old ones when the mosque was rebuilt in the eighteenth century, particularly since they have no connection with the tiles in the courtyard of the Üç Şerefeli Cami at Edirne. The problems are why there should have been only two and how the

quality could be so high in the late eighteenth century. My own suggestion is that these tiles were added in the first half of the sixteenth century as an embellishment of the courtyard of the mosque of the revered conqueror.

213 Ayverdi, *Fatih devri*, p. 146.

214 Hammer-Purgstall, *Histoire de l'Empire Ottomane*, VXIII, p. 3.

215 Kunter, 'Les Bases', pp. 229-30 says that the Fatih vakfiye ordained that this pavement was to be kept so clean that anyone who saw it could see his face as if in a mirror. La Mottraye, *Travels*, p. 184 says that in the early part of the eighteenth century the marble columns of Imperial mosques were excellently polished.

216 The türbe was damaged and the coffin destroyed when the furniture of the refugees caught fire during the conflagration of August 1782. See Cezar, 'Osmanli devrinde', p. 365.

217 Mayer, *Islamic astrolobists and their works*, p. 43. Ali al-Kuşcı.

218 See p. 394.

219 Hammer-Purgstall, *Histoire de l'Empire Ottomane*, III, p. 297.

220 Ayverdi, 'Yugoslavya 'da', p. 196.

221 Evliya, *Narrative of Travels*, I, part 1, p. 50 says that it was built on the site of the old convent.

222 Ünsal, *Turkish Islamic architecture*, p. 62.

223 Ünver, *İlim*, p. 8. Paris, Bibliothèque Nat. (Estampes).

224 It is likely to have begun at Edirne under Murat II as the natural outcome of his reorganization of the Janissaries and the devşirme system. A palace school was nothing new in Islam and both the Umayyids and Abbasids supported them as did the Selçuks.

225 Dates between 877/1472 and 883/1478 have been found on some of the doors.

226 Miller, *Beyond the Sublime Porte*, p. 141.

227 Restored in its present form by Mustafa III. Inscription.

228 The second court measures 160 × 130 metres.

229 Cezar, 'Osmanli devrinde', p. 342 says that it was burnt in the great saray fire of 24 July 1665 and rebuilt.

230 3·25 × 5·90 metres. Ayverdi, *Fatih devri*, p. 318, resim 305.

231 Erkins, *Topkapı Sarayı müzesi*, p. 43 says that it is 97 metres long.

232 Ibid., p. 14 says 1478 and that it became the Treasury when Murat III removed it from Yediküle.

233 This was the quadrangle of the palace school.

234 It could have been designed as a music gallery.

235 Because they are of the same date as the hamam else they might come from the private hamam next to the throne room within or Hünkâr sofa. Tavernier, *Nouvelle relation*, p. 43 states that the closet for depilation was 'done about with square pieces, having in them flowers of embossed work, done to the life, and covered with gold and azure'.

236 Evliya, *Narrative of Travels*, I, part 1, p. 50 calls it the Hall of Exercise. The inner hall behind may once have formed part of the hamam of Selim II. The greater hall which is now the superb museum of kaftans of the sultans was remodelled in 1859. See Erkins, *Topkapı Sarayı müzesi*, p. 11.

237 Tavernier, *Nouvelle relation*, p. 43.

238 Miller, *The palace school of Muhammed the Conqueror*, p. 67.

239 Their bases are unusually high which suggests that the columns had to be raised in order to fit where older, taller ones, possibly of wood, had stood before them. It is the columns of the loggia, rather than those of the colonnade, which make it hard to believe that a massive unrecorded eighteenth-century reconstruction took place.

240 Islamic forms recur so often that no single motif or architectural element is by itself proof of a period. Thus the circular movement in the şadırvan of the loggia links with the Mevlana Türbe, the Mama Hatun Türbe, and even Central Asia.

241 The work has been carefully done but as historical evidence can only be used with discretion.

242 Miller, *Beyond the Sublime Porte*, p. 37.

243 Square towers such as these were common in Europe. See also the observation tower of the palace at Edirne.

244 Graffiti indicate that they were used as dormitories for the more menial women of the household and also as prisons for minor delinquents.

245 Inscription. Eyice, *Istanbul: petit guide*, p. 9, sect. 4 says that it was repaired in 1682 and again in 1737 after a fire. It was further damaged or altered when made into a museum by the Roumanian architect Monterano. See the Report of 1875 and Istanbul Ansık, VII, p. 4021 et seq. It has been heavily restored in recent years. The pool and the sandy meydan in front of the kiosk have been built over.

246 Compare the plan with the Timurid base of the Ala Kapı palace at Isfahan. See Schroeder in Pope, *A Survey of Persian Art*, III, p. 964 on cross plan palaces of Horasan and Merv and Pope; ibid., p. 978 on Ghaznevid plans.

247 It was the Iranian ceramicist Şemşettin who developed inscriptive tiles with neshi script in colour and kufic in white. The dedication to the trinity of Allah, Muhammed and Ali is Sufi not Sunni but may have been due to Fatih's membership of the heretical Bektaşi order of dervishes. Yetkin, *L'architecture turque en Turquie*, p. 151 disputes Kühnel's statement that the tiles of Çinili Kiosk come from Iran, but without offering proof. However, Erdmann, 'Neue Arbeiten zur türkischen Keramik', p. 202 discussing Otto-Dorn's thesis accepts connection between these tiles and those at Bursa at least in part.

248 *Historical Monuments of Islam in the U.S.S.R.*, p. 35.

249 Ibid., p. 36.

250 Lethaby, *Architecture, nature, and magic*, p. 35. The plan of the pavilion is related to the typical form of the camekân of a hamam where the central stone is called the navel which could refer to the Navel of the World.

251 Inalcık, 'The place of the Ottoman-Turkish Empire in History', p. 57 et seq.

252 The disappearance of the wooden royal apartments at Bursa and elsewhere adds to the difficulty of tracing the origins of this form of pavilion in Turkey because there may well be a precedent to illuminate the problem. The saray of the Akkoyunlu in the citadel at Mardin of comparable date is in T-form with corner bays and is closer to Syrian than Ottoman models.

253 Recalling the apsidal form of the Yeşil Zaviye at Tire or the Hudavendigar at Bursa, etc.

254 Yetkin, *L'Architecture turque en Turquie*, p. 151 says by Mahmut I after a fire.

255 Gedik Ahmet Pasha, who was not a Turk, had risen from the ranks to become commander-in-chief and son-in-law of the Chief Vezir İshak Pasha. He was to be victorious over Cem but to earn the enmity of his sultan, Beyazit II, because he was immensely popular with the army and outspoken when drunk; so he was executed in 1482. See Fisher, *The foreign relations of Turkey*, p. 25 et seq.

256 Keppel, *Narrative of a journey across the Balcan*, p. 159 shows that the decay was already advanced in the 1820s. It is fully described, insofar as he was able, and charmingly depicted, by Tosyeri or Tosyalı (Dr Rifat Osman), *Edirne Sarayi*.

257 Godard, *L'art de l'Iran*, p. 311.

258 Joinville and Villehardouin, *Chronicles of the Crusades*, p. 141.

259 Keppel, *Narrative of a journey across the Balcan*, p. 159 says that the kiosk contained four square apartments, one over the other, reached by a narrow stone stair. It was clearly used for observation and was perhaps an actual observatory in Mehmet II's day.

260 Sand Pavilion. Probably rebuilt in the seventeenth century.

261 Arseven, *L'art turc depuis son origine jusqu'à nos jours*, p. 117 says that among the lost kiosks were the Bülbül (nightingale), İftar (Fast-breaking), Çadır (tent), of significant name, and Çıkar (hunt).

262 Kunter, 'Les bases', p. 228.

263 Kopsteg, *The Construction and use of the composite bow by the Turks*, from ms. in Robert College library, n.d. since published Illinois, 1947. P. 3 et seq. states that the Turks surpassed all others in the use of the bow and that flights of 1,200 paces were achieved.

264 The Okmeydan was not abandoned until the mid-nineteenth century.

265 Also used for ceremonial rain prayers during periods of drought.

266 Dated *810/1407*. Inscription. The cult of the open air was as strong as ever. Fisher, *The foreign relations of Turkey*, p. 73, n. 53, describes how Beyazit II received ambassadors in a tent covered in red and not in his palace. The envoys were warned not to spit.

267 Ibid., p. 16.

268 A tragedy of art history was the burning for Beyazit II, allegedly for pious reasons, of the salacious works of Bellini. The famous portrait of Mehmet II survives.

269 Like Louis XIV.

5   PRELUDE TO THE GRAND MANNER – BEYAZIT II

pages 142–195

1 Aslanapa, *Edirne'de Osmanlı devri abîdeleri*, p. 62, Hayreddin. Ünsal, *Turkish Islamic architecture*, p. 96, Hayrüddin. Mayer, *Islamic architects and their works*, p. 106 refers to Usta Murat, father of Hayrettin, who repaired the castle at Galata after the 1509 earthquake.

2 *Turkish Islamic architecture*, p. 96.

3 Aslanapa, *Edirne'de Osmanlı devri abîdeleri*, p. 162. U. Vogt-Göknil, 'Die Kulliye von Beyazit II in Edirne' in *Du/Atlantis*, Aug., 1965, no. 296, p. 612 et seq. claims this is the first külliye or social complex but this is neither true of Islamic architecture in general nor of Ottoman in particular. The Selçuk Friday mosque at Isfahan or the Orhaniye at Bursa, for example, are külliyes. Şehsuvaroğlu, 'Bîmaristân', p. 1225 says that the buildings were begun *891/1486* but that the vakfiye is dated *898/1493*.

4 Camel trains of over five hundred beasts still came every Thursday to the MacAndrew Forbes liquorice factory at Söke before World War II.

5 This subtle variation is most satisfactory but is likely, notwithstanding, to be fortuitous.

6 I am unable to see more than an attenuated connection between these two mosques, unlike Aslanapa, *Edirne'de Osmanlı devri abîdeleri*, pp. 65-7.

7 Gurlitt, 'Die Bautai Adrianopels', plate cxxiv, 21·50 metres.

8 Today there is only a marble balustrade but in a drawing dated 1830 (reproduced in Aslanapa, *Edirne'de Osmanlı devri abîdeleri*, p. 82, plate 99) a low trellis, probably added in the seventeenth century, is shown. The tribune establishes the south-east corner as the orthodox position, although at Beyazit's mosque at Istanbul it was to be set on the north-west.

9 Symbols of the pilgrimage to Mecca, but King Aziz ibn Saud exterminated the ostrich between the World Wars, massacring all game from his car. They are also fertility symbols. Sometimes these eggs are made of china but a broken example in Süleymaniye is real enough. On modern Arabian hunting methods see H. St John Philby, *Arabian Jubilee*, London, 1952, p. 101.

10 Gabriel, *Les monuments turcs d'Anatolie*, II, p. 123.

11 The stag was recurrent in Sufi symbolism.

12 See pp. 169, 184.

13 Gabriel, *Les monuments turcs d'Anatolie*, II, p. 73. Founded by the Emir Umur son of Ali Bey and built by Abu Bekir whose father came from Damascus, on the orders of Mehmet I.

14 Ibid., p. 72.

15 *Turkish Islamic architecture*, p. 40. This medrese is discussed on p. 70.

16 The curious wings of Beyazit Cami are discussed on p. 172.

17 Öz, *Istanbul camileri*, I, p. 130, is only prepared to call them portions (kısım).

18 *Turkish Islamic architecture*, p. 100. The word he uses is 'priests' which is in itself confusing.

19 *Istanbul: petit guide*, p. 128, supported by Ergin, *Türk şehirlerinde imaret sistemi*, p. 7.

20 *İlk devir Osmanlı mimarisinde cami*, p. 64.

21 It can also imply a printing house, and this has led to a curious suggestion that the Süleymaniye tabhane was a calligraphy school. I am indebted to Dr G. Lewis for the following exegesis: The primary meaning of tabhane is 'hot house' (Persian *tābkhāne*). In modern Turkish spelling it might also represent tab'khāne 'printing-office'. There is another word, tibbkhāne 'medical school' or 'office of superintendent of medical affairs', which in modern Turkish would be written tıbhane.

22 *Mahomet II, le Conquérant, et son temps*, p. 353.

23 The wise do not correct Gurlitt without good evidence.

24 The absence of lodgings for imams and, often, müezzins in mosque precincts is puzzling. In some there are rooms, such as those over the gates of Sokollu Mehmet Pasha, which may always have served this purpose but there are many without. Today, they sometimes inhabit an old tabhane room but it is unlikely that they shared them with dervishes in the sixteenth century. Moreover, at that time there must have been a porter in residence. One can only conclude that most mosque officers have always lived in homes outside the precincts.

25 Hammer-Purgstall, *Histoire de l'Empire Ottomane*, pp. 124-5.

26 Ibid., pp. 1-2 and 123.

27 Çetintaş shows two on his plan, three on his reconstructed elevation.

28 *Die Baukunst Konstantinopels*, p. 66.

29 Significantly, these have a sewer running through the middle of them just under the flagstones which is similar to the sewer at the Yıldırım hospital at Bursa. Lechevalier, *Voyage de la Propontide et du Pont-Euxin*, II, p. 238, says that the patients lay on sofas for beds all round large rooms in such hospitals.

30 *Turkish Islamic architecture*, p. 40.

31 Eyice, *Istanbul: petit guide*, pp. 125-6, and Ünsal, *Turkish Islamic architecture*, p. 100.

32 *Navigations and voyages made into Turkey*, p. 58.

33 Cf. Tom O'Bedlam's song.

34 But La Mottraye, *Travels through Europe, Asia, and into parts of Africa*, p. 187 comments on the care taken by the Turks of the insane.

35 Op. cit., p. 76.

36 Some with lands attached.

37 In 1551, over sixty years later, Sinan was to build an octagonal medrese in Istanbul for Rüstem Pasha but he made it square outside by setting triangular washrooms, etc., at the corners. See p. 243.

38 Gabriel, *Les monuments turcs d'Anatolie*, II, p. 38.

39 Relatively late for an Ottoman ruler.

40 Busbecq, *The four epistles of A. G. Busbequius, concerning his Embassy into Turkey*, p. 117.

41 Shutters in trellis form covering harem windows of a home.

42 Gabriel, *Les monuments turcs d'Anatolie*, II, pp. 56 and 65.

43 Octagonal rabats and kervansarays occur in Iran but are surely later in date.

44 It is an example of the Ottoman principle that structure should govern design down to the smallest detail.

45 Gabriel, *Les monuments turcs d'Anatolie*, II, p. 36.

46 Tritton, *Islam, belief and practices*, p. 136 says that short prayers are said over the dead, usually not inside the mosque.

47 Gabriel, *Les monuments turcs d'Anatolie*, II, p. 39.

48 Murat II Cami, Bursa, is one of the few mosques to have steps cut into the sofa to afford ease of access from the central portal to the sofas of the son cemaat yeri. Rum Mehmet at Üsküdar has an external step all the way round the portico sofas.

49 But not so fine as the example hanging on the kıble wall of the Ulu Cami at Bursa.

50 I have never found the alleged underground hamam built by Sinan at Amasya and it is not listed in the tezkere.

51 Gabriel, *Les monuments turcs d'Anatolie*, II, p. 37, n. 2.

52 Akok, 'Uşak Ulu Cami'i' in *V.D.*, III, p. 69.

53 Herzfeld, 'Damascus, studies in architecture' in *A.I.*, IX-XII, part III, p. 18.

54 See Yetkin *et al.*, *Turkish architecture*, p. 24. One of the earliest Ottoman paper mills is said to have been built near Beyazit Pasha Cami. There are extensive foundations there.

55 Gabriel, *Les monuments turcs d'Anatolie*, II, p. 39 calls the imaret a calligraphy school, again owing to confusion over the term tabhane. The muvakkithane, or house of the timekeepers, was doubtless the centre of astronomical and cosmographical studies.

56 Ibid.

57 At least in this the restoration will be traditional.

58 Ibid, p. 42.

59 See p. 116.

60 See p. 57.

61 Gabriel, *Une Capitale turque, Brousse (Bursa)*, p. 137.

62 See p. 131.

63 Ibid., p. 91. Fisher, *The foreign relations of Turkey*, p. 14 says that she came of an old Tokat family.

64 Meyer-Riefstahl, *Turkish architecture in Southwestern Anatolia*, p. 22. Oral, 'Anadolu'da san'at değeri olan ahşap mimberleri, kitabler ve tarihçeler' in *V.D.* V, pp. 75-6 gives the inscription as *893/1488*, the date of the mimber as *900/1495* and the vakfiye as *903/1497*.

65 Alderson, *The structure of the Ottoman dynasty*, table xxviii.

66 On Turkish triangles. This is a late use of an archaic support of the dome.

67 See Manisa, *Türkiye Ansik.*, IV, Ankara, 1957, p. 90. Oral, 'Anadolu'da san'at değeri', p. 75 gives the mosque date as *889/1484* and that of the vakfiye as *893/1488*.

68 Alderson, *The structure of the Ottoman dynasty*, table xxix.

69 Meyer-Riefstahl, *Turkish architecture in Southwestern Anatolia*, p. 16.

70 The central block of the Valide is very high in relation to the wings so that the windows are inset in the tympana of the flanking arches of the dome and look out over the subsidiary pairs of domes on east and west. The portico is high and the antique columns which are slim and graceful create a lively springing of the arches. The mosque is flanked by particularly tall minarets. There are two because it was built by the sultan in his mother's honour.

71 Ahmet Şehzade. The boy was nominally governor of the province but too young to exert actual power which was wielded by Mehmet Pasha. Since the latter was a lala he was also probably a white eunuch.

72 Much of the marble used to redress the façades of mosques in Amasya is freshly cut and replaces broken pieces which may have come from the Marmara quarries.

73 Dated *901/1495*.

74 Gabriel, *Les monuments turcs d'Anatolie*, II, p. 42.

75 This indicates how little their original function was understood although the chimneys have been restored externally.

76 The placing of the minaret next to the mosque proper and not beyond the tabhane foreshadows the positions at Selim I twenty-six years later.

77 They are related to those of the Sultan Beyazit Medrese and may come from the same workshop.

78 The blind central dome is only eight metres wide. It is a shock to realize how modest this mosque really is because it looks so imposing from the outside.

79 Inscription.

80 See p. 404.

81 Gabriel, *Une Capitale turque, Brousse (Bursa)*, p. 156.

82 Gabriel, *Les monuments turcs d'Anatolie*, II, p. 57.

83 It would look as if the half-cell was a conscious effort to achieve eighteen which was the orthodox number.

84 The former Miletus.

85 Mantran, *Istanbul dans la seconde moitié du XVIIe siècle*, p. 43.

86 Ibid., p. 44.

87 Babinger, *Mahomet II, le Conquérant, et son temps*, p. 128.

88 'Essai sur les donnés statistiques des registres de recensement dans l'Empire Ottoman au XV et XVI siècles' in *Journal of Economic and Social History of the Orient*, I, 1, p. 20, n. 1.

89 Mamboury, *The tourists' Istanbul*, pp. 100-1.

90 Today, the population of the city increases not by 15,000 but 100,000 every year.

91 Eyice, *Istanbul: petit guide*, p. 35, sect. 39.

92 Hammer-Purgstall, *Histoire de l'Empire Ottomane*, IV, p. 148.

93 Eyice, *Istanbul: petit guide*, p. 19, sect. 13.

94 By Buondelmonte in the British Museum.

95 Kuran, 'Edirne'de Yıldırım Camii – The Mosque of Yıldırım in Edirne' in *Belletin*, vol. xxviii, no. iii, Ankara, July 1964, pp. 429-38 argues cogently that the mosque was built by Murat I after 1361 and before 1390 and not about 1400, the accepted date. See chap. 2, n. 84.

96 Anheggar, 'Adana' in *E.I.*, I, p. 183.

97 Sixteenth-century skirting at Sokollu Mehmet imitates marble and

so do panels in the court of the Room of the Robe at Topkapısaray and also before the door of the Hünkâr oda where they imitate columns. Another example is the tile portals of the royal box of the Selimiye at Edirne where they represent the marble colonnettes inset as shafts in many mihrabs.

98 Öz, *Istanbul camileri*, p. 75.

99 Hammer-Purgstall, *Histoire de l'Empire Ottomane*, IV, p. 59 only says that he died at this time.

100 Evliya, *Narrative of travels*, I, p. 167.

101 Eyice, *Istanbul: petit guide*, p. 85, sect. 124a.

102 See p. 108. The wooden supports of the Yatağan gallery and the stairs up to it with the rail are all equally new as nail splinters make plain to see. Moreover, the carpentry is rough, and green paint covers up the crudity of the carving. The interesting long gallery serving as a mekteb retains its original and exceptional shape.

103 The eighteenth century was to install many little wooden domes in mosques and houses. A good example is the spacious, rebuilt Kapı Cami at Konya. The aisle ceilings of the Dome of the Rock, Jerusalem, which are nineteenth-century Ottoman may also be mentioned.

104 Inscription.

105 Minetti, *Osmanische provinziale Baukunst auf dem Balkan*, p. 29.

106 See p. 70.

107 Ayverdi, 'Yugoslavya'da', p. 158.

108 Akok, 'Kütahya Büyük Bedesten' in *V.D.*, III, resim ii.

109 See p. 46.

110 Inscription.

111 See p. 57.

112 See p. 151.

113 See p. 57.

114 Inscription.

115 Inscription.

116 Ayverdi, 'Yugoslavya'da', p. 157 et seq.

117 Although nowhere near as important as is implied by Arseven, *L'art turque depuis son origine jusqu'à nos jours*, p. 149. Eyice, *Istanbul: petit guide*, p. 29, sect. 34 states that the inscription is by Hamdullah, a renowned calligrapher.

118 *L'art turc depuis son origine jusqu'à nos jours*, p. 151.

119 But it is simple problems such as these which face the architect with his greatest test.

120 Cezar, 'Osmanli devrinde Istanbul', p. 387, says that it was rebuilt after the earthquake of June 1648.

121 He had to be; younger brothers did not live.

122 Evliya, *Narrative of Travels*, I, part ii, p. 3. Fisher, *The foreign relations of Turkey*, pp. 43-4 recounts a curious episode at the time of the secret negotiations between Sultan, Pope and Knights of St John: the small but attractive town of Osimo in the hills above Ancona was seized by a petty tyrant named Guzzoni who offered it to Beyazit, saying that its name derived from Osman. Just how much

intercourse there was between the Italian Renaissance and growing Ottoman culture is difficult to determine.

123 Gabriel, *Une Capitale turque, Brousse (Bursa)*, p. 188, n. 1.

124 As an offshoot of the Högg plan for the remodelling of Istanbul, the Beyazit Meydan, quaintly renamed Hürriyet (Freedom) Meydan, has been planned afresh. It was once an amiable pleasure-ground of trees and coffee houses, but for nine years the municipality have harrowed, harassed and mutilated the heart of the old city in a most uncouth manner to produce a cacophony of black rocks and concrete. Lying low, like the devil, the cistern is partly the cause of the trouble: the rest is human weakness.

125 'L'Architecte de la Mosquée de Beyazid d'Istanbul' in *1st I.C.T.A.*, pp. 264-5. He also names his successors as Ali bin Aptullah and Yusuf bin Papas, who are clearly of Greek descent. He lists a great many names of palace architects implying a very large department or fraternity including those of İlyas Suna and Usta Hayreddin. This latter name would suggest the reason for the misattribution to Hayrettin as the architect and demonstrates the need for extreme caution in calling anyone the architect of anything. A great deal more research has to be made before foothills cease to be taken for mountains. He also makes it clear that Janissaries worked on mosques.

126 Gabriel, *Une Capitale turque, Brousse (Bursa)*, p. 188. I know of no proof that Yakup Shah held the office of royal architect or Mimar-başı.

127 The name is Persian in style and does not imply that he was a prince.

128 Ünsal, *Turkish Islamic architecture*, p. 96 asserts that he was still alive in 1501, but if so he could not have been Royal Architect and this is hard to believe. Arseven says that the office was held for life and was only once resigned, which would explain why Fatih had to execute Atik Sinan if he wanted better work. However, Dalgıç Ahmet was probably dismissed without losing his life. Eyice, *Istanbul: petit guide*, p. 40, sect. 50 writing before the publication of the Meriç paper states, that according to a tradition which is insufficiently founded, the architect was Mimar Hayrettin. He ignores Kemalettin, another contender, and I doubt if the man ever existed. Öz, *Istanbul camileri*, I, p.33 has much else to say on this matter.

129 Some Turkish architectural writers seek to show that the Byzantines did not influence Ottoman architecture: as if any architecture was immaculately conceived. It has seemed to me to be a gratuitous insult to Ottoman architects to suggest that they were so blind that they never looked at major works by others, particularly since many were of Greek or Armenian origin themselves. Anyway, we know that Fatih greatly admired Sophia, while Selim II and Murat III called in Sinan to survey and preserve it. They and the redoubtable Murat IV, among other monarchs, were proud to embellish it. Ünsal, *Turkish Islamic architecture*, pp.22-3 says that the Ottomans, whom he calls Turks, had already developed the concept of a half-dome from Syrian examples, but he ignores the relationship of the Syrian half-dome to that of Sophia and also the fact that the Great Church was well known to the Ottomans before the conquest. Many had visited the city and the church, which is more than many inhabitants do today. It cannot be overlooked that the monumental conception emerged with the building of Fatih's inadequate mosque. Perhaps the dead Atık Sinan is a pathetic witness to the fact that Mehmet II could not be hoodwinked, for, however ordered the külliye may be, the stark truth is that the first Fatih was a night-light besides Sophia's midday sun. The dissolution of mediaevalism in the form of the Bursa style was clear to all who could see. Yakup Shah saw. Eyice, *Istanbul: petit guide*, p. 41, sect. 50 acknowledges the resemblances before rightly underlining the differences.

130 Arseven, *L'art turc depuis son origine jusqu'à nos jours*, p.157, fig. 307a is not a photograph of Beyazit.

131 Evliya, *Narrative of travels*, I, part 1, p. 70 says that Ibrahim I erected the gilt railing that caused it to resemble a cage, or network, or, rather, a palace of the immortals.

132 This was made all the more remarkable in the eighteenth century by the addition of a library to the west annexe by Şeyhül-Islam Veli-yüttin Efendi. It is now used as a hatipokul or school for preachers.

133 *Narrative of travels*, I, part 1, p. 70.

134 On both occasions the dome fell. The flying buttresses are baroque as a consequence.

135 No one undressed fully to go to bed in those days. Fisher, *The foreign relations of Turkey*, p. 92 says that the year 1502 saw the persecution of the heretical sects which had become a menace to the security of the state; it is therefore possible that the tabhane rooms were suppressed for political reasons after they had been started and used as oratories.

136 Yet it is said that Beyazit was a parsimonious sultan.

137 Eyice, *Istanbul: petit guide*, p. 41, sect. 50. Öz, *Istanbul camileri*, p. 34.

138 *Istanbul camileri*, I, part I, pp. 70-1. He also refers to the cemetery like the garden of Irem, adorned with various fruits and flowers, and to the precincts where under the shade of lofty trees, most of them mulberries, some thousands of people gained a livelihood by selling various kinds of things. There still is a junk bazaar.

139 Out of respect for the legend of the old woman who gave her two pigeons towards the cost of building the mosque, thus excelling her sovereign since she gave all that she had. But then she did not have to pay the salaries of the imperial civil service.

140 Evliya, *Narrative of travels*, I, part 1, p.71, states that the pipes of the basin were never closed but poured forth streams of water night and day because the congregation never failed.

141 Ibid., pp. 4 and 70.

142 Ibid., p. 67.

143 Öz, *Istanbul camileri*, p. 34.

144 Presumably this minaret snapped in the earthquake of 1766. It may also be the minaret damaged by lightning on 11 October 1746, when its cap was in flames. See Cezar, 'Osmanli devrinde Istanbul', p. 389.

145 Evliya, *Narrative of travels*, I, part 1, p. 71 says that the students received a monthly stipend plus allowances for meat and wax candles.

146 Ibid., p. 171.

147 How much Byzantine material was re-used in Ottoman foundations has been revealed by the excavations in the neighbourhood of the new underpass at Şehzadebasi where many columns were found, among them those of the Ibrahim Pasha Hamam.

148 Gyllius, *The Antiquities of Constantinople*, p. 194. It was probably of wood. There is a fine picture in the Sanat ve Heykel Müsesi attached to Dolmabahçesaray at Beşiktaş which shows this building at the turn of the century. It was probably a nineteenth-century rebuilding.

149 Evliya, *Narrative of travels*, I, part 1, p. 71. Sayili, *The Observatory in Islam*, p. 26, says astronomy was the handmaiden of religion and was carried on at the muvakkithane of certain mosques. Busbecq, *The four epistles of A.G. Busbequius, concerning his Embassy into Turkey*, p. 31, speaks of the müezzins using water clocks.

150 Eyice, *Istanbul: petit guide*, p. 82, sect. 119. The dome fell, see Cezar, 'Osmanli devrinde Istanbul', p. 390.

151 Öz, *Istanbul camileri*, p. 32.

152 Op. cit., p. 67.

153 Also of this period is the Terkem or İskender Pasha Cami, originally a mescit, dated 911/1505 – Öz, *Istanbul camileri*, p. 146. Iskender was another of Beyazit's vezirs and for a time governor of Bosnia – Eyice, *Istanbul: petit guide*, p. 80, sect. 115. The mosque built of ashlar has a porch of only three domes and a cupola on a square base inside. It is, in essence, a lofty hall and much restored.

154 Inscription.

155 Ünsal, *Turkish Islamic architecture*, pp. 24-8 states that the mosque was built in its present form by Alaüddevle. He does not seem to have visited it, since he mistakes the four lateral vaults for half-domes because of the thick plaster used in their restoration. They were originally elliptical vaults supported on squinches and the sustaining arches of the central dome.

156 The form was emergent in the Khozara mosque near Bokhara which appears to be incomplete on the north side in the manner of the İskele Cami of Sinan. It was fully developed with the ninth century Degaran mosque (if mosque it was) at Hazar, also near Bokhara according to Y. Yaralov, 'Architectural Monuments of Middle Asia of the eighth to twelfth centuries' in *1st I.C.T.A.*, p. 367; H. Field and E. Prostov, 'The Oriental Institute Report on the Near East, U.S.S.R.', in the *American Journal of Semitic Languages and Literature*, LIII, no. 2, p. 123; and Field and Prostov, 'Archaeological Investigations in Central Asia, 1917-1937' in *A.I.*, V, p. 474; Field and Prostov, (Archaeology in the Soviet Union' in the *American Anthropologist*, XXXIX, no. 3; see also Schroeder, *A survey of Persian Art*, III, p. 946 who dates it eighth- or ninth-century. Both the seventh-century Armenian church of Mastara and the tenth-century church of the Apostles at Kars have a central dome buttressed by four semi-domes but on a cruciform and not a square ground plan. The churches of Syria might also be mentioned in this context.

157 Recalling the dome of the dershane of Yıldırım's hospital at Bursa. The form recurred, for example with the Mehmet Pasha Cami, Sivas, often in elaborated form.

158 Fisher, *The foreign relations of Turkey*, p. 41, n. 82. Cezar, 'Osmanli devrinde Istanbul', p. 329 says that the Grand Vezir Mesih Pasha was killed by a stone along with the Kadı of Galata when fighting the fire.

159 He repaired the palace and walls immediately, according to Fisher, *The foreign relations of Turkey*, p. 14, n.2.

160 Sanderson, *The travels of John Sanderson*, pp. 79-80.

161 Cezar, 'Osmanli devrinde Istanbul', pp. 382-3. He left his bedroom only an hour before it fell in.

162 Hammer-Purgstall, *Histoire de l'Empire Ottomane*, IV, p. 101.

Cezar, 'Osmanli devrinde Istanbul', p. 383, says three thousand masons summoned from the provinces and eleven thousand Janissaries worked on the repairs from 29 March until 1 June 1510, and this included repairs to the castles on the Bosphorus and Galata tower.

163 Hammer-Purgstall, *Histoire de l'Empire Ottomane*, IV, p. 391. Fisher, *The foreign relations of Turkey*, pp. 111-12. He reigned for thirty-one years.

164 It was a tribute to Selim's energy and pitilessness that he won the throne although he was the youngest son. He was aided by the loyalty of the Janissaries. Beyazit's eldest son had died in 1483 and his favourite in 1503. Mahmut was poisoned at his father's orders when governor of Kaffa in the Crimea in 1505 because of rebelliousness, and Mehmet suffered the same fate when he left Manisa disguised as a sea captain to visit Istanbul. He was a troubadour by nature and had wandered as far as Kastamonu in this disguise. Şahin, who had a withered leg, drank himself to death in 1510. So Selim had only two rivals in 1511. The sultan's favourite was Ahmet but he was too pleasure-loving to withstand his brother, while Korkund was a poet and a scholar, theologian and philosopher, and equally unable to oppose his aggressive sibling.

165 1516 is the likely date.

166 Hammer-Purgstall, *Histoire de l'Empire Ottomane*, IV, p. 343.

167 Ibid., XVIII, p. 64, sect. 585.

168 Else this would be the first Ottoman mosque to be dressed with tile revetments.

169 One qualification must be made: the duodecagonal drum of the central dome is set in a shed roof which only survives at the four corners where its sharp angles are discernible. Consequently the four semi-domes are not completely contiguous with the drum.

170 Or the rigid division of the plan into sixteen sections.

171 Syrian influence which may have originated in Egypt.

172 This minaret continues to an unusual height above the gallery. High minarets are a feature of Diyarbakır.

173 Perhaps because Fatih Pasha was used as a military mosque.

174 Yalçin, *Çankırı*, p. 10.

175 Inscription.

176 See p. 368.

177 Slightly damaged in the earthquake of 1967.

178 Also known as Koca Kasım Cami. Koca means 'old' as we have seen. Cezeri signifies 'thorough' and this quality, as well as the competent workmanship which his buildings display, was the possible cause of his rise to eminence.

179 Erdmann, 'Neue Arbeiten zur türkischen Keramik', p. 203 notes also that the tiles over the windows give an inorganic impression and wonders if they were not originally from another place. The only argument against this is that there is no evidence that they were not contemporaneous with the mosque. It might be that they were not designed specifically for it but, remembering the influence of standard measurements, they might have been bought at hazard for it.

180 Miller, *The palace school of Muhammed the Conqueror*, p. 45, attributes these to Fatih but in *Beyond the Sublime Porte*, p. 74, he attributes them to Selim. Erkins, *Topkapı Sarayı müzesi*, p. 22, dates them 1478.

181 Gibb, 'Lufti Pasha on the Ottoman Caliphate' in *Oriens*, XV, pp. 287-95 establishes that the Ottoman sultans had no right to the hereditary title. See also Lewis, *Turkey*, p. 21.

182 Erkins, *Topkapı Sarayı müzesi*, p. 222 claims that the peacock tiles are sixteenth-century Iznik, yet the brown tone of the reds suggests they might date from the first period of decline, c. 1620.

183 Compare these panels with those of such Cairene mosques as those of El-Hakim, El-Azhar among many examples and note the significant lack of skirting or border at ground level.

184 Melikoff, '*Al-Battāl* Sayyid Battāl Ghazi' in *E.I.*, I, p. 1103 says that the finding of his tomb in Western Anatolia was a Selçuk legend. He was adopted by the Alevis and Bektaşis and I find it significant that the renegade Christian Mikaloğlu family were lavish benefactors of this tekke. Battal Gazi seems to have been confounded with another Islamic hero, Aptullah Battal Gazi who died in 740 according to Byzantine sources. See Canard, 'Al-Battal, 'Ab Allâh' in *E.I.*, I,

p. 1101. He says that his conquest of Gongara in Paphlagonia in 728 is a fact.

185 Öz, *Istanbul camileri*, p. 130. Evliya, *Narrative of travels*, I, part 1, p. 73 dates it 1521-7. Danişmend, *İzahlı Osman tarihi kronolojisi*, II, p. 67 says that it was begun by Sinan on 17 May 1521 and completed in October 1522. This would be record speed and defies belief. The impossible legend that Sinan built this mosque persists. He may conceivably have worked on it as an apprentice.

186 Hammer-Purgstall, *Histoire de l'Empire Ottomane*, V, p. 8 states that Süleyman laid the foundation stone almost immediately after his father's death.

187 Evliya, *Narrative of travels*, I, part 1, p. 74 clearly calls these hostels for travellers.

188 The elaborate concave and convex cusps which make such arches reflect, in silhouette, various stylized flower patterns used in books and on tiles and rugs. These show Chinese influence, as do the leaf forms. The relating of architectural forms to stylized forms in nature is, therefore, correct. Ogee and four-centred arches, or the cresting of façades, together with many alem designs, all reflect this relationship. The cresting, however, is also a Central Asian cloud head and a talisman related to celestial light as opposed to the horn symbol of the dark earth which is often used complimentarily. See Bidder, *Carpets from Eastern Turkestan*, p. 64.

189 Evliya, *Narrative of travels*, I, part 1, p.74 says that this, like other tribunes of the sultan, was caged by Ibrahim I. He was not un-justifiably paranoiac. Evliya also speaks of one thousand trophies and ornaments. None remain.

190 Selim brought seven hundred families of ceramicists back from Tabriz to work in Iznik in 1514 according to Mantran, *Istanbul dans la seconde moitié du XVIIe siècle*, p. 407; but I find this number excessive. However, even a much lesser number would have had great influence on both production and design.

191 Gabriel, 'Les mosquées de Constantinople', p. 368.

192 Evliya, *Narrative of travels*, I, part 1, p. 74.

193 İnčičean, *XVIII Asırda Istanbul*, p. 37 says that it had ninety students.

194 Cezar, 'Osmanli devrinde Istanbul', p. 379 says that it was burnt down in the great fire of 13 June 1918.

195 Öz, *Istanbul camileri*, p. 130.

196 Hammer-Purgstall, *Histoire de l'Empire Ottomane*, IV, p. 203. But the six hundred Egyptians were sent back to Egypt upon Süleyman's accession. See vol. V, p. 9.

197 Ünsal, *Turkish Islamic architecture*, p. 96 insists that he was a Turk, but, if so, he could not have been a slave nor called a Persian.

198 Ibid., and Öz, *Istanbul camileri*, p. 130. It may have been started by Selim himself as the inscription over the door implies. This has been discussed already – see Eyice, *Istanbul: petit guide*, p. 62, sect. 85. It is noteworthy that Süleyman built a grand medrese opposite Constantine of the Lips in honour of his father as late as 1562 – ibid., p. 81, sect. 117. Among others, Gabriel disposes of the attribution of the Selimiye to Sinan in 'Les mosquées de Constantinople', p. 368, n.1.

199 *Islamic architects and their works*, p. 50.

200 Ünsal, *Turkish Islamic architecture*, p. 96. Arseven, *L'art turc depuis son origine jusqu'a nos jours*, p. 160 says 1535.

201 Yalçin, *Van, Hakkarı*, p. 10.

202 Gebze had been an important station on the caravan route since Byzantine times and before. Constantine had a palace nearby and Mehmet II a kiosk at Kartal where he died.

203 Evliya, ed. Kocu, *Seyahatname*, II, pp. 70-1, says that Mustafa Pasha built the mosque at Gebze with granite columns brought from Egypt. If he is referring to those of the portico it is odd that he does not mention the gorgeous panelling. This may have been made in part of columns cut in strips by the captive Egyptian craftsmen. It would not have been the first nor the last time columns have been so used. Evliya say that the architect was Sinan, hence the persistent mis-attribution, and that Hüsam was the head Kalfa. He also says that the han was built for three thousand men and two thousand beasts, which is beyond its capacity.

204 On 4 March 1515. They were only married in 1511 – see Alderson, *The Structure of the Ottoman dynasty*, table xxix. The Grand Vezir was descended from a Frankish Duke Jean who had established himself in Albania.

205 Mayer, *Islamic Architects and their works*, p. 66.

206 This apartment has been called a library, possibly because of the eighteenth-century library over the gate at Hekimoğlu Ali Pasha in Istanbul. At this date libraries were usually inside the mosques and behind a grille if not in a gallery.

207 The placing of the türbe on the axis of the mihrab did not occur in Bursa, but it did with Mehmet II's and also Beyazit II's mausoleums and also with Süleyman's, after which the fashion appears to have died out.

208 Inscription.

209 *Turkish Islamic architecture*, pp. 67-8.

210 Some rooms were destroyed in the fire of 1660 when the Atmeydan became a refugee camp, see Cezar, 'Osmanli devrinde Istanbul', p. 335.

211 Hammer-Purgstall, *Histoire de l'Empire Ottomane*, V, p. 54 says that Ibrahim himself built it.

212 Baudier, *The History of the Serrail, and of the Court of the Grand Seigneur, Emperour of the Turks*, p. 37, for example. He states that the circumcision ceremonies in the Hippodrome were watched by the sultan from the Ibrahim Pasha Saray as can be seen from the *Surname* of Mehmet III. He also states (ibid., p. 17) that the palace in his day, the second decade of the seventeenth century, served the solemnities of the games, pomps and carousels of Turkish princes and contained an academy of four hundred pages who were there instructed in letters, arms and exercises worthy of them.

213 Sanderson, *The travels of John Sanderson*, p. 74. He married Ayşe Sultan.

214 Lybyer, *The Government of the Ottoman Empire*, p. 55. Rycault, *The history of the Turkish Empire, 1623-1677*, p. 88, states that on marrying the thirteen-year-old daughter of Murat IV in 1640, Bosnalı Mustafa Pasha was given the palace until he was executed in 1641. Alderson *The structure of the Ottoman dynasty*, table xxxvi calls him Tuccarzade Mustafa Ağa. Konyalı, *Istanbul sarayları*, p. 157 cites Evliya and states that at this date half the palace was a school and half was given over to the sultan. But the English translation of *Narrative travels*, I, part 1, p. 175 carefully states that two thousand pages were formerly educated there. They could have been moved to Galatasaray in 1675, see p. 193. In any event, the devşirme system was dying by the mid-seventeenth century.

215 Mantran, *La vie quotidienne à Constantinople*, p. 29 states that the Greek Ibrahim built Galatasaray for the devşirme. Since he had 1,500 slaves this may well be true. Konyalı, *Istanbul sarayları*, p. 155 claims that he had 6,000 at the time of his death and that his palace was given to the İçoğhlanları only after his execution.

216 Until the reign of Selim I, the devşirme was recruited in the Balkans and brought to Edirne. When the system extended to Anatolia those recruits would have been marched to Istanbul and a barracks had to be found for them. It is possible that rooms were added at the old Candarlı palace and that Evliya's figure of two thousand is therefore correct. Hammer-Purgstall, *Histoire de l'Empire Ottoman*, X, p. 192, however, states that the boys at the Ibrahim school were Bosnians and Albanians, a point which Egli, *Sinan*, who wishes to prove that Sinan was a student there, disregards. Evliya, *Narrative of travels*, I, part 1, p. 175.

217 Sanderson, *The travels of John Sanderson*, p. 74 mentions the saray which Sinan built for Rüstem Pasha but this may have been pulled down together with that of Sokollu Mehmet for the building of Ahmet I's mosque. All sadrazams' palaces were large and that of the Ağa of the Janissaries, or Commander-in-Chief, where the offices of the Mufti are now situated, was a village of apartments in phalanxes adjoining each other about a square.

218 This might explain why Nevşehirli Ibrahim Pasha repaired it. Konyalı, *Istanbul sarayları*, p. 146, plate 30.

219 Evliya, *Narrative of travels*, I, part 1, p. 178. It could be a misprint for Etmeydan.

220 This is unlikely. All that I have found to survive the destruction of Janissary monuments is one mutilated and one intact tombstone in the cemetery of the Ayasma Cami at Üsküdar.

221 Compare the bridge at Urfa with the Topkapısaray vaults.

222 In particular, Melling, *Voyage pittoresque de Constantinople et des rives du Bosphore*, plate 13.

223 Choiseul-Gouffier, *Voyage pittoresque de la Grèce*, plate 81.

224 Gibb and Bowen, *Islamic society and the West*, I, part 1, p. 81, n. 1. They list the dates of closures and re-openings.

225 H. Sumner-Boyd, in 'The seven hills of Istanbul', describes the destruction of the Delphic serpent heads erected in the Hippodrome. They were destroyed by members of the Polish delegation housed in the palace.

226 Founded by Beyazit II according to Gibb and Bowen, *Islamic society and the West*, I, part 1, p. 79.

227 Hammer-Purgstall, *Histoire de l'Empire Ottomane*, XVIII, p. 123.

228 The ruin already mentioned as lying on the other side of the Divan Yolu should be considered, but nothing appears to be documented about it.

229 Konyalı's arguments, in answer to Çetintaş, that this is not the palace of Ibrahim seem on the contrary to boomerang as soon as he has to explain the great hall. He establishes reasonably that Sinan was not the architect while showing that he effected certain additions and repairs to the palace. He gives evidence that part was used by the Mehter or military band and rebuilt, or added to, in 1828 – significantly, two years after the closing of the school. The situating of this symbolic and semi-religious band seems to have been an honour awarded by Ibrahim in the first place. The work of 1828 proves nothing about the first uses of the palace and written evidence concerning its sixteenth-century use is not at present available. Konyalı does not face the inescapable facts that the palace was used to watch celebrations in the Atmeydan, that the seats of the Hippodrome had been its quarry, and that Ibrahim set up Greek statues for his delight on the Spina opposite his windows. Thus the site must have been correct, however much time altered the function and the appearance of the buildings. The fact is that, while the hall could have served excellently for a divan, it made bad barracks. Mordtmann, in *E.I.*, II, pp. 441-2 also connects Ibrahim Pasha's saray and the military band.

230 Part of the vaults under the Sphendrome of the Hippodrome are used as such to this day.

231 The undercrofts of the Hall of the Mantle, or Room of the Robe, and the Selâmlık at Topkapısaray were dormitories for servants at one time.

232 These traditional partitions demonstrate how the division of barracks or a dormitory at the saray school related to the tents of the army in the field.

233 Choiseul-Gouffier, *Voyage pittoresque de la Grèce*, map.

234 *Histoire de l'Empire Ottomane*, V, p. 54, n. 4.

235 *Voyage du tour du monde*, p. 328.

236 Sanderson, *The travels of John Sanderson*, p. 78 states that 'many palaces were compassed by high walls and appear cities rather than seraglios: which without make no beautiful show ... for the Turks build not to pleasure the sight of those who pass by but for their own commodity; deriding the goodly shows that our palaces in Christendom make outwardly, and that within they are not very agreeable to their minds'.

237 Konyalı, *Istanbul sarayları*, p. 174 et seq., however, besides Sinan, lists many architects responsible for the repair of this palace, including Mehmet Ağa and Mimar Hasan Çavuş.

6 SINAN – THE RISE TO GREATNESS

pages 196–239

1 In Turkish: Darüs-saadet.

2 Uzunçarşılı, *Osmanlı devletinin saray teşkilatı*, pp. 375-6. In effect, Lord Privy Purse, responsible for all the saray accounts and those of the royal colleges and also the repair of state buildings. He was a minister without a seat in the cabinet ranking after defterdar, or Chancellor of the Exchequer.

3 And so clearly was he superior to the Şehr-emini, that the orders issued to Sinan show that his authority extended over Constantinople, Edirne and other towns in every physical aspect. Turan, 'Gli architteti imperiali nell'Impero Ottomano', in *2nd I.C.T.A.*, pp. 259-60 says that he had under him the Su naziri, the Master of the Waterways, mimar-i sani or auxiliary architects, Kireççibaşı or Superintendent of Supplies, Ambarbaşı or Superintendent of Depots, and Tamiratbaşı or Director of Maintenance. The Şehr-emini was at once more of a Minister of the Interior and a Minister of Finance. The Royal Architect was one of the four emin of the sultan ranking with the Procurator General and superior to the head of the civil service, Reisin-kütab, or Secretary-General. He may be seen as a Minister of Works. Most important of all was his authority over the Istanbul Ağa who controlled the acemioğlan or Janissary cadets, for there was clearly a close connection between soldiering and masonry.

4 Chronologically, the work of these two great architects overlaps. MacCurdy, *The Mind of Leonardo da Vinci*, pp. 245-6 says that Beyazit II in 1502, through envoys whom he had sent to Cesare Borgia, invited Leonardo to build a bridge across the Golden Horn and four years later he employed certain Franciscan monks to induce Michelangelo to build it instead. On Folio 66a of ms. L. of Leonardo in the Institut de France in Paris there is a note of the dimensions of the bridge of Pera at Constantinople: 'forty braccia wide, seventy braccia high above the water, six hundred braccia long, that is four hundred over the sea and two hundred on land, thus *making its own supports*' [my italics]. Vasari (ed.) *The Lives of the Painters, Sculptors and Architects*, IV, p. 122 says that when Michelangelo received his invitation he was completing work on Moses and that he nearly went to Constantinople in a fit of pique. The bridge, unfortunately, was not built but these events show that the Porte was well aware of the stature of European architects.

5 Egli, *Sinan*, p. 23 says that the first historian to mention Sinan was Cafer Çelebi who states that he died before 997/1589 at the age of one hundred in Moslem years. Evliya cheerfully claimed that he lived one hundred and seventy years. The inscription on his türbe written by his friend Mustafa Sâ'i states that he died in 996/1588 and that he was one hundred years old. It is not suggested that this entry was added until he was on his death bed. The statement is supported by the evidence of Murat III's last order to him. It was dated Monday, 28 January 1588. It was not usual to retire at this period of Ottoman history. Mayer, *Islamic Architects and their works*, p. 124 gives the date of his death as April 1588. The date of his birth may reasonably be accepted as 896/1491.

6 It is from the Tezkere-ül Bunyan and the Tezkere-ül Ebniye compiled by Mustafa Sâi in conjunction with these documents that the list of Sinan's works is known. They are reprinted by Montani Efendi, in M. de Launay, *L'Architecture Ottomane*, and by Ahmet Refik in *Mimar Sinan*. They are the only useful bases for conjecture but numerous doubtful attributions occur, nor do the two lists agree. The examples of Bali Pasha, see p. 174, and Çoban Mustafa at Gebze, see p. 189, have already been discussed.

7 Egli, *Sinan*, p. 23 et seq. He usefully disposes of a number of puerile assertions made in recent years.

8 Ibid. But he accepts the one fact that Sinan came to Istanbul from Ağırnas, now Mimarsinanköy, a village of little beauty, because an order of Selim II definitely states that he came from there.

9 See p. 192. Its opening by Candarlı Ibrahim is asserted by Mordtmann in *E.I.*, II, pp. 441-2. Uzunçarşılı, *Osmanlı devletinin saray teşkilatı*, p. 306 states that this school was a preparatory school for the other colleges or for the cavalry. One concrete fact is that the kitchens were extensively repaired in 1567. Lybyer, *The Government of the Ottoman Empire*, p. 78 says that the majority of the graduates of the Enderun College were also drafted into the cavalry.

10 Ménage, 'Devshirme' in *E.I.*, II, pp. 210-13 says that the earliest reference to the devşirme is 1395 when the Metropolitan of Thessalonika lamented the seizure of children by decree of the Emir. The second is to the exemption of Ioannina in 1430.

11 See appendix. Tritton, *Islam, belief and practices*, p. 15 says that the acceptance of Islam blots out a man's past.

12 Lybyer, *The Government of the Ottoman Empire*, p. 51 likens them to horse-dealers.

13 Miller, *The Palace School of Muhammed the Conqueror*, p. 127.

14 Lybyer, *The Government of the Ottoman Empire*, p. 75 says that the thirty-nine who were promoted personal servants of the sultan and admitted to the Hasoda were the élite of all.

15 Topkapısaray 14. 1339. miniature showing the enthronement of Selim II in the Nüzheti-Esrar el-Ehbar der Seferi Sigetvar by Ahmet Feridun Pasha, dedicated to Sokollu. This shows the sultan and his court in their order of rank, their stance symbolic of humility.

16 Busbecq, *The four epistles of A. G. Busbequius, concerning his Embassy into Turkey*, p. 36 states that the Turks esteem no man for his birth, only his accomplishments.

17 Egli, *Sinan*, p. 24 says his name is also given as Hristo and Aptullah. Ten architects witnessed Sinan's second will, nine being converts of whom eight were called Aptullahoğlu or son of Aptullah which like Abdülmenan was the anonym of fathers whose sons were Moslem converts. See Ménage, 'Seven Ottoman Documents from the reign of Mehmmed II', pp. 112 et seq.

18 It was not race but religion and culture which mattered in those days. He was an Anatolian brought up in the culture of Greece and Christianity but freely matured as a Moslem. Since he was known as Kayserli Sinan before he was awarded the title of Koca, or elder, there is no reason to doubt where he was born.

19 The first order was issued 981/1573 and was followed by a second fourteen days later, see Ahmet Refik, *Türk Mimarları*, pp. 88–90.

20 Sinan refers to his *master* who presumably taught him these skills.

21 Sanderson, *The travels of John Sanderson*, p. 73 quaintly remarks of these barracks that the Janissaries were housed like friars.

22 Ahmet Refik, *Türk Mimarları*, p. 6. The relationship between furniture and buildings is obvious; in the West, for example, there have been the brothers Adam, Le Corbusier and Mies van der Rohe. It was a rule that all students had to learn a craft and this custom extended to the sultan himself. Fatih was a gardener and Süleyman I learned to be a goldsmith from a Greek at Trabzon.

23 Ahmet Refik, *Türk Mimarları*, p. 78, sect. 8 quotes an order to the Ağa of the Janissaries to send a hundred men to Edirne to work on the Selimiye which shows that Janissaries were used as builders.

24 The Turkish work is *zenberekcibaşı*. The bow was still an important weapon. Nonetheless, the name here covers a modern development just as lancers became tank corps units. Sinan's men were tüfeciler or gunners and belonged to the 62nd Orta, see Pakalin, *Osmanlı tarih deyimleri ve terimleri sözlüğü*, III, Istanbul, 1954, p. 652. It is good training for an architect to start his career by learning how to find the weak points of structures in order to knock them down. In a bad poem, Sinan stated that he suffered many hardships until he became an infantry officer. He was very eager to fight and prepared to sacrifice himself. He became a master of archery.

25 Fischer-Galati, *Ottoman Imperialism and German Protestantism*, pp. 97–8 says that the political reason which made this appointment possible was Süleyman's need to rest his war-weary Janissaries and Spahis which led to a truce with the Hapsburg Emperor for five years in 1547 and to one indecisive battle with the Persians in 1548. Gabriel, 'Le maître-architecte Sinan' in *La Turquie Kemaliste*, XVI, December 1936, p. 2 accepts the theory that during the Persian campaign of 1534 Sinan built boats on Lake Van and that his bridging of the Danube during the Wallachian campaign established his reputation as an engineer. He was certainly proud of his bridges.

26 I accept Mustafa Sâi's records as Sinan's own.

27 Ahmet Refik, *Türk mimarları*, p. 9. It is not clear if there is any evidence except strong tradition. Egli, *Sinan*, p. 34 states that he built the ships at Van for Lutfi Pasha, an Albanian, in 1535 and a bridge for the same minister over the River Pruth in 1536. Hüsrev Gazi allegedly ordered buildings from Sinan in Sarajevo prior to his work in Aleppo in 1536, and a further patron is said to have been Hatice Sultan, aunt of the sultan. None appear on the tezkere. Sinan is not the only architect to have built ships; Pier Luigi Nervi has built at least two boats of concrete.

28 Sinan emerges as a true Ottoman – a convert and a soldier, loyal to a ruler but not to a country. The parallels with the Austro-Hungarian Empire are obvious.

29 Ahmet Refik, *Istanbul hayatı, 1553–1591*.

30 Ibid., p. 26, sect. 21. An order of the sultan in 1577 to the Kadı of Istanbul states that a letter had informed the sultan that Sinan was taking water from the fountain of his Majesty's grandfather and had built a new fountain in front of his house with a big tank, and that beside the fountain he had set a marble container. One end of this was connected, inside, with pipes to the hamam. The water of the tank was emptied twice a day and, moreover, digging a well used the waters of Kağithane which passed nearby. He cut the lead cover of the cistern and diminished the water supply of the two medreses and the Tiphane and carried it to his house. The superintendent was to examine these charges and report truthfully.

31 Allen, *Problems of Turkish power in the 16th century*, p. 52, n. 58 says that Selim II was jovial and loved by his servants, was the best poet of the dynasty and could call a halt to self-indulgence and take good advice.

32 Ahmet Refik, *Türk mimarları*, pp. 100–2, sect. 32.

33 Egli, *Sinan*, p. 39.

34 The problem has been discussed in relation to Firuz Ağa Cami, see p. 167.

35 Each has a dome of six segments which is as inelegant as it is unusual.

36 Thirty-five inches.

37 As with the Kurşunlu Cami, Kayseri, and the Selimiye at Karapinar.

38 The poor quality of much restoration and the ruthlessness of some rebuilding in Syria is deplorable.

39 Arseven, *L'art turc depuis son origine jusqu'à nos jours*, p. 160 states that Acemi İsa died in 1535. Mayer, *Islamic architects and their works*, p. 48 attributes only one mosque to him – Mimar Cami, Yenikapı.

40 Allen, *Problems of Turkish power in the 16th century*, p. 23 says that she was fat and unattractive and the daughter of a Ukrainian priest. Alderson, *The structure of the Ottoman dynasty*, table XXX says she was born in 1500 and married in 1520. Her Russian origin is reported in the records of the Bank of St George at Genoa. Lybyer, *The Government of the Ottoman Empire*, p. 58, n. 2 says that Selim I's marriage to a Tatar princess was the last free royal marriage.

41 The death of Prince Mehmet, Süleyman's beloved eldest son, in 1543 and the execution of Mustafa at Amasya in 1553 was to give Roxelane the title of Haseki, or mother of the heir apparent, the future Selim II. I have been unable to discover the original name of her foundation.

42 The imaret still serves food, mainly stewed meat and cabbage, to three hundred people each day. This fact is unknown to most Turks, who will regretfully speak of the institution of the imaret as a mark of the good old days, now extinct. There are in fact two other imarets still functioning in Istanbul, at Eyüp and Üsküdar.

43 Eyice, *Istanbul: petit guide*, p. 86, sect. 128.

44 In this mosque there is a cushion embroidered with a Persian inscription hung in a glass globe from the central arch.

45 This oblique entry recalls those of mosques in Iran whence Acemi Ali came.

46 See p. 151.

47 These rooms have been altered but one handsome double-domed chamber has a tall, slender ocak with an elegant plaster hood.

48 Inscription.

49 Hammer-Purgstall, *Histoire de l'Empire Ottomane*, V, p. 388.

50 Inscription. Ethem, *Nos mosquées de Stamboul*, pp. 67–8. Hammer-Purgstall, *Histoire de l'Empire Ottomane*, V, pp. 287, 290 and 300; also VI, p. 6. Hüsrev Pasha, brother of Lala Mustafa Pasha had been Viceroy of Europe and fell from favour partly because of the excessive revenues which he extracted from Egypt. Danişmend, *İzahlı Osman tarihi kronolojisi*, II, p. 471, lists his full career as Governor General of Karaman, 1516–17; Governor of Diyarbakır, 1527; Viceroy of Syria, 1534; and of Europe, 1541.

51 These will develop into the inner and the outer dome of the türbe of Süleyman and that of Kılıç Ali Pasha.

52 Hammer-Purgstall, *Histoire de l'Empire Ottomane*, XVIII, p. 3. Eyice, *Istanbul: petit guide*, p. 55, sect. 73. Hammer-Purgstall, VI, p. 577

states that the complex cost 300,000 ducats from the treasure of Süleyman's 9th campaign and that at the time of his death Mehmet was Viceroy of Manisa. Lybyer, *The Government of the Ottoman Empire*, p. 57 and n. 3 says that his mother, Gülbahar, the rival of Roxelane, was either Montenegran or Albanian, or Crimean. Almost all the women of the harem were from the Caucasus and Christian born.

53 Sanderson, *The travels of John Sanderson*, p. 73 says that, in 1594, Şehzade was called the New or Yeni Sultan Mehmet to differentiate it from Fatih.

54 Strictly speaking the Church of St Mary of the Mongols is quatrefoil but it has no corner areas.

55 Çıraklık.

56 They are an innovation in Ottoman architecture and conceal the lateral buttresses except at each end but they are only partially functional; the centre loggias act as porches but those on each side have no particular purpose.

57 But there is another weakness, for those which support the central dome are narrower than those supporting the lateral small domes. See Ağa-oğlu, 'The Fatih Mosque at Constantinople', p. 192.

58 Gabriel, *Voyages archéologiques dans la Turquie Orientale*, p. 80, fig. 64. Pots were used in cradle vaults in Islamic architecture as early as the convent of Imam Aptullah at Hısr Kayfa. The dome of Olcaytu's (Öljeiti) tomb at Sultaniye dated 1304 is tile on terracotta honeycombing. Their use is discussed in Vitruvius and was known to the Greeks. They improve acoustics and reduce weight. A hamam built at Siirt in 1967 has a dome of pots covered in tiles.

59 Eyice, *Istanbul: petit guide*, p. 55, sect. 73.

60 Cezar, 'Osmanli devrinde Istanbul', p. 347 says that the surroundings of this mosque, the mosque floor and the furniture of the refugees inside were burnt in the fire of 17 July 1718, and the minaret caps melted. On p. 364 he states that the fire of 22 August 1782 melted them again and burnt the royal loge and carpets inside the mosque.

61 There is a parallel here with Gothic architects who introduced buildings with multiple perspectives in which the confusion is vindicated by an order which is easily perceived when studied and which is responsible for each and every detail.

62 See p. 332.

63 Dated 950/1543–951/1544. Yetkin et al., *Turkish architecture*, p. 77.

64 Dwight, *Constantinople, old and new*, p. 61 says that this symbolizes the throne that Süleyman had hoped that his son might inherit. It might well be a pavilion for a prince in the paradisial garden.

65 Alderson, *The structure of the Ottoman dynasty*, table xxx. Mihrimah was the daughter of Süleyman and Gülbahar who died in 1558. Mihrimah was born in 1522 and married at seventeen to Rüstem by whom she had one daughter. When a widow, she lived at the saray and received her half-brother, Selim II upon his succession, see Hammer-Purgstall, *Histoire de l'Empire Ottomane*, VI, p. 292. Ibid., p. 214 he says that she died in January 1574. She was evidently a forceful personality and was lavish in her expenditure although married to a skinflint. Sinan may have designed the setting for the festivities in connection with her marriage and the circumcision of Beyazit and Cihangir which lasted a fortnight.

66 Alderson, *The structure of the Ottoman dynasty*, table xxx. Hammer-Purgstall, *Histoire de l'Empire Ottomane*, VI, p. 57 says that he was only temporarily in retirement until the anger of the Janissaries, who were fond of the prince, abated. Kara Ahmet Pasha who acted in his stead was rapidly found guilty of plotting on his own account and strangled to make way for Rüstem's return. Busbecq, *The four epistles of A. G. Busbequius, concerning his Embassy into Turkey*, p. 45 says that Rüstem was son of a shepherd. A man of wit, his sordid avarice was a blot on his escutcheon; he even taxed herbs, violets and roses. He also says (pp. 133–4) that Ahmet Pasha was suspected of plotting with Şehzade Beyazit who was eventually executed in 1561.

67 Mayer, *Islamic Architects and their works*, p. 91 says that one Mehmet Ağa was superintendent of this mosque and also erected the Taşcılar Cami in which he was buried upon his death in 1548. There is some ambiguity over the two Mihrimah mosques.

68 Hammer-Purgstall, *Histoire de l'Empire Ottomane*, VI, p. 93 says that Süleyman built both the Mihrimah mosques for his daughter, but this does not seem probable because that at Edirnekapı was founded after this Sultan's death. The imperial prerogative of two minarets does suggest that he may have built the İskele Cami for Mihrimah, however.

69 But the use of three half-domes was novel in Ottoman architecture even if his had appeared in Central Asia with the allegedly eighth-century mosque at Khozara near Bokhara. It is interesting that the two piers of the İskele Cami are related in shape to those of the mosque of Gulpaygan which is a very early Iranian type. It also owes a debt to the plan of Süleyman Pasha Cami in Cairo, dating from 1528–9. Süleyman was Viceroy of Egypt for a year and resided in the citadel. See Hautecoeur and Weit, *Les mosquées du Caire*, p. 63. This small but interesting mosque is a T-plan Bursa type reduced to three half-domed eyvans off a central domed area. There is a portico and court with revaks and what once may have been a dervish shrine and tomb on two floors on the north-east side. In it are two fascinating eighteenth-century Moslem graves with Ancient Egyptian motifs.

70 Between these is a step up to the area under the half-dome before the mihrab niche.

71 Inčičean, *XVIII asırda Istanbul*, p. 109 reports that the complex included a misafirhane (or tabhane) and a kervansaray. This, and also possibly the imaret, appears to have stood between the mosque and the landing-stage. Evliya, *Narrative of travels*, I, part 2, p. 81 says that it had a hundred hearths and stabling for a hundred horses. It would seem, therefore, to have been akin to the kervansaray at Büyükçekmice described on p. 293.

72 There had been a serious fire in 1540, see Cezar, 'Osmanli devrinde Istanbul', p. 331.

73 Bernard, *Les bains de Brousse*, p. 66 says that he suffered from gout.

74 Gibb and Bowen, *Islamic society and the West*, II, pp. 145–6 state that these medreses, together with those of Fatih and Beyazit, were the most important and all the chief members of the Ulema were trained there. Süleymaniye alone of these had a medical school and a school of tradition. The suggestion that there was a school for each of the four main Sunni sects may arise from such foundations as the Mustan Sura Medrese at Baghdad where Ibn Battuta (p. 332) reported an eyvan for each of the four schools. Evliya, *Narrative of travels*, I, part 1, p. 80 states that the Süleymaniye colleges were for the four orthodox sects. The solution is neatly put by Southgate, *Narrative of a tour*, pp. 53-4 who says that the four doctrines of the Sunni sect are equally orthodox since they agree in everything essential to the religion. They are like four paths of which one or the other is the shorter but which all lead to the same place.

75 Mayer, *Islamic architects and their works*, p. 133 cites Yetim Baba Ali Çelebi Turnaci – Master of the Cranes in the suite of the royal hunt but probably a military rank at this date (see Chap. 9, n. 89) – as Sinan's student and assistant at Süleymaniye. He became its superintendent (bina emini) in 960/1553.

76 Gyllius, *The Antiquities of Constantinople*, p. 51 reported that the mosque was expensive. Hammer-Purgstall, *Histoire de l'Empire Ottomane*, VI, p. 88 states that it cost 700,000 ducats. Evliya, *Narrative of travels*, I, part 1, p. 80 states that the endowments included the revenues of Chios and Rhodes.

77 At Santa Severina in Calabria is the modest, two-storey chapel of Sta Filomena. Briggs in *The Legacy of Islam*, p. 157 refers to the Armenians in Spain. See also Strzygowski and Focillon.

78 Eyice, *Istanbul: petit guide*, pp. 49–52, sect. 67 gives the dates as 1550–1557. Also Yetkin, et al., *Turkish architecture*, p. 57. Hagia Sophia was built in less time, and hasty workmanship resulted in structural weaknesses and incomplete decoration. Considering the size of the Süleymaniye complex, the work was speedily done.

79 The area is said to be equal to that of the mosque precinct at Mecca. Wells were specially dug all round, but this would have been customary with all mosques. The present authorities state that the foundations go down twelve metres.

80 It is striking how much is known about Sinan in comparison with the architects who preceded him or, indeed, who followed him.

81 The dome of an imperial mosque is known as the Gök Kubbe, the blue dome, and its lead painted blue on miniatures. The association of the spiritual and the blue of the sky is very old and reflected in Selçuk times by the Gök medrese. Palladio, *The four books of architecture*, Book IV, 2. But the most beautiful and most regular forms – those from which the others receive their measures – are the round, and the quadrangular: and therefore Vitruvius only mentions these two . . .

82 Sinan also uses divisions of three in his work and ratios of two to three, as with the width and height of domes such as that of Sokollu Mehmet Pasha at Kadırga.

83 The Renaissance painted its domes, on occasion, as at the Pazzi Chapel, to represent the Universe, and Selçuks and Ottomans had always done so.

84 'Cusanus . . . visualises Him as the least tangible and at the same time the most perfect geometrical figure, the centre and circumference of the circle; for in the infinite circle or sphere, centre, diameter, and circumference are identical.' (Wittkower, *Architectural principles in the Age of Humanism*, p. 28.)

85 Ibid., p. 30 for the ideas behind Alberti's work.

86 Vogt-Göknil, *Les mosquées turques*, pp. 16-17 compares the Yeşil Cami at Bursa with the Pazzi Chapel in order to emphasize its difference from the Renaissance work. She speaks of its absolute silence but I detect this in Brunelleschi's building too. She also describes it as being excavated from a single block and with this I agree.

87 See 2037, Bibl. Nat., Paris, and ms. B., Inst. de France, Paris.

88 Coomaraswamy, 'Notes on the philosophy of Persian art', p. 127, says of the ideal of architecture that the actual form reveals the essential form, and that the proportion of the one to the other is the measure of the architect's success. This seems true of Ottoman architecture.

89 Downes, *Hawksmoor*, p. 29 says that it was through Grelot that his interest in Süleymaniye was aroused, and both Hooke and Hawksmoor collected travel books. Hooke discussed Hagia Sophia in 1677. Wren was interested in the Orient. Wren and Sinan are compared in Turkish texts. Both became architects late in life after a previous, successful career, both held similar offices under the crown, and both lived to an old age. But this is all that is pertinent.

90 Mantran, *La vie quotidienne à Constantinople*, p. 268. The first coffee houses opened in Istanbul in 1558.

91 Rose, in Brown, *The dervishes*, p. 340 et seq. says that it was first used as Kaif or quiescence of the soul. The poppy is cultivated at Afyon and in the old days was grown at Bursa. The best crop, sighirma, fetched forty francs in the nineteenth century. In Egypt it was mixed with butter but in Istanbul with syrup for smoking in a naghile. The very rich could afford to add baharab, an aromatic spice, and could thus obtain visions of paradise at great expense.

92 Evliya, *Narrative of travels*, part 1, p. 80 says nothing about drugs but that the shops were let to goldsmiths and button- and boot-makers. Keppel, *Narrative of a journey across the Balcan*, p. 75 states that by 1831 opium was forbidden and that many of these coffee houses had been ruined as a consequence. This contradicts W. Colton, *A Visit to Constantinople and Athens*, p. 78 et seq. who was in Istanbul in 1836 and who says that it was smoked overtly and was legal.

93 Özdeş, *Türk çarşıları*, p. 36. He also says that all the buildings were kept low and the square narrow in proportion so that nothing could detract from the mosque.

94 Evvel and Sani are Turkish corruptions of the Arabic, awwal and thāni. The library was founded by private benefaction in the 1920s to house the libraries from some seventy mosques in Istanbul. Inčičean, *XVIII asırda Istanbul*, p. 38 says that the medreses were for two hundred students as were those on the south side, and that the Grand Vezir was Chancellor or mütevelli of the complex. Gibb and Bowen, *Islamic society and the West*, II, p. 147 et seq. state that at first some rational sciences were taught in the medreses but that they declined into theology and law and the study of mathematics and astronomy. To get a government post it was necessary to study and teach in a medrese, and the highest posts were kept for those who had passed through the chief medreses of Istanbul. In the reign of Süleyman, members of the Ulema had been first students and then teachers in twelve schools; studies could last forty years.

95 These houses are discussed further on p. 330-1.

96 A curious feature of this school is its large drainspout.

97 Ünver, 'Süleymaniye külliyesinde' in *V.F.*, II, p. 198 says that there was one doctor and one teacher and eight students or danişmends. Accounts exist for this school, the laboratories beneath, and the hospital.

98 Ibid., pp. 197-8 Ünver says that it succoured the old, sick and insane and was staffed by two doctors, two surgeons, one chemist with two assistants, a storeman, an accountant, a secretary, six servitors and a barber under the control of the Head Physician, who was the first doctor of the realm. The Director of the Ahmediye hospital was the second. There were all sorts of patients and the insane were in a special section. The poor were also admitted and out-patients attended to. The doctors worked until noon. The patients were fed, after the personnel, in the morning and at midday. It was a very rich foundation.

99 Keppel, *Narrative of a journey across the Balcan*, p. 76 states that at the end of the row of coffee houses (which had been opium dens) is a madhouse, an appropriate appendage to such a neighbourhood, and the invariable retreat of those whose intellects have been destroyed by the use of the baneful drug. It would seem placed there as if to warn them of their fate.

100 Restoration is under consideration. The area has been cleaned up but is still overgrown and many metres deep in earth and rubble.

101 Pardoe, *The city of the Sultan*, III, p. 126 et seq. says that, thanks to Mahmut II, this asylum was clean, quiet and cheerful but that it had been once filthy and neglected until Mahmut intervened. Each cell had one or two windows and there was one for each inmate. She does add, however, that there was a clanking collar and chain for each. The main disease was melancholy. She also refers to the plane trees in the second court.

102 The figure is approximate. There are also two semi-domes and many vaults.

103 Grelot, *Relation nouvelle d'un voyage de Constantinople*, p. 274 reports that bread and soup were issued and that the dogs were also lucky for they were served in the street but from plates.

104 See p. 327.

105 Evliya, *Narrative of travels*, I, part 2, p. 229 states that there was an establishment of architects at Vefa at the factory of the Doğramcıbaşı, or Chief Carpenter, and this supports the theory that architecture and carpentry went hand in hand.

106 Gravestones for men were surmounted by a turban which showed their rank; for women by flowers. Children's steles were smaller. Where colour defined a dervish sect or some special status, the turbans appear to have been painted and there is a living tradition of tombstone painting, particularly in blue or green, and the gilding or silvering of letters. Pre-Islamic steles of Central Asia were stylized figures with faces, and the tombstones of the Ottoman period would appear to have derived from these.

107 Samanyolu, literally 'Straw Road'.

108 See p. 50.

109 Eyice, *Istanbul: petit guide*, plan.

110 Glück, *Probleme des Wölbungsbaues: die Bäder Konstantinopels*, pp. 127-31.

111 See p. 50.

112 Grelot, *Relation nouvelle d'un voyage de Constantinople*, p. 279, plan, calls this a residence for mosque officers. Gibb and Bowen, *Islamic society and the West*, I, part 2, p. 151 states that the müderris of the darül-hadis of the Süleymaniye was the highest educational officer of the capital.

113 Lorichs, *Konstantinopel unter Sultan Suleiman*, shows a high wall.

114 But Grelot, *Relation nouvelle d'un voyage de Constantinople*, states that it was a chapel in which to pray for the soul of Süleyman. If so, it is odd that the door is in the middle of the south wall where a mihrab should be.

115 Lewis, *Lewis's illustrations of Constantinople,* plate 21 shows camels and tents in the outer court.

116 The mausoleum of Olcaytu at Sultaniye dated c. 1304 had eight minarets. The four turrets of the tomb of the Samanid at Bokhara and, doubtless, earlier buildings show the idea in its initial architectural form. Olcaytu's minarets were small, corresponding to stabilizing turrets marking the corners of the octagon.

117 The measurements of these minarets are: 76 metres high. Base, 11 metres; foot, 4 metres: totalling 15 metres. Trunk to first balcony, 25 metres; to second, 7·50 metres, and again to third and to the cap: this makes a total of 47·50 metres in all for the trunk. The trunk is 4·00 metres in diameter at lower level.

118 The buttresses also contain stairs to the roof.

119 Yetkin, *et al., Turkish Architecture,* p. 59. They were entirely repaired in 1660 because in the fire of that year the caps melted like wax, see Cezar, p. 238. One minaret was severely damaged by gunfire on 16 November 1808, from a warship on the Horn when the Janissaries were firing on Topkapısaray from the balconies during a rebellion.

120 The Selçuk minaret of the Ulu Cami, Bitlis, has windows at this level. The blue tiles could be the remnant of this idea or of the glazed bricks which were still in use in the Bursa period.

121 Sinan thus removed the ritual of washing from the court for the first time in Ottoman architecture and, as has been seen, freed it from the encumbrance of a şadırvan. The lateral galleries of Şehzade were decorative; at Süleymaniye they became partly functional: Evliya, *Narrative of travels,* I, part 1, p. 76 says that these galleries were used when the mosque was full, presumably in wet weather.

122 A sundial erected by Hafiz Abdurrahman in *1186/1772* in the west wall of the courtyard should be observed. See Mayer, *Islamic astrolobists and their work,* p. 31.

123 Evliya, *Narrative of travels,* I, part 1, p. 78.

124 Ibid., p. 79. This court was so well tended in his day that the window grilles were polished.

125 Tournefort, *Relation d'un voyage du Levant,* p. 195.

126 This is a truthful architectural statement and could have been defended as such by Sinan. The silhouette looks faintly like wings.

127 Columns and capitals were extravagantly used at this period as has already been noted with the Ibrahim Pasha Hamam.

128 Porphyry is the hardest of marbles. It is about two and a quarter times as hard as granite, four times as hard as concrete, six times as hard as glass and eleven to thirty times as hard as limestone. Fissures will be noted among the famous columns in the exedras of Hagia Sophia. The bronze collars there help bind cracks or cover joints.

129 Dalloway, *Constantinople.* Melling, *Voyage pittoresque de Constantinople et des rives du Bosphore,* I, p. 102 presumably repeats Grelot.

130 *The Antiquities of Constantinople,* p. 219.

131 The legends concerning the building of this great building by now exceed the tares planted by that old liar, the Anonymous of Banduri, which obscure the fertile truth of Hagia Sophia.

132 Gebhard, 'The problem of space in Ottoman architecture' in *Art Bulletin,* XLV, 1963, pp. 272-4 states the exact contrary. For him, the upward thrust of dome and drum are not dominant spatial movements and the mihrab and minber do not create directional force. It is impossible to believe that the first reaction upon entering Süleymaniye is not to look up, or that the symbol of the mihrab is not a compelling attraction for any Moslem.

133 There is still a modestly raised area before the mihrab.

134 Sixty metres at its widest.

135 Evliya, *Narrative of travels,* I, part 1, p. 76 says that the cells in this upper part of the building were used as store-rooms for the treasure of travellers and the great. They were still so used in the nineteenth century. See Pardoe, *The city of the Sultan,* II, pp. 64-6 who calls it the National Bank.

136 Yetkin *et al., Turkish Architecture,* gives the height as 47·75 metres. Comparative figures for Hagia Sophia are exact and up-to-date due to the kindness of Mr Robert L. Van Nice whose plans of the building are unique. Instalment I of his book, *Saint Sophia in Istanbul,* contains no text. The figures are: Ground plan 72·60 metres × 69·70

metres exclusive of the apse; the dome is 56·08 metres high and the width varies between 30·90 metres and 34·70 metres.

137 Kramrisch, *The Art of India,* p. 10 et seq. points out that the art of India is neither religious nor secular, and this is also true of Ottoman art. She also states that in India the square is the leading architectural symbol, having precedence over the circle of time. Like the Ottoman mosque, the Indian temple incorporates square, circle and pyramid in a complex ground plan and superstructure.

138 In the eighteenth century, the library of the mosque was installed under the west lateral gallery behind a superb bronze grille by the Grand Vezir Mustafa Pasha for Mahmut I and it was repaired by Ahmet Vefik Pasha. See Montani, *L'architecture Ottomane,* p. 34.

139 These divisions result in interesting figures for their own sakes, perhaps because of the mystique of numbers at this period. There are seven arches under the lateral galleries for example.

140 It is also a triumph for Sinan's understanding of acoustics that there is no echo under the dome. At Üç Şerefeli, for example, the echo is very bad.

141 At Hagia Sophia, Anthemius of Tralles and Isidore of Miletus hid the problem behind the columns of the exedra. They were also helped by the gallery which follows the contours of the nave. Because there was no call for such a gallery in his mosque, Sinan could not escape the problem in this way.

142 They are now plain glass with lamp bulbs inside. Lechevalier, *Voyage de la Propontide et du Pont-Euxin,* p. 308 reported in about 1800 that there was an infinite number of little lamps made of metal.

143 Baudier, *Histoire générale du Serrail,* p. 7 states that Süleymaniye surpasses Hagia Sophia in marbles and jewels.

144 Evliya, *Narrative of travels,* I, part 1, p. 76 deems these worthy of mention as taps for refreshment.

145 Staude, 'Le Caractère turc dans l'ornementation des faïences Osmanlies' in *Syrie,* 1934, p. 376 referring also to H. Glück, 'Türkische Dekorationskunst' in *Kunst und Kunsthandwerk,* Vienna, 1920, p. 1 et seq. says that 'juxtaposition of details is the principle most important in Turkish art. Each form has equal value and each should be equally clear . . . This is true of the Süleymaniye of Sinan where the supports and the stresses are not differentiated but where each element is an equal part of the architectural unity.' The niches and the lateral arches described do not fit in with this theory.

146 The voussoirs of the Great Mosque at Cordova are painted.

147 Cezar, 'Osmanli devrinde Istanbul', p. 390.

148 From the Koran, iii, 32 as always because it is the only authority for the existence of a mihrab, though the term *mihrāb* in this Koranic passage connotes some sort of inner room and has no connexion with mosque architecture.

149 Vast as they are, they would have had to have been used sparingly to last the 350 years prior to the introduction of electric light. Candle grease, however, was collected and re-used. The lampblack from this mosque, and doubtless others, was used to make ink. Electricity has deprived the mosques of half their quality after dark. Evliya, *Narrative of travels* I, part 1, p. 76 says only that the candles were made of camphorated bees-wax and that a ladder of fifteen steps was needed to light them every night.

150 J. de Thévenot, *The Travels of M. de Thévenot into the Levant,* p.21 speaks of chained Korans in the türbe of Süleyman.

151 Sinan was aware that he worked for a prince with an exact eye, trained by a goldsmith, who would view the slipshod with horror.

152 Eyice, *Istanbul: petit guide,* p.51, sect. 67.

153 Arseven, *Les Arts décoratifs turcs,* p.184, fig. 456 shows a fragment of plaster obtained during one such redecoration. To appreciate Ottoman stained glass one should stand as far back from the window as it is high from the ground and so look up at it from an angle of forty-five degrees. At a distance, the glass of Süleymaniye is fine; seen close to from the proper angle, the richness is intensified. This is because the glass fragments are set in plaster and not in lead as they are in the West whence the Ottomans imported the glass itself. The ribs are therefore thicker and deeper, and so obscure the glass design which in this instance is of fields of flowers of paradise and geometric devices of great intricacy.

154 The Earl of Carlisle, *Diary in Turkish and Greek Waters*, p. 41 says that 'there were two mausoleums of Soleyman and the late Sultan Mahmoud, in the pattern of which I recognised a great likeness to our own of Castle Howard'.

155 *The Antiquities of Constantinople*, p. 51.

156 Alderson, *The structure of the Ottoman dynasty*, table xxx.

157 Ahmet Refik, *Istanbul hayati: 1553-1591*, p.15, sect. 3 transliterates an order of Selim II to the kadıs of Bursa, Amasya, Kastamonu and Merzifon to send qualified stonemasons immediately with their tools to build the tomb of his dead father and to be careful not to send any unqualified people. It is dated 1567. Mango, 'The conciliar edict of 1166' in D.O.P., XVII, p. 315 et seq. corroborates this conclusively. The edict was written on marble slabs and erected in Hagia Sophia. The slabs were removed in 1567 according to an eye-witness, Pigafetta, and found by Mango in the ceiling of the porch of the türbe. This throws interesting light on how building materials were noted by Ottoman architects and then re-employed when opportune. It would also suggest that Ottoman proportions were related to Byzantine. The re-use of columns makes this logical when one recalls how in the Western tradition the column width was the module of the whole building.

158 Ünver, 'Süleymaniye kulliyesinde', p. 195 says that the mosque was completed in 964/1556 while' the tabhane, tımarhane, imaret and hamam had been completed the year before; but the vakfiye of the medical school, the hostel and the hospital date from 1557. He concludes (p. 196) that 14 March 1557 is the acceptable date for the completion of the complex. Both türbes and their domes can clearly be seen in Lorichs' panorama of 1559.

159 Thévenot, *The travels of M. de Thévenot into the Levant*, p. 21 says that the turban still had two heron feathers in the seventeenth century and Gurlitt, *Die Baukunst Konstantinopels*, p.19 says that they were there at the beginning of the twentieth.

160 Thévenot, *The travels of M. de Thévenot into the Levant*, p. 21. He also mentions a carpet from Medina and lamps and candles burning.

161 Grelot, *Relation nouvelle d'un voyage de Constantinople*, p. 275.

162 Montani, *L'architecture Ottomane*, p. 52 states that they were plain glass.

163 *Güzel Sanatlar*, No. VI, Istanbul, 1949, p. 96, plate.

164 See p. 209.

165 Sanderson, *The travels of John Sanderson*, pp. 70-1. Sinan merely called it the work of a journeyman (kalfalik).

7 SINAN – THE MASTER

pages 240–283

1 Eyice, *Istanbul: petit guide*, p. 103, sect. 159, says between 1544 and 1550.

2 Konyali, *Abideleri ve kitabeleri ile Erzurum tarihi*, pp. 287-8.

3 Mordtmann, 'Eregli' in *E.I.*, II, p. 705.

4 Or perhaps the symbol of his or Rüstem's old Janissary ocak.

5 Inscription. Hammer-Purgstall, *Histoire de l'Empire Ottomane*, XVIII, p.113, gives 968/1560 as the date.

6 Inscription.

7 Basically this mosque is a square block like many other sixteenth-century examples including that of Çoban Mustafa at Gebze, and both the Mihrimah mosques.

8 Cezar, 'Osmanli devrinde Istanbul', p. 386, says that it had been damaged in the earthquake of June 1648.

9 Eyice, *Istanbul: petit guide*, p. 110, sect. 178.

10 The late-nineteenth-century interior decoration is so flamboyant that it has its own vitality, and therefore value, although it mutilates Sinan's mosque still more.

11 Yaltakaya, 'Kara Ahmet Paşa vakfiyesi' in *V.D.*, II, p. 83 et seq. Vakfiye dated 21 July 1555.

12 The mosque was completed after his death. Kara Ahmet was an Albanian. He had been Ağa of the Janissaries and Viceroy of Europe. In 1548 he had been commander-in-chief in Iran and was later to be in command in Hungary.

13 It is to be remembered that Ahmet Pasha is a much smaller mosque than the Üç Şerefeli.

14 Compare this with the use of columns by Palladio in the Redentore in Venice. Ackerman, *Palladio*, p. 137, says of the tempietto at Maser that it was motivated by the Roman conception of the wall as plastic structural mass rather than a screen at the limits of space. Here is a direct parallel with Ottoman thinking.

15 The south end of the east gallery could be partitioned off for the vezir and his family. The rest along with the west gallery may have been used for a gynaeceum.

16 Eyice, *Istanbul: petit guide*, p. 84, sect. 124.

17 Ibid. Cezar, 'Osmanli devrinde Istanbul', p. 392, says that the dome fell on 28 June 1894.

18 Hammer-Purgstall, *Histoire de l'Empire Ottomane*, XVIII, p. 29. He surely meant brother-in-law. He says that Rüstem completed the complex – which was the least he could do.

19 Ibid. He also completed the türbe of Ahmet Pasha's wife, Fatima Sultan.

20 Inscription.

21 Eyice, *Istanbul: petit guide*, p. 18, sect. 10.

22 The façade has one course of cut stone alternating with two of brick, and the cornice two rows of crisp vandyking, now restored. Lateral walls and the west end are rough stone in mortar indicating that these three sides of the building were hemmed in by houses.

23 Sanderson, *The travels of John Sanderson*, p. 76, implies that a pit existed there in the sixteenth century. In the Aslanhane he saw elephants and panthers. Lechevalier, *Voyage de la Propontide et du Pont-Euxin*, p. 228, states that at the end of the eighteenth century there were lions, tigers, panthers, wolves and foxes, not strongly caged. It was dark inside and torches were needed, which scattered sparks on the straw. This ancient church of the Chrysostomos probably burnt down.

24 Inscription.

25 Inscription.

26 The Church of the Pammacaristos, Fethiye Cami, is an obvious example in Istanbul.

27 Küçük Aya Sofya Cami.

28 Some of the more abstract are Chinese in feeling.

29 There were Persians on the roll of Palace architects.

30 Inscription. Rüstem died hated by the populace. Busbecq, *The four epistles of A.G. Busbequius concerning his Embassy into Turkey*, p. 281, says that he died of dropsy; his conferences were short and concise and he appears to have been an able minister (p. 292). However, Lybyer, *The Government of the Ottoman Empire*, p. 116, holds him responsible for setting up a tariff for the procurement of office.

31 *Istanbul: petit guide*, p. 70, sect. 100.

32 Cezar, 'Osmanli devrinde Istanbul', p. 389. The dome fell on 24 May 1719.

33 Hammer-Purgstall, *Histoire de l'Empire Ottomane*, XVIII, p. 5, says that there were two medreses.

34 In the classical period windows were used to distribute the maximum quantity of light evenly which was democratic but could be boring.

35 Gabriel, 'Les mosquées de Constantinople', p. 388.

36 Alderson, *The structure of the Ottoman dynasty*, table xxx. Ahmet Pasha was married to Mihrimah's sister.

37 Aktansel, *Istanbul Ansiklopedisi*, I, p. 440 calls him Damad Ahmed Pasha and states that the türbe was domed.

38 Inscription on stele.

39 Eyice, *Istanbul: petit guide*, p. 98, sect. 148.

40 Damascus in *Encyclopaedia Britannica*, 9th ed., VI, p. 791 says that the Tekkiye was founded by Selim I in 1516. Briggs, *Muhammedan architecture in Egypt and Palestine*, p. 136 dates it 1517 and says that it was for dervishes. Hartmann, 'Damascus' in *E.I.*, I, (1913 edition), p. 908 says Damascus was captured 24 August 1516 and that the Tekkiye was not built until 962/1554 on the site of the ruins of Kasr al-Ablak.

41 Hautecoeur and Weit, *Les mosquées du Caire*, p. 136 says that this is an Egyptian technique.

42 The pounces may have been sent from the saray studio just as they were to Iznik.

43 The large casements recall the Kara Ahmet and Rüstem Pasha mosques while the dome is truly Ottoman and not Syrian like that of the tekke. But the elaboration of their corners is identical. The mosque is faced in striped marble, whereas the tekke is only of stone. It is obvious that, although local men were employed, for craftsmen were valuable and hard to find, wherever the Ottoman Empire extended, its architectural style extended also and the overall plan was distinctly Ottoman and not local. To a certain extent, this is true of the Adliye mosque at Aleppo and the citadel at Niş just as it is of the mosque of Sinan Pasha at Cairo. The details were another matter.

44 Only the voussoirs of the other buildings alternate and thus the striped paving is united with the mosque of which it is an extension.

45 Today there is no ventilator, only tall ocak chimneys, because the domes have been brutally restored in concrete.

46 Damascus had an architectural establishment and the mosques of the pashas appear to have been built by local men and are much less Ottoman in plan than the tekkes. Sinan surely sent an important assistant to carry out the royal commission; he had seventeen to select from. See Turan, 'Gli architetti imperiali nell'Impero Ottomano', p. 260.

47 See p. 303.

48 The mosque of Kara Mustafa is modest but his cloth market was of grand dimensions, see Lewis, 'A Karaite Itinerary through Turkey' in *V.D.*, III, p. 321.

49 He strangled Mahmut Sultan at Amasya.

50 Eyice, *Istanbul: petit guide*, p. 99, sect. 151.

51 'Les mosquées de Constantinople', p. 388.

52 *Istanbul camileri*, I, p. 157.

53 Sumner-Boyd, *The Seven Hills of Istanbul*. This work is still in manuscript, but Professor Boyd has kindly given me access to it.

54 It has a delightful minaret, now completely restored, without a şerefe but with a lantern of open arches instead. This belongs to the minaret-minber type and was rare in the sixteenth century. Other examples of the period are the Atta Halil Mescit and Kücük Piyale Pasha. Much taller is the minaret of Sinan's own mescit which, with a wall and a çeşme, is all that still stands of his modest complex. A seventeenth-century example is the Melek Hatun Mescit, and eighteenth-century examples include the Beşir Ağa Mescit in Topkapisaray which is related to the little minaret of Timurtaş Ağa (see p. 109), the oldest of the type remaining in Istanbul, and the Dervish Ali Mescit. A very late example is the nineteenth-century minaret of the Arpacılar Mescit which simply has a balcony.

55 They have pretty lead caps very similar to those of the same period elsewhere such as the Tudor turrets of Hampton Court, the Tower of London, or Hatfield House.

56 Eyice, *Istanbul: petit guide*, p. 99, sect. 151.

57 Something of this effect occurs at Kılıç Ali Pasha and at Azapkapı.

58 Eyice, *Istanbul: petit guide*, pp. 67-8, sect. 97, states that the mosque may be Sinan's.

59 See p. 287.

60 See p. 277.

61 Aslanapa, *Edirne'de Osmanlı devri abîdeleri*, p. 52 states that they are 70·89 metres high. Çetintaş, 'Minarelerimiz' in *Güzel Sanatlar*, IV p. 72 also gives this figure which exceeds 80 metres when the cap is included, 82·90 metres to be exact. The diameter is given as 3·80 metres. Sanderson, *The travels of John Sanderson*, p. 71 states that Selim II built his mosque at Edirne for want of space in Istanbul. Gökbilgin, 'Edirne', in *E.I.*, II, 1965, p. 685 says that the mosque was paid for out of the booty of Cyprus.

62 Aslanapa, *Edirne'de Osmanlı devri abîdeleri*, p. 34 gives 31·28 metres as the width of this dome. The height is disputed but 42 metres is an acceptable estimate.

63 Ibid., p. 32. 976-982 of the Hegira. Ahmet Refik, *Türk Mimarları*, p. 87, sect. 21 reports the dome finished, and sect. 28 shows all work complete on 16 Recep, 982.

64 Selimiye can be seen as the ultimate descendant of SS Sergius and Bacchus which had octagonal supports, galleries cut off from the central area when seen from below yet spacious above, and a deep apse.

65 When the mosque is empty in winter the music of the fountain is as much a delight as that of the garden court of the church of Santissimi Quattro Coronati in Rome.

66 Ahmet Refik, *Türk mimarları*, pp. 83-4, sect. 16 gives an order in council sending Hattat Molla Hasan to Edirne to be shown where he is to make inscriptions in various styles of calligraphy. Those on the plaster walls today are nineteenth-century as are those in the dome.

67 They date from 982/1574 and are fully discussed in Sakisian, 'Les faïences du bain de Selim II au harem du Vieux Sérail'. The baths have been demolished, unfortunately, since with a central cage for the sultan they were unusual in design. The hamam was completed in November, 1574 and Selim II had his fatal fall there a month later.

68 The Altin Yolu, which is the thoroughfare of the harem and selâmlık, from which they are now removed.

69 They attracted the attention of the Russians when they took Edirne in 1878, for a panel was removed to the Leningrad Museum.

70 Gemelli-Careri, *Voyage du tour du monde*, p. 263 says that the dome and subsidiary domes were full of inscriptions. He also reports five iron wheels from which hung innumerable lamps.

71 The precinct measures 132m. × 190m. (432′ × 628′), the courtyard 46m. × 60m. (148′ × 196′), the interior without apse or gallery area is 41·5m. × 47m. (128′ × 152′) and with apse and gallery is 49m. × 53·5m. (160′ × 172′). These measurements are my own and only approximate.

72 When it rains at Edirne, and it does, these gutters project waste water with a force that sends it three metres clear of the foundations.

73 Materials were collected from far and wide for this mosque. Sanderson, *The travels of John Sanderson*, p. 76, says four columns in the Hippodrome near the Brass Pillar with their capitals and bases were sent to Edirne.

74 It has been extensively restored recently.

75 Turan, 'Gli architetti imperiali nell'Impero Ottomano', p. 260. Ahmet Refik, *Türk Mimarları*, p. 114, sect. 46, orders Sinan to estimate the cost of repair due to damage by lightning. Ibid., pp. 115-16, sect. 48, orders that Yörüks, Gypsies and Canbaz be put to work on the building. In 1967 the south-west minaret, which was out of alignment, was rebuilt.

76 Ibid., pp. 96-7, sect. 28, states that work was completed on the Selimiye 16 Recep, 982/1574. It was, as Sinan said, his masterpiece (ustalik).

77 Tavaş Mesih Pasha appears to have been taken from the kiler class of the Enderun college to be Governor of Egypt. Hammer-Purgstall, *Histoire de l'Empire Ottomane*, VII, p. 165, says that he was a eunuch.

78 Inscription.

79 Erdogan, 'Mimar Davut Ağa'nın hayatı ve eserleri' in *Türkiyat Mecmuası*, XII, 1955, p. 187.

80 This mosque and that of Nişancı Mehmet Pasha are rivals for the claim to be the first vezir's mosque to have an arcaded avlu.

81 Hammer-Purgstall, *Histoire de l'Empire Ottomane*, VII, p. 63.

82 He was known as Şahin or Falcon, thus combining in a word his nose, his piercing glance, his family emblem, his first office of state, his swift mind and regal bearing in a way few nicknames succeed in doing.

83 Alderson, *The structure of the Ottoman dynasty*, table XXXI. Allen, *Problems of Turkish power in the 16th century*, p. 60, n. 53, says that she was forty years his junior, small and very ugly. He was born in 1505, she in 1545.

84 Inscription.

85 The dome is approximately 25·5 × 14·5 metres high; a proportion of three to two frequently used by Sinan.

86 Grosvenor, *Constantinople*, II, p. 419, in 1881.

87 Turan, 'Gli architetti imperiali nell'Impero Ottomano', p. 260, states that Sinan went on the Hajj.

88 Whereas at Rüstem Pasha the panels hang like rugs, tiles for tiles' sake, and so are unrelated to the structure but merely a cladding for it.

89 The stairway enhances the height of the mosque when one is ascending from street level.

90 Gabriel, 'Les mosquées de Constantinople', pp. 394-5, says that these tiles do not appear to belong to the original construction, perhaps because they look as if set into the arch above the casement, an impression also given inside. This effect occurs in other mosques and it would look as if the indication of the arch form was deliberately retained. The panels are exact in their measurements in relation to width and, as at Bozüyük, draw attention to the standardization of measurements. I am indebted to Mr Özer Kabaş for pointing out the effect on domestic architecture of standard lengths of timber.

91 See p. 175.

92 Alderson, *The structure of the Ottoman dynasty*, table XXXI, says that he was the son of Abdurrahman, which would suggest that he had been a devşirme. Hammer-Purgstall, *Histoire de l'Empire Ottomane*, VII, p. 58, says that he was the son of a Hungarian shoemaker.

93 Ibid., p. 193 et seq.

94 At the Enderun College.

95 Inscription.

96 Alderson, *The structure of the Ottoman dynasty*, chart XXXI.

97 Dwight, *Constantinople, old and new*, pp. 103-4, says it closed in 1846.

98 Evliya, *Narrative of travels*, I, part 2, p. 43. He also says that twelve thousand prisoners were employed on the building. However, on p. 45 he says that the mosque has twelve domes.

99 Ibid., p. 45. Evliya attributes the inscription over the door to Karahisarı. It reads, 'Salutations to ye who are good; enter it and remain there for ever'.

100 The tile lunettes from the interior windows, stolen by M. Bapst, are now in Cologne, Lisbon, Paris and Boston. Together with the theft of the panel of the revak of the Selim II türbe, they rank as the major Western desecrations of Ottoman art. The inscription is in Naskhi and quotes the 62nd and 112th suras of the Koran. It is by Çerkeş Hasan Çelebi, a Circassian pupil of Karahisarı Ahmet Efendi. Martigay, 'Die Piyale Pasha Moschee' in *A.I.*, I, p. 31 et seq. But the Hadika attributes them to Karahisarı himself, see Hammer-Purgstall, *Histoire de l'Empire Ottomane*, XVIII, p. 70.

101 If it has significance, this has been forgotten. The myth that the mosque was built to look like a ship is untrue unless it was meant to resemble an aircraft carrier.

102 They do occur. There is one in the east porch of Mihrimah at Edirnekapı and the open türbe of the Defterdar Cami on the road to Eyüp. This mosque was built by Sinan but is in bad repair. They are also inset under the gallery of the Muradiye at Manisa.

103 An old recipe for Ottoman mortar is made up of one part sand, two parts wood ashes, and three of lime beaten well together with wooden mallets and sprinkled frequently with oil and water until of the required consistency. For joining boards together, they also used an ancient composition consisting of a preparation of cheese and fine lime which, when properly mixed and quickly applied, renders the joints inseparable even by moisture.

104 Hammer-Purgstall, *Histoire de l'Empire Ottomane*, XVIII, p. 70.

105 The Pilgrim Butcher Evhat.

106 Eyice, *Istanbul: petit guide*, p. 94, sect. 143. He also mentions the lost tiles of the façade. Inscription.

107 Ibid.

108 Öz, *Istanbul camileri*, I., p. 64. He erroneously dates the mosque 1575.

109 Hammer-Purgstall, *Histoire de l'Empire Ottomane*, XVIII, p. 70.

110 It awaits the detailed publication of the researches of Mr Robert Van Nice.

111 Ahmet Refik, *Istanbul hayatı, on altıncı asırda (1553-1591)*, p. 21, sect. 14 gives an order to Mehmet (Ağa) to repair the foundation footings of Hagia Sophia and to replace wood superstructures with stone, while the wooden minaret was to be rebuilt in brick. Ibid., p. 22, sect. 18 reports the order to remove the redundant houses round the mosque and punish those making use of the building. It also covers the report of Mehmet who had enlisted Sinan's help in surveying the mosque, stating that the minaret on the half-dome should be removed and a new one built, that a buttress was needed, and that the building should be cleaned inside and out. He also reported that the squatters round the mosque were to be expelled by a fetva or edict issued by the Seyhül-Islam.

112 Van Nice and Emerson, 'Hagia Sophia and the first minaret erected after the conquest of Istanbul', pp. 39-40.

113 Eyice, *Istanbul: petit guide*, p. 99, sect. 149 gives no date.

114 Inscription on tombstone. It was the year of his death.

115 From Şams, or the Sun which replaces the moon on the alem of this mosque by way of allusion.

116 Allen, *Problems of Turkish power in the 16th century*, pp. 27-9 says that Sokollu's unpopularity stemmed partly from his Eastern policy of expansion into Russia.

117 Inscription.

118 There is a pleasant myth that this mosque was built by Süleyman for his daughter Mihrimah when she was a child as a superior dollshouse. They were both dead in 1580.

8   THE POWERS DECLINE

pages 284–333

1 Eyice, *Istanbul: petit guide*, p. 101, sect. 155.

2 Eyice, 'Istanbul minareleri', p. 72 gives the date 1826 for this minaret, but Evliya, *Narrative of travels*, I, part 2, p. 51 states that it was already detached in his time. It probably always stood where it does and was rebuilt on its original foundation.

3 Walsh, *Constantinople and the Scenery of the Seven Churches of Asia Minor*, II, p. 58, plate.

4 Eyice, *Istanbul: petit guide*, p. 106, sect. 165 gives 1580 as the date of completion. Ahmet Refik, *Istanbul hayatı, on altıncı asırda (1553-1591)*, pp. 26-8, sections 22, 25 and 27 shows that work on the complex continued until 1583 at least. The first of these orders, dated 986/1578, states that iron is to be sent to Tophane so that work may start. It is possible but unlikely that Ahmet Refik mistranscribed the date. No. 25 requires financial support for the mosque from the guild of butchers, an interesting sidelight on how funds were raised for such projects.

5 Kılıç Ali was born in Calabria, taken prisoner at the age of twenty and a galley slave for fourteen years. His brilliance as a naval commander was balanced by his mild disposition towards his three thousand slaves who were treated well, as is attested by Cervantes who was his prisoner. Until he became Governor-General of Algiers it had been the practice to cut off the ears of galley slaves, hang them, or impale them. Yet he was unkindly called Fartax or the Scabby Renegade. Also he had favourites like Azan Ağa who began his successful career in the Ottoman navy as Kılıç Ali's cabin boy. Kılıç succeeded Piyale as Grand Admiral in 1571 when the latter was disgraced after Querini's relief of Famagusta. It was then that he changed his name from Uluç to Kılıç Ali. In 1573 he raided Puglia and burnt Cesto. Perhaps the loot of these towns helped pay for his mosque.

6 Evliya, *Narrative of travels*, I, part 2, p. 58 makes a point of this likeness and so do most of the travellers.

7 The court has been altered by the widening of the road, and the shops in front of the mosque have been lost. Some of the fine trees survive.

8 But not quite. The portico is inset in its own wall, a frequent Ottoman recourse. As at Zal Mahmut, there are double windows in the three main walls, one on two of the subsidiary walls, leaving the other two walls blind. Inside, the inner dome is supported on four columns and the outer by the walls, thus creating a vaulted ambulatory round the sarcophagus.

9 She was an Italian of the Basso family and a commanding personality. See Alderson, *The structure of the Ottoman dynasty*, table xxxi. Ahmet Refik, *Istanbul hayatı, on altıncı asırda (1553-1591)*, p. 21, sect. 15 dated 978/1570, which is surprisingly early, orders marble for this mosque from the kadıs of Iznik and Sapanca to be taken from old buildings in their district. They were also to supply lime and timber and defray the costs of transportation. There appears to have been friction with the locals over the requisitioning of marble. Ibid., p. 115, sect. 23, an order dated 983/1575 concerns the supply of the mumhane

or candle shop and the debbakhane or tannery with fat and skins of sheep from the royal kitchen. Presumably, these enterprises were to help support the mosque.

10 Hammer-Purgstall, *Histoire de l'Empire Ottomane*, XVIII, pp. 89–90.

11 It would therefore appear that the complex took thirteen years to build. See n. 9, above.

12 There is a huge symbolical arrow in Beyazit Cami in Istanbul and a bow hung on the balustrade of the minber of the Ulu Cami at Birgi.

13 There is an early example of a hospital and tekke combined at Çankırı.

14 Öz, *Istanbul camileri*, II, pp. 24–5 dates it as late as 1589. Hammer-Purgstall, *Histoire de l'Empire Ottomane*, XVIII, p. 79 merely gives this as the date of his death. Both works are drawn directly from the Hadika.

15 Ibid., XVIII, p. 12. Öz, *Istanbul camileri*, I, p. 116. Popularly known as Ramazan Efendi, the mosque's correct name is Bezirgân Mescit. Ramazan Efendi was the first Şeyh of the tekke which was founded by Hüsrev Ağa whose name is almost forgotten. Perhaps he was a friend of Sinan and Sâi Çelebi.

16 See p. 165.

17 It probably had a wooden cupola under a tile roof like Takkeci İbrahim Cami. There are traces of the former triple-domed portico. The tekke once had thirteen cells.

18 Heyd, *Ottoman documents on Palestine*, XXVIII, no. 101, p. 156 gives 986/1574; either August or October, unclear. It states that iron, steel, lead, copper and first-rate marble (LIII, no. 367 also mentions kaşi – glazed tiles) brought with government funds for the repair of the Aksa Mosque and Dome of the Rock have been stored in Jerusalem since the days of Sultan Süleyman (d. 1566). The inspector (nazir) in charge of this material gave some of the timbers to Süleyman, ex-Bey of Jerusalem, who used it for the construction of his house. Doc. 16, p. 62 states that this bey was notorious and accused of various illegal and atrocious acts including the killing of many moslems. An enquiry was ordered on 15 May 1576. LXI, nos. 256 and 298, dated 994/1586-995/1587 state that one reason for the delay in carrying out the repairs may have been the shortage of builders, stone cutters, carpenters and other skilled workers in Jerusalem; such people had to be sent from Damascus. P. 157, no. 2, XXXIX, nos. 33 and 103, 987/Dec. 1579. An order to the Defterdar of Damascus and Beylerbey of Tripoli says the lead of the Dome of the Rock and Aksa mosques is in need of repair which is to cost six thousand florins. But Zi'amat-Idden Da'ud who is chief architect (mimarbaşı) at Damascus is prepared to undertake the work for two hundred gold pieces, which indicates a major repair to the lead of the domes. Part of the lead that had been sent from Istanbul to Tripoli for the repair of these mosques and the Umayyid mosque at Damascus is to be transported to Jerusalem and to be delivered to the above-mentioned Da'ud. It would look, therefore, as if Murat III deserves the actual credit for repairing the Dome of the Rock whatever his grandfather's intention may have been. Da'ud could be the architect of the two pasha's mosques in Damascus.

19 Ikram, *Muslim civilization in India*, p. 245 et seq. says that Babur summoned students of Sinan to Fathipur Sikri in the 1560s and that although the architecture of the Taj Mahal is Iranian and Usta Isa came of a Shiraz family settled in Lahore, Ismail Han Rumi from Constantinople appears to have built the dome. Arseven, *L'art turc depuis son origine jusqu'à nos jours*, says that Sinan's favourite pupil, Yusuf, was sent to India at the request of Babar.

20 In the Topkapısaray collection.

21 The difference in rank of a patron could have made a difference quite apart from questions of personality and sensitivity.

22 See p. 222. Begun probably in 1566, it was completed in 975/1567. The bridge is inscribed with the name of the ameli (builder), Yusuf bin Abdullah. The inscription mentions both Süleyman and Selim II. It is signed by Dervish Mehmet.

23 Aslanapa, *Edirne'de Osmanlı devri abîdeleri*, p. 134, says that it is also known as the Ayşe Kadın Han because of the mosque beside it.

24 See Busbecq, *The four epistles of A. G. Busbequius concerning his Embassy into Turkey*, p. 26 et seq. For a description of the similar kervansaray at Niş, see n. 27 below.

25 Özdes, *Türk çarşıları*, p. 55.

26 Covel, 'Extracts from the diaries of Jo. Covel (1670–9)' in J. T. Brent (ed.), *Early voyages and travels in the Levant*, praises the fine mosque and says that the han could lodge one thousand men with their beasts nearby.

27 Busbecq, *The four epistles of A. G. Busbequius concerning his Embassy into Turkey*, pp. 26–8, describing the kervansaray at Niş, says that it was longer than wide and had a yard for carriages, wagons and mules, surrounded by a wall which was three feet high and four feet broad. Here were ocaks for cooking and room for the traveller to spread his saddle cloth for a mattress and place his saddle as a pillow, and the animals were fed from their master's hand. There were several distinct rooms for high officers who lodged as well as they would in a palace. Guests could receive three days' victuals and Busbecq particularly praises a mess of meat and honey. The stables had hearths, and shepherds and flocks shared the same room. Elsewhere, he found the houses so small that he could not get his bed inside and he preferred to lodge in hospitals instead.

28 Inscription. The sultan died before the complex was completed. Payas was badly damaged during the suppression of a rebellious Derebey early in the nineteenth century. Kinneir, *Journey through Asia Minor, Armenia, and Koordistan in the years 1813–14*, pp. 136–7, says Payas had a handsome medrese with a fine fountain in the court and gilded inscriptions. It had been abandoned by the dervishes, so a local ağa had taken up residence there, for it was the only habitable place in the recently ruined, abandoned town.

29 Heyd, *Oriental documents on Palestine*, p. 104 says it was garrisoned by ten foot-soldiers, usually Janissaries, and forty mounted musketeers.

30 Inscription.

31 Where shepherds and flocks slept together in the stable.

32 Sauvaget, 'Les caravansérails Syriens du Hadjdj de Constantinople' in *A.I.*, IV, p. 120.

33 Also used as latrines.

34 See p. 87.

35 Op. cit., p. 111.

36 Gabriel, *Voyages archéologiques dans la Turquie Orientale*, p. 239. He refers in n. 2 to Lynch, *Armenia, travels and studies*, II, p. 155, who describes a han with two snarling lions each side of a fine doorway. Gabriel could not find the building which, however, sounds very much like a now ruined han in Muş.

37 Inscription. Tekin, *Fotograflarla Diyarbakır*, p. 10. Badger, *The Nestorians and their ritual*, says that the han was damaged partly by use as a barrack. Hans in the eastern provinces are still so used.

38 Tekin, *Fotograflarla Diyarbakır*, p. 11. Gabriel, *Voyages archéologiques dans la Turquie Orientale*, p. 203 dates this han as either sixteenth- or seventeenth-century because of the lack of an inscription. Local tradition gives 934/1527.

39 See p. 108.

40 See p. 213.

41 Inscription.

42 Inscription.

43 See p. 257.

44 Egli, *Sinan, der Baumeister osmanischer Glanzzeit*, p. 125 suggests a period between 1561 and 1565 for this mosque and gives the same dates for his mosque at Ereğli, which is also by Sinan. This is because these were the years when Ali Pasha was Grand Vezir. He also built a medrese for the complex, a market and a kervansaray at Edirne and another at the Bitpazar at Istanbul, each of which appears on the Tezkere.

45 See p. 244.

46 The room over the gate has been lost and the şadırvan badly restored.

47 See p. 257.

48 According to the board outside.

49 Inscription. It is a long one and set west of the north door instead of over it. The inscription on the mihrab is dated a year earlier. A problem is why Lala Mustafa built in Erzerum at this late date when he was Beylerbey from 1540–2.

50 Various inscriptions in the mosque testify to repairs, including one in 1268/1851.

51 Konyali, *Abideleri ve kitabeleri ile Erzurum tarihi*, pp. 231-2 argues that this is a precaution in a district where earthquakes are frequent.

52 The mosque of Kara Ahmet Pasha at Topkapı has its minaret inset but without the ugly protuberance.

53 Inscription. The calligraphy of the Erzerum inscriptions at this period was closely knit and rich in texture.

54 Gabriel, *Voyages archéologiques dans la Turquie Orientale*, p. 250.

55 Ibid., p. 251.

56 Among other similarities, because of the cutting of stone blocks, the plan of the portico and the design of the minaret.

57 Inscription.

58 The minaret of the Artukoğulları (Ortokid) Ulu Cami dating from the twelfth century has a much simpler base but the same thick trunk divided by two bands and supporting an unusual lantern above the gallery. It would appear to be the precursor of this type of minaret, but it is later than the foundation of the mosque.

59 Gabriel, *Voyages archéologiques dans la Turquie Orientale*, p. 200.

60 Inscription.

61 Inscription.

62 Major repairs were carried out in 1756, 1868 and 1915 and after the earthquake of 26-27 November 1943, when the minaret and two domes of the west portico collapsed.

63 See p. 000.

64 Briggs, *Muhammadan architecture in Egypt and Palestine*, p. 138. Hautecoeur and Weit, *Les mosquées du Caire*, p. 352.

65 From the Halil mausoleum – in a crude form – to the turrets of the Hasan Medrese dome, this was a feature already existing in Cairo but previously less elaborately expressed. In terms of Sinan it is related to the stabilizing turrets serving as buttresses at the Selimiye and common with late sixteenth-century mosques in Istanbul.

66 Hartman, 'Damascus' in *E.I.*, I, p. 908. Elisséeff, 'Dimashk' in *E.I.*, II, p. 287 gives the date of Dervish Pasha as 981/1574.

67 Like that of Melek Ahmet Pasha, Diyarbakır.

68 The architecture of Diyarbakır recalls the parallel use of vividly contrasting black and white stripes at Siena and elsewhere in Italy.

69 Feher, 'Macristan'da Türk mimarı eserleri' in *Akademi*, V, March, 1966, pp. 50-1.

70 Mayer, *Islamic architects and their works*, attributes this to Hayrettin Mimar, 974/1566-7. Sinan ordered him to build fortifications at Makarska the following year. Ayverdi, 'Yugoslavya'da Türk âbideleri de vakıfları', p. 190 confirms this and gives the date as between 965/1557-974/1566.

71 Ibid., p. 180.

72 Inscription.

73 Gabriel, *Les monuments turcs d'Anatolie*, II, p. 92, n. 1 states that Halil Ethem believed this Ali Pasha to be a descendant of Eretna, the Mongol overlord of this area in the fourteenth century. He may have been related to the Ottoman house by marriage and also may have been executed by Selim II.

74 The inserting of the stair in the wall was a common practice which produces a natural pattern. It can be seen at the Ibrahim Bey Imaret at Karaman, the Dış Cami outside Niğde (ill. 314) with approximately two rings of yellow stone to one of black alternately, and the Sara Hatun Cami at Harput; different coloured rings occur in lavish profusion at Samarkand and Bokhara. The Eski Alaca Cami, also at Harput, has a minaret with a shaft of alternating black and white rings and a chequerboard effect above the gallery.

75 Chronogram. Gabriel, *Les monuments turcs d'Anatolie*, I, pp. 56-7. Egli, *Sinan, der Baumeister osmanischer Glanzzeit*, p. 102 gives the date as 989/1581.

76 See p. 158.

77 Murat was half Italian by his mother who was a cousin of the victor of Lepanto, Admiral Vernier. He married the Italian Safiye Baffo who was a strong character. She corresponded with Elizabeth of England with whom she exchanged magnificent gifts. Murat had blue eyes and a red beard like his half-Russian father, Selim II, and was slightly built but strong, to which over forty children testify. It is said that he was a good judge of character. See Allen, *Problems of Turkish power in the 16th century*, p. 74.

78 'Muradiye Cami' in *Türkiye Ansiklopedisi*, IV, Ankara, 1957, p. 235. Konyali, *Mimar Koca Sinan. Vakfiyyeleri, hayır eserleri, hayatı*, p. 160 says that Sinan went on the pilgrimage in 992/1584 although he gives the Christian year as 1586.

79 Ibid. Also, Ahmet Refik, *Türk mimarları*, p. 118, sect. 51 publishes the order that replaced the dead Mahmut with Mehmet. The assumption that this Mehmet may be Mehmet Ağa is reasonable. Mayer, *Islamic architects and their works*, pp. 85 and 89 is uncertain.

80 Meyer-Riefstahl, *Turkish architecture in Southwestern Anatolia*, p. 17 quotes the inscription which gives the date 991/1583 for when it was begun. Egli, *Sinan, der Baumeister osmanischer Glanzzeit*, p. 107 gives 1586.

81 Ahmet Refik, quoted in 'Manisa' in *Türkiye Ansiklopedisi*, IV, p. 235, says that this kütüphane or kitabevi was built before the mosque. It is of rubble and in too poor a state to suggest a firm date.

82 *Turkish architecture in Southwestern Anatolia*, p. 22. This may be due to Chandler, *Travels in Asia Minor*, pp. 207-9 who says that Murat III built a türbe, tekke and timarhane at Manisa. He further says that the saray was plundered in 1633. I am inclined to believe that Chandler was confusing Murat III with Murat II whose monuments at Manisa are lost. See Minorsky, 'Manisa' in *E.I.*, III, p. 246.

83 Meyer-Riefstahl, *Turkish architecture in Southwestern Anatolia*, p. 21 suggests that this work has Selçuk influences and compares them with the door knocker designed by Al Cezari for the palace gate at Diyarbakır.

84 These openwork screens, which are so important because they moderate the strong light which would otherwise flood the interior, have already been noted in such later sixteenth-century mosques as Rüstem Pasha, Mesih Pasha, Azapkapı and Kılıç Ali Pasha.

85 Those under the other gallery are also good. Their paintwork is finer than that at Sokollu Mehmet Pasha and far excels that of Kılıç Ali. Meyer-Riefstahl, p. 20, reports that before the mosque of Rüstem Pasha was barbarously painted brown and that of Takkeci Ibrahim green their paint was of this quality.

86 See p. 325.

87 It has been purged of the nineteenth-century vulgar fake marbling.

88 Miller, *Beyond the Sublime Porte*, p. 105.

89 Cezar, 'Osmanli devrinde Istanbul', pp. 333-4.

90 Ibid., p. 342.

91 Inscription, 1078/1667.

92 Eyice, *Istanbul: petit guide*, p. 6, sect. 1. Hünkâr sofası, Divan yeri, or Muayede yeri.

93 Inscription, 1077/1666.

94 Inscription, 987/1579.

95 Lybyer, *The Government of the Ottoman Empire*, p. 243 says that two pages with torches guarded the sultan at night and two dressed him each morning. Public as life was in those days, one supposes that these young men sometimes stayed outside in the anteroom.

96 Since Mehmet III does not appear to have altered much at the saray. Ahmet I spared the life of his brother but kept him a prisoner on his accession and it would seem likely, therefore, that he would have constructed a special apartment for this brother.

97 *Topkapı Sarayı müzesi*, p. 21.

98 Miller, *Beyond the Sublime Porte*, p. 76, says the mescit was called the Winter Chamber and that the sultan slept there on occasion.

99 See p. 181.

100 Sanderson, *The travels of John Sanderson*, p. 72 states that Murat III built more of the saray than all his predecessors. Rosedale, *Queen Elizabeth and the Levant company*, p. 22, says that Murat III did a great deal to the interior of the palace, more than all the kings preceding him had carried out. He ordered it with state rooms, baths, and fountains, porticoes and loggias and gardens, and decorated it with gilding and with royal magnificence.

101 And Rome before her.

102 But only two or three feet deep.

103 It is natural that the lascivious side of harem life should be over-emphasized, but it must be remembered that the girls were students, just as were the pages, and that they were trained to be the wives of officials graduating from the Enderun College to whom they were

married upon leaving at the age of twenty-five. See Lybyer, *The Government of the Ottoman Empire*, p. 79.

104 Evliya, *Narrative of travels*, I, part 1, p. 175, still calls it his saray in the mid-seventeenth century.

105 The gate probably gave the name of the Porte to the government or more particularly the Foreign Ministry from this period, but it could also be confused with the Topkapısaray gate, the Sublime Porte, and was a controversial subject even in the nineteenth century, see Elliott, *Travels in the three great empires*, p. 191. Ramberti, in his appendix to Lybyer, *The Government of the Ottoman Empire*, p. 243, says that Topkapısaray was called the Porte. The Baron de Tott, *Mémoires du Baron de Tott sur les Turcs et les Tartares*, I, p. 143, n, says that the gate of the first minister was so called.

106 Inscription.

107 There is limitless fine limestone in Anatolia, especially round Niğde. The problem was one of transportation.

108 Lybyer, *The Government of the Ottoman Empire*, p. 164.

109 Ibid., p. 58, n. 4 quotes a number of sources for 1537 listing slave households of 600 for Ayas Pasha, 150 for Kasim Pasha, and 100 for Barbaros. Another list gives Ibrahim 1,500 slaves in 1526 which is just credible; but a third is not, for it says that in 1534 he had 6,000, Ayas Pasha had 200 and Kasim Pasha had 1,500 which is certainly an exaggeration.

110 Ibid., p. 234 quoting Spandugno.

111 Ahmet Refik, *Istanbul hayatı, hicrî onbirinci asırda (1000–1100)*, p. 36, sect. 70. *1022/1613*.

112 Ibid., p. 9, sect. 17.

113 See p. 191.

114 *The Antiquities of Constantinople*, p. 40.

115 Evliya, *Narrative of travels*, I, part 2, p. 103.

116 See p. 86.

117 Özdeş, *Türk çarşıları*, p. 76a.

118 Ibid., p. 13, plan.

119 Gyllius, *The Antiquities of Constantinople*, p. 49.

120 Özdeş, *Türk çarşıları*, p. 35.

121 Emler, 'Topkapı Sarayı restorasyon çalışmaları' in *Türk San'atı Tarihi Araştırma ve İncelemeleri*, p. 227, who also reports on the excellence of the water and drainage system at Topkapısaray which consists of large cisterns underground and stone conduits. Hot water was supplied from huge copper cauldrons which were kept boiling on big ranges.

122 Recent work on the underpass has revealed that the ground level has risen and obscures the first fourteen feet of the piers of this aqueduct.

123 Dalman, *Der Valens-Aquädukt in Konstantinopel*, Bamberg, 1933, pp. 49-50. Sanderson, *The travels of John Sanderson*, pp. 78-9, has much praise for Süleyman's waterworks.

124 Toy, 'The Aqueducts of Constantinople' in *Journal of the Royal Institute of British Architects*, 24.11.1928, p. 49 et seq.

125 I have not heard of any elsewhere.

126 Examples include Ahmet Refik, *Istanbul hayatı, on altıncı asırda 1553–1591*, p. 14, sect. 1, an order of 1558 on checking the tank of the waterways of Süleymaniye; this was addressed to the Kadı, the treasurer of the foundation, and the architect. A long order of 1577, p. 25, sect. 20, accuses the present and former Masters of the Waterways of taking bribes and letting the rich and the hamam owners tap the Kağıthane stream to the deprivation of the fountains of the villagers. Even the Chief Justice of Asia had tapped water for a fountain of his own. The Kadı of Istanbul, the Treasurer, and Sinan had to investigate. The Master of the Waterways who had succeeded one Hasan was Davut Ağa, soon to be Architect of the Empire in succession to Sinan. Sinan was himself accused in the same year, see p. 201. A special order allowed the Kızlarağa to tap the water of the Süleymaniye imaret for his fountain near the Beyazit Mosque in 1585, see p. 29, sect. 29; and p. 30, sect. 31, dated the same year (1585) is an order to Sinan and Davut Ağa, still Master of the Waterways, to inspect the waterworks of the Süleymaniye and the Şehzade as a result of this permission. Hasan Ağa, the Master under Selim II, appears to have been a bad lot or else very lax.

127 Sayılı, *The Observatory in Islām*, p. 289 et seq.

128 There was a sub-office of the architects' department at Süleymaniye which may have had lodging for officials. The türbe was restored in 1922, see Konyalı, *Sinan*, p. 126.

129 See p. 222.

130 Villagers still paint stone from time to time; for example, in the Digor region near Kars.

9 PRELUDE TO CHANGE

pages 334–379

1 Whose grand türbe at Eyüp (discussed on page 282) and beautiful hunting lodge Davut Ağa may have built. Davut Ağa may have been appointed simply because of seniority.

2 *Istanbul: petit guide*, p. 74, sect. 106.

3 Erdoğan, 'Mimar Davut Ağa'nin hayatı ve eserleri', p. 187.

4 Boyalı Mehmet Pasha died in 1592 after holding various second-grade posts and escaping the burdens of the highest office. Boyalı (painted) implies that he was of perverted tastes; but he had a son who was Kadı or Eyüp, Mehmet Nutki. When he died in 1648 he was buried in his father's türbe nearby.

5 'Mimar Davut Ağa'nin hayatı ve eserleri', p. 187. Begun 992/1584.

6 It would be pleasant to discover who the architect really was because this mosque is certainly a masterpiece.

7 Eyice, *Istanbul: petit guide*, p. 74, sect. 107 says that it was completed in 996/1588.

8 Evliya, *Narrative of travels*, I, part 1, p. 169 says that it was built in an elegant style like those of the sultan.

9 Eyice, *Istanbul: petit guide*, p. 74, sect. 107, says that two major restorations were carried out in 1766 and 1835.

10 Sanderson, *The Travels of John Sanderson*, p. 73 speaks specifically of the new mosque of Sinan Pasha near Çembelitaş – the Red Column – where there is the lodging of the Emperor's ambassador, i.e. the Elchi Han.

11 At the age of ninety-five.

12 Eyice, *Istanbul: petit guide*, p. 39, sect. 47.

13 A Hungarian and Chief White Eunuch. It was during his term of office that control of the Evkaf revenues passed into the hands of the Black Eunuch.

14 Erdoğan, 'Mimar Davut Ağa'nin hayatı ve eserleri', p. 187.

15 Ahmet Refik, *Turk mimarları*, p. 27.

16 Ahmet Refik, *Istanbul hayatı, hicrî onbirinci asırda, (1000–1100)*, p. 135, sect. 11 et seq.

17 Eyice, *Istanbul: petit guide*, p. 17, sect. 9b gives the completion date as 1599.

18 *Istanbul Ansiklopedisi*, I, p. 320. The inscription mentions him as the ameli or builder implying that he was not the actual architect.

19 Rosedale, *Queen Elizabeth and the Levant Company*, p. 27.

20 *The Travels of John Sanderson*, p. 141.

21 They were circumcised first. Rosedale, *Queen Elizabeth and the Levant Company*, p. 27 says that their excessive numbers required the building of an annexe to the main türbe.

22 Ibid., p. 39. Mehmet III wore purple for the funeral of his father.

23 Ahmet Refik, *Turk mimarları*, p. 141, sect. 19, gives an order dated 1595 for a total of 250 to be ready with their tools. They are listed as 10 architects, 3 hydraulic engineers, 40 ironmasters, 87 masons, 100 sappers and 10 horsemen. The figures reveal a love of round numbers which one associates with a military caste.

24 Lewis, *A Karaite itinerary through Turkey in 1641–2*, p. 315, n. 1.

25 Hammer-Purgstall, *Histoire de l'Empire Ottomane*, XVIII, p. 43, sect. 419.

26 *Istanbul: petit guide*, p. 22, sect. 19.

27 It will be further discussed on p. 357.

28 Ünal, 'Türklerde sedefçilik' in *Güzel Sanatlar*, pp. 138-40.

29 Ahmet Refik, *Istanbul hayatı hicrî onbirinci asırda (1000–1100)*, p. 26, sect. 54.

30 Çiğ, *Treasury: Guide, Topkapı Palace Museums*, pp. 27 and 29.

31 Arseven, *L'Art turc depuis son origine jusqu'à nos jours*, p. 172. Also quoted by Mayer, *Islamic architects and their works*, p. 91.

32 Salignac, *Ambassade en Turquie, 1605–1610*, p. 78.

33 Ibid., p. 182.

34 Naima, *Annals of the Turkish Empire from 1591 to 1659 of the Christian era*, pp. 405-6.

35 Ibid., p. 452 and Evliya, *Narrative of travels*, I, part 1, p. 112.

36 Gibb, *The Travels of Ibn Battuta*, II, p. 277.

37 Salignac, *Ambassade en Turquie, 1605–1610*, p. 313.

38 Sandys, *A relation of a journey begun An. Dom. 1610*, p. 22, says that the '. . . island, formerly called Proconessus . . . celebrated for the excellent quarries of white marble, and thereof now called Marmara. Where a number of poor Christian slaves do hew stones daily for that magnificent mosque which is now building at Constantinople by this sultan.'

39 Öz, 'Sultan Ahmet Camii' in *V.D.*, I, p. 25.

40 Sandys, *A relation of a journey begun An. Dom. 1610*, p. 74 says that Ahmet first broke the earth and 'wrought three hours in person. The like did the pashas; bringing with them presents of money and slaves to further the building'.

41 Öz, 'Ahmet Camii' in *V.D.*, I, p. 26.

42 This cistern, which Evliya, *Narrative of travels*, I, part 1, p. 114, emphasizes was only for drinking, is closely related to the columned sebil of Sinan Pasha by Davut Ağa and the fountain in the Valide court at Eminönü.

43 *Annals of the Turkish Empire from 1591 to 1659 of the Christian era*, p. 452. Evliya, *Narrative of travels*, I, part 1, p. 114, says that they were lit for festivals.

44 Ibid. The lateral galleries were for the overflow of the congregation and Indian fakirs also took refuge there.

45 Salignac, *Ambassade en Turquie, 1605–1610*, p. 372 says, on 24 August 1610, that all Ahmet's efforts 'are devoted to the mosque which he is having built with remarkable diligence. Indeed, to spur on the work he has been lodging on the spot for the last seven or eight days and longs to see it finished. The gossips of Constantinople say he won't succeed and the expression on his face makes me think that they are right'. This may mean that the royal kiosk was the first building to be completed.

46 See the account of the suppression in Esad Efendi, *Précis historique de la destruction du Corps des Janissaires par le Sultan Mahmoud en 1826*, Paris, 1833.

47 Significantly known as the Çadladı or Tent Gate.

48 The setting of mektebs on high foundations occurs at the Selimiye at Edirne and Pertev Pasha Cami at Izmit and later with that of Ali Pasha at Çorlu and the Recai Mehmet Mekteb, among others.

49 Bolak, *Hastahanelerimiz*, p. 39 has a picture showing how extensive a hospital this was and he also states that hospital, imaret and tabhane were grouped as a single unit. Lechevalier, *Voyage de la Propontide et du Pont-Euxin*, pp. 237-8 says that this hospital was for men and had large rooms with sofas round them to serve as beds. There was good, clean food, many servants; but not much use of medicine.

50 Evliya, *Narrative of travels*, I, part, 1, p. 114 says that there was a daruziyafet or dining hall attached.

51 Ibid., p. 113 notes that here there were no columns as at Hagia Sophia or the Süleymaniye.

52 Eyice, *Istanbul: petit guide*, pp. 32-4, sect. 37. Gabriel, 'Les mosquées de Constantinople', p. 380.

53 Sandys, *A relation of a journey begun An. Dom. 1610*, p. 57, says that Ahmet I was a maker of ivory rings by trade. As a master craftsman himself he may have been an exacting critic of the work of others.

54 Salignac, *Ambassade en Turquie, 1605–1610*, p. 32, says that he had not reached twenty-two years and was nearly as fat as a barrel.

55 Ibid., p. 349, in a letter dated the end of April, 1610.

56 Mantran, *Istanbul, dans la seconde moitié du XVIIe siècle*, p. 617.

57 Op. cit., p. 300. However, on p. 298 he calls it the most beautiful mosque in the Orient.

58 Öz, 'Sultan Ahmet Camii', p. 26, says that the mosque was well lit in order to reveal the ornaments.

59 *Visit to Constantinople and Athens*, I, part 1, pp. 112-15. Where his statements can be checked they appear to be true except in regard to numbers.

60 Derviş Mehmet. See Evliya, *Narrative of travels*, I, part 1, p. 114, where he says that the great gate was plated with brass and inset with silver and precious stone.

61 Öz, 'Sultan Ahmet Camii' speaks of the jade (yesim) rose in the royal mihrab. He says that a notebook concerning the building of the Ahmediye says that jade was used in the dome as it was before in the dome of the Muradiye at Manisa against lightning, presumably like the blue bead against the evil eye until this day.

62 *Narrative of travels*, I, p. 100.

63 *The travels of M. de Thévenot into the Levant*, p. 22.

64 *Annals of the Turkish Empire from 1591-1659 of the Christian era*, p. 452.

65 Öz, 'Sultan Ahmet Camii', p. 26.

66 Dwight, *Constantinople, old and new*, p. 53.

67 Öz, 'Sultan Ahmet Camii', p. 27.

68 Ahmet Refik, *Istanbul hayatı, hicrî onbirinci asırda, (1000–1100)*, p. 33, sect. 64 and 65.

69 Ibid., p. 34, sect. 66.

70 Ibid., pp. 36-7, sect. 70.

71 Öz, 'Sultan Ahmet Camii', p. 27. Only 4,338 tiles were used in the Süleymaniye, including the türbes.

72 Ibid.

73 Ünver, 'Davut paşa Sarayı' in *Türkiye Turing ve Otomobil Kurumu*, Dec. 1961.

74 Dr Oktay Aslanapa, unpublished lecture.

75 Ünver, 'Davut paşa Sarayı'.

76 Rycaut, *The history of the Turkish Empire from the year 1623 to the year 1677*, p. 31 says that in 1631 Murat IV was frightened by lightning which scorched his bed and shirt in this kiosk. It must, therefore, have been used as a lodging and not just as a pavilion.

77 Eyice, *Istanbul: petit guide*, p. 45, sect. 59. The pasha was sadrazam to Ahmet I and died in 1611.

78 See p. 337.

79 See p. 338.

80 Possibly Kasım Ağa. One central cell is turned into a vestibule to the latrines, as was done at the Rüstem Pasha Medrese of Sinan. See p. 243.

81 Naima, *Annals of the Turkish Empire from 1591 to 1659 of the Christian era*, p. 464 says that he died in 1026/1617 and was buried in the türbe of Mahmut Efendi at Üsküdar. He held the office of Nişanci among others.

82 Ibid. It was not completed. Aslanapa, *Edirne'de Osmanlı devri abîde-leri*, p. 134, says, giving as his authority Osman Nuri Peremeci, *Edirne tarihi*, p. 89, that the architects were Sedefkar Mehmet Ağa with Edirneli Hacı Şaban. If this is correct it is a good example of collaboration between the royal architect and a local man.

83 See p. 293.

84 Aslanapa, *Edirne'de Osmanlı devri abîdeleri*, p. 134.

85 By Mehmet Memi Bey.

86 Inscription. Elmali was the old Tekke capital and notorious for Shi'ite woodcutters in the area in Ottoman times. It still is a centre of mysticism.

87 See p. 337.

88 Arseven, *L'art turc depuis son origine jusqu'à nos jours*, p. 173. The mid-sixteenth-century superintendent of Süleymaniye was Yetim Ali Baba (see Chap. 6, n. 75) which adds to one's incredulity even in a state as full of old men as the Ottoman. The Janissary Corps comprised a part at least of the Sultan's hunt service and the Turnacıbaşı was the lowest rank of the three commanders of 'hunting' regiments. See Gibb and Bowen, *Islamic society and the West*, p. 315 and p. 318, note. Pakalin, *Osmanlı tarih devimleri ve terimleri sözlüğü*, III, p. 535 says that he was responsible for the devşirme but this seems doubtful.

89 Arseven, *L'art turc depuis son origine jusqu'à nos jours*, p. 169 and note.

90 Mayer, *Islamic architects and their works*, p. 114. Kasım may have been a political appointee, not an architect.

91 See p. 320.

92 Eyice, *Istanbul: petit guide*, p. 4, sect. 1.

93 The so-called Damascus Period. Erdmann, 'Neue Arbeiten zur türkischen Keramik', p. 210, says that they are only copies, yet the Sunnet Oda was built later.

94 Miller, *Beyond the Sublime Porte*, p. 79.

95 Iftariye Kasrı of the bower of the Sundown Feast during the fast of Ramazan. Its four gilded supporting poles have at some period been moved out of alignment with the finials above the roof.

96 Mayer, *Islamic architects and their works*, p. 114 gives the date as 1642.

97 Cezar, 'Osmanlı devrinde Istanbul', p. 342 says that on the 24 July the fire was intentionally started by a woman of the harem. It burnt the greater part of the harem, Kübbe altı, Darül-Saadet Gate, rooms of the ağas, Valide apartment and the kitchens, among other rooms. There is an element of exaggeration here. The harem was lodged in the Eski Saray until repairs and rebuilding were completed.

98 See p. 368.

99 Uzunçarşılı, *Osmanlı devletinin saray teşkilatı*, p. 14. This was the origin of the saray at Beylerbey.

100 Evliya, *Narrative of travels*, I, part 2, pp. 118-19.

101 Ibid., p. 58. He calls it an incomparable mosque.

102 Ibid., I, part 2, p. 89.

103 The sacred bow and the sacred tureen spring from Mongol beliefs. The arrow in the mosque of Beyazit and the bow in the Atık Valide are significant. The great cauldrons of the Janissaries – that Sufi freemasonry – were symbols of loyalty and when the kettles were overturned it was the gauge thrown down, the challenge of mutineers to their emperor.

104 Hasluck, *Christianity and Islam under the Sultans*, I, p. 325. Wheeler, *Journey into Greece*, p. 325 also says that it was associated with Khidr.

105 With Ibrahim Ağa as treasurer.

106 Yücel, 'Yeni Camii hünkâr kasrı' in *Arkitekt*, 320, 1965, p. 115 et seq. points out that the ramp was for the Valide's carriage and the Sultan's horse.

107 Elliot, *Travels in the three great empires*, p. 176.

108 There are fine inscriptions on the doors of this mosque and a pretty faience design of three lamps together with a fine pair of balconies onto the courtyard.

109 *Istanbul dans la seconde moitié du XVIIe siècle*, p. 212.

110 The royal loge has two fine jaune antique columns which were noticed by Dalloway, *Constantinople ancient and modern*, I, p. 105.

111 Montani, in M. de Launay, *L'Architecture Ottomane*, p. 46.

112 It is exceptionally high; the proportions are 1 to 3·5.

113 *Complete Letters*, I, p. 400. It is still the fourth mosque in size.

114 Magni, *Quanto di più curiosi*, p. 179. On p. 181, he speaks of a crystal lamp, the gift of the Republic of Genoa. Tournefort and others all remark on the fine lamps and crystal and ivory globes. Evliya, *Narrative of travels*, I, part I, p. 165, speaks of rich furnishings and trappings and Persian and Egyptian carpets.

115 Inscription.

116 Slimane, 'Des aspects tunisiens de l'art turc' in *1st I.C.T.A.*, p. 381.

117 Pertusier, *Promenades pittoresques dans Constantinople et sur les rives du Bosphore*, p. 187.

118 Or Valide Çarşi or Spice Bazaar.

119 Rosedale, *Queen Elizabeth and the Levant company*, p. 31.

120 Dwight, *Constantinople, old and new*, p. 17.

121 Eyice, *Istanbul: petit guide*, p. 22, sect. 19.

122 Montani, in M. de Launay, *L'Architecture Ottomane*, p. 47. Turhan Sultan died in *1074/1682*.

123 Özdeş, *Türk çarşıları*, p. 35.

124 Mayer, *Islamic architects and their works*, p. 114.

125 Ibid., p. 114. See also p. 25.

126 Ibid., p. 111.

127 Eyice, *Istanbul: petit guide*, p. 26, sect. 28.

128 Gabriel, *Voyages archéologiques dans la Turquie Orientale*, p. 275.

129 Ibid., p. 274, fig. 201.

130 They recall the open cells of Beyazit Pasha at Amasya.

131 It dates from *1040/1630*, inscription.

132 Inscription.

133 *Les monuments turcs d'Anatolie*, II, p. 69.

134 Ibid., p. 168.

135 Completed in 1672. See Bobowski (Bobovio), *Serrai Enderum*, and Magni, *Quanto di più curiosi*, p. 209.

136 Gemelli-Careri, *Voyage du tour du monde*, p. 327 says that it was full of shops from top to bottom. These are now workshops.

137 This was the first major library formed for use by the public in Istanbul which is still open. Galland, *Journal d'Antoine Galland pendant son séjour à Constantinople, 1672-3*, p. 77 n. 2 notes its rich collection of Arabic manuscripts celebrated for their antiquity and rarity, and also of European works; above all Latin books carried off from Hungary.

138 Sauvaget, 'Les caravansérails Syriens du Hadjdj de Constantinople', pp. 111-12 suggests that it dates from the late sixteenth or early seventeenth centuries. The Kuloğlu Cami at Ohrid is also octagonal but of uncertain date. Of the türbe, Wheeler, *Journey into Greece*, p. 182 et seq., recounts that the lead was removed from the roof of Mehmet's tomb because the Grand Signior and the Grand Vezir dreamt that he begged for water since he was in burning heat. They consulted muftis who told them to remove the lead and let rain quench the flames tormenting his body.

139 Abbott, *Under the Turk in Constantinople*, p. 193, says that he was dark of face and a kinsman of the Köprülüs (p. 325). He had 1,500 concubines and 750 eunuchs.

140 Eyice, *Istanbul: petit guide*, p. 40, sect. 49 gives his name with a query.

141 The dome of this şadırvan was gaily painted inside at the beginning of the present century with views of Istanbul and its life. It is dated *1292/1875*.

142 Built *1077/1666* – inscription.

143 Gabriel, *Les monuments turcs d'Anatolie*, II, p. 65.

144 Yetkin *et al.*, *Turkish architecture*, p. 40.

145 Pococke, *A description of the East and some other countries*, p. 534, describes it as beautiful in the 1730s. The date *1129/1717* appears over the doors.

146 Gabriel, *Voyages archéologiques dans la Turquie Orientale*, pp. 283-5. The mescit domes are not Ottoman in form.

147 Inscription, *1112/1700*.

148 Inscription, *1120/1708*. See p. 366.

149 Miller, *Beyond the Sublime Porte*, p. 125. Mamboury, 'L'Art turc du 18e siècle' in *La Turquie Kemaliste*, no. 19, June, 1937, p. 3. The tulips were replanted from Mehmet IV's garden at Edirne. Perry, *A View of the Levant*, p. 70 notes that Bosphorus gardens were planted with onions and tulips. Vandal, *Une Ambassade française en Orient sous Louis XV; la Mission du Marquis de Villeneuve, 1728-41*, p. 87 says that tulips were everywhere, even in apartments. At the festival they were cunningly lit from inside. Flowers from France were asked for from Villeneuve and Bonnac reports gifts of double hyacinths from Holland in 1722; see Schefer, *Mémoire historique sur l'ambassade de France à Constantinople par le Marquis de Bonnac*, p. xlv.

150 Miller, *Beyond the Sublime Porte*, p. 223. Hyacinths were also imported from Aleppo.

151 Eyice, *Istanbul: petit guide*, p. 118, sect. 197.

152 Ibid., p. 113, sect. 183.

153 Both in execution and design.

154 Inscription.

155 Inscription.

156 Eyice, *Istanbul: petit guide*, p. 63, sect. 87.

157 Inscription.

158 Ahmet Refik, *Istanbul hayatı hicrî onikinci asırda (1100–1200)*, p. 65, sect. 90 quotes an order of *1131/1718* for experts with their tools to come from Iznik to instruct the workers in Istanbul. In his note he says that the potteries were ready to produce titles by 1724.

159 Inscription.

160 See Appendix II on the vakfiye of this endowment.

161 Inscription. Gabriel, *Les monuments turcs d'Anatolie*, I, p. 156 states that the columns for this mosque are supposed to come from the Sungur Bey Cami in Niğde.

162 The oblique approach is a feature of this period.

163 See p. 133.

164 Ahmet Refik, *Istanbul hayatı, hicrî onikinci asırda (1100–1200)*, p. 56,

sect. 80, quotes an order of *1129/1716* for the books of Şehit Ali Pasha, killed in action, to be sent to the saray. They would appear to have been added to the Enderun Collection.

165 Yenal, 'Topkapı sarayı müzesi Enderun kitapliği' in *Güzel Sanatlar*, VI, 1949, p. 87, plan 1.

166 Kuban, *Türk barok mimarısı hakkında bir deneme*, p. 25. Mayer, *Islamic architects and their works*, p. 57, calls this architect Bekir and says that he was also Bina emini or Superintendent of the building and the architect of the darül-hadis of Nevşehirli Damat İbrahim Pasha.

167 Eyice, *Istanbul: petit guide*, p. 3, sect. 1.

168 Schefer, *Mémoire historique sur l'ambassade de France à Constantinople*, p. xliii says that Yermisekiz (meaning Twenty-Eight) Mehmet Sayid Efendi was so-called after his Janissary orta. He was appointed Ambassador to France in August, 1718. Ibid., pp. xlv and xlvi, states that the gifts which he brought back included wigs, commodes, 1,000 bottles of champagne and 500 of Burgundy, plans and engravings of the gardens of France. Vandal, *Une Ambassade française en Orient sous Louis XV; la mission du Marquis de Villeneuve 1728-41*, p. 85 says that architects came from many countries at this time and that the pavilions of the Sweet Waters were modelled on those of Isfahan as well as Versailles. Schefer, p. xlvi, reports the pillaging and burning of these pleasure houses.

169 Inscription.

170 Inscription. Ahmet Refik, *Istanbul hayatı, hicrî onikinci asırda (1100–1200)*, p. 101, sect. 129, quotes an order for pure white marble without veins from Marmara, dated *1141/1728*. His note says that Mehmet Ağa was the architect. See also, Mayer, *Islamic architects and their works*, p. 80.

171 Kuban, *Türk barok mimarisi hakkında bir deneme*, p. 105, suggests that the first appearance of a foreign element in Ottoman decoration is the leaf frieze under the eaves of this fountain. I find this less evocative of Louis XV than of Hellenistic or even Byzantine decoration, but the pattern certainly re-appears in varying forms in both the baroque and the so-called Ampir (Empire) periods.

172 Pococke, *A Description of the East and some other countries*, p. 723 writing in the 1730s says that the decoration of the fountains was gilded and Melling's plate, no. 12, of this fountain shows the details as sparkling.

173 See Chap. 2, n. 93.

174 Eyice, *Istanbul: petit guide*, p. 111, sect. 180.

175 Ibid., p. 105, sect. 164.

176 Inčičean, *Villeggiature de'Bizantini sul Bosforo Tracio*, p. 162.

177 Eyice, *Istanbul: petit guide*, p. 101, sect. 156.

178 Ibid., p. 108, sect. 169.

179 Ibid., pp. 119-20, sect. 198.

180 Ibid., p. 16, sect. 8.

181 Inscription.

182 Eyice, *Istanbul: petit guide*, p. 91, sect. 136.

183 Unfortunately, the elegant portico of this charming baroque pavilion has been glazed in.

184 It is surprising that the mosque of Hekimoğlu Ali Pasha has one of the largest areas of tile of any mosque save that of Ahmet I.

185 Inscription.

186 Inscription.

187 Eyice, *Istanbul: petit guide*, p. 79, sect. 114.

188 Inscription.

189 Konyalı, *Âbideleri ve kitabeleri ile Erzurum tarihi*, pp. 525-6.

190 Eyice, *Istanbul: petit guide*, p. 19, sect. 12.

191 Inscription.

192 It was built to support the royal library at Hagia Sophia, and a whole series of orders for marble and water, and concerning trouble over wages for quarry workers for 1740 are quoted by Ahmet Refik, *Istanbul hayatı, hicrî onikinci asırda (1100-1200)*, pp. 142-5, 147-8, 150 and 152, sect. 173-4, 176, 179-80.

193 Kuban, *Türk barok mimarisi hakkında bir deneme*, p. 105. Attributed to Mehmet Tahir. Mayer, *Islamic architects and their works*, p. 104.

194 The ultimate form of this union occurs where grave and çeşme are combined as, for example, in the graveyard of the Emir Sultan Cami at Bursa.

10 BAROQUE AND AFTER

pages 380–427

1 Inscription.

2 One regrets the lack of records of the names of individual architects; though some buildings look as if they are the work of the same man there is no proof of this.

3 Inscription.

4 Inscription. Eyice, *Istanbul: petit guide*, p. 27, sect. 30, states that it was begun in 1748. Ahmet Refik, *Istanbul hayatı, hicrî onikinci asırda (1100-1200)*, pp. 168-9, sect. 201, quotes an order dated *1162/1749* for marble columns 18 parmak in circumference, capitals, and slabs or panels 14 × 18 parmak from the Marmara Island quarries. La Mottraye, *Travels through Europe, Asia, and into parts of Africa*, I, p. 344, says that marble was extracted in large quantities on Marmara Island and that twenty ships plied to and from Palatya.

5 Ibid., I, p. 111. Grenville, *Observations sur l'état actuel de l'empire Ottomane*, pp. 1-2, says that the Şehir Emini maintained the fortifications; the Mimar Ağa was in charge of building fortifications – there being no other engineer.

6 Ibid., p. 6. He remarks somewhat scornfully that the Grand Admiral was more of a sailor than the Mimar Ağa was an architect.

7 Eyice, *Istanbul: petit guide*, p. 113, sect. 184, says that it was also in memory of his brother, Süleyman.

8 Inscription. There are also verses by the poet-sadrazam, Ragıp Pasha, who was a leading patron of the baroque movement.

9 This contains the two Janissary tombs which survived the destruction following the dissolution of the corps in 1826. The intact headstone had the sleeve of the corps and of the Bektaşi erect above a turban set on a tall square plinth.

10 But this is not at all as certain as is generally supposed, see Chap. 10, n. 18. This mosque does contain some imported Italian tiles which were also used in the saray and elsewhere at this period; they are incongruous in most Ottoman settings.

11 Öz, *Istanbul camileri*, II, p. 7, attributes this building to Mehmet Tahir Ağa. Kuban, *Türk barok mimarisi hakkında bir deneme*, p. 29 simply cites Ishak Ağa as the bina nazırı or superintendent of works. Neither Eyice nor Mayer suggest an architect. The Chief Architect or Sermimar at this date was Hacı Ahmet Ağa who succeeded Hacı Mustafa in 1756 and who was not succeeded by Mehmet Tahir until 1764. Mehmet Tahir then held office until 1779. While it might be supposed that the chief architect would be responsible for the royal foundation at Üsküdar, there is no evidence to support the theory while Grenville's report casts considerable doubt.

12 Inscription published by Meyer-Riefstahl, *Turkish architecture in Southwestern Anatolia*, p. 108, n. 28 showing the builder to be Cihanzade Abdülâziz Efendi; no mention is made of the name of the architect; the details are uncompromisingly Greek in style.

13 The idea was not new but common to market mosques. The Cihanzade had a second arcade at street level outside below the precinct because of the steep slope of the hill.

14 Kuban, *Türk barok mimarisi hakkında bir deneme*, p. 30. Ahmet Refik, *Istanbul hayatı, hicrî onikinci asırda (1100-1200)*, p. 191, sect. 231 quotes an order for iron for Laleli Cami dated *1173/1759*. An order of 1763 for a carpet for Uşak urges haste. Ibid., p. 201, sect. 244. It would appear that Uşak rugs were considered the best and were ordered for major mosques and for the saray.

15 Eyice, *Istanbul: petit guide*, p. 45, sect. 58.

16 *Istanbul camileri*, I, p. 96.

17 *Türk barok mimarisi hakında bir deneme*, p. 30.

18 Ahmet Refik, *Istanbul hayatı, hicrî onikinci asırda (1100-1200)*, p. 200, sect. 243, quotes an order dated *1176/1762* for black, yellow, red and other marbles from Bandırma for this mosque, indicating that the inlaid panels are Ottoman, not Italian work.

19 The court of Laleli Cami is 26 × 30 metres and the interior ground plan is 15 × 19·5 metres, achieving an overall area approximately 25 × 50 metres. The basic proportions are therefore the very conservative two to one. This is true of Nuruosmaniye court where

the width and length are 31 metres at the widest points and the son cemaat yeri is 15·5 metres high, or exactly half. The dome of Laleli Cami, however, is close to that of Sokollu Mehmet Cami at Kadırga which measures 13·50 × 25·50 metres.

20 Kuban, *Türk barok mimarisi hakkında bir deneme*, pp. 70-1 dates the hamam about 1740 and the school in the mid-1750s on stylistic grounds. The latter had previously been attributed to the reign of Abdülhamit I, that is to say, twenty years later. The earlier dating is acceptable but not definitive.

21 The Church of Santa Maria della Salute in Venice is an example.

22 Inscriptions.

23 Eyice, *Istanbul: petit guide*, p. 76, sect. 110. Kuban, *Türk barok mimarisi hakkında bir deneme*, p. 32. The work was completed in *1185/1771*. Ahmet Refik, *Istanbul hayatı, hicrî onikinci asırda (1100-1200)*, pp. 215-17, sect. 260 et seq., shows that Hasim Efendi and Sarım Ibrahim Efendi were put in charge of the work by an order of *1180/1767*, that work on the türbe began the same year and that all work was completed by 1771; also that the marble was ordered from Marmara Island.

24 *Istanbul camileri*, I, p. 57.

25 *Islamic architects and their works*, pp. 104 and 43.

26 'Osmanli devrinde Istanbul', p. 390. Following on Ahmet Refik. See n. 23 above.

27 Eyice, *Istanbul: petit guide*, p. 77, sect. 110. Öz, *Istanbul camileri*, I, p. 58, dates it *1177/1763*.

28 Eyice, *Istanbul: petit guide*, pp. 52-3, sect. 69.

29 *Islamic architects and their works*, p. 104.

30 Kuban, *Türk barok mimarisi hakkında bir deneme*, p. 76.

31 A Western innovation belonging to this period.

32 Eyice, *Istanbul: petit guide*, pp. 63, sect. 88.

33 *Turk barok mimarisi hakkında bir deneme*, p. 31.

34 *Istanbul camileri*, I, p. 158. Ahmet Refik, *Istanbul hayatı hicrî onikinci asırda (1100-1200)*, p. 215, sect. 259, quotes an order of *1182/1768* which expressly states that he is in charge of the building.

35 Inscription.

36 During the restoration of the Hünkâr oda, a leaf from a calendar for 1904 was conveniently found under the plaster of the pendentive.

37 Inscription.

38 *Istanbul camileri*, II, p. 2. He states that the overseer of the building was Emini Mustafa Efendi.

39 Miller, *Beyond the Sublime Porte*, p. 127, lists the palaces of Mahmut I of which those on the water were at Üsküdar, Beşiktaş, Dolmabahçe, Bebek and Çubuklu besides others in the Belgrade Forest or at Sütluce, Balta Liman, Bahçeköy, Eyüp, Kağithane, and Hasköy.

40 The sultan was rowed in state in his barge on Fridays, and fleets of lesser craft followed creating a picturesque scene of gilding and trailing silk and painted oars.

41 The Ottomans admired beautiful views and buried their dead where they might find peace of soul at some of the finest vantage points. Sailors, like the Grand Admirals Barbaros or Kılıç Ali, had their türbes built by the shore.

42 I have been unable to trace any record of the name of the architect of the Beylerbey mosque which pre-dates the work of the Balians (or Balyans), the Armenian clan which dominates nineteenth-century Istanbul.

43 Among others Öz, *Istanbul camileri*, II, p. 12 states that the second minaret was added, together with the muvakkithane, by Mahmut II in *1226/1811*.

44 They are said to come from the Istaroz Sarayı – the original palace at Beylerbey – according to Öz, ibid. Ahmet Refik, *Istanbul hayatı, hicrî onikinci asırda (1100-1200)*, p. 139, sect. 170, reports an order of *1151/1738* to the effect that the tiles in the palace at Edirne on the walls of the Valide's bedchamber should be carefully taken down, packed one by one in boxes of soft vegetation, and sent in carts to Istanbul. These were not important tiles for they are simply described as white, so the order underlines the care taken with old tiles all of which had to be accounted for.

45 The calligraphy at Emirgân is good although looser than that of the classical period.

46 Inscription.

47 Inscription.

48 See p. 376.

49 Balducci, *Rodosta Türk mimarısı*, pp. 58-9.

50 Inscription. The kitabe over the north and only door is a pleasing example of the decorative style of the period.

51 See p. 222.

52 From the ruins of Tavium on Çapanoğlu or Çobanoğlu land.

53 This rich and powerful family was still only nominally under Ottoman rule. Mordtmann, 'Derebey' in *E.I.*, II, 1965, pp. 206-8, lists the leading members of the Çapanoğlu family of derebeys or overlords of Bozok (Yozgat) as Ahmet Pasha of Bozok, deposed by the Porte in *1148/1764*, and succeeded by his son, Mustafa Bey, who was murdered by his guard and succeeded by his brother Süleyman who died in *1229/1814*.

54 Inscription.

55 Inscription.

56 The Ulu Cami at Çorum is an example but the Sinan Pasha Cami at Beşiktaş, see p. 244, is more spectacular.

57 Inscription.

58 Inscription.

59 Inscription.

60 Inscription.

61 Inscription.

62 Inscription. İzzet Pasha, among other endowments, also built a mosque at Sivas.

63 Inscription.

64 Inscription.

65 Selim III's. These devices were attractively baroque in form from the first.

66 Inscription.

67 Inscription. A later example is the Köftüncü Mehmet Ağa fountain at Haydarpaşa, dated *1263/1847*, which is crowned with a large sun disc. See Tanışık, *Istanbul çeşmeleri*, II, pp. 442-5.

68 Inscription.

69 See p. 140.

70 Although enlarged in 1780.

71 Allen, *A history of the Georgian people*, pp. 187-8, says that he was a Moslem of Georgian descent from the Jaqeli princely house, but Safrastian, *Kurds and Kurdistan*, p. 47, states that Bahlul (Beylül) Pasha was an Armenian by origin.

72 See p. 307.

73 Over the harem gate is an inscription dated *1194/1780* wishing long life and power to the İshak Pasha dynasty. *Türkiye Ansiklopedisi*, II, p. 186, states that İshak Pasha was the son of Beylül Pasha and only completed the work begun by his father in about 1800. It included a medrese and a dungeon. *E.I.*, I, p. 684, says that Beylül Pasha built the mosque.

74 I am indebted for these details to Dr Erol İnelman. Locally, Çolak Abidin Pasha is stated to be İshak Pasha's father. Çolak implies a paralysed or missing arm. İshak Pasha belonged to the Çildiroğlu family whose founder ruled Çildir and Tiflis, dying in 1748. His son was appointed his successor but led a revolt in the next year. However, his own son, Hasan Pasha, was appointed Governor General of Georgia. İshak Pasha was made a vezir in 1789.

75 This was not new but had antecedents before Islamic times. In the Beylik period, simple ducts in the brick occur at the Gazi Ahmet complex at Peçin.

76 The rooms do effectively form a medrese or zaviye.

77 Balducci, *Rodos'ta Türk mimarisi*, p. 119.

78 Beybars, 1630, Hüseyn Kethuda, 1646; see Pauty, 'L'architecture au Caire depuis la conquête Ottomane' in *Bulletin de l'Institut Français d'Archéologie Orientale*', XXXVI, p. 22 et seq.

79 Ibid., Abdul Ikbal, 1713.

80 Ibid.

81 Ibid.

82 Ayverdi, 'Yugoslavia' da Türk âbıdeleri ve vakıfları', p. 154.

83 Ibid., p. 199.

84 Ibid., p. 209.

85 Inscription.
86 Gabriel, *Bursa*, p. 161.
87 Ibid., pp. 197-9.
88 See p. 403.
89 Gabriel, *Une Capitale turque, Brousse (Bursa)*, p. 197. A sebil means a way or path to God and therefore is associated with death and memorials.
90 Inscription.
91 Eyice, *Istanbul: petit guide*, p. 118, sect. 195, gives the date as 1806.
92 Ibid., p. 98, sect. 147.
93 Kuban, *Türk barok mimarisi hakkında bir deneme*, p. 109.
94 Tanişik, *Istanbul çeşmeleri*, II, pp. 16 and 26.
95 Ibid., pp. 151-70, 386-7, 402-5. Inscriptions.
96 Kuban, *Türk barok mimarisi hakkında bir deneme*, p. 34.
97 Öz, *Istanbul camileri*, I, p. 54.
98 Gabriel, *Une Capitale turque, Brousse (Bursa)*, pp. 131-4.
99 The dome is elliptical, measuring 14·60 × 15·20 metres approximately.
100 Gabriel, *Une Capitale turque, Brousse (Bursa)*, pp. 131-4.
101 Eyice, *Istanbul: petit guide*, p. 115, sect. 187.
102 Allom and Walsh, *Constantinople and the scenery of the Seven Churches of Asia Minor*, p. 74.
103 Eyice, *Istanbul: petit guide*, p. 115, sect. 187. Allom and Walsh, op. cit., p. 75 say that the top section of one was blown down in a gale but lay undamaged on the ground.
104 Alderson, *The structure of the Ottoman dynasty*, table xliii.
105 See p. 397.
106 Eyice, *Istanbul: petit guide*, p. 59, sect. 79.
107 See p. 108.
108 Inscription.
109 Kuran, 'Küçük Efendi manzumesi' in *Belletin*, XXVII, p. 467.
110 The Kapı Cami was first built in 1658 by the dervish Pir Hüseyn Çelebi and rebuilt in 1811 by Seyit Abdurrahman Efendi; later it was restored afresh in 1867, and it has been recently refurbished (inscriptions). See also Önder, *Konya*, p. 56. It is now a sparkling rectangular interior full of white and gold and green paint, and a little red, and beautifully kept up. The long seventeenth-century portico onto the market is incongruous.
111 It is effectively a son cemaat yeri.
112 Eldem, *Nos mosquées de Stamboul*, p. 129, sect. 54.
113 Kuban, *Türk barok mimarisi hakkında bir deneme*, p. 37.
114 Inscription.
115 Pamukciyan, *Istanbul Ansiklopedisi*, IV, pp. 2090-2, gives Kirkor A. Balian, 1764-1831.
116 See p. 397.
117 See p. 340.
118 It is a large but less prominent version of the cantilevered loge of the mosque of Hekimoğlu Ali Pasha which has only two lattice windows in front but also narrow ones each side.
119 The eighteenth century had also seen an unprecedented influx of foreign artists. It also saw a fashion for things Turkish in Europe which resulted in such pictures as Liotard's portrait of the Countess of Coventry; the nineteenth century saw the appearance of tiled rooms, such as those at Rhinefield House in the New Forest and Leighton House in Kensington. The influence of Islamic tiles on de Morgan there and at Battersea House or at Blackwell House near Windermere was considerable.
120 Walsh, *Constantinople and the Scenery of the Seven Churches of Asia Minor*, I, p. 75.
121 Ibid.
122 *Istanbul Ansiklopedisi*, IV, p. 2095.
123 Eyice, *Istanbul: petit guide*, p. 47, sect. 62. He resolutely refuses to name the architects of this period.
124 Inscription.
125 Reference should be made to the beautiful cavalry barracks at Kuleli, the present Military Academy, on the Bosphorus, probably dating from 1184/1770; see Kuban, *Türk barok mimarisi hakkında bir deneme*, p. 77; its twin towers with their elegant baroque spires which were demolished when the building was enlarged in the last century have

been faithfully rebuilt. In the centre of the long façade are fine twin flights of stairs leading to the main entry over the arcade of the basement. Engaged piers divide the façade in the early nineteenth-century manner.
126 Eyice, *Istanbul: petit guide*, p. 115, sect. 88.
127 Levinge, *The traveller in the East*, pp. 308-9 calls it the noblest military establishment in Turkey and says that it contained three thousand soldiers. Everyone entering was fumigated against the plague. There were twenty soldiers to a room. Pardoe, *The city of the Sultan*, I, p. 280, said that it had the appearance of a palace.
128 Eyice, *Istanbul: petit guide*, p. 28, sect. 31.
129 Ibid., p. 20, sect. 16.
130 Ibid., p. 21, sect. 18. Allom, in Walsh, *Constantinople and the Scenery of the Seven Churches of Asia Minor*, shows one of the many earlier doors; that of 1826 varies only in detail from the present gate.
131 Eyice, *Istanbul: petit guide*, p. 29, sect. 33.
132 Tanısık, *Istanbul çeşmeleri*, II, p. 184.
133 Inscription.
134 Inscription.
135 Inscription.
136 Pamukciyan, *Istanbul Ansiklopedisi*, IV, p. 2090.
137 Ibid., p. 2090 and p. 2093. This vast hall measures 44 × 46 metres and the central chandelier, made in Britain, has 750 lights and weighs four and a half tons.
138 Ibid.
139 Ibid., p. 2093.
140 Eyice, *Istanbul: petit guide*, p. 118, sect. 195.
141 I am indebted to Colonel Zeki Akmanalp, former director of the palaces of Istanbul, for this information. The staircases at Beylerbey in particular appear to support this theory, but no written record is available for inspection so no attribution can be made.
142 Pamukciyan, *Istanbul Ansiklopedisi*, IV, p. 2095.
143 Ibid., p. 2089.
144 Eyice, *Istanbul: petit guide*, p. 83, sect. 121.
145 Other nineteenth-century mosques have this character of a mansion, such as the Teşvikiye Cami founded in 1209/1796 but heavily rebuilt.
146 Inscription.
147 The nineteenth-century use of hooded şerefes is not uncommon in Anatolia because of the heat, and even small village mosques like that at Sarayönü or Arzupınar have elaborate forms of them. There are several nineteenth-century examples in Istanbul including the Babı-Ali Mescit, the neo-Gothic Hacı Küçük Cami, and the Dizdariye Mescit.
148 At Konya, this is due to a deliberate and foolish policy of secrecy intended to mislead.
149 See p. 15.
150 Taeschner, 'Çorum' in *E.I.*, I, p. 62 says that the Selçuk minber may be from Karahisar. His date, 1909, would appear to refer to extensive rebuilding and additions rather than the erection of a totally new mosque.
151 *Istanbul: petit guide*, p. 87, sect. 130.
152 Pamukciyan, 'K.A. Balyan' in *Istanbul Ansiklopedisi*, IV, p. 2089.
153 The so-called Gothic elements in the windows are close to the Niğde tradition.
154 Not all building at this period was moribund. A fascinating late nineteenth-century troglodyte mosque dug out of the rock by its imam and his friends, complete with freestanding minaret on the crag before the door, is still used at Taşhanköy north of Kayseri. This is not revivalism but genuine folk art.
155 Öz, *Istanbul camileri*, II, pp. 63-4.
156 Endless examples would be pointless, but the Önekerler Cami at Kayseri and the rebuilt mosque at Veyselkarani on the Bitlis–Silvan road, in spite of its fine carpets and mystical associations, can be cited. The latter is a very ugly mosque in a very holy place.

11 THE OTTOMAN HOUSE

pages 428–453

1 With the exception of the manor of Haydar Bey near Kayseri, if this is a house and not a tekke.

2 Rycaut, *The history of the Turkish Empire from the year 1623 to the year 1677*, p. 30, writing in the seventeenth century, describes the camp, probably at Davutpaşa, and states that there were about two thousand tents in no order, but the Grand Signior's appeared to be in the midst and to overtop all the rest, well worth observation, since it cost $180,000, was richly embroidered inside with gold and supported with pillars plated with gold. 'Within the walls of this tent (as I may so call them) are all sorts of offices belonging to the Seraglio, all retirements and apartments for pages, kiosks or summer houses for pleasure; . . . sumptuous beyond comparison of any in use amongst the Christian princes, erected with marble and mortar.' A splendid royal awning or shade is now on view at Topkapısaray.

3 Lybyer, *The Government of the Ottoman Empire*, p. 110, n. 1, quoting Peacocke, says that the Turks lodge more grandly in the field than in peace at home.

4 I would suggest that the Altın Yolu of Topkapısaray may have got its name from the gold embroidered hangings rather than the custom for the sultan to throw gold coins to the women upon his succession after being girded with the sword of Osman by the Grand Master of the Mevlevi Order of Dervishes at Eyüp. Vandal, *Une Ambassade française en Orient sous Louis XV*, p. 72 shows that Nointel saw the Imperial Tent in the Atmeydan; it was a war tent of silk, velvet and brocade which had taken eighteen months to adorn.

5 Marek and Knížková, *The Jengiz Khan miniatures*, plate 28.

6 Mezeray, *Histoire des Turcs*, II, p. 70, says that the Ottoman camp was like a town and thronged. For plans of Ottoman camps see Marsigli, *Stato Militare dell'Impero Ottomanno*.

7 *The four epistles of A. G. Busbequius concerning his Embassy in Turkey*, part 1, p. 91.

8 Or classical column.

9 In the south the roofs sprout bedsteads of iron and brass in warm weather.

10 Vambéry, *Sketches of Central Asia, additional chapters*.

11 Tam.

12 Akçub.

13 In regions subject to heavy falls of snow, such as Ağrı, these flat roofs require clearing after every fall and the job is a recognized trade. Every year, in the spring, they have to be renewed.

14 Çatakköy produces a form of kilim with a design, alien to the Turkish tradition, of large flowers on a black ground in a style more suited to needlework.

15 As with the Hungarian konak at Tekirdağ.

16 Konyalı, *Âbideleri ve kitabeleri ile Karaman tarihi*, p. 603.

17 The ceiling bosses have a rich foliate and floral design. The house is likely to date from the mid-nineteenth century.

18 Meyer-Riefstahl, *Turkish architecture in Southwestern Anatolia*, p. 32 thinks that this konak dates from the reign of Ahmet III and local tradition puts it as early as the sixteenth century which is preposterous. The style of the plaster imposts of the upper floor eyvan is late baroque and the light treatment of the floral designs does not correspond to the tight, richly painted stylizations of the Tulip Period.

19 Gabriel, *Une Capitale turque, Brousse (Bursa)*, p. 200, claims that it could possibly be seventeenth-century.

20 Jackson, *Journey from India towards London in 1797*, pp. 206 and 213.

21 Gabriel, *Une Capitale turque, Brousse (Bursa)*, p. 202.

22 Eser, *Kütahya evleri*, p. 54.

23 Kömürcüoğlu, *Ankara evleri*, p. 31.

24 *Constantinople and the Scenery of the Seven Churches of Asia Minor*, II, p. 2.

25 Esin, 'An eighteenth century yalı' in *2nd I.C.T.A.*, pp. 83 et seq. The subject achieves an exaggerated importance in this paper including, p. 103, the mystical shooting of seagulls from yalı windows.

26 This type is a fıskıye, the common Ottoman fountain made up of upturned, pierced stalactites from which thin jets of water spout into an elegant basin below. Examples are those of the Baghdad Kiosk, the imaret of Beyazit, Aynalı Kiosk, and the terrace of the saray beside the Köprülü salon.

27 Like the drips of the fountain in the inner cloister of ss Quattro Coronati at Rome.

28 Walsh, *Constantinople and the Scenery of the Seven Churches of Asia Minor*, I, p. 69.

29 Melling, *Voyage pittoresque de Constantinople et des rives du Bosphore*, plate 32.

30 Walsh, *Constantinople and the Scenery of the Seven Churches of Asia Minor*, II, p. 2.

31 They were always red in the seventeenth century, but due to Western influence many were painted white in the eighteenth according to Esin, 'An eighteenth century yalı', p. 105. But Hervé, *A Residence in Greece and Turkey*, II, p. 65, writing in the 1830s, noted that the privileged colour of Istanbul was still red and it was denied to non-Moslems. There are still red yalıs on the Bosphorus, the best kept of which is the property of Comte Jean Osterog.

32 Çakiroğlu, *Kayseri evleri*, p. 33.

33 Ibid., p. 48.

34 Erginbaş, *Diyarbakır evleri*, pp. 23–4, levha 12–14.

35 The rooms measure thirty and twenty-six feet by thirteen, approximately; the mabeyin, twenty-seven by eighteen feet; the winter saloon thirty by thirteen feet, as does the west saloon; the south saloon sixty by thirteen feet.

36 Houses of cooler regions look out; the meandering lanes of Tire are overlooked by windows and green with trees.

37 See p. 391–92.

38 Certainly it was used in Byzantine and Selçuk times, but rarely in the latter period. An example is the royal bower or belvedere of the palace of the citadel near the Alaettin Cami at Konya which projected from the top of a bastion. Berry, 'The development of the bracket support in Turkish domestic architecture in Istanbul' in *A.I.*, V, p. 272 et seq., gives examples of wooden bracket supports dating back to Mistra. He also suggests that the Turks built wooden structures on Byzantine ruins. If the walls were already there to supply such a substructure it was intelligent to take advantage of them.

39 *The four epistles of A. G. Busbequius, concerning his Embassy into Turkey*, p. 60.

40 B. Ramberti, Venice, 1543, as an appendix to Lybyer, *The Government of the Ottoman Empire*, p. 239, also speaks of the wretched walls. Gyllius, *The Antiquities of Constantinople*, p. 277, says that all the buildings of Constantinople were low and many not two storeys high and built of rough stone and burnt or unburnt bricks.

41 Burbury, *A relation of a journey*, p. 194. Planhol, *The world of Islam*, p. 15, states that even the Divan yolu was only nine to ten feet wide in places. Blount, in 'A Voyage into the Levant' in Pinkerton, *A general collection of the best and most interesting voyages*, X, p. 261, says that the streets were not broad but paved with a high foot causeway on each side.

42 Pococke, *A description of the East and some other countries*, III, p. 722.

43 Lechevalier, *Voyage de la Propontide et du Pont-Euxin*, p. 198.

44 Levinge, *The traveller in the East*, pp. 259–60.

45 Bassano da Zara, *I Costumi et i modi particolari della vita de' Turchi*, p. 44a, says that the houses, other than those of the sultan and the nobles, were badly built with no windows that opened because glass was costly.

46 Southgate, *Narrative of a tour through Armenia, Kurdistan, Persia and Mesopotamia*, I, pp. 86–7.

47 Elliott, *Travels in the three great empires*, p. 185. The streets, he says, were narrow, ill-paved and dirty, and he adds that no carriage could be got.

48 Ahmet Refik, *Istanbul hayatı, on altıncı asırda (1553–1591)*, p. 66, sect. 14.

49 Ahmet Refik, *Istanbul hayatı, hicrî onbirinci asırda (1000–1100)*, p. 13, sect. 25. This was bad, and the culprits were to be exposed to public view.

50 Mantran, *La vie quotidienne à Constantinople*, p. 45, says that the exteriors of the konaks were modest for politic reasons but rich

within. Esad, *Précis historique de la destruction du corps des Janissaires par le Sultan Mahmoud en 1826*, p. 293, talks of the vastness of the sumptuously furnished ancient palace of Ağa of the Janissaries which was given by Mahmut II to the Şeyhül-Islam in 1826; previously he had had to rent a house for entertaining.

51 Cezar, 'Osmanli devrinde Istanbul', p. 372, reports Bâbi-Âli as having been burnt three times in the first thirty years of the nineteenth century. It was first called Bâbi-Âli in 1718, that is to say, the Porte or government which was wherever the Divan met. See Deny, 'Tughra', in *E.I.*, I, p. 836. Heyd, 'Bab-i Humayun', *E.I.*, I, pp. 836-7, makes a clear distinction between it and the Bâbi Humayun, the Gate of Majesty, or entry to the saray. Hence the confusion over the term, Sublime Porte, since the Divan sat at both the Topkapı-saray and the residence of the Sadrazam. Lewis, 'Divan-i humayun', *E.I.*, II, pp. 337-9, says that Mehmet IV transferred the Divan to Bâbi-Âli in 1054/1654.

52 Miniature No. 14.1339, among others, in the Topkapısaray – 'The Enthronement of Selim II' from Nüzheti-Esrar al-Bahar, dated 1658, by Ahmet Feridun Pasha shows a splendid example of a royal tent.

53 Rycaut, *The history of the Turkish Empire from the year 1623 to the year 1677*, p. 228. At Dimetoka in June.

54 See p. 327.

55 Ahmet Refik, *Istanbul hayatı, hicrî onikinci asırda (1100–1200)*, p. 35, sect. 53.

56 Ibid., p. 66, sect. 92.

57 Ibid., p. 83, sect. 112. Cantemir, *The History of the growth and decay of the Othman Empire*, part 2, book IV, pp. 294-5, n. 32, writing of the Mimar Ağa, says that a man cannot build what he pleases unless he has first bribed him with presents. 'For, though the measure of all buildings be settled by orders from the Sultan, so that a Christian's house is to be thirteen, and a Turk's fifteen yards high, yet as Constantinople is mostly built upon hills, the Mimar Ağa may, if he is well bribed, permit a building to rise to a very considerable height; namely by taking the dimension from the brow of the hill; by which means, a house that will be in the back part according to the stated measure, may, on the forepart rise to thirty yards, and more.'

58 Evliya, *Narrative of travels*, part 2, pp. 619-20, lists only five hundred brickmakers with straw as opposed to fifteen hundred without. The proportions, not the actual figures, are important. War also created shortages of masons and builders. Ahmet Refik, *Istanbul hayatı, on altıncı asırda (1553–1591)*, p. 29, sect. 28 gives an order of 1583 requiring the Kadı of Midilli to send six hundred workers immediately to Sinan for work on Evkaf buildings since Istanbul workers were away at the Eastern War.

59 Ramberti, the Venetian traveller, had been impressed by the trees in 1543. In the nineteenth century, Ebersolt stated that gardens and trees gave the city a fresh aspect. See, Ebersolt, *Constantinople byzantine et les voyageurs du Levant*.

60 See p. 109.

61 Mantran, *Istanbul dans la seconde moitié du XVIIe siècle*, p. 165. He reports the whitewashing of the walls by the kaymakam for the triumphal return of Murat IV in 1635.

62 Palladio, *The Four Books of Architecture*, book IV, p. 2 says '. . . of all colours, none is more proper for churches than white; since the purity of colour, as of life, is particulary grateful to God'. Byzantine churches, which were usually built of brick, were colour-washed in many different colours.

63 Planhol, *The world of Islam*, pp. 31-2.

64 Tiers of seats forming a temporary grandstand were built in the Atmeydan in front of the Ibrahim Pasha saray from which festivities could be watched by dignitaries on special occasions. It had nothing in common with the splendid meydan at Isfahan where the boxes were architecturally conceived in relation to the mosques, etc.

APPENDIX I – THE JANISSARIES

pages 454–455

1 Barthold, *Turkestan down to the Mongol invasion*, p. 227.

2 Hussey, in *The Cambridge Medieval History*, IV, part I, II, p. 210, says that the first reference to the devşirme is by Isidore Glabas, Metropolitan of Thessalonika, who lamented the seizure of children by decree of the Emir. Inalcik, 'Ghulam' in *E.I.*, II, p. 1085, says that slave boys were trained in the saray in Selçuk times and that the devşirme descended from the practice of taking sons from members of the military caste in a conquered area.

3 Lybyer, *The Government of the Ottoman Empire*, p. 51. He states that Armenians were later recruited, but city dwellers remained exempt although a levy was drawn from Athens. Children of craftsmen were exempt because they were less likely to be sturdy than peasant boys. Bosnia was an exceptional province because the peasants there were rapidly converted to Islam and so in that region only Turks were exempt but Moslems might be levied.

4 Ménage, 'Devshirme' in *E.I.*, II, pp. 210-11 reports a complaint about the levy of children from the west coast of Anatolia as early as 1456, but this could refer to acts of piracy.

5 Kocu, *Yeniçeriler*, p. 25. Lybyer, *The Government of the Ottoman Empire*, p. 48, says ten to twenty and those between fourteen and eighteen preferred. Djevad Bey, *État militaire ottoman*, does not give exact ages.

6 Fisher, *The foreign relations of Turkey*, p. 97.

7 Gibb and Bowen, *Islamic society and the West*, I, part 1, p. 66, n. 1.

8 Ibid., I, part 2, p. 152.

9 Esad, *Précis historique de la destruction du corps des Janissaires par le Sultan Mahmoud en 1826*, pp. 300-2. But he was writing immediately after the suppression of the Janissaries and the Bektaşi tekkes.

10 Sometimes called a yayabaşi.

11 Kocu, *Yeniçeriler*, p. 25 et seq. Lybyer, *The Government of the Ottoman Empire*, p. 49, says that they were given as tribute or simple presents and also purchased.

12 Kocu, *Yeniçeriler*, p. 28. Ménage, 'Seven Ottoman documents from the reign of Mehemmed II', pp. 112-18.

13 Kocu, *Yeniçeriler*, p. 33.

14 Djevad Bey, *État militaire ottoman*, p. 241 et seq., says that the acemioğlans at Gelibolu (Gallipoli) and Edirne were trained as gardeners and guards to be called Bostancı. He reports that six hundred worked in the shipyards. Kocu, *Yeniçeriler*, p. 34, says the boys at Gelibolu were trained to work in the shipyards or Tershane at Istanbul. Uzunçarşili, 'Bōstāncı' in *E.I.*, I, p. 1277, says that the Bostancıs were only two ocaks of the fittest boys. They worked on the royal estates at Amasya, Manisa, Bursa, Izmit, etc., and transported material for royal constructions, working on the timber boats from Izmit to Istanbul. In 984/1576 there were 645 working on the flower gardens and 971 on the vegetable gardens of the sultan. They looked after the boathouses and twenty-four rowed the royal barge.

15 Djevad Bey, *État militaire ottoman*, p. 244. But Nicolay, *Navigations and voyages made into Turkey*, p. 81, writing in the mid-sixteenth century says that in his day only the less handsome acemioğlans became farmhands.

16 Djevad Bey, *État militaire ottoman*, p. 244.

17 Esad, *Précis historique de la destruction du corps des Janissaires par le Sultan Mahmoud en 1826*, p. 194.

18 Ibid., p. 314, he says that tekkes over sixty years old were to be preserved and put to other uses. Bowen, 'Baltadjis', in *E.I.*, I, p. 1004, states that both the Ibrahim and Galata schools were closed in 1675.

19 Gibb and Bowen, *Islamic society and the West*, I, part 1, p. 58 and p. 41n.

20 Djevad Bey, *État militaire ottoman*, p. 28.

21 Ibid., p. 27 says that an orta consisted of between one hundred and five hundred men. Kocu, *Yeniçeriler*, p. 54 says that an orta was divided into four dormitories.

22 Djevad Bey, *État militaire ottoman*, chart, p. 90. See also Geuffroy, *Briefve description de la court du Grant Turc*.

23 Djevad Bey, *État militaire ottoman*, chart, p. 90. But the decline began at the end of Süleyman I's reign, see Lybyer, *The Government of the Ottoman Empire*, p. 50, when sons of Janissaries and some adults were admitted.

24 Gibb and Bowen, *Islamic society and the West*, I, part 1, p. 181.

25 Djevad Bey, *État militaire ottoman*, p. 29.

26 Ibid., p. 31.

27 Ibid., p. 47.

28 Ibid., p. 46. Zülfikar, or the cleft sword of Ali.

29 Meriç, 'L'architecte de la mosquée Beyazid d'Istanbul', p. 264 states that the Janissaries worked on the mosque of Beyazit II, and Djevad Bey, *État militaire ottoman*, p. 243 reports that acemioğlans were rewarded for good work on the mosque of Haseki.

30 Gibb and Bowen, *Islamic society and the West*, I, part 1, pp. 42-5. Rosenthal, *The Moslem concept of Freedom*, p. 30, says that a slave could not be called a slave but 'my young man'. Ménage, 'The Mission of an Ottoman secret agent in France in 1486', *Journal of the Royal Asiatic Society*, parts 3 and 4, pp. 114-15 says that Barak met Ottoman merchants in Genoa who said that they were sultans' *kul*. Barak was also a slave of the sultan because, although Turkish born, he was the son of a slave; (p. 120) the merchants were buying cloth for Janissary units.

31 Tritton, *Islam, belief and practices*, p. 67 quotes: 'I saw in the memoranda of the Treasurer "400,000 dinars for a robe of honour for Jafar the Barmaki", a few days later I saw below it, "10 kirat for oil and needs for burning the body of Jafar"'.

APPENDIX II – THE VAKFIYE AND IMARET SYSTEMS

pages 455–457

1 Köprülü, 'L'institution du Vakouf' in *V.D.*, II, supp., p. 9, states that there were many motives for giving and that a fetva had to be issued against debtors founding vakıfs. Minorsky, *The Chester Beatty Library. A catalogue of the Turkish manuscripts and miniatures*, sect. 442, p. 76, F. 30a of the 'Vaqf-nāma of Princess Fātıma and Ibrāhīm Pasha' states that 'the son of the founder Dāmād Muhammad-pasha is appointed to be the manager (*mütevelli*) of the vaqf and will receive 120 aqchas daily; after his death the office will pass in turn to the eldest and worthiest of the male and female descendants of Ibrāhīm pasha, preference *ceteris paribus* being given to a man. Eventually, if the scissors of destruction cut the cord of descent, the management will pass to manumitted slaves of the family ('*utaqā va 'atīqāt*) and even in the case of their extinction the vaqf must be used for the benefit of poorer muslims'.

2 Köprülü, 'L'institution du Vakouf', p. 37 states that clearly revenues did accrue to the crown and a memorandum of Koca Bey to Murat IV makes clear that these practices were illegal. On p. 38 he gives examples of properties given to Mihrimah and Rüstem Pasha by Süleyman I which were endowed for the benefit of their children because their worldly goods would revert to the crown. Minorsky, *The Chester Beatty Library. A catalogue of the Turkish manuscripts and miniatures*, sect. 422, p. 42, shows that with a vakıfname another Fatıma Sultan in *1006/1597* left her palace at Kasım Pasha, which had a yearly ground rent of 500 akşas, to her husband Ibrahim Pasha the Grand Vezir of Mehmet III, and to her descendants. If the family died out, the specially appointed mütevelli was to lease the property to a bidder ready to pay 200 akşas daily. Of these, he and his assistants were to get 10, 40 were to be used on the upkeep of the palace, and the remaining 150 akşas were to be divided between 75 worthy persons who were to read a portion of the Koran for the rest of the princess's soul. It seems a blatant way of avoiding death duties.

3 Ergin, *Türk şehirlerinde imaret sistemi*, p. 21 et seq.

4 Mantran, *La vie quotidienne à Constantinople*, p. 182, says between three hundred and two thousand.

5 Ergin, *Türk şehirlerinde imaret sistemi*, p. 25.

6 Mayer, *Islamic architects and their works*.

7 Kunter, 'Les bases appliquées dans l'administration, la conservation, l'entretien et les réparations des monuments turcs', p. 231.

8 Ibid., pp. 229-30.

9 Ibid., pp. 232-3.

10 Ibid., p. 228.

11 Ibid., p. 230.

12 Hence, presumably, the reason for installing the library inside the Süleymaniye, and as an appendage which could only be reached from the interior at Hagia Sophia.

13 Ünver, 'Fatih külliyesine ait diğer mühim bir vesika' in *V.D.*, I, p. 40 et seq.

14 Ibid., p. 42.

15 Yaltakaya, 'Kara Ahmed Paşa vakfiyesi', p. 92 et seq.

16 Minorsky, *The Chester Beatty Library. A catalogue of the Turkish manuscripts and miniatures*, sect. 442, p. 75 et seq.

17 Ibid.

Bibliography

THIS BIBLIOGRAPHY is divided into a section of works to which I refer in the text and a second section of some of the books consulted or studied to which no direct reference is made. The second list is not exhaustive since many works on Western architecture and aesthetics have prepared the way for the exploration of the Ottoman school. The importance of the buildings themselves as the prime source material cannot be overemphasized.

Source material on Ottoman architecture is varied in its extent and its depth. The contribution of Turkish scholars of the older generation is considerable. Such pioneers as Konyalı and Ayverdi have patiently accumulated stores of facts, while Ahmet Refik's researches into the archives represent a lifetime of labour, for scores of orders in council were issued daily over the centuries and filed chronologically – not by subject – and there is no catalogue. If the work of men like Arseven and Çetintaş is dated, and largely superseded, they still deserve to be read. At the present moment, three men are making fresh studies of Ottoman architecture; they are Kuran, Kuban and Eyice.

Among many other scholars who have made important contributions there is A. Gabriel, who has devoted a long lifetime to the subject and who can claim to have founded the proper study of Selçuk and Ottoman buildings. Vogt-Göknil and Egli have established reputations as scholars, while Grube has recently written a brilliant chapter on Ottoman architecture in his remarkable brief work on Islamic architecture in general. Outstanding work in depth has been produced by such authorities as Anheggar and Erdmann. Many other names could be selected, such as Diez and Riefstahl or Gebhard. The work of Sumner-Boyd on Istanbul, still in manuscript, will be outstanding.

The travellers and the gossips of many different periods are useful, even when their references to buildings are brief and often infuriatingly vague. The letters of diplomats such as Salignac are often informative. However, all the writers listed are not necessarily reliable and the work of a Hervé, for example, should be read with circumspection. Ottoman political history is not the subject of this book and only a few general works are listed here. Heyd's remarkable book on Palestine gives some idea of the immensity of the subject. I have had the privilege of talking with a number of Ottoman historians such as Dr Kemal Karpat and Mrs Stanford Shaw as well as with Mr James Mellaart whose unique vision is as illuminating in respect of Selçuk monuments as it is in his chosen archaeological fields.

I make no apology for the critical use made of established texts. The study of Ottoman architecture is recent and too many who have written on it have not visited buildings outside the major cities. To write on the subject is to be constantly in error even now, and there must be a constant dialogue of revision for years to come.

While working on this book I have had to use various editions of certain works and in the bibliography those listed are not always the best. On occasion, such as with the monumental work of Creswell, only the abridged edition has been available; but this occurs only with works which are outside the immediate scope of this book.

BOOKS AND ARTICLES REFERRED TO IN THE TEXT

ABBOTT, G. F., *Under the Turk in Constantinople. A record of Sir John Finch's Embassy, 1674–1681*, London, 1920.
ACKERMAN, J. S., *Palladio*, Harmondsworth, 1966.
AĞA-OĞLU, M., 'The Fatih Mosque at Constantinople' in *Art Bulletin*, vol. xii, no. 4, December 1930.
    'Note about one of "The two questions on Moslem Art"' in *Ars Islamica*, III, part 1, Michigan, 1936.
AHMET REFIK, *İstanbul hayatı, on altıncı asırda (1553–1591)*, Istanbul, 1935.
    İstanbul hayatı, hicrî onbirinci asırda (1000–1100), Istanbul, 1930–1.
    İstanbul hayatı, hicrî onikinci asırda (1100–1200), Istanbul, 1930–5.
    İstanbul hayatı, hicrî on üçüncü asırda (1200–1255), Istanbul, 1930–5.
    Mimar Sinan, Istanbul, 1931.
    Türk mimarları, Istanbul, 1936.

AKOK, M., 'Kütahya Büyük Bedesten' in *Vakıflar Dergisi*, III, Ankara, 1956.
    'Uşak Ulu Cami'i' in *Vakıflar Dergisi*, III, Ankara, 1956.
AKTANSEL, S. T., 'Kara Ahmet Paşa' in *İstanbul Ansiklopedisi*, I, Istanbul, 1959.
AKURGAL, E., *The Art of the Hittites*, trans. McNab, London and N.Y., 1962.
ALDERSON, A. D., *The structure of the Ottoman dynasty*, Oxford, 1956.
ALLEN, W. E. D., *A history of the Georgian people . . .*, London, 1932.
    Problems of Turkish power in the 16th century, London, 1963.
ALLOM, T., see Walsh.
ANHEGGAR, R., 'Adana' in *Encyclopaedia of Islam*, I, London and Leiden, 1960.

ARBERRY, A. J., *The Koran interpreted*, Oxford, 1964.

AREL, M., 'Muttaki Karamanoğulları devri eserleri' in *Vakıflar Dergisi*, V, Ankara, 1962.

ARSEVEN, C. E., *L'art turc depuis son origine jusqu'à nos jours*, Istanbul, 1939. *Les arts décoratifs turcs*, Istanbul, 1952.

ASLANAPA, O., *Edirne'de Osmanlı devri abîdeleri*, Istanbul, 1949.

ATABINEN, R. S., *Les Turcs occidentaux et la Méditerranée*, Istanbul, 1956.

AYTÖRE, A., 'Turkish water architecture' in *1st I.C.T.A.*, Ankara, 1961.

AYVERDİ, E. H., 'Dimetoka'da Çelebi Sultan Mehmed Camii' in *Vakıflar Dergisi*, III, Ankara, 1956.
Fatih devri mimarı eserleri, Istanbul, 1953.
'Le premier siècle de l'architecture ottomane' in *1st I.C.T.A.*, Ankara, 1961.
'Orhan Gazi devrinde mimari' in *Yilik Araştırmalar dergisi*, I, Ankara, 1956.
Osmanli mi'mârîsinin ilk devri, Istanbul, 1966.
'Yugoslavya'da Türk âbideleri ve vakıfları' in *Vakıflar Dergisi*, III, Ankara, 1956.

BABINGER, F., *Mahomet II, le Conquérant, et son temps*, Paris, 1954.
'Nilüfer Khatum' in *Encyclopaedia of Islam*, III, London and Leiden, 1936.

BADGER, G. P., *The Nestorians and their ritual*, London, 1852.

BALDUCCI, H., *Rodos'ta Türk mimarîsi*, Ankara, 1945.

BARKAN, Ö. L., 'Essai sur les données statistiques des registres de recensement dans l'empire Ottomane au XVe et XVIe siècles' in *Journal of the Economic and Social History of the Orient*, I, Leiden, 1958.
'Les fondations pieuses comme méthode de peuplement et de colonisation' in *Vakıflar Dergisi*, II, Ankara, 1942.

BARTHOLD, W., *Turkestan down to the Mongol invasion*, trans. author, asst. Gibb, Oxford, 1928.

BASSANO DA ZARA, L., *Costumi, et i modi particolari della vita de' Turchi*, Rome, 1545.

BAUDIER, M., *Histoire generalle du serrail et de la Cour du Grand Seigneur empereur des Turcs*, two parts, Paris, 1624.
The History of the Serrail, and of the Court of the Grand Seigneur, Emperour of the Turks, London, 1635. Translation by Edward Grimestone of the original French edition.

BAYSUN, M. C., 'Ahmad Pasha, Kara' in *Encyclopaedia of Islam*, I, London and Leiden, 1960.

BELL, G., *The Thousand and one churches*, London, 1909.

BERNARD, C. A., *Les bains de Brousse, en Bithynie (Turquie d'Asie) avec une vue des bains . . .*, Constantinople, 1842.

BERRY, B. Y., 'The development of the bracket support in Turkish domestic architecture in Istanbul' in *Ars Islamica*, V, Michigan, 1938.

BIDDER, H., *Carpets from Eastern Turkestan known as Khotan, Samarkand and Kansu carpets*, trans. Allen, New York, 1964.

BIRGE, J. K., *The Bektashi order of dervishes*, London, 1937.

BLOUNT, SIR H., *A Voyage into the Levant*, London, 1638. See also Pinkerton.

BOBOWSKI, A. (Ali bey), see Magni.

BOLAK, O., *Hastahanelerimiz*, Istanbul, 1950.

BOWEN, H., 'Ahmad III' and 'Baltadjis' in *Encyclopaedia of Islam*, I, London and Leiden, 1960.

BRIGGS, A., 'Timurid carpets' in *Ars Islamica*, XI-XII, Michigan, 1946.

BRIGGS, M. S., 'Architecture' in *The legacy of Islam*, ed. Arnold and Guillaume, Oxford, 1931.
Muhammadan architecture in Egypt and Palestine, Oxford, 1924.

BROWN, J. P., *The darvishes; or Oriental spiritualism*, ed. with introduction and notes by H. A. Rose, London, 1927.

BURBURY, J., *A relation of a journey of the Rt. Hon. My Lord Henry Howard from London to Vienna and thence to Constantinople*, London, 1671.

BUSBECQ, O. G., *Turkish letters of Ogier Ghiselin de Busbecq . . .*, translated from the Elzivir edition of 1633 by Edward Seymour Foster, Oxford, 1927.
The four epistles of A. G. Busbequius, concerning his Embassy into Turkey . . . To which is added his Advice how to manage war against the Turks, London, 1694.

CANARD, M., 'Al-Battāl, 'Abd Allâh' in *Encyclopaedia of Islam*, I, London and Leiden, 1960.

CANTEMIR, see Demetrius.

CARLISLE, EARL OF, *Diary in Turkish and Greek Waters*, London, 1854.

CEVAT, see Djevad.

CEZAR, M., 'Osmanli devrinde Istanbul yapılarında tahribat yapan yangınlar ve tabiî âfetler' in *Türk San'atı Tarihi Araştırma ve İncelemeleri*, I, Istanbul, 1963.

CHANDLER, R., *Travels in Asia Minor . . .*, London, 1776.

CHOISEUL-GOUFFIER, COMTE DE, *Voyage pittoresque de la Grèce*, 2 vol., Paris, 1782.

COLTON, W., *A Visit to Constantinople and Athens*, New York, 1836.

COOK, A. B., *Zeus. A Study in Ancient Religion*, 3 vol., Cambridge, 1914–1940.

COOMARASWAMY, A., 'Notes on the philosophy of Persian art' in *Ars Islamica*, XV-XVI, Michigan, 1951.

COVEL, J., 'Extracts from the diaries of Jo. Covel (1670–9)' in *Early voyages and travels in the Levant*, ed. J. T. Bent, London, 1893.

CRESWELL, K. A. C., *A short account of early Muslim architecture*, Harmondsworth, 1958.

ÇAKIROĞLU, N., *Kayseri evleri*, Istanbul, 1952.

ÇETİNTAŞ, S., 'Mimarelerimiz' in *Güzel Sanatlar*, IV, Istanbul, 1942.
Türk Mimarî anıtları Osmanlı devri; I. Bursa'da ilk eserler, Istanbul, 1946.

ÇİĞ, K., *Treasury: guide, Topkapı Palace Museums*, Istanbul, 1966.

DALLOWAY, J., *Constantinople ancient and modern with excursions to the shores and islands of the Archipeligo and to the Troad*, London, 1797.

DALMAN, K. O., *Der Valens-Aquädukt in Konstantinopel*, Bamberg, 1933.

DANIŞMEND, I. H., *İzahli Osman tarihi kronolojisi*, I-IV, Istanbul, 1947–55.

DEMETRIUS (Kantemir), Hospodar of Moldavia, *The history of the growth and decay of the Othman empire*, trans. Tindal, London, 1734.

DENY, J., 'Tughra' in *Encyclopaedia of Islam*, IV, London and Leiden, 1934.

DIEHL, C., in A. U. Pope (ed.), *A Survey of Persian Art from Prehistoric Times to the Present*, III, London, 1938.

DIEZ, E., 'L'emblème dans le.palais byzantin et la grande-mosquée turque' in *1st I.C.T.A.*, Ankara, 1961.
'Masdjid' in *Encyclopaedia of Islam*, III, London and Leiden, 1936.

DIEZ, E., with O. ASLANAPA, M. M. KORMAN, *Karaman devri sanatı*, Istanbul, 1950.

DIEZ, E., with O. ASLANAPA, *Türk sanatı . . .*, Istanbul, 1946.

DJEVAD BEY, A. (Ahmad Jewād), *État militaire ottoman depuis la fondation de l'empire jusqu'à nos jours*, Constantinople and Paris, 1882.

DOWNES, K., *Hawksmoor*, London, 1959.

DWIGHT, H. G., *Constantinople, old and new*, New York, 1915.

EBERSOLT, J., *Constantinople byzantine et les voyageurs du Levant*, Paris, 1918.

EDHEM, E., see H. E. Eldem.

EDHEM PAŞA, see Montani.

EDIB, H., *The Conflict of East and West in Turkey*, Lahore, 1935.

EGLI, E., *Sinan, der Baumeister osmanischer Glanzzeit*, Zurich, 1954

EISLER, R., *The royal art of astrology*, London, 1946.

ELDEM, H. E., *Nos mosquées de Stamboul*, trans. E. Mamboury, Istanbul, 1934.

ELISSÉEFF, N., 'Dimashk' in *Encyclopaedia of Islam*, II, London and Leiden, 1965.

ELLIOTT, C. B., *Travels in the three great empires of Austria, Russia, and Turkey*, London, 1838. Philadelphia, 1839.

EMLER, S., 'Topkapı Sarayı restorasyon çalışmaları' in *Türk San'ati Tarihi Araştırma ve İncelemeleri*, Istanbul, 1963.

ERDMANN, K., 'Neue Arbeiten zur türkischen Keramik' in *Ars Orientalis*, V, Michigan, 1963.

ERDOČAN, M., 'Mimar Davut Ağa'nin hayatı ve eserleri' in *Türkiyat Mecmuası*, December, 1955.

ERGIN, O., *Türk şehirlerinde imaret sistemi*, Istanbul, 1939.

ERGINBAŞ, D., *Diyarbakır evleri*, Istanbul, 1954.

ERKINS, Z., *Topkapı Sarayı müzesi*, Istanbul, 1965.

ESAD EFENDI, *Précis historique de la destruction du corps des Janissaires par le Sultan Mahmoud en 1826*, trans. Caussin de Perceval, Paris, 1833.

ESER, L., *Kütahya evleri*, Istanbul, 1955.

ESIN, E., 'An eighteenth century yalı' in *2nd I.C.T.A.*, Naples, 1965.
'Influences de l'art nomade et de l'architecture de Turkistan pré-Islamique sur les arts plastiques et pictureaux turcs' in *1st*

I.C.T.A., Ankara, 1961.

Mecca, the blessed; Madinah, the radiant, New York, 1963.

Turkish miniature painting, Japan, 1960.

ETHEM, H., see H. E. ELDEM.

EUDES DE MÉZERAY, F., *Histoires des Turcs*, II, 1612–49, Paris, 1667.

EVLIYA EFENDI (Evliya Çelebi), *Narrative of travels in Europe, Asia, and Africa in the seventeenth century*, trans. Hammer-Purgstall, London, 1846. See also Kocu.

EYİCE, S., 'Les "Bedestens" dans l'architecture turque' in *2nd I.C.T.A.*, Naples, 1965.

Istanbul: petit guide à travers les monuments byzantins et turcs, Istanbul, 1955.

'Istanbul minareleri' in *Türk San'atı Tarihi Araştırma ve Incelemeleri*, Istanbul, 1963.

'Two Byzantine pavements in Bithynia' in *Dumbarton Oaks Papers*, 17, Washington, 1963.

'Un type de mosquée de style turc-ottomane ancien' in *1st I.C.T.A.*, Ankara, 1961.

FEHER, G., 'Macristan'da Türk mimarı eserleri' in *Akademi*, V, Istanbul, March, 1966.

FIELD, H., and E. PROSTOV, 'Archaeological investigations in Central Asia, 1917–37' in *Ars Islamica*, V, Michigan, 1938.

'Archaeology in the Soviet Union . . .' in *American Anthropologist*, XXXIX, No. 3, 1937.

'The Oriental Institute Report on the Near East, U.S.S.R.' in *American Journal of Semitic Languages and Literature*, LIII, No. 2, 1937.

FIRATLI, N., *İznik*, Istanbul, 1959 (pamphlet).

FISCHER-GALATI, S. A. *Ottoman Imperialism and German Protestantism, 1521-55*, Cambridge, Mass., 1959.

FISHER, S. N. *The foreign relations of Turkey, 1481-1512*, Urbana, 1948.

FITZGERALD, C. P., *Barbarian beds. The origins of the chair in China*, London, 1965.

GABRIEL, A., *Une Capitale turque, Brousse (Bursa)*, Paris, 1958.

La cité de Rhodes, 1310-1522, Paris, 1921.

Châteaux turcs du Bosphore, Paris, 1943.

'Le maître-architecte Sinan' in *La Turquie Kemaliste*, XVI, Ankara, December, 1936.

Les monuments turcs d'Anatolie, I, II, Paris, 1931-4.

'Les mosquées de Constantinople', extract from the review, *Syrie*, Paris, 1926.

Voyages archéologiques dans la Turquie Orientale, Paris, 1940.

GALLAND, A., *Journal d'Antoine Galland pendant son séjour à Constantinople, 1672-3*, 2 vol., ed. Schefer, Paris, 1881.

GEBHARD, D., 'The problem of space in Ottoman architecture' in *Art Bulletin*, XLV, no. 3, New York, September, 1963.

GEMELLI-CARERI, G.F., *Voyage du tour du monde*, trans. from the Italian by M.L.N., 6 vol., Paris, 1719.

GEUFFROY, A., *Briefve description de la court du Grant Turc . . .*, Paris, 1546.

GIBB, H. A. R., 'Lufti Pasha on the Ottoman Caliphate' in *Oriens*, XV, Leiden, 1962.

See also Ibn Battuta.

GIBB, H. A. R., and H. BOWEN, *Islamic society and the West*, 2 vol., Oxford, 1950.

GIBBONS, H. A., *The Foundation of the Ottoman Empire*, Oxford, 1916.

GIDE, A., *Journal, 1889-1939*, Paris, 1955.

GILLES, P. (Gyllius), *The Antiquities of Constantinople*, trans. Ball, London, 1729.

GLÜCK, H., *Probleme des Wölbungsbaues: die Bäder Konstantinopels*, Vienna, 1921.

'Türkische Dekorationskunst' in *Kunst und Kunsthandwerk*, Vienna, 1920.

GODARD, A., *L'art de l'Iran*, Paris, 1962.

'L'origine de la madrasa, de la mosquée et du caravansérail à quatre ivâns' in *Ars Islamica*, XV-XVI, Michigan, 1951.

GÖKBILGIN, M. T., 'Edirne' in *Encyclopaedia of Islam*, II, London and Leiden, 1965.

XV-XVI asırlarda Edirne ve Paşa livâsi; vakıflar, mülkler, mukataalar, Istanbul, 1952.

GRAY, B., *Persian painting*, New York, 1961.

GRELOT, G. J., *Relation nouvelle d'un voyage de Constantinople*, Paris, 1680.

GRENVILLE, H., *Observations sur l'état actuel de l'Empire Ottoman*, ed. Ehrenkreutz, Michigan, 1965.

GROSVENOR, E. A., *Constantinople*, 2 vol., London 1895.

GRUBE, E. J., *The world of Islam*, New York, 1967.

GURLITT, C., *Die Baukunst Konstantinopels*, 4 portfolios, Berlin, 1912.

'Die Bautai Adrianopels', *Orient Archives*, I, Leipzig, 1910.

GYLLIUS, see Gilles.

HAMLIN, C., *Among the Turks*, London, 1878.

HAMMER-PURGSTALL, J. VON, *Histoire de l'Empire Ottomane*, 18 vol., including a translation of the 'Hadika ül-Cevami', Paris, 1835-43. This is a translation by J. J. Hellert of *Geschichte des Osmanischen Reiches*, 10 vol., Pest/Vienna, 1827-35.

See also Evliya Efendi.

HARTMAN, R., 'Damascus' in *Encyclopaedia of Islam*, I, London and Leiden, 1913.

HASLUCK, F. W., *Christianity and Islam under the Sultans*, ed. M. S. Hasluck, Oxford, 1929.

HAUTECOEUR, L. , and G. WEIT, *Les mosquées du Caire*, Paris, 1932.

HERVÉ, F. *A residence in Greece and Turkey . . .*, London, 1837.

HERZFELD, E., 'Damascus: studies in architecture, I-III', in *Ars Islamica*, IX-XII, Michigan, 1942-6.

HEYD., U., 'Bab-i Humāyūn' in *Encyclopaedia of Islam*, I, London and Leiden, 1960.

Oriental documents on Palestine, 1552-1615. A study of the firman according to the Mühimme defteri, Oxford, 1960.

HUSSEY, J. M., ed., *The Byzantine Empire. I: Byzantium and its neighbours. The Cambridge Medieval History*, IV, Cambridge, 1966.

IBN BATTUTA, *The Travels of Ibn Battuta, A.D. 1325-54*, translated by H. A. R. Gibb, Cambridge, 1958.

IKRAM, S. M., ed. Embree, *Muslim civilization in India*, New York, 1964.

INALCIK, H., 'Ghulăm, IV. Ottoman Empire' in *Encyclopaedia of Islam*, II, London and Leiden, 1965.

'The place of the Ottoman-Turkish Empire in History', in *Cultura Turcica*, Ankara, 1964.

INČIČEAN, L. (P. L. Ingigi), *XVIII asırda Istanbul*, ed. and trans. Andreasyan, Istanbul, 1956.

Villeggiature de' Bizantini sul Bosforo Tracio, trans. Aznavor, Venice, 1831.

İPSIROĞLU, M. S., and S. EYÜBOĞLU, *Fatih albümüne bir bakıs*, Istanbul, 1955.

İZ, F., 'Ashık Pasha' in *Encyclopaedia of Islam*, I, London and Leiden, 1960.

JACKSON, J., *Journey from India towards England*, London, 1799.

JOINVILLE AND VILLEHARDOUIN, *Chronicles of the Crusades*, trans. M. R. B. Shaw, Harmondsworth, 1963.

KEPPEL, MAJOR THE HON. G. (Earl of Albemarle), *Narrative of a journey across the Balcan*, London, 1831.

KINNEAR, J. M., *Journey through Asia Minor, Armenia, and Koordistan in the years 1813-14*, London 1818.

KIZILTAN, A., *Anadolu Beyliklerinde cami ve mescitler*, Istanbul, 1958.

KLOPSTEG, P. E., *The construction and use of the composite bow by the Turks*, ms. in Robert College library since published, Illinois, 1947.

KOCU, R. E., *Evliya Efendi, ca.1611-ca.1669. Evliya Çelebi seyahatnamesi*, Istanbul, 1949.

Yeniçeriler, Istanbul, 1964.

KONROFF, M., ed., *Contemporaries of Marco Polo*, New York, 1928.

KONYALI, I. H., *Âbideleri ve kitabeleri ile Erzurum tarihi*, Istanbul, 1960.

Âbideleri ve kitabeleri ile Karaman tarihi, Istanbul, 1967.

Âbideleri ve kitabeleri ile Konya tarihi, Istanbul, 1964.

Azadlı Sinan (Sinan-ı Atík) vakfiyeleri, eserleri, hayatı, mezarı, Istanbul, 1953.

İstanbul sarayları: Atmeydanı sarayı, Perteve Paşa sarayı, Çinili köşk, Istanbul, 1943.

Mimar Koca Sinan'ın eserleri, Istanbul, 1950.

Mimar Koca Sinan. Vakfiyyeleri, hayır eserleri, hayatı . . ., Istanbul, 1948.

Söğüt'de Ertuğrul Gazi türbesi ve ihtifalı, Istanbul, 1959.

KÖMÜRCUOĞLU, E., *Ankara evleri*, Istanbul, 1950.

KÖPRÜLÜ, F., 'L'institution du Vakouf' in *Vakıflar Dergisi*, II, Ankara, 1942.

KRAMRISCH, S., *The art of India*, London, 1954.

KRITOVOULOS, M., *History of Mehmed the Conqueror*, trans. Charles T. Riggs, Princeton, 1954.

KUBAN, D., *Anadolu-Türk mimarisinin kaynak ve sorunları*, Istanbul, 1965.
'Une analyse stylistique de l'espace dans l'architecture ottomane' in *1st I.C.T.A.*, Ankara, 1961.
Türk barok mimarisi hakkında bir deneme, Istanbul, 1954.

KUNTER, H. B., 'Les bases appliquées dans l'administration, la conservation, l'entretien et les réparations des monuments turcs' in *1st I.C.T.A.*, Ankara, 1961.

KUNTER, H. B., and A. S. ÜLGEN, 'Fatih Camii' in *Vakıflar Dergisi*, I, Ankara, 1938.

KURAN, A., *İlk Devir Osmanlı mimarisinde cami*, Ankara, 1964.
Küçük Efendi manzumesi, offprint of Belleten, XXVII, Ankara, 1963.
The mosque of Yıldırım in Edirne, offprint of Belleten, XXVIII, Ankara, 1964.

KURAN, E., 'Babaeski' in *Encyclopaedia of Islam*, I, London and Leiden, 1960.

LA MOTTRAYE, A. DE, *Travels through Europe, Asia, and into parts of Africa*, trans. from the French, 3 vol., London, 1723-32.

LANE, A., 'The Ottoman pottery of Iznik' in *Ars Orientalis*, II, Michigan, 1957.

LECHEVALIER, J. B., *Voyage de la Propontide et du Pont-Euxin*, 2 vol., Paris, 1800.

LE CORBUSIER, (C. E. Jeanneret-Gris), *My Work*, trans. Palmes, London, 1960.

LETHABY, W. R., *Architecture, nature, and magic*, London, 1956.

LEVINGE, G., *The traveller in the East*, London, 1839.

LEVY, R., trans., *A mirror for princes – The Qābūs nāma' of Kai-Kā'ūs ibn Iskandar, called 'Unşur ul-Ma'ālī, Amir of Dailam*, London, 1951.

LEWIS, B., 'Divan-i humayun' in *Encyclopaedia of Islam*, II, London and Leiden, 1965.
'A Karaite itinerary through Turkey in 1641-2' in *Vakıflar Dergisi*, III, Ankara, 1956.

LEWIS, G., *Turkey*, London, 1955.

LEWIS, J. F., *Lewis's illustrations of Constantinople . . . 1835-6*, London, 1837.

LORICHS, M., *Konstantinopel unter Sultan Suleiman dem Grossen aufgenommen im Jahre 1559 durch Melchior Lorichs aus Flensburg*, Munich, 1902.
121 plates . . . by M. Lorichs, 1570-83 in the British Museum Library, London.

LYBYER, A. H., *The Government of the Ottoman Empire in the time of Suleiman the Magnificent*, Cambridge, Mass., 1913.

LYNCH, H. F. B., *Armenia, travels and studies*, London, 1901.

MacCURDY, E., *The mind of Leonardo da Vinci*, London, 1928.

MacNEICE, L., *Astrology*, New York, 1964.

MAGNI, C., *Quanto di più curiosi, e vago ha potuto raccorre C. M. nel primo biennio da esso consumato in viaggi, e dimore per la Turchia . . . aggiontavi la relazione del Serraglio del Gran Signore . . . distesa de A. Bobovio, etc.*, Parma, 1704.

MAMBOURY, E., 'L'art turque du 18e siècle' in *La Turquie Kemaliste*, XIX, Ankara, June, 1937.
The tourists' Istanbul, Istanbul, 1953.

MANGO, C., 'The conciliar edict of 1166' in *Dumbarton Oaks Papers*, XVII,

MANTRAN, R., 'Les inscriptions arabes de Brousse' in *Bulletin d'Etudes Orientales*, XIV, Damascus, 1952-4.
Istanbul dans la seconde moité du XVIIe siècle . . ., Paris, 1962.
La vie quotidienne à Constantinople au temps de Soliman le Magnifique et ses successeurs, XVIe et XVIIe siècles, Paris, 1965.

MARÇAIS, C., 'Binā' in *Encyclopaedia of Islam*, I, London and Leiden, 1960.

MAREK, J., and H. KNÍŽKOVÁ, *The Jenghiz Khan miniatures for the court of Akbar the Great*, trans. Kuthanová, London, 1963.

MARSIGLI, CONTE L. F. DE, *Stato militare dell'Impero Ottomanno*, The Hague, 1732.

MARTIGNY, G., 'Die Piyale Pasha Moschee' in *Ars Islamica*, I, Michigan, 1934.

MATHEW, G., *Byzantine aesthetics*, London, 1963.

MAYER, L. A., *Islamic architects and their works* and *Islamic astrolobists and their works*, Geneva, 1956.
Saracenic heraldry, Oxford, 1933.

MELIKOFF, I., 'Al-Battāl (Sayyıd Battāl Ghazi)' in *Encyclopaedia of Islam*, I, London and Leiden, 1960.

MELLING, A. I. *Voyage pittoresque de Constantinople et des rives du Bosphore*, 2 vols., Paris, 1819.

MÉNAGE, V. L., 'Devshirme' in *Encyclopaedia of Islam*, II, London and Leiden, 1965.
'The mission of an Ottoman secret agent in France in 1486' in *Journal of the Royal Asiatic Society*, parts 3 and 4, London, 1965.
'Seven Ottoman documents from the reign of Mehemmed II' in *Documents from Islamic chanceries. Oriental Studies*, 1st series, III, ed. Stern, Oxford, 1965.

MENAVINO, G. A., *I costumi, et la vita de Turchi*, Florence, 1551.

MERIÇ, R. M., 'L'architecte de la mosquée Beyazid d'Istanbul' in *1st I.C.T.A.*, Ankara, 1961.
'Edirne'nin tarihi ve mimari eserleri hakkında' in *Türk San'atı Tarihi Araştırma ve İncelemeleri*, Istanbul, 1963.

MEYER-RIEFSTAHL, R., 'Early Turkish tile revetments in Edirne' in *Ars Islamica*, IV, Michigan, 1937.
'Selimiyeh in Konya' in *Art Bulletin*, XII, No. 4, New York, December, 1930.
Turkish architecture in Southwestern Anatolia, Cambridge, Mass., 1931.

MEZERAY, F. DE, *Histoire des Turcs*, II: 1612-1649, Paris 1667.

MILLER, B., *Beyond the Sublime Porte, the Grand Seraglio of Stambul*, New Haven, 1931.
The palace school of Muhammed the Conqueror, Cambridge, Mass., 1941.

MINETTI, H., *Osmanische provinziale Baukunst auf dem Balkan . . .* Hanover, 1923.

MINORSKY, V., *The Chester Beatty Library. A catalogue of the Turkish manuscripts and miniatures*, Dublin, 1958.
'Manisa' in *Encyclopaedia of Islam*, III, London and Leiden, 1936.

MORDTMANN, J. H., (Rev. B. Lewis), 'Derebey' in *Encyclopaedia of Islam*, II, London and Leiden, 1965.
'Eregli' *ibid*.

MONTANI EFENDI, *L'architecture Ottomane*, ed. Edhem Paşa, text by M. de Launay, Constantinople, 1873.

NAIMA, M., *Annals of the Turkish Empire from 1591 to 1659 of the Christian era*, trans. Frazer, London, 1832.

NICOLAY, N. DE, Sieur d'Arfeuille, *Navigations and voyages made into Turkey*, London, 1585.

ORAL, M. Z., 'Anadolu'da san'at değeri olan ahşap minberleri, kitabler ve tarihçeler' in *Vakıflar Dergisi*, V, Ankara, 1962.

OSMAN, R., (Dr. R. O. Tosyeri or Tosyalı), *Edirne sarayı*, Ankara, 1957.

OTTO-DORN, K., *Das Islamische Iznik*, Berlin, 1941.

ÖNDER, M. *Konya*, Konya, 1962.

ÖZ, T., *Istanbul camileri*, 2 vol., Ankara, 1962-5.
Mimar Mehmet Ağa ve risalei mimarîye, Istanbul, 1944.
'Sultan Ahmet Camii' in *Vakıflar Dergisi*, I, Ankara, 1938.

ÖZDEŞ, *Türk çarşıları*, Istanbul, 1953.

PAKALIN, M. Z., *Osmanlı tarih devimleri ve terimleri sözlüğü*, 3 vol., Istanbul, 1946-56.

PALEN, K. K., *Mission to Turkestan; being the memoirs of Count K. K. Palen, 1908-9*, ed. Pierce, Oxford, 1964.

PALLADIO, A., *The Four Books of architecture*, ed. Placzek, New York, 1965.

PAMUKCIYAN, K., 'K. A. Balyan', etc. in *Istanbul Ansiklopedisi*, IV, Istanbul, 1960.

PARDOE, J., *The city of the Sultan, and domestic manners of the Turks in 1836*, 3 vol., London, 1838.

PARRY, V. J., 'Čanak-kale Boghazi' in *Encyclopaedia of Islam*, II, London and Leiden, 1965.

PARVILLÉE, L., *Architecture et décorations turques au XVe siècle*, Paris, 1874.

PAUTY, E., 'L'architecture au Caire depuis la conquête ottomane' in *Bulletin de l'Institut français d'Archéologie orientale*. XXXVI, Cairo, 1936.

PERRY, C., *A view of the Levant: particularly of Constantinople, Syria, Egypt, and Greece*, London, 1743.

PERTUSIER, C., *Promenades pittoresques dans Constantinople et sur les rives du Bosphore . . .*, Paris, 1815.

PINKERTON, J., *A general collection of the best and most interesting voyages . . .*, London, 1811.

PLANHOL, X. DE, *The world of Islam*, New York, 1954.

POCOCKE, R., *A description of the East and some other countries*, London, 1743. See also Pinkerton.

PORADA, E., *et al.*, *The art of Ancient Iran*, New York, 1965.

PRESCOTT, H. F. M., *Jerusalem journey, pilgrimage to the Holy Land in the fifteenth century*, London, 1954.

RAMSEY, SIR W., and G. BELL, *The Thousand and one churches*, London, 1909.

RIEFSTAHL, R., see Meyer-Riefstahl.

ROSE, H. A., see J. P. Brown.

ROSEDALE, H. E., *Queen Elizabeth and the Levant company . . .* , London, 1904.

ROSENTHAL, F., *The Muslim concept of freedom prior to the nineteenth century*, Leiden, 1960.

RUNCIMAN, SIR S., *A history of the Crusades*, 3 vol., Harmondsworth, 1965.

RYCAUT, SIR P., *The history of the Turkish Empire from the year 1623 to the year 1677*, London, 1680.

SAFRASTIAN, A., *Kurds and Kurdistan*, London, 1948.

ST JOHN PHILBY, H., *Arabian Jubilee*, London, 1952.

SAKISIAN, A., 'Les faïences du bain de Selim II au harem du Vieux Sérail' extract from *Mélanges Syriens offerts à M. R. Dussaud*, Gembloux, n.d.

SALADIN, H., *Manuel d'art musulman: l'architecture*, Paris, 1907.

SALIGNAC, J. DE GORTAUT BIRON, BARON DE, *Ambassade en Turquie, 1605-1610*, Archives historiques de la Gascogne, ed. Comte Théodore de Gortaut, Paris/Auch, 1888.

SANDERSON, J., *The travels of John Sanderson in the Levant, 1584-1602*, ed. Foster, London, 1931.

SANDYS, G., *A relation of a journey begun An. Dom. 1610*, London, 1627.

SARRE, F., *Islamic bindings*, London, n.d.

SARTON, G., *Introduction to the history of science*, 3 vol., Baltimore, 1927-48.

SAUVAGET, J., 'Les caravansérails Syriens du Hadjdj de Constantinople' in *Ars Islamica*, IV, Michigan, 1937.

SAYILI, A. *The Observatory in Islâm, and its Place in the General History of the Observatory*, publications of the Turkish Historical Society, series VIII, no. 38, Ankara, 1960.

SCERRATO, V., 'An early Ottoman han near Lake Apolyant' in *2nd I.C.T.A.*, Naples, 1965.

SCHACHT, J., 'Ein archaischer Minaret-Typ in Ägypten und Anatolien' in *Ars Islamica*, V, Michigan, 1938.
    'The staircase minaret' in *1st I.C.T.A.*, Ankara, 1961.

SCHEFER, C., *Mémoire historique sur l'ambassade de France à Constantinople par le Marquis de Bonnac*, Paris, 1894.

SCHROEDER, E., *A survey of Persian Art*, III, ed. Upham-Pope, Oxford, 1937.

SCHUYLER, E., *Turkestan; notes of a journey in Russian Turkestan, Korkand and Kuldja*, ed. Wheeler, New York, 1966.

SOUTHGATE, H., *Narrative of a tour through Armenia, Kurdistan, Persia and Mesopotamia*, New York, 1840.

STAUDE, W., 'Le caractère turc dans l'ornementation des faïences Osmanlies' extract from revue *Syrie*, Paris, 1934.

STRZYGOWSKI, J., *Origin of Christian Church Art*, trans. Dalton and Braunholtz, Oxford, 1923.

SUMNER-BOYD, H., 'The seven hills of Istanbul', manuscript.

SEHSUVAROĞLU, B. N., 'Bīmāristān, III. Turkey' in *Encyclopaedia of Islam*, I, London and Leiden, 1960.

TAESCHNER, F., 'Čorum' in *Encyclopaedia of Islam*, II, London and Leiden, 1965. Also 'Elbistan', *ibid.*

TALBOT RICE, D., *The Great Palace of the Byzantine emperors*, I, Oxford, 1947.

TANIŞIK, I. B., *Istanbul çeşmeleri*, 2 vol., Istanbul, 1943.

TAVERNIER, J. B., Baron d'Aubonne, *Nouvelle relation de l'intérieur du Serail du Grand Seigneur*, Cologne, 1675.

TEKIN, A., *Fotoğraflarla Diyarbakır*, Diyarbakır, 1964.

TEMPLE, SIR G., *The shores and islands of the Mediterranean*, London, n.d.

TEXIER, C. F. M., *Asie Mineure*, 2 vol., Paris, 1863.

THÉVENOT, J. DE, *The travels of M. de Thévenot into the Levant*, trans. by D. Lovell, London, 1687.

TOSYALI, see Osman.

TOSYERI, see Osman.

TOTT, BARON DE, *Mémoires du Baron de Tott sur les Turcs et les Tartares*, 4 vol., Amsterdam, 1784.

TOURNEFORT, J. P. DE, *Relation d'un voyage du Levant*, Amsterdam, 1718.

TOY, S., 'The aqueducts of Constantinople' extract from the *Journal of the Royal Institute of British Architects*, London 1928.

TRITTON, A. S., *Islam, belief and practices*, London, 1966.

TURAN, S., 'Gli architteti imperiali (Hassa mimarlari) nell'Impero Ottomano' in *2nd I.C.T.A.*, Naples, 1965.

UPHAM-POPE, A., *A survey of Persian Art from prehistoric times to the present*, 6 vol., London, 1938.

UTKULAR, I., *Çanakkale boğazında Fatih kaleleri*, Istanbul, 1954.

UZUNÇARŞILI, I. *Osmanlı devletinin saray teşkilatı*, Ankara, 1945.
    'Bōstāncı' in *Encyclopaedia of Islam*, I, London and Leiden, 1960.

ÜLGEN, A. S., 'Le décor intérieur de l'architecture turque au XVIe siècle' in *1st I.C.T.A.*, Ankara, 1961.
    'Inegöl' de İshak Paşa mimari mansumesi' in *Vakıflar Dergisi*, IV, Ankara, 1958.

ÜNAL, I., 'Türklerde sedefçilik' in *Güzel Sanatlar*, VI, Istanbul, 1949.

ÜNSAL, B., *Turkish Islamic architecture in Seljuk and Ottoman times*, London, 1959.

ÜNVER, A. S., 'Davut paşa Sarayı' in *Türkiye Turing ve Otomobil Kurumu*, Istanbul, December 1961.
    Edirne Muradiye cami'i . . ., Istanbul, 1953.
    'Fatih külliyesine ait diğer mühim bir vesika' in *Vakıflar Dergisi*, I, Ankara, 1938.
    İlim ve sanat bakımından Fatih devri albümü, I, Istanbul, 1943.
    'Süleymaniye külliyesinde' in *Vakıflar Dergisi*, II, Ankara, 1942.

VAMBÉRY, A., *Sketches of Central Asia, additional chapters*, London, 1868.

VANDAL, A., *Une Ambassade française en Orient sous Louis XV; la mission du Marquis de Villeneuve, 1728–41*, Paris, 1887.

VAN NICE, R. L., *Saint Sophia in Istanbul*, I, Cambridge, Mass., 1967.

VAN NICE, R. L., and W. EMERSON, 'Hagia Sophia and the first minaret erected after the conquest of Istanbul' in *American Journal of Archaeology*, LIV, 1, January, 1950.
    'The structure of Saint Sophia' in *Architectural Forum*, XVIII, 5, May 1963.

VASARI, G., *The Lives of the Painters, Sculptors and Architects*, IV, ed. Gaunt, London and New York, 1963. (The translation by A. B. Hinds revised.)

VOGT-GÖKNIL, U., 'Die Kulliye von Beyazit II in Edirne' in *Du/Atlantis*, CCXCIV, Zurich, August 1965.
    Les mosquées turques, Zurich, 1953.

WALSH, R., *Constantinople and the Scenery of the Seven Churches of Asia Minor*, illustrated by T. Allom, 2 series, London, 1838.

WHEELER, SIR G., *Journey into Greece by G. W. Esq. in company of Dr. Spon of Lyons*, London, 1682.

WILBER, D. N., *The architecture of Islamic Iran: the Il Khānid period*, Princeton, 1955.

WILLIAMS, D. S. M., 'The traditional Muslim schools of the settled regions of Central Asia during the Tsarist period' in *Central Asian Review*, XIII, 4, London, 1965.

WITTEK, P., *Menteşe beyliği*, trans. Gökyay, Ankara, 1944.
    The rise of the Ottoman Empire, London, 1938.

WITTKOWER, P., *Architectural principles in the Age of Humanism*, London, 1962.

WORTLEY-MONTAGUE, LADY MARY, *Complete Letters of Lady Mary Wortley-Montague*, ed. Robert Halsband. Vol. I, 1708–20, London, 1965.

WULZINGER, K., *Die Pirus-Mosche zu Milas*, Karlsruhe, 1925.

YAHIA, B. BEN, 'Science in the Muslim world' in *History of Science: science in the Nineteenth century*, ed. Taton, London, 1965.

YALÇIN, O., *Çankırı*, Istanbul, 1961.
    Van, Hakkarı, Istanbul, 1961.

YALTAKAYA, S., 'Kara Ahmed Paşa vakfıyesi' in *Vakıflar Dergisi*, II, Ankara, 1942.

YARALOV, Y., 'Architectural monuments in Middle Asia of the 8th to 12th centuries' in *1st I.C.T.A.*, Ankara, 1961.

YENAL, Ş., 'Topkapı sarayı müzesi Enderun kitapliği' in *Güzel Sanatlar*, VI, Istanbul, 1949.

YETKIN, S. K., *L'architecture turque en Turquie*, Paris, 1962.

YETKIN, S. K. *et al.*, *Turkish architecture*, trans. Üysal, Ankara, 1965.

YÜCEL, E., 'Yeni Camii hünkâr kasrı' in *Arkitekt*, 320, 3 April 1965.

ZBISS., S.-M., 'Des aspects tunisiens de l'art turc' in *1st I.C.T.A.*, Ankara, 1961.

FURTHER READING

AHMET REFIK, *Eski Istanbul, 1553–1839*, Istanbul, 1931.

AKOK, M., 'Merzifon 'da Çelebi Mehmet medresesi' in *Mimarlık*, 9 (1-2), Ankara, 1952.

AKOZAN, F., 'Türk han ve kervansarayları' in *Türk San'atı Tarihi Araştırma ve İncelemeleri*, Istanbul, 1963.

AKYURT, Y., 'Konya asarıatika müzerinde Mevlana Celalattin Ruminin sandirkasi' in *Türk Tarih Arkeologya ve Etnografya Dergisi*, III, Ankara, 1936.

ANHEGGAR, R., 'Eski Fatih Camii meselesi' in *Istanbul Üniversitesi Edibiyat Fakültesi Tarih Dergisi*, 6 (9), Istanbul, March, 1954.

ARSEVEN, C. E., *Constantinople de Byzance à Stamboul*, Paris, 1909.

AYANOĞLU, F. I., 'Vakıflar idaresince tanzim ettiriler tarihi makbereler' in *Vakıflar Dergisi*, II, Ankara, 1942.

AYAŞLIOĞLU, M., 'Istanbulda Mahmut Paşa türbesi' in *Güzel Sanatlar*, VI, Istanbul, 1949.

AYVERDI, E. H., 'Gazenfer Ağa manzumesi' in *Istanbul Enstitüsu Dergisi*, III, Istanbul, 1957.
'I Murad devrinde Asılhan Bey minarî manzumesi' in *Vakıflar Dergisi*, III, Ankara, 1956.
'Yine Fatih Camii' in *Istanbul Üniversitesi Edibiyat Fakültesi Tarih Dergisi*, 7 (10), Istanbul, September 1954.

BATUR, M., 'Fatih Camii çinileri' in *Arkitekt*, V (243-4), Istanbul, 3 April 1952.
'Sultanselim Camii çinileri' in *Arkitekt*, XXI (5/8), Istanbul, 6 September 1952.

BAYKAL, I., 'Hat sanatı' in *Güzel Sanatlar*, II, Istanbul, 1940.
'Topkapi sarayı müzesi kitapları' in *Güzel Sanatlar*, VI, Istanbul, 1949.

BEYLIÉ, L. DE, *L'habitation byzantine . . .*, Paris, 1902.

BOMBACI, A., 'Gazne'deki kazılara giriş', trans. Türker, in *Türk San'atı Tarihi Araştırma ve İncelemeleri*, Istanbul, 1963.
'Les Turcs et l'art Ghaznavide' in *1st I.C.T.A.*, Ankara, 1961.

BOZKURT, O., *Koca Sinan'in köprüleri*, Istanbul, 1952.

CHAGATAI, M. A., 'Turkish architectural ornaments in Indo-Pakistani architecture' in *1st I.C.T.A.*, Ankara, 1961.

CHARDIN, SIR J., see Sykes.

CHARLES, M. A., 'Hagia Sophia and the great Imperial mosques' in *Art Bulletin*, XII, 4, New York, December 1930.

CLAVIJO, R. G. DE, *Constantinople, ses sanctuaires et ses reliques au commencement du XVe siècle*, trans. Braun, Odessa, 1883.
Embassy to Tamerlane, 1403-6, trans. Le Strange, London, 1928.

ÇETINTAŞ, S., 'Mimar Kemalettin mesleği ve san'at ülküsü', in *Güzel Sanatlar*, V, Ankara, 1944.
'Türklerde su, çeşme, sebil', *ibid*.
Türk mimarî anıtları Osmanlı devri, II. *Bursa'da Murad I ve Beyazid I binaları*, Istanbul, 1952.
Saray ve kervansaraylarımız arasında İbrahimpaşa sarayı, Istanbul, 1939.

DAĞLIOĞLU, H. T., 'Les Janissaires' in *La Turquie Kemaliste*, 32-40, Ankara, August 1939–December 1940.

DALLAM, T., 'The diary of Master Thomas Dallam, 1599–1600' in *Early voyages and travels in the Levant*, ed. Bent, London, 1893.

DAY, F. E., 'Two reviews of the Ceramic Arts in a Survey of Persian Art' in *Ars Islamica*, VIII, Michigan, 1941.

DEMIRASLAN, Ü., 'Odalar üzerine' in *Akademi*, Istanbul, March 1964.

DIEHL, C., *Constantinople*, Paris, 1924.

DIEZ, E., and H. GLUCK, *Alt Konstantinopel*, Munich, 1920.

DIEZ, E., 'A stylistic analysis of Islamic art' in *Ars Islamica*, V, Michigan, 1938.
'Simultaneity in Islamic art' in *Ars Islamica*, IV, Michigan, 1937.

DIMAND, M. S., 'Studies in Islamic ornament' in *Ars Islamica*, IV, Michigan, 1937.

DIYARBEKIRLI, N., 'Halk sanatlarımızın değeri' in *Akademi*, Istanbul, March 1964.

D'OSSEVILLE, COMTE L., *Un voyage officiel à Constantinople en 1721*, n.p., n.d.

DUTEMPLE, E., *En Turquie d'Asie*, Paris, 1883.

EDHEM, H., see H. E. Eldem.

ELDEM, H. E., 'Madenden üç türc eseri' in *Türk Tarih Arkeologya ve Etnografya Dergisi*, III, Ankara, 1936.
Topkapı Sarayı, Istanbul, 1931.

ERDENEN, O., *Istanbul çarşıları ve kapalıçarşı*, Istanbul, 1965.

ERDMANN, K., 'Das Anatolische Karavansaray des 13. Jahrhunderts', in *2nd I.C.T.A.*, Naples, 1965.
'Die Sonderstellung der Anatolischen Moschee des XII. Jahrhunderts' in *1st I.C.T.A.*, Ankara, 1961.
'Neuere Untersuchungen zur Frage der Kairener Teppiche' in *Ars Orientalis*, IV, Michigan, 1961.

ERDOĞAN, A., 'Mehmet Tahir Ağa' in *Istanbul Üniversitesi Edibiyat Fakültesi Tarih Dergisi*, 7 (10), Istanbul, September 1954.
'Silivrikapı'da Hadım İbrahim Paşa Camii' in *Vakıflar Dergisi*, I, Ankara, 1938.

ERGIN, O., *Fatih imareti vakfiyesi*, Istanbul, 1945.

ETHEM, F., and I. STCHOUKINE, *Les manuscrits orientaux illustrées de la bibliothèque de l'Université de Stamboul*, Paris, 1933.

ETTINGHAUSEN, R., *Turkey: the ancient miniatures*, UNESCO, New York, 1961.

EYICE, S., 'Fatih devri mimarısı' in *Bilgi*, 11 (122), Istanbul, May 1957.
'Gebze'de Mustafa Paşa külliyesi' in *Bilgi*, 10 (119), Istanbul, February 1957.
'İznik'te İsmail Bey hamamı' in *Bilgi*, 10 (120), Istanbul, March 1957.
'Kayseri'de Köşk Medrese' in *Bilgi*, 11 (129), Istanbul, December 1957.
'Demirciler ve Fatih darüşşifa mescidleri hakkında . . .' in *Istanbul Üniversitesi Edibiyat Fakültesi Tarih Dergisi*, 6 (9), Istanbul, March 1954.
'Sur l'archéologie de l'édifice dit "Aslanhane" et de ses environs', in *Istanbul Arkeologi Müzerleri Yilliği*, XI-XII, Istanbul, 1963.
'Le Château des Sept Tours et la mescid de Fatih' in *Istanbul Arkeologi Müzeleri Yilliği*, X, Istanbul, 1961.
'Ilk Osmanlı devrimi dini-içtimaî bir müessesesi: zaviyeleri ve zaviye-camiler' in *Istanbul Üniversitesi Iktisat Fakültesi Mecmuası*, XXIII, 1-2, Istanbul, February 1963.
'Ohri'nin Türk devrine ait eserleri' in *Vakıflar Dergisi*, VI, Ankara, 1965.
'Yunanistanda Türk mimarî eserleri' in *Türkiyat Mecmuası*, 963 (11), 1954.

FRYE, R. N., *Bukhara, the medieval achievement*, Oklahoma, 1965.
'Notes on the history of architecture in Afghanistan' in *Ars Islamica*, XI-XII, Michigan, 1946.

GABRIEL, A., 'Le masdjid-i Djum'a d'Isfahan' in *Ars Islamica*, II, Michigan, 1935.
En Turquie, Paris, 1935.

GERÇEK, S. N., 'Yabancı göziyle sivil mimarımız' in *Güzel Sanatlar*, V, Istanbul, 1944.

GERLACH, S., *Stepan Gerlach's dess Aeltern Tage-Buch . . . an die Ottomanische Pforte . . .*, Frankfurt, 1674.

GODARD, A., 'L'architecture iranienne à l'époque islamique' in *Jardin des Arts*, Paris, October 1961.
'The architecture of the Islamic period; A survey of Persian Art; compte-rendu' in *Ars Islamica*, VIII, Michigan, 1941.

GURLITT, C., *Antike Denkmalsäulen in Konstantinopel*, Munich, n.d.

HASLUCK, F. W., 'Dr Covel's notes on Galata' in *Annual of the British School at Athens*, London, 1906.

HEARSEY, J. E. N., *City of Constantinople, 324–1453*, London, 1963.

HOAG, J. D., *Western Islamic architecture*, New York, 1963.

HUART, M. C., *Konia, la ville des derviches tourneurs . . .*, Paris, 1897.

İZZET, *The chamber of Hekim-Bashi, the first pharmacy, the tower of Bash-Lala*, Istanbul, 1933.

KOCAINAN, Z., *Mimar Sinan ve XX asir mimarîsi*, Istanbul, 1939.

KOŞAY, H. Z., 'Les interdépendances des éléments culturels et les empreintes des civilisations sur l'art et la culture populaires' in *1st I.C.T.A.*, Ankara, 1961.

'Tekke ve türbeler kapandıktan sonra' in *Güzel Sanatlar*, VI, Istanbul, 1949.

KUBAN, D., 'Atık Valide Camii' in *Mimarlık ve Sanat*, II, Istanbul, 1961. 'Beşiktaşta Sinan Paşa Camii' in *Mimarlik ve Sanak*, III, Istanbul, 1961. 'Osmanlı dini mimarisinde iç mekân teşekkülü' in *Studia Islamica*, Istanbul, 1958.

KUHNEL, E., *Die Sammlung türkischer und islamischer Kunst im Tschinili Köschk*, Berlin and Leipzig, 1938.

KUNTER, H. B., 'L'aspect national des fondations pieuses turques (vakoufs)' in *Vakıflar Dergisi*, III, Ankara, 1956. 'Emir Sultan vakıfları' in *Vakıflar Dergisi*, IV, Ankara, 1958. 'Türk Spor mimarîsine dair' in *Güzel Sanatlar*, V, Istanbul, 1944. 'Türk vakıflarının milliyetçilik cephesi' in *Vakıflar Dergisi*, III, Ankara, 1956.

KUNTER, H. B., and A. S. ÜLGEN, *Fatih cami'i ve Bizans sanıcı*, Istanbul, 1939.

KURAL, M. R., 'Çelebi Mehmet' in Yeşil türbesi ve 1941–3 restorasyonu' in *Güzel Sanatlar*, V, Istanbul, 1944.

KURAN, A., 'A study of Turkish architecture of modern times' in *1st I.C.T.A.*, Ankara, 1961.

LABARTE, J., *Le Palais impérial de Constantinople*, Paris, 1861.

LARSEN, S., 'Ser Mimar Sinan' in *Yeşilay*, 232, Istanbul, April 1952.

LEE, S. E., *A history of Far Eastern art*, New York, 1964.

LEROY, J., *Monks and monasteries of the Near East*, trans. Collin, London, 1963.

LETHERBY, W. R., and H. SWAINSON, *The church of Sancta Sophia . . .*, London and New York, 1894.

LLOYD, S., and S. RICE, *Alanya*, Ankara, 1964.

MAINSTONE, R. J., 'Structural theory and design before 1742' in *Architectural Review*, CXLIII, 854, London, April 1968.

MARÇAIS, G., *Manuel d'art musulman – l'architecture*, Paris, 1926. *L'architecture musulmane d'Occident . . .*, Paris, 1955.

MARTINOVITCH, R. M., 'Two questions in Moslem art' in the *Journal of the Royal Asiatic Society*, London, 1955.

MERIÇ, R. M., *Mimar Sinan, hayatı, eseri*, Ankara, 1965.

MÉRY, F. J. P. A., *Constantinople et la Mer Noire*, Paris, 1855.

OČAN, A., 'Aydın Oğullarından İsa Bey Cami'i' in *Vakıflar Dergisi*, III, Ankara, 1956. 'Quelques chefs d'œuvres de l'art turque ancien' in *La Turquie Kemaliste*, 43, Ankara, June 1941.

OLIVIER, G. A., *Voyage dans l'Empire Othoman, l'Égypte et la Perse*, 6 vol., Paris, 1801–7.

ORGUN, Z., 'Kubbealtı ve yapılan merasim' in *Güzel Sanatlar*, Istanbul, 1949.

OTTO-DORN, K., 'Die Kunst des Islam', Baden-Baden, 1964.

ÖZ, T., 'Hünername ve minyaturleri' in *Güzel Sanatlar*, I, Istanbul, 1939. 'Tavanlarımız' in *Güzel Sanatlar*, V, Istanbul, 1944. 'La bibliothèque du palais de Topkapı' in *La Turquie Kemaliste*, 45, Ankara, October 1941. 'Topkapı sarayı müzesi onarımları' in *Güzel Sanatlar*, VI, Ankara, 1949. *Turkish textiles and velvets*, Ankara, 1950. 'Türk el işlemeleri ve resim dairesi' in *Güzel Sanatlar*, IV, Istanbul, 1942.

ÖZDEŞ, G., *Edirne . . .*, Istanbul, 1951.

SALADIN, H., *Le yalı des Keupruli à Anatoli-Hissar . . .*, n.p., 1915.

SARACOĞLU, N., *Türk mezarlarına dair araştırma*, Istanbul, 1950.

SCHNEIDER, A. M., and M. Is. NOBIDIST, *Galata: Topographisch-Archäolog-Plan mit erläuterndem Text*, Istanbul, 1944.

SMITH, A., *A month at Constantinople*, London, 1860.

SMITH, B., *The dome. A study in the history of ideas*, New Haven, 1950.

SÖYLEMEZOGLU, H. H. K., *Islam dini, ilk camiler ve Osmanlı camileri*, Istanbul, 1954.

SUDALI, M., *Hünkâr mahfilleri*, Istanbul, 1958.

SWIFT, E. H., *Hagia Sophia*, New York, 1940.

SYKES, SIR P., *Sir John Chardin's travels in Persia*, London, 1927.

TAESCHNER, F., 'Akhi', in *Encyclopaedia of Islam*, I, London and Leyden, 1960.

TAMER, C., 'Quelques recherches sur les décorations turques' in *1st I.C.T.A.*, Ankara, 1961.

TAVERNIER, J. B., *Les six voyages de J.B.T. en Turquie, en Perse, et aux Indes*, 2 vol., Amsterdam, 1678.

TEKINER, E., *The Great Bazaar of Istanbul*, Istanbul, 1949.

UPHAM-POPE, A., *An introduction to Persian art since 7th century A.D.*, London, 1937. *Persian architecture*, London, 1965.

ULUENGIN, F., 'La configuration géométrique des plans des stalactites' in *1st I.C.T.A.*, Ankara, 1961.

ÜLGEN, A. S., *Anıtların koruması ve onarılması*, Ankara, 1943. 'Le caractère philosophique et esthétique de l'architecture turque' in *1st I.C.T.A.*, Ankara, 1961. *Constantinople during the era of Mohammed the Conqueror, 1453–81*, Ankara, 1939. 'İnegöl'ün kurşunlu âbideleri' in *Türk San'at Tarihi Araştırma ve İncelemeleri*, Istanbul, 1963. 'Şehzade' in *Mimarlik*, 5/6, Ankara, April 1952. 'İznik ciniciliğine dair' in *Meslekî ve teknik öğretim*, 4 (37/38), March/April 1956. 'Niğde'de Akmedrese' in *Vakıflar Dergisi*, II, Ankara, 1942.

ÜNSAL, B., 'Topkapı sarayı arşivinde bulunan mimarî plânlar üzerine' in *Türk San'at Tarihi Araştırma ve İncelemeleri*, Istanbul, 1963. *Mimarî tarihi*, Istanbul, 1949.

ÜNVER, A. S., 'Fatih külliyesi ait diğer mühim bir vesika' in *Vakıflar Dergisi*, I, Ankara, 1938. 'Iznik'te Türk eserleri' *ibid.* 'Süsleme sanatı bakımından Topkapı Sarayı müzesi' in *Güzel Sanatlar*, VI, Istanbul, 1949. 'Türk ressamı ve içtimaî yaşayışımız' in *Güzel Sanatlar*, I, Istanbul, 1939.

VANDAL, A., *L'odyssée d'un ambassadeur. Les voyages du Marquis de Nointel, 1670–80*, Paris, 1900.

VAN MILLIGEN, A., *Constantinople*, London, 1906.

VOGT-GÖKNIL, U., *Turquie ottomane*, Fribourg, 1965.

WILDE, H., *Brussa*, Berlin, 1909.

YÜCEL, E., 'Bursa Ulucami'i restorasyonu' in *Arkitekt*, no. 312, Istanbul, 1963.

ZEREN, L., *Ocaklar*, Istanbul, 1955.

List, by towns, of
major Ottoman monuments
mentioned in the text

(*Abbreviations* Bed: bedesten; C: cami; Ham: hamam; K: külliye; Kütüp: kütüphane; Med: medrese; P: Pasha; Tek: tekke; T: türbe; Zav: zaviye.)

ADANA – *C: Nur Mehmet P., Ulu, Yağ, Yeni; clock tower.* AFYONKARAHISAR – *C, K: Ak, Gedik Ahmet P., Kubbeli.* AHLAT – *C: İskender P., Kadı Mahmut; Med. & T: Bayındır.* ALEPPO – *C: Adliye; Med: Osmaniye.* AMASYA – *Bed; C, K: Beyazit P., Burmalı Minare, Fetihye, Mehmet P., Sultan Beyazit, Yürgüç P.; Med: Kapıağa.* ANADOLUHISAR – *Castle; namazgâh.* ANKARA – *Bed: Mahmut P.; C: Ahi Elvan; T: Ahi Şerefettin.* AYASLUĞ – *C: İsa Bey.* AYDIN – *K: Cıhanzade.* BABAESKI – *C: Ali P.* BALAT (Miletus) – *C: İlyas Bey.* BEHREMKALE – *C: Hudavendigâr.* BEŞIKTAŞ – *K: Sinan P.; T: Barbaros.* BEYLERBEY – *K: Beylerbey; saray.* BEYŞEHIR – *Bed; C, T: Eşrefoğlu.* BILECIK – *C: Orhaniye.* BIRGI – *C, K: Ulu; konak.* BITLIS – *C, K: Şerefiye, Ker; Hüsrev P.* BOR – *K: Sokollu Mehmet P.* BOZÜYÜK – *C: Cezeri Kasım P.* BURSA – *Bazaar; Bed; Bridge: Meksem; C, K: Abdal Mehmet, Alaettin, Bascı Ibrahim, Emir Sultan, Hacılar, Mamza Bey, Hudavendigâr, Karaca Bey, Molla Arab, Muradiye, Orhaniye, Ömer Bey, Timurtaş, Ulu, Yeşil, Yıldırım; clock tower; Ham: Bekârlar, Bey, Eski, Eski Kaplıca, Gönlüferah, Meyhaneli, Yeni Kaplıca; Hans: Bey, Emir, Fidan, Hacı İvaz, Koza; Konak: Murat II; Med: Geyikli Ahmet P, Lala Sahin; namazgâh; Tek: İsmail Hakkı, Mevlevi; T: Cariyelar, Cam, Devlet Hatun, Murat II, Mustafa Sultan, Orhan, Osman.* CAIRO – *C, K: Abu Dahab, Hasan Rumi, Sinan P., Süleyman P.* ÇANKIRI – *C: Ulu.* ÇORUM – *C: Ulu; clock tower; Hans: Sulu, Veli P.* DAMASCUS – *C: Derviş P., Sinan P.* DIMETOKA – *C: Murat I, Sultan Mehmet.* DIYARBAKIR – *C, K: Bayram P., Fatih P., Hüsrev P., Kasım Padişah, Melek Ahmet P., Peygamber; Hans: Deliller, Hasan P.* DOĞUBAYEZIT – *C: Selim I; Saray: İshak P.* EDIRNE – *Bed; C, K: Ayşe Kadın, Beyazit II, Beylerbey, Eski, Gazi Mihal, Kasım P., Kuş Doğan, Murat II, Selçuk Hatun, Selimiye, Sittişah, Üc Şerefeli, Yıldırım; darül-hadis; Ham: Sokollu Mehmet P.; Han: Rüstem P.; Ker: Ali P., Ekmecioğlu Ahmet P.; Med: Saatlı; saray.* ELBISTAN – *C: Himmet Baba, Ulu.* ELMALI – *C: Omer P.* EMIRGÂN – *K.* EREĞLI – *C: Ali P.; Han: Rüstem P.* ERMENAK – *Bridges: Ala, Bıcakcı; C: Akça, Kemerosu Kebir, Sipas, Ulu.* ERZERUM – *C: Ayazpaşa, Bardız Nahilyesi, Ibrahim P., Kurşunlu, Lala Mustafa P., Mehdi Efendi, Şeyhler; Han: Taş.* EYÜP – *C, K: Cezeri Kasım P., Mihrişah Sultan, Sokollu Mehmet P., Sultan; T: Ferhat P., Mehmet V, Pertev P., Siyavuş P., Sokollu Mehmet P.* GALATA – *Bed.; bridge; C: Azapkapı; castle; Han: Rüstem P.* GEBZE – *Ker: Çoban Mustafa P.* GELIBOLU – *Bed.; namazgâh.* GÜLŞEHIR – *K: Sayit Kara Mehmet.* GÜMÜŞHACIKÖY – *Han: Köprülü.* HASKÖY – *C: Piri Mehmet P.; Konak: Aynalı Kavak.* HAYDARPAŞA – *K: Selim III.* ILGIN – *K: Lala Mustafa P.* INEGÖL – *K. İshak P.* INÖNÜ – *C: Hoca Yardigar.* ISTANBUL – *Bazaar; Bed: Eski, Sandaliye; Bridges: Atatürk, Galata; C, K: Amacazade, Atik Ali P., Eali P., Bayram P.,*

Beşir Ağa, Bodrum, Burmalı Minare, Cerrah P., Çorlulu Ali P., Davut P., Defterdar, Fetihye, Firuz Ağa, Gazanfer Ağa, Gül. Hacı Evhad, Hacı Küçük, Hadım Ibrahim, Haseki Hürrem, Hekinoğlu Ali P., Hırkai-Şerif, Ibrahim P., İskender P., İsmail Efendi, İvaz Efendi, Kara Ahmet P., Köprülü Mehmet P., Kuyucu Murat P., Kumrulu, Küçük Efendi, Laleli, Mahmut P., Mehmet Ağa, Merdivenli, Merzifonlu Kara Mustafa P., Mesih P., Mihrimah Sultan, Murat P., Nakşıdıl, Nisancı Mehmet P., Nuruosmaniye, Pertevniyal Valide, Piyale P., Ramazan Efendi, Rüstem P., Samanveren, Sinan P., Sokollu Mehmet P., Sultan Ahmet, Sultan Beyazit, Sultan Selim, Süleymaniye, Şah Sultan, Şebsafa Kadın, Şehzade, Takkeci Ibrahim Ağa, Timurtaş Ağa, Yarhisar, Yatağan, Yemeni Fatih Koca Sinan P., Yeni Valide, Yer Altı, Zal Mahmut P., Zeynep Sultan, Zincirlikuyu; Darül-hadis: Nevşehirli Ibrahim P.; Fountains: Abdülhamit I, Ahmet III, Hacı Mehmet Emin Ağa, Hasan P., Halit Efendi, Recai Mehmet Efendi, Sadettin Efendi; Hans: Büyük Valide, Büyük Yeni, Çukurçesme, Elci, Hasan P., Küçük Yeni, Şimkeş, Vakif, Vezir. Kütüp: Arif Efendi, Murat Molla, Ragıp P., Sayıt Ali P.; Saray: Topkapı; T: Abdülhamit I, Fuat P., Hüsrev P., Mahmut II, Mehmet III, Murat III, Selim II; Yediküle. IZMIT – *C, K: Orhan, Pertev P.* IZNIK – *C, K: Hacı Hamza, Hacı Özbek, Mahmut Çelebi, Yeşil; Hamam: İsmail Bey; Med: Süleyman P.; T: Candarlı, Kirk Kizlar, Yakup Çelebi; Zav: Nilüfer Sultan, Yakup Çelebi.* KANLICA – *C: İskender P.; Yalis: Köprülü, Sarfat P.* KARAMAN – *C: Akcasar, Arapzade, Davgandos, Hacıbeyler, Yunus Emre; Houses: Hasam, Kavasun Aptullah; İmarets: Ibrahim Bey, Şeyh Alaettin Karabaş Veli.* KARAPINAR – *K: Selim II.* KARS – *Citadel.* KASTAMONU – *Bed; C, K: Halil Bey, İbni Neccar, Mahmut Bey, Nasrullah; İmaret: Yakup Ağa.* KAYSERI – *Bazaar; Bed; C, K: Kurşunlu; Konaks: Mollaoğullar, Zennecioğlu.* KIRŞEHIR – *Med: Cacabey; T: Aşık P.* KONYA – *C, K: Abdülâziz, Alaettin, Kapı, Meram, Selimiye, Şerefettin; Kütüp: Yusuf P.; Tek: Mevlana.* KÜTAHYA – *Bed; C, K: Ali P., Demirtaş P., Karagöz Ahmet P., Kurşunlu, Ulu; Konaks: Ali P., Bandımzade, Hacı Çakır, Macar; Zav: Yakup Bey.* LÜLEBURGAZ – *K: Sokollu Mehmet P.* MANISA – *C, K: Çeşnegir, Hatuniye, İvaz P., Muradiye, Ulu, Valide; Zav: İshak Bey, Mevlevi.* MARDIN – *C: Abdul Latif.* MERZIFON – *C, K: Kara Mustafa P., clock tower; Han: Taş; Med: Çelebi Mehmet, Küçük Ağa.* MILAS – *C: Ahmet Gazi, Firuz Ağa, Hacı İlyas.* MUT – *C: Lâl Ağa.* NEVŞEHIR – *K: Ibrahim P.* NIĞDE – *C: Alaettin, Sungur Bey; clock tower; Med: Ak.* NIKSAR – *Med: Böreği Büyük.* OSMANCIK – *bridge.* PAYAS – *Ker: Selim II.* RUMELI HISAR – *castle.* SAFRANBOLU – *C: İzzet P., Köprülü.* SIVAS – *Bazaar; C: Hacı İshak, Mehmet Bey; Fountain: Orhan Tüncöz; Han: Yeni.* SÖĞÜT – *C: Abdülâziz, Ertuğrul; T: Ertuğrul.* TEKIRDAĞ – *Bed; C: Ayas P., Rüstem P.* TIRE – *Bed; Kütüp: Bagdati Necip P.; Zav: Yeşil.* TOKAT – *C: Ali P., Güdük Minare, Hatuniye; clock tower.* TOSYA – *C: Yeni.* URFA – *bridge; C: Yusuf P.; Med: Abdurrahman.* ÜSKÜDAR – *C, K: Atik Valide, Ayasma, Cinili, Mihrimah, Rum Mehmet, Şemşi Ahmet, Yeni Valide; Fountain: İskele.* VAN – *C, K: Hüsrev P., Kaya Celebi.* YOZGAT – *C: Ulu.*

Acknowledgments

All photographs are by the author, with the exception of the following: 255, Adil Arıkan (Istanbul-Beşiktaş); 56, 156, 157, 192, 194, 229, 232, 235, 265, 266, 268, 276–278, 280, 329, 368, 370, 375, 390, 405, 411, 420, 453, 454, 464, 505, 519, The Artomonov Collection, Freer Gallery of Art, Washington; 478, Bildarchiv der Öst. Nationalbibliothek, Vienna; 81, 261, 262, 319, The Hon. R. R. E. Chorley; 346, Olga Ford; 190, Sonia Halliday; 123, 133, 193, 195, 203, 206, 353, 415, Martin Hürlimann; 324, 413, Sedat Pakay; 270, 331, 428, 510, Antonello Perissinotto; I, II, IV, Othmar Pferschy; 152, 182, 223, 366, 435, 479, Josephine Powell; III, Fulvio Roiter; 514, Executors of the late Professor D. Storm Rice; 99, Thames and Hudson archive; 1, 5, 6, 13, 14, 16–20, 22, 26, 27, 37, 41, 51, 68, 69, 71, 73, 75, 84–86, 88, 89, 95, 100, 101, 110, 111, 113–115, 117, 120, 131, 134, 136–139, 141–143, 146, 148, 150, 158, 166, 168, 170–178, 180, 197, 201, 218–220, 224, 225, 228, 230, 245, 247–249, 251, 253, 254, 256–258, 267, 271, 273, 286, 291–293, 304, 306, 308, 313, 314, 318, 321–323, 326, 327, 332, 334, 336, 339, 347, 348, 355, 357, 359, 361, 362, 364, 367, 369, 378, 380, 393, 400, 402, 403, 408, 409, 412, 418, 421–428, 449, 452, 456, 461, 472, 475–477, 481, 483, 485–488, 490, 492–495, 497–501, 504, 512, 515, 516, 520, Michael Stewart Thompson; frontispiece, 11, 15, 23, 25, 43, 45–47, 54, 57, 58, 60, 61, 64–66, 78, 80, 87, 91, 92, 96, 102, 132, 149, 162, 167, 198, 213, 217, 222, 241, 252, 275, 281, 294, 302, 316, 317, 320, 325, 342, 349, 397, 414, 419, 436, 450, 457, 465–470, 473, 484, Turkish Ministry of Tourism; 53, 199, 255, Eduard Widmer, Zurich.

Engravings were photographed from the following books: Comte de Choiseul-Gouffier, *Voyage pittoresque de la Grèce* (Paris, 1782), 188, 227, 372; Pierre Coeck, *Les mœurs et fachons de faire de Turcs* (1533), 160; G. J. Grelot, *Relation nouvelle d'un voyage de Constantinople* (Paris, 1680), 269, 338, 354; M. Lorichs, *Konstantinopel unter Sultan Suleiman dem Grossen* (Munich, 1902), 155, 244; A. I. Melling, *Voyage pittoresque de Constantinople et des rives du Bosphore* (Paris, 1819), 126, 189, 508; J. Pardoe, *Beauties of the Bosphorus* (London, 1838), 330, 384, 440, 441, 509, 517; R. Walsh, *Constantinople and the Scenery of the Seven Churches of Asia Minor* (London, 1838), endpapers, 377, 392, 394, 399, 442, 445.

The plans have been specially drawn by Christopher Woodward Dip. A.A. (Hons) after the following sources (for details see bibliography): C. E. Arseven, 502; O. Aslanapa, 70; E. H. Ayverdi, 31, 67, 82, 122, 124, 127, 128, 130; M. Charles, 315; N. Çakıroğlu, 511; E. Egli, 289; Nezih Fıratlı, 38; A. Gabriel, 42, 49, 62, 72, 77, 97, 103, 140, 178, 274, 309, 312, 333, 341, 360, 363, 379, 496, 503; H. Glück, 105; A. Közen, 358; D. Kuban, 396, 406, 417, 429; A. Kuran, 2, 4, 7, 9, 10, 34, 35, 50, 52, 90, 93, 94, 106, 107, 112, 124, 147, 161, 163, 365, 451; Patricolo, 307; N. M. Penzer, 328; A. S. Ülgen, 108, 119, 287, 288, 340, 356; M. Vogt-Göknil, 135; S. Yenal, 381; S. K. Yetkin, 28.

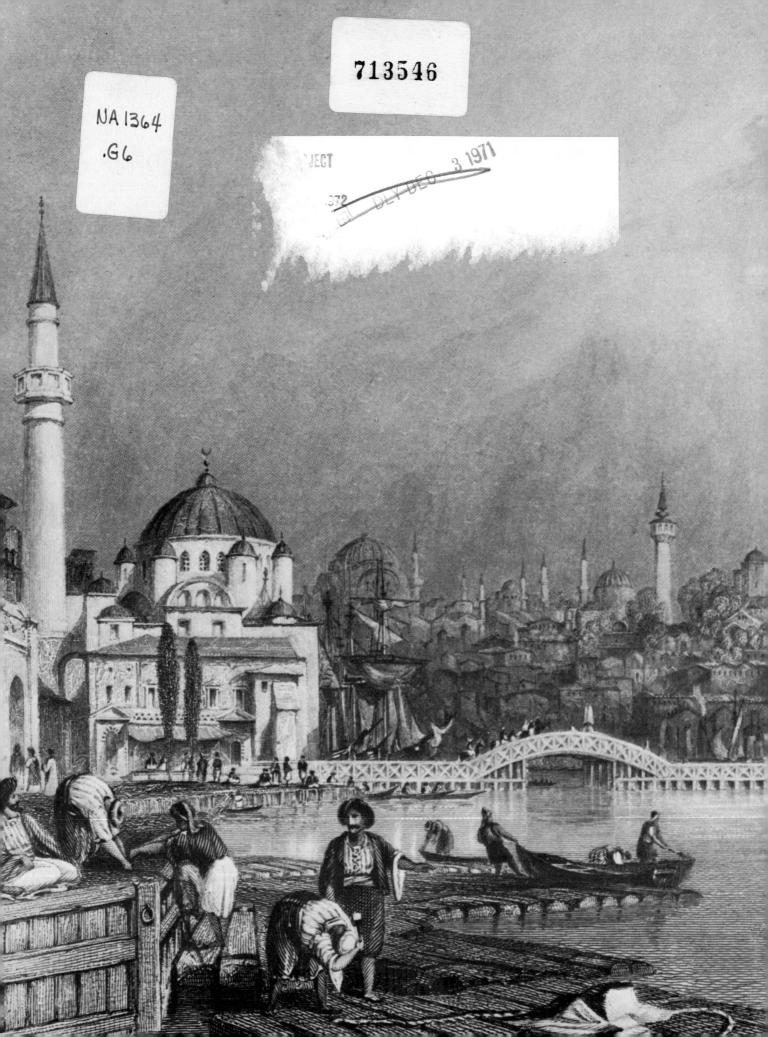

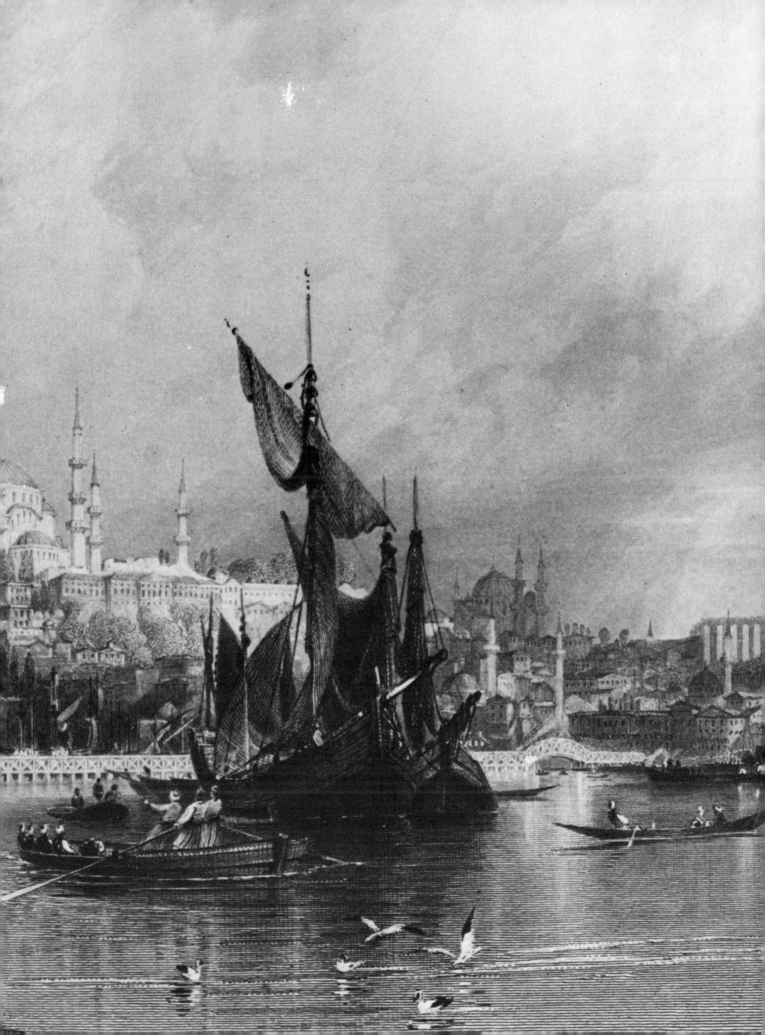